M. Bruynooghe M. Wirsing (Eds.)

Programming Language Implementation and Logic Programming

4th International Symposium, PLILP '92
Leuven, Belgium, August 26-28, 1992
Proceedings

Springer-Verlag
Berlin Heidelberg New York
London Paris Tokyo
Hong Kong Barcelona
Budapest

Series Editors

Gerhard Goos
Universität Karlsruhe
Postfach 69 80
Vincenz-Priessnitz-Straße 1
W-7500 Karlsruhe, FRG

Juris Hartmanis
Department of Computer Science
Cornell University
5149 Upson Hall
Ithaca, NY 14853, USA

Volume Editors

Maurice Bruynooghe
Catholic University of Leuven, Dept. of Computer Science
Celestijnenlaan 200 A, B-3001 Heverlee, Belgium

Martin Wirsing
University of Munich, Institute of Computer Science
Leopoldstr. 11 B, W-8000 Munich 40, FRG

QMW LIBRARY
(MILE END)

CR Subject Classification (1991): F.4.1-2, D.3.1, D.3.4, F.3.3, I.2.3

ISBN 3-540-55844-6 Springer-Verlag Berlin Heidelberg New York
ISBN 0-387-55844-6 Springer-Verlag New York Berlin Heidelberg

This work is subject to copyright. All rights are reserved, whether the whole or part of the material is concerned, specifically the rights of translation, reprinting, re-use of illustrations, recitation, broadcasting, reproduction on microfilms or in any other way, and storage in data banks. Duplication of this publication or parts thereof is permitted only under the provisions of the German Copyright Law of September 9, 1965, in its current version, and permission for use must always be obtained from Springer-Verlag. Violations are liable for prosecution under the German Copyright Law.

© Springer-Verlag Berlin Heidelberg 1992
Printed in Germany

Typesetting: Camera ready by author/editor
Printing and binding: Druckhaus Beltz, Hemsbach/Bergstr.
45/3140-543210 - Printed on acid-free paper

Preface

This volume contains the papers which have been accepted for presentation at the Fourth International Symposium on Programming Language Implementation and Logic Programming (PLILP'92) held in Leuven, Belgium, August 26–28, 1992. The Symposium was preceded by three meetings which took place in Orléans, France May 16–18, 1988, in Linköping, Sweden, August 20–22, 1990 and in Passau, Germany, August 26–28, 1991 (their proceedings were published by Springer-Verlag as Lecture Notes in Computer Science, volumes 348, 456, and 528 respectively).

The aim of the Symposium was to explore new declarative concepts, methods and techniques relevant for implementation of all kinds of programming languages, whether algorithmic or declarative. The intention was to gather researchers from the fields of algorithmic programming languages as well as logic, functional and object-oriented programming.

In response to the call for papers, 82 papers were submitted. The Program Committee met in Leuven on April 27 and selected 29 papers, chosen on the basis of their scientific quality and relevance to the Symposium. At the Symposium, two invited talks were given by Michael Hanus and Patrick Cousot. Several software systems were presented, showing new developments in the implementation of programming languages and logic programming.

This volume contains the two invited presentations, the selected papers and abstracts of the system demonstrations.

On behalf of the Program Committee the Program Chairmen would like to thank all those who submitted papers and the referees who helped to evaluate the papers.

The support of

Association for Logic Programming,
Belgian National Fund for Scientific Research,
BIM,
Katholieke Universiteit Leuven

is gratefully acknowledged. Bart Demoen, Brigitte Gelders, Gerda Janssens, Baudouin Le Charlier, Bern Martens, Anne Mulkers and several other members of the department provided invaluable help throughout the preparation and organization of the Symposium. We also would like to thank Springer-Verlag for their excellent cooperation concerning the publication of this volume.

June 1992
Leuven
München

Maurice Bruynooghe
Martin Wirsing

Conference Chairmen

Maurice Bruynooghe, K.U. Leuven (Belgium)
Martin Wirsing, Univ. of München (Germany)

Program Committee

Maurice Bruynooghe, K.U. Leuven (Belgium)
John Darlington, Imperial College, London (UK)
Saumya Debray, Univ. of Arizona, Tucson (USA)
Wlodek Drabent, Linköping Univ. (Sweden) and Warsaw Univ. (Poland)
Gérard Ferrand, Université d' Orléans (France)
Stefan Jähnichen, TU Berlin (Germany)
Bharat Jayaraman, State Univ. of New York, Buffalo (USA)
Claude Kirchner, INRIA Lorraine & CRIN, Nancy (France)
Feliks Kluźniak, Warsaw Univ. (Poland)
Heikki Mannila, Univ. of Helsinki (Finland)
Torben Mogensen, Univ. of Copenhagen (Denmark)
Alan Mycroft, Cambridge (UK)
Lee Naish, Univ. of Melbourne (Australia)
Jaan Penjam, Estonian Academy of Science, Tallinn (Estonia)
Jiro Tanaka, Fujitsi Laboratories, Tokyo (Japan)
Franco Turini, Universita di Pisa (Italy)
Andrei Voronkov, Novosibirsk (Russia) and ECRC, München (Germany)
Reinhard Wilhelm, Univ. des Saarlandes, Saarbrücken (Germany)
Martin Wirsing, Univ. of München (Germany)

Organizing Committee

Maurice Bruynooghe, K.U. Leuven
Bart Demoen, K.U. Leuven
Gerda Janssens, K.U. Leuven (organizing chairman)
Baudouin Le Charlier, F.U.N.D.P. (Namur)
Bern Martens, K.U. Leuven
Anne Mulkers, K.U. Leuven

List of Referees

Many other referees helped the Program Committee in evaluating papers. Their assistance is gratefully acknowledged.

M. Alt
N. Andersen
J.-M. Andreoli
M. Anlauff
F. Baiardi
A. Bansal
R. Barbuti
F. Barthélemy
R.N. Bol
S. Bonnier
D. Boulanger
A. Brogi
M.V. Cengarle
M.M.T. Chakravarty
M. Codish
P. Codognet
P. Dague
B. Demoen
A. De Niel
P. Deransart
D. De Schreye
R. Dietrich
E. Domenjoud
M. Dorochevsky
H. Emmelmann
C. Fecht
C. Ferdinand
U. Fraus
L. Fribourg
M. Fujita
S. Gastinger
M. Gengenbach
U. Geske
R. Giacobazzi
J. Grosch
Y. Guo
G. Gupta
J. Hannan
F. Henglein
A.V. Hense
L. Hermosilla
A. Herold
W. Hesse
K. Hirano
K. Hirata
J.-M. Hufflen
J. Hughes
H. Hußmann
N. Ichiyoshi
J.-P. Jacquot
D. Jana
G. Janssens
P. Kilpeläinen
H. Kirchner
F. Klay
E. Klein
M. Koshimura
U. Lechner
H.C.R. Lock
M. Maeda
J. Małuszyński
P. Mancarella
R. Manthey
L. Maranget
B. Martens
M. Meier
A. Mück
F. Nickl
U. Nilsson
A. Ohsuga
J. Paakki
C. Palamidessi
D. Parigot
R. Paterson
D. Pedreschi
H. Perkmann
H. Peterreins
S. Prestwich
M. Raber
I. Ramakrisnan
B. Reus
O. Ridoux
M. Rittri
H. Rohtla
K.H. Rose
G. Sander
P.-Y. Schoebbens
K. Sieber
M. Simons
R. Stabl
H. Sugano
A. Takeuchi
T. Tammet
H. Tsuda
H. Ueda
E. Ukkonen
P. Van Hentenryck
M. Vittek
M. Weber

QMW Library
23 1036849 X

Lecture Notes in Computer Science

Edited by G. Goos and J. Hartmanis

Advisory Board: W. Brauer D. Gries J. Stoer

QA66.5 LEC/631

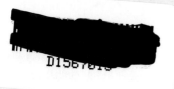

WITHDRAWN
FROM STOCK
QMUL LIBRARY

DATE DUE FOR RETURN

NEW ACCESSION
CANCELLED

13 MAR 1996

18. JUN. 1993

08. NOV 93

17 JUN 1994

30 SEP 1994

13 MAY 1997

WITHDRAWN
FROM STOCK
QMUL LIBRARY

Table of Contents

Integration

System Demonstrations

Improving Control of Logic Programs by Using Functional Logic Languages

Michael Hanus

Max-Planck-Institut für Informatik
Im Stadtwald
W-6600 Saarbrücken, Germany
e-mail: michael@mpi-sb.mpg.de

Abstract. This paper shows the advantages of amalgamating functional and logic programming languages. In comparison with pure functional languages, an amalgamated functional logic language has more expressive power. In comparison with pure logic languages, functional logic languages have a better control behaviour. The latter will be shown by presenting methods to translate logic programs into a functional logic language with a narrowing/rewriting semantics. The translated programs produce the same set of answers and have at least the same efficiency as the original programs. But in many cases the control behaviour of the translated programs is improved. This requires the addition of further knowledge to the programs. We discuss methods for this and show the gain in efficiency by means of several examples.

1 Introduction

Many proposals have been made to integrate functional and logic programming languages during the last years (see [3, 11] for surveys). Recently, these proposals became relevant for practical applications because efficient implementations have been developed [5, 8, 19, 33, 35, 48]. This raises the natural question for the advantages of such amalgamated languages. In comparison with pure functional languages, functional logic languages have more expressive power due to the availability of features like function inversion, partial data structures and logic variables [42]. In comparison with pure logic languages, functional logic languages allow to specify functional dependencies and to use nested functional expressions. Although this improves the readability of logic programs, it is not clear whether this is only a minor syntactic improvement (which can be added to logic languages by a simple preprocessor [37]) or there is a genuine advantage of functional logic languages compared to pure logic languages. In this paper we show that the latter is true: functional logic languages have a better operational behaviour than logic languages. We show this by presenting methods to translate logic programs into a functional logic language. These methods ensure that the translated programs produce the same set of answers and have at least the same efficiency as the original programs. But in many cases the translation improves the control behaviour of logic programs which will be demonstrated by several examples.

```
sort(L,M) :- perm(L,M), ord(M).

perm([],[]).
perm([E|L],[F|M]) :- del(F,[E|L],N), perm(N,M).

del(E,[E|L],L).
del(E,[F|L],[F|M]) :- del(E,L,M).

ord([]).
ord([E]).
ord([E,F|L]) :- le(E,F), ord([F|L]).

le(0,E).
le(s(E),s(F)) :- le(E,F).
```

Figure 1. Permutation sort (natural numbers are represented by s-terms)

Logic programming allows the specification of problems at an abstract level and permits the execution of the specifications. However, these specifications are often very slowly executed because a lot of search is performed under the standard Prolog computation rule. For instance, Figure 1 specifies the notion of a sorted list (cf. [44], p. 55): a list `M` is a sorted version of a list `L` if `M` is a permutation of `L` and all elements of `M` are in ascending order. We can use this Prolog program to sort the list `[4,3,2,1]` by solving the query `?- sort([4,3,2,1],S)`. But this runs very inefficiently under the standard computation rule because all permutations must be enumerated and tested in order to solve this goal.

Therefore several proposals have been made in order to improve the control of Prolog programs. Naish [36] has extended the standard computation model of Prolog by a coroutining mechanism. He allows the addition of "wait" declarations to predicates. Such declarations have the effect that the resolution of a literal is delayed until the arguments are sufficiently instantiated. If a variable of a delayed literal is bound to a non-variable term, this literal is woken and executed in the next step if it is now sufficiently instantiated. In the permutation sort example, the programmer can add a wait declaration to the predicate `ord` and change the ordering in the first clause into

```
sort(L,M) :- ord(M), perm(L,M).
```

Now the goal `?- sort([3,2,1],S)` is executed in the following way: After the application of the first clause to this goal the literal `ord(S)` is delayed and the literal `perm([3,2,1],S)` will be executed. If `S` is bound to the first part of a permutation of `[3,2,1]` (i.e., a list with two elements and a variable at the tail), then `ord(S)` is activated. If the first two elements of `S` are in the wrong order, then the computation fails and another permutation is tried, otherwise `ord` is delayed again until the next part of the permutation is generated. Thus with this modification not *all* permutations are completely computed and therefore the execution time is better than in the naive approach. Naish has also presented an algorithm which generates the wait declarations from a given program and transforms the program by reordering the goals in a clause. Although this approach seems to be attractive, it has some problems. For instance, the generation of wait declarations is based on heuristics and therefore it is unclear whether these heuristics are generally successful. Moreover, it is possible that the annotated program flounders, i.e., all goals are delayed which is considered as a run-time error. Hence completeness of SLD-resolution can be lost when transforming a logic program into a program with wait declarations (see example at the end of Section 3.3 or the `goodpath` example in [46]).

Another approach to improve control has been developed by Bruynooghe's group [7]. They try to avoid the overhead of coroutining execution by transforming a logic program with coroutining into a logic program with an equivalent behaviour executed under the standard computation rule. The transformation is done in several steps. In the first step a symbolic trace tree of a goal is created where the user has to decide which literal is selected and whether a literal is completely executed or only a single resolution step is made, i.e., the user must supply the system with a *good computation rule*. If a goal in the trace tree is a renaming of a goal in an ancestor node, an arc from this goal to the ancestor node is inserted. This results in a symbolic trace graph which is then reduced and in the last step translated into a logic program simulating the symbolic trace under the standard computation rule. The crucial point in this approach is to find a *good* computation rule for the program with respect to the initial goal. In a recent paper [46] a method for the automated generation of an efficient computation rule is presented. The method is based on a global analysis of the program by abstract interpretation techniques in order to derive the necessary information. Since the arguments for choosing a "good" computation rule are heuristics, it is unclear whether the transformed programs are in any case more efficient than the original ones. Another problem is due to the fact that their method uses a given call pattern for the initial goal. Therefore different versions of the program are generated for different call modes of the goal.

In this paper we propose a much simpler method to improve control of logic programs. This method ensures that the new programs have at least the same efficiency as the original ones. But for a large class of programs ("generate-and-test" programs like permutation sort) we obtain a better efficiency similar to other approaches to improve control. The basic idea is to use a functional logic language and to translate logic programs into functional programs (without considering the initial goal). The motivation for the integration of functional and logic programming languages is to combine the advantages of both programming paradigms in one language: the possibility of *solving* predicates and equations between terms together with the efficient *reduction* paradigm of functional languages. A lot of the proposed amalgamations of functional and logic languages are based on Horn clause logic with equality [40] where the user can define predicates by Horn clauses and functions by (conditional) equations. Predicates are often omitted because they can be represented as Boolean functions. A complete operational semantics is based on the narrowing rule [14, 29, 30]: *narrowing* combines unification of logic languages with rewriting of functional languages, i.e., a narrowing step consists of the unification of a subterm of the goal with the left-hand side of an equation, replacing this subterm by the right-hand side of the equation and applying the unifier to the whole goal. Since we have to take into account *all* subterms of a goal in the next narrowing step, this naive strategy produces a large search space and is less efficient than SLD-resolution (SLD stands for selecting *one* literal in the next resolution step). Also the advantage of functional languages, namely the deterministic reduction principle, is lost by this naive approach.

Therefore a lot of research has been done to improve the narrowing strategy without loosing completeness. Hullot [29] has shown that the restriction to *basic* subterms, i.e., subterms which are not created during unification, is complete. Fribourg [15] has proved that the restriction to subterms at innermost positions is also complete provided that all functions are reducible on all ground terms. Finally, Hölldobler [28] has proved completeness of the combination of basic and innermost narrowing where a so-called innermost reflection rule must be added for partially defined functions. But innermost basic narrowing is not better than SLD-resolution since it has been shown that innermost basic narrowing corresponds to SLD-resolution if a functional program is translated into a logic program by flattening [6]. On the other hand, we can also translate a logic program into a functional one without loosing efficiency if we use the innermost basic narrowing strategy. But now we are able to improve the execution by simplifying the goal by deterministic rewriting before a narrowing step is applied (rewriting is similar to reduction in functional languages with the difference that rewriting is also applied to terms containing variables). The simplification phase cuts down the search space without loosing completeness [28, 39].

We will see in the next sections that the operational behaviour of innermost basic narrowing combined with simplification is similar to SLD-resolution with a particular dynamic control rule. Hence we get an improvement in the execution comparable to previous approaches [7, 36] but with the following advantages:

- The translation technique from logic programs into functional logic programs is simple.
- It is ensured that the translated programs have at least the same efficiency as the original ones. For many programs the efficiency is much better.
- It is ensured that we do not loose completeness: there exists an answer w.r.t. the translated program iff there exists an answer w.r.t. the original program.

The last remark is only true if we use a fair computation strategy. If we use a backtracking implementation of SLD-resolution as in Prolog, the completeness may be lost because of infinite computations. However, infinite paths in the search tree can be cut by the simplification process [15], i.e., it is also possible that we obtain an answer from the functional logic program where the original logic program does not terminate.

These theoretical considerations are only relevant if there is an implementation of the functional logic language which has the same efficiency as current Prolog implementations. Fortunately, this is the case. In [19, 21, 24] it has been shown that it is possible to implement a functional logic language very efficiently by extending the currently known Prolog implementation techniques [47]. The language

ALF ("**A**lgebraic **L**ogic **F**unctional language") is based on the operational semantics sketched above. Innermost basic narrowing and simplification is implemented without overhead in comparison to Prolog's computation strategy, i.e., functional programs are executed with the same efficiency as their relational equivalents by SLD-resolution (see [21] for benchmarks). Therefore it is justified to improve the control of logic programs by translation into a functional logic language.

In the next section we give a precise description of ALF's operational semantics and in Section 3 we present our approach to improve control of logic programs in more detail.

2 Operational semantics of ALF

As mentioned in the previous section, we want to improve the control behaviour of logic programs by translating them into a functional logic language. We have also mentioned that in order to compete with SLD-resolution we have to use a functional logic language with a refined operational semantics, namely innermost basic narrowing and simplification. Hence the target language of the translation process is the language ALF [19, 21] which is based on this semantics. ALF has more features than actually used in this paper, e.g., a module system with parameterization, a type system based on many-sorted logic, predicates which are resolved by resolution etc. (see [25] for details). In the following we outline the operational semantics of ALF in order to understand the translation scheme presented in the next sections.

ALF is a constructor-based language, i.e., the user must specify for each symbol whether it is a constructor or a defined function. Constructors must not be the outermost symbol of the left-hand side of a defining equation, i.e., constructor terms are always irreducible. Hence constructors are used to build data types, and defined functions are operations on these data types (similarly to functional languages like ML [27] or Miranda [45]). The distinction between constructors and defined function symbols is necessary to define the notion of an *innermost position* [15].

An ALF program consists of a set of (conditional) equations which are used in two ways. In a narrowing step an equation is applied to *compute a solution* of a goal (i.e., variables in the goal may be bound to terms), whereas in a rewrite step an equation is applied to *simplify* a goal (i.e., without binding goal variables). Therefore we distinguish between *narrowing rules* (equations applied in narrowing steps) and *rewrite rules* (equations applied in rewrite steps). Usually, all conditional equations of an ALF program are used as narrowing and rewrite rules, but it is also possible to specify rules which are only used for rewriting. Typically, these rules are inductive axioms or CWA-valid axioms (see below). The application of such rules for simplification can reduce the search space and is justified if we are interested in ground-valid answers [15, 39] (i.e., answers which are valid for each ground substitution applied to it).

Figure 2 shows an ALF module to sort a list of naturals. Naturals are represented by the constructors `0` and `s`, `true` and `false` are the constructors of the data type

```
module isort.

  datatype bool = { true ; false }.
  datatype nat  = { 0 ; s(nat) }.
  datatype list = { '.'(nat,list) ; [] }.

  func isort  : list      -> list;
       insert : nat, list -> list;
       le     : nat, nat  -> bool.
rules.
  isort([])     = [].
  isort([E|L]) = insert(E,isort(L)).

  insert(E,[])      = [E].
  insert(E,[F|L]) = [E,F|L]              :- le(E,F) = true.
  insert(E,[F|L]) = [F|insert(E,L)]  :- le(E,F) = false.

  le(0,N)          = true.
  le(s(N),0)       = false.
  le(s(M),s(N)) = le(M,N).

end isort.
```

Figure 2. ALF program for insertion sort

`bool` and lists are defined as in Prolog. The defined functions of this module are `isort` to sort a list of naturals, `insert` to insert an element in an ordered list, and `le` to compare two naturals.

The *declarative semantics* of ALF is the well-known Horn clause logic with equality as to be found in [40]. The *operational semantics* of ALF is based on innermost basic narrowing and rewriting.[1] Before a narrowing step is applied, the goal is simplified to normal form by applying rewrite rules. We will distinguish two kinds of nondeterminism by the keywords "don't know" and "don't care": *don't know* indicates a branching point in the computation where all alternatives must be explored (in parallel or by a backtracking strategy in a concrete implementation); *don't care* indicates a branching point where it is sufficient to select (nondeterministically) one alternative and disregard all other possibilities.

In order to give a precise definition of the operational semantics, we represent a goal (a list of equations to be solved) by a skeleton and an environment part [28, 39]: the *skeleton* is a list of equations composed of terms occurring in the original program, and the *environment* is a substitution which has to be applied to the equations in order to obtain the actual goal. The initial goal G is represented by the pair $\langle G; id\rangle$ where id is the identity substitution. The following scheme describes the operational semantics (if π is a position in a term t, then $t|_\pi$ denotes the subterm of t at position π and $t[s]_\pi$ denotes the term obtained by replacing the subterm $t|_\pi$ by s in t [12]; π is called an *innermost position* of t if the subterm $t|_\pi$ has a defined function

[1] Similarly to EQLOG [18], ALF allows also the definition of predicates which are solved by resolution, but we omit this aspect in the current paper.

symbol at the top and all argument terms consist of variables and constructors). Let $\langle E_1, \ldots, E_n ; \sigma \rangle$ be a given goal ($E_1, \ldots, E_n$ are the skeleton equations and σ is the environment):

1. Select *don't care* a non-variable position π in E_1 and a new variant $l = r \leftarrow C$ of a rewrite rule such that σ' is a substitution with $\sigma(E_1|_\pi) = \sigma'(l)$ and the goal $\langle C ; \sigma' \rangle$ can be derived to the empty goal without instantiating any variables from $\sigma(E_1)$. Then
$$\langle E_1[\sigma'(r)]_\pi, E_2, \ldots, E_n ; \sigma \rangle$$
is the next goal derived by **rewriting**; go to 1.[2] Otherwise go to 2.
2. If the two sides of equation E_1 have different constructors at the same outer position (a position not belonging to arguments of functions), then the whole goal is **rejected**, i.e., the proof fails. Otherwise go to 3.
3. Let π be the leftmost-innermost position in E_1 (if there exists no such position in E_1, go to 4). Select *don't know* (a) or (b):
   (a) Select *don't know* a new variant $l = r \leftarrow C$ of a narrowing rule such that $\sigma(E_1|_\pi)$ and l are unifiable with mgu σ'. Then
   $$\langle C, E_1[r]_\pi, E_2, \ldots, E_n ; \sigma' \circ \sigma \rangle$$
   is the next goal derived by **innermost basic narrowing**; go to 1. Otherwise: fail.
   (b) Let x be a new variable and σ' be the substitution $\{x \mapsto \sigma(E_1|_\pi)\}$. Then
   $$\langle E_1[x]_\pi, E_2, \ldots, E_n ; \sigma' \circ \sigma \rangle$$
   is the next goal derived by **innermost reflection**; go to 3 (this corresponds to the elimination of an innermost redex [28] and is called "null narrowing step" in [6]).
4. If E_1 is the equation $s = t$ and there is a mgu σ' for $\sigma(s)$ and $\sigma(t)$, then
$$\langle E_2, \ldots, E_n ; \sigma' \circ \sigma \rangle$$
is the next goal derived by **reflection**; go to 1. Otherwise: fail.

The attribute *basic* of a narrowing step emphasizes that a narrowing step is only applied at a position of the original program and not at positions introduced by substitutions [29]. The innermost reflection rule need not be applied to completely defined functions, i.e., functions which are reducible on all ground terms of appropriate sorts [15, 28]. Therefore the innermost reflection rule can be avoided by using types and checking whether each function is sufficiently defined for all constructors of their argument types. Since ALF is a typed language and allows such tests, we implicitly assume in this paper that the sufficiently definedness tests are performed

[2] Rewriting is only applied to the first literal, but this is no restriction since a conjunction like E_1, E_2, E_3 can also be written as an equation $and(E_1, and(E_2, E_3)) = true$. This technique will be used in the following sections.

at compile time in order to avoid unnecessary applications of the innermost reflection rule at run time.

This operational semantics is sound and complete if the term rewriting relation generated by the conditional equations is *canonical* (i.e., confluent and terminating [12]) and the condition and the right-hand sides of the conditional equations do not contain *extra-variables* [28]. Moreover, the conditional equations must be *reductive*, i.e., the conditions must be smaller than the left-hand side w.r.t. some termination ordering (otherwise basic conditional narrowing may be incomplete as Middeldorp and Hamoen [34] have pointed out).[3] If a program has conditional equations with extra-variables, there may be other criteria to ensure completeness (e.g., level-confluence [17] or decreasing rules [13]) or it may be possible to transform the program into an equivalent program for which this operational semantics is complete (e.g., Bertling and Ganzinger [4] have proposed such a method). Therefore we allow extra-variables in conditional equations which is the reason for the instantiation condition in the rewrite step.

Rewriting in ALF is applied from innermost to outermost positions, i.e., rewriting corresponds to eager evaluation in functional languages. Similarly to Prolog, ALF uses a backtracking strategy to implement the choices of different clauses in a narrowing step. Hence the theoretical completeness will be lost due to infinite computations, but for finite search trees the operational semantics is complete. Due to the requirement for a canonical and reductive set of equations, the normal form of a term uniquely exists and can be computed by rewriting with an arbitrary matching equation in a rewrite step. Therefore the creation of choice points is only necessary in narrowing steps.

We have mentioned in the introduction that it is also possible to translate functional programs into logic programs by flattening and to execute these programs by SLD-resolution [6]. ALF's operational semantics has the following advantages in comparison to that and other techniques:

- Since rewriting is a deterministic process (or it can be also seen as "don't care" nondeterminism) and rewriting is done before narrowing, deterministic computations are performed whenever it is possible. This avoids superfluous creation of choice points. Nondeterministic computations are only performed if it is necessary, i.e., if a solution (binding of a goal variable) must be guessed by an application of a narrowing rule.
- A similar behaviour can be achieved in Prolog by inserting delays [36, 37]. But this has the disadvantage that the program with delays may flounder which corresponds to incompleteness. This cannot be the case in ALF because of ALF's complete operational semantics.
- The residuation principle of Le Fun [1] is also related to ALF's operational semantics: If a Le Fun function is applied to a variable argument, the application is delayed until the variable becomes bound to a non-variable term. But this

[3] The requirement for reductive conditional equations is not a real restriction since tools for checking canonicity of conditional equations usually have this requirement [16].

semantics is also incomplete in some cases. For instance, if **append** is a function that concatenates two lists, we can extract the last element `E` of a given list `L` by solving the equation

```
append(_,[E]) = L
```

Residuation will delay this computation (since the first argument is always unbound) and we obtain no result for `E`. But ALF will solve this goal by narrowing and rewriting and delivers the unique solution for `E`. Moreover, the residuation principle of Le Fun may produce an infinite search space for examples where ALF's or Prolog's operational semantics has a finite search space [23].

- Similarly to ALF, the Andorra computation model [26] prefers deterministic computations before nondeterministic ones. However, the rewriting mechanism of ALF yields deterministic computations also when more than one clause matches (see **max** example in section 3.3) and may *delete* goals with infinite or nondeterministic computations. E.g., if `X*0=0` is a defining equation for the function `*`, then a term like t`*0` will be simplified to `0`, i.e., the entire subterm t will be deleted. This is important if t contains unevaluated functions with variable arguments. The same is true for the relation of ALF and Prolog with Simplification [9]: ALF's rewriting mechanism is more general than simplification because unifiable (but confluent) equations, equations with deleting left-hand side variables and conditional equations are admissible rewrite rules in ALF.
- It is also important to note that ALF's operational semantics can be implemented with the same efficiency as current Prolog implementations [21]. The overhead of searching the next innermost subterm can be avoided by using a stack of references to subterms in the goal (see [19] and [21] for details).

These arguments gives us the feeling that the computation principle of ALF is more efficient than Prolog's SLD-resolution. In the next section we will show how logic programs can be translated into ALF programs and what we gain from such a translation.

3 Translating logic programs into functional programs

There are two principle ways to translate a logic program into a functional one:

1. We consider each predicate as a Boolean function and translate the Horn clauses of each predicate into a functional expression over the Booleans.
2. We try to find out functional dependencies between the arguments of a predicate. If there is such a dependency, we transform the predicate into function from input to output arguments, otherwise we transform the predicate into a Boolean function.

The second method is clearly an extension of the first one. The first method is very simple and always applicable, but we will also show techniques for the second translation method.

Example: The predicates **member** and **append** are defined by the following logic program:

```
member(E,[E|L]).
member(E,[F|L]) :- member(E,L).
append([],L,L).
append([E|R],L,[E|RL]) :- append(R,L,RL).
```

We can translate this program into a functional program by the first method:

```
func member: term, term → bool
member(E,[E|L]) = true.
member(E,[F|L]) = true :- member(E,L) = true.
func append: term, term, term → bool
append([],L,L) = true.
append([E|R],L,[E|RL]) = true :- append(R,L,RL) = true.
```

But we can also perceive that the first and the second argument of **append** determine the value of the third argument, i.e., there is a functional dependency between the arguments of **append**. Therefore it is possible to translate **append** into the following function definition:

```
func append: term, term → term
append([],L)      = L.
append([E|R],L) = [E|append(R,L)].
```

In the following we will discuss both methods in more detail.

3.1 Translating all predicates into Boolean functions

In this section we discuss the simple approach where each n-ary predicate is translated into an n-ary Boolean function. We define the translation of logic programs into functional programs by the following rules:

Facts:	L.	⇒	L = true.
Clauses:	L :- $L_1,\ldots,L_n$.	⇒	L = true :- (L_1 and ⋯ and L_n) = true.
Goals:	?- $L_1,\ldots,L_n$.	⇒	?- (L_1 and ⋯ and L_n) = true.

The Boolean values together with the function **and** are defined in Figure 3.[4] Since the right-hand side of each equation in the translated program is the constant `true`, we get immediately the following property of the translated programs:[5]

[4] The declaration "`infixright 650`" defines the symbol "and" as a right-associative infix operator with priority 650. This has the similar effect as the declaration `op(650,xfy,and)` in Prolog.

[5] In this paper we do not deal with the problem of proving termination of the narrowing/rewrite rules since ALF's operational semantics does also work for nonterminating programs. Moreover, the correspondence of narrowing and resolution derivations [6] is also valid for nonterminating programs. But note that the operational semantics may be incomplete for some nonterminating programs and therefore we implicitly assume that the rewrite relation is terminating and all conditional rules are reductive.

```
module bool.

  datatype bool = { true ; false }.

  func and : bool, bool -> bool infixright 650.
rules.
  false and B       = false.
  true  and B       = B.
  B     and false = false.
  B     and true  = B.
end bool.
```

Figure 3. Module for Boolean values

Proposition 1. *If R is the set of conditional equations obtained by translating a logic program with the above translation scheme, then R is confluent.*

Hence we can use the translated equations as narrowing rules and solve the translated goals by innermost basic narrowing. But what is the relation between narrowing derivations of the functional program and resolution derivations of the original logic programs? Bosco et al. [6] have shown that there is a strong relationship between these derivations, i.e., every innermost basic narrowing derivation of a functional program corresponds to an SLD-resolution derivation with the leftmost selection rule if the functional program is appropriately flattened into a logic program. Applying their result to our framework we obtain the following proposition (actually, they have proved the correspondence for unconditional equations but it is not difficult to extend it to the conditional case):

Proposition 2. *Let P be a logic program and R be the set of conditional equations obtained by translating P. For each goal G and each SLD-resolution with the leftmost selection rule there is a corresponding innermost basic narrowing sequence for the translated goal G' where each resolution step corresponds to an innermost basic narrowing step together with at most one application of the equation "*`true and B = B`*".*

Hence the logic program and its functional version have the same efficiency (if we neglect the simple application of the equation "`true and B = B`") and produce the same set of answers. But the efficiency of the functional version can be improved by adding rewrite rules. We know from Section 2 that we can add the narrowing rules also as rewrite rules and perform rewriting between narrowing steps without loosing completeness. Rewriting can be done in a deterministic way, i.e., it is not necessary to generate choice points during rewriting and therefore rewriting may reduce the search space. For instance, if the functional program contains the equations

```
member(E,[E|L]) = true.
member(E,[F|L]) = true :- member(E,L) = true.
```

both as narrowing rules and rewrite rules, the goal

```
?- member(2,[1,2,3]) = true.
```

is proved by rewriting without generating any choice point. Note that two choice points are generated during the corresponding SLD-resolution (using standard implementation techniques [47]).

Since rewriting cannot bind any goal variable (a rewrite rule is applicable if the left-hand side of the equation *matches* the current subterm), it can only be applied as a *test* and then it avoids the search for alternative proofs of this test. This is a slight improvement and does not justify the translation from the well-known Prolog framework into the new functional logic framework. For instance, if we translate the permutation sort program in Figure 1, the functional version is executed in the same slow way as the relational version. The improvement of the control behaviour in the framework of Naish [36] or Bruynooghe [7] is due to the fact that the failure of a goal is detected early in the computation. Therefore we must add negative information to our functional program. This will be outlined in the next section.

3.2 Adding negative information

For the case that we are interested in valid answers w.r.t. the least Herbrand model, which is a natural assumption in logic programming [32], Fribourg [15] has shown that we can add equations which are valid w.r.t. the so-called "Closed World Assumption" (*CWA-valid*) as rewrite rules to our program. The operational semantics is still sound w.r.t. ground-valid answers, i.e., answers which are valid for each ground substitution applied to it. A conditional equation

$$L \texttt{ = false :- } L_1 \texttt{ and } \cdots \texttt{ and } L_n \texttt{ = true.}$$

is called *CWA-valid* w.r.t. a set of conditional equations R if for any ground constructor substitution σ

$$R \models \sigma(L) \texttt{ = true :- } \sigma(L_1) \texttt{ and } \cdots \texttt{ and } \sigma(L_n) \texttt{ = true}$$

does not hold (later we will also allow equations of the form L`=false` in the condition part; CWA-validity of such clauses is similarly defined). If we rewrite a literal L`=true` to the equation `false=true` by CWA-valid rewrite rules, we can immediately reject the whole goal (compare the "rejection" rule in Section 2). This technique does not affect the completeness of the operational semantics but can be an essential improvement. For instance, consider the following clauses [15] (`a`, `b` and `c` are constructors):

```
on(a,b) = true.
on(b,c) = true.
above(X,Y) = true :- on(X,Y) = true.
above(X,Y) = true :- above(X,Z) and on(Z,Y) = true.
```

The execution of the goal `?- above(a,a) = true` leads to an infinite loop. If the CWA-valid equation `above(X,X) = false` is inserted into the set of rewrite rules, the goal `?- above(a,a) = true` is first rewritten into `?- false = true` and then it fails by the rejection rule.

As a further example, consider the following set of rules defining the predicates **even** and **le** (less-or-equal):

```
even(0) = true.
even(s(s(N))) = true :- even(N) = true.
le(0,N) = true.
le(s(M),s(N)) = true :- le(M,N) = true.
```

The execution of the goal **?- even(N) and le(N,s(s(0))) = true** leads to an infinite loop after producing the answers **N=0** and **N=s(s(0))**, because the predicate **even** generates an infinite number of even naturals. In order to avoid this loop, we may add the CWA-valid equation **le(s(N),0) = false**. But this does not solve the problem because there is the following infinite derivation (the narrowed subterms are underlined):

```
?- even(N) and le(N,s(s(0))) = true.
?- even(N1) = true, true and le(s(s(N1)),s(s(0))) = true.
?- even(N2) = true, true = true,
                    true and le(s(s(s(s(N2)))),s(s(0))) = true.
...
```

The reason for this infinite derivation is that only the first literal of a goal is simplified by rewriting (cf. Section 2).[6] But this is no real problem since we can also translate the original logic program for **even** and **le** in the following way:

```
even(0) = true.
even(s(s(N))) = even(N).
le(0,N) = true.
le(s(M),s(N)) = le(M,N).
```

Now we obtain the following derivation with the additional CWA-valid rewrite rule **le(s(N),0) = false**:

```
?- even(N) and le(N,s(s(0))) = true.
        narrowing with the second equation for even
?- even(N1) and le(s(s(N1)),s(s(0))) = true.
        simplifying the goal
?- even(N1) and le(N1,0) = true.
        narrowing with the second equation for even
?- even(N2) and le(s(s(N2)),0) = true.
        simplifying the goal:
?- false = true.
        failure by rejection
```

Hence the search space of this goal is finite in contrast to the original Prolog program. In order to implement the improved proof strategy, we simply modify our translation scheme for clauses:

---

[6] This is for the sake of an efficient implementation [21] because rewriting the whole goal allows less optimizations during the compilation phase.

```
sort(L,M) = perm(L,M) and ord(M).
perm([],[])         = true.
perm([E|L],[F|M]) = del(F,[E|L],N) and perm(N,M).
del(E,[E|L],L)      = true.
del(E,[F|L],[F|M]) = del(E,L,M).
ord([])       = true.
ord([E])      = true.
ord([E,F|L]) = le(E,F) and ord([F|L]).
le(0,E)          = true.
le(s(E),s(F)) = le(E,F).
```

Figure 4. Functional version of permutation sort

Translation of clauses: Let L `:-` L_1`,`...`,`L_n be a clause for which one of the following conditions holds:

1. L is not unifiable with the head of any variant of another clause of the logic program.
2. If there are a variant of another clause L' `:-` L'_1`,`...`,`L'_m and a unifier σ for L and L', then the goals `?-` $\sigma(L_1$ `and` $\cdots$ `and` $L_n)$ `= true` and `?-` $\sigma(L'_1$ `and` $\cdots$ `and` $L'_m)$ `= true` can be rewritten to the same goal using the rewrite rules corresponding to the logic program w.r.t. the old translation scheme (*confluence of clauses*).

Then the clause is translated into the equation

L `= (`L_1 `and` $\cdots$ `and` L_n`).`

otherwise it is translated into the conditional equation

L `= true :- (`L_1 `and` $\cdots$ `and` L_n`) = true.`

Note that this modified translation is only necessary because of the restricted rewriting in ALF. If we use another functional logic language which performs rewriting on the whole goal (like SLOG [15]), this modification is superfluous. The conditions guarantee that the translated program is confluent, i.e., Proposition 1 holds also for the modified translation scheme. Figure 4 shows the translation of the logic permutation sort program of Figure 1. Note that this is nearly the same program which Fribourg [15] has presented in a rather ad-hoc manner.

The final problem is the generation of CWA-valid rules for rewriting. For instance, from the given rules

```
le(0,E) = true.
le(s(E),s(F)) = le(E,F).
```

we have to generate the CWA-valid rule

```
le(s(E),0) = false.
```

In this case it can be done by inspecting the constructors of the argument terms of the left-hand side, and then generating `false` rules for all constructor terms on which `le` is not reducible. Fortunately, there is also a systematic method for doing this in general. *Intensional negation* [2] is a transformation technique which synthesizes clauses for new predicates p'_i from a given logic program for the predicates p_i. The new predicates p'_i describe the finite failure set of the original predicates p_i and hence they are a computable approximation of the CWA-valid literals [32]. E.g., given the clauses

```
even(0).
even(s(s(X))) :- even(X).
```

intensional negation generates the new clauses

```
even'(s(0)).
even'(s(s(X))) :- even'(X).
```

which define the odd numbers. If we translate the predicate `even'(···)` into `even(···) = false`, we obtain the CWA-valid rewrite rule used in our `even` example above.

We do not propose to compute the intensional negation of all defined predicates since this leads to a large number of additional rewrite rules. Moreover, intensional negation does not generate Horn clauses for the negated predicates if the original clauses contain local variables in their bodies (see [2] for details). But in most cases it is possible and sufficient to compute the negation of some *base predicates.* For instance, from the given definition of the less-or-equal predicate `le` in Figure 1 we obtain by intensional negation the CWA-valid rule

```
le(s(X),0) = false.
```

If we add this single rule as a rewrite rule to the narrowing/rewrite rules of Figure 4, the computation is automatically optimized without control instructions: as soon as the variable `M` in the goal `perm([···],M) and ord(M) = true` is bound to a partial list `[`a`,`b`|L]` with a greater than b, the goal is simplified by rewriting as follows:

```
perm([···],[a,b|L]) and ord([a,b|L]) = true
⟹ perm([···],[a,b|L]) and le(a,b) and ord([b|L]) = true
⟹ perm([···],[a,b|L]) and false and ord([b|L]) = true
⟹ perm([···],[a,b|L]) and false = true
⟹ false = true
```

Hence not all permutations are enumerated but the computation of a permutation immediately stops if two consecutive elements are in the wrong order. Thus we have obtained the same improved operational behaviour as in related approaches [7, 36] in a simple and declarative way. The following table shows the execution times in seconds to sort the list `[`n`,...,2,1]` for different values of n:

Length of the list:	5	6	7	8	9	10
Original logic program (Figure 1)	0.10	0.65	4.63	37.92	348.70	3569.50
Translated functional program (Figure 4)	0.10	0.27	0.61	1.43	3.28	7.43

Both the original logic version and the functional version were executed by the ALF system since ALF also allows the definition of predicates which are executed as in

Prolog (pure logic ALF programs are translated into code of an abstract machine as described in [47]).

Using our method we can translate arbitrary logic programs into functional programs. An essential speeding up will be obtained for the class of "generate-and-test" programs like the permutation sort above, the classical 8-queens problem or the goodpath program of [46].

3.3 A more sophisticated translation scheme

Until now we have simply translated predicates into Boolean functions. But it is often the case that a programmer has a function in mind but must write it down as a predicate in a logic program. Any n-ary function can be expressed as a $(n+1)$-ary relation by adding the result as an additional argument. For instance, the concatenation of two lists is a function from two list arguments into another list. It can be defined in a functional language with pattern-matching by the equations

```
conc([],L)     = L.
conc([E|R],L) = [E|conc(R,L)].
```

Since Prolog does not allow the definition of functions and nested expressions, a Prolog programmer must express the concatenation as a predicate with three arguments and writes down the following clauses:

```
append([],L,L).
append([E|R],L,[E|RL]) :- append(R,L,RL).
```

Innermost basic narrowing execution of the first program is equivalent to the Prolog execution of the append clauses. But the additional simplification mechanism of the functional evaluation can avoid infinite loops which may occur in the relational evaluation. For instance, Naish [36] has noted that the following goal causes an infinite loop under the standard Prolog evaluation rule for any order of literals and clauses:

```
?- append([1|V],W,X), append(X,Y,[2|Z]).
```

But the evaluation of the equivalent conc equation causes a fail and does not loop:

```
?- conc(conc([1|V],W),Y) = [2|Z].
```

simplifying the goal by two applications of the second conc *rule:*

```
?- [1|conc(conc(V,W),Y)] = [2|Z].
```

failure by rejection since 1 *and* 2 *are different constructor terms*

Note that the failure situation is detected without any additional CWA-valid rule. The only knowledge used here is the fact that constructor terms are irreducible and therefore different constructor terms cannot denote the same object. This knowledge is expressed by the rejection rule (Section 2).

We see from this example that it is desirable to declare predicates with functional dependencies between arguments as functions from input to output arguments and not as Boolean functions. Since we use a functional logic language with a complete operational semantics, this does not restrict the class of evaluable goals.

If a programmer writes down a program, he has the functional dependencies between data in mind. Thus he can directly define the functions if he uses a functional logic language like ALF. But it is also possible to find functional dependencies in a given Prolog program. In general, a functional dependency is an undecidable property of a logic program [38]. However, in particular cases one can find sufficient criteria for that. For instance, Reddy [41] has proposed a technique for transforming logic programs into functional ones. However, his technique is based on modes for the predicates in the logic program which obviously restricts the application of his method (e.g., if a predicate is called in two different modes, two different functions are generated for that predicate). Debray and Warren [10] have proposed a technique to detect functional computations in logic programs. It is also based on modes and tries to find out mutual exclusions between different clauses of a predicate. We do not want to discuss the detection of functional dependencies in more detail but give another sufficient criterion for this property.

Let p be an n-ary predicate. If we suppose that the first $n-1$ arguments determine the value of the last argument (the generalization to other argument combinations is straightforward), we modify our translation scheme of Section 3.1 in the following way. Instead of defining p as an n-ary Boolean function, we define p as an $(n-1)$-ary function and perform the following transformation steps:

1. Every literal $p(t_1, \ldots, t_n)$ in a clause or in the goal is replaced by the equation $p(t_1, \ldots, t_{n-1}) = t_n$.
2. If we have generated an equation $p(t_1, \ldots, t_{n-1}) = X$ in the body of a clause and X is a variable which does not occur in the left-hand side of the clause head, all occurrences of X in the clause are replaced by the term $p(t_1, \ldots, t_{n-1})$ and the equation is deleted
3. If we have generated an equation $p(t_1, \ldots, t_{n-1}) = X$ in the goal and X is a variable, then all occurrences of X in the goal are replaced by the term $p(t_1, \ldots, t_{n-1})$ and the equation is deleted.

It is easy to see that this transformation is the inverse of flattening the clauses (compare [6]). Since Bosco et al. [6] have shown the correspondence of innermost basic narrowing derivations and SLD-resolution derivations w.r.t. the flattened clauses, we immediately obtain the following proposition:[7]

Proposition 3. *If the set of rules after the transformation steps is canonical and reductive, then the functional program has the same set of answers as the original logic program.*[8]

[7] The requirement for canonical and reductive rules is not essential for the correspondence of narrowing and resolution derivations, but it is important for the unique termination of the rewriting process between the narrowing steps.

[8] Actually, the functional program may compute more answers than the original logic program since it can "skip" calls to partially defined functions by the innermost reflection

Hence, if we have a supposition about the functional dependencies of the arguments of the predicates, we apply the above transformation and then check the resulting program for canonicity which can often be done by simple syntactic criteria (e.g., the arguments of the left-hand side are constructor terms and two different left-hand sides are not unifiable) or by special completion procedures for conditional equations [16]. For instance, the logic program of **append** is transformed into the functional **conc** program above which is obviously canonical. As a further example take the following logic program:

```
max(X,Y,Y) :- le(X,Y).
max(X,Y,X) :- ge(X,Y).
le(0,X).
le(s(X),s(Y)) :- le(X,Y).
ge(X,0).
ge(s(X),s(Y)) :- ge(X,Y).
```

The clauses for **max** are not mutually exclusive and therefore the algorithm in [10] does not detect a functionality in these clauses. However, if we suppose that the third argument of predicate **max** is functional dependent on the first and the second argument, we apply our transformation above and obtain the following rules:

```
max(X,Y) = Y :- le(X,Y) = true.
max(X,Y) = X :- ge(X,Y) = true.
le(0,X) = true.
le(s(X),s(Y)) = le(X,Y).
ge(X,0) = true.
ge(s(X),s(Y)) = ge(X,Y).
```

Now we can construct a successful proof of the canonicity of these rules using the completion procedure in [16] (this can be easily done since there is an interface between the ALF system and the completion system). Hence the canonicity criterion is more general than other more syntactically oriented criteria [10, 41].

The transformation of predicates into functions has at least two advantages. Firstly, the search space can be reduced because more terms can be evaluated by rewriting (e.g., the term `conc([1],[2])` is evaluable by rewriting where `append([1],[2],L)` must be evaluated by narrowing/resolution) and thus the rejection rule is applicable in more cases (see the above example for **conc** and **append**). Secondly, the execution is more efficient because less nondeterminism must be implemented. For instance, the execution of the goal `add(s(s(0))),s(s(0)))) = L` w.r.t. the functional program

```
add(0,N) = N.          add(s(M),N) = s(add(M,N))
add(N,0) = N.          add(N,s(M)) = s(add(N,M))
```

---

rule. An innermost reflection step for the subterm $p(t_1,\ldots,t_k)$ corresponds to resolution with the unit clause $p(X_1,\ldots,X_k,p(X_1,\ldots,X_k))$ in the logic program. To state the exact equivalence of the functional and the logic program, these facts must be added to the logic program for functions which are not completely defined.

does not create any choice point since the goal is fully evaluated by rewriting and not by nondeterministic narrowing, whereas the execution of the goal `add(s(s(s(0))),s(s(s(0))),L)` w.r.t. the Prolog program

```
add(0,N,N).              add(s(M),N,s(L)) :- add(M,N,L).
add(N,0,N).              add(N,s(M),s(L)) :- add(N,M,L).
```

creates at least three choice points. The concrete effect of this behaviour on the execution time and memory usage can be found in [21].

Our final example demonstrates the advantage of our approach in comparison to other proposals to improve control. In this example we combine the advanced translation scheme with the addition of negative information. Consider the following Prolog program for the definition of mobiles (a *mobile* is a *fish* with a fixed positive weight, or a *bridge* of weight 1 (=`s(0)`) where two mobiles of the same weight hang at the left and right end):

```
mobile(fish(_)).
mobile(bridge(M1,M2)) :-
        mobile(M1), mobile(M2),
        weight(M1,W1), weight(M2,W2), equal(W1,W2).
weight(fish(s(W)),s(W)).      % a fish has a positive weight
weight(bridge(M1,M2),s(W)) :-
                      weight(M1,W1), weight(M2,W2), add(W1,W2,W).
add(N,0,N).
add(0,N,N).
add(N,s(M),s(Z)) :- add(N,M,Z).
add(s(M),N,s(Z)) :- add(M,N,Z).
equal(0,0).
equal(s(M),s(N)) :- equal(M,N).
```

If we want to know whether a given `fish/bridge`-structure is a mobile, we prove the goal

```
?- mobile(bridge(fish(s(s(s(0)))),bridge(fish(s(0)),fish(s(0))))).
```

which yields the answer `yes`. If we want to get all mobiles of weight 3, we prove

```
?- mobile(M), weight(M,s(s(s(0)))).
```

This query goes into an infinite loop after enumerating all solutions because it generates bigger and bigger mobiles which are not of weight 3. If we want to avoid this under the standard computation rule, we have to restructure the whole program.[9] Hence we need another program for another mode of predicate `mobile` which is

[9] Note that Naish's algorithm for generating wait declarations [36] does not help because it generates waits for the first arguments of `mobile` and `weight`; hence the goal immediately flounders. The method of [46] depends on a given call pattern of the initial goal, i.e., it would generate two programs for the two modes of `mobile`. Generally, if the modes of the initial goal are not known in advance, it is necessary to generate a program for *each* possible mode of the goal.

clearly unsatisfactory from a logical point of view. This problem can be avoided using our translation scheme. It is easy to see that **weight** and **add** are functions where the last argument depends on the other arguments. Hence we obtain the following functional program using our translation method:

```
mobile(fish(_)) = true.
mobile(bridge(M1,M2)) =
      mobile(M1) and mobile(M2) and equal(weight(M1),weight(M2)).
weight(fish(s(W)))       = s(W).
weight(bridge(M1,M2)) = s(add(weight(M1),weight(M2))).
add(N,0) = N.
add(0,N) = N.
add(N,s(M)) = s(add(N,M)).
add(s(M),N) = s(add(M,N)).
equal(0,0) = true.
equal(s(M),s(N)) = equal(M,N).
```

This program is canonical which can be easily checked by standard completion procedures for equational specifications. In order to avoid the infinite loop, we simply add negative information about unequal numbers. Intensional negation generates the following rules (among others):

```
equal(0,s(M)) = false.
equal(s(M),0) = false.
```

After adding these equations as rewrite rules, **mobile** has a finite search tree for all modes, i.e., the following queries terminate after enumerating all solutions:

```
?- mobile(bridge(fish(s(s(s(0)))),bridge(fish(s(0)),fish(s(0)))))=B.
?- mobile(M) and equal(weight(M),s(s(s(0)))) = true.
```

The termination of the last goal is due to the fact that the generation of mobiles **M** with weight greater than 3 is prevented by rewriting

```
equal(weight(M),s(s(s(0))))
```

to **false**.

4 Conclusions

We have presented a technique to translate logic programs into programs of the functional logic language ALF. This translation ensures that the set of answers to a goal remains the same and the translated programs have at least the same efficiency (search space) as the original programs. This is due to the correspondence between SLD-derivations and innermost basic narrowing derivations. However, in many cases the search space is reduced by simplifying goals (rewriting) and comparing both sides of an equation (rejection) which is effective for the class of generate-and-test programs. This improved control behaviour requires the addition of negative knowledge or the transformation of predicates into functions between arguments. Fortunately, there are well-known tools for both tasks. The necessary negative knowledge can be derived by intensional negation of the program, and the validity of a functional transformation can be checked by completion procedures for equational specifications.

Of course, similar effects or, in some cases, better effects can be obtained by other methods to influence the control of logic programs, e.g., delay declarations for predicates or inserting cuts. But the advantage of our transformation method is the declarative nature of the approach. Since ALF's proof strategy is complete, any solution to the original logic program is also computed w.r.t. the new strategy. This may be not the case in other methods where goals can flounder (because of delay declarations) or solutions are lost (because of inserting "red" cuts).

We do not propose to use our method for the automatic translation of logic programs into functional logic programs. The motivation for our method was to show that functional logic languages are superior to pure logic languages since it is possible to translate any logic program into a functional equivalent which has the same set of answers but is often more efficient. Hence we should directly use functional logic languages instead of pure logic languages. Nevertheless, the presented transformation techniques point to important aspects for improving the efficiency of functional logic programs: functional dependencies reduce the number of possible search paths, and negative knowledge supports the early detection of failures.

In order to increase the power of logic programming, it is necessary to improve the operational behaviour in a declarative way such that logic programs become more deterministic without loosing logically important answers. The integration of functions is one possibility as shown in this paper. Further improvements can be achieved by including constraints over specific domains [31] or type information which influences the search space [20, 22, 43].

Acknowledgements. The author is grateful to Andreas Schwab for improving and debugging the current implementation of ALF, and to Alexander Bockmayr, Rita Loogen and Michael Gollner for their comments on a previous version of this paper.

References

1. H. Aït-Kaci, P. Lincoln, and R. Nasr. Le Fun: Logic, equations, and Functions. In *Proc. 4th IEEE Internat. Symposium on Logic Programming*, pp. 17–23, San Francisco, 1987.
2. R. Barbuti, P. Mancarella, D. Pedreschi, and F. Turini. A Transformational Approach to Negation in Logic Programming. *Journal of Logic Programming (8)*, pp. 201–228, 1990.
3. M. Bellia and G. Levi. The Relation between Logic and Functional Languages: A Survey. *Journal of Logic Programming (3)*, pp. 217–236, 1986.
4. H. Bertling and H. Ganzinger. Completion-Time Optimization of Rewrite-Time Goal Solving. In *Proc. of the Conference on Rewriting Techniques and Applications*, pp. 45–58. Springer LNCS 355, 1989.
5. P.G. Bosco, C. Cecchi, and C. Moiso. An extension of WAM for K-LEAF: a WAM-based compilation of conditional narrowing. In *Proc. Sixth International Conference*

on Logic Programming (Lisboa), pp. 318–333. MIT Press, 1989.

6. P.G. Bosco, E. Giovannetti, and C. Moiso. Narrowing vs. SLD-Resolution. *Theoretical Computer Science 59*, pp. 3–23, 1988.
7. M. Bruynooghe, D. De Schreye, and B. Krekels. Compiling Control. *Journal of Logic Programming (6)*, pp. 135–162, 1989.
8. M.M.T. Chakravarty and H.C.R. Lock. The Implementation of Lazy Narrowing. In *Proc. of the 3rd Int. Symposium on Programming Language Implementation and Logic Programming*, pp. 123–134. Springer LNCS 528, 1991.
9. P.H. Cheong and L. Fribourg. Efficient Integration of Simplification into Prolog. In *Proc. of the 3rd Int. Symposium on Programming Language Implementation and Logic Programming*, pp. 359–370. Springer LNCS 528, 1991.
10. S.K. Debray and D.S. Warren. Functional Computations in Logic Programs. *ACM Transactions on Programming Languages and Systems*, Vol. 11, No. 3, pp. 451–481, 1989.
11. D. DeGroot and G. Lindstrom, editors. *Logic Programming, Functions, Relations, and Equations.* Prentice Hall, 1986.
12. N. Dershowitz and J.-P. Jouannaud. Rewrite Systems. In J. van Leeuwen, editor, *Handbook of Theoretical Computer Science, Vol. B*, pp. 243–320. Elsevier, 1990.
13. N. Dershowitz and M. Okada. Conditional Equational Programming and the Theory of Conditional Term Rewriting. In *Proc. Int. Conf. on Fifth Generation Computer Systems*, pp. 337–346, 1988.
14. M.J. Fay. First-Order Unification in an Equational Theory. In *Proc. 4th Workshop on Automated Deduction*, pp. 161–167, Austin (Texas), 1979. Academic Press.
15. L. Fribourg. SLOG: A Logic Programming Language Interpreter Based on Clausal Superposition and Rewriting. In *Proc. IEEE Internat. Symposium on Logic Programming*, pp. 172–184, Boston, 1985.
16. H. Ganzinger. A Completion Procedure for Conditional Equations. *J. of Symb. Computation*, Vol. 11, pp. 51–81, 1991.
17. E. Giovannetti and C. Moiso. A completeness result for E-unification algorithms based on conditional narrowing. In *Proc. Workshop on Foundations of Logic and Functional Programming*, pp. 157–167. Springer LNCS 306, 1986.
18. J.A. Goguen and J. Meseguer. Eqlog: Equality, Types, and Generic Modules for Logic Programming. In D. DeGroot and G. Lindstrom, editors, *Logic Programming, Functions, Relations, and Equations*, pp. 295–363. Prentice Hall, 1986.
19. M. Hanus. Compiling Logic Programs with Equality. In *Proc. of the 2nd Int. Workshop on Programming Language Implementation and Logic Programming*, pp. 387–401. Springer LNCS 456, 1990.
20. M. Hanus. A Functional and Logic Language with Polymorphic Types. In *Proc. Int. Symposium on Design and Implementation of Symbolic Computation Systems*, pp. 215–224. Springer LNCS 429, 1990.
21. M. Hanus. Efficient Implementation of Narrowing and Rewriting. In *Proc. Int. Workshop on Processing Declarative Knowledge*, pp. 344–365. Springer LNAI 567, 1991.
22. M. Hanus. Parametric Order-Sorted Types in Logic Programming. In *Proc. of the TAPSOFT '91*, pp. 181–200. Springer LNCS 494, 1991.
23. M. Hanus. An Abstract Interpretation Algorithm for Residuating Logic Programs. Technical Report MPI-I-92-217, Max-Planck-Institut für Informatik, Saarbrücken, 1992.
24. M. Hanus. Incremental Rewriting in Narrowing Derivations. In *Proc. of the 3rd International Conference on Algebraic and Logic Programming.* Springer LNCS, 1992.
25. M. Hanus and A. Schwab. ALF User's Manual. FB Informatik, Univ. Dortmund, 1991.

26. S. Haridi and P. Brand. Andorra Prolog: An Integration of Prolog and Committed Choice Languages. In *Proc. Int. Conf. on Fifth Generation Computer Systems*, pp. 745–754, 1988.
27. R. Harper, D.B. MacQueen, and R. Milner. Standard ML. LFCS Report Series ECS-LFCS-86-2, University of Edinburgh, 1986.
28. S. Hölldobler. *Foundations of Equational Logic Programming.* Springer LNCS 353, 1989.
29. J.-M. Hullot. Canonical Forms and Unification. In *Proc. 5th Conference on Automated Deduction*, pp. 318–334. Springer LNCS 87, 1980.
30. H. Hussmann. Unification in Conditional-Equational Theories. In *Proc. EUROCAL '85*, pp. 543–553. Springer LNCS 204, 1985.
31. J. Jaffar and J.-L. Lassez. Constraint Logic Programming. In *Proc. of the 14th ACM Symposium on Principles of Programming Languages*, pp. 111–119, Munich, 1987.
32. J.W. Lloyd. *Foundations of Logic Programming.* Springer, second, extended edition, 1987.
33. R. Loogen. From Reduction Machines to Narrowing Machines. In *Proc. of the TAPSOFT '91*, pp. 438–457. Springer LNCS 494, 1991.
34. A. Middeldorp and E. Hamoen. Counterexamples to Completeness Results for Basic Narrowing. In *Proc. of the 3rd International Conference on Algebraic and Logic Programming.* Springer LNCS, 1992.
35. A. Mück. Compilation of Narrowing. In *Proc. of the 2nd Int. Workshop on Programming Language Implementation and Logic Programming*, pp. 16–29. Springer LNCS 456, 1990.
36. L. Naish. *Negation and Control in Prolog.* Springer LNCS 238, 1987.
37. L. Naish. Adding equations to NU-Prolog. In *Proc. of the 3rd Int. Symposium on Programming Language Implementation and Logic Programming*, pp. 15–26. Springer LNCS 528, 1991.
38. K. Nakamura. Control of logic program execution based on the functional relation. In *Proc. Third International Conference on Logic Programming (London)*, pp. 505–512. Springer LNCS 225, 1986.
39. W. Nutt, P. Réty, and G. Smolka. Basic Narrowing Revisited. *Journal of Symbolic Computation*, Vol. 7, pp. 295–317, 1989.
40. P. Padawitz. *Computing in Horn Clause Theories*, volume 16 of *EATCS Monographs on Theoretical Computer Science.* Springer, 1988.
41. U.S. Reddy. Transformation of Logic Programs into Functional Programs. In *Proc. IEEE Internat. Symposium on Logic Programming*, pp. 187–196, Atlantic City, 1984.
42. U.S. Reddy. Narrowing as the Operational Semantics of Functional Languages. In *Proc. IEEE Internat. Symposium on Logic Programming*, pp. 138–151, Boston, 1985.
43. G. Smolka. *Logic Programming over Polymorphically Order-Sorted Types.* Dissertation, FB Informatik, Univ. Kaiserslautern, 1989.
44. L. Sterling and E. Shapiro. *The Art of Prolog.* MIT Press, 1986.
45. D. Turner. Miranda: A non-strict functional language with polymorphic types. In *Conference on Functional Programming Languages and Computer Architecture, Nancy, France*, pp. 1–16. Springer LNCS 201, 1985.
46. K. Verschaetse, D. De Schreye, and M. Bruynooghe. Generation And Compilation of Efficient Computation Rules. In *Proc. Seventh International Conference on Logic Programming*, pp. 700–714. MIT Press, 1990.
47. D.H.D. Warren. An Abstract Prolog Instruction Set. Technical Note 309, SRI International, Stanford, 1983.
48. D. Wolz. Design of a Compiler for Lazy Pattern Driven Narrowing. In *Recent Trends in Data Type Specification*, pp. 362–379. Springer LNCS 534, 1990.

Independent AND-Parallel Implementation of Narrowing

Herbert Kuchen* Juan José Moreno-Navarro** Manuel V. Hermenegildo**

Abstract. We present a parallel graph narrowing machine, which is used to implement a functional logic language on a shared memory multiprocessor. It is an extension of an abstract machine for a purely functional language. The result is a programmed graph reduction machine which integrates the mechanisms of unification, backtracking, and independent and-parallelism. In the machine, the subexpressions of an expression can run in parallel. In the case of backtracking, the structure of an expression is used to avoid the reevaluation of subexpressions as far as possible. Deterministic computations are detected. Their results are maintained and need not be reevaluated after backtracking.

1 Introduction

During the past few years, several attempts have been made to achieve an integration of functional and logic programming languages, trying to combine the advantages of both paradigms. *Functional logic languages*, one class of such languages, have functional syntax and use narrowing, an evaluation mechanism that uses unification for parameter passing, as operational semantics [21]. Babel [19,20,11,12] is a functional logic language based on a constructor discipline defined in a simple, flexible, and mathematically well-founded way.

A natural way of implementing these languages is to extend functional programming techniques. A couple of graph narrowing machines have been defined for the sequential implementation of Babel. [11,12] follow an innermost strategy, while [18] uses lazy evaluation. All of them have been designed by extending a graph reduction machine for a functional language [15] with those features that are necessary for executing functional logic programs, i.e. unification, backtracking, and logical variables. The mechanisms used for both are inspired by the techniques used in the implementation of Prolog, mainly the ideas present in the Warren Abstract Machine (WAM) [24]. The approach contrasts with others, normally termed *Logic functional languages*, such as e.g. K-LEAF [1], where the converse solution of adding support for functional characteristics to a logic language is taken both at the language and implementation levels. One advantage of the functional logic language approach, is that it guarantees that purely functional programs can be executed almost as efficiently as in the original functional machine, although some overhead due to the different parameter passing mechanism cannot be completely avoided.

* RWTH Aachen, Lehrstuhl für Informatik II, Ahornstraße 55, 5100 Aachen, Germany, email: herbert@zeus.informatik.rwth-aachen.de

** Universidad Politécnica de Madrid, Facultad de Informática, Campus de Montegancedo, Boadilla del Monte, 28660 Madrid, Spain, email: {jjmoreno, herme}@fi.upm.es

In this paper the subject of parallel execution in the context of the functional logic language Babel is treated. A particular form of parallelism is presented and an abstract machine for its implementation, which is essentially a parallel variant of the BAM [11], is then described. The parallelism exploited allows subexpressions of an expression to run in parallel, if they do not share a logical variable. This is essentially a generalization of the concept of independent and-parallelism, known from logic programming [6,3,10], where AND is the only "function" combining subexpressions. As in [15], we allow n expressions e_i $(1 \leq i \leq n)$ to run in parallel with the expression e that uses it. The synchronization is, however, different from the usual one in independent and-parallel implementations of Prolog. In most such implementations, and due to the lack of information on directionality of arguments in logic programs (unless extensive global analysis is performed or the program is annotated), a computation e, which combines the results of some parallel computations e_i $(1 \leq i \leq n)$, has to be placed and evaluated after them. In a language of the type being considered we can take advantage of functional dependencies so that the synchronization of e and each e_i is performed when e really needs the e_i. This increases the degree of parallelism because $n + 1$ tasks (instead of n, where the extra task could in turn generate more parallel tasks) run in parallel. The ability of the abstract machine of keeping multiple environments is used to take advantage of the structure of e to avoid reevaluations. When some e_i produces a new solution, only the work made after the use of this e_i needs to be redone, while for several reasons in Prolog implementations the evaluation of e generally restarts from the beginning.

Moreover, it is possible to keep some results of the parallel tasks, avoiding reevaluations. Since Babel is a functional language a Babel function maps each sequence of (ground) arguments to exactly one result. This property can be used to dynamically detect so-called *deterministic computations* [12,16]. Such a computation cannot produce an alternative result. If it is involved in a parallel execution, it is not affected by backtracking. Its result is kept and can be used later on, when the reexecution of the previous expressions is successful and the value is needed again.

This paper is organized as follows. In Section 2, we briefly introduce the language Babel and discuss extensions to Babel in order to be able to express parallelism. Section 3 presents the independent and-parallel Babel machine. Section 4 focuses on the backtracking mechanism of this machine. Section 5 presents some related work. Finally, in Section 6, we conclude and point out future work.

2 The Functional Logic Language Babel

The language Babel integrates functional and logic programming in a flexible and mathematically well-founded way. It is based on a constructor discipline and uses narrowing as evaluation mechanism [21]. Babel has a Miranda-like polymorphic type system [23]. Since herein we want to focus on the issue of parallel implementation, we will not consider higher order functions throughout this paper (although including them presents no additional problem). Also, rather than giving a precise description of the syntax and semantics of Babel (which can be found in [19,20,11,12]) we will present Babel in an intuitive way by first using a small example program for the well-known *towers* of Hanoi problem and then presenting some basic concepts:

datatype pin := a | b | c.
datatype nat := 1 | (suc nat).
datatype list α := nil | (cons α (list α)).
fun *towers*: pin → pin → pin → nat → (list (list pin)) → (list (list pin)).
  towers Source Help Dest 1 L := [[Source, Dest] | L].
  towers Source Help Dest (suc M) L :=
    towers Source Dest Help M [[Source,Dest] | (*towers* Help Source Dest M L)].

A Babel *program* consists of a sequence of datatype definitions and a sequence of function definitions. The program can be queried with a goal expression. For example, a valid query for the previous program can be

solve *towers* a b c N [ ].

which would return the list of moves for each value of N (number of disks) starting with 1, i.e. the first solution is the value [[a,c]] with binding {N/1}.

A *datatype* definition introduces a new ranked *type constructor* (e.g. pin, nat (both of arity 0), list (of arity 1)) and a sequence of *data constructors* (separated by |). If an n-ary type constructor ($n \geq 0$) is applied to n argument types (including *type variables* –like α– representing any valid type) the resulting type expression is a valid type, e.g. "list pin" and "list α". A consistent replacement of type variables in a *polymorphic type* (i.e. a type including type variables) by other types yields an *instance* of the polymorphic type.

A *data constructor* is an uninterpreted function mapping an instance of its argument type (given behind the name of the constructor) to the corresponding instance of the type on the left hand side of the datatype definition. For example, the most general type of "cons" is cons: $\alpha \rightarrow$ (list α) $\rightarrow$ (list α). But "cons" may also be applied to arguments which have a more specific type (i.e. an instance of the argument type), e.g. "cons 1 nil" is of type "list nat" (α is replaced by nat).

A Prolog-like syntax for lists is allowed, i.e. [e | e'] is equivalent to "cons e e'", [e, e'] represents "cons e (cons e' nil)" and [ ] is the empty list "nil".

For each function, its type and a sequence of defining rules are specified. A *rule* for a function f has the form

$$\underbrace{f\ t_1 \ldots t_m}_{\text{left hand side}} \ := \ \underbrace{\underbrace{\{b \rightarrow\}}_{\text{optional guard}} \ \underbrace{e}_{\text{body}}}_{\text{right hand side}}$$

where $t_1, \ldots, t_n$ are terms, b is a boolean expression, and e is an arbitrary expression. A *term* is either a (logical) *variable* (denoted by an identifier beginning with a capital letter) or an application of an n-ary data constructor ($n \geq 0$) to n argument terms. An *expression* has the form:

$e ::= t$	% term
$\mid (c\ e_1 \ldots e_n)$	% application of a n-ary data constructor c ($n \geq 0$)
$\mid (f\ e_1 \ldots e_n)$	% application of a n-ary function f ($n \geq 0$)
$\mid (b \rightarrow e)$	% guarded expression, meaning "if b then e else undefined"
$\mid (b \rightarrow e_1 \,\Box\, e_2)$	% conditional expression, meaning "if b then e_1 else e_2"

All expressions have to be well typed. For an application this means that the types of the arguments have to be (consistent) instances of the argument type of the function. We assume that application associates to the left and omit parentheses accordingly.

Babel functions are functions in the mathematical sense, i.e. for each tuple of (ground) arguments, there is only one result. This is ensured by syntactic restrictions for the rules (see [12]). In order to simplify the translation of Babel, no variable may occur more than once on the left hand side (left linearity). The type bool is predefined in Babel: **datatype** bool := true | false. Moreover, several basic operations like equality (=), conjunction (,), disjunction (;) and so on are predefined. In [12], a straightforward translation of Prolog rules to Babel rules is shown.

2.1 Narrowing Semantics

The operational semantics of Babel is based on *narrowing.* To use narrowing as the operational semantics of (syntactically) functional languages was first proposed by Reddy [21]. An expression e is narrowed by applying the minimal substitution that makes it reducible, and then reducing it. The minimal substitution is found by unifying e with the left hand side of a rule. A new expression e' and an *answer substitution* σ binding some variables from e are the *outcome* of one narrowing step (denoted by $e \Rightarrow_\sigma e'$). If, after several steps, an expression e is narrowed to a term t, we speak of a *computation* for the *goal* e with *result* t and *answer* σ, where σ is the composition of the answer substitutions of all the individual steps. If e cannot be narrowed further, but it is not a term, then the computation *fails.* The machine will backtrack in such a situation. The rules are tried in their textual order.

The goal in the *towers* of Hanoi example can be narrowed as follows:

1. solution: *towers* a b c N [ ] $\Rightarrow_{\{N/1\}}$ [[a,c]]
2. solution: *towers* a b c N [ ] $\Rightarrow_{\{N/suc\ M\}}$
   towers a c b M [[a,c] | *towers* b a c M [ ]] $\Rightarrow_{\{M/1\}}$
   towers a c b 1 [[a,c],[b,c]] $\Rightarrow$
   [[a,b],[a,c],[b,c]]
3. solution: ...

The outcome of the second solution consists of the result [[a,b],[a,c],[b,c]] and the answer {N/ suc 1}.

2.2 Extensions of Babel to Express Parallelism

An (intermediate) goal usually contains several subexpressions, which can in principle be narrowed in parallel. In the above example, the expression

towers a c b M [[a,c] | *towers* b a c M [ ]]

contains two applications of the function *towers*, namely e_1 := *towers* a c b M [...] and e_2 := *towers* b a c M [ ]. The resulting parallelism is a generalization of the and-parallelism of Prolog. While in Prolog the conjunction is the only way to connect applications of predicates, Babel allows arbitrarily nested function applications. Although the notion *subexpression parallelism* might be more appropriate, we will still call it and-parallelism.

Explicit Parallelism. Clearly, it is not always advisable to narrow subexpressions in parallel. First of all, there is the issue of "granularity" (we will deal with other issues in the following section): for a "small" expression (in terms of execution time) it may be the case that spawning a process to evaluate it is more expensive than evaluating the expression sequentially. Although some work has been done on automatic granularity analysis [2,14] available results still need to be extended to functional logic languages and there are still few practical analysis tools. In this paper we adopt the solution of providing a special syntax which allows the expression of the desired parallelism. This allows the user, who is in the best position to determine which expressions are complex enough, to do so. Alternatively, if an automatic parallelization of the program is possible based on techniques capable of predicting the granularity of the subexpressions, the proposed language can serve as the intermediate language to which these tools translate.[3]

First, we will extend the syntax of expressions with what will be termed a letpar-expression: e ::= letpar X_1 := e_1 & ... & X_n := e_n in e
where e_i has to be an application of a defined function to terms ($1 \leq i \leq n$) and e may contain the new auxiliary variables $X_1, \ldots, X_n$. To simplify the implementation, we allow at most one letpar-expression in each rule. This is no real restriction, since it is always possible to decompose an expression by introducing new functions.

The meaning of a letpar-expression is that e_1,...,e_n, and e (!) will be narrowed in parallel. e will be evaluated using a leftmost innermost strategy. If e needs the outcome of some e_i, it has to wait (suspension) until the corresponding process is ready (synchronization), at which point it can continue (reactivation). The outcome of e_i is *needed* if an X_i or a variable Y, occurring in e and e_i, is accessed during the narrowing of e. In order to facilitate backtracking (to be discussed in Section 4), we will require that the outcomes of e_1, ..., e_n are always needed in the same order. If some outcomes are needed in a runtime dependent order, we say that all of them are needed, when the first of them is needed. For example in

letpar X_1 := e_1 & X_2 := e_2 in h ($b \rightarrow X_1 \,\Box\, X_2$) X_1 X_2

the outcomes of e_1 and e_2 are both needed after the narrowing of b.

In order to make the parallelism in the *towers* example explicit, we can change the function *towers* as follows:

fun *towers*: pin → pin → pin → nat → (list (list pin)) → (list (list pin)) → bool.
    towers Source Help Dest 1 L R := R = [[Source, Dest] | L].
    towers Source Help Dest (suc M) L R :=
        letpar L_1 := *towers* Help Source Dest M L R_1 &
            L_2 := *towers* Source Dest Help M X R
        in [[Source,Dest] | R_1] = X
        → true.

Note that the type of *towers* had to be changed in order to enable the decomposition of the nested application of *towers* using the free variable X. Remember that free variables are only allowed in the guard. The goal has to be changed correspondingly:

solve *towers* a b c N [ ] R.

R will be bound to the old result.

[3] This is the approach taken in the &-Prolog system [9], which has allowed a concurrent but rather independent development of the parallel language implementation and the automatic parallelization tools.

Independent And-Parallelism. Even if two expressions are of adequate granularity there is still another issue, the existence of dependencies among the expressions to be executed in parallel, which may make it not always advisable to do so. In general, if two expressions which are narrowed in parallel have an unbound variable in common, this may lead to problems. Consider the following simple rules:

$$f\ a := g\ a \qquad f\ b := 1 \qquad g\ b := 1$$

If the goal is $f\ X = g\ X$, the two expressions $e_1 := f\ X$ and $e_2 := g\ X$ can be narrowed in parallel. Suppose that the narrowing of e_1 binds X to a and reduces $f\ a$ to $g\ a$. Now, the narrowing for e_2 may want to try the rule for g. This fails because X is already bound to a and it cannot be bound to b. After this, the narrowing of e_1 fails because there is no rule for $g\ a$. Hence, X is unbound and later bound to b, in order to try the second rule for f. But this is already too late for the narrowing of e_2, since it has already discarded the rule for g.

This example shows only one possible problem which may arise when dependent expressions are narrowed in parallel. Other more complicated situations can occur. A general solution ensuring that the correct result is always computed would arguably require a very complicated backtracking mechanism which would be a source of large overheads. Furthermore, there is an additional complication related to efficiency in ensuring that the search space to be explored by the program is not enlarged [10]. Due to these problems we take the approach, inspired by the theoretical results obtained for independent and-parallelism in Prolog [10] (ensuring correctness and "no-slowdown" properties for parallel execution), that subexpressions will only be narrowed in parallel if they are *independent*, i.e. they do not share unbound variables. As in [10], we offer two built-in (pseudo-)functions

$$\textit{ground}: \alpha \rightarrow \text{bool}. \qquad \textit{independent}: \alpha \rightarrow \beta \rightarrow \text{bool}.$$

ground e delivers the result *true*, if e is a ground term (i.e. a term without unbound variables) and *false* otherwise. *independent e e'* delivers the result *true*, if e and e' do not contain a common unbound variable and *false* otherwise. As in [3,8] the implementation of *ground* and *independent* may decide to deliver the value *false*, if it is too expensive to compute the exact value, e.g. if *ground* is applied to a very long list. These pseudo-functions may be used to guard a letpar-expression:

$$\text{e} ::= \text{letpar } grd \Rightarrow X_1 := e_1 \ \& \ \ldots \& \ X_n := e_n \text{ in } e$$

where *grd* is a conjunction of pseudo-function applications. The meaning of such a letpar-expression is that e_1, ..., e_n, and e will be narrowed in parallel, if *grd* evaluates to *true*. Otherwise, they will be evaluated sequentially.

Accordingly, the second rule of the *towers* example might be modified to:

towers Source Help Dest (suc M) L R :=
  letpar (*ground* [Source, Dest, Help, M]), (*independent* L R) ⇒
    L_1 := *towers* Help Source Dest M L R_1,
    L_2 := *towers* Source Dest Help M X R
  in [[Source,Dest] | R_1] = X → true.

For the goal "*towers* a b c N [ ] R", this results in a sequential evaluation, since N is not ground. But e.g. "*towers* a b c (suc 1) [ ] R" would be narrowed in parallel.

In many cases, global program analysis [17] can detect that a variable is always bound to a ground term or that two variables are always independent. In those cases, the corresponding checks can be omitted at runtime. For the second goal, for instance, and for a given query pattern, it is possible to infer that Source, Dest, Help, and M are always bound to ground terms and that L and R will be independent, and all checks can be removed. Note that this type of program analysis is easier in Babel than in Prolog, due to the presence of types and nested function applications in Babel. In Prolog, nested function applications need to be flattened by introducing new variables, and it may take some effort to rediscover the structure which the programmer originally had in mind.

2.3 Deterministic Computations

In order to apply a rule, the arguments of a function are unified with the corresponding patterns on the left hand side and the guard is evaluated. Often, no variables of the rule are bound during the unification and the evaluation of the guard. We call this a *deterministic computation* [16,12], since the syntactic restrictions on Babel rules (Section 2) imply that no other rule for the same function needs to be tried. Hence, no choice point is needed in this case. Note that this optimization is more difficult in Prolog, since it uses relations rather than functions.

3 The And-Parallel Babel Machine

The PBAM is a parallel abstract graph narrowing machine that has been designed for the implementation of Babel on a shared memory multiprocessor. It has a decentralized organization of the runtime structures in a graph instead of a stack.

The graph component of the PBAM contains, among others, so-called task nodes which correspond to ordinary activation records of function calls, but which for decentralization purposes contain all the information needed to execute a function call, e.g. a stack for data manipulations and a local program counter. Some information for parallel execution is also needed.
The store of the PBAM consists of these components:

- the *program store* containing the translation of the Babel rules into PBAM code,
- the *graph*, which may contain task-, variable-, and constructor nodes,
- for each processor, one *active task pointer*, which points to the task node corresponding to the currently executed function call,
- a task queue, containing pointers to task nodes, ready to be executed.

3.1 The Graph

The graph consists of several nodes which are accessed via their addresses. Figure 1 shows the structure of such nodes. The computation is controlled by the *task nodes*, which represent function applications. Each task node contains:

- the *code address* of the code for the corresponding function symbol,
- pointers to the graph representations of the *arguments*,
- a list of pointers to initially unbound variable nodes representing *local variables*,

– Task Node:

TASK	code address	argument list	local variables
program counter	local stack	father pointer	
backtracking information	parallelism information		

backtracking information:

local trail	determ. flag	backtracking pointer	last descendant pointer
backtracking address	program counter and local stack of the father		

parallelism information:

parallelism flag	T_1	state T_1	...	T_n	state T_n

– Constructor Node:

CONSTR	constructor name	list of components

– Variable Nodes: unbound: | UBV | or bound: | VAR | Graph-address |

Fig. 1. Structure of graph nodes.

– the *program counter*,
– the *local stack*, needed for accessing and building structures in the graph,
– the *father pointer*, pointing to the node by which the current node has been created (this pointer is used when a task finishes successfully and control has to be returned to the father task), and
– the *return flag* indicating whether the task is looking for its first solution.

The task nodes contain also certain *backtracking* information. This consists of

– a *local trail* which keeps track of variable bindings to be removed in case of backtracking,
– a *determinism flag* used to discover whether the current function call is a deterministic computation,
– a *backtracking pointer* indicating the task that has to be forced to backtrack in case of a failure,
– a *last descendant pointer* indicating the last successful descendant of the current task (used to initialize the backtracking pointer of newly generated subtasks),
– a *backtracking address*, which is the program address of the next alternative rule of the current function call, and, finally,
– safe copies of the *program counter* and *the local stack of the father task* which have to be restored upon successful termination after backtracking has occurred.

All this will be explained in more detail in the following section, where the organization of backtracking is shown.

In order to control parallel execution, task nodes contain also some *parallelism* information. This consists of

– a *parallelism tag* indicating whether subtasks shall be evaluated in parallel,
– pointers to the tasks involved in the parallel execution,
– a *status tag* for each of these tasks, which should contain the values READY, DETERMINISTIC, EXECUTING, or DORMANT.

In addition to the task nodes, the graph contains *constructor* and *variable nodes. Constructor nodes* represent structured data. They contain the constructor name and a list of pointers to the graphs representing the components of the structure.

Variable nodes are needed for the organization of unification. We distinguish nodes for unbound and bound variables. Unbound variable nodes only consist of the tag (UBV). When a variable is bound, the corresponding node is changed into a bound variable node pointing to the node representing its binding.

3.2 Translation

Next, we show how a Babel program is translated into PBAM-code and sketch the behaviour of the machine instructions. Due to lack of space, we will only treat the translation of a letpar expression in detail. The general translation scheme will be sketched using an example. An expression:

letpar $grd \Rightarrow X_1 := f_1\ t_{1,1} \ldots t_{1,m_1}\ \& \ldots \&\ X_n := f_n\ t_{n,1} \ldots t_{n,m_n}$ in e

produces the following code

code for grd
code for $\mathrm{t}_{1,1} \ldots \mathrm{t}_{1,m_1}$
PCALL (ca(f_1), m_1, k_1, 1)
⋮
code for $\mathrm{t}_{n,1} \ldots \mathrm{t}_{n,m_n}$
PCALL (ca(f_n), m_n, k_n, n)
code for e

where k_i is the number of local variables of f_i $(1 \leq i \leq n)$.

grd is some test for independence and is translated by using the instructions GROUND and INDEPDNT. The code for evaluating the expression e has the following properties:

- Before the first appearance of each X_i or of a variable Y occurring in the terms $t_{i,1}, \ldots, t_{i,m_i}$, where Y is not guaranteed to be bound to a term, the instruction WAIT i is inserted.
- Each consultation of X_i is done by the instruction LOADR i.

In Figure 2, the translation of the *towers* example and of the goal (*towers* a b c (suc 1) [ ] R) is given. The first CALL instruction generates a task node for the goal and starts its evaluation. After a successful evaluation, the programmer is asked by the instruction MORE, whether more solutions are wanted. If this is the case, the FORCE instruction is executed and the task for the goal is forced to backtrack. Otherwise, control jumps to the STOP instruction at the end of the code. The translation of the functions follows after this preliminary code.

The *towers* example contains only one function with two rules. Since the first rule does not contain any parallelism, we omit its code due to the lack of space. The code for the second rule starts with an UNDO instruction that deletes the bindings that should have been produced by the first rule. Then, the backtracking address *fail* is stored in the actual task node (TRY_ME_ELSE *fail*). This label will be used if the rule fails. After this, the non-variable arguments of the actual task are unified with the corresponding terms on the left hand side of the rule. The 4th argument must consist of an application of the unary constructor *suc*. If this is the case, the UNIFYCSTR command leaves a pointer to the substructure (argument) of this argument on the stack. It is unified with the corresponding part of the term on the left hand side of the rule (UNIFYVAR). If the 4th argument is an unbound variable, this variable is bound to the appropriate term (by the three commands following *bind*). These possible actions correspond to the read and write mode of the WAM [24], respectively. If the 4th argument starts with another constructor than *suc* the rule fails.

```
          CALL (goal, 0, 1)
          MORE
          JPF stop
  force:  FORCE
 towers:  TRY_ME_ELSE rule2
          ... code for the first rule
          RET
 rule2 :  UNDO
          TRY_ME_ELSE fail
          LOAD 4
          UNIFYCSTR (suc,1,bind)
          UNIFYVAR 1
          JMP rhs_2
   bind:  LOADX 1
          CNODE (suc,1)
          BIND
  rhs_2:  CUT fail
          GROUND 1
          GROUND 3
          GROUND 2
          GROUNDX 1
          INDEPDNT (5,6)
          LOAD 2
          LOAD 1
          LOAD 3
          LOADX 1
          LOAD 5
          LOADX 2
          PCALL (towers,6,3,1)
          LOAD 1
          LOAD 3
          LOAD 2
          LOADX 1
          LOADX 3
          LOAD 6
          PCALL (towers,6,3,2)
          LOAD 1
          LOAD 3
          CNODE (nil,0)
          CNODE (cons,2)
          CNODE (cons,2)
          WAIT 1
          LOADX 2
          CNODE (cons,2)
          WAIT 2
          LOADX 3
          CHECKEQ
          RET
   fail:  UNDO
          FAILRET
   goal:  TRY_ME_ELSE end
          CNODE (a,0)
          CNODE (b,0)
          CNODE (c,0)
          CNODE (1,0)
          CNODE (suc,1)
          CNODE (nil,0)
          LOADX 1
          CALL (towers,6,3)
          RETURNRESULT
    end:  PRINTFAILURE
   stop:  STOP
```

Fig. 2. PBAM-code for the towers example.

The translation of the body of the rule starts at label *rhs_2*. The CUT instruction at the beginning of the code for the body is used to detect deterministic computations, as mentioned in Subsection 2.3. If the current computation is deterministic this instruction sets the backtracking address to the fail label of the considered function. The technical details of the CUT instruction can be found in [12,16].

The top expression on the right hand side is a letpar construction. First, code is generated to check the groundness of the arguments Source, Dest, and Help (using GROUND instructions) and of the local varible M (using GROUNDX 1). Then, code to check the independence of L and R (instruction INDEPDNT (5,6)) is appended. GROUND, GROUNDX, and INDEPDNT set the parallelism flag (initially *true*) to *false*, if the corresponding check fails. If the parallelism flag is *false*, subsequent GROUND, INDEPDNT, and WAIT instructions will be ignored and PCALLs are handled like CALLs.

Using LOAD (to load an argument) and LOADX instructions (to load a local variable) the arguments for the call to towers are pushed on the stack. A task for the first call to *towers* is produced with a PCALL instruction, moving the arguments to the new task node. The second call to *towers* is handled analogously. The code for the main expression in the letpar, an equality, follows next. First the arguments of the equality are constructed on the stack using LOAD, LOADX, and CNODE instructions. CNODE (c,k) takes k components from the stack and inserts them into a new constructor node for constructor c.

However, before the use of R_1 (LOADX 2), the first parallel task needs to be finished. The instruction WAIT 1 is used to wait for this event. Similarly, WAIT 2 is placed before the use of X (LOADX 3).

Finally, control is given back to the calling task by RET. If the second and last rule also fails a jump to the command referenced by the current backtrack address (*fail*) is performed. All bindings produced by the rule are deleted (by UNDO) and backtracking is initiated (by FAILRET).

The translation of the goal appears after the code for the *towers* function. This translation is done analogously to the translation of the right hand side of a rule. A RETURNRESULT is included at the end in order to print the result after a successful termination. This instruction terminates the evaluation of the goal and gives control back to the top level task which continues with the MORE instruction. If the evaluation of the goal ultimately fails this is reported by the PRINTFAILURE command.

4 Backtracking

This section describes the management of backtracking both in the sequential and in the parallel case. Although the components of the backtracking information have already been sketched previously, we now explain their behaviour in detail. The local *trail* is a list of graph addresses indicating bound variable nodes, which have to be replaced by unbound variable nodes when an UNDO instruction is executed. The management of backtracking is mainly controlled by two pointers: a so-called *backtracking pointer* to the *predecessor task* and a so-called *last descendant pointer* to the most recently generated task, i.e. the last successor task generated by the task or one of its descendants.

The notion of a *predecessor task* needs a precise definition. If a task is the first child of its father the predecessor task is the father. Otherwise, in the sequential case, it is the last task that terminated successfully before the currently executed task was generated.

In the parallel case, the predecessor task is initially the task finished before the code for the letpar was started. When WAIT i is executed, the backtracking pointer of the i-th parallel task is set to (the last descendant of) the previously finished task (if it is a sequential one), or to the $(i-1)$-th parallel task, if there is no call to a task between the use of task $i-1$ and i, i.e. between WAIT $i-1$ and WAIT i. Furthermore, the last descendant pointer of the father is updated with the last descendant pointer of the parallel task. By using this mechanism, the last descendant pointer of a task contains the most recently used task and it can help to set the backtracking pointer of the next task.

The backtracking pointers determine an implicit stack of nodes that reflects the order in which the nodes have been activated. While the father pointers are used to control the forward computation, the backtracking pointers determine the order of backward computation:

- A task returning with success (RET command) gives control to the father task (indicated by the father pointer) which continues its execution.
- A task returning with failure (FAILRET command) gives control to the predecessor task in the implicit stack (indicated by the backtracking pointer).

Here, it is important to point out that a deterministic task without children cannot give any new result, and it is not included in the backtracking chain. Any parallel task of this kind has the status DETERMINISTIC.

Some additional information for handling backtracking is needed in the task nodes. The *backtracking address* is the program address where the task must continue in case of backtracking (i.e. the address of the next rule). The backtracking information contains also a safe copy of the state of the father: a copy of the program counter and the stack. It is used to restore the state of the father in case of termination of a subtask after some backtracking has occurred. In this case the father must redo all evaluation that was done after the previous successful termination of the subtask. The copy is made during the execution of the CALL or PCALL command and the restoration is made after the successful reevaluation of a subtask, by the RET instruction in the sequential case and by the WAIT instruction in the parallel case. This situation is detected by checking the *return flag*.

Now, we can explain an instance of backward execution using an example. We want to evaluate the body of the rule:

$$f\ X\ :=\ g\ e_0\ (\text{letpar}\ X_1 := e_1\ \&\ X_2 := e_2\ \&\ X_3 := e_3\ \text{in}\ (b\ X_1\ e_4\ X_2\ \rightarrow\ h\ X_3))$$

The structure of the graph after the evaluation of this expression is shown in Fig. 3.[4]

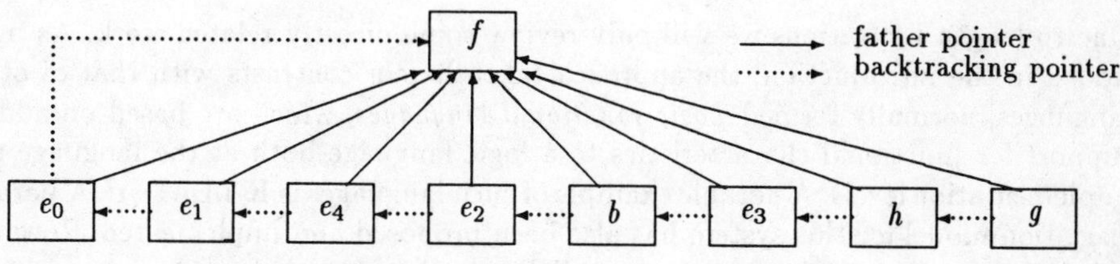

Fig. 3. Structure of the graph.

There are three situations when a task fails:

Sequential backtracking to the predecessor task appears, if the failing task was not spawned by a letpar (e.g. when backtracking from g to h, h to e_3, b to e_2 (e_3 may still be running), e_4 to e_1, and e_0 to f).

Parallel inside backtracking occurs when a task fails during its execution in parallel with other tasks. In this case, *intelligent backtracking* can be performed. Since we use independent and-parallelism, the failure is certainly not caused by a bad binding of a parallel sibling. Hence, the parallel sibling tasks and the intermediate sequential tasks (like e_4 and b) are removed and their bindings are undone (by the FAILRET instruction of the failing task). In our example, this kind of backtracking occurs if e_1, e_2 or e_3 fail, looking for their first solution. They will backtrack to e_0.

Sequential inside backtracking occurs when the reevaluation of an originally parallel task T_i fails. If it is not the first one, it backtracks to the predecessor task like in sequential backtracking (e.g. from e_3 to b, e_2 to e_4), but it is converted into a dormant task (which can be reexecuted). If it is the first one, the complete letpar expression fails and all the parallel tasks are disposed. If T_i returns with success, the rest of the dormant tasks are evaluated from scratch (in parallel).

[4] Note that the order in which the expressions are linked in the backtracking chain is the order in which they are used, rather than that in which they are generated or specified.

Returning to the example: if the reevaluation of e_1 fails, the whole letpar expression fails and all the parallel tasks e_1, e_2, and e_3 are deallocated. However, when a new solution is generated, e_2 and e_3 are started again, and e_4 is executed. After this, the corresponding WAIT command before the use of X_2 ensures the synchronization with e_2 and the execution of b is started. The synchronization with e_3 can wait until b finishes.

Note that e_2 and e_3 are only restarted when e_4 has produced a new result. The policy is to restart the execution of parallel tasks only in the case of a forward execution and not in a backward one.[5]

Recall that deterministic tasks are not included in the backtracking chain. Therefore, they are not affected by the backtracking mechanism and, hence, they are not reevaluated. However, the result is kept for later use. Suppose that, in our example, e_2 is a deterministic task. A failure in b yields backtracking to e_4, but the result of e_2 can be accessed after a successful reevaluation of e_4.

5 Some Related Work

Due to length limitations we will only review some directly related work. As mentioned in the introduction, the approach taken herein contrasts with that of other languages, normally termed *Logic functional languages*, which are based on adding support for functional characteristics to a logic language both at the language and implementation levels. A notable example of such languages is K-LEAF [1]. A parallel execution model for this system has also been proposed and implemented. However, it is based on the exploitation of or-parallelism and its abstract machine is an extension of a logic abstract machine, rather than a functional one. Thus, the solutions presented herein are different and complementary to those presented for K-LEAF. Since there is also backtracking in Babel, or-parallelism can also be exploited by extending the PBAM with either the environment sharing or the environment copying techniques used in the combination of and- and or-parallelism in Prolog, or, perhaps, with the techniques used in K-LEAF.

Some authors have proposed or implemented functional logic systems which support dependent And-parallelism (e.g. [13]). In [13] every variable belongs to a process, and only the owner may bind it. Usually, the extended synchronization in such systems imposes more overhead. It is not clear at this point whether this overhead would be worthwhile. An interesting logic programming system which does support dependent and-parallelism is the Andorra-I system [4], which allows (in addition to or-parallelism) dependent and-parallelism but only for goals which can be found to be deterministic. A similar approach could be taken in the PBAM, with the advantage of being able to more easily detect determinism. This deterministic dependent and-parallelism could be combined with the non-deterministic independent and-parallelism presented in the spirit of the combination of the Andorra-I and &-Prolog systems presented in the IDIOM model [22].

The approach presented in this paper borrows similarities from the independent and-parallelism found in Prolog [3,6,9,10] and exploited in &-Prolog. The main difference is that in that scheme the processes for some expressions e_1 & ...& e_n are not

[5] This corresponds to "point backtracking" as opposed to "streak backtracking" [6].

linked by an expression e in a letpar expression. Rather, the evaluation of e would have been placed after that of e_1, ..., e_n. This leads to a simpler backtracking mechanism, but it requires the complete reevaluation of e, if some e_i has to produce a new solution. Many of the compile-time techniques developed in the context of this work could be extended to be useful for the model presented in this paper.

The idea of running e_1, ..., e_n, and e in parallel, and to synchronize e and e_i, when e needs the result of e_i, was used for the implementation of a purely functional language in [15]. In their framework, the order of the processes is not important, since in a functional language there is no backtracking.

The idea of allowing parallel expressions to proceed until their results are required, although developed independently, is reminiscent of Halstead's multilisp "future" construct [5]. However, the reasons for which synchronization is imposed are quite different in Babel, since they are related to nondeterminism and the partly logical nature of the language.

6 Conclusions and Future Work

We have presented some techniques for the parallel implementation of narrowing, by integrating mechanisms used in functional and logic programming implementations. We propose a new synchronization model, where it is only necessary to wait for the value of a parallel subexpression, if the result is needed. The approach increases the parallelism and decreases the reevaluation effort, especially in the case of deterministic computations. We have also presented an abstract machine, the PBAM, capable of implementing the model of parallelism, sketched the translation process from Babel to PBAM instructions, and discussed in detail the more involved issues, such as backtracking.

Currently we are developing a concrete Babel implementation on a Sequent shared-memory multiprocessor, based on the approach presented. We hope to have a complete running prototype and some performance measurements in the near future. As future work, we plan to investigate the efficient management of the stopping of processes in order to implement the intelligent backtracking, and efficient groundness and independence tests. We also plan to develop a parallel machine for lazy narrowing, extending the design presented in [18]. Moreover, we wish to integrate the machine in a distributed environment. The graph structure will support this.

Acknowledgements. We thank all the members of the Babel teams in Aachen and Madrid as well as the anonymous referees for helpful comments. Manuel Hermenegildo is supported in part by ESPRIT project "PEPMA" and CICYT project TIC90-1105-CE.

References

1. P. Bosco, C. Cecchi, C. Moiso, M. Porta, G. Sofi: Logic and Functional Programming on Distributed Memory Architectures, Proc. 7th ICLP, 325-339,(1990).
2. S. Debray, N.-W. Lin, M. Hermenegildo: Task Granularity Analysis in Logic Programs, Proc. ACM Conf. on Programming Language Design and Implementation, 1990.

3. D. DeGroot: Restricted And-parallelism, Conf. on 5th Generation Comp. Syst., 1984.
4. G. Gupta, V. Santos Costa, R. Yang, M.V. Hermenegildo: IDIOM: A Model Integrating Dependent-, Independent-, and Or-parallelism, Proc. of the 1991 Int'l. Logic Programming Symposium, MIT press.
5. R. Halstead: Multilisp: A Language for Concurrent Symbolic Computation, ACM Trans. on Prog. Languages and Systems 7:4, October 1985, pp. 501-538
6. M.V. Hermenegildo: An Abstract Machine for Restricted And Parallel Execution of Logic Programs, 3rd Int. Conf. on Logic Programming, LNCS 225, 25-39 (1986).
7. M.V. Hermenegildo, R.I. Nasr: Efficient Management of Backtracking in And-parallelism, 3rd Int. Conf. on Logic Programming, LNCS 225, 40-50 (1986).
8. M.V. Hermenegildo, M. Carro: Experimenting with Independent And-Parallel Prolog using Standard Prolog, Proc. PRODE'91, and Tech. Report, UP Madrid.
9. M.V. Hermenegildo, K.J. Green: &-Prolog and its performance: Exploiting Independent And-Parallelism, Proc. 7th ICLP, 253-268, (1990).
10. M. Hermenegildo, F. Rossi: Strict and Non-Strict Independent And-Parallelism in Logic Programs: Correctness, Efficiency, and Compile-Time Conditions, Journal of Logic Programming, to appear (1992).
11. H. Kuchen, R. Loogen, J.J. Moreno Navarro, M. Rodríguez Artalejo: Graph-Based Implementation of a Functional Logic Language, ESOP, LNCS 432:271–290 (1990).
12. H. Kuchen, R. Loogen, J.J. Moreno Navarro, M. Rodríguez Artalejo: Graph-Narrowing to Implement a Functional Logic Language, Technical Report, UP Madrid (1992).
13. H. Kuchen, W. Hans: An And-Parallel Implementation of the Functional Logic Language Babel, Aachener Informatik-Bericht 91/12:119–139, RWTH Aachen (1991).
14. A. King and P. Soper, Granularity Analysis of Concurrent Logic Programs, 5th Int. Symp. on Computer and Information Sciences, Nevsehir, Turkey, 1990.
15. R. Loogen, H. Kuchen, K. Indermark, W. Damm: Distributed Implementation of Programmed Graph Reduction, PARLE, LNCS 365:136–157(1989).
16. R. Loogen, S. Winkler: Dynamic Detection of Determinism in Functional Logic Languages, 3rd PLILP, LNCS 528:335–346 (1991).
17. K. Muthukumar, M.V. Hermenegildo: The CDG, UDG and MEL methods for Automatic Compile-time Parallelization of Logic Programs for Independent And-Parallelism, Proc. ICLP, (1989).
18. J.J. Moreno Navarro, H. Kuchen, R. Loogen, M. Rodríguez-Artalejo: Lazy Narrowing in a Graph Machine, 2nd ALP, LNCS 456:298–317 (1990).
19. J.J. Moreno Navarro, M. Rodríguez-Artalejo: Babel: A Functional and Logic Programming Language Based on Constructor Discipline and Narrowing, Int. Conf. on Algebraic and Logic Programming (ALP), LNCS 343:223–232 (1989).
20. J.J. Moreno Navarro, M. Rodríguez Artalejo: Logic Programming with Functions and Predicates: The Language Babel, J. of Logic Programming:12: 191–223 (1992).
21. U.S. Reddy: Narrowing as the Operational Semantics of Functional Languages, IEEE Int. Symp. on Logic Progr., IEEE Computer Society Press, 138–151 (1985).
22. V. Santos Costa, D.H.D. Warren, R. Yang: Andorra-I: A Parallel Prolog system that transparently exploits both And- and Or-Parallelism, Proc. Principles and Practices of Parallel Programming, to appear.
23. D.A. Turner: Miranda: A Non-Strict Functional Language with Polymorphic Types, ACM Conf. on Functional Languages and Computer Arch., LNCS 201:1–16 (1985).
24. D.H.D. Warren: An Abstract Prolog Instruction Set, Technical Note 309, SRI International, Menlo Park, California, October 1983

This article was processed using the LaTeX macro package with LLNCS style

Binding Techniques and Garbage Collection for OR-Parallel CLP Systems

Michel Dorochevsky, André Véron

European Computer-Industry Research Center
Arabellastr. 17
D-8000 Munich 81
email:{veron,michel}@ecrc.de

Abstract. ElipSys is the first system combining in one environment OR-parallel execution facilities, advanced AND-execution paradigms such as coroutining and constraints satisfaction on finite domains and a complete garbage collector. This paper reports on the issues involved in combining these features into one system. A data structure called consecutively updatable field is depicted which fulfills the concomitant requirements of OR-parallelism, non left-to-right computation rules and garbage collection.

1 Introduction

Parallel logic programming and constraint logic programming have been two active fields of research in the past years ([LBD+88, AK90] and [Col90, JL87, DSV90]) and ECRC has succesfully contributed to both of them [BdKH+88, DVS+88]. At their common frontier ElipSys is the first logic programming system providing in one unified environment specialized computation domains such as finite domains of integers or atoms, builtin arithmetic constraints, advanced coroutining and suspensions mechanisms together with an OR-parallel execution machinery and a complete garbage collector.

ElipSys departs significantly from a Prolog system, its implementation required the use of non standard implementation techniques. We focus in this paper on the memory management issues in ElipSys. We address the technicalities linked to the management of a constraint programming system (suspensions, specialized domain handling) and an OR-parallel execution model. We present a data-structure called the consecutively updatable field which is used intensively in the ElipSys system and caters for the joint requirements of garbage collection, flexible computation rules and OR-parallel execution.

Together with a complete garbage collector, this data structure has made it possible to turn ElipSys into a parallel system whose internal mechanisms are of comparable quality to those of sequential systems.

This paper is built in four parts. First we sketch the internals of an OR-parallel CLP system and highlight the need for non standard implementation techniques. Second we introduce the consecutively updatable field and state its properties with respect to memory management and garbage collection. In a third part, we present the ElipSys garbage collection scheme. Finally we report on the performances of ElipSys with coroutining and domain manipulation programs and its comparison with other sequential logic programming systems.

2 Anatomy of an OR-parallel CLP system

In an OR-parallel CLP system two types of execution mechanisms cohabit: those related to AND-execution and those related to OR-parallel execution. The first deals with the calling/exiting/suspension/resumption of goals when the computation flows down *one* branch of the computation tree. The second deals with the management of inference engines which traverse in parallel *different* branches of the computation tree.

2.1 OR-execution

Conceptually when the system reaches a choice-point, it should fork itself into as many new systems as there are alternatives, each of these systems holding a copy of their parent's state.

Practically a raw copy of the state is much too costly. Instead, the same state implemented in shared memory is usually used for the different branches. Hence two workers busy with the traversal of two *different* and *independent* branches might try to modify the same location in memory. This is the so called multiple binding problem. [GJ90] is a survey of methods used to solve this problem. A recent method using incremental true copy of workers' state has been successfully implemented in the MUSE system ([AK90]). ElipSys uses the binding array technique ([War84]) of which we give an account here:

- An additional stack is allocated to each inference engine present in the OR-parallel system.
- Each worker is allocated a chunk of shared memory which it uses to allocate its stacks.
- Each newly created variable in the stacks is allocated an entry in the binding array. An unbound variable is then a linked pair of cells, one in a stack, one in the binding array:

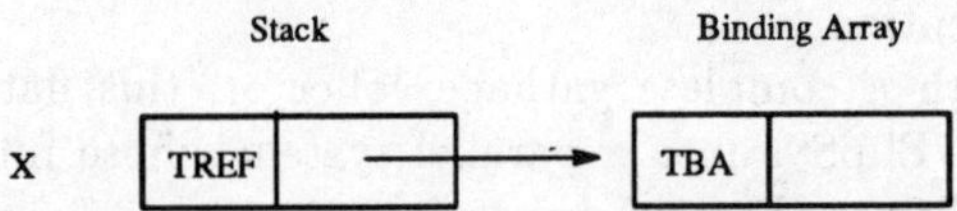

- When a worker binds a variable, it updates the cell in the stack when the binding is deterministic, it binds the cell in the binding array when the variable is non-deterministic. In the latter case, the update on the binding array is recorded in the value trail. This binding technique allows multiple workers to bind the same variable without actually modifying the data they share. It enables to fork a computation without actually having to copy its state:

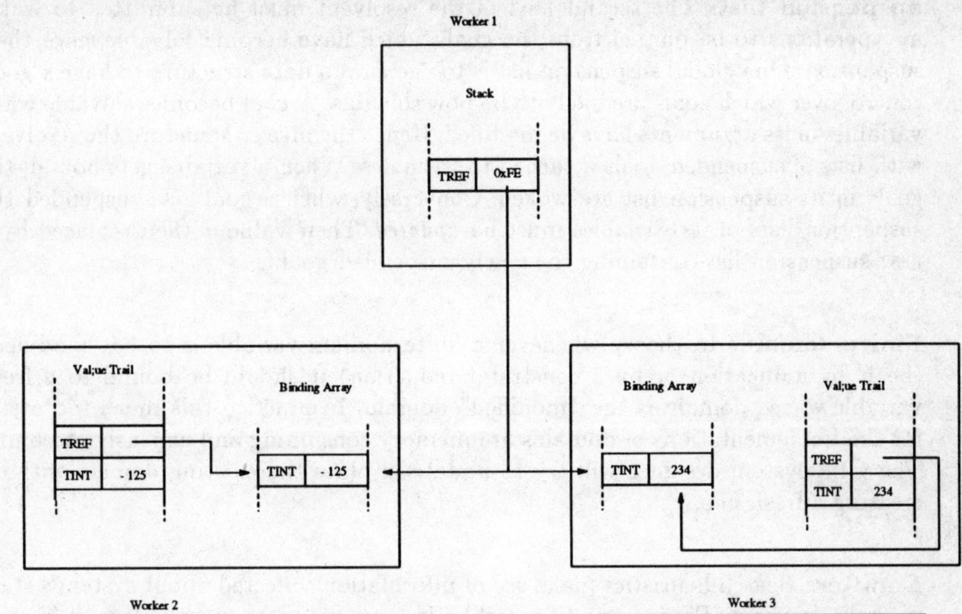

Variable X with binding array entry 0xFE is bound to -125 on the branch traversed by worker 1 and to 254 on the branch traversed by worker 2

2.2 AND-execution

In the subsequent paragraphs we highlight the importance of destructive update mechanisms for the implementation of CLP systems. All updates must be backtrackable so as to cope with non-determinism.

A global list of suspended goals Coroutining makes it possible to use non left-to-right one computation rules. The system can no longer handle the SLD-resolvent as a stack of goals. Instead the resolvent is split in two. The first part is a stack of yet unprocessed goals. The second is the set of processed but still not yet solved goals. When a goal is delayed after having been extracted from the first part it is added to the second part, by ***updating*** the data structure implementing it.

It must be noted that some systems offering coroutining like SICStus do not maintain such an explicit data structure ([Car87]). The access to suspended goals is done via a scan of the stacks. This is sufficient to detect unsolved goals at the end of a computation (floundering). This is not enough to satisfy the increasing requirements put on coroutining systems. For instance, ElipSys offers the **subcall/1, subcall/2** à la Sepia builtins enabling to execute goals and to deregister or to collect the suspended goals which remain unsolved ([ECR91]). The suspended parts of the resolvent must then first be a user level data structure and second must be quickly accessible for it can be used within heavily backtracking programs.

Suspension Lists The second part of the resolvent must be submitted to wake-up operations to be purged from the goals which have become solvable since their suspension. One global suspension list is too general a data structure to have a good control over which goals are likely to be now solvable. A goal becomes solvable when variables in its arguments have be modified. Hence the idea to structure the resolvent with lists of suspended goals attached to variables. When a variable gets bound, the goals in its suspension list are woken. Conversely, when a goal gets suspended the suspension lists of its variables must be *updated*. Their value is then replaced by a new suspension list containing the newly suspended goal.

Finite domains In theory whenever a finite domain variable is to be "modified" (be it by unification or by a constraint reduction) it should be bound to a fresh variable whose domain is the "modified" domain. In practice this much too costly for the implementations of domains are memory consuming and expensive to build. The CLP system designer will try to update in place the existing domain without creating a fresh one.

Counters Search heuristics make use of information collected about system's state to make decisions. For instance if variables in a set are to be given values, it is good practice to try to give first a value to the one which has the most goals suspended on it. Hence the need for a counter recording the number of suspended goals on a given variable. Counters are also useful to build constraints or control conditions such as "there must at least N variables with the same value". Counters are *updated* as the system's state evolves.

Status of a suspension Goals present in more than one suspension list can be be woken more than once. For side-effect prone goals this is most of the time an undesirable behaviour. For side-effect free goals this is uselessly costly.

Priority based wakening between suspended goals is a valuable mechanism. For instance it makes it possible to reorder goals according to their branching behaviour or their computation cost or to postpone the execution of suspensions such as accounting daemons which monitor the resolvent or of a constraints network.

To tackle these two cases, one often needs to associate a status to a suspended goal. The status can indicate whether the goal has already been solved (to avoid solving it more than once), that the goal has been woken and resuspended (to avoid creating a new suspension for the same goal), that the wakening of a goal has been postponed until all goals with a smaller status or priority have been woken. Statuses must then *updated* so as to reflect the computation's state.

2.3 Requirements for an OR-parallel CLP system

The cohabitation of an OR-parallel machinery with flexible AND-execution mechanism can only be set up when techniques to implement the updating mechanisms described above are available. One need to cope with multiple updates stemming from OR-parallelism and with consecutive updates due to intricate AND-computations.

Consecutively updatable data structures (Cf **setarg/3** [ECR91]) are readily available in Prolog systems and are usually implemented implemented via value trailing. With this approach a value trail frame is created for each update. Computations in CLP systems are bursts of deterministic computations (propagations) intermingled with branching operations. The propagations heavily use the suspension/resumption mechanisms and aim at reducing the scope of variables by binding them and/or reducing their domains. Creating a fresh value trail frame for each update leads to an unbearable memory consumption. A CLP implementation must therefore avoid creating a new record for each update. Furthermore due to the rate of updates, it is crucially important for a CLP system to have a constant read and write access time to consecutively updatable data structures

Pruning operations suppress alternatives in the search tree. Consequently trail information which have been recorded to enable backtracking or task-switching can become useless. The number of these trail frames and the size of the value they are holding can be arbitrarily big. Useless information appearing after pruning must imperatively be collectable via a garbage collection process. The requirements are therefore:

Requirement 1 Compliance with OR-parallelism multiple updates requirements.
Requirement 2 Reusability of trail frames in case of deterministic consecutive updates.
Requirement 3 Constant read and write access times for consecutively updatable data structures.
Requirement 4 Collectability of useless trail frames after pruning operations.

Requirements 2 and 4 have been addressed in [Hui90]. The approach relies on an intelligent memory equipped with a garbage collector and dedicated to non deterministic languages. The inference engine itself is impeded by the weight of the memory management. Properties 2 and 3 have been dealt with in the CHIP CLP system with a very efficient and successful implementation ([AB90]). Requirements 1,2 and 3 have been satisfied in the PEPSys-CHIP system using the same time stamping technique from CHIP ([Hen89b]). The Andorra-I system presented in [CWY91] relies also backtrackable updatable variables. The scheme presented there seems to satisfy requirements 1 , 2 , 3, garbage-collection and requirement 4 are not mentioned. In the following we present the implementation scheme for consecutively updatable fields used in ElipSys and show it fulfills all requirements 1, 2, 3 and 4.

3 Consecutively Updatable Fields

A Consecutively Updatable field (CU-field) is the data structure ubiquitously used in ElipSys to perform efficiently successive updates on a data structure in an OR-parallel context.

3.1 CU-field's initial value is in the trail

The binding array technique is not dedicated to the implementation of write-once data cells. It requires that what ever value is in the binding array it must also be in the value trail. Consequently when a data cell which has already been given a value through a binding array update is updated anew, the value trail must also be updated. The naïve possible solutions are:

- To create a new frame on the value trail. This does not comply with requirement 2.
- To scan the value trail to find the frame corresponding to the first update. If no choice point has been created since the last update, the trail frame can safely be modified in place to hold the new value. If a choice point has already been made public, a new trail frame for the new update must be pushed on the value trail. The scan has a non constant cost. Requirement 3 is not fulfilled.

The solution adopted in ElipSys bears much similarity with the second approach. It uses a variation of the binding array technique to implement the data cell which can be submitted to consecutive updates (CU-field). A freshly created CU-field is a quintuplet of data cells having the following format:

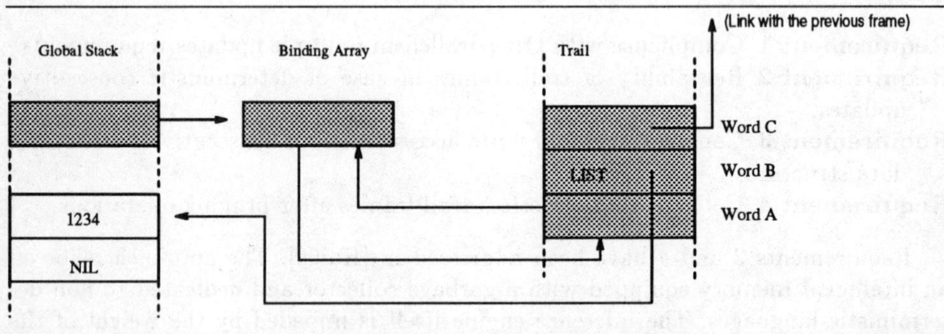

A CU-field with a list [1234] as value

The word A in the trail points to the binding array entry. It is used at task-switching or backtracking time. The word B holds the CU-field's value. The word C makes it possible to link a CU-field's trail frames and to restore the CU-field's binding array entry at backtracking time. The binding array entry points at the trail frame describing the CU-field's current value. CU-fields clearly fulfill requirement 1 for OR-parallel updates.

3.2 CU-field's new values are also in the trail

CU-fields are given a value when they are created. Their value is accessible in constant time from the trail by following the two reference chain from global stack to the trail via the binding array. Requirement 3 for read accesses is satisfied.

As usual, deterministic and non-deterministic updates are not processed in the same way:

1. The previous value is not protected by a choice point. The value can safely be updated in place (requirement 2 and 3).

2. The previous value is protected by a choice point. The update is performed by updating the binding array cell of the CU-field so that it points at a fresh CU-trail frame holding the new value. The new CU-trail frame must also be linked to the previous one. This can be done with five pointer updates (requirement 3).

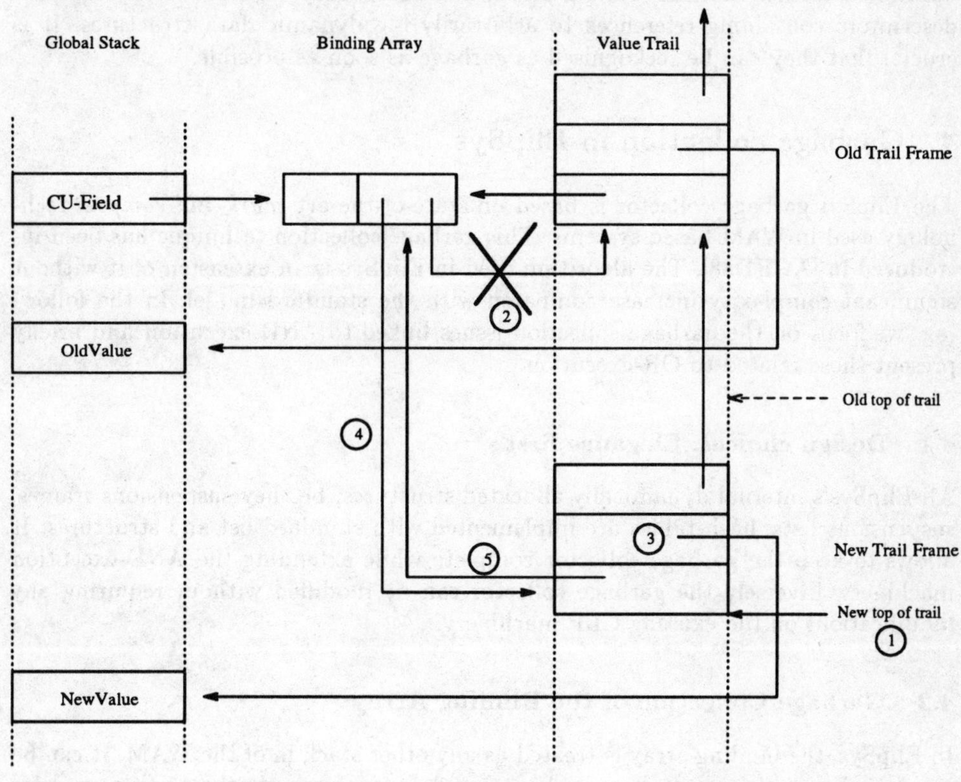

Non deterministic update of a CU-field

The most significant change with respect to the standard binding array technique is that there are pointers from the binding array to the trail. In the next section, we shall present the ElipSys garbage collector, and depict how it makes ElipSys CU-fields satisfy requirement 4.

3.3 Dvariables

Dvariables in ElipSys are all the true logical variables which are not simple free variables. They are either created implicitely - for instance a suspension occurs on a standard variable - or explicitely - for instance when a finite domain variable is introduced by the program -. CU-fields can be conveniently used to implement Dvariables. A Dvariable in ElipSys is a specially tagged CU-field whose value is a structure (descriptor) describing the variable's attributes (control information, domain description, ...).

When a Dvariable X is bound to a Dvariable Y, the descriptor of X is updated to be Y's descriptor. Besides its simplicity (no new extension is needed), this binding scheme achieves transparently a run-time shunting of Dvariables. Length reduction of dereferencing chains is not the most significant aspect of this implementation. The important fact is that after a deterministic binding the Dvariable descriptor can be smoothly garbage collected (See section 4): Depending on the computational functionalities the CLP system offers, Dvariables may have arbitrarily complex descriptors containing references to arbitrarily big dynamic data structures. It is crucial that they can be reckognised as garbage as soon as possible.

4 Garbage collection in ElipSys

The ElipSys garbage collector is based on state-of-the-art *mark-and-compact* technology used in WAM based systems. This garbage collection technique has been introduced in [ACHD88]. The algorithm used in ElipSys is an extension of it without significant complexity increase compared with the standard model. In the following, we focus on the garbage-collection issues linked to AND-execution and briefly present those related to OR-execution.

4.1 Design choices: Elegance first

All ElipSys's internal dynamically allocated structures, be they suspensions frames, suspensions lists, hash-tables are implemented with standard list and structures. It allows to keep the garbage collector complete while extending the AND-execution machinery. Inversely the garbage collector can be modified without requiring any modifications on the existing CLP machinery.

4.2 Garbage Collection of the Binding Array

In ElipSys, the binding array is treated as any other stack in of the WAM. It can be submitted to garbage collection and is treated in a manner similar to that used for the global stack. Neither the marking phase nor the compaction phase of the mark-and-compact algorithm have increased in complexity due to the separate binding area. The cells in the binding array get marked like those in the global stack. The memory compaction is done separately, first in the binding array and afterwards in the global stack. Pointers between the two memory areas are handled like pointers within the global stack in the classical scheme.

4.3 Garbage Collection of the Trail Stack

As already mentioned, the use of consecutively updatable fields allocated on the trail stack has to be viewed as one important contribution to the efficient implementation of a CLP system. This data structure introduces the only true extension to the standard scheme.

CU-fields are built with references from the binding array to the value trail. However, these references can easily be updated at trail stack compaction time using the property of consecutively updatable fields to point back to the corresponding binding array entry, as depicted in section 3.2.

The trail contains sources for marking The first implication of consecutively updatable fields is that the trail contains records for previous values of data cells. This is not the case in a standard WAM systems and the marking phase of the garbage collector must be modified accordingly:

> *Previous* values of A CU-field must be treated as sources for marking as soon as one value of such a field gets marked. Successive values of a CU-field are linked together via the field's chain of trail frames. These additional sources are therefore easily accessible.

Early reset of data cells The compaction of the trail is not affected much by the introduction of CU-fields. The technique of early reset of variables can be equally well applied to these new trail frames.

Pruning operations and consecutive updates The combination of value trailing and pruning opens opportunities for garbage collection which we consider crucial for a CLP system (requirement 4).

— Deterministic updates on CU-fields are performed in place without creating new trail frames. Hence in a segment of value trail filled between two choice point creations there must only one trail frame per updated CU-field.

— This property gets lost when a pruning operation removes choice points and merges trail segments together. Several linked trail frames of a CU-field might then fall into one segment, the most recent only being still active. The ElipSys garbage collector collapses these chains of CU-trail frames into the youngest frame of the chain. Some of the structures which were previous values of a CU-field might then ipso facto be turned into collectable garbage for one pointer at them disappear.

4.4 Garbage Collection in Parallel

ElipSys follows an independent garbage collection approach, an idea first presented by [Ali89], where neither synchronisation nor communication is necessary between parallel threads of computation. Garbage collection is done in an incremental way, i.e. garbage collection restricts itself to those parts of the stacks which have not yet been garbage-collected previously and is triggered *before* creating a parallel branch. A single, incremental garbage collection step is therefore restricted locally to one thread of sequential computation and can be performed completely independently from any other parallel work. So far the incremental and independent garbage collection approach has proven quite successful in the execution of parallel programs (more details can be found in [Dor91]).

5 Results

Once a proper binding scheme has been designed, OR-parallel execution details are orthogonal to the mechanisms related to AND-execution such as unification, suspension/resumption, specialized computation domains. Hence in the evaluation of our binding scheme with respect to memory consumption and garbage collection, we put here emphasis on the characteristics of *mono-processor* execution of our *parallel system* and the comparison with other *sequential* systems. We show that:

1. compared with other techniques designed for sequential systems, our CU-fields implementation behaves
   - as well as those for deterministic updates
   - better than those for non deterministic updates.
2. the provision for OR-parallel execution is perfectly compatible with a complete garbage-collector

CHIP CHIP is the successful forerunner of ElipSys. CHIP and ElipSys have roughly the same execution speed for standard Prolog code. CHIP is dedicated to sequential execution and uses time stamps ([AB90]) when ElipSys is an OR-parallel system using the CU-field technique together with a binding array.

To compare the efficiency of the two binding schemes we use two variants of a program which updates a domain variable (See Appendix A). In the first case the updating is deterministic and no trailing is performed. In the second all updates are trailed because the program creates protecting choice points.

ElipSys behaviour is not modified by trailing. When CHIP performs a trailed update, it has to update the domain variable in the global stack, update the corresponding time stamp *and* to trail the update. CHIP timings for trailed updates drift from those for non trailed updates:

N	50000	100000	200000	300000
Non trailed	8.5s	17s	34s	51s
Trailed	9.3s	18.8s	38.2s	57s

CHIPC3.0 Updating and trailing performances (Sun Sparc 2)

N	50000	100000	200000	300000
Non Trailed	8.8s	17.6s	35.2	52s
Trailed	8.8s	17.6s	35.2s	52s

ElipSys Updating and trailing performances (Sun Sparc 2)

PrologII/MALI In [Hui90], a program implementing an Eratosthene's sieve is proposed which makes heavy uses of coroutining. It constructs a chain of filters each of which associated with one of the already found prime numbers. A new integer is fed in at the beginning of the chain. If the proposed integer is not a multiple of a filter's prime, the filter resuspends itself and transmits the candidate to the next filter. The chain of filters is submitted to an intense rewriting which leads to an important creation of coroutining/suspension structures and makes a garbage collection mechanism necessary (See Appendix B).

The program is intended to show the garbage collection accuracy of Prolog II when coupled with the MALI memory management system ([BCRU86, Rid91]). To measure the accuracy the author proposes to record the greatest prime number the program can generate before a system runs out of memory. This a very rough measurement for it is does not take into account neither the size of abstract machine memory units nor the relative size of internal structures like suspension variables, suspended goals, suspension lists.

In this program, the suspended goals form a chain the length of which is the rank of the biggest prime found so far. Memory requirements should linearly increase with the rank of the greatest prime. The slope of increase reflects the size of internal structures which in turn depends on richness of computational mechanisms. As a matter of fact ElipSys's slope is greater than PrologII/MALI but constant. ElipSys garbage collector is as accurate as the MALI machinery.

	PrologII/MALI		ElipSys 0.3	
Memory (Kbytes)	Prime	Nth prime	Prime	Nth prime
31	683	124	173	40
38	1021	172	317	66
112	5119	685	1699	266
Slope	0.14		0.35	

Ratios (Memory consumption/nth prime number) for MALI and ElipSys

SICStus In SICStus implementation, a suspension variable is handled like a two argument structure ([Car87, SIC90]). The first argument is dedicated to the future binding of the variable; the second argument holds the list of goals suspended on that variable. This scheme's immediate consequence is that even when a suspension variable is deterministically bound and the variable is markable by the garbage collector, the list of suspended goals is also markable and can not be garbage collected although of no use to the computation.

During propagation phases (sequences of deterministic suspensions/resumptions) SICStus hence generates pseudo garbage which can not be collected with a blind mark and collect technique. As a matter of fact in [SC90] a "variable shunting" algorithm is presented to overcome this problem. The importance of the algorithm is exemplified by evaluating the amount of memory that two versions of SICStus (one with variable shunting and one without) keep active after computing the first N prime numbers.

The program highlight the influence of pruning operations on garbage generation. The propagation triggered by head unification on the second clause of *primesfrom/2*) generates data on the trail to enable backtracking if the propagation fails. The pruning performed by the cut makes these data useless.

By using CU-fields to implement suspension variables (3.3) ElipSys avoids *smoothly* these memory management difficulties and the use of an ad hoc mechanism. When a suspension variable is deterministically bound, its descriptor becomes automatically garbage. When the binding is non deterministic, the old value (the descriptor) is kept active through a fresh trail frame. If a cut ever happens, the useless trail frames are collapsed, the descriptor allocated on the stacks is not pointed at anymore and is hence collectable. The following table gives the amount of memory still active after running the queries. ElipSys with its binding scheme achieves the same effect as SICStus with variable shunting.

N first primes	SICStus 0.7 without variable shunting	SICStus 0.7 with variable shunting	ElipSys 0.3
100	0.2 M	229	717
200	1.2 M	429	1417
300	2.5 M	761	2117
400	4.5 M	961	2817
500	7 M	1161	3517

Memory consumption (in data cells)to compute the first N primes numbers

OR-parallel execution As aforementioned, OR-parallel execution evaluation is not the main topic of this paper. We nevertheless here present some timings for OR-parallel computations, to somehow justify a posteriori the ElipSys concept of integrating OR-parallel enumeration facilities together with as powerful as possible AND-execution paradigms whose usage require a garbage collector and justify this paper. The program used in here is a version of queens using generalized forward-checking with a first fail heuristic ([Hen89a]):

```
:- heuristic queens(Board, Domain) with first_fail(Board).
queens(Board, Domain) :-
        place(Board, Domain),
        safe(Board).
place([], Domain).
place([X|Y], Domain) :-
        X :: Domain,
        place(Y, Domain).
safe([]).
safe([F|T]) :- safe1(T,F,1), safe(T).
safe1([],X,Nb).
safe1([F|T],X,Nb) :-
        X =\= F, X =\= F+Nb, X =\= F-Nb,
        Nb1 is Nb+1,
        safe1(T,X,Nb1).
?- queens([X1,X2,X3,X4,X5,X6,X7,X8],1 ~~ 8).
```

The timings for all solutions queries are:

Queens	gfcff-queens(N) Workers 1	2		4		8		10	
	time	time	speedup	time	speedup	time	speedup	time	speedup
8	3.0	1.58	1.89	0.9	3.33	0.56	5.35	0.42	7.14
9	12.5	6.37	1.96	3.3	3.78	1.95	6.41	1.44	8.68
10	49.7	24.93	1.99	12.81	3.87	6.71	7.41	5.06	9.82

Timings in seconds for N-queens all-solution queries (Sequent Symmetry).

All solution queries for the queens problem where the search tree is well balanced are somehow an ideal case for ElipSys. The timings demonstrate the potential of the combination of OR-parallelism with constraints handling.

6 Conclusion

The more flexible the computation models, the less predictable are the run-time behaviour and the memory consumption and the more necessary are garbage collection mechanisms. Such has been our experience with the parallel constraint logic programming system ElipSys and we have had to use adequate memory management mechanisms.

We have depicted in this paper consecutively updatable frames, a data structure enabling to cope with the multiple binding problem due to OR-parallelism and the needs for in-place-updating-instead-of-copying required at many levels and in many places for the efficient and flexible implementation of a complex AND-execution machinery. In a complementary approach we have presented a garbage collection scheme adapted to OR-parallel execution and to the optimal management of this new data structure.

Acknowledgments

This work was partially funded by the CEC as part of ESPRIT II project EP2025, European Declarative System (EDS). We thank Mireille Ducassé for her witty comments on drafts of this paper.

References

[AB90] Abderrahmane Aggoun and Nicolas Beldiceanu. Time Stamps Techniques for the Trailed Data in Constraint Logic Programming Systems. In *Seminaire de Tregastel sur la Programmation en Logique*, France, 1990.

[ACHD88] Karen Appleby et al. Garbage Collection for Prolog Based on WAM. *Communications of the ACM*, 31(6):719–741, 1988.

[AK90] K. Ali and R. Karlsson. The Muse OR-Parallel Prolog Model and its Performance. In *NACLP'90*, Austin, Texas.

[Ali89] Khayri Ali. Incremental Gargage Collection for Or-parallel Prolog Based on WAM. In *Gigalips Workshop*, Stockholm, April 1989. SICS.

[BCRU86] Y. Bekkers, B. Canet, O. Ridoux, and L. Ungaro. MALI: A memory with a Real-Time Garbage Collector for Implementing Logic Programming Languages. In *International Symposium on Logic Programming*, Salt Lake City, 1986.

[BdKH+88] U.C. Baron et al. The parallel ECRC Prolog system PEPSys: An overview and evaluation results. In *FGCS'88*, Tokyo, November 1988.

[Car87] M. Carlsson. Freeze, indexing, and other implementation issues in the WAM. In *ICLP'87*, volume 2, pages 40–58, 1987.

[Col90] Alain Colmerauer. An introduction to prolog-III. *Communications of the ACM*, 33(7):69–90, July 1990.

[CWY91] Vitor Santos Costa, David H.D Warren, and Rong Yang. The Andorra-I Engine: A Parallel Implementation of the Basic Andorra Model. In Koichi Furokawa, editor, *ICLP'91*, Paris, 1991. MIT Press.

[Dor91] Michel Dorochevsky. Garbage Collection in the OR-Parallel Logic Programming System ElipSys. Technical Report DPS-85, ECRC, March 1991.

[DSV90] M. Dincbas et al. Solving Large Combinatorial Problems in Logic Programming. *Journal of Logic Programming*, 8(1-2):74–94, January-March 1990.

[DVS+88] M. Dincbas, P. Van Hentenryck, H. Simonis, A. Aggoun, T. Graf, and F. Berthier. The Constraint Logic Programming Language CHIP. In *FGCS'88*, Tokyo, Japan, December 1988.

[ECR91] ECRC. *Sepia 3.1 User Manual*, November 1991.

[GJ90] G. Gupta and B. Jayaraman. On Criteria for Or-parallel execution of Logic Programs. In *NACLP'90*, Austin, Texas, 1990. MIT Press.

[Hen89a] Pascal Van Hentenryck. *Constraint Satisfaction in Logic Programming.* MIT Press, 1989.

[Hen89b] Pascal Van Hentenryck. Parallel constraints satisfaction in logic programming: Preliminary results of CHIP within PEPSys. In Giorgio Levi and Maurizio Martelli, editors, *ICLP'89*, pages 165–180, Lisbon, June 1989. MIT Press.

[Hui90] Serge Le Huitouze. A new data structure for implementing extensions to Prolog. In *PLILP'91*. LNCS456, 1990.

[JL87] Joxan Jaffar and Jean-Louis Lassez. Constraint logic programming. In *POPL'87, Munich, Germany.* ACM, January 1987.

[LBD+88] R. Butler et al. The Aurora OR-parallel Prolog system. In *FGCS'88*, Tokyo, November 1988.

[Rid91] Olivier Ridoux. Mali v06 Tutorial and Reference Manual. Internal report, 611, IRISA-INRIA-CNRS, October 1991.

[SC90] Dan Sahlin and Mats Carlsson. Variable Shunting for the WAM. In *2nd NACLP Workshop on Logic Programming Architectures and Inplementations*, Austin, Texas, 1990.

[SIC90] SICS. *SICStus Prolog User's Manual*, December 1990.

[War84] David S. Warren. Efficient Prolog memory management for flexible control strategies. In *ISLP*, 1984.

A Testbench for CU-Fields

```
updates_notrail(N):-
        X :: 1 ~~ N,                % X ranges from 1 to N
        update_notrail(N,X).
update_notrail(N,X):- N =\= 1, !,          % prevents from trailing
        X ## N,                            % X is different from N
                                           % N is removed from the range of X
        M is N - 1,
        update_notrail(M,X).
update_notrail(1,_).
updates_trail(N):- X :: 1 ~~ N,            % X ranges from 1 to N
        update_trail(N,X).
update_trail(N,X):- N =\= 1,  X ## N,
        !,                      % dummy cut but necessary to have the same
                                % program structure as in the update_notrail/2
        M is N - 1,  update_trail(M,X).
update_trail(1,_).
```

B PrologII/MALI

```
prime:- freeze(L,sieve(L)), int_list(2,L).
sieve([X|L]):-
        writeln(X),
        freeze(L,filter(X,L,L1)),
        freeze(L1,sieve(L1)).
filter(F,[X|L],L1):-
        multiple(X,F),!,
        freeze(L,filter(F,L,L1)).
filter(F,[X|L],[X|L1]):- freeze(L,filter(F,L,L1)).
multiple(X,F) :- 0 is X mod F.
int_list(N,[N|L]):-
        N1 is N + 1, int_list(N1,L).
?- prime.
```

C SICSTUS

```
nprimes(N,List):- length(List,N), primesfrom(List,2).
primesfrom([],_).
primesfrom([I|Ns],I):- nomultall(Ns,I), J is I + 1, !,primesfrom(Ns,J).
primesfrom(L,I):- J is I + 1, primesfrom(L,J).
nomultall([],_).
nomultall([N|Ns],I):- freeze(N,N mod I >0), nomultall(Ns,I).
?- nprimes(N,L), garbage_collect.
```

Path Analysis for Lazy Data Structures

Carsten K. Gomard[1] and Peter Sestoft[2]

[1] DIKU, Department of Computer Science, University of Copenhagen, DK-2100 Copenhagen Ø, Denmark. E-mail: gomard@diku.dk
[2] Department of Computer Science, Technical University of Denmark, DK-2800 Lyngby, Denmark. E-mail: sestoft@id.dth.dk

Abstract. We present a method to statically infer evaluation order information for data structures in typed lazy functional programs. Our goal is to determine in what order and to what extent variables and data structures are evaluated. This subsumes backwards data structure strictness analysis and can be used to optimize the implementation of suspensions (or "thunks") in lazy languages.

The order of evaluation of the variables in an expression is described by *variable paths*, which are sequences of variables. The evaluation order of a data structure is described by a *context*. This is the type of the data structure together with path sets describing the order of evaluation of its components. Thus for the type `natlist ::= Nil | Cons nat natlist` we record the order in which the `nat` and `natlist` fields of `Cons` are evaluated (if at all).

To obtain a terminating analysis, only *uniform* contexts are allowed for recursively defined types such as `natlist`: all the recursive components (those of type `natlist`) must have the same description.

Contexts seem to be natural tools for describing and reasoning with data structure strictness. In particular, one can characterize head strictness also in the absence of tail strictness.

The main advantage of this work over previous work [2] [4] is the handling of data structures.

1 Introduction

Previous work on analysing the evaluation order of lazy functional languages has focussed on the evaluation order of variables and has not dealt with lazy data structures. Thus Bloss and Hudak would analyse an expression such as

```
letrec f(x,y,z) = if x=0 then y else z
in     f(v+5,w,u+w)
```

and find that the variables `v` and `w` may be evaluated in the following orders: First `v`, then `w`; or first `v`, then `u`, then `w`, assuming that "+" evaluates its arguments from left to right [2]. This finding would be expressed by a set of paths, where a *path* is a finite sequence of variable names. The path set for the above example is $\{\langle \texttt{v},\texttt{w}\rangle, \langle \texttt{v},\texttt{u},\texttt{w}\rangle\}$.

Bloss and Hudak's path analysis is a *forwards* analysis in which the paths for argument expressions are concatenated in the order in which the corresponding variables are used. Variables can occur at most once in a path: in a lazy language the argument expression bound to a variable is evaluated at most once.

The forwards path analysis method does not work for computations involving lazy data structures, however. The reason is that the order of evaluation of `x` and `y` in the expression `e` ≡ `(Pair x y)` depends on the context of the expression, and more specifically, on the order in which the parts of its result are required. We call this the *context* or *evaluation order type* of the expression.

Assume again that "+" evaluates its arguments from left to right. Now if the expression `e` ≡ `(Pair x y)` occurs in `(f e)` where `f z = (fst z) + (snd z)`, then `x` is evaluated before `y`. On the other hand, if `e` occurs in `(g e)` where `g z = (snd z) + (fst z)`, then `y` would be evaluated before `x`. It is also easy to construct contexts that ignore any one or both of `x` and `y`.

We therefore suggest an analysis in which one works *backwards*: from the evaluation order of the result of an expression to its subexpressions, and from these to the variables occurring in the expression.

Example 1. Consider the data type `natlist` and the function `(take xs n)` which computes the n-prefix of list `xs`:

```
natlist ::= Nil | Cons nat natlist
take :: natlist × nat → natlist

take xs n = case xs of
              Nil      => Nil
              Cons y ys => case n=0 of
                             True  => Nil
                             False => Cons y (take ys (n-1))
```

Assume that a call to `take` is to be evaluated and printed. In the `natlist` type, whose constructor `Cons` has arguments of types `nat` and `natlist`, the printer prints the `nat`-component before the `natlist` component. Thus the printer determines the evaluation order of the result, that is, its *context* or *evaluation order type*, which we denote by $\mathtt{natlist}_{\mathtt{Cons}:\{\langle 1,2\rangle\}}$.

Our analysis finds that if the context of `take xs n` is $\mathtt{natlist}_{\mathtt{Cons}:\{\langle 1,2\rangle\}}$, then `xs` will have context $\mathtt{natlist}_{\mathtt{Cons}:\{\langle 1,2\rangle,\langle\rangle\}}$. This means that whenever a `Cons` in `xs` is evaluated, then either both the head (component 1) *and* the tail (component 2) will be evaluated, in that order, or none of them will be evaluated.

If `take xs n` appears in context $\mathtt{natlist}_{\mathtt{Cons}:\{\langle 2,1\rangle\}}$ then `xs` is in context $\mathtt{natlist}_{\mathtt{Cons}:\{\langle 2,1\rangle,\langle\rangle\}}$. Again this means that whenever a `Cons` in `xs` is evaluated, then either tail *and* head are evaluated, in that order, or none of them is.

In summary, the components of each `Cons` in the argument of `take` are evaluated in the same order as the `Cons` components of the result, if at all. Also, even if the result is in a head- as well as tail-strict context (where 1 and 2 appear in all paths), the argument is not in a head- and tail-strict context.

2 A First Order Example Language

To present evaluation order analysis we use a lazy, simply typed, first order functional language with (directly or indirectly recursive) data types. Standard examples of data types are pairs, tuples, lists of naturals, lists of lists of naturals *etc*. The syntax of programs is as follows, where $m, n \geq 0$ and $N \geq 1$:

$$
\begin{array}{lll}
\textit{program} & ::= & \textit{typedef}_1 \; \ldots \; \textit{typedef}_n \; \textit{letrec} \\
\textit{typedef} & ::= & t \; \texttt{::=} \; \textit{summand}_1 \mid \ldots \mid \textit{summand}_N \\
\textit{summand} & ::= & \texttt{C} \; \textit{texp}_1 \; \ldots \; \textit{texp}_m \\
\textit{texp} & ::= & \texttt{nat} \mid t \\
\textit{letrec} & ::= & \texttt{letrec} \; \textit{def}_1 \; \ldots \; \textit{def}_n \; \texttt{in e} \\
\textit{def} & ::= & \texttt{f} \; \texttt{x}_1 \; \ldots \; \texttt{x}_n \; \texttt{=} \; \texttt{e} \\
\texttt{e} & ::= & \texttt{x} \mid \texttt{A} \; \texttt{e}_1 \ldots \texttt{e}_n \mid \texttt{C} \; \texttt{e}_1 \ldots \texttt{e}_n \mid \texttt{f} \; \texttt{e}_1 \ldots \texttt{e}_n \\
 & & \mid \texttt{case} \; \texttt{e}_0 \; \texttt{of} \; \textit{branch}_1 \; \ldots \; \textit{branch}_N \\
\textit{branch} & ::= & \texttt{C} \; \texttt{x}_1 \; \ldots \; \texttt{x}_m \; \texttt{=>} \; \texttt{e}
\end{array}
$$

A type expression is either a *base type* or the name of a *data type*. A data type is a set of *summands*, each of which consists of a *constructor* `C` and a list of type expressions. Note that data types may be recursive. All constructor names must be distinct.

Base functions `A` are strict and evaluate their (base type) arguments from left to right. The language is first order: all defined functions `f`, base functions `A`, and constructors `C` must be fully applied. A `case` expression `case` $\texttt{e}_0$ `of` $\textit{branch}_1$ ... $\textit{branch}_n$ consists of a *root expression* $\texttt{e}_0$ the type of which must be a data type t, and several *branches*, one for each constructor of t. The *body* of a program or letrec expression `letrec ... in` $\texttt{e}_0$ is the last expression $\texttt{e}_0$.

The language is simply (monomorphically) typed, and all expressions are assumed to be type correct. We do not give a formal type system here. For the extension to higher order programs, see [6].

3 Describing Evaluation Order

In any particular evaluation of a lazy program, the subexpressions of the program will be evaluated to *weak head normal form* (abbreviated *whnf*) in some order, ultimately determined by the printer's demand for a result to print. The precise order cannot be inferred unless one has the program's input data available, so that the program can be run. Our goal is to describe *approximately* the order of evaluation of variables and data structures for all possible evaluations of the program, *independently* of its concrete input data. We will give this approximate description as a set of *paths* of variables and constructor fields, each describing one possible order.

3.1 Paths and Path Sets

We use paths and path sets to describe evaluation order. A *path* π over D is a repetition-free sequence of elements of D. A *variable path* is a path over a set of variables and describes the order in which the variables are evaluated to whnf. An *argument path* is a path over a set $\{1, \ldots, n\}$ of argument positions and describes the order in which the arguments of a function or constructor are evaluated to whnf. Formally, the set of paths over D is

$$Path(D) = \{ \langle x_1, \ldots, x_n \rangle \in D^* \mid \forall i, j. \; x_i = x_j \Rightarrow i = j \}$$

Since paths are repetition-free, a variable or argument position appears at most once in a path. This reflects lazy evaluation: A variable, function argument, or data structure component is evaluated only the first time its value is required. Note also that if D is finite, then so is $Path(D)$. Typical names for paths are π and ρ.

Our static analysis is approximate and therefore works with *sets* Π of possible paths. The path set domain $PathSet(D)$ over D is

$$PathSet(D) = \{ \Pi \mid \Pi \subseteq Path(D) \}$$

When ordered by set inclusion, it is a finite lattice for finite D. The least element is the empty path set $\{\}$. This element describes the argument's context in a non-terminating function such as `f x = f x`. Compare this with the singleton path set containing only the empty path, $\{\langle\rangle\}$, which describes the argument's context in `f x = 4`, where the argument is ignored.

3.2 Path Sets and Strictness

If $\pi = \langle \mathtt{x} \rangle$ is a variable path for an evaluation of expression `e` to whnf, then `x` must be evaluated to whnf no later than `e` is. Now if `x` appears in every path in the path set for evaluation of `e` to whnf, then `x` is *needed by* `e`, or in other words `e` is *strict in* `x`. (If `e` is undefined and thus cannot be evaluated to a whnf, then the path set is empty, so `x` formally appears on every path, and thus `e` is strict in `x` as expected.)

In a similar manner, an argument path set for the constructor `Cons` of `natlist` describes how the constructor will evaluate its arguments. In other words, the path set describe the context of a constructor application, including strictness. For example, if 1 belongs to every path in the path set, then the context is *head strict*: the constructor will always evaluate its first argument to whnf in this context. Similarly, if 2 belongs to every path, then the context is *tail strict*.

3.3 Operations on Paths and Path Sets

The *repetition-free concatenation* $\pi_1 {\cdot} \pi_2$ of paths $\pi_1 = \langle x_1, \ldots, x_m \rangle$ and $\pi_2 = \langle x_{m+1}, \ldots, x_n \rangle$ is defined by

$$\begin{aligned}
\pi_1 {\cdot} \langle\rangle &= \pi_1 \\
\pi_1 {\cdot} \langle x_{m+1}, \ldots, x_n \rangle &= \langle x_1, \ldots, x_m \rangle {\cdot} \langle x_{m+2}, \ldots, x_n \rangle \quad \text{if } x_{m+1} \in \{x_1, \ldots, x_m\} \\
&= \langle x_1, \ldots, x_{m+1} \rangle {\cdot} \langle x_{m+2}, \ldots, x_n \rangle \text{ otherwise}
\end{aligned}$$

If both π_1 and π_2 contain x, then the x from π_2 will not appear in the concatenation. We also denote the elementwise concatenation of path sets Π_1 and Π_2 by $\Pi_1 {\cdot} \Pi_2 = \{\pi_1 {\cdot} \pi_2 \mid \pi_1 \in \Pi_1,\ \pi_2 \in \Pi_2\}$.

The *restriction* $\pi \restriction \sigma$ of path π to set σ is the maximal subsequence of π consisting only of elements of σ:

$$\begin{aligned}
\langle\rangle \restriction \sigma &= \langle\rangle \\
\langle x_1, \ldots, x_m \rangle \restriction \sigma &= \langle x_1 \rangle {\cdot} (\langle x_2, \ldots, x_m \rangle \restriction \sigma) \text{ if } x_1 \in \sigma \\
&= \langle x_2, \ldots, x_m \rangle \restriction \sigma \qquad \text{otherwise}
\end{aligned}$$

The *hiding* $\pi \backslash \sigma$ of a path $\pi \in Path(D)$ with respect to the set σ is defined by $\pi \backslash \sigma = \pi \restriction (D \setminus \sigma)$. For a path set Π, restriction and hiding are defined elementwise.

In the analysis below we need to describe the evaluation order of an expression $\mathsf{e} \equiv (\ldots \mathsf{e}_1 \ldots \mathsf{e}_n \ldots)$ in terms of the evaluation order of its subexpressions e_j. For this we need to combine path sets for the e_j into a path set for e. A safe but overly conservative description of e's evaluation order is obtained by simply *interleaving* all paths for the e_j.

The *interleaving* $\pi \| \rho$ of paths π and ρ is the path set defined by

$$\pi \parallel \rho = \{\ \pi_1 \cdot \rho_1 \cdot \ldots \cdot \pi_n \cdot \rho_n \mid \pi_1 \cdot \ldots \cdot \pi_n = \pi \text{ and } \rho_1 \cdot \ldots \cdot \rho_n = \rho\ \}$$

Note that any of π_j and ρ_j may be the empty path, in particular π_1 and ρ_n. The interleaving $\Pi_1 \| \Pi_2$ of path sets is defined by

$$\Pi_1 \parallel \Pi_2 = \bigcup_{\pi \in \Pi_1, \rho \in \Pi_2} (\pi \parallel \rho)$$

The simple interleaving is overly conservative since it takes into account neither the order in which the subexpressions $\mathsf{e}_1 \ldots \mathsf{e}_n$ are evaluated to whnf, nor any information about the variables needed in a subexpression e_j. A variable is *needed* in an expression if the expression cannot be evaluated to whnf unless the variable has been evaluated to whnf.

For instance, if e_1 is evaluated to whnf before e_2, and variable $\mathbf{x}$ is needed in e_1, then variable $\mathbf{x}$ must be evaluated to whnf before any variable occurrence in e_2. We therefore introduce *merging* as an improved form of interleaving that takes such information into account.

The *merging* $merge(\Pi_a)(\sigma_1 \ldots \sigma_n)(\Pi_1 \ldots \Pi_n)$ of subexpression path sets Π_j with respect to Π_a and σ_j is a path set describing the order of evaluation of expression e. The path set Π_a describes the possible orders in which the subexpressions e_i are evaluated to whnf, σ_i is the set of variables needed in e_i, and Π_i is the set of variable paths for subexpression e_i.

$$\begin{aligned}
&merge(\Pi_a)(\sigma_1 \ldots \sigma_n)(\Pi_1 \ldots \Pi_n) = \\
&\bigcup_{\pi_a \in \Pi_a, \pi_i \in \Pi_i} merge1(\pi_a)(\sigma_1 \ldots \sigma_n)(\pi_1 \ldots \pi_n)
\end{aligned}$$

$$\begin{aligned}
&merge1(\langle\rangle)(\sigma_1 \ldots \sigma_n)(\pi_1 \ldots \pi_n) \qquad\qquad = \{\langle\rangle\} \\
&merge1(\langle i_1, \ldots, i_k \rangle)(\sigma_1 \ldots \sigma_n)(\pi_1 \ldots \pi_n) = \\
&\{\pi_1 \restriction \sigma_1\} \cdot (\{\pi_1 \backslash \sigma_1\} \parallel merge1(\langle i_2, \ldots, i_k \rangle)(\sigma_1 \ldots \sigma_n)(\pi_1 \ldots \pi_n))
\end{aligned}$$

In the analysis functions presented later we shall write $\mathcal{S}[\![\,\mathsf{e}\,]\!]\zeta$ for the set of variables needed in e. The function $\mathcal{S}$ can be defined in terms of the analysis function $\mathcal{R}$ defined later; a separate neededness analysis is not required.

3.4 Evaluation Order for Variables

If the free variables of expression e are $\mathbf{x}_1, \ldots, \mathbf{x}_n$, then evaluation order information about these variables is represented by a path set in $PathSet(\{\mathbf{x}_1, \ldots, \mathbf{x}_n\})$. For example, if the free variables are $\mathbf{x}$ and $\mathbf{y}$, then the path set $\Pi = \{\langle \mathbf{x} \rangle, \langle \mathbf{x}, \mathbf{y} \rangle\}$ says that e is strict in $\mathbf{x}$, and that $\mathbf{y}$ is evaluated to whnf after $\mathbf{x}$, if at all.

3.5 Evaluation Order Types

Since the language is first-order, a value is either of base type, such as `nat`, or of a data type, such as list of `nat`. In the latter case, we want to know the extent and order in which the structure is evaluated.

A *context* or *evaluation order type* describes the evaluation order of the components of a value.

Evaluation order types over base types are simple because a base type value is atomic. If the value has been evaluated to whnf, then it has been fully evaluated: there are no components which can be evaluated independently of the others. Thus the only evaluation order types are $\{\langle\rangle\}$ which represents full evaluation, and $\{\}$ which represents the non-terminating context (this is the argument's context in `f x = f x` as previously mentioned). Let $Eot(t)$ denote the set of evaluation order types or contexts over type t. The set of evaluation order types $Eot(\texttt{nat})$ over `nat` then is:

$$Eot(\texttt{nat}) = \{\{\}, \{\langle\rangle\}\}$$

and similarly for other base types. The set of evaluation order types over a base type is isomorphic to that over a data type with a single nullary constructor.

Evaluation order types over constructed values, that is, values of a data type t, are more interesting. Let the data type t be defined by:

$$t ::= \texttt{C}_1\ t_{11} \ldots t_{1c_1} \mid \ldots \mid \texttt{C}_n\ t_{n1} \ldots t_{nc_n}$$

The m arguments of a constructor $\texttt{C}\ t_1\ \ldots\ t_m$ are evaluated to whnf in some order. The possible argument evaluation orders for `C` are described by a path set $\Pi_a \in PathSet(\{1,\ldots,m\})$. In addition, the constructor arguments are described by a tuple $(\tau_1,\ldots,\tau_m)$, where each τ_j is an evaluation order type over type t_j. Thus the constructor `C` is suitably described by the tuple $(\Pi_a,(\tau_1,\ldots,\tau_m))$. This is called an *application context* for the constructor. Application contexts are used also to describe defined functions.

The set $Actx(t_1\ \ldots\ t_m)$ of application contexts over argument types $t_1\ \ldots\ t_m$ is defined as follows:

$$Actx(t_1\ \ldots\ t_m) = PathSet(\{1,\ldots,m\}) \times \textstyle\prod_{j=1}^{m} Eot(t_j)$$

An evaluation order type over data type t now naturally consists of a tuple of application contexts, one for each constructor $\texttt{C}_i$. The set of evaluation order types over the data type t above is:

$$Eot(t) = \textstyle\prod_{i=1}^{n} Actx(t_{i1}\ \ldots\ t_{ic_i})$$

The ordering on the component lattices $PathSet(\{1,\ldots,c_i\})$ makes the set $Eot(t)$ a complete lattice. However, this definition yields infinite evaluation order types when the type t is recursive. To obtain a finite presentation of evaluation order types also for recursive types t, we require evaluation order types to be *uniform*. The idea is that all (recursive) occurrences of t in the definition of t must have the same evaluation order type as the top level one.

For a list data type, uniformity means that evaluation order information for all list elements are identified, and similarly for all tails of the list. As a consequence, our analysis can collect only information which is valid for all elements of a list. This is not a strong limitation: well-written typed functional programs usually treat all elements of recursive data types the same anyway.

3.6 Towards formalizing uniformity

The uniformity constraint is formalized by making recursion explicit in the type equations. Type equations that are mutually recursive, say $r_1 \ldots r_k$ with defining equations of form $r_i = rhs_i$, are transformed into $\mu(r_1,\ldots,r_n).(rhs_1,\ldots,rhs_n)$. Type equations that are not recursive are left as they are. For a recursively defined type, r_i, with defining equation

$$\mu(r_1,\ldots,r_n).(rhs_1,\ldots,rhs_n)$$

the set of evaluation order types is (re-)defined by:

$$\begin{aligned}
&Eot(r_i) = Mu(r_1,\ldots,r_n).(EoRhs(rhs_1),\ldots,EoRhs(rhs_n)) \\
&EoRhs(\mathtt{C}_1\ t_{11}\ldots t_{1c(1)} \mid \ldots \mid \mathtt{C}_n\ t_{n1}\ldots t_{nc(n)}) \\
&= \textstyle\prod_{i=1}^{n} (PathSet(\{1,\ldots,c(i)\}) \times \prod_{j=1}^{c(i)} RecEot(t_{ij})) \\
&RecEot(t_{ij}) = r_k, \qquad \text{if } t_{ij} = r_k \\
&\qquad\qquad\quad = Eot(t_{ij}), \text{otherwise}
\end{aligned}$$

Mu is a constructor used to build the structure that represents evaluation order types over μ-defined types. Outside this section we shall not make uniformity handling explicit. Different approaches to maintain uniformity are described in [6,9].

4 Evaluation Order Analysis

This section describes evaluation order for the lazy example language from Section 2 above, and presents a computable evaluation order analysis.

The purpose of the evaluation order analysis is to find evaluation order information about a given program `letrec ... in` $\mathtt{e}_0$. We shall represent this information as an *evaluation order description* ζ such that for every function `f` of type $t_1 \times \ldots \times t_n \rightarrow t$ in the program, $\zeta\mathtt{f}$ has type

$$\zeta\mathtt{f} : Eot(t) \rightarrow Actx(t_1 \ldots t_n)$$

The idea is that $\zeta\mathtt{f}$ maps the context $\tau \in Eot(t)$ of an application $(\mathtt{f}\ \mathtt{e}_1\ \ldots\ \mathtt{e}_n)$ into an application context $(\Pi_a, (\tau_1, \ldots, \tau_n)) \in Actx(t_1 \ldots t_n)$. This consists of a path set Π_a describing the argument evaluation order, and an evaluation order type τ_j for each argument expression $\mathtt{e}_j$.

Below we present two analysis functions, $\mathcal{R}$ and $\mathcal{T}$, which are used when finding ζ for a given program. Since ζ is defined by the functions $\mathcal{R}$ and $\mathcal{T}$, but also used in defining them, we shall define ζ as a solution to an equation (equivalently, as a fixed point of a functional) involving $\mathcal{R}$ and $\mathcal{T}$. The functions $\mathcal{R}$ and $\mathcal{T}$ are mutually recursive.

The role of the path analysis function $\mathcal{R}$ is to compute a path set describing the order in which the variables of an expression `e` are evaluated to whnf.

The role of the context analysis function $\mathcal{T}$ is to compute the evaluation order types of variables in an expression `e`.

In both cases, the evaluation order type of the expression `e` itself must be given, so the analyses work *backwards*: from the outside in.

4.1 Evaluation Order in the Example Language

For each syntactic construct of the language, we list the rule for combining variable paths found for the subexpressions. These rules form the basis of the analysis function $\mathcal{R}$. Clearly, the rules must reflect the actual order of evaluation in the language, that is, the operational aspects of lazy evaluation.

In this section Π_i denotes the path set for subexpression $\mathtt{e}_i$ for $i = 1, \ldots, n$, and Π denotes the path for $\mathtt{e}$ – the one we wish to determine.

- $\mathtt{e} \equiv \mathtt{x}$: The path for evaluating variable $\mathtt{x}$ is just $\langle \mathtt{x} \rangle$.
- $\mathtt{e} \equiv (\mathtt{A}\ \mathtt{e}_1\ \ldots\ \mathtt{e}_n)$: Base functions are strict and evaluate their base type arguments from left to right. Evaluation to whnf is complete evaluation. The combined path set is therefore the concatenation $\Pi = \Pi_1 \cdot \ldots \cdot \Pi_n$.
- $\mathtt{e} \equiv (\mathtt{C}_i\ \mathtt{e}_1\ \ldots\ \mathtt{e}_m)$: The context τ of $\mathtt{e}$ must have form $(\alpha_1,\ldots,\alpha_n)$. Constructor $\mathtt{C}_i$ is described by the application context $\alpha_i = (\Pi_a, (\tau_1, \ldots, \tau_m))$. Each $\pi_a \in \Pi_a$ describes a possible order of evaluation of C's arguments.
  If according to π_a, $\mathtt{e}_i$ is evaluated to whnf before $\mathtt{e}_j$, then those variables *needed* in $\mathtt{e}_i$ are evaluated to whnf before those in Π_j. We employ this information to combine the Π_j, using the function *merge* defined in Section 3.3 above. This is far more precise than just interleaving the argument path sets Π_j. For example, if $m = 2$, $\Pi_a = \{\langle 2, 1\rangle\}$, $\Pi_1 = \{\langle \mathtt{z}\rangle\}$, $\Pi_2 = \{\langle \mathtt{x},\mathtt{y}\rangle, \langle \mathtt{x}\rangle\}$ and $\mathtt{e}_2$ is known to be strict in $\mathtt{x}$, then $\Pi = \{\langle \mathtt{x},\mathtt{y},\mathtt{z}\rangle, \langle \mathtt{x},\mathtt{z},\mathtt{y}\rangle, \langle \mathtt{x},\mathtt{z}\rangle\}$.
- $\mathtt{e} \equiv (\mathtt{f}\ \mathtt{e}_1\ \ldots\ \mathtt{e}_n)$: From the evaluation order description ζ and the context τ of $\mathtt{e}$, we get $\mathtt{f}$'s application context $\zeta \mathtt{f} \tau = (\Pi_a, (\tau_1, \ldots, \tau_n))$. Using this, the path set Π is then composed as for constructor application.
- $\mathtt{e} \equiv \begin{pmatrix} \mathtt{case}\ \mathtt{e}_0\ \mathtt{of} \\ \quad \mathtt{C}_1\ \mathtt{x}_{11} \ldots \mathtt{x}_{1c_1}\ \mathtt{=>} \mathtt{e}_1 \\ \quad \ldots \\ \quad \mathtt{C}_n\ \mathtt{x}_{n1} \ldots \mathtt{x}_{nc_n} \mathtt{=>} \mathtt{e}_n \end{pmatrix}$:
  First the root expression $\mathtt{e}_0$ is evaluated to whnf, then *one* of the branches is evaluated. We thus combine Π_0 with Π_i for $i = 1, \ldots, n$ and take the union of these path sets. The combination is done using the *merge* function and follows the standard pattern: those variables in which $\mathtt{e}_0$ is strict come first while other variables in Π_0 are interleaved with the Π_i's.

Note the need for the evaluation order description ζ in analysing a defined function application.

4.2 The Path Analysis Function

The evaluation order analysis function $\mathcal{R}$ finds a variable path set $\Pi = \mathcal{R}[\![\mathtt{e}]\!]\zeta\tau$ for an expression $\mathtt{e}$ in a context τ. If $\mathtt{e}$ has type t and free variables $\mathit{FreeVars}(\mathtt{e})$ then:

$$\mathcal{R}[\![\mathtt{e}]\!]\zeta : \mathit{Eot}(t) \rightarrow \mathit{PathSet}(\mathit{FreeVars}(\mathtt{e}))$$

The definition of $\mathcal{R}$ is based on the rules just given in Section 4.1, and is shown in Figure 1. The function *merge* was defined in Section 3.3, and $\mathcal{S}[\![\mathtt{e}]\!]\zeta$ is the set of variables needed in expression $\mathtt{e}$. We assume that all identifiers in the program are distinct.

To find the paths through a **case** expression we analyse $\mathbf{e}_0$ in the context τ_0 found by analysing the branches, and we analyse the n branches in the same context τ as the entire **case** expression. The context τ_0 of $\mathbf{e}_0$ is found by finding the variable path sets Π_i for the $\mathbf{e}_i$ using $\mathcal{R}$. Restricting these path sets to the set $\{\mathtt{x}_{i1},\ldots,\mathtt{x}_{ic_i}\}$ of **case**-bound variables, we obtain an argument path set Π_{ai} for each constructor $\mathtt{C}_i$. The argument path set together with the constructor arguments' evaluation order types τ_{ij} gives the application contexts α_i. The context for $\mathbf{e}_0$ is the tuple $\tau_0 = (\alpha_1,\ldots,\alpha_n)$ of application contexts.

$$\mathcal{R}[\![\,\mathtt{x}\,]\!]\zeta\tau = \{\langle \mathtt{x}\rangle\}$$

$$\mathcal{R}[\![\,\mathtt{A}\ \mathtt{e}_1\ \ldots\ \mathtt{e}_n\,]\!]\zeta\tau = \mathcal{R}[\![\,\mathtt{e}_1\,]\!]\zeta\tau\cdot\ldots\cdot\mathcal{R}[\![\,\mathtt{e}_n\,]\!]\zeta\tau$$

$$\begin{aligned}\mathcal{R}[\![\,\mathtt{C}_i\ \mathtt{e}_1\ \ldots\ \mathtt{e}_m\,]\!]\zeta\tau &= \mathit{merge}(\Pi_a)(\mathcal{S}[\![\,\mathtt{e}_1\,]\!]\zeta,\ldots,\mathcal{S}[\![\,\mathtt{e}_m\,]\!]\zeta)(\mathcal{R}[\![\,\mathtt{e}_1\,]\!]\zeta\tau_1,\ldots,\mathcal{R}[\![\,\mathtt{e}_m\,]\!]\zeta\tau_m)\\ &\quad\text{where } (\Pi_a,\ (\tau_1,\ldots,\tau_m)) = \alpha_i\\ &\quad\phantom{\text{where }} (\alpha_1,\ldots,\alpha_n) = \tau\end{aligned}$$

$$\begin{aligned}\mathcal{R}[\![\,\mathtt{f}\ \mathtt{e}_1\ \ldots\ \mathtt{e}_n\,]\!]\zeta\tau &= \mathit{merge}(\Pi_a)(\mathcal{S}[\![\,\mathtt{e}_1\,]\!]\zeta,\ldots,\mathcal{S}[\![\,\mathtt{e}_n\,]\!]\zeta)(\mathcal{R}[\![\,\mathtt{e}_1\,]\!]\zeta\tau_1,\ldots,\mathcal{R}[\![\,\mathtt{e}_n\,]\!]\zeta\tau_n)\\ &\quad\text{where } (\Pi_a,\ (\tau_1,\ldots,\tau_n)) = \zeta\mathtt{f}\tau\end{aligned}$$

$$\mathcal{R}\left[\!\!\left[\begin{array}{l}\mathtt{case}\ \ \mathtt{e}_0\ \ \mathtt{of}\\ \quad \mathtt{C}_1\ \ \mathtt{x}_{11}\ldots\mathtt{x}_{1c_1}\ \mathtt{=>e}_1\\ \quad\ldots\\ \quad \mathtt{C}_n\ \ \mathtt{x}_{n1}\ldots\mathtt{x}_{nc_n}\ \mathtt{=>e}_n\end{array}\right]\!\!\right]\zeta\tau = \bigcup_{i=1}^{n} \mathit{merge}(\{\langle 1,2\rangle\})(\mathcal{S}[\![\,\mathtt{e}_0\,]\!]\zeta,\mathcal{S}[\![\,\mathtt{e}_i\,]\!]\zeta)(\Pi_0,\Pi_i{}')$$

$$\begin{aligned}\text{where } \Pi_0 &= \mathcal{R}[\![\,\mathtt{e}_0\,]\!]\zeta\tau_0\\ \tau_0 &= (\alpha_1,\ldots,\alpha_n)\\ \alpha_i &= (\Pi_{ai},\ (\tau_{i1},\ldots,\tau_{ic_i}))\\ \Pi_{ai} &= \{\langle j_1,\ldots,j_k\rangle \mid \langle \mathtt{x}_{ij_1},\ldots,\mathtt{x}_{ij_k}\rangle \in \Pi_i{\restriction}\{\mathtt{x}_{i1},\ldots,\mathtt{x}_{ic_i}\}\}\\ \tau_{ij} &= \mathcal{T}[\![\,\mathtt{e}_i\,]\!]\zeta\tau\mathtt{x}_{ij}\\ \Pi_i &= \mathcal{R}[\![\,\mathtt{e}_i\,]\!]\zeta\tau\\ \Pi_i{}' &= \Pi_i\backslash\{\mathtt{x}_{i1},\ldots,\mathtt{x}_{ic_i}\}\\ i &\in \{1,\ldots,n\},\ j\in\{1,\ldots,c_i\}\end{aligned}$$

Fig. 1. Path analysis function

4.3 The Context Analysis Function

The context analysis function $\mathcal{T}$ finds the context or evaluation order type $\tau' = \mathcal{T}[\![\,\mathbf{e}\,]\!]\zeta\mathbf{y}$ of a variable $\mathbf{y}$ in an expression $\mathbf{e}$ in a given context τ. For every expression $\mathbf{e}$ of type t,

$$\mathcal{T}[\![\,\mathbf{e}\,]\!]\zeta : \mathit{Eot}(t) \rightarrow \mathrm{Var}(t') \rightarrow \mathit{Eot}(t')$$

Here $\mathrm{Var}(t')$ denotes the set of variables of type t'.

The context or evaluation order type of variable $\mathbf{y}$ in an expression is the least upper bound of the contexts of its occurrences. Recall from Section 3.5 that the set $\mathit{Eot}(t')$ of evaluation order types over t' is a lattice. Thus function $\mathcal{T}$ works by finding the evaluation order type of every occurrence of $\mathbf{y}$. Its definition is given in Figure 2.

$$
\begin{array}{lll}
\mathcal{T}[\![\mathtt{x}]\!]\zeta\tau\mathtt{y} & = \tau & \text{if } \mathtt{x} = \mathtt{y} \\
 & = \bot_{Eot(t)} & \text{otherwise} \\
\mathcal{T}[\![\mathtt{A}\ \mathtt{e}_1 \ldots \mathtt{e}_n]\!]\zeta\tau\mathtt{y} & = \bigsqcup_{i=1}^{n} \mathcal{T}[\![\mathtt{e}_i]\!]\zeta\tau\mathtt{y} & \\
\mathcal{T}[\![\mathtt{C}_i\ \mathtt{e}_1 \ldots \mathtt{e}_m]\!]\zeta\tau\mathtt{y} & = \bigsqcup_{j=1}^{m} \mathcal{T}[\![\mathtt{e}_j]\!]\zeta\tau_j\mathtt{y} & \\
 & \text{where } (\Pi, (\tau_1,\ldots,\tau_m)) = \alpha_i & \\
 & \qquad (\alpha_1,\ldots,\alpha_n) = \tau & \\
\mathcal{T}[\![\mathtt{f}\ \mathtt{e}_1 \ldots \mathtt{e}_n]\!]\zeta\tau\mathtt{y} & = \bigsqcup_{i=1}^{n} \mathcal{T}[\![\mathtt{e}_i]\!]\zeta\tau_i\mathtt{y} & \\
 & \text{where } (\Pi, (\tau_1, \ldots, \tau_n)) = \zeta\mathtt{f}\tau &
\end{array}
$$

$$
\mathcal{T}\left[\!\!\left[\begin{array}{l}\mathtt{case}\ \ \mathtt{e}_0\ \mathtt{of} \\ \quad \mathtt{C}_1\ \mathtt{x}_{11}\ldots\mathtt{x}_{1c_1}\ \mathtt{=>e}_1 \\ \quad \ldots \\ \quad \mathtt{C}_n\ \mathtt{x}_{n1}\ldots\mathtt{x}_{nc_n}\mathtt{=>e}_n\end{array}\right]\!\!\right]\zeta\tau\mathtt{y} = \left(\bigsqcup_{i=1}^{n} \mathcal{T}[\![\mathtt{e}_i]\!]\zeta\tau\mathtt{y}\right) \sqcup \mathcal{T}[\![\mathtt{e}_0]\!]\zeta\tau_0\mathtt{y}
$$

$$
\begin{array}{lcl}
\text{where} & & \\
\tau_0 & = & (\alpha_1,\ldots,\alpha_n) \\
\alpha_i & = & (\Pi_{ai}, (\tau_{i1},\ldots,\tau_{ic_i})) \\
\Pi_{ai} & = & \{\langle j_1,\ldots,j_k\rangle \mid \langle \mathtt{x}_{ij_1},\ldots,\mathtt{x}_{ij_k}\rangle \in \Pi_i \restriction \{\mathtt{x}_{i1},\ldots,\mathtt{x}_{ic_i}\}\} \\
\tau_{ij} & = & \mathcal{T}[\![\mathtt{e}_i]\!]\zeta\tau\mathtt{x}_{ij} \\
\Pi_i & = & \mathcal{R}[\![\mathtt{e}_i]\!]\zeta\tau \\
i \in \{1,\ldots,n\},\ j \in \{1,\ldots,c_i\} & &
\end{array}
$$

Fig. 2. Context analysis function

The equations are explained as follows. If `x` and `y` are the same variable, then an occurrence of `x` contributes to the context of `y`, otherwise it does not. For a base function application the context (which must be $\{\}$ or $\{\langle\rangle\}$) is propagated to the subexpressions. For an application of constructor $\mathtt{C}_i$ the context must be an n-tuple of application contexts. For a function application, the argument contexts must first be found using ζ, then the argument expressions are analysed in these contexts. The `case` equation is similar to that in function $\mathcal{R}$ above, and the explanation is the same.

4.4 Doing Evaluation Order Analysis

The purpose of the analysis is to determine an evaluation order description ζ for the given program. For ζ to be safe, it should satisfy the simultaneous equations:

$$
\begin{array}{l}
\zeta\mathtt{f}\tau = (\Pi_a, (\tau_1, \ldots, \tau_n)) \\
\qquad \text{where } \Pi_a = \{\langle j_1,\ldots,j_k\rangle \mid \langle \mathtt{x}_{j_1},\ldots,\mathtt{x}_{j_k}\rangle \in \Pi \restriction \{\mathtt{x}_1,\ldots,\mathtt{x}_n\}\} \\
\qquad\qquad\quad \tau_i = \mathcal{T}[\![\mathtt{e}]\!]\zeta\tau\mathtt{x}_i \qquad \text{for } i = 1,\ldots,n \\
\qquad\qquad\quad \Pi = \mathcal{R}[\![\mathtt{e}]\!]\zeta\tau \\
\qquad \text{and } \ \mathtt{f}\ \mathtt{x}_1\ldots\mathtt{x}_n\ \mathtt{=}\ \mathtt{e} \text{ in the program has type } \mathtt{f} : t_1\times \ldots \times t_n \to t
\end{array}
$$

To be as precise as possible, it should be the *least* solution. This least solution exists because all possible ζ make up a finite lattice, and $\mathcal{R}$ as well as $\mathcal{T}$ are monotonic. For a defined function of type $\mathtt{f} : t_1\times \ldots \times t_n \to t$, the description $\zeta\mathtt{f}$ belongs to the set of functions $Eot(t) \rightarrow Actx(t_1 \ldots t_n)$. Since the domain and the codomain are finite lattices, this is a finite lattice too (with the pointwise ordering), and since there are finitely many functions `f`, the set of ζ's is a finite lattice.

To analyse a given program `letrec ... in` e_0 whose goal expression e_0 has type t_0, we first need to find the evaluation order type τ_0 of e_0. This is determined by the printer's order of demand on values of type t_0.

If t_0 is a base type, then this evaluation order type is $\mathtt{nat}_{\{\langle\rangle\}}$. If t_0 is `natlist`, then τ_0 is $\mathtt{natlist}_{\mathtt{Cons}:\{\langle 1,2\rangle\}}$: the printer evaluates and prints the head (component 1) before the tail (component 2). For other data types, τ_0 can be expressed similarly, reflecting that the printer evaluates and prints all data structures in preorder and from left to right.

5 Examples of Evaluation Order Analysis

In this section we show the results of applying our analysis to some small programs. The result of analysing a function `f` of type $t_1 \times \ldots \times t_n \rightarrow t$ will be shown in the following form:

$$\mathtt{f} : \Pi_a,\ \tau_1 \times \ldots \times \tau_n \rightarrow \tau$$

meaning that $\zeta \mathtt{f} \tau = (\Pi_a, (\tau_1 \ldots \tau_n))$. As usual we write evaluation order types τ as the type name with path sets for the constructors subscripted. In Π_a we will refer to the function parameters by their name instead of by their position.

The function length

```
natlist ::= Nil | Cons nat natlist
length :: natlist → nat
length xs = case xs of
                 Nil        => 0
                 Cons y ys => 1 + (length ys)
```

Analysis result:

$$\mathtt{length} : \{\langle \mathtt{xs} \rangle\},\ \mathtt{natlist}_{\mathtt{Cons}:\{\langle 2\rangle\}} \rightarrow \mathtt{nat}$$

This result is quite strong: The argument path set $\{\langle \mathtt{xs} \rangle\}$ shows that `length` is strict, and the context $\mathtt{natlist}_{\mathtt{Cons}:\{\langle 2\rangle\}}$ for `xs` means that all list elements (heads) are ignored, and that the function is tail strict.

The function sum

```
sum :: natlist → nat
sum xs = case xs of
              Nil        => 0
              Cons y ys => y + (sum ys)
```

Analysis result:

$$\mathtt{sum} : \{\langle \mathtt{xs} \rangle\},\ \mathtt{natlist}_{\mathtt{Cons}:\{\langle 1,2\rangle\}} \rightarrow \mathtt{nat}$$

The `sum` function is strict, evaluates its argument from left to right, and is head strict as well as tail strict.

The function and

```
bool     ::= False | True
boollist ::= Nil | Cons bool boollist
and :: boollist → bool
and xs = case xs of
           Nil         => True
           Cons y ys => case y of
                          False => False
                          True  => and ys
```

Analysis result:

$$\texttt{and} : \{\langle \texttt{xs} \rangle\}, \texttt{boollist}_{\texttt{Cons}:\{\langle 1\rangle,\langle 1,2\rangle\}} \rightarrow \texttt{bool}$$

The analysis result states that function **and** is strict and evaluates its argument from left to right. This function is a natural example of a function which is head strict but not tail strict: 1 is in both paths of the argument context, 2 is not.

Reverse function with accumulating parameter

```
rev :: natlist × natlist → natlist
rev xs zs = case xs of
              Nil       => zs
              Cons y ys => rev ys (Cons y zs)

reverse :: natlist → natlist
reverse ys = rev ys Nil
```

Analysis results:

$$\begin{aligned}
&\texttt{rev} : \{\langle \texttt{xs,zs} \rangle\},\\
&\quad \texttt{natlist}_{\texttt{Cons}:\{\langle 2,1\rangle\}} \times \texttt{natlist}_{\texttt{Cons}:\{\langle 1,2\rangle\}} \rightarrow \texttt{natlist}_{\texttt{Cons}:\{\langle 1,2\rangle\}}\\
&\texttt{rev} : \{\langle \texttt{xs,zs} \rangle\},\\
&\quad \texttt{natlist}_{\texttt{Cons}:\{\langle 2,1\rangle\}} \times \texttt{natlist}_{\texttt{Cons}:\{\langle 2,1\rangle\}} \rightarrow \texttt{natlist}_{\texttt{Cons}:\{\langle 2,1\rangle\}}\\
&\texttt{rev} : \{\langle \texttt{xs,zs} \rangle,\langle \texttt{xs} \rangle\},\\
&\quad \texttt{natlist}_{\texttt{Cons}:\{\langle 2\rangle,\langle 2,1\rangle\}} \times \texttt{natlist}_{\texttt{Cons}:\{\langle 1\rangle,\langle 1,2\rangle\}} \rightarrow \texttt{natlist}_{\texttt{Cons}:\{\langle 1\rangle,\langle 1,2\rangle\}}\\
&\texttt{rev} : \{\langle \texttt{xs,zs} \rangle,\langle \texttt{xs} \rangle\},\\
&\quad \texttt{natlist}_{\texttt{Cons}:\{\langle 2\rangle\}} \times \texttt{natlist}_{\texttt{Cons}:\{\langle\rangle\}} \rightarrow \texttt{natlist}_{\texttt{Cons}:\{\langle\rangle\}}
\end{aligned}$$

Function `rev` is strict in `xs` and evaluates it before `zs` in any strict context. In a head and tail strict context (two first lines), `rev` is strict in both `xs` and `zs`. In a head and tail strict context, `xs` is in a head and tail strict context which evaluates tail before head, no matter whether the context of `rev` evaluates heads or tails first.

In a context which is only head strict (third line), `rev` is tail strict in `xs`, and `rev` is tail strict in `xs` even in a context which only demands a whnf (fourth line). Intuitively, `rev` needs to traverse the whole spine of `xs` before the first constructor in the reversed list is returned.

6 Applications: Optimization of Suspensions

Bloss describes how evaluation order information can be used for optimizing suspensions in a lazy language [3] [1, Sec. 4.3]. Here we summarize Bloss's description.

When **x** is a variable, we let the symbols $\mathbf{x}^j$ and $\mathbf{x}^i$ range over occurrences of **x** in **e**. Once the evaluation order description of the functions ζ is found as described in the previous sections, it is easy to find the order(s) in which the different occurrences of a variable are accessed. Given expression **e**, define **e**$'$ to be an expression identical to **e** except that each occurrence of a free variable **x** is replaced by a unique free variable $\mathbf{x}^i$. Now compute

$$\Pi_{occ} = \mathcal{R}[\![\mathbf{e}']\!]\zeta\tau$$

to find the occurrence paths through **e** in context τ.

There are six possibilities for the status of a variable **x** at an occurrence $\mathbf{x}^i$. The six possibilities are spanned by the three possibilities for the variable's past (definitely not already evaluated, definitely already evaluated, don't know) and two possibilities for its future (definitely no later use, possibly a later use). Five of the six cases allow us to improve on the default code for a variable access, and evaluation order analysis allow us to identify such cases. The default code for a variable access is:

```
if   <status = already evaluated>
then return value
else evaluate;
     overwrite;
     return value
```

Given a path set Π_{occ} of paths of variable occurrences through an expression **e**, the code for a variable access can be optimized at compile time according to Figure 3.

Optimization of code at occurrence $\mathbf{x}^i$	**x** already evaluated	**x** not yet evaluated	**x** possibly already evaluated
No later use of **x**	No status check, No evaluation, No overwrite	No status check, No overwrite	No overwrite
Possibly a later use of **x**	No status check, No evaluation, No overwrite	No status check	No optimization possible

Fig. 3. Optimization of variable accesses

For instance, **x** is already evaluated at occurrence $\mathbf{x}^i$ if on every path $\mathbf{x}^i$ is preceded by some occurrence $\mathbf{x}^j$ of **x**. That is, if

$$\forall\ \pi \in \Pi_{occ}.\ \exists\ \mathbf{x}^j.\ \pi = \langle \ldots\ \mathbf{x}^j\ \ldots\ \mathbf{x}^i\ \ldots \rangle.$$

The assertions "**x** not yet evaluated" and "no later use of **x**" can also be expressed in terms of path sets.

7 Cost versus Precision

Some program properties are not easily deduced by backwards analysis. Our analysis is, for example, unable to find that a and b are always evaluated before z in the expression:

```
case (Pair a b) of
    Pair x y => x + y + z
```

In return, our analysis has lower complexity than, *e.g.*, the forwards analysis of Bloss and Hudak [2], but full backwards path analysis is still expensive. Witness that the height of $PathSet(D) = |Path(D)| = \sum_{i=0}^{n} \frac{n!}{(n-i)!} \geq n!$ where $n = |D|$ and $2^{n!} \leq |PathSet(D)| \leq 2^{(n+1)!}$. An evaluation order type is isomorphic to a finite product of such sets $PathSet(1 \ldots n_i)$.

Clearly, there is good reason to look for computationally cheaper analyses. A cheaper evaluation order analysis has been based on *evaluation order relations* which may be thought of as propositions about paths. For example, the assertion $e_1 \rightarrow e_2$ means: if e_2 is evaluated at all, then e_1 has been evaluated *before* e_2. That analysis has significantly lower complexity than the one presented here and is described in [7].

8 Related Work

The work on path analysis by Bloss and Hudak has served as reference and inspiration. The use of backwards analysis allowed us to extend their work to handle data structures. For first-order programs without data structures their forwards analysis is sometimes more precise, but the complexity of their analysis is higher than ours.

One may ask why an analysis for lazy data structures could not be achieved simply by applying Bloss and Hudak's higher order analysis to data structures encoded as higher order functions, thus obviating the need for a whole new theory. However, the complexity of higher order path analysis is superexponential in the depth of types in the expressions being analysed, and the encoding of data structures as functions give very complex types. Furthermore, it may be that for type reasons, higher order path analysis cannot be applied at all to recursive functions involving data structures encoded as functions [8].

Similar work, but restricted to first order languages without data structures has been reported by Draghicescu and Purushothaman [4] [5]. Their analysis can accommodate also evaluation strategies which make use of strictness information to move evaluation of arguments forwards (earlier). However, their analysis remains restricted to languages without lazy data structures.

9 Conclusion

We have presented a method and supporting concepts for inferring the order of evaluation of subexpressions in a functional language with lazy data structures.

Evaluation order information obtained using this method can be used for optimizing suspensions (or "thunks"), that is, closures representing unevaluated argument expressions. The optimization of suspensions requires detecting whether at a given occurrence of a variable, the expression is always not previously evaluated, always already evaluated, always not later used, *etc.* Detecting these situations requires precisely that one knows in which order the various occurrences of a variable are evaluated.

One restriction of our method is that it does not allow to relate the evaluation of substructures of different function arguments. Thus we cannot tell that all elements of the `xs` list must be evaluated before any element of the `zs` in the `rev` function. We only know that `xs` will be evaluated to whnf before `zs`.

We have specified the analysis in detail but we have not implemented it. It has been demonstrated on several small examples, and we have found that it produces the expected evaluation order information for these examples.

Acknowledgements

The second author was supported by a grant from the Danish Natural Science Research Council. Thanks to Neil D. Jones, Alan Mycroft, and Carolyn Talcott for comments on this work.

References

1. A. Bloss. *Path Analysis and the Optimization of Non-Strict Functional Languages.* PhD thesis, Computer Science Department, Yale University, New Haven, Connecticut, USA, May 1989. Also: Research Report YALEU/DCS/RR-704. 129 pages.
2. A. Bloss and P. Hudak. Path semantics. In M. Main et al., editors, *Mathematical Foundations of Programming Language Semantics, 3rd Workshop, New Orleans, Louisiana. (Lecture Notes in Computer Science, vol. 298)*, pages 476–489. Springer-Verlag, 1988.
3. A. Bloss, P. Hudak, and J. Young. Code optimizations for lazy evaluation. *Lisp and Symbolic Computation*, 1(2):147–164, September 1988.
4. M. Draghicescu and S. Purushothaman. A compositional analysis of evaluation-order and its application. In *1990 ACM Conference on Lisp and Functional Programming, Nice, France*, pages 242–250. ACM Press, 1990.
5. M. Draghicescu and S. Purushothaman. Static analysis of lazy functional languages. University of Massachusetts at Boston. 28 pages. Submitted to Theoretical Computer Science, 1991.
6. C.K. Gomard. *Program Analysis Matters.* PhD thesis, DIKU, University of Copenhagen, Denmark, November 1991. Also DIKU Report 91/17.
7. C.K. Gomard and P. Sestoft. Evaluation order analysis for lazy data structures. In *Preliminary Proceedings, Fifth Glasgow Functional Programming Workshop, Isle of Skye, Scotland, August 1991*, pages 125–149. Department of Computing Science, University of Glasgow, Scotland, 1991.
8. P. Hudak and J. Young. Higher-order strictness analysis in untyped lambda calculus. In *Thirteenth ACM Symp. Principles of Programming Languages, St. Petersburg, Florida, 1986*, pages 97–109, 1986.
9. P. Sestoft. *Analysis and Efficient Implementation of Functional Programs.* PhD thesis, DIKU, University of Copenhagen, Denmark, October 1991.

Why the Occur-check is Not a Problem

Krzysztof R. Apt
Centre for Mathematics and Computer Science
Kruislaan 413, 1098 SJ Amsterdam, The Netherlands
and
Faculty of Mathematics and Computer Science, University of Amsterdam
Plantage Muidergracht 24, 1018 TV Amsterdam, The Netherlands

Alessandro Pellegrini
Dipartimento di Matematica Pura ed Applicata
Università di Padova, Via Belzoni 7, 35131 Padova, Italy

Abstract

In most Prolog implementations for the efficiency reasons so-called occur-check is omitted from the unification algorithm. We provide here natural syntactic conditions which allow the occur-check to be safely omitted. The established results apply to most well-known Prolog programs and seem to explain why this omission does not lead in practice to any complications.

Note. **This research was done during the second author's stay at Centre for Mathematics and Computer Science, Amsterdam. His stay was supported by the 2060th District of the Rotary Foundation, Italy.**

1 Introduction

The occur-check is a special test used in the unification algorithm. In most Prolog implementations it is omitted for the efficiency reasons. This omission affects the unification algorithm and introduces a possibility of divergence or may yield incorrect results. This is obviously an undesired situation. This problem was studied in the literature under the name of the *occur-check problem* (see e.g. Plaisted [Pla84] and Deransart and Maluszynski [DM85b]).

The aim of this paper is to provide easy to check syntactic conditions which ensure that the occur-check can be safely omitted. We use here a recent result of Deransart, Ferrand and Téguia [DFT91] and build upon it within the context of moded programs. This allows us to extend the results of Deransart and Maluszynski [DM85b], to simplify the arguments of Chadha and Plaisted [CP91] and to offer a uniform presentation. Additionally, the results of the former paper needed here are proved directly, without resorting to the techniques of the attribute grammars theory, and the results of the latter paper are supplied with a needed justification. The established results apply to most well-known Prolog programs. In fact, we found in the book of Sterling and Shapiro [SS86] only two (sic!) programs to which these results cannot be directly applied.

In what follows we study logic programs executed by means of the *LD-resolution*, which consists of the SLD-resolution combined with the leftmost selection rule. An SLD-derivation in which the leftmost selection rule is used is called an *LD-derivation*. We allow in programs various first-order built-in's, like $=$, $\neq$, $>$, etc, and assume that they are resolved in the way conforming to their interpretation.

Throughout the paper we use the standard notation of Lloyd [Llo87] and Apt [Apt90]. In particular, given a syntactic construct E (so for example, a term, an atom or a set of equations) we denote by $Var(E)$ the set of the variables appearing in E. Given a substitution $\theta = \{x_1/t_1, ..., x_n/t_n\}$ we denote by $Dom(\theta)$ the set of variables $\{x_1, \ldots, x_n\}$, by $Range(\theta)$ the set of terms $\{t_1, \ldots, t_n\}$, and by $Ran(\theta)$ the set of variables appearing in $\{t_1, \ldots, t_n\}$. Finally, we define $Var(\theta) = Dom(\theta) \cup Ran(\theta)$.

Recall that a substitution θ is called *grounding* if $Ran(\theta)$ is empty, and is called a *renaming* if it is a permutation of the variables in $Dom(\theta)$. Given a substitution θ and a set of variables V, we denote by $\theta|V$ the substitution obtained from θ by restricting its domain to V.

2 Occur-check Free Programs

We start our considerations by recalling a unification algorithm due to Martelli and Montanari [MM82]. We use below the notions of sets and of systems of equations interchangingly. Two atoms can unify only if they have the same relation symbol. With two atoms $p(s_1, ..., s_n)$ and $p(t_1, ..., t_n)$ to be unified we associate the set of equations $\{s_1 = t_1, ..., s_n = t_n\}$. In the applications we often refer to this set as $p(s_1, ..., s_n) = p(t_1, ..., t_n)$. The algorithm operates on such finite sets of equations. A substitution θ such that $s_1\theta = t_1\theta, \ldots, s_n\theta = t_n\theta$ is called a *unifier* of the set of equations $\{s_1 = t_1, ..., s_n = t_n\}$. Thus the set of equations $E = \{s_1 = t_1, ..., s_n = t_n\}$ has the same unifiers as the atoms $p(s_1, ..., s_n)$ and $p(t_1, ..., t_n)$.

A unifier θ of a set of equations E is called a *most general unifier* (in short *mgu*) of E if it is more general than all unifiers of E. An mgu θ of a set of equations E is called *relevant* if $Var(\theta) \subseteq Var(E)$.

A set of equations is called *solved* if it is of the form $\{x_1 = t_1, ..., x_n = t_n\}$ where the x_i's are distinct variables and none of them occurs in a term t_j.

The following unification algorithm will be used in the sequel.

MARTELLI-MONTANARI ALGORITHM

Nondeterministically choose from the set of equations an equation of a form below and perform the associated action.

(1) $f(s_1, ..., s_n) = f(t_1, ..., t_n)$	*replace by the equations* $s_1 = t_1, ..., s_n = t_n$,
(2) $f(s_1, ..., s_n) = g(t_1, ..., t_m)$ where $f \not\equiv g$	*halt with failure,*
(3) $x = x$	*delete the equation,*
(4) $t = x$ where t is not a variable	*replace by the equation* $x = t$,
(5) $x = t$ where $x \not\equiv t$, x does not occur in t and x occurs elsewhere	*perform the substitution* $\{x/t\}$ *in every other equation,*
(6) $x = t$ where $x \not\equiv t$ and x occurs in t	*halt with failure.*

The algorithm terminates when no action can be performed or when failure arises. To keep the formulation of the algorithm concise we identified here constants with 0-ary functions. Thus action (2) includes the case of two different constants.

The following theorem holds (see Martelli and Montanari [MM82]).

Theorem 2.1 (Unification) *The Martelli-Montanari algorithm always terminates. If the original set of equations E has a unifier, then the algorithm successfully terminates and produces a solved set of equations determining a relevant mgu of E, and otherwise it terminates with failure.* □

The Martelli-Montanari algorithm does not generate all mgu's of a set of equations E but the following lemma, proved in Lassez, Marriot and Maher [LMM88], will allow us to cope with this peculiarity.

Lemma 2.2 *Let θ_1 and θ_2 be mgu's of a set of equations. Then for some renaming η we have $\theta_2 = \theta_1\eta$.* □

The test "x does not occur in t" in action (5) of the Martelli-Montanari algorithm is called the *occur-check*. In most Prolog implementations the occur-check is omitted. By omitting the occur-check in (5) and deleting action (6) from the Martelli-Montanari algorithm we are still left with two options depending on whether the substitution $\{x/t\}$ is performed in t itself. If it is, then divergence can result, because x occurs in t implies that x occurs in $t\{x/t\}$. If it is not (as in the case of the modified version of the algorithm just mentioned), then an incorrect result can be produced, as in the case of the single equation $x = f(x)$ which yields the substitution $\{x/f(x)\}$.

None of these alternatives is desirable. It is natural then to seek conditions which guarantee that, in absence of the occur-check, in all Prolog evaluations of a given goal w.r.t. a given program unification is correctly performed. This leads us to the following notion due to Deransart, Ferrand and Téguia [DFT91].

Definition 2.3 A set of equations E is called *not subject to occur-check* (NSTO in short) if in no execution of the Martelli-Montanari algorithm started with E action (6) can be performed. □

We now introduce the key definition of the paper.

Definition 2.4

- Let ξ be an LD-derivation. Let A be an atom selected in ξ and H the head of the input clause selected to resolve A in ξ. Suppose that A and H have the same relation symbol. Then we say that the system $A = H$ *is considered in* ξ.
- Suppose that all systems of equations considered in the LD-derivations of $P \cup \{G\}$ are NSTO. Then we say that $P \cup \{G\}$ is *occur-check free.* □

This definition assumes a specific unification algorithm but allows us to derive precise results. In contrast, no specific unification algorithm in the definition of the LD-resolution is assumed.

By Theorem 2.1 if a considered system of equations is unifiable, then it is NSTO, as well. Thus the property of being occur-check free rests exclusively upon those considered systems which are not unifiable. As in the definition of the occur-check freedom *all* LD-derivations of $P \cup \{G\}$ are considered, all systems of equations that can be considered in a possibly backtracking Prolog evaluation of a goal G w.r.t. the program P are taken into account.

In Deransart, Ferrand and Téguia [DFT91] a related concept of an NSTO program is studied which essentially states that, independently of the selection rule and the resolution strategy chosen, all considered systems are NSTO. The definition of the occur-check freedom refers to the leftmost selection rule, so the results we obtain are usually incompatible with those dealing with NSTO programs.

The aim of this paper is to offer simple syntactic conditions which imply that $P \cup \{G\}$ is occur-check free. It is useful to note the following.

Lemma 2.5 *The problem whether a set of equations is NSTO, is decidable.* □

Lemma 2.5 provides a method to determine whether a given set of equations is NSTO. However, it is not easy to apply it. Instead, we shall use a result due to Deransart, Ferrand and Téguia [DFT91]. We need some preparatory definitions first.

Definition 2.6

- We call a family of terms (resp. an atom) *linear* if every variable occurs at most once in it.
- We call a set of equations *left linear* (resp. *right linear*) if the family of terms formed by their left-hand (resp. right-hand) sides is linear. □

Thus a family of terms is linear iff no variable has two distinct occurrences in any term and no two terms have a variable in common.

Definition 2.7 Let E be a set of equations. We denote by $\rightarrow_E$ the following relation defined on the elements of E:
$e_1 \rightarrow_E e_2$ iff the left-hand side of e_1 and the right-hand side of e_2 have a variable in common. □

In particular, if a variable occurs both in the left-hand and right-hand side of an equation e of E, then $e \rightarrow_E e$.

We can now state the result proved by Deransart, Ferrand and Téguia [DFT91].

Lemma 2.8 (NSTO) *Suppose that the equations in E can be oriented in such a way that the resulting system F is left linear and the relation $\rightarrow_F$ is cycle-free. Then E is NSTO.* □

The original formulation of this lemma is slightly stronger, but for our purposes the above version is sufficient.

3 Moded Programs

For a further analysis we introduce modes.

Definition 3.1 Consider an n-ary relation symbol p. By a *mode* for p we mean a function d_p from $\{1, \ldots, n\}$ to the set $\{+, -\}$. If $d_p(i) =$ '+', we call i an *input position* of p and if $d_p(i) =$ '−', we call i an *output position* of p (both w.r.t. d_p).

We write d_p in a more suggestive form $p(d_p(1), \ldots, d_p(n))$. □

Modes indicate how the arguments of a relation should be used. This definition assumes one mode per relation in a program. Multiple modes may be obtained by simply renaming the relations. From now on we assume that *every considered relation* has a mode associated with it. This will allow us to talk about input positions and output positions of an atom. Throughout the paper, given an atom A, we denote by $VarIn(A)$ (resp. $VarOut(A)$) the set of variables occurring in the input (resp. output) positions of A. Similar notation is used for sequences of atoms.

We now introduce the following concepts.

Definition 3.2

- An atom is called *input* (resp. *output*) *linear* if the family of terms occurring in its input (resp. output) positions is linear.

- An atom is called *input-output disjoint* if the family of terms occurring in its input positions has no variable in common with the family of terms occurring in its output positions. □

The following lemma is crucial.

Lemma 3.3 (NSTO via Modes) *Consider two atoms A and H with the same relation symbol. Suppose that*

- *they have no variable in common,*

- *one of them is input-output disjoint,*

- *one of them is input linear and the other is output linear.*

Then $A = H$ is NSTO.

Proof. Suppose first that A is input-output disjoint and input linear and H is output linear. Let $i_1^A, \ldots, i_m^A$ (resp. $i_1^H, \ldots, i_m^H$) be the terms filling in the input positions of A (resp. H) and $o_1^A, \ldots, o_n^A$ (resp. $o_1^H, \ldots, o_n^H$) the terms filling in the output positions of A (resp. H).

The system under consideration is

$$E = \{i_1^A = i_1^H, \ldots, i_m^A = i_m^H, o_1^A = o_1^H, \ldots, o_n^A = o_n^H\}.$$

Reorient it as follows:

$$F = \{i_1^A = i_1^H, \ldots, i_m^A = i_m^H, o_1^H = o_1^A, \ldots, o_n^H = o_n^A\}.$$

By assumption A and H have no variable in common. This implies that

- F is left-linear (because additionally A is input linear and H is output linear),

- the equations $i_j^A = i_j^H$ have no successor in the $\rightarrow_F$ relation and the equations $o_j^H = o_j^A$ have no predecessor (because additionally A is input-output disjoint).

Thus by the NSTO Lemma 2.8 $A = H$ is NSTO. The proofs for the remaining three cases are analogous and omitted. □

We now prove two results allowing us to conclude that $P \cup \{G\}$ is occur-check free. The first one uses the following notion due to Dembinski and Maluszynski [DM85a].

Definition 3.4 We call an LD-derivation *data driven* if all atoms selected in it are ground in their input positions. □

Theorem 3.5 *Suppose that*

- *the head of every clause of P is output linear,*

- *all LD-derivations of $P \cup \{G\}$ are data driven.*

Then $P \cup \{G\}$ is occur-check free.

Proof. By the NSTO via Modes Lemma 3.3. □

The second result uses the following notion.

Definition 3.6 We call an LD-derivation *output driven* if all atoms selected in it are output linear and input-output disjoint. □

Theorem 3.7 *Suppose that*

- *the head of every clause of P is input linear,*
- *all LD-derivations of $P \cup \{G\}$ are output driven.*

Then $P \cup \{G\}$ is occur-check free.

Proof. By the NSTO via Modes Lemma 3.3. □

This theorem is implicit in Chadha and Plaisted [CP91] (see the proof of their Theorem 2.2).

So far we isolated two properties of LD-derivations, each of which implies occur-check freedom. In both cases we had to impose some restrictions on the heads of the clauses. When we combine these two properties we get occur-check freedom directly.

Theorem 3.8 *Suppose that*

- *all LD-derivations of $P \cup \{G\}$ are both data and output driven.*

Then $P \cup \{G\}$ is occur-check free.

Proof. By the NSTO Lemma 2.8. □

4 Well-moded Programs

The obvious problem with Theorems 3.5, 3.7 and 3.8 is that is is not easy to check their conditions. In fact, one can show that in general it is undecidable whether for a given program P and goal G the conditions of Theorem 3.5, 3.7 or 3.8 hold.

The aim of this section is to propose some syntactic restrictions that imply the conditions of Theorems 3.5. We then show that these restrictions are satisfied by a number of well-known programs.

We use here the notion of a well-moded program. The concept is due to Dembinski and Maluszynski [DM85a]; we use here an elegant formulation due to Rosenblueth [Ros91] (which is equivalent to that of Drabent [Dra87] where well-moded programs are called simple). The definition of a well-moded program constrains the "flow of data" through the clauses of the programs. To simplify the notation, when writing an atom as $p(\mathbf{u}, \mathbf{v})$, we now assume that $\mathbf{u}$ is a sequence of terms filling in the input positions of p and that $\mathbf{v}$ is a sequence of terms filling in the output positions of p.

Definition 4.1

- A goal $\leftarrow p_1(\mathbf{s_1}, \mathbf{t_1}), \ldots, p_n(\mathbf{s_n}, \mathbf{t_n})$ is called *well-moded* if for $i \in [1, n]$

$$Var(\mathbf{s_i}) \subseteq \bigcup_{j=1}^{i-1} Var(\mathbf{t_j}).$$

- A clause $p_0(\mathbf{t_0}, \mathbf{s_{n+1}}) \leftarrow p_1(\mathbf{s_1}, \mathbf{t_1}), \ldots, p_n(\mathbf{s_n}, \mathbf{t_n})$ is called *well-moded* if for $i \in [1, n+1]$

$$Var(\mathbf{s_i}) \subseteq \bigcup_{j=0}^{i-1} Var(\mathbf{t_j}).$$

- A program is called *well-moded* if every clause of it is well-moded. □

Note that a goal with only one atom is well-moded iff this atom is ground in its input positions. The definition of a well-moded program is designed in such a way that the following theorem due to Dembinski and Maluszynski [DM85a] holds.

Theorem 4.2 *Let P and G be well-moded. Then all LD-derivations of $P \cup \{G\}$ are data driven.* □

This theorem brings us to the following conclusion.

Corollary 4.3 *Let P and G be well-moded. Suppose that*

- *the head of every clause of P is output linear.*

Then $P \cup \{G\}$ is occur-check free.

Proof. By Theorems 3.5 and 4.2. □

This corollary can be easily applied to a number of well-known Prolog programs.

Example 4.4 Below, when presenting the programs we adhere to the usual syntactic conventions of Prolog with the exception that Prolog's ":-" is replaced by the logic programming " ← ".
(i) Consider the program append:

```
app([X | Xs], Ys, [X | Zs]) ← app(Xs, Ys, Zs).
app([], Ys, Ys).
```

with the moding `app(+,+,-)`. It is easy to check that append is then well-moded and that the head of every clause is output linear. By Corollary 4.3 we conclude that for `s` and `t` ground, append ∪ { ← `app(s, t, u)`} is occur-check free.

(ii) Consider now the program append with the moding `app(-,-,+)`. Again, by Corollary 4.3, we conclude that for `u` ground, append ∪ { ← `app(s, t, u)`} is occur-check free.

(iii) Consider the program `permutation` which consists of the clauses

```
perm(Xs, [X | Ys]) ←
    app(X1s, [X | X2s], Xs),
    app(X1s, X2s, Zs),
    perm(Zs, Ys).
perm([], []).
```

augmented by the append program.

We use here the following modings: perm(+,-), app(-,-,+) for the first call to append and app(+,+,-) for the second call to append.

It is easy to check that permutation is then well-moded and that the heads of all clauses are output linear. By Corollary 4.3 we get that for s ground, permutation $\cup$ { ← perm(s, t)} is occur-check free.

(iv) Consider now the program quicksort which consists of the clauses

```
qs([X | Xs], Ys) ←
    partition(X, Xs, Littles, Bigs),
    qs(Littles, Ls),
    qs(Bigs, Bs),
    app(Ls, [X | Bs], Ys).
qs([], []).

partition(X, [Y | Xs], [Y | Ls], Bs) ← X > Y, partition(X, Xs, Ls, Bs).
partition(X, [Y | Xs], Ls, [Y | Bs]) ← X ≤ Y, partition(X, Xs, Ls, Bs).
partition(X, [], [], []).
```

augmented by the append program.

We mode it as follows: qs(+,-), partition(+,+,-,-), app(+,+,-). Again, it is easy to check that quicksort is then well-moded and that the heads of all clauses are output linear. By Corollary 4.3 we conclude that for s ground, quicksort $\cup$ { ← qs(s, t)} is occur-check free.

(v) Finally, consider the program palindrome:

```
palindrome(Xs) ← reverse(Xs, Xs).
reverse(X1s, X2s) ← reverse(X1s, [], X2s).
reverse([X | X1s], X2s, Ys) ← reverse(X1s, [X | X2s], Ys).
reverse([], Xs, Xs).
```

We mode it as follows: palindrome(+), reverse(+,-), reverse(+,+,-). Then palindrome is well-moded and the heads of all clauses are output linear. By Corollary 4.3 we conclude that for s ground, palindrome $\cup$ { ← palindrome(s)} is occur-check free. □

5 Nicely Moded Programs

The above conclusions are still of a restrictive kind, because in each case we had to assume that the input positions of the one atom goals are ground. To alleviate this restriction we now consider some syntactic restrictions that imply the conditions of Theorem 3.7.

The following notion was introduced in Chadha and Plaisted [CP91]. (We found essentially the same concept independently, though later; the name and formulation are ours.)

Definition 5.1

- A goal $\leftarrow p_1(\mathbf{s_1}, \mathbf{t_1}), \ldots, p_n(\mathbf{s_n}, \mathbf{t_n})$ is called *nicely moded* if $\mathbf{t_1}, \ldots, \mathbf{t_n}$ is a linear family of terms and for $i \in [1, n]$

$$Var(\mathbf{s_i}) \cap (\bigcup_{j=i}^{n} Var(\mathbf{t_j})) = \emptyset.$$

- A clause $p_0(\mathbf{s_0}, \mathbf{t_0}) \leftarrow p_1(\mathbf{s_1}, \mathbf{t_1}), \ldots, p_n(\mathbf{s_n}, \mathbf{t_n})$ is called *nicely moded* if $\leftarrow p_1(\mathbf{s_1}, \mathbf{t_1}), \ldots, p_n(\mathbf{s_n}, \mathbf{t_n})$ is nicely moded and

$$Var(\mathbf{s_0}) \cap (\bigcup_{j=1}^{n} Var(\mathbf{t_j})) = \emptyset.$$

- A program is called *nicely moded* if every clause of it is nicely moded. □

Thus, assuming that in every atom the input positions occur first, a goal is nicely moded if every variable occurring in an output position of an atom does not occur earlier in the goal. And a clause is nicely moded if every variable occurring in an output position of a body atom occurs neither earlier in the body nor in an input position of the head.

Note that a goal with only one atom is nicely moded iff it is output linear and input-output disjoint. The following theorem clarifies our interest in nicely moded programs.

Theorem 5.2 *Let P and G be nicely moded. Then all LD-derivations of $P \cup \{G\}$ are output driven.*

The proof is quite complicated and requires a number of lemmas. The first one allows us to search for mgu's in an iterative fashion.

Lemma 5.3 *Let E_1, E_2 be two sets of equations. Suppose that θ_1 is a relevant mgu of E_1 and θ_2 is a relevant mgu of $E_2\theta_1$. Then $\theta_1\theta_2$ is a relevant mgu of $E_1 \cup E_2$. Moreover, if $E_1 \cup E_2$ is unifiable then θ_1 exists and for any such θ_1 an appropriate θ_2 exists, as well.* □

Lemma 5.4 *Let θ be a substitution and $\mathbf{s}$ and $\mathbf{t}$ sequences of terms such that*

- $Var(\mathbf{s}) \cap Var(\mathbf{t}) = \emptyset$,
- $Ran(\theta | Var(\mathbf{s})) \cap Ran(\theta | Var(\mathbf{t})) = \emptyset$,
- $Var(\mathbf{s}) \cap Ran(\theta | Var(\mathbf{t})) = \emptyset$,
- $Var(\mathbf{t}) \cap Ran(\theta | Var(\mathbf{s})) = \emptyset$.

Then $Var(\mathbf{s}\theta) \cap Var(\mathbf{t}\theta) = \emptyset$. □

The next two lemmas use the following notion.

Definition 5.5 A substitution $\{x_1/t_1, \ldots, x_n/t_n\}$ is called *linear* if $t_1, \ldots, t_n$ is a linear family of terms. □

Lemma 5.6 *Let θ be a substitution and $\mathbf{t}$ a family of terms. Suppose that*

- *θ is linear,*
- *$\mathbf{t}$ is linear,*
- $Ran(\theta) \cap Var(\mathbf{t}) = \emptyset$.

Then $\mathbf{t}\theta$ is a linear family of terms, as well. □

The following lemma is stated in Deransart and Maluszynski [DM85b].

Lemma 5.7 *Consider two atoms A and H with the same relation symbol. Suppose that*

- *they have no variable in common,*
- *A is linear.*

Assume that A and H are unifiable. Then there exists a relevant mgu θ of A and H such that

- *$\theta | Var(H)$ is linear,*
- *$Ran(\theta | Var(H)) \subseteq Var(A)$.* □

Finally, we establish the following lemma.

Lemma 5.8 *Consider two atoms A and H with the same relation symbol. Suppose that*

- *they have no variable in common,*
- *A is input-output disjoint and output linear.*

Assume that A and H are unifiable. Then there exists a relevant mgu θ of A and H such that for $V = VarOut(H) - VarIn(H)$, $\eta_1 = \theta | V$ and $\eta_2 = \theta | VarIn(H)$

(i) η_1 *is linear,*

(ii) $Ran(\eta_1) \subseteq Var(A)$,

(iii) $Ran(\eta_2) \cap (Ran(\eta_1) \cup V) = \emptyset$.

Proof. Let $i_1^A, \ldots, i_m^A$ (resp. $i_1^H, \ldots, i_m^H$) be the terms filling in the input positions of A (resp. H) and $o_1^A, \ldots, o_n^A$ (resp. $o_1^H, \ldots, o_n^H$) the terms filling in the output positions of A (resp. H). Let θ_1 be the relevant mgu of $\{o_1^A = o_1^H, \ldots, o_n^A = o_n^A\}$ constructed in the proof of Lemma 5.7. By the disjointness of A and H we have $\theta_1 | Var(H) = \theta_1 | VarOut(H)$, so by Lemma 5.7

$$\theta_1 | Var(H) \text{ is linear} \tag{1}$$

and

$$Ran(\theta_1 | Var(H)) \subseteq VarOut(A). \tag{2}$$

Let θ_2 be a relevant mgu of $\{i_1^A = i_1^H, \ldots, i_m^A = i_m^H\}\theta_1$. By Lemma 5.3 θ_2 exists and $\theta = \theta_1\theta_2$ is a relevant mgu of $A = H$.

By the relevance of θ_1 we have $Dom(\theta_1) \subseteq VarOut(A) \cup VarOut(H)$, so by the input-output disjointness of A and the disjointness of A and H we get $\{i_1^A = i_1^H, \ldots, i_m^A = i_m^H\}\theta_1 = \{i_1^A = i_1^H\theta_1, \ldots, i_m^A = i_m^H\theta_1\}$.

By the relevance of θ_2 we have $Var(\theta_2) \subseteq Var(\{i_1^A = i_1^H\theta_1, \ldots, i_m^A = i_m^H\theta_1\}) \subseteq VarIn(A) \cup VarIn(H) \cup Ran(\theta_1 | VarIn(H))$.

Thus, by the disjointness of A and H and (2),

$$Var(\theta_2) \cap V = \emptyset. \tag{3}$$

For the same reasons and additionally by the input-output disjointness of A and (1)

$$Var(\theta_2) \cap Ran(\theta_1 | V) = \emptyset. \tag{4}$$

Now, (3) and (4) imply that

$$\eta_1 = \theta_1 | V. \tag{5}$$

Thus $\eta_1 \subseteq \theta_1 | \mathit{Var}(H)$, so by (1) we conclude (*i*) and by (2) we conclude (*ii*).

Consider now η_2. Note that $\eta_2 \subseteq (\theta_1 | \mathit{VarIn}(H))\, \theta_2$, so

$$\mathit{Ran}(\eta_2) \subseteq \mathit{Ran}(\theta_1 | \mathit{VarIn}(H)) \cup \mathit{Var}(\theta_2). \tag{6}$$

But by (1), (4), (2), disjointness of A and H, and (3)

$$(\mathit{Ran}(\theta_1 | \mathit{VarIn}(H)) \cup \mathit{Var}(\theta_2)) \cap (\mathit{Ran}(\theta_1 | V) \cup V) = \emptyset,$$

so by (6) and (5) we conclude (*iii*). □

Note that the first atom of a nicely moded goal is output linear and input-output disjoint, and a variant of a nicely moded clause is nicely moded. Thus to prove Theorem 5.2 it suffices to prove the following lemma which shows the "persistence" of the notion of being nicely moded.

Lemma 5.9 *An LD-resolvent of a nicely moded goal and a disjoint with it nicely moded clause is nicely moded.*

Proof. We start by proving three claims.

Claim 1 *Suppose that A and H satisfy the assumptions of Lemma 5.8 and assume that θ is a relevant mgu of $A = H$ which satisfies conditions (i) – (iii) of Lemma 5.8. Let $H \leftarrow \mathbf{B}$ be a nicely moded clause with no variables in common with A. Then $\leftarrow \mathbf{B}\theta$ is nicely moded.*

Proof. Below, by the standardization apart we mean the assumption that $H \leftarrow \mathbf{B}$ and A have no variables in common. Let V, η_1 and η_2 be as in the formulation of Lemma 5.8.

Let $\theta_1 = \theta | \mathit{VarOut}(\mathbf{B})$ and $\theta_2 = \theta | (\mathit{VarIn}(\mathbf{B}) - \mathit{VarOut}(\mathbf{B}))$. We first establish some claims about θ_1 and θ_2. By the standardization apart and the definition of a nicely moded clause

$$\mathit{VarOut}(\mathbf{B}) \cap (\mathit{Var}(A) \cup \mathit{Var}(H)) \subseteq V, \tag{7}$$

so by the fact that θ is relevant

$$\theta_1 \subseteq \eta_1. \tag{8}$$

Thus by the linearity of η_1 (condition (*i*) of Lemma 5.8)

$$\theta_1 \text{ is linear.} \tag{9}$$

Moreover, by (8), (*ii*) of Lemma 5.8 and standardization apart

$$\mathit{Ran}(\theta_1) \cap \mathit{Var}(\mathbf{B}) = \emptyset. \tag{10}$$

Now, let $\theta_2' = \theta_2 | V$ and $\theta_2'' = \theta_2 | \mathit{VarIn}(H)$. We have

$$\theta_2 = \theta_2' \,\dot\cup\, \theta_2'', \tag{11}$$

$$\theta_2' \subseteq \eta_1, \tag{12}$$

and

$$\theta_2'' \subseteq \eta_2. \tag{13}$$

Consider now θ_2'. We have $Dom(\theta_1) \cap Dom(\theta_2) = \emptyset$, so $Dom(\theta_1) \cap Dom(\theta_2') = \emptyset$. Thus, by (8), (12) and the linearity of η_1

$$Ran(\theta_2') \cap Ran(\theta_1) = \emptyset \tag{14}$$

Moreover, by (12), (*ii*) of Lemma 5.8 and the standardization apart

$$Ran(\theta_2') \cap VarOut(\mathbf{B}) = \emptyset. \tag{15}$$

Consider now θ_2''. By (8), (13) and (*iii*) of Lemma 5.8 we get

$$Ran(\theta_2'') \cap Ran(\theta_1) = \emptyset. \tag{16}$$

Also, by the fact that θ is relevant $Ran(\theta_2'') \subseteq Var(A) \cup Var(H)$, so by (7) $Ran(\theta_2'') \cap VarOut(\mathbf{B}) \subseteq V$. Thus by (13) and (*iii*) of Lemma 5.8

$$Ran(\theta_2'') \cap VarOut(\mathbf{B}) = \emptyset. \tag{17}$$

Combining (14) with (16) and (15) with (17) we get by virtue of (11)

$$Ran(\theta_2) \cap (Ran(\theta_1) \cup VarOut(\mathbf{B})) = \emptyset. \tag{18}$$

Now, let us consider $\mathbf{B}$ more in detail. Suppose $\mathbf{B} = p_1(\mathbf{s_1}, \mathbf{t_1}), \ldots, p_n(\mathbf{s_n}, \mathbf{t_n})$. By assumption $\mathbf{t_1}, \ldots, \mathbf{t_n}$ is a linear family of terms and for $i \in [1, n]$ $\mathbf{t_i}\theta \equiv \mathbf{t_i}\theta_1$. So by (9), (10) and Lemma 5.6 $\mathbf{t_1}\theta, \ldots, \mathbf{t_n}\theta$ is a linear family of terms, as well.

Fix now $i \in [1, n]$ and $j \in [i, n]$. We have

$$Ran(\theta | Var(\mathbf{s_i})) \subseteq Ran(\theta_1 | Var(\mathbf{s_i})) \cup Ran(\theta_2 | Var(\mathbf{s_i})) \tag{19}$$

and

$$Ran(\theta | Var(\mathbf{t_j})) = Ran(\theta_1 | Var(\mathbf{t_j})). \tag{20}$$

$\leftarrow \mathbf{B}$ is nicely moded, so

$$Var(\mathbf{s_i}) \cap Var(\mathbf{t_j}) = \emptyset. \tag{21}$$

Thus by the linearity of θ_1 $Ran(\theta_1 | Var(\mathbf{s_i})) \cap Ran(\theta_1 | Var(\mathbf{t_j})) = \emptyset$, and consequently by (19), (20) and (18)

$$Ran(\theta | Var(\mathbf{s_i})) \cap Ran(\theta | Var(\mathbf{t_j})) = \emptyset. \tag{22}$$

Next, by (20) and (10)

$$Var(\mathbf{s_i}) \cap Ran(\theta | Var(\mathbf{t_j})) = \emptyset. \tag{23}$$

Finally, by (19), (10) and (18)

$$Var(\mathbf{t_j}) \cap Ran(\theta | Var(\mathbf{s_i})) = \emptyset. \tag{24}$$

Now, by (21), (22), (23), (24) and Lemma 5.4 we conclude that $Var(\mathbf{s_i}\theta) \cap Var(\mathbf{t_j}\theta) = \emptyset$. This proves that $\leftarrow \mathbf{B}\theta$ is nicely moded. □

Claim 2 *Let θ be a substitution and $\leftarrow \mathbf{A}$ a nicely moded goal such that $Var(\theta) \cap VarOut(\mathbf{A}) = \emptyset$. Then $\leftarrow \mathbf{A}\theta$ is nicely moded, as well.*

Proof. For any term s and a substitution σ we have $Var(s\sigma) \subseteq Var(s) \cup Var(\sigma)$. Moreover, for any term t occurring at an output position of $\mathbf{A}$ by the assumption about θ we have $t\theta = t$. The claim now follows by the definition of a nicely moded goal. □

Claim 3 *Suppose* $\leftarrow \mathbf{A}$ *and* $\leftarrow \mathbf{B}$ *are nicely moded goals such that* $VarOut(\mathbf{A}) \cap Var(\mathbf{B}) = \emptyset$. *Then* $\leftarrow \mathbf{B}, \mathbf{A}$ *is a nicely moded goal, as well.*

Proof. Immediate by the definition of a nicely moded goal. □

Consider now a nicely moded goal $\leftarrow A, \mathbf{A}$ and a disjoint with it nicely moded clause $H \leftarrow \mathbf{B}$, such that A and H unify. Observe that A and H satisfy the assumptions of Lemma 5.8. Assume now that θ is a relevant mgu of $A = H$ which satisfies conditions $(i) - (iii)$ of Lemma 5.8. By Claim 1 $\leftarrow \mathbf{B}\theta$ is nicely moded.

θ is relevant and $Var(A) \cap VarOut(\mathbf{A}) = \emptyset$, so by the standardization apart

$$Var(\theta) \cap VarOut(\mathbf{A}) = \emptyset. \tag{25}$$

By Claim 2 $\leftarrow \mathbf{A}\theta$ is nicely moded.

But (25) implies that $VarOut(\mathbf{A}\theta) = VarOut(\mathbf{A})$. Moreover, $Var(\mathbf{B}\theta) \subseteq Var(\mathbf{B}) \cup Var(\theta)$ and by the standardization apart $VarOut(\mathbf{A}) \cap Var(\mathbf{B}) = \emptyset$, so, again by (25),

$$VarOut(\mathbf{A}\theta) \cap Var(\mathbf{B}\theta) = \emptyset. \tag{26}$$

Now (26) establishes the last assumption of Claim 3 with $\leftarrow \mathbf{A}$ replaced by $\leftarrow \mathbf{A}\theta$ and $\leftarrow \mathbf{B}$ replaced by $\leftarrow \mathbf{B}\theta$. We conclude by Claim 3 that the LD-resolvent $\leftarrow (\mathbf{B}, \mathbf{A})\theta$ of the goal $\leftarrow A, \mathbf{A}$ and the clause $H \leftarrow \mathbf{B}$ is nicely moded.

θ is just one specific mgu of $A = H$. By Lemma 2.2 every other mgu of $A = H$ is of the form $\theta\eta$ for a renaming η. But a renaming of a nicely moded goal is nicely moded, so we conclude that every LD-resolvent of $\leftarrow A, \mathbf{A}$ and $H \leftarrow \mathbf{B}$ is nicely moded. □

This brings us to the following conclusion.

Corollary 5.10 *Let P and G be nicely moded. Suppose that*

- *the head of every clause of P is input linear.*

Then $P \cup \{G\}$ is occur-check free.

Proof. By Theorems 3.7 and 5.2. □

This corollary is stated in Chadha and Plaisted [CP91] as a direct consequence of Theorem 3.7 without mentioning Theorem 5.2. In our opinion the latter theorem is necessary to draw the above conclusion. Pierre Deransart (private communication) pointed out to us that this corollary is a consequence of Theorem 4.1 in Deransart, Ferrand and Téguia [DFT91] whose conditions are satisfied for a nicely moded program P and a nicely moded goal G. This actually suggests a stronger result, namely that such a P and G is NSTO.

It is worthwhile to note that to prove Corollary 5.10 it is actually sufficient to prove Lemma 5.9 under the assumption that the head of every clause of P is input linear. The proof is considerably simpler than that of Lemma 5.9.

This corollary can be easily applied to the previously studied programs.

Example 5.11
(i) Consider again the program append with the moding `app(+,+,-)`. Clearly, append is nicely moded and that the head of every clause is input linear. By Corollary 5.10 we conclude that when u is linear and $Var(\mathtt{u}) \cap Var(\mathtt{s,t}) = \emptyset$, append $\cup \{ \leftarrow \mathtt{app(s,\ t,\ u)}\}$ is occur-check free.

(ii) With the moding `app(-,-,+)` the program append is nicely moded, as well, and the head of every clause is input linear. Again, by Corollary 5.10 we conclude that when `s,t` is a linear family of terms and $Var(\mathtt{u}) \cap Var(\{\mathtt{s,t}\}) = \emptyset$, append $\cup \{ \leftarrow \mathtt{app(s,\ t,\ u)}\}$ is occur-check free.

(iii) Reconsider now the program `permutation` with the modings as before. Again, it is easy to check that `permutation` is nicely moded and that the heads of all clauses are input linear. By Corollary 5.10 we get that when `t` is linear and $Var(\mathtt{s}) \cap Var(\mathtt{t}) = \emptyset$, `permutation` $\cup$ $\{ \leftarrow \mathtt{perm(s,\ t)}\}$ is occur-check free.

(iv) Consider again the program `quicksort` with the modings as before. Again, Corollary 5.10 applies and we conclude that when `t` is linear and $Var(\mathtt{s}) \cap Var(\mathtt{t}) = \emptyset$, `quicksort` $\cup \{ \leftarrow \mathtt{qs(s,\ t)}\}$ is occur-check free.

(v) So far it seems that Corollary 5.10 allows us to draw more useful conclusions that Corollary 4.3. However, reconsider the program `palindrome`. In Chadha and Plaisted [CP91] it is shown that no moding exists in which `palindrome` is nicely moded with the heads of all clauses being input linear. Thus Corollary 5.10 cannot be applied to this program. □

Finally, let us mention that Chadha and Plaisted [CP91] proposed two efficient algorithms for generating modings with the minimal number of input positions, for which the program is nicely moded. These algorithms were implemented and applied to a number of well-known Prolog programs.

6 Strictly Moded Programs

Finally, we consider syntactic restrictions that imply the condition of Theorem 3.8. To this end it is sufficient to combine the properties of being well-moded and nicely moded.

Definition 6.1

- A goal $\leftarrow p_1(\mathbf{s_1}, \mathbf{t_1}), \ldots, p_n(\mathbf{s_n}, \mathbf{t_n})$ is called *strict* if $\mathbf{t_1}, \ldots, \mathbf{t_n}$ is a linear family of terms.
- A clause $H \leftarrow \mathbf{B}$ is called *strict* if $\leftarrow \mathbf{B}$ is strict.
- A program is called *strict* if every clause of it is strict.
- A goal (clause) (program) is called *strictly moded* if it is both strict and well-moded. □

Theorem 6.2 *Let P and G be strictly moded. Then all LD-derivations of* $P \cup \{G\}$ *are both data and output driven.*

Proof. Omitted. □

Corollary 6.3 *Let P and G be strictly moded. Then* $P \cup \{G\}$ *is occur-check free.*

Proof. By Theorems 6.2 and 3.8. □

7 Conclusions

The aim of this paper was to provide simple syntactic conditions which imply that for a given program P and goal G, $P \cup \{G\}$ is occur-check free. To apply the established results one needs to find appropriate modings for the considered relations such that the conditions of one of the established Corollaries (4.3, 5.10 or 6.3) are satisfied. In the table below several programs taken from the book of Sterling and Shapiro [SS86] are listed. (A similar analysis of the notion of a well-moded program was carried in Drabent [Dra87]). For each program it is indicated which of the relevant conditions for a given moding are satisfied. All built-in's are moded completely input.

In programs which use difference lists we replaced "\" by ",", thus splitting a position filled in by a difference list into two positions. Because of this change in some relations additional arguments are introduced, and so certain clauses have to be modified in an obvious way. For example, in the parsing program on page 258 each clause of the form `p(X)` $\leftarrow$ `r(X)` has to be replaced by `p(X,Y)` $\leftarrow$ `r(X,Y)`. Such changes are purely syntactic and they allow us to draw conclusions about the occur-check freedom of the original program.

The modings considered are usually intuitive and at least one of the Corollaries 4.3, 5.10 or 6.3 applies. This indicates that the established results are widely applicable and thus justifies the title of this paper.

program	page	moding	well-moded	heads out. lin.	nicely moded	heads in. lin.	strictly moded
member	45	(–,+)	yes	yes	yes	yes	yes
member	45	(+,+)	yes	yes	yes	no	yes
prefix	45	(–,+)	yes	yes	yes	yes	yes
prefix	45	(+,+)	yes	yes	yes	no	yes
suffix	45	(–,+)	yes	yes	yes	yes	yes
suffix	45	(+,+)	yes	yes	yes	no	yes
naive reverse	48	r(+,–) a(+,+,–)	yes	yes	yes	yes	yes
reverse-accum.	48	r(+,–) r(+,+,-)	yes	yes	yes	yes	yes
delete	53	(+,+,–)	yes	yes	yes	no	yes
select	53	(+,+,–)	yes	yes	yes	no	yes
insertion sort	55	s(+,–) i(+,+,–)	yes	yes	yes	yes	yes
tree-member	58	(–,+)	yes	yes	yes	yes	yes
tree-member	58	(+,+)	yes	yes	yes	no	yes

isotree	58	(+,+)	yes	yes	yes	no	yes
substitute	60	(+,+,+,−)	yes	yes	yes	no	yes
pre-order	60	p(+,−) a(+,+,−)	yes	yes	yes	yes	yes
in-order	60	i(+,−) a(+,+,−)	yes	yes	yes	yes	yes
post-order	60	p(+,−) a(+,+,−)	yes	yes	yes	yes	yes
polynomial	62	(+,+)	yes	yes	yes	no	yes
derivative	63	(+,+,−)	yes	no	yes	no	yes
hanoi	64	h(+,+,+,−) a(+,+,−)	yes	yes	yes	yes	yes
append_dl	241	(+,−,+,+,−,−)	yes	yes	yes	yes	yes
append_dl	241	(+,−,+,−,−,−)	no	no	yes	yes	no
flatten_dl	241	f(+,+) f_dl(+,+,−)	yes	yes	yes	no	yes
flatten	243	f(+,−) f(+,+,−)	yes	yes	yes	yes	yes
reverse_dl	244	r(+,−) r_dl(+,−,+)	yes	yes	yes	yes	yes
quicksort dl	244	q(+,+) q_dl(+,+,−) p(+,+,−,−)	yes	yes	no	yes	yes
dutch	246	dutch(+,−) di(+,−,−,−)	yes	yes	yes	yes	yes
dutch_dl	246	dutch(+,−) di(+,−,+,−,+,−,+)	yes	yes	yes	yes	yes
parsing	258	all (+,−)	yes	yes	yes	yes	yes

P.S. Of course, you would like to know to which two programs from Sterling and Shapiro [SS86] we could not apply the results of this paper. These are `flatten_dl` (program 15.2 on page 241): and `quicksort_dl` (program 15.4 on page 244).

The appropriate entry in the table above indicates that, after replacing "\" by ",", in the mode `flatten(+,+)` and `flatten_dl(+,+,-)`, `flatten_dl` is well-moded and the heads of the clauses are output linear. Thus by virtue of Corollary 4.3 for `s` and `t` ground, all LD-derivations of `flatten_dl` $\cup$ { ← `flatten(s,t)`} are occur-check free. Similar conclusion can be drawn about `quicksort_dl` moded `qs(+,+)` and `qs_dl(+,+,-)`.

However, *no* conclusion can be drawn for the modes `flatten(+,-)` and `qs(+,-)` in which these two programs are customarily used. Indeed, it is easy to check that for both programs no completion of the moding exists for which the program is well-moded, or nicely moded and with the heads of all clauses being input linear.

A solution to this problem is proposed in Pellegrini [Pel92] and for the space reasons omitted here.

Acknowledgement

We thank Pierre Deransart for constructive remarks on the subject of this paper.

References

[Apt90] K. R. Apt. Logic programming. In J. van Leeuwen, editor, *Handbook of Theoretical Computer Science*, pages 493–574. Elsevier, 1990. Vol. B.

[CP91] R. Chadha and D.A. Plaisted. Correctness of unification without occur check in Prolog. Technical report, Department of Computer Science, University of North Carolina, Chapel Hill, N.C., 1991.

[DFT91] P. Deransart, G. Ferrand, and M. Téguia. NSTO programs (not subject to occur-check). In V. Saraswat and K. Ueda, editors, *Proceedings of the International Logic Symposium*, pages 533–547. The MIT Press, 1991.

[DM85a] P. Dembinski and J. Maluszynski. AND-parallelism with intelligent backtracking for annotated logic programs. In *Proceedings of the International Symposium on Logic Programming*, pages 29–38, Boston, 1985.

[DM85b] P. Deransart and J. Maluszynski. Relating Logic Programs and Attribute Grammars. *Journal of Logic Programming*, 2:119–156, 1985.

[Dra87] W. Drabent. Do Logic Programs Resemble Programs in Conventional Languages? In *International Symposium on Logic Programming*, pages 389–396. San Francisco, IEEE Computer Society, August 1987.

[Llo87] J. W. Lloyd. *Foundations of Logic Programming.* Springer-Verlag, Berlin, second edition, 1987.

[LMM88] J.-L. Lassez, M. J. Maher, and K. Marriott. Unification Revisited. In J. Minker, editor, *Foundations of Deductive Databases and Logic Programming*, pages 587–625. Morgan Kaufmann, Los Altos, Ca., 1988.

[MM82] A. Martelli and U. Montanari. An efficient unification algorithm. *ACM Transactions on Programming Languages and Systems*, 4:258–282, 1982.

[Pel92] A. Pellegrini. Sul problema dell' "occur check" in Prolog. Technical report, Department of Computer Science, University of Padova, Padova, Italy, 1992. Tesi di Laurea, in Italian, to appear.

[Pla84] D.A. Plaisted. The occur-check problem in Prolog. In *Proc. International Conference on Logic Programming*, pages 272–280. IEEE Computer Science Press, 1984.

[Ros91] D.A. Rosenblueth. Using program transformation to obtain methods for eliminating backtracking in fixed-mode logic programs. Technical Report 7, Universidad Nacional Autonoma de Mexico, Instituto de Investigaciones en Matematicas Aplicadas y en Sistemas, 1991.

[SS86] L. Sterling and E. Shapiro. *The Art of Prolog*. MIT Press, 1986.

Incremental Evaluation of Natural Semantics Specifications*

Isabelle Attali
INRIA Sophia Antipolis - BP 93
06902 Sophia Antipolis - France
ia@trinidad.inria.fr

Jacques Chazarain
Serge Gilette
CNRS I3S - Univ. Nice Sophia Antipolis
250 Av. Einstein - 06560 Valbonne - France
{jmch,gilette}@mimosa.unice.fr

Abstract

Natural Semantics is a logical formalism used to specify semantic aspects of a language by sets of logical rules (called a Typol program) where a query is proved using Prolog. In a previous paper, we have shown how to replace, under certain hypotheses, the Prolog engine by a functional evaluator; this is possible because unification is no longer required and can be replaced by pattern matching. Starting from this previous work, we now add incremental facilities to our evaluator. That is to say, after some modification of a term whose semantic value has already been evaluated, we do not need to re-evaluate everything from scratch as it is the case with a Prolog engine.

1 Introduction

The description of semantic properties in the natural deduction style is developed by G. Kahn [8] and his group inside the Centaur Project. A semantic specification is represented by a set of inference rules which constitutes, together with type information, a Typol program [5]. The Typol formalism is based on a logical framework, as advocated by G. Plotkin [9], which makes it highly declarative and expressive.

*This work is partially supported by PRC Greco de Programmation CNRS, Opération INTERSEM

For instance,

- in a rule, the subjects of the premises do not need to be subterms of the subject of the conclusion as it must be the case with Attribute Grammars. Therefore, the proof tree of a query with an abstract syntax term as subject is not isomorphic to this abstract syntax term. This explains why this formalism can also be used for dynamic semantics;

- the relational aspect of the logical rules avoid to consider some clumsy error case as it is necessary in the Denotational Semantics framework.

Typol rules are easily translated into a set of Horn clauses, so Prolog is a natural tool for evaluation of TYPOL programs. As a matter of fact, the current implementation of the Typol formalism is based on a Prolog engine.

As a drawback to this natural implementation, Typol specifications are not evaluated in an incremental manner.

To attack this problem, we introduce a new method for evaluating Typol programs. We present this method in two steps:

The first step is described in our previous paper [2]; it consists in replacing the Prolog engine using unification by a functional evaluator based on pattern matching. We have proved this can be done under some hypotheses concerning dependencies between attributes. To provide a systematic way to translate a Typol program into a Lisp program, we introduce a Lisp special construct named **CondMatch** which is a blend of the Lisp "cond" and the ML "match".

In this paper, we consider the second step: we add an incremental strategy to our functional evaluator. When the semantics of a term is computed for the first time, the evaluation tree is saved with some information. When we need to recompute the same term after a syntactic modification, we can reuse (part of) the previous computation. This kind of incremental strategy is an extension of incremental evaluators used in Attributed Grammars [10] to logical specifications.

Section 2 briefly recalls some terminology about Typol programs, the principle of a functional evaluation for them, and the translation scheme from Typol programs to Lisp functions. In Section 3, we present an alternative technique for incremental computation of Typol specifications; we show how to link a change in an abstract syntax term, subject of a query, to its corresponding proof subtree and we describe the propagation algorithm through the proof tree. Section 4 is an evaluation of our implementation through a well-known example: the dynamic semantics of Mini-ML [3]. Section 5 concludes the paper.

2 Functional Evaluation of Natural Semantic Specifications

In this section, we first recall some definitions about Typol programs in order to explain our translation into a functional program.

2.1 Some Definitions about Typol Programs

A Typol program is essentially a collection of inference rules of the generic form:

$$\frac{H_1 \vdash T_1 : S_1 \qquad \cdots \qquad H_n \vdash T_n : S_n}{H \vdash T : S} \quad (r)$$

Each inference rule is composed of a finite set of premises (which is empty for an axiom) and a conclusion. Premises and conclusion of a rule are relations represented by sequents in the Gentzen natural deduction style [6]. The object languages are manipulated via their abstract syntax, defining a many-sorted algebra.

Roughly speaking, a sequent expresses the fact that some hypotheses H are needed to prove a particular property S about an abstract syntax term T.
A sequent $H \vdash T : S$ is generally composed of:

- a term T (the subject of the sequent)
- a tuple $H = h_1, \cdots, h_m$
- a tuple $S = s_1, \cdots, s_p$

(H and S could also be called inherited and synthesized attributes by analogy with Attribute Grammars)

Typol rules indicate how a sequent may be deduced from other sequents.
In the rule (r), the sequent $H \vdash T : S$ is named the conclusion of the rule and the sequents $H_i \vdash T_i : S_i$ are named the premises of the rule.
The subject T of the conclusion is the subject of the rule.

Example:

$$\frac{s \vdash \text{EXP} : \mathit{true} \qquad s \vdash \text{STMS} : s_1 \qquad s_1 \vdash \text{while EXP do STMS end} : s_2}{s \vdash \text{while EXP do STMS end} : s_2} \quad (\mathit{while}1)$$

This rule comes from the dynamic semantics of Asple (a small Pascal-like language). It expresses the fact that, if the test expression is evaluated to *true*, the body of the loop is to be executed once; then, the whole loop has to be evaluated again in the resulting environment.

To evaluate a Typol program means to try to prove a goal $H_0 \vdash T_0 : S_0$ within

the logic defined by the Typol program itself. Such an evaluation leads to the construction of a proof tree.
It must be noticed all Typol programs can not be translated into Attribute Grammars; the reasons are the following:

1. the subjects of the premises of a rule may be different from the sons of the subject of the rule, which may imply a difference between the abstract syntax tree and the proof tree; for example, the *while1* rule has 3 premises but the *while* operator has only 2 sons;

2. this difference can also lead to a (possibly endless) growth of the proof tree.

3. attribute values may be constrained; for example, the *while1* rule contains a constraint on the attribute value for the test expression (*true*);

We focus on the following kind of goals $H_0 \vdash T_0 : S_0$ to be proved where H_0 is given, T_0 is a closed term and S_0 is a result to be computed. This kind of goals gives an orientation to the rules during the proof process. Given this kind of goals to prove, and given a Typol program, the flow of information in the proof tree is correct only if all the Typol rules are safe, according to the following definition:

A Typol rule (r) is *safe* if :

- the set of variables which appear in the terms $S, T_1, \cdots, T_n, H_1, \cdots, H_n$ is included in the set of variables which appear in the terms $T, H, S_1, \cdots, S_n$
- the sets of variables of the terms T_i are included in the set of variables of T.

For instance, the *while1* rule is safe.

2.2 Functional Evaluation

Under some hypotheses concerning dependencies between attributes, a Typol program can be translated into a Lisp program using a new constructor so-called CondMatch. To avoid the re-definition of the notion of the "Strongly Non Circular" dependency, we briefly recall our theoretical result in a simplified case.
We assume in the following that:

- **Hyp1:** the dependency is left to right between attributes in the premises of the Typol rules; or more precisely, for each rule (r), there exists an order of the premises of (r) such that, for any indices $i < j$, the attributes S_i do not depend on the attributes S_j during the proof of a goal.
- **Hyp2:** we assume that all the rules in the Typol program are safe.

We define a new language construct, called **CondMatch**. Intuitively, the CondMatch construct is a conditional expression similar to the usual Cond construct except that the selection of a branch is based on a sequence of pattern-matchings, with backtracking when there is a failure in a branch. More precisely, we give the syntax and the semantics of the CondMatch construct.

Syntax of the CondMatch construct:

```
(CondMatch
     L1
     ...
     Lk
)
```

where each branch Lj is a list with the following structure:

```
(  ((p1 e1)
      ...
    (pn en))
 s1 ... sN
)
```

where $p1, \cdots, pn$ are terms and $e1, \cdots, en$, $s1, \cdots, sN$ are S-expressions.

Semantics of the CondMatch construct:
To compute a CondMatch form, we select the first branch in which the whole sequence of pattern-matchings between each non-evaluated pattern *pi* and expression *ei* succeeds. These matchings are done in sequence, using the local environments given by the previous matching. Then, CondMatch evaluates in sequence the expressions $s1, \cdots, sN$ in the resulting matching environment and returns the value of the last evaluation sN. If one matching fails, the next branch is examined.

Under the hypotheses Hyp1 and Hyp2 we obtain, as a particular case from our previous paper, that the evaluation of a Typol goal $H_0 \vdash T_0 : S_0$ (where H_0 is given, T_0 is a closed term and S_0 is a result to be computed) can be done by the following scheme of a Lisp function:

```
(defun FuncTypol (TO HO)
   (condMatch
                  ...
                  ( ( ((T H) (TO HO))
                      (S1 (FuncTypol T1 H1))
                       ...
                      (Sn (FuncTypol Tn Hn))
                    )
                   S
                  )
                  ...
   )
)
```

where each branch of the CondMatch construct is associated with a Typol rule of the form (r).

Fortunately, Typol programs usually satisfy the previous hypotheses: see for instance, Mini-ML dynamic semantics (cf Section 4) or static and dynamic semantics of the Asple language.

3 Incremental Evaluation of Natural Semantic Specifications

In the setting of interactive programming environments, we aim at designing tools that work well in practice for the end-user (in terms of both storage and efficiency). We focus here on the answering time of tools such as type-checkers, translators or evaluators. This kind of semantic computation on a structured object, computer program, or mathematical formula is quite complex and time consuming. We claim that incremental re-evaluation (when the end-user edits and modifies his structured object) is mandatory, for comfort and user-friendliness reasons. This need is even clearer in visual applications such as document formatting in *wysiwyg* editors: we do not want to embarass the end-user with hundreds of screen redisplays. In the context of semantic checking in programming environments, we do not want to recompute each time everything, for instance type-check the whole program each time it is edited; we want to incrementally give the user feedback on compile-time errors as the program is edited and corrected.

An incremental evaluator acts as a standard evaluator for the first computation except that it stores some results in order to re-use them for the next times.

The problem of incremental computation has been intensively studied in the case of Attribute Grammars ([10], see a complete bibliography in [4], and a survey in [1]). As we explained in Section 2, the evaluation of logical specifications is not always reducible to Attribute Grammars formalism. We provide an alternative technique for incremental computation that can be used for problems where Attribute Grammars are not suitable, such as dynamic semantics, rewriting systems and theorem proving.

3.1 A simple example

Let us give first an intuitive view of our incremental evaluator on a small example from the Mini-ML dynamic semantics.

We want to evaluate the value of the following expression:

```
let x = 5 in if x = 0 then x-1 else x * x .
```

The abstract syntax tree T of this term is given by:

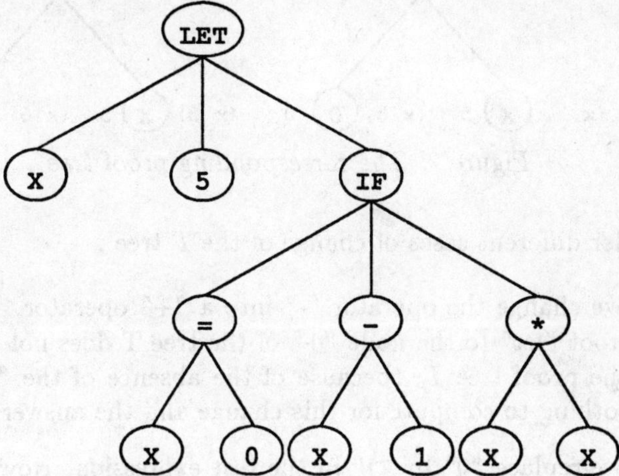

Figure 1: An abstract syntax tree

We compute its semantic value using the Typol rules for *let* and *if* abstract syntax operators:

$$\frac{\rho \vdash \mathrm{E_1} : \alpha \qquad (\rho, \mathrm{X} \mapsto \alpha) \vdash \mathrm{E_2} : \beta}{\rho \vdash \text{let } \mathrm{X} = \mathrm{E_1} \text{ in } \mathrm{E_2} : \beta} \quad (let)$$

$$\frac{\rho \vdash \mathrm{E_1} : \mathit{true} \qquad \rho \vdash \mathrm{E_2} : \alpha}{\rho \vdash \text{if } \mathrm{E_1} \text{ then } \mathrm{E_2} \text{ else } \mathrm{E_3} : \alpha} \quad (if1)$$

$$\frac{\rho \vdash \mathrm{E_1} : \mathit{false} \qquad \rho \vdash \mathrm{E_3} : \alpha}{\rho \vdash \text{if } \mathrm{E_1} \text{ then } \mathrm{E_2} \text{ else } \mathrm{E_3} : \alpha} \quad (if2)$$

The computation of a semantic value using these logical rules yields to the construction of a proof tree T_p. We decorate this proof tree with attribute values : the inherited environnement ρ on the left side of each node and the synthesized value α (or β) on the right side.

Moreover there is a natural correspondence between the nodes in the abstract syntax tree and the nodes in the proof tree (see section 3.2).

Back to our example, we get the following decorated proof tree T_p with the value 25 as result (note the absence of the "then" subterm):

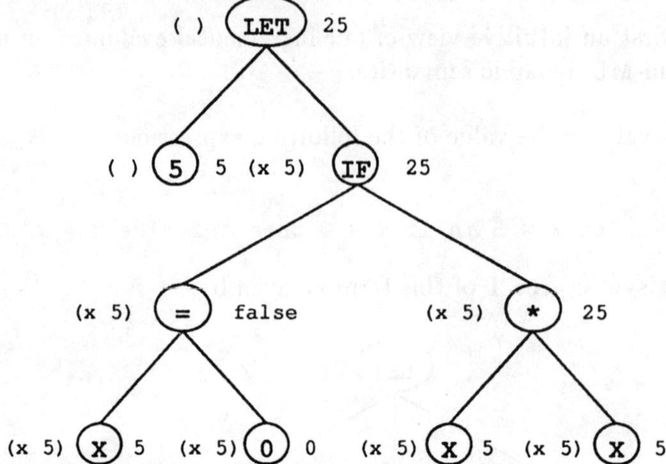

Figure 2: The corresponding proof tree

Now, we consider different cases of change of the T tree :

- **case a:** we change the operator "-" into a "+" operator. The path starting from the root "let" to the node "+" of the tree T does not correspond to any node in the proof tree T_p (because of the absence of the "then" branch), so there is nothing to compute for this change and the answer is "25".
- **case b:** we replace "0" by "1" in the test expression. Now the path starting from the root "let" to this node has a corresponding path in the proof tree T_p. So our evaluator starts from that modified node and propagates the modification to its father. But this still gives the same value "false" for the test subtree; therefore the propagation stops and the answer is "25".
- **case c:** we replace the "$\star$" operator by a "-" operator. The propagation starts from the corresponding path in the proof tree, which yields to the "x-x" subtree. We recompute the semantic value of this subtree, which is "0" and propagate "0" to its father and grand father in order to replace the old value. Now the proof tree is:

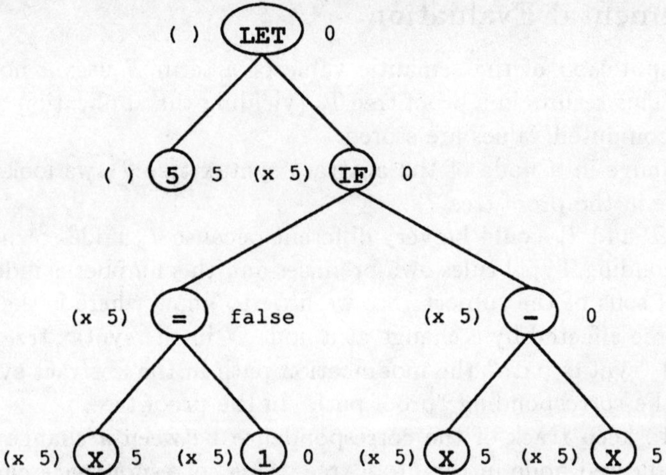

Figure 3: Proof tree after some changes

- case d: finally, we replace "1" by "5" in the test expression. The propagation starts from the corresponding path in the proof tree. First, we recompute the test expression and get the value "true"; therefore, the *(if2)* rule used in the proof tree is no longer valid, and the proof actually requires to use rule *(if1)*. This introduces a structural modification in the proof tree: replace the "else" subterm by the "then" subterm, and compute its semantic value. This results in the value "6", which is propagated up to the root. The resulting proof tree is the following:

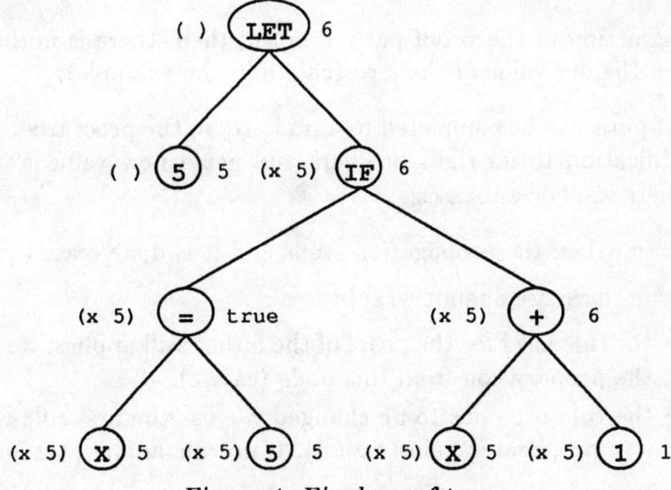

Figure 4: Final proof tree

As a conclusion, we can see on this simple example that, except for the d case, the incremental evaluator saves computation.
Here is now a more general description of our incremental evaluation.

3.2 Incremental Evaluation

The first computation of the semantic value of a term T uses a non incremental CondMatch. This results in a proof tree T_p (yielding the application of Typol rules) in which the computed values are stored.

After a change in a node of the abstract syntax tree T, we look for the corresponding node in the proof tree T_p.

The trees T and T_p could be very different because T_p nodes own as many sons as the corresponding Typol rules own premises and this number is independent from the number of sons of the subject. So, we have to know where is the first node N_p in the proof tree affected by a change at a node N in the syntax tree.

Let us call "syntax path" the modification path in the abstract syntax term; we want to find the corresponding "proof path" in the proof tree.

We need to keep track of the correspondence between a change in the syntax tree and the affected node in the proof tree. This correspondence can be statically determined on the Typol program: for each rule, we know in which premise appears which subterm of the subject. If a subterm appears in more than one premise, we choose the leftmost one: it corresponds to the first affected node in the proof tree.

For a given syntax path, we navigate in the proof tree using the static correspondences to build the proof path. If there is no proof path, the change in the syntax tree has no effect on the proof tree and there is no propagation nor recomputation. In the other case, the propagation starts from the node N_p reached by the proof path.

Here is now a sketch of the propagation algorithm after a modification at node N in the syntax tree; there are two cases:

1. the construction of the proof path aborted; then, there is nothing to do and we return the old value of the tree (case a in the example);

2. the proof path can be completed to a node N_p in the proof tree. We propagate the modification to its right brothers and get a new value v' for its father. Then, there are two subcases:

   - $v' = v$, then the propagation stops and it is done (case b);
   - $v' \neq v$ there are again two subcases :
     - the rule used for the proof of the father still applies; we simply iterate the propagation from this node (case c).
     - the rule used has to be changed; we use the first rule that can apply and propagate again (case d). If no rule applies, the proof fails.

It is necessary to find the good trade-off between time consuming and space comsuming; some times, it is clear that incremental evaluation for a given abstract syntax operator is not useful and it is better to recompute a proof subtree than to remember everything from the last computation. Therefore, the incremental re-evaluation can be switched off for a given abstract syntax operator.

We can now summarize the architecture of our implementation.

3.3 General Architecture

Given a Typol program, we associate:

- a Lisp condMatch for each set of rules (FuncTypol);
- a representation of the rules with the static dependency between attributes (Static-Dependencies).

For the first computation of the semantics of a syntax term T we associate a decorated proof tree T_p. For each modification of the syntax term T, we call our incremental evaluator whith the following arguments:

- the syntax path and the new subtree,
- the previous proof tree T_p,
- FuncTypol,
- Static-Dependencies.

Our incremental evaluator returns a modified proof tree and the new semantic value for T. This architecure is sketched in Figure 4:

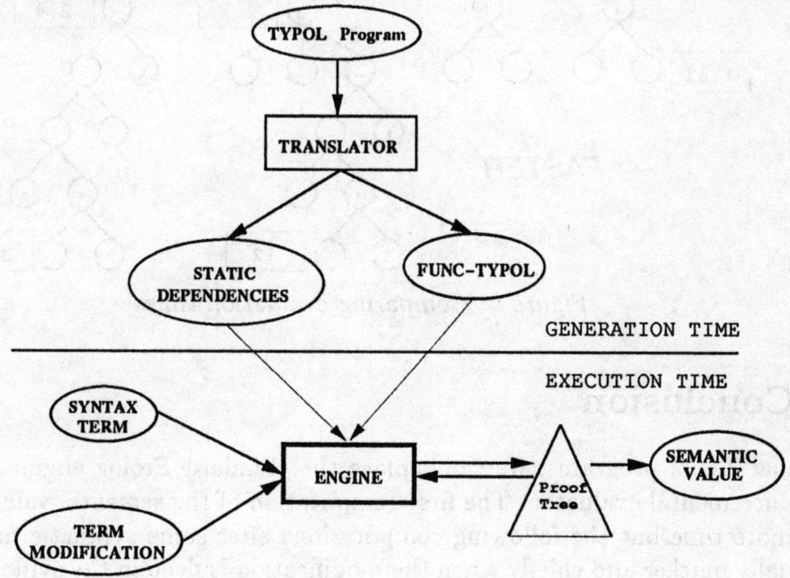

Figure 4: General architecture

4 Results and Performances

We use a variant of the well-known Typol program specifying the dynamic semantics of Mini-ML to give some performances comparisons (This variant has been designed in order to avoid circular dependencies in the *letrec* rule.)

Varied examples of Mini-ML expressions show that the incremental re-evaluation after a syntactic modification is generally faster than the Prolog evaluation (see Figure 5 for more details). As a normal drawback, the first computation is always slower than the Prolog evaluation.

The Figure 5 sketches the comparing times between Prolog and our incremental evaluator for the following expression:

```
let a = (2+1)*(3+2)
in if if a+2 = (13+1) - 1 then false else true
         then a - (1 + 1*2 + a)
         else 2 * (a - (4 + a) * 2)
```

Numbers indicate the speed factor between the time of our incremental evaluation (after a change in a given node) and the Prolog evaluation time.

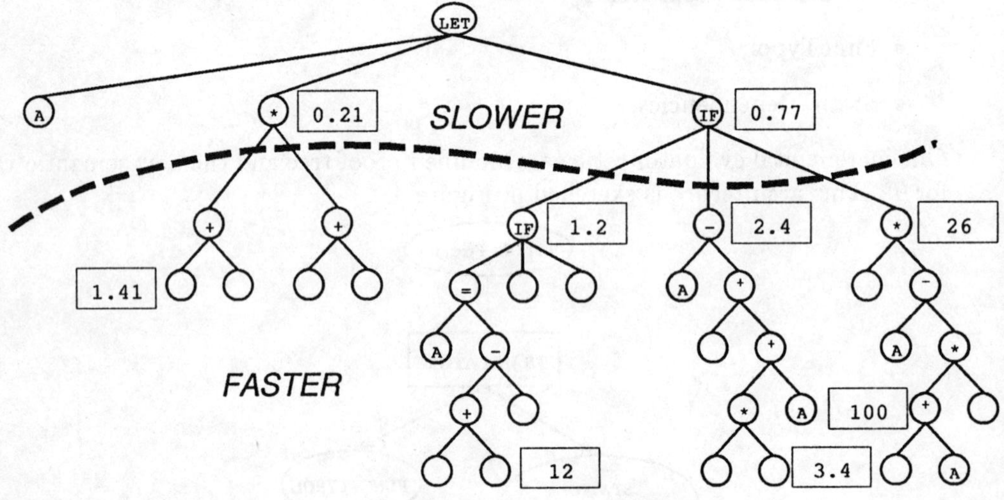

Figure 5: Comparing evaluation times

5 Conclusion

For usual Typol programs, we can replace the standard Prolog engine by a functional incremental evaluator. The first computation of the semantic value of a term takes more time but the following computations after some syntactic modification are usually quicker and chiefly when the modification is deep in the syntax tree. For this kind of logical specifications we are aware of only one other work about incremental evaluation in the case of a type-checker [7]. Hascoet had another strategy than ours: to get a given type-checker run in an incremental manner, he chose to automatically transform the Typol rules into new Typol rules that only contain synthesized attributes. These typol rules were compiled into Prolog, using the Prolog data-base (assert and retract) to store some synthesized attributes for re-evaluation.

Concerning the implementation, it mainly remains to automatically translate the Typol program into the sets of Lisp functions. This kind of translation will naturally be written in the Typol formalism.

References

[1] Alblas H. & Melichar B. "Attribute Grammars, Applications and Systems", Proc. of International summer school SAGA, Prague, 1991 LNCS 545.

[2] Attali I. and Chazarain J. "Functional Evaluation of Natural Semantics Specifications" INRIA Research Report 1218, May 1990, also in Proc. of WAGA "international Workshop on Attribute Grammars and their Applications" Paris sept 90, LNCS 461.

[3] Clément D., Despeyroux J., Despeyroux T. & Kahn G. "A simple applicative language: Mini-ML" Symp. on Functional Programming Languages and Computer Architecture, 1986

[4] Deransart P., Jourdan M., & Lorho B. "Attribute Grammars: Definitions, Systems and Bibliography" LNCS 323, Spinger Verlag, 1988

[5] Despeyroux T. "Typol: a formalism to implement Natural Semantics" INRIA research report 94, 1988

[6] Gentzen G. "Investigation into Logical Deduction" Thesis 1935, reprinted in "The collected papers of Gerhard Gentzen" E. Szabo, North-Holland, Amsterdam, 1969

[7] L. Hascoët, "Transformations automatiques de spécifications sémantiques", Thèse de Doctorat, Univ. Nice, 1987

[8] Kahn G. "Natural Semantics" Proc. of Symp on Theoretical Aspects of Computer Science, Passau, Germany, LNCS 247, 1987

[9] Plotkin G. D. "A structural approach to operational semantics" Report DAIMI FN-19, Computer Science Dpt, Aarhus Univ., Aarhus, Denmark, 1981

[10] Reps T. "Generating Language based Environments" ACM Doctoral Dissertation Award, M.I.T. Press, Cambridge, Mass, 1984

Subsumption–oriented Push–Down Automata *

F. Barthélemy and E. Villemonte de la Clergerie

INRIA Rocquencourt - BP 105
78153 LE CHESNAY
France
clerger@inria.inria.fr barthele@inria.inria.fr

Abstract. This paper presents Subsumption–oriented Push–Down Automata (SPDA), a very general stack formalism used to describe forest ("AND–OR" tree) traversals. These automata may be used for parsing or the interpretation of logic programs. SPDA allow a Dynamic Programming execution which breaks computations into combinable, sharable and storable sub–computations. They provide computation sharing and operational completeness and solves some of the problems posed by the usual depth–first, left–to–right traversals (as implemented in PROLOG). We give an axiomatization of SPDA and two examples of their use: the evaluation of logic programs and parsing with Tree Adjoining Grammars. SPDA may also serve in other areas such as Constraint Logic Programming, Abstract Interpretations, or Contextual parsing.

1 Introduction

The Push–Down Automaton (PDA) is a well–known machine that uses single stack operations for context–free parsing. B.Lang proposed in [Lan74] a technique extending *Dynamic Programming* (DP) to efficiently execute PDA, especially when they are non–deterministic. The idea consists in computing the complete set of stack tops that may appear in any calculation of the PDA. The reachable stacks, and especially success ones, can be extracted from this set of tops. Dynamic programming techniques are a good way to share sub-computations and are operationally complete.

Our purpose is to extend PDA to richer domains (Herbrand domain, constraint domains) while preserving the advantages of Dynamic Programming. These domains, in addition to a rich vocabulary, often provide a subsumption order which can be used to share computations. Dynamic Programming avoids redundancy by computing only the most general (sub-)goals. Furthermore, logic program non–determinism tends to duplicate sub–computations, making computation sharing even more interesting.

Besides computation sharing, Dynamic Programming also offers a solution to completeness problems one encounters with standard depth–first strategies (as in PROLOG). It improves termination by avoiding those loops which correspond to infinite recomputations. Our approach is related to tabulation[TS86, Vie87] or magic–set[Sek89] techniques proposed for Logic Programming, but encompasses them by being more flexible. Indeed, Dynamic Programming works for various automata which

* This work has been partly supported by the Eureka Software Factory (ESF) project.

can encode all kinds of resolution strategies (e.g. SLD, Bottom–Up, and Earley Deduction[Por86]). Extensions of tabulation or magic–set techniques have been proposed for constraint logic programming and abstract interpretation [KK90, Kan90].

The heart of this paper is devoted to a systematic axiomatization of a very general class of automata, namely Subsumption–oriented Push–Down Automata. These automata are conceived for a Dynamic Programming execution with subsumption. We give axioms to ensure the validity of such an execution.

Section 2 presents the Subsumption–oriented Push–Down Automata. In the last two sections, we give two concrete applications of these SPDA : pure Logic Programs interpretation and parsing with Tree Adjoining Grammars.

2 Subsumption–oriented Push–Down Automata

2.1 Preliminaries about Diagram Notations

In this paper, we use commutative diagrams to introduce the needed axioms and to ease proofs. These diagrams are widely used in papers which employ Category Theory. We recall basic reading conventions on the below diagram example.

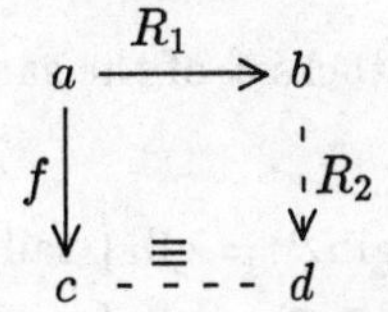

$$\begin{array}{ccc} a & \xrightarrow{R_1} & b \\ {\scriptstyle f}\downarrow & & \downarrow{\scriptstyle R_2} \\ & \equiv & \\ c & - - - - & d \end{array}$$

An arrow $a \xrightarrow{R_1} b$ states that the objects a and b are related by R_1 $(a\ R_1\ b)$. An arrow $a \xrightarrow{f} c$ where f denotes a (partial) function can be read "$a \in \mathrm{Dom}(f) \wedge c = f(a)$". Non-oriented arrows ($c \overset{\equiv}{\text{———}} d$) are used for equivalence relations. Plain arrows denote universal quantified premises while dashed arrows denote existential quantified conclusions. Thus, the previous diagram should be read :

$$\forall a, b, c : \mathit{objects},\ (a\ R_1\ b \wedge a \in \mathrm{Dom}(f) \wedge c = f(a)) \Rightarrow (\exists d : \mathit{object},\ b\ R_2\ d \wedge c \equiv d)$$

2.2 Ordered Stack Domains

Generally speaking[2], a stack is only a finite sequence of elements of a domain D. A stack ξ is noted (using a list notation) $[A_1, \ldots, A_n]$ where the top of the stack is on the left. The empty stack is noted $[]$. We use the notation $[\,A_1, \ldots, A_n \,|\, \theta]$ to describe a stack where the n first top elements are $A_1 \ldots A_n$ and the rest is the stack θ. $\mathrm{tail}\,\xi$ denotes the stack ξ minus its first top element and $h(\xi)$ denotes the height of ξ. We also introduce the cut operators π_n which return (when possible) the n first top elements.

[2] We limit our presentation to the usual stack notion, but the interested reader can find in [BVdlC] an axiomatization which allows more exotic stacks and still preserves the results of this paper.

Definition 1. $\mathrm{tail}\,[] = [] \wedge \mathrm{tail}\,[\,A\,|\,\xi] = \xi \wedge \pi_n\,[A_1 \ldots A_m] = \begin{cases} [A_1 \ldots A_n] \text{ if } m \geq n \\ [A_1 \ldots A_m] \text{ if } m < n \end{cases}$

Now, a stack domain $\mathcal{S}$ is only a set of stacks closed for the tail and π_n operators[3].

The stack domains used in this paper possess "generalization" (partial) orders which verify a minimal set of constraints relative to the tail, π_n and height operations.

Definition 2. A Generalization Stack Order (GSO) over a Stack Domain $\mathcal{S}$ is an order $\preceq$ such that :

- Two comparable stacks must have the same height.
- The following diagrams[4] hold :

$$\begin{array}{ccc}
\begin{array}{ccc} \xi & \xrightarrow{\pi_n} & \cdot \\ \downarrow\preceq & & \preceq\,\vdots \\ \xi^\circ & \xrightarrow{\pi_n} & \cdot \end{array}
&
\begin{array}{ccc} \xi & \xrightarrow{\pi_n} & \cdot \\ \vdots\,\preceq & & \preceq\downarrow \\ \cdot & \dashrightarrow_{\pi_n} & \theta^\circ \end{array}
&
\begin{array}{ccc} \xi & \xrightarrow{\text{tail}} & \cdot \\ \downarrow\preceq & & \preceq\,\vdots \\ \xi^\circ & \xrightarrow{\text{tail}} & \cdot \end{array}
\\
\textbf{[CUT1]} & \textbf{[CUT2]} & \textbf{[TAIL1]}
\end{array}$$

- Any finite or infinite set of stacks $\mathcal{E}$ of the same height has a lower bound noted glb $(\mathcal{E})$ which also satisfies

$$\mathrm{tail}(\mathrm{glb}\,\mathcal{E}) = \mathrm{glb}\,\{\ \mathrm{tail}\,\xi \mid \xi \in \mathcal{E}\ \}$$
$$\pi_n\,(\mathrm{glb}\,\mathcal{E}) = \mathrm{glb}\,\{\ \pi_n\,\xi \mid \xi \in \mathcal{E}\ \}$$

$\xi \preceq \xi^\circ$ means that "ξ generalizes ξ°" or conversely that "ξ° is an instance of ξ".

2.3 SPDA

We now generalize standard Push-Down Automata over an ordered stack domain $\mathcal{S}$.

Definition 3 SPDA. A Subsumption–oriented Push Down Automaton is a 4-tuple $(\mathcal{S}, \xi_{init}, \xi_{end}, \Theta)$ where:

- $\mathcal{S}$ is stack domain with a generalization order $\preceq$.
- ξ_{init} is the **initial stack** and $h(\xi_{init}) = 1$.
- Any instance of ξ_{end} is called a **final stack**. We require $\xi_{init} \preceq \mathrm{tail}(\xi_{end})$.
- Θ is a set of "allowed" stack transition, which will be defined precisely below as a sub–class of transitions.

---

[3] Please note that $\mathcal{S}$ may be a strict subset of the set of all stacks built on a domain D.

[4] whose meaning is given here :

[CUT1] $\forall n \in N, \forall \xi, \xi^\circ \in \mathcal{S},\ \xi \preceq \xi^\circ\ \Rightarrow\ \pi_n\,\xi \preceq \pi_n\,\xi^\circ$
[CUT2] $\forall n \in N, \forall \xi, \theta^\circ \in \mathcal{S},\ \pi_n\,\xi \preceq \theta^\circ\ \Rightarrow (\exists \xi^\circ \in \mathcal{S},\ \xi \preceq \xi^\circ \wedge \pi_n\,\xi^\circ = \theta^\circ)$
[TAIL1] $\forall \xi, \xi^\circ \in \mathcal{S},\ \xi \preceq \xi^\circ\ \Rightarrow\ \mathrm{tail}(\xi) \preceq \mathrm{tail}(\xi^\circ)$

Transitions. A stack transition τ is a partial function[5] from $\mathcal{S}$ to $\mathcal{S}$, viewed as a black-box which takes an input stack ξ and possibly returns an output stack $\tau\xi$. The transition application is externally characterized by a triple of numbers $(p_\tau, b_\tau, \delta_\tau)$. Figure 1 provides an informal interpretation of these numbers.

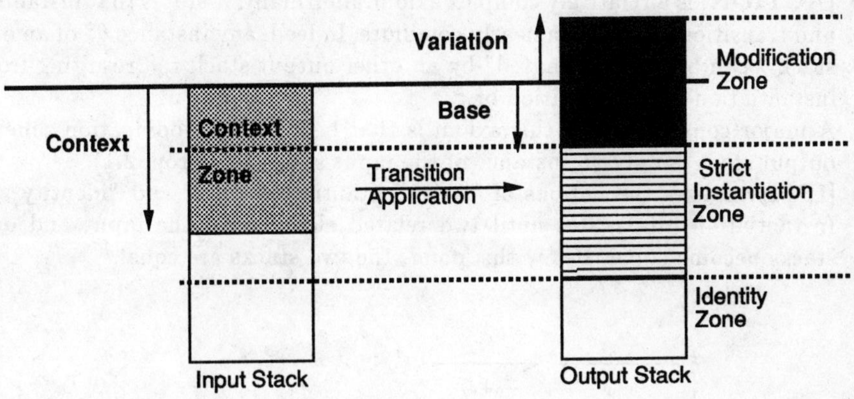

Fig. 1. How does a transition application work ? The applicability of a transition τ depends on the context elements of the input stack. The output stack is built by adding, removing or modifying the elements of the modification zone and instantiating the bottom of the input stack.

- The **context** p_τ states how many of the input stack top elements are used to apply the transition τ. It follows that the height of the input stack must be greater than or equal to p_τ and the sub–stack $(\pi_{p_\tau}\ \xi)$ of the input stack is called the *"context zone"*.
- The **base** b_τ measures the depth of the modifications resulting from the application of τ. By convention, the modifications should not propagate below the "context zone" $(b_\tau \leq p_\tau)$.
  Below the *"modification zone"* the only consequence of the application is an instantiation of the input stack[6]. The *"instantiation zone"* has itself two components : a *"strict instantiation zone"* where all stack elements are strictly instantiated and, below this zone, an *"identity zone"* where no instantiation occurs.
- The **variation** $\delta_\tau = h(\xi) - h(\tau\xi)$ represents the height variation between the input and output stacks [7]. The top of the output stack is also the top of the "modification zone" ; therefore we have $\delta_\tau \leq b_\tau$.

[5] In fact, all results are preserved when one views the transitions as partial binary relations.

[6] Instantiation is not considered as a modification but rather as an information update on the existing elements (specialization).

[7] Please note that a height increasing between the input and the output stacks will give a negative variation.

The diagrams of Fig. 2 show the set of axioms the transitions must verify:

- **[CONTEXT]** formalizes the meaning of p_τ. The application of τ only depends on the p_τ top elements of the input stack which also condition the result.
- **[GEN]** means that transition application is order compatible. Computations done on a stack are still possible on more general stacks.
- **[ACTION]** is a relatively complex axiom. Informally, it states that instantiation and transition application nearly commute. Indeed, any instance θ° of an output stack θ can be "approximated" by an other output stack $\tau\xi^\circ$ resulting from an instantiation–free application of τ.
  A major consequence of this axiom is that below the "modification zone", the output stack is only an instance of the input stack (see Prop. 2.1).
- **[ID]** formalizes the notions of "strict instantiation zone" and "identity zone". Instantiation propagates until two related elements of the input and output stacks become equal. Below this point, the two stacks are equal.

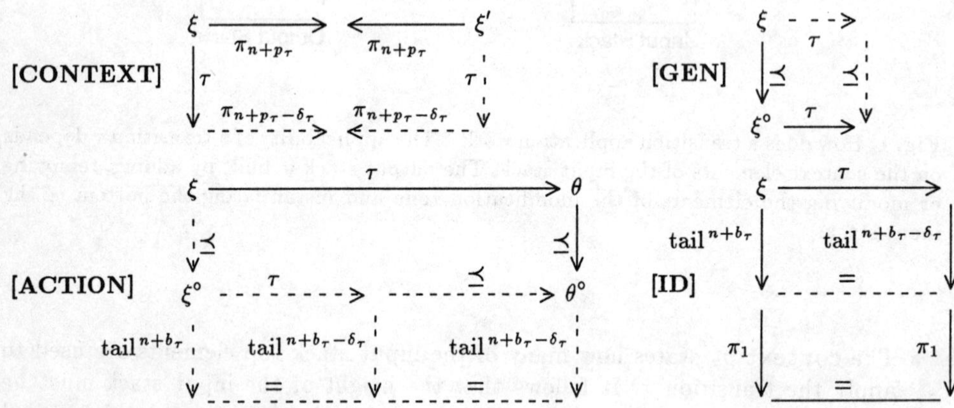

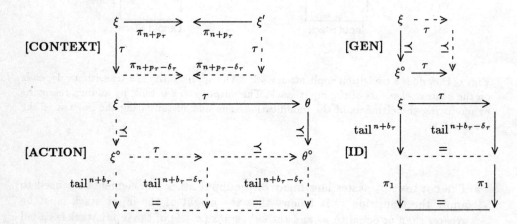

Fig. 2. Transition Application Axioms (with "n" universally quantified)

The existence of the already mentioned "instantiation zone" comes from the axiom **[ACTION]**.

Proposition 2.1 *(Instantiation zone) The diagram* **[INST]** *holds for all transition applications:*

$$\textbf{[INST]} \qquad \begin{array}{ccc} \xi & \xrightarrow{\tau} & \\ \Big\downarrow \mathit{tail}^{b_\tau} & & \Big\downarrow \mathit{tail}^{b_\tau-\delta_\tau} \\ & \xrightarrow[\preceq]{} & \end{array}$$

Proof. From **[ACTION]** with $\theta^\circ = \tau\xi$ and $n = 0$, we exhibit an instance ξ° of ξ such that tail $^{b_\tau}\xi^\circ$ = tail $^{b_\tau-\delta_\tau}(\tau\xi)$. From **[TAIL1]**, we get tail $^{b_\tau}\xi \preceq$ tail $^{b_\tau}\xi^\circ$ = tail $^{b_\tau-\delta_\tau}(\tau\xi)$. ∎

Allowed Transitions. In the rest of this paper, only three kinds of *allowed transitions* (namely HOR, PUSH and POP transitions) are used to ensure the existence of a dynamic programming interpretation. Intuitively, a transition HOR of characteristics $(p, b, \delta) = (1, 1, 0)$ replaces the input stack top element while a transition PUSH $(1, 0, -1)$ pushes a new element on the input stack and a transition POP $(2, 2, 1)$ reduces the two input stack top elements to only one [8].

Derivations. We call *derivation* any (possibly empty) transition sequence. A derivation may also be characterized by a triple of numbers which play the same role as for the transitions. Furthermore, the transition properties extend to the derivations.

Definition 4 Derivation. A derivation is a transition sequence $d = \tau_1 \dots \tau_n$. The symbol ϵ denotes the empty derivation. Concatenation of derivations is noted "." and if $d = q.r$ then q (resp. r) is a prefix (resp. postfix) derivation of d.

The symbol $\vdash$ denotes transition or derivation application. Thus, $\xi \vdash^{n}_{d} \theta$ means that the derivation d of length n applies to ξ to return θ while $\xi \vdash^{\star} \theta$ means that there exists a derivation d which transforms ξ into θ. $\vdash^{\star} \theta$ stands for $\xi_{init} \vdash^{\star} \theta$.

Definition 5. The characteristic triple (p_d, b_d, δ_d) of a derivation d is defined by

	p_d	b_d	δ_d
$d = \epsilon$	0	0	0
$d = \tau$	p_τ	b_τ	δ_τ
$d = q.r$	$max(p_q, \delta_q + p_r)$	$max(b_q, \delta_q + b_r)$	$\delta_q + \delta_r$

One can easily verify that this definition is well-founded.

We can now present the most important result of this part :

Proposition 2.2 *The diagrams* **[GEN]**, **[CONTEXT]**, **[ACTION]**, **[ID]** *and* **[INST]** *hold for the derivations.*

Proof. In fact, this proposition only states that the set of transitions is closed by composition and the proof is obtained by combining the diagrams. ∎

Basic Derivations. Informally, a **basic derivation** is a derivation which has the same characteristics as a PUSH transition (namely $(1, 0, -1)$). Proposition 2.3 founds the validity of Dynamic Programming interpretation : it allows computations to be broken into easily recombinable sub–computations.

Proposition 2.3 *For all derivation D such that $\delta_D < 0$, there exists a basic derivation d postfix of D.*

Proof. We mainly use the fact that the allowed transitions τ satisfy $|\delta_\tau| \leq 1$. It follows that we can extract postfix derivations r from D such that $\delta_r = -1$. We take for d the shortest of these derivations. It is easy to show that d is a basic derivation. ∎

[8] Some readers may expect characteristics $(0, 0, 1)$ (resp. $(1, 1, 1)$) for PUSH (resp. POP) transitions. But, SPDA transitions do not strictly coincide with usual PDA transitions which act in fact on pairs (*stack*, *state*). In the SPDA formalism, states are implicitly part of the stacks which explain PUSH and POP characteristics.

2.4 Dynamic Programming Interpretation

The aim of a Dynamic Programming interpretation is to break computations into sub–computations which validate the following requirements :

1. They may be compactly represented by storable traces called **items**.
2. The items can easily be combined to retrieve all general computations.
3. The items can be reused in various contexts to gain computation sharing.
4. The items are subject to a subsumption test to avoid redundant computations.

SPDA computations may be decomposed into such sub–computations.

Indeed, a SPDA computation is the application of a derivation d on the initial stack ξ_{init} to get a stack ξ ($\vdash_{\overline{d}} \xi$). By an iterative use of the extraction theorem 2.3, any computation $\vdash_{\overline{d}} \xi$ can be decomposed[9] into $\xi_0 \vdash_{\overline{d_1}} \xi_1 \cdots \xi_{n-1} \vdash_{\overline{d_n}} \xi_n$ where $\xi_0 = \xi_{init}$ and $\xi_n = \xi$ and the d_i are basic derivations.

A sub–computation $\xi \vdash_{\overline{d}} \theta$ is said to be *basic* when d is a basic derivation and ξ is a computable stack. Basic computations allow reductions of computation as illustrated by the following remarks:

- A computation $\xi_0 \vdash_{\overline{\tau}} \xi_1$ where τ is a PUSH transition and ξ_0 a computable stack is a basic computation.
- A computation $\xi_0 \vdash_{\overline{d}} \xi_1 \vdash_{\overline{\tau}} \xi_2$ where $\xi_0 \vdash_{\overline{d}} \xi_1$ is a basic computation and τ a HOR transition is a basic computation.
- A computation $\xi_0 \vdash_{\overline{d_1}} \xi_1 \vdash_{\overline{d_2}} \xi_2 \vdash_{\overline{\tau}} \xi_3$ where $\xi_0 \vdash_{\overline{d_1}} \xi_1$ and $\xi_1 \vdash_{\overline{d_2}} \xi_2$ are basic computations and τ a POP transition is a basic computation.

Furthermore, a successful computation $\vdash^{\star} \xi^{\circ}_{end}$ where ξ°_{end} is an instance of the final stack ξ_{end} is a basic computation.

Now, the essential information provided by a basic computation $\xi_0 \vdash_{\overline{d}} \xi_1$ concerns the existence of a computable stack whose context zone allows the application of d to give a new computable stack. Thus, a trace of a basic computation must remember the context necessary to apply d and the result. Without instantiation, one could use the pair $(\pi_1\, \xi_0, \pi_1\, \xi_1)$ to trace the computation.

The instantiation makes life more complex, but the following result (deriving from **[ACTION]** on basic computations) will help us :

$$\xi_0 \vdash_{\overline{d}} \xi_1 \Rightarrow \text{tail}\, \xi_1 \vdash_{\overline{d}} \xi_1$$

Instead of tracing the original computation, we keep a trace of the second one which does not instantiate the input stack and which is in fact a more general computation than the original one. A good representation for this trace is then given by $I = \pi_2\, \xi_1$ (*context* $= \pi_1\, \text{tail}(I)$ and *result* $= \pi_1\, I$).

Thus, we use items defined by $\pi_2\, \xi$ to represent basic computations. They are more compact than stacks and are reusable in various contexts. They are subject to subsumption because they inherit the GSO $\preceq$. The only problem concerns the

[9] We implicitly suppose that all computations will act above the initial stack and never pop the bottom element (This can always be achieved by simple transformations of the automaton).

existence of a tractable order–compatible combination mechanism to retrieve all computations.

The following part presents a DP interpretation[10] of the SPDA based on these remarks.

The Dynamic Programming Interpretation S^2. The DP interpretation S^2 we present here works on a domain of items called ITEM$_2$ isomorphic to $\pi_2(\mathcal{S})$ [11]. The items will be denoted by upper case letters (e.g. I,J). Counterparts in ITEM$_2$ for $\preceq$, tail, π_n are also noted $\preceq$, tail, π_n.

The isomorphism α_2 from $\pi_2(\mathcal{S})$ in ITEM$_2$ extends to a morphism from $\mathcal{S}$ to ITEM$_2$ also called α_2 by $\alpha_2\xi = \alpha_2(\pi_2\,\xi)$.

Now, we would like to be able to retrieve the stack which matches a tuple of overlapping items. However, a perfect match is not always possible and we use the following notion :

Definition 6. A stack ξ is *covered* by an item tuple $(I_1,\ldots,I_n)$ iff $\pi_{n+1}\xi = \xi$ and $\forall k \in [1,n]$, $I_n \preceq \alpha_2(\text{tail}^{\,k-1}\xi)$. The set of stacks covered by $(I_1,\ldots,I_n)$ is noted $C_{I_1,\ldots,I_n}$ and when this set is not empty, the most general stack covered by $(I_1,\ldots,I_n)$ is defined by $\xi_{I_1,\ldots,I_n} = \text{glb}\, C_{I_1,\ldots,I_n}$.

Using this notion of stack reconstruction, we define the following interpretation :

Definition 7. The **S^2–interpretation** of an SPDA $A = (\mathcal{S}, \xi_{init}, \xi_{end}, \Theta)$ is a 4-tuple $(\text{ITEM}_2, I_{init}, I_{end}, \Theta)$ where $I_{init} = \alpha_2\xi_{init}$ (resp. $I_{end} = \alpha_2\xi_{end}$) denotes the *initial* (resp. *final*) item.

A transition τ of Θ now applies to an item tuple $(I_1,\ldots,I_{p_\tau})$ iff $\xi_{I_1,\ldots,I_{p_\tau}}$ exists and belongs to Dom(τ). Then, we pose $\tau(I_1,\ldots,I_{p_\tau}) = \alpha_2(\tau\xi_{I_1,\ldots,I_{p_\tau}})$.

The well-foundness of this definition comes from the properties of glb and Axioms **[CONTEXT]** and **[GEN]**. It must be noted that this DP interpretation has an interest only when $\xi_{I_1,\ldots,I_{p_\tau}}$ is easily computable.

It is easy to show that a counterpart of **[GEN]** holds for items when replacing the input stacks by item tuples and using the tuple extension order $(I_1,\ldots,I_n) \preceq (I_1^\circ,\ldots,I_n^\circ) \iff \forall k \in [1,n],\ I_1 \preceq I_k^\circ$. Practically, it means that a computed item which is subsumed by another computed item can be discarded as well as its descendants.

Given a set of items $\mathcal{I}$ and an item I, $\mathcal{I} \,\overline{\vdash_{\tau}}\, I$ states that there exist $I_1,\ldots,I_{p_\tau}$ in $\mathcal{I}$ such that $\tau(I_1,\ldots,I_{p_\tau}) = I$. The notation $\mathcal{I} \,\overline{\vdash_{d}}\, I$ where $d = \tau_1.d'$ inductively means $\mathcal{I} \,\overline{\vdash_{\tau_1}}\, K \wedge \mathcal{I} \cup \{K\} \,\overline{\vdash_{d'}}\, I$. The notation $\overline{\vdash_{d}}\, I$ abbreviates $\{I_{init}\} \,\overline{\vdash_{d}}\, I$.

To compare sets of stacks (or items), we introduce the set order $\sqsubseteq$ defined by "$\forall \mathcal{E}, \mathcal{E}' \subset \mathcal{S},\ \mathcal{E} \sqsubseteq \mathcal{E}' \iff \forall \xi \in \mathcal{E}, \exists \xi' \in \mathcal{E}',\ \xi' \preceq \xi$" and the equivalence $\equiv$ derived from $\sqsubseteq$.

We can now show the equivalence of stack and items computations, both on $\mathcal{S}$ and ITEM$_2$:

---

[10] There exist several DP interpretations of the SPDA. In particular, we often uses DP interpretations on $\pi_1(\mathcal{S})$ which are only valid for a sub–class of SPDA.

[11] We use an isomorphic domain to clearly differentiate the stacks from the items.

Theorem 8. *For all SPDA A, we have,*

[on stacks] $\{\, \xi \mid \vdash^{\star} \xi \,\} \equiv \{\, \xi_{I_1,\ldots,I_n} \mid n \in N \wedge \overline{\vdash}^{\star} (I_1, \ldots, I_n) \}$

[on items] $\alpha_2\{\, \xi \mid \vdash^{\star} \xi \,\} \equiv \{\, I \mid \overline{\vdash}^{\star} I \,\}$

Proof. The proofs uses the completeness and correction lemmas 1 and 2.

$$\forall \xi \in \mathcal{S}, \vdash^{\star} \xi \Rightarrow (\exists I \in \text{ITEM}_2, \overline{\vdash}^{\star} I \wedge I \preceq \alpha_2 \xi) \quad (1)$$

$$\forall I \in \text{ITEM}_2, \overline{\vdash}^{\star} I \Rightarrow (\exists \xi \in \mathcal{S}, \vdash^{\star} \xi \wedge \alpha_2 \xi \preceq I) \quad (2)$$

Lemmas proofs are rather long and technical but can be found in [BVdlC]. They are done by induction on the derivation lengths.∎

3 Logical Push–Down Automata

We present in this section an example of Subsumption–oriented Push-Down Automata which works on Herbrand domains. They are used to evaluate Horn Clause Programs by encoding various resolution mechanisms (OLD, Bottom–Up, and Earley Deduction). They were first introduced in [Lan88] with a slightly different presentation than the one used in this paper for simplicity reasons. The reader can find in Appendix A an example of an evaluation of a tiny logic program by an automaton.

We assume the reader is familiar with the notions of free algebra $T(\Sigma, V)$, subsumption pre–order $\preceq$, substitution and unification. The stack domain $S_{\Sigma,V}$ denotes the set of the stacks formed over $T(\Sigma, V)$. The substitutions and $\preceq$ extend to $S_{\Sigma,V}$:

Definition 9. $\forall \sigma \in Subst, \forall \xi = [A_1 \ldots A_n] \in S_{\Sigma,V},\ \xi\sigma = [A_1\sigma \ldots A_n\sigma]$

Definition 10. $\forall \xi, \xi^{\circ} \in S_{\Sigma,V},\ \xi \preceq \xi^{\circ} \iff \exists \sigma \in Subst, \xi^{\circ} = \xi\sigma$

Proposition 3.1 *$\preceq$ is a generalization stack pre–order over $S_{\Sigma,V}$.*

The equivalence relation defined by "$\xi \preceq \xi' \wedge \xi' \preceq \xi$" is noted $\xi \equiv \xi'$. We can also speak of the most general unifier (mgu) of two stacks.[12].

Definition 11. A Logical Push–Down Automaton (LPDA) is defined as a 5-tuple $(\Sigma, V, \$_{init}, \$_{end}, \Theta)$ where

1. Σ is a graded alphabet and V a denumerable set of variables.
2. $\$_{init}$ is a nullary initial predicate. The initial stack is $\xi_{init} = [\$_{init}()]$.
3. $\$_{end}$ is the final predicate. The final stacks are instances of $\xi_{end} = [\$_{end}(\bar{X})\, \$_{init}()]$.
4. Θ is a finite set of HOR transitions $B \mapsto C$, PUSH transitions $B \mapsto CB$ and POP transitions $BD \mapsto C$ where $B, C, D \in T(\Sigma, V)$.

Application of a transition τ is defined, up to a fresh renaming σ_r [13], as follows:

- The transition $B \mapsto C$ applies to any stack $[\,A \,|\, \xi]$ such that $B\sigma_r$ and A are unifiable by the mgu σ. The result is $[\,C\sigma_r \,|\, \xi]\sigma$.

[12] We should work in $S_{\Sigma,V\,/\equiv}$ but we prefer stay in $S_{\Sigma,V}$ for sake of conciseness.

[13] to avoid clashes between transition and stack variables.

- The transition $B \mapsto CB$ applies to any stack $[A \,|\, \xi]$ such that $B\sigma_r$ and A are unifiable by the mgu σ. The result is $[C\sigma_r\, A \,|\, \xi]\sigma$.
- A transition $BD \mapsto C$ applies to any stack $[A\, A' \,|\, \xi]$ such that the two pairs $(B\sigma_r, D\sigma_r)$ and (A, A') are unifiable by the mgu σ. The result is $[C\sigma_r \,|\, \xi]\sigma$.

The application of a transition τ to a stack τ depends on the chosen renaming substitution σ_r but all resulting stacks $\tau_r\xi$ are in fact equivalent and are noted $\tau\xi$ without reference to the renaming.

Unfortunately, LPDA are not SPDA over the stack domain $S_{\Sigma,V}$ because **[ID]** is not verified on $S_{\Sigma,V}$ as shown by the following example.

Example 1. The transition $\tau = b(a) \mapsto c(a)$ applies to the stack $[b(X)\, r()\, p(X)]$ and returns the stack $[c(a)\, r()\, p(a)]$. The instantiation stops on atom $r()$ but restarts below on the atom $p(X)$.

However, **[ID]** is in fact satisfied on all computable stacks because of the transition renaming. We restrict our stack domain to a subdomain $RS_{\Sigma,V}$ of $S_{\Sigma,V}$ which embeds computable stacks and ensures **[ID]**.

Definition 12. $RS_{\Sigma,V}$ is the biggest subdomain of $S_{\Sigma,V}$ such that (3) holds

$$\forall \xi \in RS_{\Sigma,V}, \forall n \in N,\ \mathrm{Var}(\pi_n\, \xi) \cap \mathrm{Var}(\mathrm{tail}^{\,n+1} \xi) \subset \mathrm{Var}(\pi_1\, (\mathrm{tail}^{\,n} \xi)) \tag{3}$$

The reader can easily verify that $RS_{\Sigma,V}$ is a stack domain and that $\preceq$ is still a GSO on $RS_{\Sigma,V}$. Equation (3) intuitively states that whenever a variable X appears at two levels l_1 and l_2 of a stack ξ of $RS_{\Sigma,V}$, then X also appears at all intermediary levels between l_1 and l_2.

Example 2. The stack $[b(X)\, r()\, p(X)]$ is not in $RS_{\Sigma,V}$ (violation of (3) for $n = 1$) while stack $[b(Y)\, r()\, p(X)]$ is in $RS_{\Sigma,V}$.

Proposition 3.2 $\forall \xi \in RS_{\Sigma,V}, \forall \tau,\ \xi \in \mathit{Dom}(\tau) \ \Rightarrow\ \tau\xi \in RS_{\Sigma,V}$

Proof. The complete proof can be found in [BVdlC]. ∎

Proposition 3.3 *LPDA are SPDA on the stack domain* $RS_{\Sigma,V}$.

Proof. The complete proof can be found in [BVdlC]. ∎

3.1 S^2–Interpretation

We take for ITEM$_2$ the set of all pairs of atoms $<A|A'>$. We introduce a special symbol $\perp$ to represent the bottom of a stack. The morphism α_2 from $RS_{\Sigma,V}$ to ITEM$_2$ is defined by $\alpha_2[] = <\perp|\perp>$, $\alpha_2[A] = <A|\perp>$ and $\alpha_2[A\, A' \,|\, \xi] = <A|A'>$. Items will always be considered up to a renaming.

A transition $HOR : B \mapsto C$ (resp. $PUSH : B \mapsto CB$) applies to an item $<A|A'>$ iff $\sigma = \mathrm{mgu}(A, B)$ exists. The resulting item is $<C\sigma|A'\sigma>$ (resp. $<C\sigma|A\sigma>$).

A transition $POP : BD \mapsto C$ applies to an item pair $(<A|A'>, <E|E'>)$ iff $\sigma = \mathrm{mgu}(AA', BD)$ and $\mu = \mathrm{mgu}(A'\sigma, E)$ exist. The resulting item is $<C\sigma\mu|E'\mu>$.

Proposition 3.4 *The proposed S^2-interpretation is valid.*

Proof. The proposed application mechanism is in fact the same as the one presented in section 2.4 when noting that (with the above notation) for a PUSH or HOR transition τ we have $[A\,A']\sigma = [B\,A']\sigma = \text{Pivot}(\tau, \xi_{<A|A'>})$ and for a POP transition τ $[A\,E\,E']\sigma\mu = [A\,A'\,E']\sigma\mu = [B\,D\,E']\sigma\mu = \text{Pivot}(\tau, \xi_{<A|A'>,<E|E'>})$ where $\text{Pivot}(\tau, \xi) = \text{glb}\{\ \xi^\circ \mid \xi^\circ$ satisfies **[ACTION]** for $\theta = \theta^\circ = \tau\xi$ and $n = 0\ \}$. ∎

3.2 Extensions

A DP implementation of the LPDA, called DyALog, exists[VdlC90]. It is a correct and complete evaluator of Logic Programs and performs quite reasonably. We plan to extend the LPDA and DyALog to treat Constraint Logic Programs and abstract interpretation of Logic Programs[VdlC91]. Indeed, all these cases (among others) work on domains with similar properties (essentially the "mgu" and substitution notions).

4 A Parser for Tree Adjoining Grammars

The goal of this section is to provide an example of the use of SPDA on a non-Herbrand domain. We briefly describe Tree Adjoining Grammars and the parser. We don't claim this parser to have practical interest. We only want to give an intuitive idea. For more details see [BVdlC].

4.1 Tree Adjoining Grammars

Tree Adjoining Grammars (TAG) are a class of grammars proposed by A.K.Joshi in [JLT75]. It formalizes a particular point of structural description of natural language.

A *Tree Adjoining Grammar (TAG)* is a 5-tuple (V_N, V_T, S, I, A) where V_N and V_T are sets of respectively *non-terminal* and *terminal* symbols, I and A are sets of respectively *initial* and *auxiliary* elementary trees. Except as specified below, the leaf (resp. non-leaf) nodes of elementary trees are labelled with terminal symbols or the empty string (resp. with non-terminal symbols). The root of an initial tree is labelled with the distinguished non-terminal S. Each auxiliary tree has one distinguished leaf node called its *foot* which is labelled with the same non-terminal as the root of the tree. The path from root to foot is called the *spine* of the auxiliary tree.

Given a tree $\mathcal{T}$ containing a non-leaf node X labelled with a non-terminal N, the *adjunction* of an auxiliary tree $\mathcal{A}$ with its root also labelled by N is the following operation: *excise* the subtree $\mathcal{T}'$ of $\mathcal{T}$ occurring in X, replace it with a copy of the auxiliary tree $\mathcal{A}$, and graft the excised subtree $\mathcal{T}'$ to the foot of this copy of $\mathcal{A}$ (figure 4). We shall call (the frontier of) the excised subtree $\mathcal{T}'$ the *footer* of the adjoined auxiliary tree $\mathcal{A}$.

A tree is generated by the TAG iff it can be obtained by a succession of adjunctions of auxiliary trees to some initial tree. The language generated by the TAG is the set of terminal strings that are the frontiers of trees that the TAG can generate.

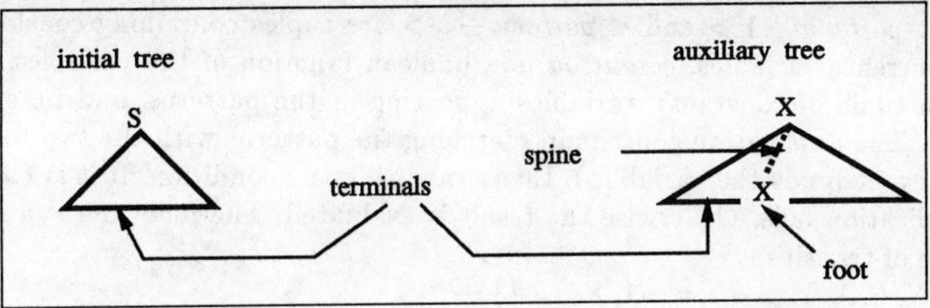

Fig. 3. TAG components

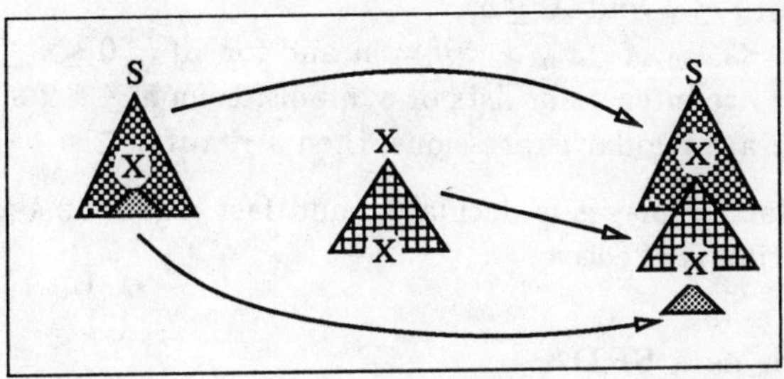

Fig. 4. Adjunction

4.2 The Parser

The parser is an Earley-like parser, that is bottom-up with a top-down predictive component. When doing the top-down filtering, one has to consider that adjunction may happen everywhere. When adjoining, one must pass along the spine the information on the node to be recognized at the foot (that is the node where the auxiliary tree was adjoined). Adjunction may arise on a spine-node. In that case one must remember what node to find at the foot of this footer. So the information to be passed is a sequence of nodes. When the foot is the leftmost leaf of an auxiliary tree, there might be an infinite number of adjunctions that are to be predicted without consuming any terminal. In order to ensure termination, this infinity must be represented finitely. Using a regular expression with the transitive closure operator $*$ is convenient here. The parser carries the contextual information coded by regular expressions along the spines.

The compilation method to obtain a SPDA out of a TAG is described in [BVdlC]. The stack domain is composed of tuples having different arities, containing symbols, symbol lists, node identifiers, integers, and regular expressions, written as terms. There are no logical variables in this domain. We write tuples as $< s_0, \ldots, s_n >$. The transitions may all be described in a functional way, using pattern matching. They don't change the stack bottom at all, even by an instanciation. The standard form for a pop is:

$$< pattern - 1 >< pattern - 2 > \{\} \mapsto \text{ IF } condition \text{ THEN } < result >$$

where $< pattern - 1 >$ and $< pattern - 2 >$ are tuples containing constants and one-occurrence variables, *condition* is a boolean function of the variables, and result is a tuple of constants, variables appearing in the patterns, and functions on integers. The application consists in matching the patterns with the two top tuples of a stack (it binds the variables), then evaluating the condition. If it is false, then the application fails. Otherwise the result is evaluated. The following is a concrete example of transition:

$< pff, N, R, X, Y >< i, n, R1, X1 > \{\} \mapsto$
IF $X = X1$ and $[N|R] \subset R1$ THEN $< p(n), R, X, Y >$

The subsumption relation $\preceq$ is defined by:

- $[] \preceq []$.
- $[t|X] \preceq [u|Y]$ if $t \preceq u$ and $X \preceq Y$.
- $< s_0, \ldots, s_n > \preceq < z_0, \ldots, z_m >$ if $n = m$ and for all i, $0 \leq i \leq n$, $s_i \preceq z_i$.
- When s and z are integers or lists or symbols, then $s \preceq z$ if $s = z$.
- When s and z are regular expressions, then $s \preceq z$ if $z \subset s$.

Inclusion of regular languages is decidable, and fast algorithms are known, so this subsumption relation is effective.

4.3 The Parser as a SPDA

In order to use dynamic programming with subsumption to execute our automata, we have to prove the validity of the axioms from section 2. We give the intuition and the main principles of the proof rather than a complete one. In this particular case of TAG parsers, they are quite simple.

First of all, there are the axioms on the stack domain. They are trivially verified because there is no link between the stacked symbols. There are no variables relating objects. They are completely independant. Any projection applied on stacks preserves the subsumption relation. This makes **[CONTEXT]**, **[ACTION]**, and **[ID]** trivial. The transitions preserve the subsumption relation since their right hand side is built using the symbols and regular expressions of left hand side and constants. If R_1, R_2, R_3 are regular languages such that $R_1 \preceq R_2$, then $R_1 R_3 \preceq R_2 R_3$. This property implies the property **[GEN]** for the automaton. Dynamic programming with subsumption is applicable to the TAG parser.

5 Conclusion

In this paper, we have described a general framework for the use of dynamic programming with subsumption for various stack-based computations in a wide set of domains. Dynamic programming is used to share computations and thus to increase the termination and/or the operational completeness. Two applications are provided for Logic Programming and Parsing with Tree Adjoining Grammars.

These theoretical results are validated by existing implementations for Logic Programming (DyALog) and Contextual Parsing (APOC). Using our results and the experience of our implementations, various extensions (Constraint Logic Programming, Abstract Interpretation, Higher–Order Logic Programming, "exotic" grammars) are planned.

6 Acknowledgments

We are grateful to P. Codognet for his helpful comments. A special thanks to Paul Taylor for his "Commutative Diagrams in TEX" package.

References

[BVdlC] François Barthélemy and Eric Villemonte de la Clergerie. Subsumption–oriented push–down automata and dynamic programming with subsumption. Technical report, INRIA. to appear.

[JLT75] A. K. Joshi, L. Levy, and M. Takahashi. Tree adjunct grammars. *Journal of the Computer and System Science*, 10(1):136–163, Feb 1975.

[Kan90] Tadashi Kanamori. Abstract interpretation based on alexander templates. TR-549, ICOT, March 1990.

[KK90] Tadashi Kanamori and Tadashi Kawamura. Abstract interpretation based on OLDT resolution. Research report, ICOT, Tokyo, July 1990.

[Lan74] Bernard Lang. Deterministic techniques for efficient non-deterministic parsers. In *Proc. of the 2nd Colloquium on automata, languages and Programming*, pages 255–269, Saarbrücken (Germany), 1974. Springer-Verlag (LNCS 14).

[Lan88] Bernard Lang. Complete evaluation of Horn clauses: an automata theoretic approach. Technical Report 913, INRIA, Rocquencourt, France, nov 1988. to appear in Int. Journal of Foundations of Computer Science.

[Por86] Harry H. III Porter. Earley deduction. Technical Report CS/E-86-002, Oregon Graduate Center, Beaverton, Oregon, March 10 1986.

[Sek89] H. Seki. On the power of alexander templates. In *Proc. of the 8th ACM symps. on principles of Databases Systems*, 1989.

[TS86] H. Tamaki and T. Sato. OLD resolution with tabulation. In E Shapiro editor, editor, *Proc. of Third Int. Conf. on Logic Programming*, pages 84–98, London, 1986. Springer–Verlag.

[VdlC91] Eric Villemonte de la Clergerie. A tool for abstract interpretation : Dynamic programming. In *Actes JTASPEFL'91*, pages 151–156, Bordeaux (FRANCE), Octobre 1991.

[VdlC90] Eric Villemonte de la Clergerie. DyALog: une implantation des clauses de horn en programmation dynamique. In *Proc. of the 9th Séminaire de Programmation en Logique*, pages 207–228. CNET, May 90.

[Vie87] Laurent Vieille. Database-complete proof procedures based on SLD resolution. In *Proc. of the 4 int. Conf. on Logic Programming*, May 1987.

A An example of a Logical Push–Down Automaton

We describe in this section the evaluation of a tiny logic program by the S^2-interpretation of a LPDA A which encodes an OLD-like resolution strategy. In the automaton, the new atoms `c_q(X)` (resp. `r_q(X)`) denote calls (resp. returns from calls) to `q(X)`.

```
 Program                                         LPDA
q(X) :- q(f(X)).       Initial Pred. : start()     Final Pred. : r_q(U)
q(f(f(a))).            Transitions :   [a] start() -> c_q(U) start()
                                       [b] c_q(X) -> c_q(f(X)) c_q(X)
```

```
[c] c_q(f(f(a))) -> r_q(f(f(a)))
[d] r_q(_) c_q(X) -> r_q(X)
```

For the goal `?-q(U).`, a standard PROLOG evaluator loops and does not return any answers. However, the answers `U=a`,`U=f(a)` and `U=f(f(a))` are expected.

Figure 5 shows a stack computation line for A. There also exists an infinite computation line obtained by iteratively applying Transition [b] to the initial stack. Now, the DP interpretation S^2 (Fig. 6) avoids the loop because of a subsumption test on the computed items. DyALog uses a fair selection order to schedule the transition applications (to ensure that no application is eternally ignored).

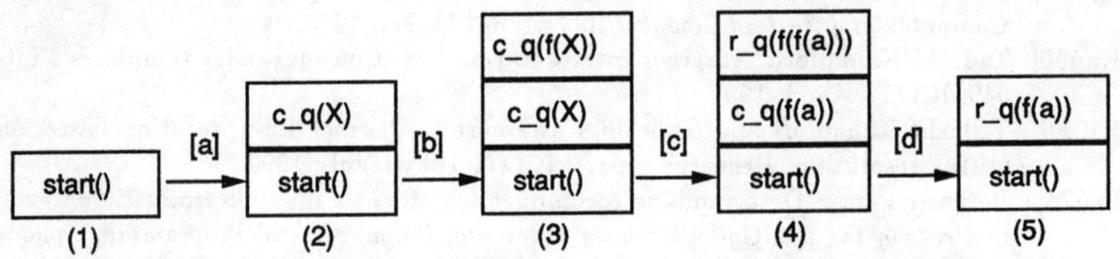

Fig. 5. A LPDA computation line for SPDA A. An instantiation $X = f(a)$ arises when applying Transition [c] to stack (3).

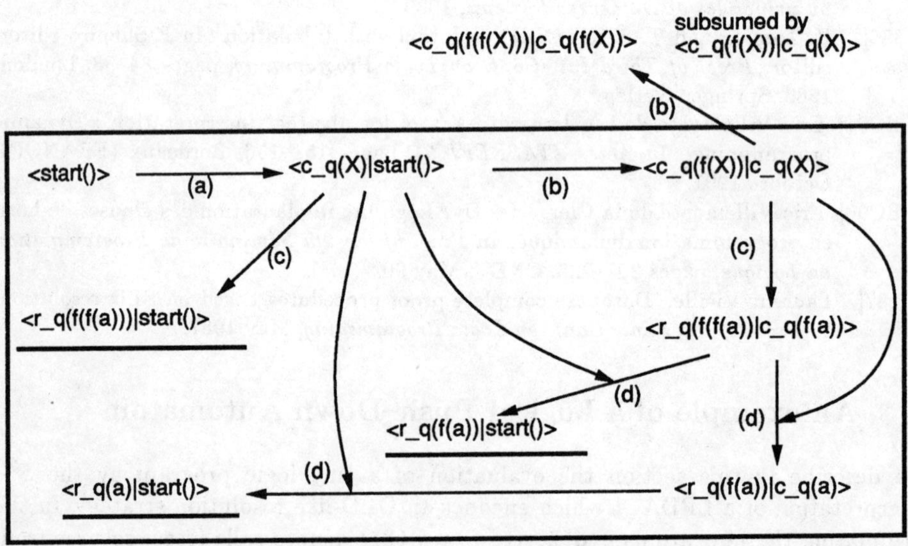

Fig. 6. a S^2 computation : The items inside the box are the most general computed items, the one outside the box is rejected by the subsumption test. The final items are underlined.

This article was processed using the LaTeX macro package with LLNCS style

Unlimp
Uniqueness as a Leitmotiv for Implementation

Stefan Kahrs*

University of Edinburgh
Laboratory for Foundations of Computer Science
King's Buildings, EH9 3JZ
email: smk@dcs.ed.ac.uk

Abstract. When evaluation in functional programming languages is explained using λ-calculus and/or term rewriting systems, expressions and function definitions are often defined as terms, that is as *trees*. Similarly, the collection of all terms is defined as a *forest*, that is a directed, acyclic graph where every vertex has at most one incoming edge. Concrete implementations usually drop the last restriction (and sometimes acyclicity as well), i.e. many terms can share a common subterm, meaning that different paths of subterm edges reach the same vertex in the graph.
Any vertex in such a graph represents a term. A term is represented uniquely in such a graph if there are no two different vertices representing it. Such a representation can be established by using *hash-consing* for the creation of heap objects. We investigate the consequences of adopting uniqueness in this sense as a leitmotiv for implementation (called Unlimp), i.e. not *allowing* any two different vertices in a graph to represent the same term.

1 Introduction

The definition of most programming languages is or can be based on some notion of term, e.g. the abstract syntax of the language. It is convenient to express properties of such terms as properties of tree-like objects, similarly as it is convenient to represent (in an implementation) a collection of terms as a directed acyclic graph, allowing the violation of the property that each vertex has an *indegree* of at most 1, i.e. that each vertex has at most one incoming edge.

If the language satisfies *referential transparency* for those terms, i.e. if the meaning of (closed) terms is context-independent and if this meaning is expressible as a term, one can moreover exploit the internal representation and destructively replace subgraphs by their results, even if their indegree is greater than 1.

Such graph reduction is the standard technique for implementing lazy languages, see [15, 4], because under lazy evaluation unevaluated subterms naturally occur. For implementing (general) term rewriting systems, graph reduction may lose confluence and weak normalisation, see [8], but rewriting systems in programming languages normally satisfy further properties that make graph reduction a correct implementation.

* The research reported here was partially supported by SERC grant GR/E 78463.

While acyclic graphs seem to be a natural choice for the internal representation of terms (cyclic graphs are not easily handled by a reference-counting garbage collector), one might also look at the extreme cases of this representation. There are two of particular interest: (i) the indegree of every vertex is at most 1 (trees and forests); (ii) the function that maps vertices to the terms they represent is injective, i.e. each represented term is represented uniquely.

The disadvantage of proper trees (i) is obviously the waste of space, but it also has advantages: memory management becomes easy, and sharing analysis [22] comes for free. For example, concatenation of two lists *xs* and *ys* in a graph representation usually works by copying *xs* and drawing an edge from the last vertex in the copy to *ys*, i.e. *ys* may become a shared object. In representation (i) however, it is known that *xs* and *ys* are uniquely used for the concatenation, hence it is not only possible to avoid copying *ys*, but also to avoid copying *xs*, using LISP's NCONC for list concatenation.

At first glance, the advantage of unique representation (ii) seems to be compactness, a further gain of space. But actually, it is more the uniqueness of representation itself, i.e. the property that a term can be uniquely identified by the root vertex of its representation, that turns out to be the major plus. The disadvantage is the effort needed to preserve this uniqueness under rewriting.

In this paper, we study this representation, how to get it and how to exploit it under the slogan "Uniqueness as a Leitmotiv for Implementation", short: Unlimp.

The examples are written in Haskell and in SML. Readers not familiar with these languages may consult [10] and [14].

2 Preliminaries

Instead of considering ordinary directed graphs, we deal with directed hypergraphs, i.e. we have directed hyperedges instead of ordinary edges. A hyperedge has in general more than one target (and also more than one source), we adopt a formal definition from [9]:

Definition 1. A *hypergraph* $G = (V_G, E_G, s_G, t_G, l_G, m_G)$ over Σ consists of a finite set V_G of *vertices*, a finite set E_G of *hyperedges*, two mappings $s_G : E_G \to V_G^*$ and $t_G : E_G \to V_G^*$, assigning a string of *source vertices* and a string of *target vertices* to each hyperedge, and two mappings $l_G : V_G \to \mathrm{S}$ and $m_G : E_G \to \mathrm{OP}$, labelling vertices with sorts, and hyperedges with operation symbols.

The definition was originally intended for first-order signatures, $\Sigma = (\mathrm{S}, \mathrm{OP})$, but it can also be used in the higher-order case, simply by allowing non-elementary sorts in S, adding apply-symbols to OP, etc.

We also use some other standard graph-theoretic notions: $\mathrm{indegree}_G(v)$ denotes the sum (over all $e \in E_G$) of the number of occurrences of v in $t_G(e)$, analogously $\mathrm{outdegree}_G(v)$ for the $s_G(e)$. The subterm relation $\to_G$ (on vertices) is defined as follows:

$$v \to_G v' \quad \Leftrightarrow \quad \exists e \in E_G \; \exists a, a', b, b' \in V_G^* : s_G(e) = a \cdot v \cdot b \wedge t_G(e) = a' \cdot v' \cdot b'$$

A hypergraph is *acyclic* if the transitive closure of $\rightarrow_G$ is irreflexive. Notice that irreflexivity of $\rightarrow_G$ also implies that it is strongly normalising, as we have assumed a *finite* set of vertices.

Definition 2. A hypergraph G is a *jungle*, iff (i) it is acyclic, (ii) $\text{outdegree}_G(v) = 1$ for all $v \in V_G$ and (iii) for all $e \in E_G$, $m_G(e) = f : s_1 \cdots s_n \rightarrow s$ implies $l^*_G(s_G(e)) = s$ and $l^*_G(t_G(e)) = s_1 \cdots s_n$.

l^*_G is the homomorphic extension of l_G to strings of vertices.

Acyclicity is useful for maintaining uniqueness of representation (see below), the restriction for the outdegree is motivated by the analogy between addresses and vertices, and the third condition is well-typedness.

The reason for this choice for the representation of terms is the very close correspondence between a jungle, vertices and hyperedges on the one hand, and a heap, addresses (pointers) and storage cells on the other, i.e. hypergraphs model implementations more faithfully than ordinary directed graphs. Therefore we will also freely intermix these notions, depending on whether it is in a particular case more intuitive or useful to talk about, say, a pointer rather than a vertex.

Given a jungle G, we define a function $\mathsf{term}_G : V_G \rightarrow \mathsf{Ter}(\Sigma)$ that assigns any vertex (address) the term it represents:

$$\mathsf{term}_G(v) \;=\; m_G(e) \cdot \mathsf{term}^*_G(t_G(e)) \;\; \textit{where}\; s_G(e) = v \;.$$

The $*$ again denotes homomorphic extension to strings. Note that e is unique because of the outdegree restriction.

A jungle is a called *fully collapsed*, if term_G is injective. Because of this one-to-one correspondence we choose fully collapsed jungles to represent terms in Unlimp.

For any jungle there exists a (unique) fully collapsed jungle that represents the same set of terms. For this and some other results about representing terms by jungles and term rewriting by graph grammars, see [6, 9].

3 Hash Consing

Suppose we already have a fully collapsed jungle; then we have the problem of preserving this property each time we change the jungle, that is when we:

- create new objects
- evaluate an object
- delete an object

An object is anything represented by a vertex in a jungle. For the implementation of a functional programming language, objects could be values (elementary and composed values, functions), expressions yet to be evaluated, even non-closed expressions and type expressions (in an interpreter or compiler), etc.

How do we *create* a composed value $\mathsf{op}(x_1, ..., x_n)$ in a fully collapsed jungle (for some n-ary operation op)? Since we need a vertex that represents this value, there are two cases: either there is already a vertex v in V_G with $\mathsf{term}_G(v) = \mathsf{op}(x_1, ..., x_n)$, then we have to "find" it; or, if there is not, then we have to create a new cell (add a vertex and a hyperedge) and make sure that future searches can find it.

Typically, each x_i is already represented in the jungle, i.e. there is a vertex v_i in V_G with $\mathsf{term}_G(v_i) = x_i$. Because of Unlimp v_i is uniquely determined, as two vertices represent the same term iff they are identical. So any other hyperedge (in the jungle) pointing at a vertex that represents the same term as x_i, actually points at v_i.

To search for a cell $\mathsf{op}(x_1, ..., x_n)$ we could scan the entire heap, but that would be horribly inefficient. Since such a cell is uniquely determined by the vertices v_i and the operation op, these could give us a hint *where* we have to search. In other words, we can compute a search key from them, a value which is (almost) unique for the cell to be constructed. Because of the "almost" we still have to search, but our search space is very restricted.

Such a method is known as "hash consing", see [21, 17], because CONS is the only cell-constructing operation in LISP. It does not only apply for creating composite *values*, but for any kind of composite heap object, for example terms representing the application of a function to some other terms, also type expressions, etc. For the implementation of op, it is only a minor difference whether the cell to be created is supposed to be a value or some other heap object. We can even apply this method for creating λ-abstractions: If we lambda-lift [15, 4] all nested abstractions (such that any abstraction becomes a closed term) and then rename its variables[2] to x_0, x_1, etc., then α-congruence becomes trivial (pointer comparison).

In implementations of strict languages, one usually tries to avoid to create heap objects whenever possible, i.e. a term like `length [6,3,4]` would never exist as a vertex in the jungle. For reasons which become apparent later, we do not follow this line.

The author experimented with several ways to organize the heap. The method finally chosen (surely not the best one) is a combination of digital search trees and double hashing (see [5, 18] or some other standard book on data structures and algorithms): the search tree has hash tables as its leaves; searching an entry is done by using the leading bits of the key to branch in the tree, and finally the remaining bits are used for double hashing at a leaf.

4 Reduction

The second way to change the hypergraph is to *evaluate* a term.

Evaluation usually refers to the evaluation in the language itself, but we may apply it to a more general setting: the evaluation result of a type expression is the type expression one gets after substituting all type synonyms (e.g. in Haskell), the evaluation result of function definition is the code the compilation produces for it.

In a strict language implementation, an evaluation simply creates some new objects and makes some other objects (probably) obsolete. For Unlimp this view is harmless, because it reduces the problem of keeping the uniqueness to the previous one, to the creation of new objects.

[2] SML and Haskell have a generalised λ-abstraction (patterns instead of variables) that allows to abstract more than one variable in a single abstraction.

In an ordinary implementation of a lazy language the following happens: if a term t is evaluated to u, then the subhypergraph reachable from the vertex t is deleted and replaced by the subhypergraph reachable from u. This method is usually called ***graph reduction*** [4].

In Unlimp, this would not work well. Firstly, we might lose the injectivity of term_G, because if t is a subterm of some $C[t]$ then the vertex representing $C[t]$ now represents $C[u]$, but this term might already be represented by another vertex. For the implementation the situation is worse, because even if the jungle remains fully collapsed, the term $C[u]$ would be located at the wrong place in the search tree in our sketched implementation method. One could repair this mess by relocating all those terms in the search tree that have t as a direct[3] subterm, but then all (direct) superterms of t have to be found. Moreover, this method can introduce cycles[4], i.e. it may destroy our jungle structure. Allowing cycles would lead to (some restrictions for garbage collection and) the Unlimp problem for cycles, i.e. having a unique representation for any infinite term that can be expressed by a cyclic graph.

For these reasons, we do not replace t by u. On the other hand, we do not want to evaluate t a second time, staying as lazy as possible. Therefore, we draw an additional edge from t to u, a result edge. The hypergraph containing all the edges (hyperedges and result edges) may now be cyclic, but the result edges form a kind of second layer for the graph and both layers are in themselves acyclic.

A very simple example:

```
cycle xs = xs ++ cycle xs
```

A one-step evaluation for `cycle xs` (for an arbitrary `xs`) leads to the hypergraph in figure 1.

The three small circles are the vertices, the marked ellipses together with all incoming and outgoing arrows the hyperedges. The dotted arrow from the left to the right circle is a result edge. Looking just at the ordinary hyperedges, the picture says: "the result of `cycle xs` is `xs++cycle xs`", but thinking of the result edge as an indirection pointer, we have the full result `xs++xs++xs++`.... These result edges are not only a natural way to perform lazy evaluation; they are also useful for certain debugging tasks, like tracing a function, because the unevaluated expression and the evaluation result are available at the same time.

To allow these result edges in our hypergraph model, we add another component, a set of result edges to it:

Definition 3. A *result jungle* $J = (G, R_J, s_J, t_J)$ consists of a jungle G, a set of result edges R_J and two mappings $s_J, t_J : R_J \to V_G$, such that s_J is injective and $\forall e \in R_J : \; l_G(s_J(e)) = l_G(t_J(e))$.

Furthermore we call a result jungle *loopless* if the subterm relation $\to_H$ of any hypergraph $H = (V_G, R_J, s_J, t_J, \_, \_)$ is strongly normalising.

Result edges of the above form are simply partial, sort-preserving functions on vertices, but the above encoding within the hypergraph world preserves the close

[3] Example: t is a direct subterm of $f(t)$, but not of $f(f(t))$.

[4] According to [8], theorem 5.5, jungle reduction cannot introduce cycles, due to the realisation of rewrite steps chosen there. We do not consider this here, because it violates the Unlimp principle in a different way.

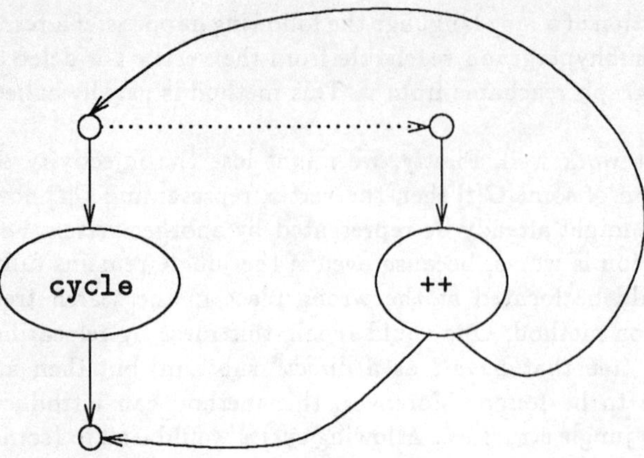

Fig. 1. Term with Result Edge

correspondence to implementations. For example, the storage cell corresponding to a result edge could be located at the address corresponding to its source vertex, either before or after the storage cell corresponding to the "ordinary" hyperedge going from there.

For loopless result jungles, we have another mapping term_J from vertices to terms, but the terms might be of infinite size, see [12]:

$$\mathsf{term}_J : V_G \rightarrow \mathsf{Ter}^\infty(\Sigma)$$
$$\mathsf{term}_J(s_J(r)) = \mathsf{term}_J(t_J(r))$$
$$\mathsf{term}_J(s_G(e)) = m_G(e) \cdot \mathsf{term}_J^*(t_G(e)), \text{ if } \neg\exists r \in R_J :\ s_J(r) = s_G(e)$$

For any vertex v, $\mathsf{term}_G(v)$ is the (finite) term before evaluation and $\mathsf{term}_J(v)$ the (possibly infinite) term after it. The result jungle J has to be loopless to make the above definition of term_J well-defined. In figure 1, we have $\mathsf{term}_G(v) =$ `cycle xs` where v is top left vertex and `xs` the term represented by the bottom vertex, and $\mathsf{term}_J(v) =$ `xs'++xs'++...` where `xs'` is the term_J-value of the bottom vertex.

The definition of result jungles still allows chains of result edges. We can propagate results by the following relation $\trianglerighteq$ between result jungles:

$$(G, R_J, s_J, t_J) \trianglerighteq (G, R_J, s_J, t'_J) \text{ iff}$$
$$\forall r \in R_J :\ t_J(r) = t'_J(r) \vee \exists r' \in R_J :\ s_J(r') = t_J(r) \wedge t_J(r') = t'_J(r)$$

For loopless result jungles, the irreflexive part $\triangleright$ of $\trianglerighteq$ is strongly normalising. Its (unique) normal forms are the result jungles with fully propagated result edges. The relation $\trianglerighteq$ does not change term_J, i.e. if $J \trianglerighteq J'$, $J = (G, R_J, s_J, t_J)$, then $\forall v \in V_G :\ \mathsf{term}_J(v) = \mathsf{term}_{J'}(v)$.

5 Memoization by Memo Tables

Memoization (sometimes called function caching) is a method to store evaluation results such that they can be reused if the same evaluation is required again later.

The traditional approach [13] uses memo tables, i.e. hash tables that store pairs of argument and result for those functions that are supposed to be memoized. From the hypergraph point of view, this method corresponds to a slightly different encoding of result edges, see [7]: a result hyperedge has then n sources (the n arguments of the function), one label (the function symbol) and one target, the result. One disadvantage, which is immediately obvious from the encoding itself, is a certain waste of space: the information the hyperedge has to carry comprises the function symbol, all the argument vertices and the result vertex.

Hughes [11] generalised memoization appropriately for lazy evaluation, storing as argument the (pointer to the) unevaluated argument in such a table. Pugh and Teitelbaum [16] showed how to widen the application of memoization to incremental computations (like attribute grammars) by carefully selecting the representation of the involved data types.

Beside the mentioned disadvantage that is apparent just by looking at the hypergraph encoding, memo tables have certain other drawbacks:

- they may overflow,
- they may be nearly unused,
- entries have to be searched for,
- they are oriented towards a first-order programming style.

In other words: they need some administration.

The last point refers to the problem: Where do we store the result of $(f \circ g)(x)$? The natural solution "in the memo table of $\circ$" seems fairly unreasonable, because it then heavily depends on the programming style whether the memo table for a combinator like $\circ$ is nearly empty, for programs written in first-order style, or totally overcrowded, as would be typical for programs developed in the Bird-Meertens formalism [2].

Figure 1 suggests a natural place for the result edge; it is the storage cell of the (unevaluated) expression. This means to make storage cells of expressions bigger (space for an additional pointer), provided the expression can have a value. This proviso is simply the negation of "is in weak head normal form" (for the terminology, see [15]), and this property is known when the cell is created.

This approach has a neat side-effect. Suppose, we create a cell $\mathsf{op}(t_1, \ldots, t_n)$. If a cell of this form already exists somewhere in the heap, Unlimp guarantees (and forces) us to find it, and if it has already been evaluated before, we will moreover find the result in this very cell. A memo table approach requires some further search: look up the memo table for op and then search for the appropriate n-tuple.

Similarly, if we store the compiled code of a λ-abstraction as its result, then creating the same (an α-congruent) λ-abstraction would find this compilation result, avoiding a superfluous recompilation. One could even give a pattern a value: the code to match it; this would not only guarantee to avoid recompilation of patterns, it might also ease the task of creating a decision tree[1] for pattern matching compilation.

6 Dealing with Side-Effects

Occasionally, the effect of memoization is unwanted, particularly in the presence of side-effects of various kinds, e.g. assignment and I/O, or – in an interpreter – a change of the rule base. To allow this in an Unlimp framework, one has to distinguish between applicative expressions, expressions that may depend on the state, and expressions that may change the state.

Expressions that may *change* the state have to be re-evaluated each time their value is required, hence we do not need a result edge for them. Expressions that may *depend on* the state but do not change it (like access to variables) have to be re-evaluated each time the state changes, hence result edges have to be time-stamped, *time* being a kind of side-effect counter. If the considered side-effects include the change of the rule base in an interpreter, every expression is state dependent and so each result edge needs a time stamp.

The properties "may change state" and "may depend on state" can be seen as simple syntactic properties of certain elementary operations (e.g. assignment the former, variable access the latter). But it is not quite obvious how they should be inherited by other operations or composite expressions. An abstract interpretation would probably provide a good approximation to the required information. But even in the absence of such an analysis, one can do the following:

For each expression (except whnf's), space for a result edge *and* its time stamp has to be provided. There are global counters for state changes and state accesses. If the evaluation of an expression t to some result u increases neither of the counters, we can draw an unstamped result edge. If the state change counter was increased, we do not draw a result edge; if the state remains unchanged but was accessed, the result edge gets the actual "time" (state change counter) as a stamp.

In the hypergraph world, we can encode this as follows:

Definition 4. A *changeable jungle* $C = (J, T, p)$ consists of a result jungle J, a number $T \in \omega$ (the time), and a mapping $p : R_J \longrightarrow \omega + 1$ (the time stamp), such that $\forall r \in R_J : p(r) = \omega \vee p(r) \leq T$.

The effect of the time stamp can be described by a forgetful map from changeable jungles to result jungles, which maps $((G, R_J, s_J, t_J), T, p)$ to (G, R'_J, s_J, t_J), R'_J being the set $\{r \in R_J | \, p(r) \geq T\}$, i.e. the map forgets the expired result edges. The stamp ω indicates that the result edge is not state-dependent.

Result propagation for changeable jungles is slightly trickier than for result jungles, because instead of simply redirecting the target of certain result edges, we may have to add further result edges:

$$
\begin{array}{l}
((G, R_J, s_J, t_J), T, p) \quad \trianglerighteq \quad ((G, R_J \cup R'_J, s_J \cup s'_J, t'_J), T, p \cup p') \text{ iff} \\
\forall r \in R'_J : \, p'(r) = T \;\wedge\; \exists a, b \in R_J : \, p(a) = \omega \;\wedge\; p(b) = T \;\wedge \\
\qquad s'_J(r) = s_J(a) \;\wedge\; t'_J(r) = t_J(b) \;\wedge\; s_J(b) = t_J(a) \\
\forall r \in R_J : \, t_J(r) = t'_J(r) \quad \vee \quad p(r) = T \;\wedge \\
\qquad \exists r' \in R_J : \, p(r') \geq T \;\wedge\; s_J(r') = t_J(r) \;\wedge\; t_J(r') = t'_J(r)
\end{array}
$$

What this rather lengthy formula is all about can be seen in figure 2.

If an unmarked result edge is followed by a marked one, we can propagate the result as shown by the dotted line, but it would be a pity to overwrite the unmarked

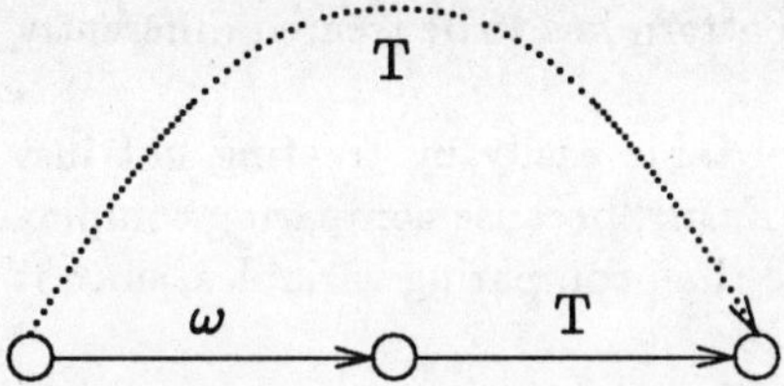

Fig. 2. Result Propagation for Changeable Jungles

edge: if there is a further change of state, the unmarked result is still valid while the marked result information expires. Therefore we have an additional set of result edges R'_J created in situations as above.

For the implementation this suggests the need to provide space for two result edges, a marked and an unmarked one, but this is not really necessary. If we restrict $\trianglerighteq$ to the case where R'_J is empty, then chains of (non-expired) result edges in the normal forms of $\triangleright$ have length at most 2.

Intuitively, this means the following. Suppose we have an evaluation sequence $t_0 \Rightarrow_1 t_1 \Rightarrow_2 \ldots \Rightarrow_n t_n$. We draw an unstamped result edge from t_0 to the last t_i, such that all the $\Rightarrow_j, j \leq i$ are applicative, and mark t_i as an *applicative normal form*. If $i < n$, we draw a stamped result edge from t_i to t_n, provided no $\Rightarrow_l, l \leq n$ changed the state.

Notice that this affects the notion of value: in addition to weak head normal forms there are now *applicative normal forms*.

The concept of a monolithic state is a bit strict, because it does not reflect locality of variables, e.g. (in SML):

```
fun fac n =
    let val p = ref (n,1) in
        while #1(!p) > 0
        do p := (#1(!p)-1, op * (!p));
        #2(!p)
    end;
```

The lifetime of the variable p does not exceed any call of fac and it is not accessible outside of fac – a dataflow analysis could easily detect this. We could exploit information of this kind for a more sophisticated concept of time and time stamp, but this goes beyond the scope of this paper.

7 Compilation

One subtask of compiling a function definition in a language that supports pattern matching is the management of a symbol table for the pattern variables. It assigns to each variable name a relative address (relative to the stack) and can furthermore be used to detect free variables, anonymous variables and non-linear patterns. Non-linear patterns are forbidden in most languages (not all), but even when they are allowed, the second occurrence of a variable in a pattern has to be treated differently from its first occurrence.

Under Unlimp, we can generalise the symbol table easily by treating not just variables, but arbitrary non-ground expressions. *Easily*, because comparing complex expressions is here not more difficult or expensive than comparing variables, since it is just the comparison of addresses.

The generalisation to non-ground expressions (nge) works as follows:

- An nge is allocated space on the stack, if and only of it occurs more than once in the left-hand or right-hand side of the definition.
- If an nge occurs a second time, we do not count its subterms as second occurrences.

Variables are also nge's, and in this special case the first point is the detection of anonymous variables, because variables occurring only once do not need to be stored on the stack. For composite expressions it is a common subexpression elimination, because we put them onto the stack if they occur more than once, which corresponds to the introduction of a let-expression. An example (in Haskell), taken from [10]:

```
dropWhile p []     = []
dropWhile p (x:xs)
          | p x       = dropWhile p xs
          | otherwise = x:xs
```

For the first rule, there are 3 nge's, but none of them requires space on the stack, p occurs only once and is hence anonymous. In the second rule, we have 8 nge's and 5 of them are allocated space on the stack, see table 1.

Table 1. Generalised Symbol Table

nge	occurrences
dropWhile p (x:xs)	1
dropWhile p	2
p	2
x:xs	2
x	2
xs	2
p x	1
dropWhile p xs	1

In this example, each nge which is to be stored on the stack is a subexpression of the left-hand side of the rule. Hence, when an expression matches the left-hand side, each nge to be stored on the stack is a subterm of this expression and can be stored during the matching process. One can argue about nge's like dropWhile p; it depends on other implementation details (representation of function application) whether they should count or not.

Some care is necessary to treat conditional expressions properly, e.g. common subexpressions of the then- and else-parts of a conditional expression are not really common. It is harmless to put them onto the stack, but harmful to expect them to be there.

8 Garbage Collection

... is a weak point of Unlimp.

The problem is that there is very little *proper* garbage. Deallocating an unreferenced cell would also throw away its result edge and hence a bit of useful information, so that only unreferenced weak head normal forms (have no result edge) and former K-redexes[5] (result edge remains NIL under lazy evaluation) are proper garbage. Unfortunately, almost no weak head normal form will be unreferenced, at least there is the result edge from some (perhaps unreferenced) vertex, and K-redexes are more the exception than the rule. Only in the presence of side-effects can we expect some unreferenced weak head normal forms, because the time stamps of the result edges pointing to them may have expired.

For this reason, a garbage collector would need to collect improper garbage, which is against the spirit of Unlimp, of course. Each unreferenced vertex is (im)proper garbage. Even vertices only referenced by result edges could be treated as improper garbage, but this would require some additional administration, e.g. the garbage collection has to be treated as a global side-effect.

9 Programming Style

Working with an Unlimp implementation can influence programming style. First let us look at a similar influence of lazy evaluation.

Lazy and strict evaluation do not have the same computational power (in a *practical* sense), because lazy evaluation can deal with (conceptually) infinite objects, whereas strict evaluation cannot. Thus, when the natural solution of a problem requires the intermediate creation of an object of infinite size, solving the problem with a strict language means looking for a less natural way.

But such an influence on programming style is also present when there is no such principal difference in computational power, because for certain programming styles, strict evaluation is very inefficient. Typical for this are backtracking algorithms, see [20]; one example is the following simplified version (in Haskell) of the pairing algorithm used for Swiss System chess tournaments:

```
type Entry a = (a,[a])
type Pairing a = [(Entry a,Entry a)]
pairing :: (Eq a) => [Entry a] -> Pairing a
pairing table = if allpairs==[] then error "no pairing"
                else head allpairs
                where allpairs = fullpairs table
```

[5] In λ-calculus, $(\lambda x.t)u$ is a K-redex if x is not free in t.

```
fullpairs :: (Eq a) => [Entry a] -> [Pairing a]
fullpairs [] = [[]]
fullpairs (x:xs) = [ (x,y):zs | y <- xs, condition x y,
                                zs <- fullpairs (xs\\[y]) ]
condition :: (Eq a) => Entry a -> Entry a -> Bool
condition (x,xs)(y,ys) = notElem x ys
```

The function pairing is applied to the actual table of the players (which is supposed to be a list of even length) and produces a list of pairs (the pairing for the next round), such that each pair fulfills the condition. Moreover, the table leader should play (if possible) against the second, the third against the fourth, etc. The entries in the table consist of the player and his or her opponents so far, which is sufficient for the condition "haven't already played against each other".

The above algorithm is expressed in terms of computing all possible pairings and then selecting the first one, which – because of the structure of the algorithm – tends to pairs first with second etc. This is fine for lazy evaluation, but under strict evaluation it is very inefficient, because the number of all possible pairings usually (depending on condition) grows very fast. Table 2 shows the number of reduction steps (successful rule applications) executed to evaluate `pairing tab`, for five different examples[6], depending on whether the evaluation strategy is strict or lazy and whether full memoization is used or not.

Table 2. Reduction Steps for a Backtracking Algorithm

strategy	stab	mtab1	mtab2	ltab1	ltab2
strict, nomemo	347	16,401	18,211	1,776,421	1,865,213
strict, memo	184	2,133	2,068	84,117	84,361
lazy, nomemo	110	134	474	238	2,276
lazy, memo	88	128	240	230	540

Clearly, strict evaluation is inappropriate for this program. Although the algorithm is correct for strict evaluation too, a programmer using a strict language is encouraged to solve the problem on a lower level, e.g. by making the backtracking strategy explicit.

The impact of memoization on the program is characteristic: the "better" the algorithm is, the less is the effect of memoization. It cannot turn a horribly slow program into a fast one, but it can reduce the horror drastically. The drastic improvement under strict evaluation, and the slight but significant improvement for the heavy backtrackers (mtab2 and ltab2) under lazy evaluation are rather surprising, as the pairing program does not appear to be a prime candidate for memoization.

Full memoization can work together with lazy as well as strict evaluation, but it does not affect the computational power of either strategy. Therefore, there is no

[6] The chosen examples were lists of length 6 after 2 rounds (stab), of length 10 after 3 rounds (mtab1 and mtab2), and of length 14 after 4 rounds (ltab1 and ltab2). The examples mtab2 and ltab2 were chosen to require a lot of backtracking, in contrast to mtab1 and ltab1.

principle need to change the programming style when memoization is absent, but we do have similar kinds of unpleasant encouragement to solve problems at a lower level.

Some further examples (and references) can be found in [11]. We do not have to look for examples that are contrived to support this argument – the following piece of program (in SML) to compute the nth prime number was taken from [19]:

```
fun prime n =
    let fun next(k,i) =
            if n<=i then k
            else if divides(prime i,k) then next(k+1,0)
            else next(k,i+1)
    in
        if n=0 then 2
        else next(prime(n-1)+1,0)
    end
```

It was considered there to be "rather inefficient". In a traditional implementation it is indeed, but under Unlimp it turns out to be fairly reasonable, because memoizing `prime` makes the algorithm behave like a (rather naïve) variation of the sieve of Eratosthenes.

10 Speed-Up in the Small

Most examples people mention when they promulgate memoization are like the naïve version of the Fibonacci function or the above version of `prime` - without memoization terribly inefficient and - since they are naïve - only naïve people would write the function this way, unless it is known that the implementation supports memoization[7].

But memoization also has great effects in the small, as in the `pairing` program. Sometimes they appear very unexpectedly, like the following one:

As their favoured benchmark test for functional programs, Jörn von Holten and Richard Seifert at the University of Bremen took arithmetic on natural numbers represented as successor terms. To make the task hard, the following version of arithmetic was used:

```
data Nat     = Z | S Nat
add Z     x = x
add (S x) y = S (add x y)
mul Z     x = Z
mul (S x) y = add (mul x y) y
pow x     Z = S Z
pow x (S y) = mul (pow x y) x
```

This version is supposed to make arithmetic expensive, because (minor reason) add is not tail recursive and (major reason) the right-hand sides of the last rules for

[7] Another less well-known example of this kind is model checking with binary decision diagrams, see [3].

mul and pow have their recursive calls in the first rather than the second argument of add and mul. Note that add n m is linear in n and constant in m.

However, the response time of an Unlimp implementation turned out to be fairly stable under switching the arguments of add and mul in the mentioned rules. The reason is that several addition terms reappear in this process, because computing $n + m$ involves also the computation of $k + m$ for all k less than m.

The following table compares the number of evaluation steps to compute 4^2, 4^3, and 4^4. The left figures show the number of steps for the above definition, the right figures refer to the version obtained by switching the arguments of the mentioned calls of add and mul.

Table 3. Reduction Steps for a Successor Arithmetic

strategy	4^2		4^3		4^4	
strict, nomemo	40	42	554	116	8748	382
strict, memo	22	40	83	109	324	358
lazy, nomemo	96	195	444,678	1,611	too many	13,123
lazy, memo	27	42	192	116	2295	382

The suspected bad behaviour of exponentiation does not appear under memoization and strict evaluation, here it is even slightly better than the ordinary definition. Only for lazy evaluation, memoization cannot fully compensate for the "bad" algorithm.

As in the pairing example, we can again observe different kinds of improvement, depending on how "badly" the algorithm behaves. In both cases, the effects appeared in the small, i.e. they had no fancy recursive structure (as the prime example), the functions were linear recursive.

11 Conclusion

A unique representations for expressions can affect compilation, execution and usage of functional languages.

We tried to convey the spirit of thinking in unique representations and of exploiting it for different purposes, e.g. for compilation. The given modelling by hypergraphs stays close to the machine level and allows several meta-observations on a rather abstract level. We showed how memoization and side-effects can happily coexist, even in the hypergraph modelling.

The effect of memoization on program execution seems to be well-known, but the analysis of the given examples suggest that it is not well-known enough. When using full memoization, i.e. storing *every* evaluation result, an important and often unexpected phenomenon appears: a cumulative speed-up by saving minor, but numerous computations. This phenomenon encourages a more problem-oriented programming style.

References

1. Marianne Baudinet and David MacQueen. Tree pattern matching for ML. In *Conference on Functional Programming Languages and Computer Archtitecture*, 1987. LNCS 274.
2. Richard Bird. Lectures on Constructive Functional Programming. Technical Monograph PRG-69, Programming Research Group, Oxford University Computing Laboratory, 1988.
3. Reinhard Enders, Thomas Filkorn, and Dirk Taubner. Generating BDDs for symbolic model checking in CCS. In *Third Workshop on Computer Aided Verification*, pages 263–278, Aalborg, 1991.
4. A. J. Field and P. G. Harrison. *Functional Programming*. Addison-Wesley, 1988.
5. G. H. Gonnet. *Handbook of Algorithms and Data Structures*. Addison-Wesley, 1984.
6. Annegret Habel, Hans-Jörg Kreowski, and Detlef Plump. Jungle Evaluation. *Fundamentae Informaticae*, 15(1):37–60, 1991.
7. Berthold Hoffmann. Term Rewriting with Sharing and Memoïzation, 1992. (to appear in: Proceedings, Algebraic and Logic Programming 1992).
8. Berthold Hoffmann and Detlef Plump. Jungle Evaluation for Efficient Term Rewriting. Technical Report 4/88, Universität Bremen, Studiengang Informatik, 1988. (short version in LNCS 343).
9. Berthold Hoffmann and Detlef Plump. Implementing Term Rewriting by Jungle Evaluation. *Informatique théorique et Applications*, 25(5):445–472, 1991.
10. P. Hudak, S. Peyton Jones, and P. Wadler. Report on the Programming Language Haskell, a Non-strict, Purely Functional Language. Technical report, University of Glasgow, 1991. (version 1.2 to appear in SIGPLAN notices).
11. R. J. M. Hughes. Lazy memo functions. In *Conference on Functional Programming and Computer Architecture*, pages 129–146. Springer, 1985. LNCS 201.
12. Jan Willem Klop and Roel de Vrijer. Extended Term Rewriting Systems. Technical Report CS-R9107, Centrum voor Wiskunde en Informatica, January 1991.
13. D. Michie. Memo functions and machine learning. *Nature*, 218:19–22, 1968.
14. Laurence C. Paulson. *ML for the Working Programmer*. Cambridge University Press, 1991.
15. Simon Peyton Jones. *The Implementation of Functional Programming Languages*. Prentice-Hall, 1987.
16. William Pugh and Tim Teitelbaum. Incremental computation via function caching. In *Symposion on Principles of Programming Languages*, pages 315–328, 1989.
17. Masataka Sassa and Eiichi Goto. A hashing method for fast set operations. *Information Processing Letters*, 5(2):31–34, June 1976.
18. Robert Sedgewick. *Algorithms*. Addison-Wesley, 1988.
19. Stefan Sokołowski. *Applicative High Order Programming*. Chapman & Hall Computing, 1991.
20. Philip Wadler. How to replace failure by a list of successes. In *Functional Programming Languages and Computer Architecture*, pages 113–128, 1985. LNCS 201.
21. Ben Wegbreit and Jay M. Spitzen. Proving properties of complex data structures. *Journal of the ACM*, 23(2):389–396, 1976.
22. Burkhart Wolff. Sharing-Analyse in funktionalen Sprachen. Technical Report 6/91, Universität Bremen, Studiengang Informatik, 1991. (in German).

This article was processed using the LaTeX macro package with LLNCS style

Using Cached Functions and Constructors for Incremental Attribute Evaluation

Maarten Pennings, Doaitse Swierstra and Harald Vogt

Department of Computer Science, Utrecht University,
P.O. Box 80.089, 3508 TB Utrecht, The Netherlands,
E-Mail: `maarten@cs.ruu.nl`, `doaitse@cs.ruu.nl` and `harald@cs.ruu.nl`.

Abstract. This paper presents a technique for the efficient incremental evaluation of Attribute Grammars. Through its generality, the applied approach may be affective too in the evaluation of Higher order Attribute Grammars. Our approach is an extension of a simpler algorithm for incremental evaluation, where functions, corresponding to visit sequences, are cached. Consequently, attributes are now either found in the cache or they are recomputed, so there is no longer need to represent the attributed tree explicitly. We may share common subtrees, avoiding repeated attribute evaluation, thus solving a typical HAG problem.

We propose the following change: instead of explicitly representing the tree and calling visit sequence functions to compute the attributes, the tree is represented *through* a set of visit functions corresponding to the successive visits. These functions are constructed using the visit sequences as building blocks.

This technique has two major advantages. Firstly, a visit function characterizes precisely that part of the tree that would actually have been visited in the previous approach, thus increasing the number of cache hits. Secondly, copyrules may be removed during the construction phase. This results in shortcircuiting copychains and in minimizing the number of recomputed functions.

1 Introduction

Attribute Grammars (AGs) [Knu68, Knu71] describe the computation of attributes: values associated with the nodes of a tree. Trees are described with a context free grammar and the attribute computation is defined through semantic functions. Attribute grammars are used to define languages and form the basis of compilers, language-based editors and other language based tools [DJL88, DJ90, Alb91].

Higher order attribute grammars (HAGs) [VSK89] remove the artificial distinction between the syntactic level (context free grammar) and the semantic level (attributes) in attribute grammars. This strict separation is removed in two ways: trees can be defined through attribution, and such trees may be instantiated (and attributed!). Trees defined through attribution are known as non-terminal attributes. A non-terminal attribute occurs both as a non-terminal on the right hand side of a production rule and as an attribute on the left hand side of an attribution rule of that production, thus promoting trees to first class citizens.

Our new evaluation technique is based on an efficient algorithm for ordered HAGs which is presented in the next section. In Sect. 3 the new technique is explained with an informal example. Section 4 presents a detailed example using the old algorithm and in Sect. 5 the new technique is applied to it. Finally, Sect. 6 contains the conclusions.

2 Introduction to the Old Algorithm

The new algorithm presented in this paper resulted from our research on efficient incremental evaluators for higher order attribute grammars. Typical HAG features make the standard AG evaluators unsuitable.

Attribute evaluators for ordered AGs [Kas80, Yeh83, TC90] can be trivially adapted to handle ordered HAGs [VSK89]. However, the adapted evaluator attributes instances of non-terminal attributes with the same inherited attributes separately. This leads, amongst others, to a non-optimal incremental behavior after a change to such an attribute, as can be seen in the recently published algorithm of [TC90]. A better technique is the evaluation algorithm for ordered HAGs in [VSK91, SV91]. It handles multiple occurrences of the same subtree efficiently. This algorithm is based on the combination of the following ideas:

Visit sequence functions. Attribute values are computed by visit sequence functions. Such functions take as parameter a tree and a subset of inherited attributes of the root of that tree and they return a subset of the synthesized attributes (of the root). The entire evaluator consists of visit sequence functions that recursively call each other in order to attribute the tree.

Caching. In a conventional incremental treewalk evaluator a partially attributed tree can be considered as a very efficient caching mechanism—where caching is replaced by explicit navigation—for the semantic functions. Instead of using a separate cache for the results of semantic functions, as was done in [Pug88], only visit sequence functions are cached: one uniform treatment of semantic functions and attribute evaluation. Furthermore, we have no separate administration on whether attributes have changed and further visits are necessary.
This approach is more efficient because a cache hit of a visit sequence function means that the entire visit to the (possibly large) tree can be skipped. Furthermore, a visit sequence function may return the results of several semantic functions at a time.

Memoed constructors. Since attributes may be found in the cache, there is no longer need to store them in the tree. This allows us to share multiple instances of the same tree. As in [TC90], we use memoed treeconstructors. A memoed (cached) constructor is called a 'hashing cons' in [Hug85].

Bindings. Although the above ideas seem appealing at first sight, a complication is that attributes computed in an earlier visit may have to be preserved for use in later visits. Normally, this is no problem since attributes are stored in the tree. Now these values, called *bindings*, must be passed explicitly to the future visits. Each visit sequence function therefore not only computes synthesized attributes but also bindings for subsequent visits. Bindings computed by earlier visits are passed as parameters to later visit sequence functions.

3 Introduction to the New Algorithm

The original visit sequences of [Kas80] were designed with the goal to minimize the number of visits to each node. In the case of incremental evaluation, however, one's goal will be to maximize the number of cache hits for the visit sequence functions. The parameters of these functions—the tree, the inherited attributes and the bindings—form the cache key.

An essential property of the construction of bindings is that when calling a visit sequence function with its bindings, these bindings contain *precisely* that information that will be used in this visit. This is a direct result of the fact that these bindings were constructed during earlier visits, at which time it was known what productions had been applied and what actual dependencies are occurring in the subtrees. Thus there is little room for improvement here. The same holds for the inherited attributes.

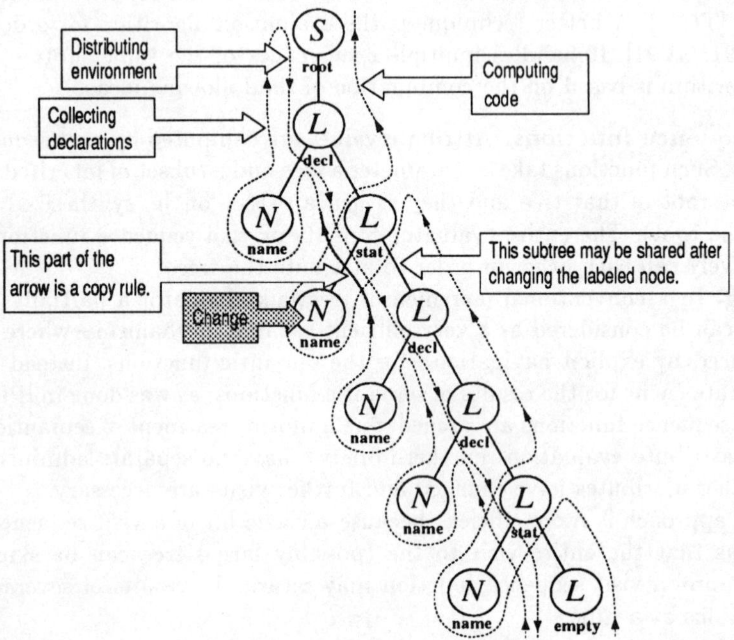

Fig. 1. Dataflow analyses.

The situation is different however, when we inspect the role of the tree as parameter to the visit sequence functions. The complete tree is passed and not only those parts that will actually be traversed by the called visit sequence function. Since the complete tree is used as part of the key in the function cache, unnecessary visit calls may be performed. *Splitting* eliminates these shortcomings: instead of having a single large tree, we represent the tree by a tuple of terms, one for each visit. Each of these terms includes only those parts of the abstract tree that are traversed in the visit they are meant for. In this way, more cache hits will occur.

Let us have a look at an example where we have visits which pass through different parts of the subtree. We model a language which does not demand identifiers to be declared before they are used. This naturally leads to a two-pass algorithm: one pass for constructing the environment and a second pass for actually compiling the statements. In Fig. 1 an example tree is given. The dashed arrows indicate the dataflow: the leftmost for collecting the declarations, the middle one for distributing the environment and the rightmost for computing the code. Notice that for collecting the declarations only the identifiers of the declaration nodes are passed whereas for computing the code only the identifiers of the statement nodes are visited.

What happens when we change a using occurrence? Suppose we change the N-node labeled with Change. Due to constructor memoing, the newly constructed tree shares the lower part (the four L-nodes and three N-nodes) with the old tree. But there is more: since the first visit subsequence of a **stat** production does not refer to the N-son (a **stat** production doesn't add a declaration), the term representing the first visit isn't changed. So the *entire* first visit of the new tree (called from the **root**) is found in the cache and hence may be skipped.

We could do even better. The first visit to a **stat** node simply copies values. Rephrased, it consists of so called *copyrules* only. Therefore, if we add another statement just above the one we just changed, some useless copyrules are inserted. This means that the first-visit term has changed, so no cache hit will occur. In this simple example, we could remove the **stat** nodes from the first-visit term so that even after inserting a statement, the entire first visit will still hit. To be able to eliminate copyrules in more elaborated grammars, we do not represent the tree by a tuple of *terms* but by a tuple of *functions* (one for each visit), simply by applying the visit sequence function to the terms (partial parameterisation).

The next section explains the old algorithm by using the above example in detail. This example will also be used in the explanation of the new algorithm in Sect. 5.

4 The Old Algorithm: an Example

We present a simple grammar implementing the "programming language" from the previous section. To illustrate all aspects of the algorithm we made the grammar two-pass. In pass one the definitions will be collected, so that in pass two the actual translation may take place. Thus the "main" non-terminal (L) has two visits, so that the visit sequences [Kas80] associated with the production rules that may be applied to L (**stat**, **decl** and **empty**) consist of two subsequences.

We now define visit sequence functions corresponding to these visit subsequences. For each non-terminal we construct one function for each visit. The ith visit sequence function of a non-terminal is applied to the inherited attributes which have newly become available for visit i and it returns the synthesized attributes for that visit.

This doesn't differ too much from Kastens' approach. But Kastens uses the abstract tree as a repository in which attributes are stored between defining and using visits. As we do not have an explicit tree representation we must store these intermediate results somewhere else. The problem is solved by introducing so called *bindings*, their usage is illustrated further on.

4.1 The Example Grammar

A program in the example grammar is a list of "declarations" (such as `var x`) and "statements" (like `use x`). They may be mixed freely, and we do not require *definition before use.* In the translation process, each variable is mapped onto a number. The resulting list will contain this number for each using occurrence, and the negation of it for the defining occurrence. Hence

```
(use x;use y;var y;use x;use y;use z;var z;var x;use x;)
```

is mapped onto the list

```
3, 1, -1, 3, 1, 2, -2, -3, 3 .
```

The grammar of our language has the following (labeled) production rules:

$$\begin{array}{ll}\textbf{root}: & S \rightarrow (L)\\ \textbf{decl}: & L \rightarrow \texttt{var}\ N; L\\ \textbf{stat}: & L \rightarrow \texttt{use}\ N; L\\ \textbf{empty}: & L \rightarrow \epsilon\\ \textbf{name}: & N \rightarrow str\end{array}$$

Since we are using trees as arguments for our visit sequence functions, we need a concise notation for trees. We will follow a MIRANDA-like notation [Tur85] for terms. So, the above grammar is transformed (leaving out the terminals ('(', ')', '`var`', '`use`', and ';') since they are not of interest to us) to:

$$\begin{array}{rl}S = & \textbf{root}(L)\\ L = & \textbf{decl}(N, L)\\ \mid & \textbf{stat}(N, L)\\ \mid & \textbf{empty}()\\ N = & \textbf{name}(str)\end{array}$$

This grammar is as follows augmented with attributes. Apart from the already introduced type *str* (representing identifiers) we distinguish $env = [str]$ and $code = [num]$ where type *num* represents the natural numbers (with square brackets we denote "list-of"). The startsymbol S has a single (synthesized) attribute returning the code whereas the listsymbol L has three attributes: one that collects the declarations (synthesized), one that distributes the environment (inherited) and one that synthesizes the code. See Fig. 2 for the complete attribute grammar.

We have written a small compiler for this grammar using the techniques described in this paper. The compiler is written in a special version of GOFER [Jon91], a large subset of the functional language Haskell [HF92, HPW92], to which we added the polymorphic function memo :: $(\alpha \rightarrow \beta) \rightarrow (\alpha \rightarrow \beta)$ that implements memoisation for functions (and thus constructors). We used this system to test the various optimizations.

Signature
$S\langle\uparrow code\rangle$
$L\langle\uparrow env, \downarrow env, \uparrow code\rangle$
$N\langle\uparrow str\rangle$

$S\langle\uparrow c_0\rangle$ = **root**$(L\langle\uparrow d, \downarrow e, \uparrow c_1\rangle)$
$\quad e := d;$
$\quad c_0 := c_1$
$N\langle\uparrow n\rangle$ = **name**(str)
$\quad n := str$

$L\langle\uparrow d_0, \downarrow e_0, \uparrow c_0\rangle$ = **decl**$(N\langle\uparrow n\rangle, L\langle\uparrow d_1, \downarrow e_1, \uparrow c_1\rangle)$
$\quad d_0 := [n] +\!\!+\, d_1;$
$\quad e_1 := e_0;$
$\quad c_0 := [-\ \mathsf{lookup} \cdot e_0 \cdot n] +\!\!+\, c_1$
| **stat**$(N\langle\uparrow n\rangle, L\langle\uparrow d_1, \downarrow e_1, \uparrow c_1\rangle)$
$\quad d_0 := d_1;$
$\quad e_1 := e_0;$
$\quad c_0 := [\mathsf{lookup} \cdot e_0 \cdot n] +\!\!+\, c_1$
| **empty**()
$\quad d_0 := [\,];$
$\quad c_0 := [\,]$

Fig. 2. The attribute grammar.

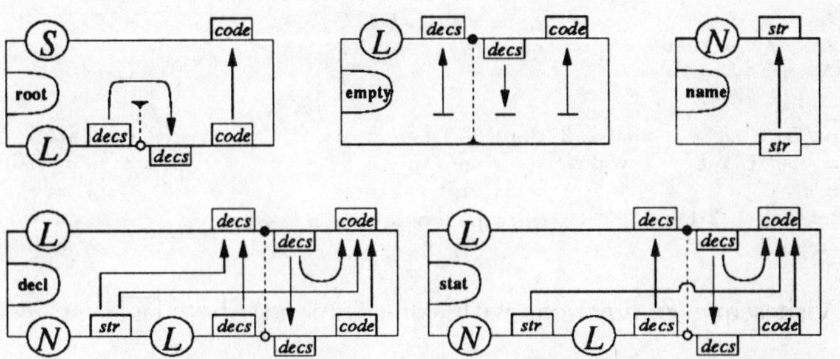

Fig. 3. Attribute dependencies in a production rule.

4.2 Visit (sub)Sequences

In Fig. 3 the attribute dependencies are presented graphically. The attributes of the symbols are topologically sorted according to their (indirect) dependencies. The dashed lines indicate a visit border: attributes to the left of it are evaluated during the first visit and attributes to the right of it during the second.

Note that when a tree is constructed from these productions, the "pieces" fit nicely together. This does not only hold for the non-terminals, the inherited and synthesized attributes, but also for the visit borders: a solid disk hooks into an open circle splitting the entire tree. With this division it is fairly simple to determine suitable visit (sub)sequences: see Fig. 4 in which **name** and **empty** are omitted for brevity.

4.3 From Visit (sub)Sequences to a Functional Program

We will not show the mapping from visit (sub)sequences to visit sequence functions. This is a straightforward process: each visit(X, i) instruction is mapped to a visit-X-i function call with the tree (X) as first parameter and the appropriate inherited attributes as the next parameters. The function returns the computed

```
VS(root(L))                  VS(decl(N, L))                    VS(stat(N, L))
 = VSS(root(L), 1)            = VSS(decl(N, L), 1)              = VSS(stat(N, L), 1)
   = visit(L, 1) {ret d}        = visit(N, 1) {ret n}             = visit(L, 1) {ret d1}
   ; e := d                     ; visit(L, 1) {ret d1}            ; d0 := d1
   ; visit(L, 2) {ret c1}       ; d0 := [n] ++ d1                 ; return(1)
   ; c0 := c1                   ; return(1)                     ; VSS(stat(N, L), 2)
   ; return(1)                ; VSS(decl(N, L), 2)                = visit(N, 1) {ret n}
                                = e1 := e0                        ; e1 := e0
                                ; visit(L, 2) {ret c1}            ; visit(L, 2) {ret c1}
                                ; c0 := [- lookup·e0·n] ++ c1     ; c0 := [lookup·e0·n] ++ c1
                                ; return(2)                       ; return(2)
```

Fig. 4. The visit (sub)sequences for productions **root**, **decl** and **stat**.

```
Signature                        visit-L-1· decl(N, L) = d0         visit-L-1· stat(N, L) = d0
visit-S-1 :: S         → code      where [n] := visit-N-1·N           where d1 := visit-L-1·L
visit-L-1 :: L         → env         ; d1 := visit-L-1·L                ; d0 := d1
visit-L-2 :: L × env   → code        ; d0 := [n] ++ d1
visit-N-1 :: N         → str

visit-S-1· root(L) = c0          visit-L-2· decl(N, L)·e0 = c0      visit-L-2· stat(N, L)·e0 = c0
  where d := visit-L-1·L           where e1 := e0                     where n := visit-N-1·N
    ; e := d                         ; c1 := visit-L-2·L·e1             ; e1 := e0
    ; c1 := visit-L-2·L·e            ; c0 := [- lookup·e0·[n]] ++ c1    ; c1 := visit-L-2·L·e1
    ; c0 := c1                                                          ; c0 := [lookup·e0·n] ++ c1
```

Fig. 5. Visit sequence functions with side-effects: attribute [n] is stored in the tree.

synthesized attributes. In Fig. 5 the visit sequence functions are given. Observe that these functions are strict and therefore efficient computation is possible.

The reader may have noticed that we use · for function application. We do this in order not to confuse functions and constructors. Note also that we overload the symbols S, L and N; they are used as type identifiers as well as dummies in the patterns.

4.4 Bindings

One of the major drawbacks of the visit sequence functions presented in Fig. 5 is that they have side-effects. Some attributes must remain known over several visits. In our example $N.\mathit{str}$—in Fig. 5 these occurrences are boxed—needs to be stored in the tree.

Taking another look at the attribute dependencies of production **decl** in Fig. 3, we observe that one arrow—from $N.\mathit{str}$ to $L_0.\mathit{code}$—is crossing a visit border. Attribute $N.\mathit{str}$ is evaluated (and needed) in the first visit but it is also needed in the second one. Therefore it can not be deleted when returning from the first visit. The conventional solution is to store the attribute in the tree, but we take a different approach. The later needed values are passed to the father, and we rely on him to pass them down for the next visit. Such a link from visit-X-i to visit-X-j via a parent is called a binding from i to j for symbol X.[1]

[1] By the way, if attribute a is computed in visit i and $f{\cdot}a$ is needed in visit j ($i < j$),

In Fig. 6 the production rules are enhanced with bindings, in our simple example we have *bind* = **stack of** *str*. Note that there is no need to bind *N.str* in production **stat**: *N.str* is not used in the first visit to *L*, so *N* is visited in *L*s second visit. That an arrow is still crossing the visit border in production **stat** is just a consequence of the limited possibilities of 2D drawings: see Fig. 7 for the 3D version. The visit sequence functions enhanced with bindings are given in Fig. 8.

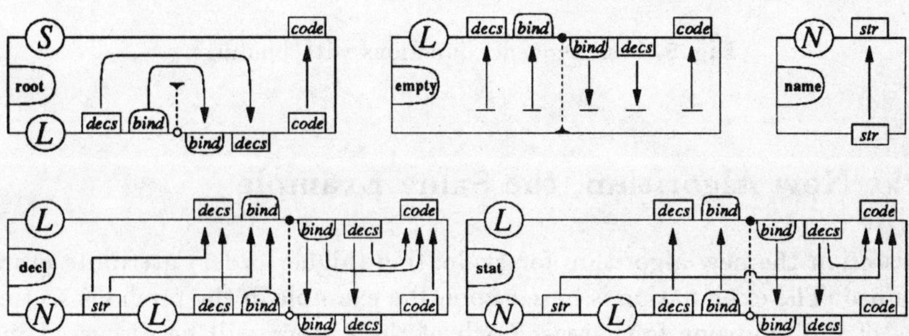

Fig. 6. Introduction of bindings.

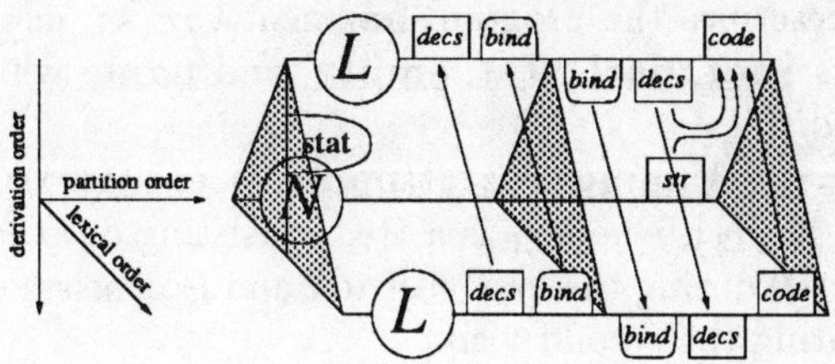

Fig. 7. A 3D drawing of production **stat**.

When we memo these visit sequence functions and use them to evaluate the program `pr1=(use z;use x;use y;var y;use z;var z;var x;use y;use x;use z;)`,33 visit sequence function calls are made; 7 of them (visit-N-1) are hits. After compiling the program `pr0=(use x;use y;var y;use z;var z;var x;use y;use x;use z;)`, the incremental compilation of `pr1` (note: `pr1` is `pr0` prefixed with `use z`) costs only 6 calls. Changing, inserting or deleting **decl** nodes is inherently hard since this not only changes the tree, but also the *env* attributes that are passed all over the tree. But as we will see later, these operations on **stat** nodes can be handled rather efficiently.

then it is better to compute and bind $f{\cdot}a$ than to bind a and compute $f{\cdot}a$ in visit j. The reason for this is that f need not be injective so that in the former case there is a chance that the binding does not change, even if a does. And since bindings are part of the cache key in incremental evaluation, this means more cache hits.

Signature
visit-S-1 :: $S \rightarrow code$
visit-L-1 :: $L \rightarrow env \times bind$
visit-L-2 :: $L \times env \times bind \rightarrow code$
visit-N-1 :: $N \rightarrow str$

visit-L-1 · **decl**$(N, L) = \langle d_0, b_0 \rangle$
  where $n :=$ visit-N-1 $\cdot N$
  ; $\langle d_1, b_1 \rangle :=$ visit-L-1 $\cdot L$
  ; $d_0 := [n] +\!\!+\ d_1$
  ; $b_0 :=$ push $\cdot n \cdot b_1$

visit-L-1 · **stat**$(N, L) = \langle d_0, b_0 \rangle$
  where $\langle d_1, b_1 \rangle :=$ visit-L-1 $\cdot L$
  ; $d_0 := d_1$
  ; $b_0 := b_1$

visit-S-1 · **root**$(L) = c_0$
  where $\langle d, b \rangle :=$ visit-L-1 $\cdot L$
  ; $e := d$
  ; $c_1 :=$ visit-L-2 $\cdot L \cdot e \cdot b$
  ; $c_0 := c_1$

visit-L-2 · **decl**$(N, L) \cdot e_0 \cdot b_0 = c_0$
  where $e_1 := e_0$
  ; $\langle n, b_1 \rangle :=$ pop $\cdot b_0$
  ; $c_1 :=$ visit-L-2 $\cdot L \cdot e_1 \cdot b_1$
  ; $c_0 := [-$ lookup $\cdot e_0 \cdot n] +\!\!+\ c_1$

visit-L-2 · **stat**$(N, L) \cdot e_0 \cdot b_0 = c_0$
  where $n :=$ visit-N-1 $\cdot N$
  ; $e_1 := e_0$
  ; $b_1 := b_0$
  ; $c_1 :=$ visit-L-2 $\cdot L \cdot e_1 \cdot b_1$
  ; $c_0 := [$lookup $\cdot e_0 \cdot n] +\!\!+\ c_1$

Fig. 8. Visit sequence functions with bindings.

5 The New Algorithm, the Same Example

In this section the new algorithm for evaluating (higher order) attribute grammars is explained. The explanation is based upon the example in the previous section and consists of the following four steps. Each of these steps will be discussed in more detail in the next sections.

Splitting Consider the tree l = **decl(name(A), stat(name(A), empty()))**, which has type L. It describes the program fragment `var A; use A;`. We will define new constructors $\underline{\textbf{root}}$, $\underline{\textbf{decl}}$, $\underline{\textbf{stat}}$, $\underline{\textbf{empty}}$, and $\underline{\textbf{name}}$ which are used in constructing splitted trees.
For example, $\underline{l}$ = $\underline{\textbf{decl}}$($\underline{\textbf{name}}$(A), $\underline{\textbf{stat}}$($\underline{\textbf{name}}$(A), $\underline{\textbf{empty}}$())), which has type $\underline{L}$, is the two tuple $\langle \underline{l}_1, \underline{l}_2 \rangle$, where $\underline{l}_1$ is a tree consisting of exactly those parts of l which are traversed during the first visit to l and $\underline{l}_2$ consists of those parts which are traversed during the second visit.

Memoing In order to have efficient incremental construction and efficient incremental evaluation of splitted trees, constructors will be memoed.

Elimination Splitting allows for an important optimization: the elimination of some tree nodes that consist of copyrules only.

Parameterisation To attribute the splitted tree $\underline{l}$ from above, we would call functions visit-L-1 $\cdot\, \underline{l}_1$ and visit-L-2 $\cdot\, \underline{l}_2$. So why not parameterise right away? The constructors $\underline{\underline{\textbf{root}}}$, $\underline{\underline{\textbf{decl}}}$, $\underline{\underline{\textbf{stat}}}$, $\underline{\underline{\textbf{empty}}}$, and $\underline{\underline{\textbf{name}}}$ are used in constructing a tuple of visit functions out of the tuples of visit functions of its sons.
For example, $\underline{\underline{l}}$ = $\underline{\underline{\textbf{decl}}}$($\underline{\underline{\textbf{name}}}$(A), $\underline{\underline{\textbf{stat}}}$($\underline{\underline{\textbf{name}}}$(A), $\underline{\underline{\textbf{empty}}}$())), which has type $\underline{\underline{L}}$, is the two tuple $\langle \underline{\underline{l}}_1, \underline{\underline{l}}_2 \rangle$, where $\underline{\underline{l}}_1$ = visit-L-1 $\cdot\, \underline{l}_1$ and $\underline{\underline{l}}_2$ = visit-L-2 $\cdot\, \underline{l}_2$; i.e. reduction at construction time.

5.1 Splitting

The first step is to split the tree. Each node (non-terminal) X is represented by a tuple of type $\underline{X} = \langle \underline{X}_1, \ldots, \underline{X}_{|X|} \rangle$ where $|X|$ is the number of visits to X. So, in our running example, we have $\underline{S} = \langle \underline{S}_1 \rangle$, $\underline{L} = \langle \underline{L}_1, \underline{L}_2 \rangle$ and $\underline{N} = \langle \underline{N}_1 \rangle$.

In order to be able to build trees with the splitted nodes $\underline{S}_1$, $\underline{L}_1$, $\underline{L}_2$ and $\underline{N}_1$, we have to split the constructors too. For each constructor **prod** on node X we define the splitted constructors $\underline{\mathbf{prod}}_1, \ldots, \underline{\mathbf{prod}}_{|X|}$ on respectively $\underline{X}_1, \ldots, \underline{X}_{|X|}$ such that $\underline{\mathbf{prod}}_i(\ldots \underline{Y}_j \ldots) :: \underline{X}_i$ if visit(Y, j) occurs in VSS(**prod**$(\ldots Y \ldots), i)$.

For example, the second visit to a **stat** node, visits its N son for the first time and its L son for the second. So, $\underline{\mathbf{stat}}_2 :: \underline{N}_1 \times \underline{L}_2 \rightarrow \underline{L}_2$. An important observation is that each visit i to a tree X occurs exactly once. This forms the basis for splitting:

$$
\begin{array}{lll}
\underline{S}_1 = \underline{\mathbf{root}}_1(\underline{L}_1, \underline{L}_2) & & \\
\underline{L}_1 = \underline{\mathbf{decl}}_1(\underline{N}_1, \underline{L}_1) & \qquad & \underline{L}_2 = \underline{\mathbf{decl}}_2(\underline{L}_2) \\
\quad\ \mid\ \underline{\mathbf{stat}}_1(\underline{L}_1) & & \quad\ \mid\ \underline{\mathbf{stat}}_2(\underline{N}_1, \underline{L}_2) \\
\quad\ \mid\ \underline{\mathbf{empty}}_1() & & \quad\ \mid\ \underline{\mathbf{empty}}_2() \\
\underline{N}_1 = \underline{\mathbf{name}}_1(str) & &
\end{array}
$$

The visit sequence functions from Fig. 8 are now easily transformed to visit sequence functions for the splitted tree: see Fig. 9. The original tree constructors have been replaced by tuple constructors which encapsulate the splitted constructors:

$$
\begin{array}{llll}
\underline{\mathbf{root}} & :: \underline{L} & \rightarrow \underline{S} & \underline{\mathbf{root}}([\underline{L}_1, \underline{L}_2]) = [\underline{\mathbf{root}}_1(\underline{L}_1, \underline{L}_2)] \\
\underline{\mathbf{decl}} & :: \underline{N} \times \underline{L} & \rightarrow \underline{L} & \underline{\mathbf{decl}}([\underline{N}_1], [\underline{L}_1, \underline{L}_2]) = [\underline{\mathbf{decl}}_1(\underline{N}_1, \underline{L}_1), \underline{\mathbf{decl}}_2(\underline{L}_2)] \\
\underline{\mathbf{stat}} & :: \underline{N} \times \underline{L} & \rightarrow \underline{L} & \underline{\mathbf{stat}}([\underline{N}_1], [\underline{L}_1, \underline{L}_2]) = [\underline{\mathbf{stat}}_1(\underline{L}_1), \underline{\mathbf{stat}}_2(\underline{N}_1, \underline{L}_2)] \\
\underline{\mathbf{empty}} & :: & \rightarrow \underline{L} & \underline{\mathbf{empty}}() = [\underline{\mathbf{empty}}_1(), \underline{\mathbf{empty}}_2()] \\
\underline{\mathbf{name}} & :: str & \rightarrow \underline{N} & \underline{\mathbf{name}}(str) = [\underline{\mathbf{name}}_1(str)]
\end{array}
$$

Higher order attributes should be built using the above tuple constructors. If a non-terminal attribute $\overline{X}$ is computed in VSS$(Y, 1)$ but visit$(\overline{X}, 1)$ occurs in VSS$(Y, 2)$ and visit$(\overline{X}, 2)$ occurs in VSS$(Y, 3)$, then naturally, $\overline{X}$ must be passed in a binding $Y^{1\rightarrow 2}$ and in a binding $Y^{1\rightarrow 3}$. But since $\overline{X}$ is splitted, it is much better to pass $\overline{\underline{X}}_1$ in $Y^{1\rightarrow 2}$ and $\overline{\underline{X}}_2$ in $Y^{1\rightarrow 3}$.

Signature

$$
\begin{array}{lll}
\text{visit-S-1} & :: \underline{S}_1 & \rightarrow code \\
\text{visit-L-1} & :: \underline{L}_1 & \rightarrow env \times bind \\
\text{visit-L-2} & :: \underline{L}_2 \times env \times bind & \rightarrow code \\
\text{visit-N-1} & :: \underline{N}_1 & \rightarrow str
\end{array}
$$

$$
\begin{array}{l}
\text{visit-L-1} \cdot \underline{\mathbf{decl}}_1(\underline{N}_1, \underline{L}_1) = [d_0, b_0] \\
\quad \text{where } n := \text{visit-N-1} \cdot \underline{N}_1 \\
\quad\quad ;\ [d_1, b_1] := \text{visit-L-1} \cdot \underline{L}_1 \\
\quad\quad ;\ d_0 := [n] +\!\!+\ d_1 \\
\quad\quad ;\ b_0 := \text{push} \cdot n \cdot b_1
\end{array}
$$

$$
\begin{array}{l}
\text{visit-L-1} \cdot \underline{\mathbf{stat}}_1(\underline{L}_1) = [d_0, b_0] \\
\quad \text{where } [d_1, b_1] := \text{visit-L-1} \cdot \underline{L}_1 \\
\quad\quad ;\ d_0 := d_1 \\
\quad\quad ;\ b_0 := b_1
\end{array}
$$

$$
\begin{array}{l}
\text{visit-S-1} \cdot \underline{\mathbf{root}}_1(\underline{L}_1, \underline{L}_2) = c_0 \\
\quad \text{where } [d, b] := \text{visit-L-1} \cdot \underline{L}_1 \\
\quad\quad ;\ e := d \\
\quad\quad ;\ c_1 := \text{visit-L-2} \cdot \underline{L}_2 \cdot e \cdot b \\
\quad\quad ;\ c_0 := c_1
\end{array}
$$

$$
\begin{array}{l}
\text{visit-L-2} \cdot \underline{\mathbf{decl}}_2(\underline{L}_2) \cdot e_0 \cdot b_0 = c_0 \\
\quad \text{where } e_1 := e_0 \\
\quad\quad ;\ [n, b_1] := \text{pop} \cdot b_0 \\
\quad\quad ;\ c_1 := \text{visit-L-2} \cdot \underline{L}_2 \cdot e_1 \cdot b_1 \\
\quad\quad ;\ c_0 := [-\ \text{lookup} \cdot e_0 \cdot n] +\!\!+\ c_1
\end{array}
$$

$$
\begin{array}{l}
\text{visit-L-2} \cdot \underline{\mathbf{stat}}_2(\underline{N}_1, \underline{L}_2) \cdot e_0 \cdot b_0 = c_0 \\
\quad \text{where } n := \text{visit-N-1} \cdot \underline{N}_1 \\
\quad\quad ;\ e_1 := e_0 \\
\quad\quad ;\ b_1 := b_0 \\
\quad\quad ;\ c_1 := \text{visit-L-2} \cdot \underline{L}_2 \cdot e_1 \cdot b_1 \\
\quad\quad ;\ c_0 := [\text{lookup} \cdot e_0 \cdot n] +\!\!+\ c_1
\end{array}
$$

Fig. 9. Visit sequence functions for splitted trees.

Splitting allows us to evaluate *changes* to **stat** nodes efficiently. Compiling the program `pr3=(use x;use y;var y;use z;var z;var x;use y;use x;use x;)` using memoed visit sequence functions for splitted trees costs 30 calls (6 hits for visit-N-1). If we evaluate **pr3** after **pr0** (for **pr0** see page 8; note: the last **use z** is changed to a **use x**), we only need 18 calls: 1 call for visit-L-1 which hits, 10 for visit-L-2 of which only the last hits, 6 hits for visit-N-1 and 1 miss for visit-S-1.

5.2 Memoing Constructors

Terms are often implemented by means of pointer structures. In order to save space, memoed constructors can be used: equal structures are shared. This has another major advantage: the term equality test reduces to fast pointer comparison. The effect of memoing constructors on the PASCAL-like program fragment

```
x:=x xor y; y:=x xor y; x:=x xor y
```

is illustrated in Fig. 10. This figure just illustrates the basic idea. The main advantage of memoing constructors is not the sharing of subtrees within a single tree (for example, multiple **name**(**x**) trees) although we do need this in order to have efficient evaluation of multiple instances of the same non-terminal attribute, but the sharing of subtrees between the old version and the updated version of the tree in an incremental environment.

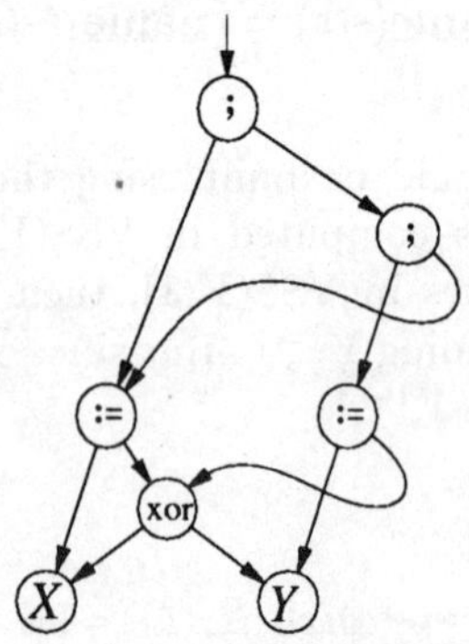

Fig. 10. Memoing constructors for statements and expressions.

Memoing is implemented as a "shell" around the constructor. Each constructor has its own memoed constructor; for efficiency reasons, the caches (hash tables) may be merged. As an example, see the memoed concat constructor on statements in Fig. 11.

Figure 12.**a** shows a sample tree for our grammar. Each circle represents a tree-node and the names below it label the tree constructors used. Figure 12.**b** shows an equivalent but splitted version. In order to make full use of splitting, not the tuple constructors but the splitted constructors themself should be memoed. Although a tuple of terms is generated instead of one tree, equal trees in the old case yield equal tuples in the splitted case. Memoing is not spoiled by splitting.

```
function memo–concat(s0 : stat, s1 : stat) : stat
  var s2 : stat
  begin
    if InHashtable("concat", s0, s1)
      then s2 := GetFromHashtable("concat", s0, s1)
      else s2 := concat(s0, s1); InsertInHashtable(s2)
    fi;
    return(s2)
  end
```

Fig. 11. The memoed concat constructor

5.3 Elimination of Copyrules

We already noticed noticed that a change to an N-son of a **stat** node doesn't change the term for the first visit: a **stat** production adds nothing to the first visit; it inserts some copyrules. This is an important observation: we may eliminate a $\underline{\mathbf{stat}}_1$ constructor altogether! To see this, we derive

$$
\begin{aligned}
& \text{visit-L-1}\cdot \underline{\mathbf{stat}}_1(\underline{L}_1) \\
= \quad & \quad \{ \text{ for definition of visit-L-1 see Fig. 9 } \} \\
& [d_0, b_0] \text{ where } [d_1, b_1] := \text{visit-L-1}\cdot \underline{L}_1;\ d_0 := d_1;\ b_0 := b_1 \\
= \quad & \quad \{ \text{ pairing } \} \\
& [d_0, b_0] \text{ where } [d_1, b_1] := \text{visit-L-1}\cdot \underline{L}_1;\ [d_0, b_0] := [d_1, b_1] \\
= \quad & \quad \{ \text{ substitution } \} \\
& [d_0, b_0] \text{ where } [d_0, b_0] := \text{visit-L-1}\cdot \underline{L}_1 \\
= \quad & \quad \{ \text{ substitution } \} \\
& \text{visit-L-1}\cdot \underline{L}_1
\end{aligned}
$$

This means that we may change the tuple constructor $\underline{\mathbf{stat}}$ to

$$\underline{\mathbf{stat}} :: \underline{N} \times \underline{L} \to \underline{L} \quad \underline{\mathbf{stat}}([\underline{N}_1], [\underline{L}_1, \underline{L}_2]) = [\underline{L}_1, \underline{\mathbf{stat}}_2(\underline{N}_1, \underline{L}_2)]$$

incorporating the elimination of copyrules. Figure 12.c shows a resulting tree. We now not only have cache hits for the first visit when we *change* the identifier of a **stat** node; we even have cache hits for the first visit after *adding* new **stat** productions, or *removing* existing **stat** productions! And in addition to this speed-up, we also gain in memory usage.

The number of calls in non-incremental compilation of the aforementioned programs `pr1` and `pr3` decreases from 33 to 26 respectively from 30 to 24. This is due to the absence of 7 respectively 6 $\underline{\mathbf{stat}}_1$ nodes. In the incremental compilation of these programs the extra gain is neglectable. However, for program `pr5=(use x;use y;var y;use z;var z;var x;use y;use x;use z;use x;)` (note: `pr5` is `pr0` postfixed with `use x`) the situation is different. Due to the elimination of 7 $\underline{\mathbf{stat}}_1$ nodes, there is a drop from 33 to 26 in non-incremental evaluation. But there is another drop till 20 for incremental compilation after `pr0`: 1 call for visit-L-1 which hits, 11 for visit-L-2 of which only the last hits, 7 hits for visit-N-1 and 1 miss for visit-S-1.

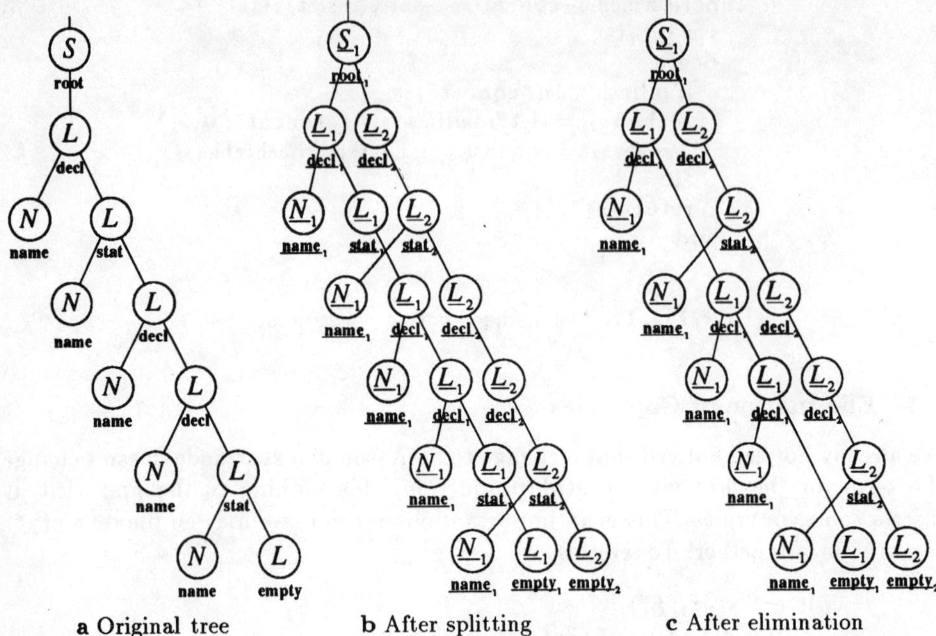

a Original tree **b** After splitting **c** After elimination

Fig. 12. The transformation.

5.4 Partial Parameterisation

In the previous section we discussed the elimination of $\underline{\mathbf{stat}}_1$ nodes. Although it is a succesful optimization, its applicability is limited since only nodes of the form $\underline{\mathbf{prod}}_i(\underline{X}_i)$ :: $\underline{X}_i$ may be eliminated.

The approach in this paragraph relaxes this constrain. The main idea is that the tree is no longer represented by a tuple of terms—one for each visit—but by its visit functions. So, each node (non-terminal) X is represented by a tuple of type $\underline{X} = [\underline{X}_1, \ldots, \underline{X}_{|X|}]$ where $\underline{X}_i$ is the type of visit-X-i· $\underline{X}_i$.
The types in our example are now easily deduceable:

$$
\begin{array}{lll}
\underline{S}_1 :: & & \rightarrow code \\
\underline{L}_1 :: & & \rightarrow env \times bind \\
\underline{L}_2 :: & env \times bind & \rightarrow code \\
\underline{N}_1 :: & & \rightarrow str
\end{array}
$$

The tuple constructors have the same structure as before:

$$
\begin{array}{llll}
\underline{\mathbf{root}} & :: \underline{L} & \rightarrow \underline{S} & \underline{\mathbf{root}}([\underline{L}_1, \underline{L}_2]) = [\underline{\mathbf{root}}_1(\underline{L}_1, \underline{L}_2)] \\
\underline{\mathbf{decl}} & :: \underline{N} \times \underline{L} & \rightarrow \underline{L} & \underline{\mathbf{decl}}([\underline{N}_1], [\underline{L}_1, \underline{L}_2]) = [\underline{\mathbf{decl}}_1(\underline{N}_1, \underline{L}_1), \underline{\mathbf{decl}}_2(\underline{L}_2)] \\
\underline{\mathbf{stat}} & :: \underline{N} \times \underline{L} & \rightarrow \underline{L} & \underline{\mathbf{stat}}([\underline{N}_1], [\underline{L}_1, \underline{L}_2]) = [\underline{L}_1, \underline{\mathbf{stat}}_2(\underline{N}_1, \underline{L}_2)] \\
\underline{\mathbf{empty}} & :: & \rightarrow \underline{L} & \underline{\mathbf{empty}}() = [\underline{\mathbf{empty}}_1(), \underline{\mathbf{empty}}_2()] \\
\underline{\mathbf{name}} & :: str & \rightarrow \underline{N} & \underline{\mathbf{name}}(str) = [\underline{\mathbf{name}}_1(str)]
\end{array}
$$

The constructors for visit functions, like $\underline{\textbf{stat}}_2$, may be thought of as an incomplete data flow graphs. These graphs have holes, where other graphs need to be pasted in. For example, in production **stat** the graph for the second visit sequence function has two holes. One for a complete graph visit-N-1$\cdot \underline{N}_1$ and one for a complete graph visit-L-2$\cdot \underline{L}_2$. Formulated differently visit function constructor $\underline{\textbf{stat}}_2$ is the graph of the combinator:

$$\begin{aligned} \underline{\textbf{stat}}_2(f,g) = [&\lambda \text{ v-N-1} :: \underline{N}_1 \text{ , v-L-2} :: \underline{L}_2 \text{ , } e_0 :: \mathit{env} \text{ , } b_0 :: \mathit{bind} \\ &: c_0 \text{ where } n := \text{v-N-1}; \; e_1 := e_0; \; b_1 := b_0; \\ &\qquad\qquad c_1 := \text{v-L-2}\cdot e_1 \cdot b_1; \; c_0 := [\text{lookup} \cdot e_0 \cdot n] + c_1 \\ ]&\cdot f \cdot g \end{aligned}$$

This approach has several advantages. First of all, a constructor that consists of copyrules only, may now be eliminated even if the underlying terms differ. To be more precise $\underline{\textbf{prod}}_i(\underline{Y}_j) :: \underline{X}_i$ may be eliminated if $\underline{Y}_j$ and $\underline{X}_i$ designate the same signatures $(\alpha \rightarrow \beta)$.

Furthermore, in the old case, the visit functions had to determine on which kind of node they were applied. For example, visit-L-1 could be applied to $\underline{\textbf{decl}}_1$ to $\underline{\textbf{stat}}_1$, and to $\underline{\textbf{empty}}_1$. The run-time case analyses is no longer needed since the correct graphs are combined during tree construction time.

Finally, it might even be possible to fold 0-airy visit functions, like $\underline{L}_1$, during tree construction time, thereby saving even more evaluation time.

6 Conclusions

We have presented a new evaluation technique for attribute grammars based on a functional approach. One large evaluation function is constructed for a given tree. This evaluation function can be efficiently incrementally updated using memoed constructors for visit functions. Efficient incremental evaluation is achieved by caching these functions.

The two uses of the abstract tree—a guide for the evaluator and a cache for the attributes—are separated this way, allowing us to optimize both aspects separately. Visit functions are made to depend only on that part of the tree which is actually visited by them, in order to generate more cache hits. Secondly, copyrules may be removed, thus saving visits and maximizing cache hits.

References

[Alb91] Alblas, Henk. *Introduction to Attribute Grammars.* In H. Alblas and B. Melichar (Eds.) *Attribute Grammars, Applications and Systems (SAGA '91)*, Lecture Notes in Computer Science, Vol. **545**, pages 1–15, Springer-Verlag, June 1991.

[DJL88] Deransart, Pierre, Martin Jourdan and Bernard Lorho. *Attribute Grammars. Definitions, Systems and Bibliography.* Lecture Notes in Computer Science, Vol. **323**, Springer-Verlag, August 1988.

[DJ90] Deransart, P, M Jourdan (Eds.). *Attribute Grammars and their Applications (WAGA '90).* Lecture Notes in Computer Science, Vol. **461**, Springer-Verlag, September 1990.

[HF92] Hudak, Paul and Joseph H. Fasel. *A Gentle Introduction to Haskell.* In ACM SIGPLAN Notices *Haskell special issue*, Vol. **27**, No. 5, May 1992.

[HPW92] Hudak, P., S. Peyton-Jones and P. Wadler (Eds.). *Report on the Programming Language Haskell, A Non-strict Purely Functional Language (Version 1.2).* In ACM SIGPLAN Notices *Haskell special issue*, Vol. **27**, No. 5, May 1992.

[Hug85] Hughes, John. *Lazy memo-functions.* In Jean-Pierre Jouannaud (Ed.) *Functional Programming Languages and Computer Architecture*, Lecture Notes in Computer Science, Vol. **201**, pages 129–146, Springer-verlag, 1985.

[Jon91] Jones, Mark P. *Introduction to Gofer 2.20*, Oxford Programming Research Group, November 1991.

[Kas80] Kastens, Uwe. *Ordered Attributed Grammars.* In Acta Informatica, Vol. **13**, pages 229–256, 1980.

[Knu68] Knuth, Donald E. *Semantics of context-free languages.* In Mathematical Systems Theory, Vol. **2**, No. 2, pages 127–145, Springer-Verlag, 1968.

[Knu71] Knuth, Donald E. *Semantics of context-free languages (correction).* In Mathematical Systems Theory, Vol. **5**, No. 1, pages 95–96, Springer-Verlag, 1971.

[Pug88] Pugh, W.W. *Incremental Computation and the Incremental Evaluation of Functional Programs.* Technical Report 88-936 and Ph.D. Thesis, Department of Computer Science, Cornell University, Ithaca, N.Y., August 1988.

[SV91] Swierstra, S.D. and H.H. Vogt. *Higher Order Attribute Grammars.* In H. Alblas and B. Melichar (Eds.) *Attribute Grammars, Applications and Systems (SAGA '91)*, Lecture Notes in Computer Science, Vol. **545**, pages 256–296, Springer-Verlag, June 1991.

[TC90] Teitelbaum, Tim and Richard Chapman. *Higher-Order Attribute Grammars and Editing Environments.* In Proceedings of the SIGPLAN '90 Conference on Programming Language Design and Implementation, Vol. **25**, No. 6 (proceedings), pages 197-208, June 1990.

[Tur85] Turner, D.A. *Miranda: A non-strict functional language with polymorphic types.* In Jean-Pierre Jouannaud (Ed.) *Functional Programming Languages and Computer Architecture*, Lecture Notes in Computer Science, Vol. **201**, pages 1-16, Springer-Verlag, 1985.

[VSK89] Vogt, H.H., S.D. Swierstra and M.F. Kuiper. *Higher Order Attribute Grammars.* In Proceedings of the SIGPLAN '89 Conference on Programming Language Design and Implementation, Vol. **24**, No. 7 (proceedings), pages 131-145, June 1989.

[VSK91] Vogt, Harald, Doaitse Swierstra and Matthijs Kuiper. *Efficient Incremental Evaluation of Higher Order Attribute Grammars.* In J. Maluszyński and M. Wirsing (Eds.) *Programming Language Implementation and Logic Programming (PLILP '91)*, Lecture Notes in Computer Science, Vol. **528**, pages 231–242, Springer-Verlag, 1991.

[Yeh83] Yeh, D. *On incremental evaluation of ordered attributed grammars.* In BIT, Vol. **23**, pages 308-320, 1983.

Strictness Analysis for Attribute Grammars

Mads Rosendahl

DIKU, University of Copenhagen
Universitetsparken 1, DK-2100 Copenhagen Ø
Denmark

E-mail rose@diku.dk

Abstract. Attribute grammars may be seen as a (rather specialised) lazy or demand-driven programming language. The "programs" in this language take text or parse trees as input and return values of the synthesised attributes to the root as output. From this observation we establish a framework for abstract interpretation of attribute grammars. The framework is used to construct a strictness analysis for attribute grammars. Results of the analysis enable us to transform an attribute grammar such that attributes are evaluated during parsing, if possible. The analysis is proved correct by relating it to a fixpoint semantics for attribute grammars. An implementation of the analysis is discussed and some extensions to the analysis are mentioned.

1 Introduction

As pointed out by Jourdan [1984] there are broadly speaking two approaches to attribute evaluation: either one restricts the class of attribute grammars and makes it possible to use an efficient evaluation strategy or one allows any well-defined attribute grammar but reduces the efficiency of the evaluation method. A large part of the work in Attribute Grammars has been concentrated on defining classes or subclasses of attribute grammars with special evaluation properties, or constructing and analysing classification methods (Deransart, Jourdan and Lorho [1988]).

We follow a different line by analysing attribute grammars rather than classifying them. Hence, the aim is to locate those parts of an attribute grammar for which more efficient implementation techniques are available. This approach has mainly been pursued with a view to optimising the storage management in attribute grammars (Kastens [1987] and Christiansen [1988]) but it has also been used for analysing the order of evaluation in an attribute grammar (see Jones and Madsen [1980] and Sassa, Ishizuka and Nakata [1987]).

In this paper we provide a semantic basis for this type of analysis based on abstract interpretation (Cousot and Cousot [1977] and Mycroft [1980]). The framework is based on a fixpoint semantics for attribute grammars in the style of Chirica and Martin [1979] which is then changed to give non-standard interpretations for static analysis of attribute grammars. Results from this kind of interpretations may be used to answer certain questions about the runtime behaviour of attribute grammars.

Attribute Grammars as a language has many similarities with lazy or demand-driven functional languages. From a parse tree an evaluator computes values of the synthesised attributes of the root symbol. The order of evaluation of attribute values is determined by "demand" or dependencies rather than the order in which they occur in the grammar. This resembles the situation for lazy functional languages where expressions and arguments are only computed when needed for evaluating the result of function calls.

Lazy functional languages seem very well suited for static analysis; strictness analysis, one of the most successful abstract interpretations, is designed for such languages. Much attention has been given to extending the original definition (Mycroft [1980]), to higher-order functions, lazy data structures, polymorphic type systems, and to finding efficient implementations of the analysis. In this paper, however, strictness analysis in the first-order case suffices for the application to attribute grammars.

Strictness analysis may be used to find arguments to functions which may be evaluated prior to the call, so as to change call-by-need to call-by-value. By doing this one may save both time and space as one does not need to build suspensions for expressions which may be evaluated later. Strictness analysis for attribute grammars enable us to find attributes which may be evaluated during parsing. By this, one may eliminate the need for symbolic expressions for attributes or parts of the parse tree. In this way one is likely to save both time and space during evaluation.

2 Notation and terminology

Most of the notation in this paper is standard. The semantic framework uses fixpoint semantics based on the theory of complete partial orders and continuous functions. Grammars are as usual context-free grammars.

We will make a few restrictions on the specification of grammars and attribute grammars to simplify the semantic description. The two main restrictions imposed here are that all productions should have a right hand side of a single terminal symbol or of n nonterminals for some fixed n, and that each nonterminal has exactly two attributes: one synthesised and one inherited. Any actual implementation of an analysis should not of course impose such restrictions on attribute grammars. These restrictions can in practice be made without loss of generality. The extension to allow m inherited and synthesised attributes ($m > 1$) is straightforward, as the evaluation of arguments in a fixpoint semantics is done lazily. Furthermore we allow several common extensions to the original definition of attribute grammars (Knuth [1968]) as expressions may contain conditionals (Gallier [1984]) and the root symbol may have an inherited attribute. In this way the analysis should be applicable to a very large class of attribute grammars.

2.1 Definitions

A *context-free grammar* (or *grammar*, for short) is a four-tuple $G = (R, P, N, T)$ of a root symbol $R \in N$, a finite set of productions $P = \{p_1, \ldots, p_k\}$, a finite set of nonterminals N, and a finite set of terminals T. To each production $p \in P$ there will be associated a left hand side symbol $\mathsf{lhs}(p) \in N$ and a right hand side of either n nonterminals: $\mathsf{rhs}(p) \in N^n$ or a terminal: $\mathsf{rhs}(p) \in T$. We assume that $N^n \cap T = \varnothing$. We may further assume (without loss of generality) that all nonterminals occurring in a production are distinct and distinct from the nonterminal on the left hand side.

The set of *parse trees* $\mathcal{T}_G$ for a grammar G is the smallest set such that

$$\begin{aligned}
\langle p, q\rangle \in \mathcal{T}_G \quad & \Leftrightarrow q \in T \wedge \mathsf{rhs}(p) = q \\
\langle p, t_1, \ldots, t_n\rangle \in \mathcal{T}_G & \Leftrightarrow t_j \in \mathcal{T}_G,\ j = 1, \ldots, n \wedge \\
& \qquad \mathsf{rhs}(p) = \langle q_1, \ldots, q_n\rangle \wedge \\
& \qquad \mathsf{lhs}(t_j \downarrow 1) = q_j,\ j = 1, \ldots, n
\end{aligned}$$

Notice that as parse trees we allow any tree built from productions in the grammar. We may from this define the subset of parse trees with the root symbol as the left hand side of the outermost production.

Let V be a set of values which includes numbers and boolean values. Let $\underline{c}_j, j \in \mathbb{N}$ be names for constants $c_j \in V$ and $\underline{a}_j, j \in \mathbb{N}$ be names for m-ary partial functions over V: $a_j : V^m \xrightarrow{p} V$.

An *attribute expression* (or *expression*, for short) is a string in the language

$$\begin{aligned}
e \rightarrow\ & \underline{c}_j \\
\mid\ & q_j.s\ , \quad j = 1, \ldots, n \\
\mid\ & q_0.i \\
\mid\ & \underline{a}_j(e_1, \ldots, e_m) \\
\mid\ & \textbf{if } e_1 \textbf{ then } e_2 \textbf{ else } e_3
\end{aligned}$$

The meaning or semantics of expressions will be defined later.

An *attribute grammar* is a context-free grammar G with a list of expressions associated with each production. For a production with n nonterminals on the right hand side, there will be $n + 1$ expressions, and for productions with one terminal symbol on the right hand side there will be one expression.

2.2 Notation

An attribute grammar may be specified as a list of *attributed productions* of the form

$$p : q_0 ::= q_1 \cdots q_n\ \{q_1.i := e_1;\ \ \ldots;\ q_n.i := e_n;\ \ q_0.s := e_{n+1}\}$$

where $\mathsf{rhs}(p) = \langle q_1, \ldots, q_n\rangle$ and $\mathsf{lhs}(p) = q_0$ and $[e_1, \ldots, e_n, e_{n+1}]$ is the list of expressions associated with production p. For productions with a single terminal symbol on the right hand side the form is

$$p : q_0 ::= q_1\ \{q_0.s := e\}$$

where e is the expression associated with production p.

The purpose of the $n + 1$ expressions in the first form of attributed productions is that expressions e_1 to e_n define the inherited attributes of the n nonterminals on the right hand side of the production, and that the expression e_{n+1} defines the synthesised attribute of the nonterminal on the left hand side. In the notation for attributed productions this is indicated by "$.i$" for inherited attributes and "$.s$" for synthesised attributes. This is made precise by the fixpoint semantics below.

The attributed productions may be seen as an abstract syntax for some other kind of notation of attribute grammars. Whether the attribute grammar is defined in OLGA (Jourdan, Bellec and Parigot [1990]), Aladin (Kastens [1984]), or as an extended attribute grammar (Watt and Madsen [1983]) is not central to this work.

3 Fixpoint semantics

The meaning of an attributed production is a function which maps a parse tree and the value of its inherited attribute to the value of its synthesised attribute. The meaning of an attribute grammar is an environment of such maps. The semantics follows the usual pattern for recursion equation systems (see Gordon [1979] and Schmidt [1986]).

The description differs from Chirica and Martin [1979] in that the semantics is given directly as an interpretation of the attribute grammar rather than as rules to construct a recursion equation system which defines the meaning. In spirit it is similar to the recursive evaluation method for attribute grammars (Engelfriet [1984] and Jourdan [1984]).

3.1 Semantic rules

In the semantics the domain of attribute values is $D = V_\perp$. An attributed production is given a meaning as a function of type $T_G \rightarrow D \rightarrow D$ which maps a parse tree and its inherited attribute to the value of its synthesised. An attribute expression in a production may depend on the inherited attribute to the nonterminal on the left hand side and to the synthesised attributes to the (at most) n nonterminals on the right hand side. For this reason the semantic function for expressions uses an environment of $n+1$ attribute values.

The semantics consists of three semantic functions, one for each of the syntactic categories in the language.

Syntactic categories

$ag \in AG$	$: ap_1 \cdots ap_k$	*attribute grammar*
$ap \in AP$		*attributed production*
$e \in Exp$		*expressions*

Semantic domains

$v \in D$	$: V_\perp$	*attribute values*
$t \in T_G$		*parse trees*
$\rho \in Env$	$: (T_G \rightarrow D \rightarrow D)^k$	*production environment*

Semantic functions

$\mathsf{M} : AG \rightarrow Env$

$\mathsf{P} : AP \rightarrow Env \rightarrow T_G \rightarrow D \rightarrow D$

$\mathsf{E} : Exp \rightarrow D^{n+1} \rightarrow D$

Semantic rules

$$\mathsf{M}\,[\![ap_1 \ldots ap_n]\!] = \\ \quad \mathsf{fix}(\lambda\rho.\ \langle \mathsf{P}\,[\![ap_1]\!]\,\rho, \ldots, \mathsf{P}\,[\![ap_k]\!]\,\rho\rangle\,)$$

$$\mathsf{P}\,[\![p : q_0 ::= q_1 \cdots q_n\ \{q_1.i := e_1;\ \ldots;\ q_n.i := e_n;\ q_0.s := e_{n+1}\}]\!]\,\rho\ t\ v = \\ \quad \mathbf{let}\ \langle p, t_1, \ldots, t_n\rangle = t\ \mathbf{and} \\ \qquad \langle p_{j_1}, \ldots\rangle = t_1\ \mathbf{and} \cdots \mathbf{and}\ \langle p_{j_n}, \ldots\rangle = t_n \\ \quad \mathbf{in}\ \mathsf{E}\,[\![e_{n+1}]\!]\,(\mathsf{fix}\,\lambda\xi.\langle((\rho{\downarrow}j_1)t_1)(\mathsf{E}\,[\![e_1]\!]\,\xi), \ldots, ((\rho{\downarrow}j_n)t_n)(\mathsf{E}\,[\![e_n]\!]\,\xi), v\rangle)$$

$$\mathsf{P}\,[\![p : q_0 ::= q_1\ \{q_0.s := e\}]\!]\,\rho\ t\ v = \mathsf{E}\,[\![e]\!]\,(\,\langle\bot, \ldots, \bot, v\rangle\,)$$

$$\begin{aligned} \mathsf{E}\,[\![q_j.s]\!]\,\xi &= \xi{\downarrow}j\ ,\ j = 1, \ldots, n \\ \mathsf{E}\,[\![q_0.i]\!]\,\xi &= \xi{\downarrow}(n+1) \\ \mathsf{E}\,[\![\underline{c}_j]\!]\,\xi &= c_j \\ \mathsf{E}\,[\![\underline{a}_j(e_1, \ldots, e_m)]\!]\,\xi &= \mathit{lift}(a_j)(\mathsf{E}\,[\![e_1]\!]\,\xi, \ldots, \mathsf{E}\,[\![e_m]\!]\,\xi) \\ \mathsf{E}\,[\![\mathbf{if}\ e_1\ \mathbf{then}\ e_2\ \mathbf{else}\ e_3]\!]\,\xi &= \mathbf{if}\ \mathsf{E}\,[\![e_1]\!]\,\xi = \mathit{true}\ \mathbf{then}\ \mathsf{E}\,[\![e_2]\!]\,\xi\ \mathbf{else} \\ &\ \mathbf{if}\ \mathsf{E}\,[\![e_1]\!]\,\xi = \mathit{false}\ \mathbf{then}\ \mathsf{E}\,[\![e_3]\!]\,\xi\ \mathbf{else}\ \bot \end{aligned}$$

where

$$\mathit{lift}(f) = \lambda\vec{x}.\ \mathbf{if\ some}\ x_j = \bot\ \mathbf{then}\ \bot\ \mathbf{else} \\ \qquad\qquad \mathbf{if}\ f(\vec{x})\ \mathbf{undefined\ then}\ \bot\ \mathbf{else}\ f(\vec{x})$$

The semantic function $\mathsf{P}\,[\![ap]\!]$ takes a production environment $\rho \in \mathit{Env}$, a tree $t \in T_G$, and an inherited value $v \in D$ and returns the value of the synthesised attribute.

The semantic function $\mathsf{E}\,[\![e]\!]$ evaluates an expression from an environment of values of the $n+1$ attributes it may depend on: the n synthesised attributes to nonterminals on the right hand side and the inherited to left hand side.

The innermost fixpoint iteration is not as unpleasant as it may look: it is over the domain D^{n+1} which with D as a flat cpo will have a finite height of $n+2$. The fixpoint can be found using a lazily evaluated *letrec*-expression.

By allowing conditional expressions in attribute expressions one may have attribute grammars with circular dependency graphs but where no attributes in practice are circularly defined. If an attribute is circularly defined the semantics will give the value $\bot$. The bottom element $\bot$ is used both for runtime errors and for circularly defined attributes.

4 Strictness analysis

Strictness analysis (Mycroft [1981]) was developed as a method to detect when call-by-value could be used instead of call-by-need in lazy functional languages. In this section we will recall the central definitions in strictness analysis and show how they may be applied to attribute grammars.

4.1 Strictness of functions

Let f be a function of type $D^n \to D$. If the function satisfies

$$\forall \vec{v} \in D^n . f(v_1, \ldots, v_{j-1}, \bot, v_{j+1}, \ldots, v_n) = \bot$$

for some j then we know that at calls of f, the jth argument may be evaluated prior to calling f. This is because nontermination of the argument would have resulted in nontermination of f anyway and we may therefore use call-by-value instead of call-by-need in function calls. We then say that f is *strict* in its jth argument.

Strictness, however, is not a decidable property but by analysis we may find a sufficient condition for strictness. In this analysis we represent values in D in a two-point domain $\mathbb{2}$ of the values 0 and 1

$$\mathbb{2} = \{0, 1\}, \qquad 0 \sqsubseteq 1$$

where $\bot$ in D is represented by 0 and all other values are represented by 1.

$$\alpha_1 \ : D \to \mathbb{2} \qquad\qquad \alpha_1(d) = \textbf{if } d = \bot \textbf{ then } 0 \textbf{ else } 1$$

We may now construct a function $f^\sharp$ with the property

$$\forall \vec{v} \in D^n . \alpha_1(f(\vec{v})) \sqsubseteq f^\sharp(\alpha_1(v_1), \ldots, \alpha_1(v_n))$$

This is always possible as the constant function 1 is a candidate but better alternatives may be constructed with a little bit of ingenuity. If this function has the property that $f^\sharp(1, \ldots, 1, 0, 1, \ldots, 1) = 0$ where all arguments are 1 except at the jth place then f is strict in its jth argument. We may say that for $f^\sharp$ a value of 1 means *possibly* defined while a value of 0 means *definitely* undefined.

The function $f^\sharp$ gives an upper bound to the termination properties of f. In a similar fashion we may give a lower bound with a function $f^\flat$ with the property

$$\forall \vec{v} \in D^n . \alpha_1(f(\vec{v})) \sqsupseteq f^\flat(\alpha_1(v_1), \ldots, \alpha_1(v_n))$$

For this function a value of 1 means *definitely* defined while a value of 0 means *possibly* undefined. The function $f^\flat$, however, is not quite as important when analysing functional programs.

4.2 Abstract domains

Below we define an interpretation for attribute grammars which evaluates the strictness properties of attribute expressions. As for functional programs it is based on abstractions of the values in the usual fixpoint semantics. We will use three abstraction functions, one for each of the arguments to the semantic function **P**.

Attribute values are abstracted as the values 0 or 1 in the two-point domain $\mathbb{2}$ using the abstraction function α_1 defined above.

Parse trees my be abstracted as productions where a production denotes the set of parse trees with the given production in the root node. When necessary productions may be abstracted as nonterminals where a nonterminal denotes the set of production with the nonterminal on the right hand side. The abstraction function for parse trees is:

$$\alpha_2 \; : \mathcal{T}_G \rightarrow P \qquad \alpha_2(t) = t \downarrow 1$$

Production environments of type $(\mathcal{T}_G \rightarrow D \rightarrow D)^k$ can be abstracted in two ways to abstract environments $Env' = (P \rightarrow 2 \rightarrow 2)^k$. The first will give an upper bound to the strictness properties of an environment and the other will give a lower bound.

$$\begin{aligned} \alpha_3^\sharp \; &: Env \rightarrow Env' & \alpha_3^\sharp(\rho) &= \langle \alpha_4^\sharp(\rho \downarrow 1), \ldots, \alpha_4^\sharp(\rho \downarrow k)\rangle \\ & & \alpha_4^\sharp(f) &= \lambda p.\lambda v, \bigsqcup\{\alpha_1(f\, t\, d) | \alpha_2(t) = p,\, \alpha_1(d) = v\} \\ \alpha_3^\flat \; &: Env \rightarrow Env' & \alpha_3^\flat(\rho) &= \langle \alpha_4^\flat(\rho \downarrow 1), \ldots, \alpha_4^\flat(\rho \downarrow k)\rangle \\ & & \alpha_4^\flat(f) &= \lambda p.\lambda v, \bigsqcap\{\alpha_1(f\, t\, d) | \alpha_2(t) = p,\, \alpha_1(d) = v\} \end{aligned}$$

The abstraction functions $\alpha_3^\flat$ and $\alpha_3^\sharp$ are defined as the usual lifting of abstraction functions to function domains.

$$\forall \rho : \alpha_3^\flat(\rho) \sqsubseteq \alpha_3^\sharp(\rho)$$

We will also need an abstraction function for attribute value environments:

$$\alpha_5 \; : D^{n+1} \rightarrow 2^{n+1} \qquad \alpha_5(\xi) = \langle \alpha_1(\xi \downarrow 1), \ldots, \alpha_1(\xi \downarrow (n+1))\rangle$$

Using these abstraction functions we may define two new semantic functions $\mathbf{P}^\sharp$ and $\mathbf{P}^\flat$ which satisfy the following properties:

$$\forall \rho, t, v : \mathbf{P}^\sharp \, [\![ap]\!]\, \alpha_3^\sharp(\rho)\, \alpha_2(t)\, \alpha_1(v) \sqsupseteq \alpha_1(\mathbf{P}\, [\![ap]\!]\, \rho\, t\, v)$$
$$\forall \rho, t, v : \mathbf{P}^\flat \, [\![ap]\!]\, \alpha_3^\flat(\rho)\, \alpha_2(t)\, \alpha_1(v) \sqsubseteq \alpha_1(\mathbf{P}\, [\![ap]\!]\, \rho\, t\, v)$$

It is now possible to define the various semantic functions and establish their relationship with the standard semantics.

4.3 Analysis

We will here only define the semantic function $\mathbf{M}^\flat$ (with $\mathbf{P}^\flat$ and $\mathbf{E}^\flat$). The semantic function $\mathbf{M}^\sharp$ follows a similar pattern.

$$\begin{aligned} &\mathbf{M}^\flat \, [\![ap_1 \ldots ap_n]\!] = \\ &\quad \mathsf{fix}(\lambda\rho.\, \langle \mathbf{P}^\flat \, [\![ap_1]\!]\, \rho, \ldots, \mathbf{P}^\flat \, [\![ap_k]\!]\, \rho\rangle\,) \end{aligned}$$

$$\begin{aligned} &\mathbf{P}^\flat \, [\![p : q_0 ::= q_1 \cdots q_n \; \{q_1.i := e_1; \;\; \ldots; \; q_n.i := e_n; \; q_0.s := e_{n+1}\}]\!]\, \rho\, p'\, v = \\ &\quad \mathbf{E}^\flat \, [\![e_{n+1}]\!] (\mathsf{fix}\, \lambda\xi.\langle \bigsqcap\{\rho \downarrow \ell(p_\ell)\, (\mathbf{E}^\flat \, [\![e_1]\!]\, \xi) | \ell : \mathsf{lhs}(p_\ell) = \mathsf{rhs}(p) \downarrow 1\}, \ldots, \\ &\quad\quad \bigsqcap\{\rho \downarrow \ell(p_\ell)\, (\mathbf{E}^\flat \, [\![e_n]\!]\, \xi) | \ell : \mathsf{lhs}(p_\ell) = \mathsf{rhs}(p) \downarrow n\}, v\rangle) \\ &\mathbf{P}^\flat \, [\![p : q_0 ::= q_1 \; \{q_0.s := e\}]\!]\, \rho\, p'\, v = \mathbf{E}^\flat \, [\![e]\!] (\, \langle \bot, \ldots, \bot, v\rangle\,) \end{aligned}$$

$$\begin{aligned} \mathbf{E}^\flat \, [\![q_j.s]\!]\, \xi &= \xi{\downarrow}j \\ \mathbf{E}^\flat \, [\![q_0.i]\!]\, \xi &= \xi{\downarrow}(n+1) \\ \mathbf{E}^\flat \, [\![\underline{c}_j]\!]\, \xi &= 1 \\ \mathbf{E}^\flat \, [\![\underline{a}_j(e_1, \ldots, e_m]\!]\, \xi &= min(\mathbf{E}^\flat \, [\![e_1]\!]\, \xi, \ldots, \mathbf{E}^\flat \, [\![e_m]\!]\, \xi) \\ \mathbf{E}^\flat \, [\![\mathbf{if}\; e_1 \;\mathbf{then}\; e_2 \;\mathbf{else}\; e_3]\!]\, \xi &= min(\mathbf{E}^\flat \, [\![e_1]\!]\, \xi, \mathbf{E}^\flat \, [\![e_2]\!]\, \xi, \mathbf{E}^\flat \, [\![e_3]\!]\, \xi) \end{aligned}$$

4.4 Correctness

As correctness proof for this analysis we will prove that for any attribute grammar *ag* the following condition holds.

$$\mathsf{M}^\flat [\![ag]\!] \sqsubseteq \alpha_3^\flat(\mathsf{M} [\![ag]\!])$$

There are two levels of fixpoint induction involved in the proof since the semantics contains two nested fixpoints.

Correctness for the inner level is obtained automatically as the interpretation of the basic operations can be induced using the abstraction function α_1:

$$\forall \xi.\ \mathsf{E}^\flat [\![e]\!] \alpha_5(\xi) \sqsubseteq \alpha_1(\mathsf{E} [\![e]\!] \xi)$$

In the next level we will prove that:

$$\forall \rho, t, v. \mathsf{P}^\flat [\![ap]\!] \alpha_3^\flat(\rho)\, \alpha_2(t)\, \alpha_1(v) \sqsubseteq \alpha_1(\mathsf{P} [\![ap]\!] \rho\, t\, v)$$

This requires fixpoint induction. The proof requires the following relationship.

$$\begin{aligned} \forall \rho, \xi, t, j.\ & \bigsqcap\{\alpha_3^\flat(((\rho) \downarrow \ell\,) p_\ell)\, (\mathsf{E}^\flat [\![e_j]\!] \alpha_5(\xi)) | \ell : \mathsf{lhs}(p_\ell) = \mathsf{rhs}(p) \downarrow j\} \\ & \sqsubseteq \alpha_1(((\rho \downarrow i_j)\ t_j)(\mathsf{E} [\![e_j]\!] \xi)) \\ \text{where} \quad & \langle \mathrm{p}, \mathrm{t}_1, \ldots, \mathrm{t}_n \rangle = \mathrm{t} \textbf{ and } \langle \mathrm{p}_{\mathrm{i}_j}, \ldots \rangle = \mathrm{t}_j \end{aligned}$$

For a start we notice that

$$\mathsf{rhs}(p) \downarrow j = \mathsf{lhs}(t_j \downarrow 1) = \mathsf{lhs}(p_{i_j})$$

This means that

$$\begin{aligned} & \bigsqcap\{\alpha_3^\flat(((\rho) \downarrow \ell\,) p_\ell)\, (\mathsf{E}^\flat [\![e_j]\!] \alpha_5(\xi)) | \ell : \mathsf{lhs}(p_\ell) = \mathsf{rhs}(p) \downarrow j\} \\ & \sqsubseteq\ \alpha_3^\flat(((\rho) \downarrow i_j\,) p_{i_j})\, (\mathsf{E}^\flat [\![e_j]\!] \alpha_5(\xi)) \\ & =\ \bigsqcap\{\alpha_1((\rho \downarrow i_j) t'\ d) | \alpha_2(t') = p_{i_j},\ \alpha_1(d) = \mathsf{E}^\flat [\![e_j]\!] \alpha_5(\xi)\} \\ & \sqsubseteq\ \alpha_1(((\rho \downarrow i_j)\ t_j)(\mathsf{E} [\![e_j]\!] \xi)) \end{aligned}$$

Both levels of fixpoint induction follow now directly.

4.5 Using the analysis

Strictness analysis for attribute grammars can give two kinds of information. It can identify those productions where the inherited attribute is definitely needed to evaluate the synthesised attribute, and it can find the productions where the synthesised attribute can be evaluated without using the inherited attribute.

This may be expressed using the semantic functions as

$$(\mathsf{M}^\sharp [\![ag]\!] \downarrow j) p_j 0 = 0$$

which states that the inherited attribute is needed to evaluate the synthesised in the jth production; and

$$(\mathsf{M}^\flat [\![ag]\!] \downarrow j) p_j 0 = 1$$

which says that the inherited attribute is not used for evaluating the synthesised in the jth production.

An attributed production in a grammar may not satisfy either of these properties as the inherited attribute may be needed for some input but not used for other input. As an example consider

$$\begin{array}{ll} A \rightarrow \text{“a”}\, B\, \text{“d”} & \{\, A.s := 3 + B.s \\ & \phantom{\{\,} B.i := A.i + 2\} \\ B \rightarrow \text{“b”} & \{\, B.s := B.i + 1\} \\ B \rightarrow \text{“c”} & \{\, B.s := 0\} \end{array}$$

where the inherited attribute to A is needed for the string “**abd**” but not used for the string “**acd**”.

5 Evaluation order

From the strictness analysis we may derive other interpretations which analyse the order of evaluation in an attribute grammar. One example of this type of analysis is given below. It will enable us to determine when attributes can be evaluated during left-to-right parsing and it is obtained from the strictness analysis by ensuring that expressions defining inherited attributes may not use the values of the synthesised attribute to the right in a production.

$$\begin{array}{l} \mathsf{M}^{\triangleright}[\![ap_1 \ldots ap_n]\!] = \\ \quad \mathsf{fix}(\lambda\rho.\, \langle \mathsf{P}^{\triangleright}[\![ap_1]\!]\rho, \ldots, \mathsf{P}^{\triangleright}[\![ap_k]\!]\rho\rangle\,) \end{array}$$

$$\begin{array}{l} \mathsf{P}^{\triangleright}[\![p : q_0 ::= q_1 \cdots q_n\ \{q_1.i := e_1;\ \ldots;\ q_n.i := e_n;\ q_0.s := e_{n+1}\}]\!]\,\rho\ p'\ v = \\ \quad \mathsf{E}^{\triangleright}[\![e_{n+1}]\!](\mathsf{fix}\,\lambda\xi.\langle \bigsqcap\{\rho \downarrow \ell(p_\ell)\,(\mathsf{E}^{\triangleright}[\![e_1]\!]\,\mathit{strip}_1(\xi)) | \ell : \mathsf{lhs}(p_\ell) = \mathsf{rhs}(p) \downarrow 1\}, \ldots, \\ \qquad\qquad\qquad\qquad \bigsqcap\{\rho \downarrow \ell(p_\ell)\,(\mathsf{E}^{\triangleright}[\![e_n]\!]\,\mathit{strip}_n(\xi)) | \ell : \mathsf{lhs}(p_\ell) = \mathsf{rhs}(p) \downarrow n\}, v\rangle) \end{array}$$

$$\mathsf{P}^{\triangleright}[\![p : q_0 ::= q_1\ \{q_0.s := e\}]\!]\,\rho\ p'\ v = \mathsf{E}^{\triangleright}[\![e]\!](\,\langle \bot, \ldots, \bot, v\rangle\,)$$

$$\mathsf{E}^{\triangleright}[\![e]\!]\xi = \mathsf{E}^{\flat}[\![e]\!]\xi$$

where

$$\mathit{strip}_j(\,\langle v_1, \ldots, v_n, v_{n+1}\rangle\ = \ \langle v_1, \ldots, v_{j-1}, \bot, \ldots, \bot, v_{n+1}\rangle$$

The soundness of this analysis follows directly from the strictness analysis due to the monotonicity of the semantic functions:

$$\mathsf{M}^{\triangleright}[\![ag]\!] \sqsubseteq \mathsf{M}^{\flat}[\![ag]\!]$$

5.1 Using the analysis

Using the result of this analysis we may identify the productions where the synthesised attribute may be evaluated during LR-parsing if the inherited attribute is evaluated.

In the semantics this may be expressed as the condition

$$(\mathbf{M}^{\triangleright}\, [\![ag]\!] \downarrow j)p_j 1 = 1$$

which says that in the jth production the synthesised attribute may be evaluated if the inherited is defined.

5.2 Comparison

Our analysis may be seen as an extension to the concept of an L-attribute grammar (Aho, Sethi and Ullman [1986]). Whether it is possible to insert semantic actions into productions and preserve LR(1) (or LALR(1)) properties is not expressed by this analysis. That has been addressed by Purdom and Brown [1980] where they find safe positions in productions for such actions to be inserted.

The analysis in Jones and Madsen [1980] examines the structure of the LR-parse table and the attribute grammar and it can be used to find a list of attributes which can be evaluated (known) during LR-parsing. If this list contains all attributes one may conclude that it is an L-attribute grammar.

The life time analysis in Kastens [1987] can be used to identify attributes which can be stored in a global variable or using a stack. The analysis is applicable to ordered attribute grammars and is based on transformations of the visit-sequences for the attribute grammar.

In both Jones and Madsen [1980] and Kastens [1987] the analysis will associate properties with each attribute in the grammar. Our analysis may give a finer grained information in that it examines the attributes in each production. It may be possible to evaluate an attribute during parsing in one production but not in other productions.

5.3 Example

A number of questions about the computational behaviour of an attribute grammar can be expressed using these interpretations.

In the attribute grammar below we will allow two synthesised attributes and two inherited attributes to the nonterminal Y.

$$\begin{array}{ll}
S \rightarrow Y & \{\, Y.a := 1 \\
 & \;\; Y.c := f_1(Y.b) \\
 & \;\; S.x := Y.d \} \\
Y_1 \rightarrow \text{“}\mathbf{x}\text{”}\ Y_2 & \{\, Y_1.b := f_2(Y_1.a,\ Y_2.b) \\
 & \;\; Y_2.a := f_3(Y_1.a) \\
 & \;\; Y_2.c := f_4(Y_1.c,\ Y_2.b) \\
 & \;\; Y_1.d := f_5(Y_2.d,\ Y_1.c) \} \\
Y \rightarrow \text{“}\mathbf{z}\text{”} & \{\, Y.b := f_6(Y.a) \\
 & \;\; Y.d := 3 \}
\end{array}$$

In this example the attribute $Y_1.b$ can be evaluated during LR-parsing in the second production and the attributes $Y.b$ and $Y.d$ can be evaluated during LR-parsing in the third production. This is under the assumption that the inherited attribute a to Y can be evaluated during parsing. Using the semantic function $\mathsf{M}^{\triangleright}$ this may be expressed as

$$(\mathsf{M}^{\triangleright}[\![..]\!] \downarrow 2)(Y_1 \rightarrow \text{“}\mathbf{x}\text{”}\ Y_2)\,\langle 1,0\rangle \;=\; \langle 1,0\rangle$$

and

$$(\mathsf{M}^{\triangleright}[\![..]\!] \downarrow 3)(Y \rightarrow \text{“}\mathbf{z}\text{”})\,\langle 1,0\rangle \;=\; \langle 1,1\rangle$$

5.4 Implementation

The strictness and evaluation order analyses have been implemented in a demonstrator system. The system uses a DAG-based strategy for attribute evaluation and the analyses can decrease the size of the DAG by allowing evaluation of some attribute values during parsing.

6 Further work

The analyses described here can be extended in several ways. It is not possible in this framework to give a satisfactory analysis of storage management in attribute grammars. Doing that using abstract interpretation is likely to require an instrumented standard semantics. Such extensions are frequently seen in analysis of functional and logic programming languages.

The treatment of inherited and synthesised attributes in this framework is somewhat asymmetrical. A better analysis of inherited attributes may be obtained if the semantics is based on a minimal function graph framework (Jones and Mycroft [1986]). This, however, is not easy as that technique was developed for an eager language and attribute evaluation uses laziness. The extension of the minimal function graph framework to a first-order lazy functional language is considered by Rosendahl and Mycroft [1992].

Resent work in strictness analysis have examined extensions of the analysis to languages with higher-order functions and lazy data structures. Whether such results may be applicable to attribute grammars seems to be an open question. Attribute values are normally considered to be simple values in sets but the extension to allow higher-order functions and lazy data structures as attribute values is semantically well understood.

7 Conclusion

In this paper we have presented a framework for semantically based analysis of attribute grammars. The framework is used to define a strictness analysis for attribute grammars which is proved correct with respect to a standard fixpoint semantics. The analysis has been implemented as part of an attribute evaluation system.

The framework may be the basis for a number of analyses of attribute grammars. Attributes that may be evaluated during LR-parsing may be identified by an evaluation-order analysis for attributes.

Perhaps the most surprising result of this work is that Attribute Grammars as a language is well suited to semantic-based program analysis. It is a clean and relatively simple language with a tractable fixpoint semantics. Furthermore, "programs" in Attribute Grammars are typically run frequently enough for nearly any type of program optimisation to be profitable.

Acknowledgements. Thanks to Alan Mycroft, Gordon Gran, Helen Hansen, Troy Ferguson and the anonymous referees for comments on drafts of this paper. This work was partly supported by the Danish SNF Dart grant.

References

Aho, A. V, Sethi, R, and Ullman, J. D. *Compilers: Principles, Techniques, and Tools.* Addison Wesley, [1986].

Chirica, L. M and Martin, D. F. *An Order-Algebraic Definition of Knuthian Semantics.* Math. Systems Theory **13**, pp. 1–27, [1979].

Christiansen, H. *Structure Sharing in Attribute Grammars.* In *Programming Languages Implementation and Logic Programming, Orléans* (Deransart, P, Lorho, B, and Maluszynski, J, eds.), pp. 180–200. Volume 348 of LNCS. Springer-Verlag, May, [1988].

Cousot, P and Cousot, R. *Abstract Interpretation: A Unified Lattice Model for Static Analysis of Programs by Construction or Approximation of Fixpoints.* In *4th POPL, Los Angeles, CA*, pp. 238–252, Jan., [1977].

Deransart, P, Jourdan, M, and Lorho, B. *Attribute grammars. Definitions, systems, and bibliography.* Volume 323 of LNCS. Springer-Verlag, [1988].

Engelfriet, J. *Attribute Grammars: Attribute Evaluation Methods.* In *Methods and Tools for Compiler Construction* (Lorho, B, ed.), pp. 103–138. Cambridge Univ. Press, [1984].

Gallier, J. *An Efficient Evaluator for Attribute Grammars with Conditionals.* Tech. Rep. MS-CIS-83-36. Philadelphia, PA, May, [1984].

Gordon, M. J. C. *The Denotational Description of Programming Languages: An Introduction.* Springer-Verlag, [1979].

Jones, N. D and Madsen, M. *Attribute-influenced LR parsing.* In *Semantics-Directed Compiler Generation* (Jones, N. D, ed.), pp. 393–407. Volume 94 of LNCS. Springer-Verlag, [1980].

Jones, N. D and Mycroft, A. *Data Flow Analysis of Applicative Programs using Minimal Function Graphs.* In *13th POPL, St. Petersburg, Florida*, pp. 296–306, Jan., [1986].

Jourdan, M. *Recursive Evaluators for Attribute Grammars: An Implementation.* In *Methods and Tools for Compiler Construction* (Lorho, B, ed.), pp. 139–163. Cambridge Univ. Press, [1984].

Jourdan, M, Bellec, C. L, and Parigot, D. *The OLGA Attribute Grammar Description Language.* In *WAGA'90* (Deransart, P and Jourdan, M, eds.), pp. 222–237. Volume 461 of LNCS. Springer-Verlag, Oct., [1990].

Kastens, U. *The GAG-System—A Tool for Compiler Construction.* In *Methods and Tools for Compiler Construction* (Lorho, B, ed.), pp. 165–182. Cambridge Univ. Press, [1984].

Kastens, U. *Lifetime Analysis for Attributes.* Acta Inf. **24**(6), pp. 633–652, Nov., [1987].

Knuth, D. E. *Semantics of Context-Free Languages.* Math. Systems Theory **2**(2), pp. 127–145, June, [1968]. Correction ibid 5(1):95–96 Mar. 1971.

Mycroft, A. *The Theory and Practice of Transforming Call-by-Need into Call-by-Value.* In *International Symposium on Programming'80, Paris, France* (Robinet, B, ed.), pp. 269–281. Volume 83 of LNCS. Springer-Verlag, Apr., [1980].

Mycroft, A. *Abstract Interpretation and Optimising Transformations for Applicative Programs.* Ph.D. Thesis. Univ. of Edinburgh, Dec., [1981].

Purdom, P. W and Brown, C. A. *Semantic routines and LR(k) parsers.* Acta Inf. **14**(4), pp. 299–316, Oct., [1980].

Rosendahl, M. *Abstract Interpretation and Attribute Grammars.* PhD thesis. Cambridge University, [1991].

Rosendahl, M and Mycroft, A. *Lazy minimal function graphs,* [1992]. Under preparation.

Sassa, M, Ishizuka, H, and Nakata, I. *ECLR-attributed Grammars: a Practical Class of LR-attributed Grammars.* Inform. Process. Lett. **24**(1), pp. 31–41, Jan., [1987].

Schmidt, D. A. *Denotational Semantics: A Methodology for Language Development.* Allyn and Bacon, Newton, MA, [1986].

Watt, D. A and Madsen, O. L. *Extended Attribute Grammars.* Comput. J. **26**(2), pp. 142–153, [1983].

Checking and Debugging of Two-level Grammars

Sadegh SAIDI and Jean-Francois BOULICAUT

Ecole Centrale de Lyon
Département Mathématiques-Informatique-Systèmes
BP 163
F-69131 Ecully cedex
e-mail : saidi@cc.ec-lyon.fr

Abstract. An extension of PROLOG which supports software specification by means of a class of two-level grammars is presented. AFFLOG logic programs are typed and modes can be specified if desired. By examining their underlying grammatical properties, a static analysis is performed. Our purpose is to support translator writing starting from a grammatical model that has been checked and debugged.

1 The context

Data processing can be viewed fundamentally as the transformation of data delivered as character strings into results which are character strings too. Therefore, programs should be designed as translators of the language defining the input data into the language defining the output data. Processing steps are considered as semantic computations on some intermediate languages.

Typical approaches of the so-called *grammatical programming framework* have been described e.g. in [Hehner-83,Torii-84]. However, these works are limited from the following points of view :

- the grammatical formalisms which are used. In general, only the context-free approximation of the input language is formalized.
- the static checks which are performed on the definitions. Few works emphasize the need to check and debug the specifications.

Our goal is to propose a powerful grammatical formalism (Chomsky's class 0) that helps to write readable specifications which can still be machine-oriented and automatically evaluated (e.g. to produce parsers or translators). We investigate the use of two-level grammars and in particular the Extended Affix Grammar formalism (EAG) [Watt-74].

In [Boulicaut-92], a Wide Spectrum Grammatical Programming Framework is proposed. Starting from formal specification by means of an EAG, a program (i.e. a translator) is considered as a device that computes tuples from a characteristic relation of this EAG. In this framework, the refinement of the specification, from prototyping through efficient implementation relies on affix grammars. A compiler compiler like STARLET [Beney-90] is used when we have to compute deterministic translations (a realistic need).

Besides, there is a close relationship between context-sensitive grammar processing and logic programming [Kowalski-79,Colmerauer-75,Deransart-88]. Chomsky's class 0 languages can be defined by logic grammars such as Metamorphosis Grammars [Colmerauer-75] or Definite Clause Grammars (DCG) [Pereira-80], which are easily compiled into PROLOG programs.

However, experiences show that a PROLOG translator writer needs to define "metastructures" to improve the readability of written translators and to check well-formedness conditions. Even during the prototyping phase, efficiency has to be improved by a backtracking control and an informed use of unification (taking concatenation associativity into account...). The production of more reliable PROLOG programs is made easier by using systems which have explicit type definitions. Two-level grammars like EAG provide a mean of expression for these metastructures and their relationships with PROLOG are well-known [Maluszynski-82a].

The main goal of our current research is to support the specification process by means of EAG. J. Maluszynski studied the question of programming with transparent W-grammars [Maluszynski-82ab,84] and the first experimental implementation of a logic programming language that should support these ideas [Maluszynski-82c,Näslund-87]. Then, our purpose is to explore the methodological impact of multiple transfers between grammatical and logic programming using EAG instead of transparent W-grammars.

From a methodological point of view (see Fig. 1), our approach aims to take the most of grammatical modelling and logic programming. There are three important relations during the life-cycle of a program : the *intended relation*, (the intended declarative semantics), the *specified relation* (what is stated by the specification) and the *computed relation* (what the programming system computes). A program design method must supply systematic design elements for these three relations, in particular help to debug computed and specified relations.

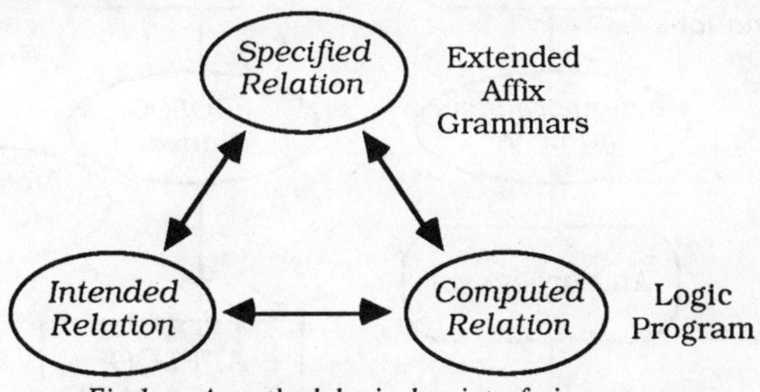

Fig 1 : A methodological point of view

Since programs are considered as translators, the specification method relies on techniques borrowed from compiler design (the specified relation is described by an EAG) while the relation is computed through logic programming. We also write logic programs which do not generate a language (the specified relation is described by Horn clauses and the language generated by the underlying grammar is reduced to the empty string). Informations can be extracted from these logic programs provided one consider them as two-level grammars.

As a first step towards computer-assisted grammatical modelling, we propose the experimental tool AFFLOG.

AFFLOG can be considered to be :

• A two-level grammatical formalism. A text is a two-level grammar which borrows concepts from extended affix grammars and logic grammars. Thus, such a text will generate a language. The AFFLOG formalism aims to bridge the gap between the informal specification of a problem and its formal one by enhancing readability (the use of strings instead of compound terms).

• An extension of PROLOG. A PROLOG program is a special case of an AFFLOG program where a (meta) grammar specifies the structure of the terms and where the terminal vocabulary is empty (i.e. its language is reduced to the empty string).

2 The AFFLOG Programming Tool

2.1 An overview

An AFFLOG program mainly consists of a metagrammar (CF-rules describing intermediate languages i.e. the syntax of the terms which will be used) and a hypergrammar which is the definition of a context-sensitive grammar.

Figure 2 illustrates the processing done by the AFFLOG logic programming system.

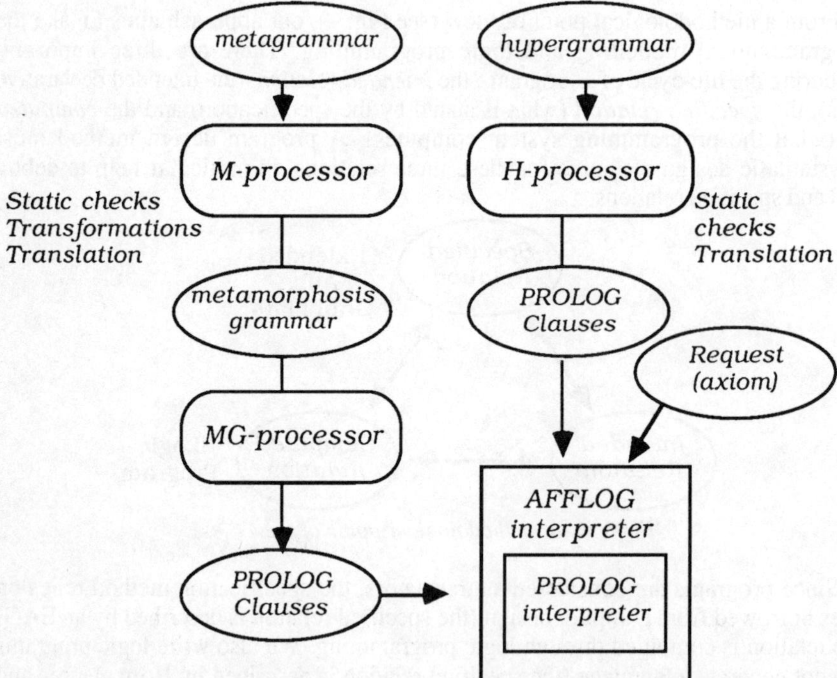

Fig. 2 : An overview of the AFFLOG two-level grammar processor

The M-processor compiles the metagrammar when it is well-formed (see § 2.2.3). The H-processor compiles the hypergrammar provided that the static analysis is successful (see § 2.3).

Let us introduce AFFLOG semantics thanks to a self-explanatory program. We consider the question of an environment construction in a small programming language.

E1 (comments in italic style)

The metagrammar is :

DECS <= DEC DECS ; EMPTY.
one DECS is a list of DEC which may be reduced to EMPTY
DEC <= IDF TYPE.
one DEC is an IDF followed by a TYPE
TYPE <= "ref" TYPE ; BASIC.
BASIC <= "int" ; "bool".
a BASIC is the string ""int" or the string "bool"
IDF <= "i" ; "j" ; "k" .

The hypergrammar is :

declarations (DEC DECS) <- declaration (DEC), more_declarations (DECS).
declaration (IDF TYPE) <- ?IDF, type (TYPE).
more_declarations (DECS) <- ?";", declarations (DECS).
type (ref TYPE) <- ?"ref" , type (TYPE).
type (BASIC) <- ?BASIC.

The axiom is S : declarations(DECS).

?X reads a symbol (PROLOG term) on input and unifies it with X.

Given the *query* : <- declarations (DECS1).
If the input string is "k bool ; j ref ref int" then the provided answer is declarations(k bool j ref ref int), a variable-free instance of the axiom S.

Let us introduce more precisely AFFLOG semantics.

2.2 AFFLOG Semantics

An AFFLOG text can be considered either as an extended affix grammar or as a logic program. We will define its semantics from both points of view.

Formal definition of AFFLOG grammars

An AFFLOG grammar is a 8-uple $(M_n,M_t,M_r,H_n,H_t,H_r,T,S)$

Here, (M_n,M_t,M_r) is called a *metagrammar* where M_n is a finite set of *non-terminal affixes*, M_t is a finite set of *terminal affixes* and M_r is a finite set of context-free *affix rules* i.e. a subset of $M_n \otimes (M_n \cup M_t)^*$ and M_n and M_t are assumed to be disjoint.

A variable is an element of M_n possibly concatenated to a natural number. If V_m is the set of variables which are built on the nonterminal m, V is the union of the sets V_m, $m \in M_n$. For all m in M_n, the language generated by the CF-grammar (M_n,M_t,M_r,m) defines the domain for the variables of V_m.

Then, $Hg=(H_n,H_t,H_r,T,S)$ is called an *hypergrammar*.

H_n is a set of (basic) *hypernotions*. These hypernotions are built with a functor name and parameters which are *grammatical terms* (sentential forms of a CF-grammar (M_n,M_t,MR,m)). We use the following syntax :

functor_name $(e_1,...,e_n)$ where $\exists m_i \in M_n,\ m_i \Rightarrow^* e_i$ (by application of affix rules)

H_t is a set of *predicates*. The right-hand side of a predicate definition contains only PROLOG predicate calls and thus can not generate a language.

H_r is a finite subset of $H_n \otimes (H_n \cup H_t \cup T)^*$ called the set of *hyperrules*.

$T=TT \cup TM$ is the *terminal alphabet* (whose symbols are prefixed by '?') where TT is a finite set of terminal symbols which appears in the right-hand side of the hyperrules while TM is a finite set of terminal symbols which belong to the domains of the variables (terminal affixes which are terminal symbols). For the above example E1, T={";","ref"}$\cup$ L(IDF)$\cup$L(BASIC).

$S \in H_n$ is the *axiom*.

The *uniform replacement rule* is the basic mechanism for language production in a two-level grammar. Following [Maluszynski-84], an hyperreplacement is any string homomorphism θ on $(V \cup M_t)^*$ which replaces variables occurring in the grammati-cal terms by legal productions according to the metarules.

The images of hypernotions under hyperreplacements are called hypernotion instances. A ground instance is called a protonotion (a variable-free instance of an hyper-notion). The set of protonotions is the nonterminal alphabet of a CF-grammar which generates a language : the *protogrammar*. Considering the extension of hyperreplacements to hyperrules (hyperrules instances), the set of ground hyperrules is the possibly infinite set of (context-free) rules of the protogrammar. Ground instances of the axiom constitute the set of axioms of the protogrammar.

L(G), the *language* generated by an AFFLOG grammar G is a set of terminal strings whose elements are derived from ground instances of S (using protorules).

In fact, we work with partially instanciated hypernotions and hyperrules and construct a stepwise refinement of hyperrules in order to find derivations in G. Thus, the problem of *grammatical unification* must be solved : how can we compute an hyper-replacement θ such that $\theta(h)=\theta(h')$ where h and h' are hypernotions ?

When it exists, θ is called a grammatical unifier for h and h' and is given as a set of substitutions. The grammatical unification problem is a kind of string equation problem where the domains of variables are context-free languages [Maluszynski-82b]. The AFFLOG grammatical unification procedure is presented in § 2.2.3.

Let us consider a second example, E2, whose axiom is instr (ENV,TYPE). This AFFLOG program assigns a type to a simple assignment instruction given an environ-ment produced by E1.

E2		*Context-free definition*	*Static semantics*
INSTR	::	ID , ":=" , EXPR.	int ⊗ int -> int & bool ⊗ bool -> bool
EXPR	::	PRIM , "+", EXPR ;	int ⊗ int -> int
		"(", EXPR, "=", EXPR,")";	bool ⊗ bool -> bool & int ⊗ int -> bool
		PRIM.	bool -> bool & int -> int
PRIM	::	ID ; NBR.	

Metagrammar

```
ENV    <= ITEM ENV ; EMPTY.
ITEM   <= ID TYPE.
TYPE   <= 'int' ; 'bool' ; 'ref' TYPE .
PRIM   <= ID ; NBR.
ID     <= "i"; "j"; "k";....
NBR    <= "1"; "2"; "3";....
```

Hypergrammar

```
(h1)  instr (ENV, TYPE) <-
              ?ID, ?':=', type (ID,ENV,TYPE), expr (ENV,TYPE).
(h2)  expr (ENV, 'int')    <-
              ?PRIM , ?'+' , type (PRIM,ENV,'int'), expr (ENV,'int').
(h3)  expr (ENV,TYPE)   <- ?PRIM , type (PRIM,ENV,TYPE) .
(h4)  expr (ENV, 'bool')   <-
              ?'(', expr (ENV,TYPE) , ?'=' , expr (ENV,TYPE)  , ?')' .
(h5)  type (NBR,ENV,'int').
(h6)  type (ID, ID  TYPE  ENV, TYPE) .
(h7)  type (ID, ID1  TYPE1  ENV, TYPE)  <-
              dif (ID,ID1),  type (ID,ENV,TYPE).
```

Axiom

S : instr (ENV,TYPE).

Query : <- type (i int k int, j bool,TYPE)
If the input string is "j := (i +1 = k)", we get TYPE=bool.

Grammatical semantics

The *specified relation* of a grammar G whose axiom S is the hypernotion $A(t_1,...,t_n)$ is the set of S instances which can produce some terminal strings of L(G) : that is $\exists\omega\in T^*$ such that $A(t'_1,...,t'_n)\Rightarrow^*\omega$ where t'_i is an instance of t_i.

Example :
instr (i int j int, int) belongs to the specified relation for E2 (ω = "i:=j").

A term t'_i may contain variables in which case $A(t'_1,...,t'_n)$ describes a relation where t'_i would not be variable-free. Hence, these terms define a subset of the language generated by the metagrammar. For example, instr (ID int ID1 int, int) describes the set of tuples associated to the generic assignment "ID := ID1 ".

The *characteristic relation* of G is a binary relation which links the specified relation to the generated sentences ($\omega\in$ L(G)). The couple <instr(i int j int, int), "i:=j"> is an example of tuples over the characteristic relation defined by E2.

Thus, one may associate a subset of the specified relation to each sentence of L(G). String ω is called the *control*. It allows language-controlled computations of a specified relation subset.

Example : noun ("mal","sing") <- ?"bob"

Arguments "mal" and "sing" are the properties of the noun "bob". But "bob" is used as a control string which selects the instance noun("mal",sing") among the possible instances of noun(tp,nb) (tp∈{"mal","fem"}, nb∈{"sing","plur "}).

Operational semantics

The operational semantics of an AFFLOG program is described by the procedure which computes instances of the axiom S for a given goal or query i.e. which computes a subset of the characteristic relation. Let us introduce some auxiliary concepts and discuss the problem of grammatical unification in AFFLOG.

We write $\theta_1(N)$ to denote that a grammatical unifier θ_1 is applied to the hypernotion N ; $\theta_1 \circ \theta_2$ denotes the composition of θ_1 and θ_2 ; MGGU denotes the most general grammatical unifier for two grammatical terms t_1 and t_2. If θ is the MGGU of t_1 and t_2, then θ is given as a set of substitution pairs [x/y].

$N =_g N'$ means that $N=A(t_1,...,t_n)$ and $N'=A(t'_1,...,t'_n)$ can be grammatically unified. We write that $N \in_g Ns$, $N \in H_n$, $Ns=(H_n)^+$ (N grammatically belongs to the set Ns) if at least one hypernotion $N' \in Ns$ such that $N =_g N'$ exists.

Unification in AFFLOG

Grammatical unification is the basic mechanism for context transmission. In AFFLOG, it works on the syntactic structures of the grammatical terms i.e. trees whose nodes are labelled by nonterminal affixes and whose leaves are terminal affixes. These representations are abstractions of grammatical terms presented as terms of an initial algebra associated to the metagrammar. By considering a CF-grammar as a specification whose equation set is empty, the initial algebra operators are defined by the production rules of the CF-grammar [Goguen-77] and the mapping between strings and algebraic terms is performed by classical parsing technics [Saidi-92a].

Hence, we must check that for each grammatical term, there exists a CF-grammar (M_n,M_t,M_r,m) which generates it. The unification of two terms produces a set of pairs [x/y] where x is a variable whose associated nonterminal symbol in the metagrammar derives y. The efficiency of the unification algorithm can be improved by user-defined modes associated to the hypernotions. The following notations are used : '+' for ground, '-' for free and '?' for any (e.g. for E2 instr(+,-), expr (+,-)...).

Given the following (meta)grammar and two grammatical terms T_1 and T_2

```
INSTR <= ID, ":=", EXPR.
EXPR <= PRIM, "+",  EXPR ; "(", EXPR, "=",  EXPR, ")"; PRIM.
PRIM <= ID ; NBR.
```

T_1 :   k := (PRIM = EXPR)
T_2 :   ID := (x = j + 1)

Tree(T_1)= instr(id("k"), ":=", expr("(", expr(prim(PRIM)), "=", expr(EXPR), ")"))
Tree(T_2)= instr(id(ID), ":=" , expr ("(", expr(prim(id("x"))),
"=" , expr(prim(id("j"))), "+", expr(prim(nbr("1"))), ")"))

We must perform the following confrontations : ID v. k, id("x") v. PRIM and EXPR v. expr(prim(id("j"))), "+", expr(prim(nbr("1")))). These are terms of the algebra associated to the CF-grammar.

A function from these terms onto $(T \cup V)^*$ gives the following MGGU :
θ=[ID/k, PRIM/x, EXPR/ j+1]

In order to compute unifiers, the metagrammar must not contain ε-rule and must not be "infinitely ambiguous" to enable our non-deterministic parser to find a finite set of parse trees [Saidi-92ab]. A well-formed metagrammar is compiled into definite clauses and the programmer gets a parser for it.

Resolution in AFFLOG

The AFFLOG operational device uses the SLD-resolution whose unification part is extended to grammatical unification and a PROLOG-like strategy ($\mathcal{R}$) (considering hypernotions as predicates and hyperrules as definite clauses).

A query consists of (B,δ) where B is the goal and δ a control string.

For a program P and a goal B such that $S=_g B$, a SLD-derivation of $P \cup \{B\}$ following $\mathcal{R}$ consists of a sequence B, B_1 ... of goals, a sequence H_1, H_2 ... of hyperrules from P and a sequence θ, θ_1... of MGGU such that B_{i+1} can be derived from B_i and H_{i+1} by using θ_{i+1} according to $\mathcal{R}$.

The first unification between axiom S and goal B (the question) gives $\theta(B)=\theta(S)$ where θ is the MGGU of B and S. The resulting goal is $(\theta(S),\delta)$ with $\delta \in T^*$.

Let $\delta=\omega\alpha$ where $\omega,\alpha \in T^*$, $\omega=\omega_1...\omega_k$ is the string already parsed while $\alpha=\alpha_1...\alpha_p$ is the string to be parsed.

If at step i, we have $B_i=\theta_i(A)$ $(A \leftarrow A_1,...,A_m.\ A_j \in (H_n \cup H_t))$ and the control string $\omega\alpha$, then we can produce $B_{i+1}=\theta_{i+1}(A')$ and the control string $\omega'\alpha'$ from B_i by using the MGGU θ_{i+1} via $\mathcal{R}$ by one of the following rules :

① If A_1=?X, X is a variable, if X and α_1 can be grammatically unified and $[X/\alpha_1]$ is the resulting unifier
then $\theta_{i+1}=\theta_i o[X/\alpha_1]$, $\omega'=\omega\alpha_1$, $\alpha'=\alpha_2...\alpha_p$, $A'=A_2,...,A_m$.

② If A_1=%q, and if the PROLOG predicate q succeeds (the empty string is derived) producing θ_{i+1} as resulting unifier
then $\omega'=\omega$, $\alpha'=\alpha$, $A'=A_2,...,A_m$.

③ If $A_1 \in H_n$ and if $H \leftarrow H_1,...,H_q$. is the hyperrule chosen following $\mathcal{R}$ and if θ_{i+1} is the MGGU of A_1 and H
then $\theta_{i+1}(A_1)=\theta_{i+1}(H)$
$\omega'=\omega$, $\alpha'=\alpha$, $A'=H_1,...,H_q,A_2,....,A_m$.

2.3 Checking and debugging AFFLOG programs

Construction and use of a Pattern Grammar

A parse in an AFFLOG grammar G is directed by a context-free parse of the input using a *pattern grammar* G_S such that $L(G_S) \supseteq L(G)$ [Maluszynski-84]. Derivation trees in G_S could be used when trying to build derivations in the AFFLOG program. Note that this process may not terminate.

Let us call *definition hypernotion* (resp. *application hypernotion*) an hypernotion which occurs on the left-hand side (resp. right-hand side) of the hyperrules. Let H_D be the set of definitions and H_A be the set of applications. Clearly $S \in H_A$. Let $\equiv$ be the binary relation on H (subset of H_n) defined as follows :

$h \equiv h'$ if $h =_g h'$ and $h \in H_D$ and $h' \in H_A$ or $h \in H_A$ and $h' \in H_D$.

This relation is called the cross-reference relation and its transitive closure is an equivalence relation on H. We denote by [h] the equivalence class of h.

In order to produce the pattern grammar $G_S=(N_S,T,R_S,S_S)$ we proceed as follows : the set N_S of the equivalence classes [h] is computed ; T is the terminal alphabet ; S_S is the equivalence class [S] and in each hyperrule $r \in H_r$, we replace each hypernotion $h \in H_n$ by [h]. Predicate symbols for which the generated language is empty are then removed from N_S and metarules associated to the variables which occur on the right-hand side of the hyperrules (prefixed by '?') are added to R_S. Finally, G_S is translated into a metamorphosis grammar [Colmerauer-75].

For E2, we produce the following grammar :

```
A      ::   ID, ':=' , C , B.
B      ::   PRIM, '+', C, B.
B      ::   PRIM, C.
B      ::   '(', B, '=', B, ')'.
C      ::   C ; .
ID     ::   ...
NBR    ::   ...
PRIM   ::   ...
```

where A = {instr (ENV, TYPE)}
B = {expr (ENV,TYPE), expr (ENV,'int'), expr (ENV,'bool')}
C = {type (ID,ENV,TYPE), type (ID, ID TYPE ENV, TYPE)...}

$S \in_g A$

Note that before looking for a derivation which might produce an instance of S, the input string could be parsed according to G_S by bottom-up parsing methods [Nilsson-86].

A special case of AFFLOG program must be reported : if $T=\varnothing$ and $S \Rightarrow^* \varepsilon$ we have a PROLOG program for which there is no user-defined language control. Grammatical unification enables typed PROLOG programming and in that case every instance of the specified relation can be computed.

E3 : List concatenation
L <= EMPTY ; X L.
X <= symbol.
conc (EMPTY,L,L) .
conc (X L,L1, X L2) <- conc (L,L1,L2).
S=conc (L1,L2,L3).
The pattern grammar is : A .
A :: A .
with A={ conc(EMPTY,L,L), conc(X.L1,L2,X.L3), conc(L1,L2,L3) }, $S \in_g A$.

Pattern grammar construction provides a grammar whose language is a super set of the one generated by the original AFFLOG grammar. Experimentations might be done to check if a given string belongs to the language generated by the pattern grammar. Some special conditions are required to get a one-to-one correspondence between the derivations in both grammars [Wegner-80]. Another use of the pattern grammar is to enable an off-line derivation. One may extract all dependencies between grammatical terms and build an equational system to be solved when a derivation is constructed in the pattern grammar [Maluszynski-82a, Isakowitz-91].

A first check on the hypergrammar consists in considering an application hypernotion (h) and looking for some definition hypernotion (h') which is grammatically unifiable to h. We check that the axiom is grammatically unifiable with the query before the activation of the derivation procedure. If user-defined modes are associated to the hypernotions, the above checks take them into account.

Construction and use of a Hypernotion schematas

Being given the equivalence classes, an algorithm computes a *most specific generalizer* (MSG) for each of them. This algorithm is a kind of anti-unification algorithm [Plotkin-69]. Informally, the MSG for a set of hypernotions is an hypernotion such that all the elements of the set are particular instances.

For E2, we get MSG(A) = instr (ENV, TYPE)
MSG(B) = expr (ENV,TYPE)
MSG(C) = type (ID,ENV,TYPE)

In [Saidi-92b], we propose an algorithm which computes the MSG and guaranties that for each equivalence class, the MSG is unique under some conditions. We also check whether there exists an unique derivation for each member of a given equivalence class (starting from the associated MSG).

This helps the translation of AFFLOG programs into DCGs and may provide the transparency condition to EAG (see bellow).

Grammatical consequence and use of Hypernotion schematas

For an AFFLOG program whose pattern grammar is $G_S=(N_S,R_S,T,S_S)$, the following sets are built recursively :

$L_0=T$

$L_{n+1}=L_n \cup \{A \,/\, (A :: W) \in R_S,\ W=w_1,...,w_k\ ,\ k \geq 0,\ w_i \in (N_S \cup T), w_i \in L_n\}$

So, $\forall n$, if $A \in L_n$ with $n>0$ then $A \Rightarrow^* x,\ x \in T^*$

The algorithm stops at step k if it does not add any new element to L_{k-1}. Thus, k is such that $L_k=L_{k-1}$, while for n<k, $L_{n-1} \neq L_n$ and L_n contains at least one more symbol (a nonterminal $\in N_S$) than L_{n-1}. Since N_S is finite, clearly k is finite and we have $k \leq card(N_S)$.

$X \in N_S$ is called a *grammatical consequence* of P if $X \in L_k$. This concept is naturally extended to every hypernotion occurring in P.

For E2, we get (see equivalence classes A,B and C previously given) :
L_0 = { ID, NBR, PRIM, ":=", "+", "=", "(", ")"}
$L_1 = L_0 \cup \{C\}$
$L_2 = L_1 \cup \{B\}$
$L_3 = L_2 \cup \{A\}$
k=3 , $S_S \in L_3$.

For E3 we get : $L_0=\varnothing$, $L_1=L_0 \cup \{A\}$, k=1, $S_S \in L_1$

The grammatical consequence concept is used to perform some static checks : the set $L=L_k-L_0$ is computed and then used to build a metarule whose right-hand side is the disjunction of MSGs associated with the equivalence classes represented by L elements. This metarule (called ATOM in [Maluszynski-84]) is very close to the "PREDICATES" definitions section in Turbo Prolog [Borland-86]. If the programmer specifies it, the consistency between the specified rule and the computed one is checked : the right-hand side elements of the specified rule must belong to the computed equivalence classes.

For E2, having L={A,B,C}, we get :
ATOM <= instr (ENV, TYPE) ; expr (ENV,TYPE) ; type (ID,ENV,TYPE).

The construction of the ATOM metarule could provide a transparency condition [Maluszynski-84] for AFFLOG grammars provided that the following open problem is solved :

If there is a unique derivation for every equivalence class elements starting from the corresponding MSG then the metagrammar whose axiom is ATOM is not ambiguous.

Static analysis is finished by checking whether all hypernotions can be derived from ATOM and whether for each application there exists at least one definition which can be grammatically unified with it. The hypergrammar is then translated into PROLOG clauses.

From AFFLOG grammars to Definite Clause Grammars

AFFLOG grammars can be translated to DCGs if we succeed in computing the MSGs. In this case, grammatical terms are replaced by their termal representations which are parse trees. MSGs guide this translation since they provide informations about the derivation tree roots, that is, functional symbols are known when rewriting strings into compound (PROLOG) terms.

The following DCG is generated for E2 :

```
(r1)    instr(env(ENV), type(TYPE))         -->
                [ID], [':='], type(prim(id(ID)),env(ENV),type(TYPE)),
                expr(env(ENV),type(TYPE)), {id(ID)}.
```

```
(r2)    expr(env(ENV), type(ent))          -->
                 [PRIM] , ['+'] , type(prim(id(PRIM)),env(ENV),type(int)) ,
                 expr(env(ENV),type(int)) , {prim(PRIM)}.

(r3)    expr(env(ENV), type(ent))          -->
                 [PRIM] , ['+'] , type(prim(nbr(PRIM)),env(ENV),type(int)) ,
                 expr(env(ENV),type(int)) , {prim(PRIM)}.

(r4)    expr(env(ENV), type(TYPE))         -->
                 [PRIM], type(prim(id(PRIM)),env(ENV),type(TYPE)),
                 {prim(PRIM)}.

(r5)    expr(env(ENV), type(TYPE))         -->
                 [PRIM] , type(prim(nbr(PRIM)),env(ENV),type(TYPE)) ,
                 {prim(PRIM)} .

(r6)    expr(env(ENV), type(bool))         -->
                 ['('] , expr(env(ENV), type(TYPE)) , ['='] ,
                 expr(env(ENV), type(TYPE)) , [')'] .

(r7)    type(prim(nbr(NBR)), env(ENV), type(int)) --> [].

(r8)    type(prim(id(ID)), env([item(id(ID), type(TYPE)), env(ENV)]),
                         type(TYPE))       --> [] .

(r9)    type(prim(id(ID)), env([item(id(ID1), type(TYPE1)), env(ENV)]),
                         type(TYPE))       -->
                 {dif(prim(id(ID)), prim(id(ID1)))} ,
                 type(prim(id(ID)), env(ENV), type(TYPE)).

id(X)            :- X=i ; X=j ; X=k.
dif(X,Y)         :- X \=Y.
prim(X)          :- id(X) ; nbr(X).
nbr(X)           :- X=1 ; X=2 ; X=3 .
```

Note that rules (r1)...(r5) take into account the fact that the H-schemata for *type* (i.e. type(PRIM, ENV, TYPE)) represents all the possible configurations of parse trees associated to ID and NBR. These trees have PRIM at their roots and either a number (NBR) or an identifier (ID) as their leaves.

Query example :
If the input string is "j:=(i+1=k)" and if the value of ENV is <i int k int j bool>, the query instr (ENV, TYPE) is submitted to PROLOG as the following term :

```
?- instr(env([item(id(i),type('int')),env([item(id('k'),type('int')),
                         env([item(id('j'),type('bool')),env('empty')])])])]),
                 type(TYPE),[j, :=, '(',i,'+',1,'=',k,')'], []).
```

The computed value for TYPE is given by type (TYPE)=type (bool) meaning that TYPE value is "bool".

3 Conclusion

We presented some of our current work on AFFLOG programs static analysis. The AFFLOG interpreter has been implemented in PROLOG (2500 lines). A grammatical unification algorithm as well as a grammatical resolution procedure have been developed. The resolution can be controlled by terminal string derivations belonging to the language specified by the program. We emphasize the static checks, not only those which are related to type-sensitive string unification but also to hypergrammar checking.

AFFLOG has been designed to study program construction by means of two-level grammars (in particular the extended affix grammars). It supports specification debugging within a Wide Spectrum Grammatical Programming Framework [Boulicaut-92]. These specifications can be used (and transformed) when we want to produce translators using the STARLET/GL compiler compiler [Beney-90].

Apart from this interpreter, we have also implemented various logic grammar processors : Definite Clause Grammars, Metamorphosis Grammars, Definite Clause Translation Grammars [Abramson-84] and Gapping Grammars [Dahl-84]. This toolbox is used to develop experimental systems in order to study two-level grammar properties from both the theoretical and the practical points of view. For instance, partial specification of modes and automatic error processing are actually studied.

References

Abramson-84 ABRAMSON (H.). Definite Clause Grammars and the Logical Specification of Data Types as Unambiguous CF- Grammars. Proc. of Int. Conf. of FGCS, Tokyo (J), 1984, p. 678-685.

Beney-90 BENEY (J.), BOULICAUT (J.F.). STARLET : an affix-based compiler compiler designed as a Logic Programming System. In : Proceedings of the Third International Workshop on Compiler Compilers CC'90, October 22-24, 1990, Schwerin (G), D. HAMMER Ed., Springer-Verlag, LNCS 477, p. 71-85.

Borland-86 BORLAND Int. Turbo Prolog Owner's Handbook, Scott Valley (USA), 1986.

Boulicaut-92 BOULICAUT (J.F.). Towards a Wide Spectrum Grammatical Programming Framework. Ph-D Thesis: INSA Lyon, february 1992, 320 p. (in French)

Colmerauer-75 COLMERAUER (A.). Metamorphosis Grammars. Research Report GIA (Aix-Marseille II, Luminy), november 1975.

Dahl-84 DAHL(V.), ABRAMSON(H.). On Gapping Grammars. in : Proceedings of the 2nd. ICLP, Uppsala (S), 1984.

Deransart-88 DERANSART (P.), MALUSZYNSKI (J.). A Grammatical View of Logic Programming. in : Proceedings of the 1st Int. Workshop PLILP 88, Orléans, mai 1988, (P. DERANSART, B. LOHRO, J. MALUSZYNSKI Eds), Springer-Verlag, LNCS 348, p. 219-251.

Goguen-77 GOGUEN (J.A.) & al. Initial Algebra Semantics and Continuous Algebras. JACM Vol. 24, n°1, january 1977, pp. 68-95.

Hehner-83 HEHNER (E.C.R.), SILVERBERG (B.A.). Programming with Grammars : An Exercise in Methodology-Directed Language Design. The Computer Journal, Vol.26, 1983, p. 277-281.

Isakowitz-91 ISAKOWITZ (T.). Can we transforme logic programms into attribute grammars ? RAIRO Informatique Théorique et Applications. Vol. 25, n° 6,1991, p. 499-543.

Kowalski-79 KOWALSKI (R.). Logic for Problem Soving. North-Holland, 1979.

Maluszynski-82a MALUSZYNSKI (J.), NILSSON(J.F). A comparison of the logic programming language Prolog with two-level grammars. in : Proceedings of the 1st ICLP, Marseille (F), 1982, M. van CANEGHEM Ed., p. 193-199.

Maluszynski-82b MALUSZYNSKI (J.), NILSSON (J.F.). Grammatical Unification. Information Processing Letters, Vol.15, n°4, 1982, p.150-158.

Maluszynski-82c MALUSZYNSKI (J.) , NILSSON(J.F). A version of Prolog based on the notion of two-level grammars. Working paper at the "Prolog programming environments workshop", Linköping Institute of Technology (S), march 1982, 15 p.

Maluszynski-84 MALUSZYNSKI (J.). Towards a programming language based on the notion of two-level grammars. TCS, Vol.28, 1984, p.13-43.

Näslund-87 NASLUND (T.). An experimental implementation of a compiler for two-level grammars. in : Proceedings of the 2nd int. symp. on methodologies for intelligent systems, (Z.W.RAS & M. ZEMANKOVA Eds.), pp.424-431.

Nilsson-86 NILSSON (U.). AID : an Alternative Implementation of Definite Clause Grammars. New Generation Computing, 1986, p. 385-398.

Pereira-80 PEREIRA (F.C.N.), WARREN (D.H.D.). Definite Clause Grammars for Language Analysis : a survey of the formalism and a comparison with ATN. Artificial Intelligence, Vol 13, 1980, p. 231-278.

Plotkin-69 PLOTKIN(G.) A Note on Inductive Generalization. Machine intelligence 5, 1969, p.153-163.

Saidi-92a SAIDI (S.). Associative Unification in the AFFLOG Grammatical Logic Programming System. in : Proceedings of JFPL'92, 25-27 may 1992, Lille (F), (J.P Delahaye Ed.), p.107-126 (in french)

Saidi-92b SAIDI (S.). Grammatical Extensions to Logic Programming. Ph-D Thesis : Ecole Centrale de Lyon, may 1992, 172 p. (in french).

Torii-84 TORII (K.), MORISAWA (Y.), SUGIYAMA (Y.), KASAMI (T.). Functional programming and logical programming for the telegram analysis problem. in : Proceedings of 1st IEEE Int. Symp. on Logic Programming, Atlantic City (USA),1984, p. 463-472.

Watt-74 WATT (D.A.). Analysis-oriented two-level grammars. Ph.D. thesis : University of Glasgow, 1974, 285 p.

Wegner-80 WEGNER (L.M.). On Parsing Two-Level Grammars Acta Informatica,Vol.14, 1980, p. 175-193.

Ecully, june 5th, 1992

On Safe Folding *

Annalisa Bossi, Nicoletta Cocco, Sandro Etalle

Dipartimento di Matematica Pura ed Applicata,
Università di Padova,
Via Belzoni 7, 35131 Padova, Italy.
email: bossi,cocco,etalle@pdmat1.unipd.it
fax: ++-49-8758596

Abstract. In [3] a general fold operation has been introduced for definite programs wrt computed answer substitution semantics. It differs from the fold operation defined by Tamaki and Sato in [26,25] because its application does not depend on the transformation history. This paper extends the results in [3] by giving a more powerful sufficient condition for the preservation of computed answer substitutions. Such a condition is meant to deal with the critical case when the atom introduced by folding depends on the clause to which the fold applies. The condition compares the "dependency degree" between the fonding atom and the folded clause, with the "semantic delay" between the folding atom and the ones to be folded. The result is also extended to a more general replacement operation, by showing that it can be decomposed into a sequence of definition, general folding and unfolding operations.
Keywords: Program transformation, folding, computed answer substitution semantics.

1 Introduction

The operations of *fold* and *unfold* are the basis of many program transformation techniques [6,13,15,26,11,18,2,21,7,4]. In logic programming unfold consists in having an atom substituted by its definition, namely by the bodies of the clauses that define it. This corresponds to an evaluation step. Fold is the inverse operation: a conjunction of literals is substituted (folded) by an atom. Folding is generally used to terminate the unfolding process and to detect and express implicit recursion. Transformations are required to be *safe*, which means that the initial and the final programs have to be equivalent wrt some semantics. Depending on the choice of the semantics, which corresponds to the features of the program we focus on, the requirement for safeness may restrict more or less the transformation. Unrestricted unfold is safe for semantics corresponding to a complete search for solutions [16,25, 26,14,24,3,18]. Order constraints on its application become necessary when Prolog semantics is considered [18]. Fold is more complex. It requires the folding atom and the folded conjunction of atoms to be equivalent wrt the chosen semantics. This ensures soundness, but it is not sufficient to guarantee completeness. In fact

* This work has been partially supported by "Progetto Finalizzato Sistemi Informatici e Calcolo Parallelo" of CNR under grant n. 89.00026.69

by folding we can introduce recursion and this can lead to nontermination. The study of conditions sufficient to ensure fold safeness is a major topic in program's transformation, as a rich literature shows, see, for example, [25,26,19,20,14,12,23, 22,3,24]. Most proposed conditions depend on the transformation history. In [3] the safeness of a set of basic transformation operations, including fold and unfold, wrt S-semantics [9,10], is studied. This fold is more general in the sense that it does not depend on any previous transformation sequence. A set of definitions is associated to the program for collecting the information useful to transformations. Equivalences among predicates are also expressed by means of such definitions. A necessary and sufficient condition for safe folding is given, but it requires to check some property on the minimal S-model of both the initial and the final programs.

In this paper we supply a new sufficient condition for completeness of folding, based only on the S-semantics of the initial program. The S-semantics corresponds to the *computed answer substitution semantics* and it seems to be particularly interesting for logic programs transformations. It is declarative and in has pleasant theoretical properties, namely the existence of a minimal S-model and the coincidence of model-theoretic and fixpoint characterization. Moreover, it is the strongest semantics which is invariant under unrestricted unfolding [16]. We give a condition which characterizes when an infinite loop cannot be introduced by folding. We define:

- a *semantic delay* between the folding atom and the folded ones. It corresponds to the difference in the number of steps of their bottom-up derivations.
- a *dependency degree* of the folding atom on the clause to be folded.

When the semantic delay is less or equal to the dependency degree, no infinite loop can be introduced by folding and then completeness is ensured. These ideas were originally devised in [8,5] for ensuring safeness of *replacement* (a more general transformation operation than folding), wrt Fitting's, Kunen's and the Well-Founded semantics of normal programs.

The structure of the paper is the following. In section 2 we give some notation and basic definitions. The semantic delay and the dependency degree are also defined. In section 3 we recall the definition of folding and the results on its safeness given in [3]. In section 4 the new sufficient condition for completeness of folding wrt computed answer substitution semantics is defined and proved. A few examples are also given. Section 5 concludes by defining the replacement operation and the corresponding completeness condition.

2 Preliminaries

2.1 Basic definitions

In the following we assume the standard terminology of logic programs to be well-known, for further details see [17] or [1]. We briefly recall here some definitions and notations. We consider definite programs, a definite clauses is written as

c: $A \leftarrow A_1, \ldots, A_n$.

head(c) denotes the consequent A and *body(c)* the set of atoms in the antecedent $\{A_1, \ldots, A_n\}$. *A substitution* is a finite set of pairs (*variable*, *terms*), such that no two pairs share a common variable part. *A ground substitution* is a substitution with all the terms ground. A *renaming* is a substitution where all the terms are distinct variables. The *domain*, $D(\theta)$, of a substitution $\theta = \{(x_i, t_i) | \ i = 1, \ldots, n\}$ is the set $\{x_i | \ i = 1, \ldots, n\}$. The result of applying a substitution θ to a term t, denoted by $t\theta$, is t in which, for every pair (x_i, t_i) in θ, each occurrence of x_i is replaced by t_i, $\{x_i := t_i\}$. A term t is *an instance* of a term t' if there is some substitution θ such that $t = t'\theta$. A substitution θ is called *a unifier* of two terms t_1 and t_2 if $t_1\theta = t_2\theta$. It is *a most general unifier (mgu)* if any unifier θ' of t_1 and t_2 can be represented as $\theta \cdot \sigma$ by some substitution σ. *The domain of a most general unifier* of two terms is a subset of the set of all the variables occurring in the two terms. Note that we can speak of "the" most general unifier only up to renaming of variables. For this reason, we denote by ε both the empty substitution and a renaming. Substitutions and unifiers for atoms are defined similarly. In what follows we assume that all the mgu's are idempotent and mainly use the notation $\theta = mgu((A_1, \ldots, A_n), (B_1, \ldots, B_n))$ instead of $\theta = mgu((A_1, B_1), \ldots, (A_n, B_n))$. With overlines we denote tuples of objects, hence we often write also $\theta = mgu(\bar{A}, \bar{B})$. Analogously, $var(\bar{A})$ denotes the set of variables occurring in the tuple $\bar{A}$; if S is a set of atoms and $\bar{A} = (A_1, \ldots, A_n)$, we use the notation $\bar{A} \in S$ as an abbreviation for $A_i \in S$, for each i, $1 \leq i \leq n$.

We also assume [18] to be well-known and particularly the definitions of *resultant* and *partial evaluation*.

Let G, G' be goals in a logic program P, $G \overset{\theta}{\longmapsto} G'$ denotes an SLD-derivation of G' from G with computed answer substitution θ, which corresponds to the resultant $G\theta \leftarrow G'.$, $\Box$ denotes the empty clause and $G \overset{\theta}{\longmapsto} \Box$ denotes an SLD-refutation of G with computed answer substitution θ. $Ans(G, P)$ denotes the set of computed answer substitutions of the atom G in the program P: $Ans(G, P) \overset{\text{def}}{=} \{\theta | \ G \overset{\theta}{\longmapsto} \Box\}$. We omit the reference to P when no confusion arises. Moreover, if V is a set of variables we denote by $Ans(G, P) \mid_V$ the set obtained by restricting all the substitutions in $Ans(G, P)$ to V.

2.2 S-semantics

We refer to the semantics for logic programs given in [9,10]. Such a semantics, in our opinion, is particularly interesting for logic programs transformations. On one hand, it is still declarative (it corresponds to a complete SLD-resolution) and it has all the pleasant theoretical properties of the standard least Herbrand model semantics, namely the existence of a minimal S-model and its correspondence with a fixpoint semantics. On the other hand its operational characterization is more expressive than the standard one, since all computed answer substitutions are captured and not only ground ones. Moreover it is the strongest semantics which is invariant by unrestricted unfolding [16]. We give here only the notation and some of the results in [9,10].

The S-semantics of logic programs is based on interpretations containing also non ground atoms. *A new Herbrand universe*, U_S, is defined as the set of equivalence classes of terms with respect to the equivalence relation induced by renaming (two terms are in the same equivalence class if and only if they are equal up to renaming). Similarly, *a new Herbrand base*, B_S, is defined as the set of equivalence classes of atoms with respect to the equivalence induced by renaming. For the sake of simplicity, the equivalence class of an atom A will be represented by A itself.

A *preorder*, $\leq$, on B_S can be defined by: $A \leq A'$ (A is less instantiated than A') if and only if there exists a substitution θ such that $A\theta = A'$.

An extension of the standard definition of truth in a Herbrand interpretation is also given. Let I be an S-interpretation, then:

- an atom A is *S-true* in I iff $\exists A' \in I.\ A' \leq A$;

- a definite clause $A \leftarrow B_1, \ldots, B_n.$ is *S-true* in I iff for each $B'_1 \ldots, B'_n \in I$ and θ, if $\theta = mgu((B_1, \ldots, B_n), (B'_1 \ldots, B'_n))$, then $A\theta \in I$.

An *S-model* of a logic program P is any S-interpretation, M, in which all the clauses of P are S-true. For any program P there exists a *minimal S-model, MS(P)*, which is the intersection of all the S-models of P [9,10].

The S-semantics fully characterizes the computed answers substitutions associated to a goal. In fact $MS(P)$ is equal to $O_S(P)$, where: $O_S(P) = \{A | \exists \bar{x}\ A = p(\bar{x})\theta$ and $\theta \in Ans(p(\bar{x}), P)\}$. The set of ground instances of $MS(P)$ is equal to the least Herbrand model of P.

Example 1. Let us consider the program

$$
\begin{aligned}
P = \{\ & c1\colon r(a). \\
& c2\colon p(X, pair(a,a)). \\
& c3\colon q(X) \leftarrow r(X), p(a,Y).\}.
\end{aligned}
$$

The interpretation $I = \{r(a),\ p(Z, pair(a,a)),\ q(a),\ p(a,W)\}$ is an S-model of P, but it is not the minimal one which is $MS(P) = \{r(a),\ p(Z, pair(a,a)),\ q(a)\}$.

In [9,10] beside the model-theoretic and the operational semantics, analogously to the standard declarative approach, a fixpoint semantics is given and the equivalence of the three semantics is proved. Let I be an S-interpretation, then

$$
\begin{aligned}
TS_P(I) = \{A\theta \in B_S \mid\ & \exists A \leftarrow B_1, \ldots, B_n. \in P. \\
& \exists B'_1, \ldots, B'_n \in I. \\
& \theta = mgu((B_1, \ldots, B_n), (B'_1, \ldots, B'_n))\}.
\end{aligned}
$$

TS_P is the immediate consequence operator for the S-semantics. Its least fixed point is reached in ω steps and it coincides with MS(P).

In the sequel we will adopt the following standard notation: $TS_P^0(I) = I$, $TS_P^{n+1}(I) = TS_P(TS_P^n(I))$; $TS_P^\omega(I) = \cup\, TS_P^n(I)$; $TS_P^\alpha = TS_P^\alpha(\emptyset)$; when the argument is omitted, $\emptyset$ is assumed.

2.3 Semantic equivalence and Delay

In order to define safe program transformations it is necessary to express program equivalence with respect to S-semantics. Namely two programs P_1 and P_2 are *S-equivalent* when they have the same minimal S-model: $MS(P_1) = MS(P_2)$. For dealing with folding we need to define some relations among goals in a program P.

Definition 1 (S-equivalence of conjunctions of atoms). Let P be a definite program, $\bar{C}$ and $\bar{D}$ be two arbitrary conjunctions of atoms, Y a subset of $var(\bar{D})$ such that $Y \cap var(\bar{C}) = \emptyset$, X a subset of $var(\bar{C})$ such that $X \cap var(\bar{D}) = \emptyset$ and Z the set of remaining variables: $Z = (var(\bar{D}) \backslash Y) \cup (var(\bar{C}) \backslash X)$.
$\exists X \bar{C}$ *is equivalent to* $\exists Y \bar{D}$ *in* $MS(P)$, $\exists Y \bar{D} \cong_{MS(P)} \exists X \bar{C}$, iff

(i) for each $\bar{C}' \in MS(P)$ and θ such that $\theta = \text{mgu}(\bar{C}, \bar{C}')$, there exists $\bar{D}' \in MS(P)$ and ϕ such that $\phi = \text{mgu}(\bar{D}, \bar{D}')$ and $\phi\,|_Z = \theta\,|_Z$;
(ii) for each $\bar{D}' \in MS(P)$ and θ such that $\theta = \text{mgu}(\bar{D}, \bar{D}')$, there exists $\bar{C}' \in MS(P)$ and ϕ such that $\phi = \text{mgu}(\bar{C}, \bar{C}')$ and $\phi\,|_Z = \theta\,|_Z$.

Note that this definition of equivalence basically means that the set of computed answers for $(\leftarrow \bar{D}.)$ restricted to Z is equal to the ones for $(\leftarrow \bar{C}.)$: $\text{Ans}(\bar{D}, P)\,|_Z = \text{Ans}(\bar{C}, P)\,|_Z$.

Example 2. Let P be the following program:

$$
\begin{aligned}
P = \{\ & member2(El, List) && \leftarrow member(El, List, Place).\\
& member(El, [El|Tail], s(0)).\\
& member(El, [Head|Tail], s(N)) && \leftarrow member(El, Tail, N).\ \}
\end{aligned}
$$

member differs from *member2* only because it 'reports' the position where element *El* has been found in the list.

$member(El, List, Place)$ is *not* equivalent to $member2(El, List)$ in $MS(P)$. In fact, if we consider the substitution $\theta = \{(El, a), (List, [a]), (Place, 0)\}$, we have that $member2(El, List)\theta$ is *true* in $MS(P)$, while $member(El, List, Place)\theta$ is not. Viceversa, it is easy to check that:

$\exists Place\ \ member(El, List, Place) \cong_{MS(P)} member2(El, List)$.

That is, an instance of $member2(El, List)$ is *true* in $MS(P)$ if and only if there exist a term t such that the corresponding instance of $member(El, List, t)$ is *true* in $MS(P)$.

Lemma 2. *If cl : $A \leftarrow \bar{C}$. is the only clause in program P defining the predicate symbol of A, and X is the set of variables local to $\bar{C}$, $X = var(\bar{C}) \backslash var(A)$, then $A \cong_{MS(P)} \exists X\, \bar{C}$.*

Consider now the following definite program:

$$
\begin{aligned}
P = \{\ & m(X) \leftarrow n(s(X)).\\
& n(0).\\
& n(s(X)) \leftarrow n(X).\ \ \}
\end{aligned}
$$

The predicates $m(X)$ and $n(X)$ have exactly the same meaning, they are, in fact, *equivalent* in $MS(P)$ but in order to build the proof of $m(s(0))$, we need four inference steps, while for $n(s(0))$, two steps are sufficient, as $m(t)$ belongs to TS_P^4, while $n(t)$ belongs to TS_P^2. In general, $n(t)$ occurs in TS_P^j iff $m(t)$ occurs in TS_P^{j+2}. We can formalise this idea by saying that the *semantic delay of $m(X)$ wrt $n(X)$* is two.

Definition 3 (S-delay). Let P be a definite program, $\bar{C}$ and $\bar{D}$ be two conjunctions of atoms, Y a subset of $var(\bar{D})$ such that $Y \cap var(\bar{C}) = \emptyset$, X a subset of $var(\bar{C})$ such that $X \cap var(\bar{D}) = \emptyset$ and Z the set of remaining varibles: $Z = (var(\bar{D})\backslash Y) \cup (var(\bar{C})\backslash X)$. Suppose that $\exists Y \bar{D} \cong_{MS(P)} \exists X \bar{C}$.
The S-delay of $\exists Y \bar{D}$ wrt $\exists X \bar{C}$ is the least integer n such that, for each natural m, and each substitution θ:
if $\bar{C}' \in TS_P^m$ and $\theta = \text{mgu}(\bar{C}', \bar{C})$, then there exists $\bar{D}' \in TS_P^{m+n}$ and a substitution ϕ such that $\phi = \text{mgu}(\bar{D}', \bar{D})$ and $\theta\,|_Z = \phi\,|_Z$.

2.4 Dependency degree

We now need to define the *dependency degree* of a predicate on a program clause. Let us consider the following program:

$$
\begin{aligned}
P = \{\ & c1 : p \leftarrow q, s. \\
& c2 : q \leftarrow r. \\
& c3 : r. \\
& c4 : s \leftarrow q. \quad \}
\end{aligned}
$$

The definitions of the atoms p, q, s and r, all depend from clause $c3$. Informally we could say that *the dependency degree of the predicate p over clause c3 is two*, as the shortest derivation path from a clause having head p to $c3$ contains two arcs: the first from $c1$ to $c2$, through the atom q; the second from $c2$, to $c3$, through r. In a similar way, *the dependency degree of q and s on c3* are respectively one and two and *the dependency degree of r on c3 is zero.*
The next definition formalises this intuitive notion. The atom A and the clause cl are assumed to be standardized apart.

Definition 4 (dependency degree). Let P be a program, cl a clause of P and A an atom. *The dependency degree of A on cl*, $dep_P(A, cl)$, is

- 0 if A unifies with head(cl);
- n+1 if A does not unify with head(cl) and n is the least integer such that there exists a clause $C \leftarrow C_1, \ldots, C_k$. in P, whose head unifies with A via mgu, say, θ, and, for some i, $dep_P(C_i\theta, cl) = n$.

A is independent from cl when no such n exists.

The definition can be extended to conjunctions of atoms. The conjunction $(A_1 \wedge \ldots \wedge A_n)$ is *independent* from cl iff all its components are *independent* from cl; otherwise the *dependency degree* of $(A_1 \wedge \ldots \wedge A_n)$ on cl is equal to the least dependency degree of one of its elements on cl, $dep_P((A_1 \wedge \ldots \wedge A_n), cl) = \inf\{dep_P(A_i, cl)\}$, where $1 \leq i \leq n$.

Lemma 5. *Let A and B be atoms and cl a clause in a program P. If* $B \leq A$ *and* $dep_P(B, cl) \geq k$ *then either A is independent from cl or* $dep_P(A, cl) \geq k$.

3 The Fold Operation

The fold operation consists in substituting an atom for an equivalent conjunction of atoms, in the body of a clause. This operation is generally used in all the transformation techniques in order to pack back unfolded clauses and to detect implicit recursive definitions. In the literature we find different definitions for this operation. The differences mainly depend on how we derive the equivalence between the conjunction of atoms to be folded and the folding one. The simpler case is when such equivalence derives directly from a clause, the folding clause, which belongs to the same program where the fold operation is performed [12,19]. This is often too restrictive as the folding clause could have been modified or eliminated from the program by some previous transformation. Hence in many proposals [25,26,22,23,24] the folding and the folded clause do not belong to the same program, more precisely, the folding clause belongs to the first program of a *transformation sequence*. In [3], no transformation sequence is considered; instead a set of definitions is associated to the program in order to record the information useful for future transformations. The equivalence among an atom and a conjunction of atoms is represented by a definition which must be consistent with the program's semantics.

In this section we recall the general definition of folding given in [3] and its properties.

In order to characterize the correctness of a transformation operation wrt to the S-semantics we adopt the following terminology.

Definition 6. Let P' be the result of applying a transformation operation to a program P. The transformation is *sound* if $MS(P) \supseteq MS(P')$, *complete* if $MS(P) \subseteq MS(P')$, *safe* if $MS(P) = MS(P')$.

We give here a definition of *consistency* of a definition wrt a program which is equivalent to the one given in [3].

Definition 7 (consistency of definitions). Let P be a logic program, $D, D_1, \ldots, D_m$ be atoms, Y the set of local variables of D, $Y = var(D) \backslash var(D_1, \ldots, D_m)$, X the set of local variables of $(D_1, \ldots, D_m)$, $X = var(D_1, \ldots, D_m) \backslash var(D)$.
The definition $D \stackrel{\text{def}}{=} (D_1 \wedge \ldots \wedge D_m)$ is *consistent* with P iff
$\exists Y D \cong_{MS(P)} \exists X (D_1 \wedge \ldots \wedge D_m)$.

Definition 8 (folding). Let $c : A \leftarrow D_1, \ldots, D_m, A_1, \ldots, A_n$. be a clause in a logic program P, $(D \stackrel{\text{def}}{=} D_1 \wedge \ldots \wedge D_m)$ a definition consistent with P.
Let $Y = var(D) \backslash var(D_1, \ldots, D_m)$ and $X = var(D_1, \ldots, D_m) \backslash var(D)$ be the sets of variables local respectively to D and $D_1, \ldots, D_m$.
If $(X \cup Y) \cap var(A, A_1, \ldots, A_n) = \emptyset$ then *folding* D in c in P consists in substituting c' for c in P, where

$head(c') \stackrel{\text{def}}{=} A$, $body(c') \stackrel{\text{def}}{=} (body(c) - \{A_{i_1}, \ldots, A_{i_m}\}) \cup \{D\}$.

$\text{fold}(P, D, c) \stackrel{\text{def}}{=} (P - \{c\}) \cup \{c'\}$.

The consistency of the definition wrt P guarantees the soundness of the folding operation, as is proven in [3].

Lemma 9 (soundness of folding). *If* $P' = fold(P, D, c)$, *then* $MS(P) \supseteq MS(P')$.

Completeness is not always guaranteed as it is shown by the following example.

Example 3. Let P be the following program: $P = \{ \quad p \leftarrow r. \quad r \leftarrow q. \quad q. \quad \}$.
$MS(P) = \{p, q, r\}$; p, q and r are all *equivalent* in $MS(P)$, the definition $p \stackrel{\text{def}}{=} q$ is consistent with P, but, if we fold p in the body of *cl* we obtain:

$P' = \{ \quad p \leftarrow r. \quad r \leftarrow p. \quad q. \quad \}$

which is by no means equivalent to the previous program. In fact $MS(P') = \{q\}$. We have introduced a loop and p and r are no more *true*.

The consistency of the definition wrt both P and P' guarantees the safeness of the folding operation.

Proposition 10. *Let* $D \stackrel{\text{def}}{=} (D_1 \wedge \ldots \wedge D_m)$ *be a definition consistent with a program* P *and* P' *=fold*(P, D, c). *The folding operation is safe,* $MS(P) = MS(P')$, *iff the definition* $D \stackrel{\text{def}}{=} (D_1 \wedge \ldots \wedge D_m)$ *is also consistent with* P'.

Proposition 10 requires the knowledge of $MS(P')$, the minimal S-model of P', the program resulting from the transformation. This is not very practical, hence, in [3], other sufficient conditions, simpler to verify, are also given.

Proposition 11. *In the hypothesis of the definition of the folding operation, with* $D = d(t_1, \ldots, t_n)$, *each of the following conditions guarantees that* $MS(P) = MS(P')$:

1. $MS(P) \mid_{instances\ of\ d(x_1,\ldots,x_n)} = MS(P - \{c\}) \mid_{instances\ of\ d(x_1,\ldots,x_n)}$;
2. $c_D : D \leftarrow D_1, \ldots, D_m.$ *is in* P *and* $c_D \neq c$.

The first condition is trivially satisfied when D is independent from c. The second one, when $c_D : D \leftarrow D_1, \ldots, D_m.$ is the only clause defining the predicate symbol $d(x_1, \ldots, x_n)$ in P, guarantees also that $D \stackrel{\text{def}}{=} (D_1 \wedge \ldots \wedge D_m)$ is consistent wrt P.

4 Safe Folding

In this section we give a new sufficient condition for safe folding that depends on the *delay* of D wrt $(D_1, \ldots, D_m)$. In particular we prove that, if the delay of of D wrt $(D_1, \ldots, D_m)$ in $MS(P)$ is "small enough", then the S-semantics of the program is not affected by the fold operation. In order to formalise the concept of "small enough delay" we compare it to the dependency degree of D on the clause to which we want to apply the fold operation.

4.1 A sufficient condition

Example 3 shows that the equivalence of p and q is not sufficient to guarantee the preservation of the semantics after folding. This happens when the definition of p depends on the clause cl and the folding operation modifies the meaning of p in the program. In fact proposition 11.1 guarantees that, when the folding predicate is independent from the folded clause, then the operation is safe. Consider now the following program:

$$P = \{\ d : p(X) \leftarrow q(X). \qquad cl : A \leftarrow \ldots, q(X), \ldots \qquad \ldots \qquad \}$$

where d is the only clause defining the predicate symbol p. $p(X)$ and $q(X)$ are *equivalent* in $MS(P)$ and the definition $p(X) \cong_{MS(P)} q(X)$ is then consistent with P. Now, if we fold $p(t)$ in cl, we obtain the following program:

$$P' = \{\ d : p(X) \leftarrow q(X). \qquad cl : A \leftarrow \ldots, p(X), \ldots \qquad \ldots \qquad \}$$

which, by proposition 11, has the same S-semantics of the previous one, $MS(P) = MS(P')$. This holds even if the definition of p is dependent from cl. The point is that here "there is no room for introducing a loop".

Let us consider the differences between this program and the one in example 3 in

terms of semantic delay and dependency degree. In example 3 the semantic delay of p wrt q is *two*, while the dependency degree of p on the folded clause is one, $\text{dep}_P(p, cl) = 1$, here the delay of $p(X)$ wrt $q(X)$ in $MS(P)$ is *one*, while $\text{dep}_P(p(X), cl) \geq 1$, in fact d is the only clause defining predicate p and $d \neq cl$, it follows that $dep_P(p(X), cl) > 0$.
We now prove that, in any program P, replacing an atom $q(X)$ by another one $p(X)$ in a clause cl preserves the S-semantics of the initial program if

- either p *does not depend on* cl or
- *the dependency level of* p *on* cl (i.e. the size of the possible loop) *is greater or equal to the semantic delay of* $p(X)$ *wrt* $q(X)$ *in* $MS(P)$ (i.e. the space where the loop should fit).

We list here the notation used in the proof:
P is a definite program;
$d : D \stackrel{\text{def}}{=} (D_1 \wedge \ldots \wedge D_m)$ is a definition consistent with P;
Z is the set of variables common to the left and the right part of the definition,
$Z = var(D) \cap var(D_1, \ldots, D_m)$;
Y is the set of local variables of D, $Y = var(D) \backslash Z$;
X is the set of local variables of $(D_1, \ldots, D_m)$, $X = var(D_1, \ldots, D_m) \backslash Z$;
$cl : A \leftarrow A_1, \ldots, A_l, D_1, \ldots, D_m$ is a clause of P;
P' is the program obtained by folding D in cl in P, $P' = \text{fold}(P, D, cl)$;
cl' is the clause resulting from the folding operation,
$cl' : A \leftarrow A_1, \ldots, A_l, D.$, hence $P' = P \backslash \{cl\} \cup \{cl'\}$.

The following lemma is necessary in the proof.

Lemma 12. *Let B, B' be two unifiable atoms, I an S-interpretation, k a natural number such that:*
- $B' \in TS_P^k(I)$;
- *either* $dep_P(B, cl) \geq k$, *or B is independent from cl;*

then $B' \in TS_{P'}^k(I)$.

Proof. By induction on k.
Base: $k = 0$. Trivial, since $TS_{P'}^0(I) = TS_P^0(I) = I$.
Induction step: $k > 0$. Since $B' \in TS_P^k(I)$, there exists $c : C \leftarrow C_1, \ldots, C_n. \in P$ and γ such that $C\gamma = B'$ and $\gamma = mgu((C'_1, \ldots, C'_n)\ (C_1, \ldots, C_n))$, where, for each i, $C'_i \in TS_P^{k-1}(I)$.
Let us consider an element $C_i\gamma$ of body$(c)\gamma$. We have to consider two cases:
(1) $C_i\gamma$ is independent from cl. Then by inductive hypothesis: $C'_i \in TS_{P'}^{k-1}(I)$;
(2) $C_i\gamma$ is not independent from cl. Let $\phi = \text{mgu}(B, B') = \text{mgu}(B, C\gamma)$. If $C_i\gamma\phi$ is independent from cl then, by inductive hypothesis (applied to $C_i\gamma\phi$ and C'_i), $C'_i \in TS_{P'}^{k-1}(I)$. If $C_i\gamma\phi$ is not independent from cl then B cannot be independent from cl. Hence from our hypothesis $dep_P(B, cl) \geq k$, and, consequently, $dep_P(C_i\gamma\phi, cl) \geq k - 1$. By the hypothesis (applied to $C_i\gamma\phi$ and C'_i) it follows that $C'_i \in TS_{P'}^{k-1}(I)$.
Hence, for each i, $C'_i \in TS_{P'}^{k-1}(I)$.
Since $dep_P(B, cl) \geq k > 0$, B cannot be an instance of the head of cl, hence $c \neq cl$.
Then c belongs to both P and P', which gives the thesis. □

Theorem 13. *If either*

1. *D is independent from cl; or*
2. *the dependency degree of D on cl is greater or equal to the S-delay of* $(\exists Y D)$ *wrt* $(\exists X(D_1, \ldots, D_m))$;

then $MS(P) = MS(P')$.

Proof. By lemma 9, $MS(P') \subseteq MS(P)$. We need to show that $MS(P) \subseteq MS(P')$.
If D is independent from cl then the result follows from proposition 11.1.
By contradiction, let us suppose $MS(P) \not\subseteq MS(P')$. Since TS_P^n is monotonically increasing and $\emptyset = TS_P^0 \subseteq MS(P')$, there has to be a natural j such that:

$MS(P') \supseteq TS_P^j$
$MS(P') \not\supseteq TS_P^{j+1}$.

Let C be an atom belonging to $TS_P(TS_P^j) \backslash MS(P')$.
There has to be a clause in $P \backslash P'$ which allows to infer C from TS_P^j. Since, $P \backslash P' = \{cl\}$, there exist $(A'_1, \ldots, A'_l, D'_1, \ldots, D'_m) \in TS_P^j$ and θ such that:

$\theta = \text{mgu}((A'_1, \ldots, A'_l, D'_1, \ldots, D'_m), (A_1, \ldots, A_l, D_1, \ldots, D_m))$ and $C = A\theta$.

Hence there exist a ϕ. such that

$$\phi = mgu((D'_1, \ldots, D'_m), (D_1, \ldots, D_m)). \tag{1}$$

Let k be $dep_P(D, cl)$. From (1) and the hypothesis it follows that, by definition 3, there exists $D' \in TS_P^{k+j}$ and a substitution γ such that: $\gamma = \text{mgu}(D, D')$ and $\gamma|_Z = \phi|_Z$. Since $TS_P^{j+k} = TS_P^k(TS_P^j)$, it follows that $D' \in TS_P^k(TS_P^j)$.
$dep_P(D, cl) \geq k$, D and D' are unifiables; by lemma 12: $D' \in TS_{P'}^k(TS_P^j)$.
$TS_P^j \subseteq MS(P')$ and $TS_{P'}$ is monotone, then $D' \in TS_{P'}^k(MS(P'))$
And since $MS(P') = lfp(TS_{P'})$ $D' \in MS(P')$.
But then there exists θ' such that: $\theta' = \text{mgu}((A'_1, \ldots, A'_l, D'), (A_1, \ldots, A_l, D))$ and $\theta|_Z = \theta'|_Z$, that is $A\theta' = A\theta = C$.
Since $(A'_1, \ldots, A'_l)$ are already in $TS_P^j \subseteq MS(P')$, and cl' in P', it follows that:

$C = A\theta' \in TS_{P'}(MS(P')) = MS(P')$

which contradicts the fact that C belongs to $TS_P(TS_P^j) \backslash MS(P')$. □

4.2 Examples

Example 4. Let us consider the program:

$P = \{\ c1 : m(X) \leftarrow n(X).$
$\quad c2 : n(0).$
$\quad c3 : n(s(X)) \leftarrow n(X).\ \}$

together with the following set of definitions:

$\{\quad d1 : m(X) \stackrel{\text{def}}{=} n(X). \quad d2 : m(s(X)) \stackrel{\text{def}}{=} n(X).\ \}$

Both d1 and d2 are consistent with P; but while d1 can safely be used for folding in c3, $d2$ would introduce a loop, leading to the program:

$P' = \{\ c1 : m(X) \leftarrow n(X).$
$\quad c2 : n(0).$
$\quad c3' : n(s(X)) \leftarrow m(s(X)).\ \}$

In fact, when using $d1$ for folding in $c3$, the conditions in theorem 13 are met as the delay of $m(X)$ wrt $n(X)$ is one, equal to $dep_P(m(X), c3)$. When using $d2$ the conditions are not satisfied, since the delay of $m(s(X))$ wrt $n(X)$ is two. Similarly, the conditions are not satisfied if we want to use either of the definitions for folding in $c1$.

Example 5 (suggested by M.J.Maher). Let P_0 be the following program where, for simplicity, we use s as a prefix operator.

$$\begin{aligned} P_0 = \{ & c1 : divbytwo(0). \\ & c2 : divbytwo(ssX) \leftarrow divbytwo(X). \\ & c3 : divbythree(0). \\ & c4 : divbythree(sssX) \leftarrow divbythree(X). \\ & c5 : divbysix(X) \leftarrow divbytwo(X), divbythree(X).\} \end{aligned}$$

Since $c5$ is the only clause defining predicate $divbysix(X)$, by lemma 2 the definition $(divbysix(X) \stackrel{\text{def}}{=} divbytwo(X) \wedge divbythree(X))$ is consistent with P_0.
Let us now unfold $divbytwo(X)$ in the body of $c5$; we obtain:

$$\begin{aligned} P_1 = P_0 \backslash \{c5\} \cup \{ & c6 : divbysix(0) \leftarrow divbythree(0). \\ & c7 : divbysix(ssX) \leftarrow divbytwo(X), divbythree(ssX).\} \end{aligned}$$

We can now unfold $divbythree$ in the bodies of $c5$ and $c7$, thus obtaining respectively $c8$ and $c9$ and the following program:

$$\begin{aligned} P_2 = P_1 \backslash \{c6, c7\} \cup \{ & c8 : divbysix(0). \\ & c9 : divbysix(sssX) \leftarrow divbytwo(sX), divbythree(X).\} \end{aligned}$$

Again, we can unfold $divbytwo$ in the body of $c9$:

$$P_3 = P_2 \backslash \{c9\} \cup \{ c10 : divbysix(ssssX) \leftarrow divbytwo(X), divbythree(sX).\}$$

By unfolding $divbythree$ in the body of $c10$ and then again $divbytwo$ in the resulting clause, we obtain:

$$P_4 = P_3 \backslash \{c10\} \cup \{ c11 : divbysix(ssssssX) \leftarrow divbytwo(X), divbythree(X).\}$$

Since unfolding is a safe operation wrt the S-semantics, [14,16,3], it follows that $MS(P) = MS(P_1) = \ldots = MS(P_4)$.
Hence the definition $(divbysix(X) \stackrel{\text{def}}{=} divbytwo(X) \wedge divbythree(X))$ is consistent with P_4 and it can be used to perform a fold operation in the body of $c11$, since the applicability conditions in definition 8 are trivially satisfied. By theorem 13 this is a safe operation, in fact:

- $dep_P(divbysix(X), c11) = 0$;
- the S-delay of $divbysix(X)$ wrt $(divbytwo(X) \wedge divbythree(X))$ is zero too; in fact each time that, for some τ and k, $\{divbytwo(X)\tau, divbythree(X)\tau\} \subseteq TS_P^k$, then also $divbysix(X)\tau \in TS_P^k$. This is due to the fact that all the atoms in the body of $c5$ have been unfolded at least once.

After the fold operation, we end up with the final program:

$$
\begin{aligned}
P_5 = \{\, & c1: && divbytwo(0). \\
& c2: && divbytwo(ssX) && \leftarrow divbytwo(X). \\
& c3: && divbythree(0). \\
& c4: && divbythree(sssX) && \leftarrow divbythree(X). \\
& c8: && divbysix(0). \\
& c12: && divbysix(ssssssX) && \leftarrow divbysix(X).\}
\end{aligned}
$$

This example shows a typical application of folding in a transformation sequence as defined by Tamaki and Sato [25,26] and successively modified by Seki [24].

5 From Fold to Replacement

The conditions of theorem 13 for a safe folding have been originally designed in [8,5] for a more general case, namely for safeness of replacement in normal programs. Replacement is a very general transformation operation which substitutes a conjunction of atoms for another conjunction. In [8,5] we study safeness of replacement wrt Fitting's and the Well-Founded semantics.

Definition 14 (replacement). Let $cl: A \leftarrow C_1, \ldots, C_k, A_1, \ldots, A_l.$ be a clause in a definite program P and $(D_1, \ldots, D_m)$ a conjunction of atoms.
Let $X = var(C_1, \ldots, C_k) \backslash var(D_1, \ldots, D_m)$ and $Y = var(D_1, \ldots, D_m) \backslash var(C_1, \ldots, C_k)$ be the sets of variables local respectively to $(C_1, \ldots, C_k)$ and $(D_1, \ldots, D_m)$.
If $(X \cup Y) \cap var(A, A_1, \ldots, A_l) = \emptyset$ then *replacing* $(C_1, \ldots, C_k)$ with $(D_1, \ldots, D_m)$ consists in substituting cl' for cl, where $cl': A \leftarrow D_1, \ldots, D_m, A_1, \ldots, A_l$.
$P' = \text{replace}(P, cl, (C_1, \ldots, C_k), (D_1, \ldots, D_m)) \stackrel{\text{def}}{=} P \backslash \{cl\} \cup \{cl'\}$.

We give now the safeness conditions for replacing. We use the same notation as in the previous definition.

Theorem 15. *If*

R1 $\exists X(C_1 \wedge \ldots \wedge C_k) \cong_{MS(P)} \exists Y(D_1 \wedge \ldots \wedge D_m)$;
R2 *either:*

1. $(D_1, \ldots, D_m)$ *is independent from cl; or*
2. *the delay of* $\exists Y(D_1 \wedge \ldots \wedge D_m)$ *wrt* $\exists X(C_1 \wedge \ldots \wedge C_k)$ *is not greater than the dependency degree of* $(D_1, \ldots, D_m)$ *on cl;*

then $MS(P) = MS(P')$.

Proof. The proof could be given directly, but here we prefer to use our previous safeness result for folding. We simulate replacement by a three steps process which uses only fold, unfold, and new predicates definition. Let $B_S(P)$ be the *new* Herbrand base of P.

Step 1. Introducing a new predicate.
Let $P_1 = P \cup \{c_p : \ p(\bar{Z}) \leftarrow D_1, \ldots, D_m\}$, where p is a new predicate symbols, $Z = var(D_1, \ldots, D_m) \backslash Y$ is the set of variables common to the left and right part of the definition d. Note that $MS(P_1) \cap B_S(P) = MS(P)$, that is, $MS(P_1)$ and $MS(P)$ coincide on the predicates defined in P.

Step 2. Folding.
$P_2 = \text{fold}(P_1, p(\bar{Z}), cl) = P_1 \backslash \{cl\} \cup \{cl_2 : A \leftarrow p(\bar{Z}), A_1, \ldots, A_l.\}$.
In order to ensure that the operation is sound, we have to show that the definition $(p(\bar{Z}) \stackrel{\text{def}}{=} (C_1, \ldots, C_k).)$ is consistent with P_1 and that conditions on the local variables given definition 8 are met. To ensure that it is also complete wrt S-semantics, we make use of theorem 13.

Soundness. Since c_p is the only clause defining the predicate p, by lemma 2 we have that $p(\bar{Z}) \cong_{MS(P_1)} \exists Y(D_1, \ldots, D_m)$, from this and (R1) it follows that $p(\bar{Z}) \cong_{MS(P_1)} \exists X(C_1, \ldots, C_k)$, hence $(p(\bar{Z}) \stackrel{\text{def}}{=} C_1, \ldots, C_k.)$ is consistent wrt P_1. Hence, by lemma 9, it follows that $MS(P_1) \supseteq MS(P_2)$.

Completeness We apply theorem 13, in fact:
a) p is independent from cl iff $(D_1, \ldots, D_m)$ is independent from cl.
b) If p is not independent from cl, then $dep_{P_1}(p(\bar{Z}), cl) = 1 + dep_{P_1}((D_1, \ldots, D_m), cl)$. But also the delay of $p(\bar{Z})$ wrt $\exists X(C_1, \ldots, C_k)$ is 1+(delay of $\exists Y D_1, \ldots, D_m$ wrt $\exists X(C_1, \ldots, C_k)$). Hence, if condition (R2) is met, then the conditions in theorem 13 are satisfied.

Step 3. Unfolding.
We can now unfold $p(\bar{Z})$ in cl_2:
$P_3 = \text{unfold}(P_2, cl, p(\bar{Z})) = P_2 \backslash \{cl_2\} \cup \{cl_3 : A \leftarrow D_1, \ldots, D_m, A_1, \ldots, A_l.\}$
The clause defining predicate p can be removed, being now superfluous. In fact the predicate symbol p does not occur in the body of any clause in P_3. The resulting program is identical to P'. We have: $MS(P') = MS(P_3) \cap B_S(P) = MS(P_1) \cap B_S(P) = MS(P)$. □

Example 6 (Sorting by Permutation and Check). The following program is borrowed from [26]. Here we assume that the predicate $smallereq(x, y)$ is defined in the program by a finite set of ground facts. Let P_0 be the following program:

$$
\begin{array}{lll}
P_0 = \{ & c1 : perm([\,],[\,]). & \\
& c2 : perm([A \mid X], Y) & \leftarrow perm(X, Z), ins(A, Z, Y). \\
& c3 : ins(A, X, [A \mid X]). & \\
& c4 : ins(A, [B \mid X], [B \mid Y]) & \leftarrow ins(A, X, Y). \\
& c5 : ord([\,]). & \\
& c6 : ord([A]). & \\
& c7 : ord([A, B \mid X]) & \leftarrow smallereq(A, B), ord([B \mid X]). \\
& c8 : sort(X, Y) & \leftarrow perm(X, Y), ord(Y). \\
& \ldots & \qquad \}
\end{array}
$$

Let us unfold $perm(X, Y)$ in the body of $c8$; the resulting program is:

$$
\begin{array}{lll}
P_1 = P_0 \backslash \{c8\} \cup \{ & c9 : sort([\,],[\,]) & \leftarrow ord([\,]). \\
& c10 : sort([A \mid X], Y) & \leftarrow perm(X, Z), ins(A, Z, Y), ord(Y).\}
\end{array}
$$

Let us unfold $ord([\,])$ in the body of $c9$:
$P_2 = P_1 \backslash \{c9\} \cup \{c11\} = P_0 \backslash \{c8\} \cup \{c10\} \cup \{ c11 : sort([\,],[\,]).\ \}$
We can now replace $(ins(A, Z, Y), ord(Y))$ with $(ord(Z), ins(A, Z, Y), ord(Y))$ in the body of $c10$. In fact:
a) each time that, for some τ, $\{ins(A, Z, Y)\tau, ord(Y)\tau\} \subseteq MS(P_2)$; then $(ord(Z))\tau \in$

$MS(P_2)$; hence $(ins(A,Z,Y), ord(Y)) \cong_{MS(P_2)} (ord(Z), ins(A,Z,Y), ord(Y))$;
b) The conjunction $(ord(Z), ins(A,Z,Y), ord(Y))$ is independent from $c10$.
Let P_3 be the resulting program: $P_3 = P_2 \backslash \{c10\} \cup \{c12\} = P_0 \backslash \{c8\} \cup$

$\{\ c11 : sort([\,],[\,]).$
$\ \ c12 : sort([A \mid X], Y) \leftarrow perm(X,Z), ord(Z), ins(A,Z,Y), ord(Y).\}$

With a fold operation we can now change $(perm(X,Z), ord(Z))$ with $sort(X,Z)$ in the body of $c12$. In fact:
a) the definition $sort(X,Z) \stackrel{\text{def}}{=} perm(X,Z), ord(Z)$ is consistent with P_3;
b) the S-delay of $sort(X,Z)$ wrt $perm(X,Z), ord(Z)$ is zero.
Hence folding can be applied and the conditions of theorem 13 are satisfied; the resulting program is: $P_4 = P_3 \backslash \{c12\} \cup \{c13\} = P_0 \backslash \{c8\} \cup$

$\{\ c11 : sort([\,],[\,]).$
$\ \ c13 : sort([A \mid X], Y) \leftarrow sort(X,Z), ins(A,Z,Y), ord(Y).\}$

This is an $O(n^3)$ sorting program while P_0 runs in $O(n!)$.

References

1. K. Apt. Introduction to logic programming. In *Handbook of Theoretical Computer Science*, pages 493–574. Elsevier Science Publishers B.V., 1990.
2. D. Bjørner, A. Ershov, and N. Jones, editors. *Partial Evaluation and Mixed Computation. Proceedings of the IFIP TC2 Workshop, Gammel Avernæs, Denmark, October 1987.* North-Holland, 1988. 625 pages.
3. A. Bossi and N. Cocco. Basic transformation operations for logic programs which preserve computed answer substitutions. Technical Report 16, Dip. Matematica Pura e Applicata, Università di Padova, Italy, April 1990. to appear in Special Issue on Partial Deduction of the Journal of Logic Programming.
4. A. Bossi, N. Cocco, and S. Dulli. A method for specializing logic programs. *ACM Transactions on Programming Languages and Systems*, 12(2):253–302, April 1990.
5. A. Bossi, N. Cocco, and S. Etalle. Transforming normal program by replacement. In *Third Workshop on Metaprogramming in Logic, META92: Uppsala, Sweden*, June 1992.
6. R. Burstall and J. Darlington. A transformation system for developing recursive programs. *Journal of the ACM*, 24(1):44–67, January 1977.
7. Y. Deville. *Logic Programming. Systematic Program Development.* Addison-Wesley, 1990.
8. S. Etalle. Transformazione dei programmi logici con negazione, Tesi di Laurea, Dip. Matematica Pura e Applicata, Università di Padova, Padova, Italy, July 1991.
9. M. Falaschi, G. Levi, M. Martelli, and C. Palamidessi. Declarative modelling of the operational behavior of logic languages. *Theoretical Computer Science*, 69(3):289–318, 1989.
10. M. Falaschi, G. Levi, M. Martelli, and C. Palamidessi. A model-theoretic reconstruction of the operational semantics of logic programs. Technical Report 32/89, Dipartimento di Informatica, Universitá di Pisa, Italy, September 1989. to appear in Information and Computation.
11. J. Gallagher. Transforming logic programs by specialising interpreters. In *ECAI-86. 7th European Conference on Artificial Intelligence, Brighton Centre, United Kingdom*, pages 109–122, 1986.

12. P. Gardner and J. Shepherdson. Unfold/fold transformations of logic programs. In J.-L. Lassez and e. G. Plotkin, editors, *Computational Logic: Essays in Honor of Alan Robinson.* 1991.
13. C. Hogger. Derivation of logic programs. *Journal of the ACM*, 28(2):372–392, April 1981.
14. T. Kawamura and T. Kanamori. Preservation of stronger equivalence in unfold/fold logic program transformation. In *International Conference on Fifth Generation Computer Systems, Tokyo, Japan, November 1988*, pages 413–421. ICOT, 1988.
15. H. Komorowski. Partial evaluation as a means for inferencing data structures in an applicative language: A theory and implementation in the case of Prolog. In *Ninth ACM Symposium on Principles of Programming Languages, Albuquerque, New Mexico*, pages 255–267, 1982.
16. G. Levi and P. Mancarella. The unfolding semantics of logic programs. Technical Report 13/88, Dipartimento di Informatica, Universitá di Pisa, Italy, September 1988.
17. J. Lloyd. *Foundations of Logic Programming.* Springer-Verlag, 1987.
18. J. Lloyd and J. Shepherdson. Partial evaluation in logic programming. Technical Report CS-87-09, Department of Computer Science, University of Bristol, England, 1987. to appear in Journal of Logic Programming.
19. M. Maher. Correctness of a logic program transformation system. IBM Research Report RC13496, T.J. Watson Research Center, 1987.
20. M. Maher. A transformation system for deductive databases with perfect model semantics. *Theoretical Computer Science*, to appear.
21. M. Proietti and A. Pettorossi. The synthesis of eureka predicates for developing logic programs. In N. Jones, editor, *ESOP'90, (Lecture Notes in Computer Science, Vol. 432)*, pages 306–325. Springer-Verlag, 1990.
22. T. Sato. An equivalence preserving first order unfold/fold transformation system. In *Second Int. Conference on Algebraic and Logic Programming, Nancy, France, October 1990, (Lecture Notes in Computer Science, Vol. 463)*, pages 175–188. Springer-Verlag, 1990.
23. H. Seki. A comparative study of the well-founded and stable model semantics: Transformation's viewpoint. In D. P. W. Marek, A. Nerode and V. Subrahmanian, editors, *Workshop on Logic Programming and Non-Monotonic Logic, Austin, Texas, October 1990*, pages 115–123, 1990.
24. H. Seki. Unfold/fold transformation of stratified programs. *Journal of Theoretical Computer Science*, 86:107–139, 1991.
25. H. Tamaki and T. Sato. A transformation system for logic programs which preserves equivalence. Technical Report ICOT TR-018, ICOT, Tokyo, Japan, August 1983.
26. H. Tamaki and T. Sato. Unfold/fold transformation ol logic programs. In S. Tarnlund, editor, *2nd International Logic Programming Conference, Uppsala, Sweden, July 1984*, pages 127–138, 1984.

This article was processed using the LaTEX macro package with LLNCS style

Unfold/fold Transformations Preserving Termination Properties

Torben Amtoft *

Computer Science Department, Aarhus University
Ny Munkegade, DK-8000 Århus C, Denmark

Abstract. The unfold/fold framework constitutes the spine of many program transformation strategies. However, by unrestricted use of folding the target program may terminate less often than the source program. Several authors have investigated the problem of setting up conditions of syntactic nature, i.e. not based on some well-founded ordering of the arguments, which guarantee preservation of termination properties. These conditions are typically formulated in a way which makes it hard to grasp the basic intuition why they work, and in a way which makes it hard to give elegant proofs of correctness. The aim of this paper will be to give a more unified treatment by setting up a model which enables us to reason about termination preservation in a cleaner and more algebraic fashion. The model resembles a logic language and is parametrized with respect to evaluation order, but it should not be too difficult to transfer the ideas to other languages.

1 Introduction

The unfold/fold framework for program transformation dates back to (at least) [BD77] and has since been the subject of much interest, primarily aimed at making the process of finding "eureka"-definitions more systematic, e.g. [Wad90], [NN90], [PP91b]. Also supercompilation [Tur86] can be seen as a variant over the concept.

A major problem with the technique is that one, due to "too much folding", may risk that the program resulting from transformation (the *target program*) loops while the original (the *source program*) does not. A classical example is the following, expressed in a logic language:

Example 1. Suppose we have a source program S_1 containing the clauses

$p(X) \leftarrow q(X);\ q(a) \leftarrow \Box$

Here the query $p(X)$ will succeed with answer substitution $\{X \rightarrow a\}$. However, if one *folds* the first clause of the program against itself, the target program T_1 will contain the clause

$p(X) \leftarrow p(X)$

and now the query $p(X)$ will loop (i.e. neither succeed or fail). □

* internet: tamtoft@daimi.aau.dk

By innocent abuse of terminology, we will say that a transformation is partially correct iff each time the target program terminates with some result also the source program terminates and with the same result; whereas we will define total correctness to mean partial correctness together with the condition that if the target program does not terminate then neither does the source program. Whether a transformation process itself terminates is beyond the scope of this paper, but e.g. [Wad90], [PP91b] address this problem for certain transformation strategies. For the related technique of *partial evaluation* (cf. [JSS89], [BD91]), the problem of ensuring termination of the partial evaluation process is addressed in [Hol91]. Upper bounds for the speed-up possible by applying unfold/fold transformations have been given in [Han91], [Hon91].

Several ways to guarantee total correctness have been proposed in the literature, e.g. [TS84], [KK90], [Sek91], [Kot85], [GS91], [PP91a]. They all work by putting forward some restrictions on the types of foldings allowed. For a more detailed description (and comparison with our approach), see Sect. 5.

The purpose of this paper is to present a model for unfold/fold-transformations which enables one to express conditions which are provably sufficient for total correctness. We want the model to include (most of) the results from the literature as special cases (after the frameworks in question have been encoded into our framework); and we want the model to have a clean algebraic structure.

Lack of space prevents us from giving detailed descriptions of how to translate other formalisms into our model - however, we hope our examples will provide the reader with sufficient intuition.

Our framework is primarily aimed at modeling logic programming - even though the machinery differs from the one usually used when treating logic languages, as done in e.g. [Llo84], [Søn89]. However, we believe that the main ideas can be carried over to other types of languages as well.

1.1 Two-level Transitions

The meaning of programs will be defined in terms of a transition semantics (cf. [Plo81]). The reason for this is that we feel this is more appropriate for capturing the essence of unfolding and folding: unfolding corresponds to a transition being made in the "right" direction; folding corresponds to a transition being made in the "wrong" direction. By using a denotational approach, this cannot be expressed directly. We believe that the reason why conditions for unfold/fold transformations to be termination preserving apparently is a more hot topic in the logic programming community than in the functional community is that in the former operational semantics (typically derivation trees) has a more respectable status than in the latter.

Main Idea. We will now, in a *very informal and simplified* way, present the basic intuition underlying this work. Execution of the source program on a goal configuration C_1 corresponds to a transition sequence

$$C_1 \rightarrow C_2 \rightarrow C_3 \rightarrow \ldots$$

where each $C_i \rightarrow C_{i+1}$ corresponds to an atom in C_i being unfolded. For the transition system in question, a "Church-Rosser property" says that if there is a transition from C to C_1 using n_1 inference steps (i.e. unfoldings), and also a transition from C to C_2 using n_2 inference steps, then there exists a configuration C' and numbers n'_1 and n'_2 such that there is a transition from C_1 to C' using n'_1 inference steps, and a transition from C_2 to C' using n'_2 inference steps. Moreover, it will hold that $n_1 + n'_1 = n_2 + n'_2$ [2]

A clause in the target program takes the form

$$C_1 \xrightarrow{u} C' \xleftarrow{f} C_2$$

This means that first we have unfolded C_1 into C' (using u inference steps), and then folded back into C_2 - or equivalently unfolded C_2 into C', using f inference steps.

Now suppose the target program loops. This means that there exists an infinite sequence $C_1 \ldots C_i \ldots$ where each step from C_i to C_{i+1} represents an application of a clause in the target program, i.e. for all i there exists C'_i, u_i, f_i such that

$$C_i \xrightarrow{u_i} C'_i \xleftarrow{f_i} C_{i+1}$$

In order for the transformation in question to be termination preserving, we must demand the source program to loop on C_1 as well. Our task is to find sufficient conditions for this. First we can draw the Church-Rosser completion of the situation, as sketched in Fig. 1. Now, if for all i we have $u_i > f_i$ then the path

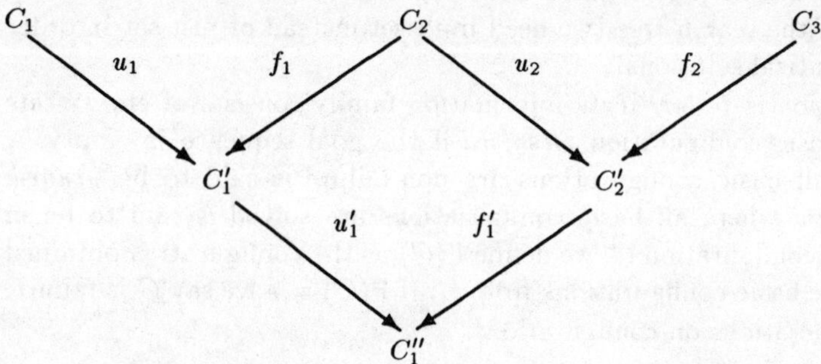

Fig. 1. A Church-Rosser completion.

$$C_1 \rightarrow C'_1 \rightarrow C''_1 \rightarrow \ldots$$

will represent infinitely many inference steps - too see this, note that e.g.

$$\begin{aligned} u_1 + u'_1 &> f_1 + u'_1 = u_2 + f'_1 \\ &> f_2 + f'_1 \end{aligned}$$

[2] In order for such a simple relation to hold one must, of course, assume that no copying or destruction of "redices" takes place.

Observe that the u_i's and f_i's do not necessarily have to denote the total number of inference steps. By e.g. letting them denote only the number of steps where certain predicates are unfolded, the same reasoning applies. More generally, one can - as will be done in this paper - assign a *weight* to each predicate symbol.

Of course, several features are not accounted for in the treatment above - we will repair on this in the following.

Configurations. A *basic configuration* is a sequence of goals together with some information about which values the variables in the goals can assume. One usually represents this information as a substitution, cf. [Llo84]. As substitutions are hard to reason about from an algebraic point of view (even though e.g. [Søn89] and [Pal89] show that certain sets of substitutions carry some structure), we will represent the information as a family of sets of ground values. As an example take the goal sequence $(p(X),q(Y),r(Z))$ together with the substitution $\{X \rightarrow f(Y),\ Z \rightarrow \mathrm{a}\}$ Assuming that $\mathcal{D}$ is a universal data domain, this in our framework could be represented as the goal sequence (p,q,r) together with the $\mathcal{D}$-indexed family where the d'th element is the singleton set $\{(f(d), d, \mathrm{a})\}$ - on the other hand, one might also use the family consisting of one element only, namely the set $\{(f(d), d, \mathrm{a}) | d \in \mathcal{D}\}$. The latter representation will be needed for dealing with "variables occurring on the right hand side but not on the left hand side"; we will elaborate on this issue later in this section.

A *configuration* is a multiset of basic configurations (whose "information families" are indexed over the same set). A configuration can be thought of as representing the current frontier of the search tree (we need multiset instead of just set in order to model multiple identical solutions).

A basic configuration is *failure* if its information family consists of empty sets only. A non-failure basic configuration is *solved* if the goal sequence is empty. A configuration where all basic configurations are non-failure is said to be *pruned.* A pruned configuration where all basic configurations are solved is said to be in *normal form.* Given a configuration C, we define $\mathsf{P}(C)$ as the configuration obtained by removing all failure basic configurations from C. If $\mathsf{P}(C) = \emptyset$ we say C is failure.

We define some operations on configurations:

+: C_1+C_2 is just the union (taken as multisets) of C_1 and C_2 (only defined if the information families are indexed over the same set). Intuitively, this models "or".

&: Intuitively, this models "and". On basic configurations, this is defined as follows: let B_i, $i = 1, 2$, consist of goal sequence H_i and an information family Q_i indexed over K_i. Now $B_1 \& B_2$ consists of the goal sequence $H_1 H_2$ together with an information family Q indexed over $K_1 \times K_2$, where Q is given by

$$Q(k_1, k_2) = \{d_1 \times d_2 | d_1 \in Q(k_1), d_2 \in Q(k_2)\}$$

The extension to (non-basic) configurations is determined by the desire to make & distributive over +.

$\mathcal{U}\_(\_)$: Intuitively, this models instantiation. Let B be a basic configuration with goal sequence H and an information family Q indexed over K. Let s be a mapping from some other index set K' into $\mathcal{P}(K)$. Then $\mathcal{U}_s(B)$ is the goal sequence H together with the K'-indexed information family Q', where

$$Q'(k') = \bigcup_{k \in s(k')} Q(k)$$

As an example of how these operations work together, consider how the goal sequence *p(X),q(X)* will be represented in our framework. Define B_1 as the basic configuration consisting of goal sequence p and $\mathcal{D}$-indexed information family Q_1 given by $Q_1(d) = \{d\}$; and let B_2 consist of goal sequence q and (again) Q_1. Now $B = B_1 \& B_2$ will consist of goal sequence *(p,q)* and $\mathcal{D} \times \mathcal{D}$-indexed family Q, where $Q(d_1, d_2) = \{(d_1, d_2)\}$. Define $s : \mathcal{D} \rightarrow \mathcal{D} \times \mathcal{D}$ by $s(d) = (d, d)$. Then $B' = \mathcal{U}_s(B)$ will contain goal sequence *(p,q)* and $\mathcal{D}$-information family Q', where

$$Q'(d) = \bigcup_{(d_1,d_2) \in s(d)} Q(d_1, d_2) = Q(d, d) = \{(d, d)\}$$

enabling us to conclude that *p(X),q(X)* can be represented as $\mathcal{U}_s(B_1 \& B_2)$.

Transitions. If there is a transition between configurations C and C', the index sets of the information families of C and C' must be isomorphic. There exist some operations on transitions:

+: If t_1 is a transition from C_1 to C_1', and if t_2 is a transition from C_2 to C_2', then $t_1 + t_2$ will be a transition from $C_1 + C_2$ to $C_1' + C_2'$. This models "or-parallelism", cf. [Gre87].

&: If t_1 is a transition from C_1 to C_1', and if t_2 is a transition from C_2 to C_2', then $t_1 \& t_2$ will be a transition from $C_1 \& C_2$ to $C_1' \& C_2'$. This models "and-parallelism".

$\mathcal{U}\_(\_)$: If t is a transition from C_1 to C_2, and s is a function (having an appropriate functionality), $\mathcal{U}_s(t)$ will be a transition from $\mathcal{U}_s(C_1)$ to $\mathcal{U}_s(C_2)$.

$\star$: If t_1 is a transition from C_1 to C_2, and t_2 is a transition from C_2 to C_3, then $t_1 \star t_2$ is a transition from C_1 to C_3. This modeles sequential execution.

*Id_*: For all configurations C, there exists an identity transition Id_C from C to C.

P(_): If t is a transition from C_1 to C_2, then $\mathsf{P}(t)$ (the pruning of t) is a transition from $\mathsf{P}(C_1)$ to $\mathsf{P}(C_2)$.

Not all transitions are valid. We have a hierarchy as follows:

1. The source program is represented as *rules at level 0*. For instance, if p is defined by the clauses

   p(a) $\leftarrow \square$ *and p(X)* $\leftarrow$*q(f(X,Y))*

   then this will be represented as a transition from the configuration *[p]*,$\{\{d\} | d \in \mathcal{D}\}$ to the configuration consisting of the basic configurations B_1 and B_2, where $B_1 = ([], Q_1)$, $B_2 = ([q], Q_2)$ and where the information families Q_1 and Q_2, both indexed by $\mathcal{D}$, are defined by $Q_1(\mathrm{a}) = \{()\}$, $Q_1(d) = \emptyset$ for $d \neq \mathrm{a}$, $Q_2(d) = \{f(d, d') | d' \in \mathcal{D}\}$.

2. As soon as the rules at level 0 have been given, the *valid transitions at level 1* (also called the 1-valid transitions) and the *t-valid transitions at level 1* (also called the 1t-valid transitions) will be fixed. The intuition behind the 1-valid transitions is that they should model standard execution of the source program; therefore the set of 1-valid transitions is defined to be the closure of the set of level 0 rules wrt. the operations $+$, &, $\mathcal{U}_{\_}(\_)$, $\star$, $Id_{\_}$ and P(_).
   The intuition behind the 1t-valid transitions is that they should model transformation ("symbolic evaluation") of the source program, thus the set of 1t-valid transitions will be the closure (wrt. the operations $+$, &, $\mathcal{U}_{\_}(\_)$, $\star$, $Id_{\_}$, P(_)) of the set consisting of the level 0 rules *together with* "legal reversals" of those. What constitutes a legal reversal will be defined in the following.
   If there is a 1-valid transition from C to D we write $1 \vdash_u C \rightarrow D$; if there is a 1t-valid transition from C to D we write $1 \vdash C \rightarrow D$. One can also define the closure of the set of legal reversals of level 0 rules (without the level 0 rules themselves); if there is a transition in this set from C to D we write $1 \vdash_f C \rightarrow D$.
3. Among all the 1t-valid transitions, some are chosen to be *rules at level 1.* These rules can be interpreted as the target program.
4. As soon as the rules at level 1 have been given, the *valid transitions at level 2* (also called the 2-valid transitions) will be fixed as the closure of the level 1 rules (wrt. the operations $+$, &, $\mathcal{U}_{\_}(\_)$, $\star$, $Id_{\_}$, P(_)). Intuitively, 2-valid transitions model (standard) execution of the target program. If there is a 2-valid transition from C to D, we write $2 \vdash C \rightarrow D$.

A key point of our approach is that "standard evaluation" (the 1-valid transitions) is a special case of "symbolic evaluation" (the 1t-valid transitions) - this greatly facilitates reasoning about the properties of the target program. This lack of distinction between standard evaluation and symbolic evaluation comes almost for free in a logic language, but also in the functional world one gains from viewing the latter as a generalization of the former [DP88]. However, an important difference between standard and symbolic evaluation is that during symbolic evaluation any atom in the goal sequence may be unfolded, whereas during standard evaluation one for efficiency reasons often chooses a fixed strategy, typically the strategy always to unfold the leftmost goal - this strategy will be denoted $\mathcal{LR}$.

Legal Reversals. We are left with the question of what constitutes a legal reversal of a level 0 rule. Let the level 0 rule (defining p) be a transition from basic configuration $B = ([p], \{\{d\} | d \in \mathcal{D}\})$ to configuration $B_1 + \ldots + B_n$. Now suppose $s(p, i)$ (a function of p and i) is such that

- the information family of $\mathcal{U}_{s(p,i)}(B_i)$ consists of non-empty sets only
- $\mathcal{U}_{s(p,i)}(B'_i)$ is failure for all $i' \neq i$.

Then there will be a transition (a legal reversal) from $\mathcal{U}_{s(p,i)}(B_i)$ to $\mathcal{U}_{s(p,i)}(B)$.
Some noteworthy points:

- To motivate why we demand the information family of $\mathcal{U}_{s(p,i)}(B_i)$ to consist of non-empty sets only, observe that otherwise there might be a fold transition from a failure configuration into a non-failure configuration, something which would render our theorems about termination preservation void: referring back to Fig. 1, this corresponds to e.g. C_1'' being failure while C_3 not. In the standard framework, the condition can be explained as follows: if there is a program clause $p(a) \leftarrow q(a)$ and one encounters the goal $q(a)$, one should fold it back into $p(a)$ and not into $p(X)$ - even though unifying the goal $p(X)$ against the above clause gives us the goal $q(a)$ as result.

- To motivate why we demand that $\mathcal{U}_{s(p,i)}(B'_i)$ is failure for all $i' \neq i$, observe that otherwise we would have a 1t-valid transition from $\mathcal{U}_{s(p,i)}(B_i)$ to $\mathcal{U}_{s(p,i)}(B_i)$ + $\mathcal{U}_{s(p,i)}(B'_i)$ the latter basic configuration *not* being failure. In the standard framework, this is modeled by the requirement that only one clause defining the predicate folded against should match.
- Recall that e.g. the clause $p(X) \leftarrow q(f(X,Y))$ is translated into a transition from $([p], \{\{d\} | d \in \mathcal{D}\}$ to $([q], Q)$, where $Q(d) = \{f(d,d') | d' \in \mathcal{D}\}$. Thus Q does *not* consist of singletons only, and hence - switching back and forth between our framework and the standard framework - it will be impossible to instantiate Y by means of the $\mathcal{U}_{\_}(\_)$-operation. This gives a nice solution to the problems arising when folding against a clause containing variables not occurring in the head - a problem to which some incorrect solutions have been proposed in the literature (and yet proved correct!), for a survey see [GS91].

1.2 An Overview of This Paper

In Sect. 2 we give a semantics for the language sketched above and state some of its properties. In Sect. 3 we state some conditions ensuring preservation of semantics. These conditions will be "global", i.e. not relate to a single rule at level 1. In Sect. 4 we for each such global condition states a local condition, i.e. a condition concerning the form of a level 1-rule, which implies the global condition (and hence termination preservation). In Sect. 5 we discuss other approaches to the problem of ensuring total correctness and relate them to our model. Section 6 concludes. Some important theorems will, due to lack of space, be given without proof (or only a loose sketch of such); these will appear in [Amt92].

2 Two-level Semantics

First the Church-Rosser property can be formulated:

Theorem 1. *If* $1 \vdash_u C \rightarrow C_1$ *and* $1 \vdash_u C \rightarrow C_2$*, with* C_1 *and* C_2 *pruned, then there exists* D *such that* $1 \vdash_u C_1 \rightarrow D$ *and* $1 \vdash_u C_2 \rightarrow D$.

This proposition only holds because we imposed no ordering on the elements of a configuration, which thus is a *multiset* and not a *sequence* of basic configurations. In [PP91a] one wants to model the fact the standard PROLOG explores the branches in sequential order, and therefore unfolding of the *leftmost* atom only is allowed (unless extra conditions are satisfied).

Suppose we have a function $\mathcal{E}$ which from a *basic* configuration B and a configuration C in normal form (where there is a transition from B to C) extracts the "final result" $\mathcal{E}(B,C)$. $\mathcal{E}(B,C)$ will correspond to the multiset of answer substitutions. For instance, if C is a singleton and contains a $\mathcal{D}$-indexed information family Q, then we would naturally define

$$\mathcal{E}(B,C) = \{d|Q(d) \neq \emptyset\}$$

Let $\mathcal{V}$ be the codomain of $\mathcal{E}$, extended with a bottom element $\perp$ such that for all $v \in \mathcal{V}$, $\perp \leq v$ - thus making $\mathcal{V}$ a flat domain.

Definition 2. If there exists a pruned C in normal form such that there is a 1-valid transition from B to C, then $[\![\mathrm{B}]\!]_1 = \mathcal{E}(B,C)$. If there exists no such C, $[\![\mathrm{B}]\!]_1 = \perp$.

Exploiting Theorem 1, one can easily check that this is well-defined. Notice that a program which e.g. returns an answer and then loops is identified with a program which loops without producing any answer. It should not be too hard to modify the semantics so it distinguishes between such programs.

The following theorem comes almost immediately from the definitions:

Theorem 3. *If* $2 \vdash C \rightarrow D$, *then also* $1 \vdash C \rightarrow D$.

Next comes a most crucial theorem, stating that an arbitrarily mixed sequence of unfoldings and foldings is equivalent to a sequence of unfoldings followed by a sequence of foldings - this bears some similarities to proof normalization [GLT89].

Theorem 4. *If* $1 \vdash C \rightarrow D$ *with* C,D *pruned, there exists* E *such that* $1 \vdash_u C \rightarrow E$, $1 \vdash_f E \rightarrow D$ *(and then also* $1 \vdash_u D \rightarrow E$*).*

Proof. (A sketch only) Consider the transition sequence leading from C to D (which we can assume leads through pruned configurations only). If no folding precedes an unfolding, we are through. Otherwise, the situation is that some C_i has been folded into C_{i+1} and then unfolded into C_{i+2}. As a folding represents an inverse unfolding, we can apply theorem 1 to find C'_{i+1} such that C_i and C_{i+2} both can be unfolded into C'_{i+1}. Moreover, it is not too hard to see that the latter unfolding can be reversed into a folding from C'_{i+1} into C_{i+2}.

By repeating the process above, we eventually gets a transition sequence in the desired form. □

If D is in normal form, we from $1 \vdash_u D \rightarrow E$ conclude $D = E$. We then, by combining with Theorem 3, get

Corollary 5. *If* $2 \vdash C \rightarrow D$, *with* C *pruned and* D *in normal form,* $1 \vdash_u C \rightarrow D$.

Definition 6. If there exists a C in normal form such that there is a 2-valid transition from B to C, then $[\![\mathrm{B}]\!]_2 = \mathcal{E}(B,C)$. If there exists no such C, $[\![\mathrm{B}]\!]_2 = \perp$.

Using Corollary 5 we see that this is well-defined. Moreover, we get a theorem expressing that transformation is *partial correct*:

Theorem 7. *If* $[\![B]\!]_2 = v \neq \perp$, *then also* $[\![B]\!]_1 = v$ *- i.e. for all* B, $[\![B]\!]_2 \leq [\![B]\!]_1$.

In order to give conditions for *total correctness* we need some definitions. We say that B *loops at level 1* iff there exists an infinite sequence of pruned, non-empty configurations $C_1 \ldots C_n \ldots$ with $B = C_1$ such that for all i there exists a 1-valid transition from C_i to C_{i+1} where this transition represents (at least) one unfolding step. Similarly, we can define that B loops at level 2.

Notice that it does not necessarily hold that $[\![B]\!]_2 = \perp$ (or $[\![B]\!]_1 = \perp$) implies that B loops at level 2 (level 1), since a given configuration may be *stuck*, i.e. it is not in normal form but it is not possible to unfold any goals. However, we shall assume that the rules are "exhaustive", excluding such behavior.

As is well known, it may happen that B loops at level 1 (due to some ineffective strategy) while $[\![B]\!]_1 \neq \perp$. On the other hand, if we (cf. [Llo84]) define a *fair* strategy as a strategy which sooner or later unfolds any goal, we have

Fact 8. *If B loops at level 1 (2) by a fair strategy, then $[\![B]\!]_1 = \perp$ ($[\![B]\!]_2 = \perp$).*

3 Global Conditions for Total Correctness

We start by proposing some conditions which may be helpful for proving total correctness. Here B will be a basic configuration.

Definition 9. We say that $\mathcal{F}$ (for *F*air) is satisfied iff for any B it holds that if B loops at level 2 by a fair strategy then it also loops at level 1 by a fair strategy.

We say that $\mathcal{L}$ (for *L*eftmost) is satisfied iff for any B it holds that if B loops at level 2 by the $\mathcal{LR}$ strategy then it also loops at level 1 by the $\mathcal{LR}$ strategy.

We say that $\mathcal{A}$ (for *A*ny) is satisfied iff for any B it holds that if B loops at level 2 by some strategy then it also loops at level 1 by some strategy.

Theorem 10. *Suppose $\mathcal{F}$ holds. Then for any B, $[\![B]\!]_2 = [\![B]\!]_1$.*

Proof. Suppose $[\![B]\!]_2 = \perp$. Then B loops at level 2 by a fair strategy, and by $\mathcal{F}$ also at level 1 by a fair strategy. By Fact 8, $[\![B]\!]_1 = \perp$. Now combine with Theorem 7. □

In order to model e.g. PROLOG, a semantics capturing that evaluation employs the $\mathcal{LR}$ strategy seems better suited:

Definition 11. If there exists a C in normal form such that there is a 1-valid (2-valid) transition, using the $\mathcal{LR}$ strategy, from B to C, then $[\![B]\!]_1^{\mathcal{L}} = \mathcal{E}(B, C)$ ($[\![B]\!]_2^{\mathcal{L}} = \mathcal{E}(B, C)$). If there exists no such C, $[\![B]\!]_1^{\mathcal{L}} = \perp$ ($[\![B]\!]_2^{\mathcal{L}} = \perp$).

Fact 12. *For all B, $[\![B]\!]_1^{\mathcal{L}} \leq [\![B]\!]_1$, $[\![B]\!]_2^{\mathcal{L}} \leq [\![B]\!]_2$.*

As is well known, we cannot hope for $[\![B]\!]_2^{\mathcal{L}} \leq [\![B]\!]_1^{\mathcal{L}}$ to hold in general (unless some tight restrictions are made). This corresponds, in the functional world, to the fact that the call-by-name nature of symbolic evaluation may increase the domain of termination in a call-by-value language. Now let us consider what must be fulfilled in order for the opposite inclusion to hold:

Theorem 13. *Suppose $\mathcal{L}$ is fulfilled. Then for all B, $[\![B]\!]_1^{\mathcal{L}} \leq [\![B]\!]_2^{\mathcal{L}}$.*

Proof. If $[\![B]\!]_2^L = v \neq \perp$, then by Fact 12 $[\![B]\!]_2 = v$. By Theorem 7, $[\![B]\!]_1 = v$; so by Fact 12 $[\![B]\!]_1^L \leq v$. If $[\![B]\!]_2^L = \perp$, the result follows from the assumption. □

Finally, one may ask what use the condition $\mathcal{A}$ is. Now, suppose B is such that if B loops at level 1 by some strategy then B loops at level 1 by any strategy (we say that B is strategy-independent). Then we can reason as follows: Suppose $[\![B]\!]_2 = \perp$. Therefore B loops at level 2 by any strategy. If $\mathcal{A}$ holds, B loops at level 1 by some strategy. By assumption, B loops at level 1 by any strategy; thus $[\![B]\!]_1 = \perp$. We have shown

Theorem 14. *If $\mathcal{A}$ holds, and B is strategy-independent, then $[\![B]\!]_2 = [\![B]\!]_1$.*

4 Local Conditions for Total Correctness

This section will be devoted to formulating conditions F, L, A for the 1t-valid transition sequences leading to the level-1-rules, such that F implies $\mathcal{F}$, L implies $\mathcal{L}$ and A implies $\mathcal{A}$.

In order to reason about 1t-valid transition sequences we represent them as *U-mirrors,* which models the fact (cf. Theorem 4) that such a sequence is equivalent to a sequence of unfoldings followed by a sequence of foldings. Before stating a formal definition we will give an example.

Example 2. Let the source program S_2 be given by (as it is the control aspect which has our primary interest, we use substitutions to describe data)

$p(X) \leftarrow q(X), r(X);\ q(a) \leftarrow q(a);\ r(b) \leftarrow \Box$

We can transform the definition of p by *first* unfolding q (into q) and *then* fold back into p. By leaving q and r unchanged, we arrive at the target program T_2:

$p(a) \leftarrow p(a);\ q(a) \leftarrow q(a);\ r(b) \leftarrow \Box$

In Fig. 2 is depicted a U-mirror u corresponding to the transformation on p.

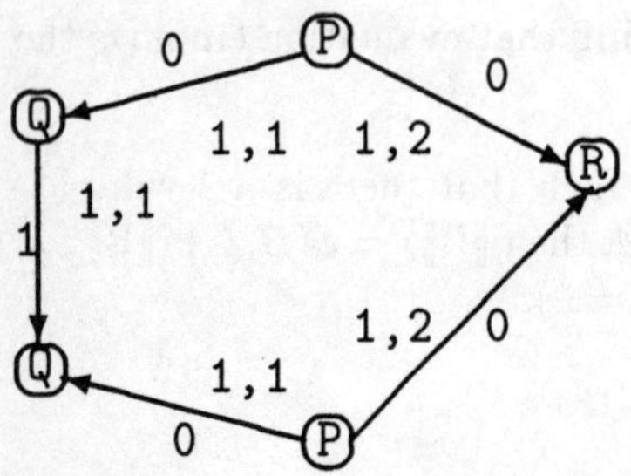

Fig. 2. The U-mirror u, corresponding to T_2.

We see that u has an arrow from the topmost node labeled q to the node below (representing the unfolding of q), and the folding step is represented by the arrows going *up* from the bottom node.

As can be seen, also the arcs are labeled. For instance the arc from p to r is labeled with $(1,2)$ (inside the diagram) and with 0 (outside the diagram). The label $(1,2)$ means that the 2nd conjunct in the 1st rule (in this case, there are no other rules) for p is r. The label 0 is the *weight* of the arc, more about that later. □

Now we will embark on giving a formal definition of U-mirrors. First, the control aspect (ctr. the data aspect) of a source program must be represented:

Definition 15. A control representation of a source program consists of

- A universe U of predicate symbols. Let $U' = U \cup \{\Box\}$
- A function OI (for Or Indices) which for each $G \in U$ returns a non-empty index set $OI(G)$.
- A function AI (for And Indices) which for each $G \in U$ and each $i \in OI(G)$ returns a non-empty index set $AI(G,i)$. This set must be equipped with a total order $\prec$, $j_1 \prec j_2$ modelling "j_1 is to the left of j_2".
- A function P which for each $G \in U$, each $i \in OI(G)$ and each $j \in AI(G,i)$ returns $P(G,i,j) \in U'$. If $P(G,i,j) = \Box$, then $AI(G,i)$ is a singleton.
- A function W which for each $G \in U$, each $i \in OI(G)$ and each $j \in AI(G,i)$ returns $W(G,i,j)$, a non-negative integer.

Except for the weight part it is rather obvious how one, given a source program, arrives at a control representation:

Example 3. For the source program S_2 from Example 2 we have among others $U = \{p,q,r\}$, $OI(p) = \{1\}$ (or any one-element set), $AI(p,1) = \{1,2\}$ (or any two-element set) with $1 \prec 2$, $P(p,1,1) = q$, $P(p,1,2) = r$, $P(r,1,1) = \Box$. □

The weights, on the other hand, can be assigned in a completely arbitrary fashion - but if one wants to prove that a given transformation is correct using the techniques given in this paper, one may have to be a bit clever about the assignment. In Fig. 2, one has e.g. made the choices $W(p,1,2) = 0$, $W(q,1,1) = 1$.

Definition 16. A *goal sequence* (J,H) is a totally ordered index set J and a mapping H from J to U.

Definition 17. A U-forest over a goal sequence (J,H) is a J-indexed family of trees where

- All nodes are labeled by a member of U'.
- All arcs are labeled by a direction label (i,j) and a weight label w.
- For all $j \in J$, the root of the j'th tree must be labeled by $H(j)$
- Let N be a node which is not a leaf. Then its label G must belong to U (i.e. not be □), and there must exist an $i' \in OI(G)$ such that (i,j) is the label of an arc from N if and only if $i = i'$, $j \in AI(G,i)$. The arcs from N inherit the ordering of $AI(G,i)$.
- If a is an arc with direction label (i,j) from a node labeled G to a node N, then the label of N must be $P(G,i,j)$, and the weight label of a must be $W(G,i,j)$
- There is a total ordering among the leaves (and thus also among the paths, where a path starts at a root and ends at a leaf), determined in the "natural way" by the ordering on J and the ordering on the arcs leaving each node.

We say that a U-forest is *foldy* iff no nodes are labeled □. The intuition is that if one has a clause say $r \leftarrow \Box$ then one is not allowed to make a fold transition from p to p,r.

We define the *weight* of a path as the sum of the weight labels encountered when walking along the path. We define the *weight* of a U-forest as the sum of all the weight labels occurring in the tree.

Definition 18. A U-mirror $(u, v, \sim)$ over goal sequences H and H' consists of a U-forest u over H, a foldy U-forest v over H', and a bijection $\sim$ between the paths of u *not* containing □ and the paths of v which preserves the ordering on these, and which satisfies that if $p \sim q$ then p and q end with the same symbol.

A path in $(u, v, \sim)$ is *either* of the form (p, q) with $p \in u$, $q \in v$ and $p \sim q$ *or* is of the form p, where $p \in u$ and p ends with □. There is a natural total order on paths. Referring back to Fig. 2, it can be checked that u is a U-mirror over (p) and (p).

We can assign weights to paths in a U-mirror as follows: if the path is of form (p, q), the weight is the difference between the weight of p and the weight of q; otherwise the path is of form p and its weight is simply the weight of p. Likewise, we can define the weight of the U-mirror as the difference between the weight of u and the weight of v.

Finally, we are in position to formulate F, L and A:

Definition 19. Given a U-mirror m. Then

- m satisfies F iff all paths have weight ≥ 1
- m satisfies L iff the leftmost path has weight ≥ 1
- m satisfies A iff m has weight ≥ 1.

Example 4. Referring back to Fig. 2, u satisfies L and A but not F.

We say that a transition from B to $B_1 + \ldots + B_n$ satisfies F if for all $i \in \{1 \ldots n\}$, the U-mirror representing how to get from B to B_i satisfies F. Similarly for L and A.

Theorem 20. *Suppose all rules at level 1 satisfy* F. *Then $\mathcal{F}$ holds, and thus* $[\![B]\!]_2 = [\![B]\!]_1$ *for all B, cf. Theorem 10.*

This theorem is essentially the main content of (but is more general than) [Sek91]

Theorem 21. *Suppose all rules at level 1 satisfy* L. *Then $\mathcal{L}$ holds, and thus* $[\![B]\!]_2^L \geq [\![B]\!]_1^L$ *for all B, cf. Theorem 13.*

More specific versions of this theorem are stated in [PP91a] and [Han91].

Theorem 22. *Suppose all rules at level 1 satisfy* A. *Then $\mathcal{A}$ holds, and thus* $[\![B]\!]_2 = [\![B]\!]_1$ *for all* strategy-independent *B, cf. Theorem 14.*

As the correctness condition for folding, [TS84] and [KK90] essentially use (a special case of) A.

For proofs of Theorem 20, 21 and 22 (which all elaborate on the intuition presented in section 1), see [Amt92].

Example 5. Continuing from Example 4, we by Theorem 21 can conclude that $\mathcal{L}$ holds - which is as expected since S_2 loops on $p(t)$ by the $\mathcal{LR}$ strategy iff t unifies with a iff T_2 loops on $p(t)$ by the $\mathcal{LR}$ strategy.

On the other hand, our theorems do not allow us to conclude that $\mathcal{F}$ holds - and neither it does, since S_2 terminates by a fair strategy on $p(t)$ for any t while T_2 loops (by any strategy) on e.g. $p(a)$.

Notice that if we e.g. had chosen $W(q, 1, 1) = 0$, we had not been able to infer that $\mathcal{L}$ holds.

5 Related Work

- In the literature on unfold/fold transformations in logic languages transformation typically proceeds in a "step by step fashion"; after a goal in the body of a clause has been unfolded the clause is *deleted* from the program and *replaced* by the clause resulting from the unfolding - this is the approach taken in e.g. [GS91], [KK90], [PP91a], [Sek91], [TS84]. As pointed out in [GS91], one by applying this method loses some power - to see this, consider the clause $C = p(f(X)) \leftarrow p(X)$. By our or similar techniques one is able to derive the clause $C' : p(f(f(f(X)))) \leftarrow p(X)$ but this is impossible by the step-by-step method, since one - after having unfolded C against itself obtaining $p(f(f(X))) \leftarrow p(X)$ - has lost C. Aside from being less powerful, we also think that the step-by-step strategy conceptually is much less clean than our approach - a similar view being held in [Tur86].
- In the literature, one is typically (contrary to our framework) not allowed to fold against a (direct or indirect) recursive predicate [KK90], [PP91a], [Sek91], [TS84]. This mirrors the view that folding corresponds to abbreviation, a view also held in [Han91]. On the other hand, as pointed out in [PP91b] this is essentially no restriction for applications.
- [TS84] and [KK90] divide the predicates into two classes: the *new* (corresponding to "eureka-definitions") and *old*, where folding is allowed against new predicates only. In order for folding to be valid, they require that in the body of the clause defining a new predicate (where only old predicates can occur) at least one predicate must have been unfolded. We can translate this into our framework: new predicates are assigned weight 0, old predicates are assigned weight 1, and A must hold. As we have seen in Sect. 3, this condition is (too) weak, since failing branches may convert to loops.
- [Sek91] improves on the above, essentially by demanding that F must hold (still when new predicates have been assigned weight 0 and old predicates weight 1).
- [Kot85] treats a functional language, where there apparently is no branching. The situation is that first a number of unfoldings are made, then some laws are applied (not catered for by our framework), then some foldings are made. It is claimed that folding is safe if the number of unfoldings is greater than the number of foldings. In some sense, this can be modeled in our framework by assigning all predicates weight 1.
- [GS91] allows folding against *existing* clauses (recall clauses are deleted after having been unfolded) only (not allowing a clause to be folded against itself).

This greatly limits the applications, since it seems impossible to arrive at recursive definitions of eureka-predicates. On the other hand, it becomes possible to give a relatively simple proof of termination preservation.

- In contrast to the authors mentioned so far, [PP91a] impose an order on a sequence of goals, i.e. consider PROLOG's $\mathcal{LR}$ strategy. The crucial condition on folding is that the leftmost atom has been unfolded. Again by assigning the predicates folded against weight 0 and the others 1, the essence of this translates into our condition L.

6 Final Remarks

We hope this paper has contributed to giving a better understanding of the notion of folding, making the duality between folding and unfolding more explicit. Still, not every unfolding can be reversed into a folding, and even though we cannot hope for this, the set of legal reversals might be extended:

- If there is a transition from B to B_1+B_2, we in order to make a fold step from B_1 to B had to ensure that B_2 was failure. Under some conditions it will be enough if there is a transition from B_2 to a failure configuration - such an extension is essential if one is to model folding against clauses derived during transformation but not present in the original source program.
- If there is a transition from B to B_1+B_2, we may even consider folding the *non-singleton* configuration B_1+B_2 back into B - this bears some similarity to the process of converting a nondeterministic automaton into a deterministic equivalent.

Work in progress includes setting up a model for a *functional* language in which results similar to the ones presented here can be obtained.

Thanks are due to Jens Palsberg, Jesper Träff and Brian Mayoh for reading drafts of this paper; also thanks to the anonymous referees for useful suggestions.

References

[Amt92] Torben Amtoft. Unfold/fold transformations preserving termination properties. To appear as a technical report from DAIMI, University of Aarhus, Denmark, 1992.

[BD77] R.M. Burstall and John Darlington. A transformation system for developing recursive programs. *Journal of the ACM*, 24(1):44–67, January 1977.

[BD91] Anders Bondorf and Olivier Danvy. Automatic autoprojection of recursive equations with global variables and abstract data types. *Science of Computer Programming*, 16(2):151–195, 1991.

[DP88] John Darlington and Helen Pull. A program development methodology based on a unified approach to execution and transformation. In D. Bjørner, A.P. Ershov, and N.D. Jones, editors, *Partial Evaluation and Mixed Computation*, pages 117–131. North-Holland, 1988.

[GLT89] Jean-Yves Girard, Yves Lafont, and Paul Taylor. *Proofs and Types*. Cambridge University Press, 1989.

[Gre87] Steve Gregory. *Parallel Logic Programming in PARLOG - the language and its implementation.* Addison-Wesley, 1987.

[GS91] P. A. Gardner and J. C. Shepherdson. Unfold/fold transformations of logic programs. In *Computational Proofs: Essays in honour of Alan Robinson.* 1991.

[Han91] Torben Amtoft Hansen. Properties of unfolding-based meta-level systems. In *Partial Evaluation and Semantics-Based Program Manipulation, New Haven, Connecticut. (Sigplan Notices, vol. 26, no. 9)*, 1991.

[Hol91] Carsten Kehler Holst. Finiteness analysis. In John Hughes, editor, *International Conference on Functional Programming Languages and Computer Architecture.* Springer Verlag, LNCS no 523, August 1991.

[Hon91] Zhu Hong. How powerful are folding/unfolding transformations. Technical Report CSTR-91-2, Department of Computer Science, Brunel University, January 1991.

[JSS89] Neil D. Jones, Peter Sestoft, and Harald Søndergaard. Mix: A self-applicable partial evaluator for experiments in compiler generation. *Lisp and Symbolic Computation*, 2(1):9–50, 1989.

[KK90] Tadashi Kawamura and Tadashi Kanamori. Preservation of stronger equivalence in unfold/fold logic program transformation. *Theoretical Computer Science*, 75:139–156, 1990.

[Kot85] Laurent Kott. Unfold/fold program transformations. In Maurice Nivat and John C. Reynolds, editors, *Algebraic Methods in Semantics*, chapter 12. Cambridge University Press, 1985.

[Llo84] J.W. Lloyd. *Foundations of Logic Programming.* Springer-Verlag, 1984.

[NN90] Hanne Riis Nielson and Flemming Nielson. Eureka definitions for free! or disagreement points for fold/unfold transformations. In Neil D. Jones, editor, *ESOP 90, Copenhagen, Denmark. LNCS 432*, pages 291–305, May 1990.

[Pal89] Catuscia Palamidessi. Algebraic properties of idempotent substitutions. Technical Report TR-33/89, University of Pisa, 1989.

[Plo81] Gordon D. Plotkin. A structural approach to operational semantics. Technical Report FN-19, DAIMI, University of Aarhus, Denmark, September 1981.

[PP91a] Maurizio Proietti and Alberto Pettorossi. Semantics preserving transformation rules for Prolog. In *Partial Evaluation and Semantics-Based Program Manipulation, New Haven, Connecticut. (Sigplan Notices, vol. 26, no. 9)*, 1991.

[PP91b] Maurizio Proietti and Alberto Pettorossi. Unfolding - Definition - Folding, in this order, for avoiding unnecessary variables in logic programs. In *Proceedings of PLILP 91, Passau, Germany (LNCS 528)*, August 1991.

[Sek91] Hirohisa Seki. Unfold/fold transformations of stratified programs. *Theoretical Computer Science*, 86(1):107–139, 1991.

[Søn89] Harald Søndergaard. Semantics-based analysis and transformation of logic programs. Technical Report 89/22, DIKU, University of Copenhagen, Denmark, 1989.

[TS84] Hisao Tamaki and Taisuke Sato. Unfold/fold transformation of logic programs. In *Proceedings of 2nd International Logic Programming Conference, Uppsala*, pages 127–138, 1984.

[Tur86] Valentin F. Turchin. The concept of a supercompiler. *ACM Transactions on Programming Languages and Systems*, 8(3):292–325, July 1986.

[Wad90] Philip Wadler. Deforestation: Transforming programs to eliminate trees. *Theoretical Computer Science*, 73:231–248, 1990.

This article was processed using the LaTeX macro package with LLNCS style

A Technique for Transforming Logic Programs by Fold-Unfold Transformations

Francis Alexandre

Centre de recherches en informatique de Nancy - CNRS - INRIA Lorraine
BP 239, 54506 Vandœuvre lès Nancy Cedex, FRANCE
e-mail : alexandr@loria.fr
Fax : 83-41-30-79

Abstract. This paper deals with the logic program transformation using the fold-unfold technique. The major problem in the strategies using fold-unfold transformation is to find a sequence of unfolding that permits the folding. In this paper we propose a technique that solves this problem for a particular class of logic programs. This technique consists in studying the possibility of folding for some simple or basic programs and then to apply these results for some more general logic programs. This technique permits to compute the sequence of unfolding to achieve a folding or to detect the impossibility of a folding, in the latter case the technique permits the invention of new predicates.
Key words : program transformation, definite program, fold-unfold, schema.

1 Introduction

The general aim of our researches is the derivation of programs using transformations. This method is fruitful for producing correct and efficient programs [8].

Within this context we use the fold-unfold transformations. Fold-unfold is a well known program transformation technique, in the case of functional programs this technique has been initiated by Burstall and Darlington [5], in the case of logic programming Sato and Tamaki were the initiators [13], many researches has been devoted to the logic programs transformations using fold-unfold technique, let us cite Debray [7] and Pettorossi and Proietti [11], [12] whose researches concern the strategies.

Within this context our initial specification is a definite program, our objective is to get by transformation a more efficient program. Our transformations are the folding, the unfolding and the definition of a new predicate, they are the same as those defined by Tamaki and Sato [13].

The major difficulty in program transformation using fold-unfold technique is to find a sequence of unfolding that allows us the folding and when it is not possible the problem is to invent a new predicate.

It has been shown in [11] that the problem of the folding (i.e. the possibility to find a recursive definition) is not decidable, on the other hand it has been shown that for a class of programs (the unilinear programs) the problem is decidable and a decision procedure is given (i.e. defined by a SDR-rule). A SDR-rule is a rule that selects the more instantiated atom in the bodies of the clauses. The strategies of transformation are also studied in [12], they are based on the loop absorption technique and on the SDR-rule these strategies allow to invent some new predicate.

In [4] and [3], the approach consists in analyzing an example or a trace of an execution, then these informations are used to compile the control.

Our approach can also be regarded as a compilation of the control because we study for some basic programs the possibility to fold and then we deduce the results for more general programs (i.e. linear recursive programs). A system of linear equations is associated with every program, the possibility of folding is deduced by solving these systems, if the system has no solution the folding is impossible, in this case a new predicate is invented, the technique can be compared with this one called "forced folding" for the functional programs in [6].

The paper is organized as follows. In section 2 we give some preliminary definitions and notations. In section 3, we define some schemas for the program, section 4 is devoted to results about basic programs. Section 5 is a description of the technique and its application to several examples. Section 6 is the conclusion.

2 Definitions and notations

We assume that the reader is familiar with the basic terminology of first order logic such as term, atom, formula, substitution, matching, most general unifier (m.g.u) and so on, (see [9], [1]), and also with the fold-unfold transformations for logic programs.

We adopt the following notations:

- $\mathcal{V}(e)$ is the set of the variables occurring in the expression e (i.e. a term, atom or clause).
- Let be t and t' two terms, $t' \ll t$ holds if t' is a subterm of t and if $t' \neq t$.
- If V is a countable set of variables and F a finite set of function symbols, $T(F, V)$ is the set of the terms built with the symbols of F and the symbols of V.
- $\bar{t}$ denotes a vector of terms, $\bar{x}$ denotes a vector of variables.
- We denote a substitution σ by a set of $\{(x_1/t_1), \ldots, (x_n/t_n)\}$, where every x_i is a variable and every t_i is a term.

A definite program is a sequence of definite clauses (Horn clauses). A definition of predicate p is the set of the clauses of a program whose the heads are constructed with the symbol p.

3 Schema of clauses

To illustrate the definitions we give some examples from the following program (DIV) that specifies the Euclidean division.

(DIV)

(1) $div(x_1, x_2, y_1, y_2) \leftarrow\ times(y_1, x_2, z_1)\ plus(z_1, y_2, x_1)\ inf(y_2, x_2)$

(2) $plus(0, x, x) \leftarrow$
(3) $plus(s(x), y, s(z)) \leftarrow plus(x, y, z)$

(4) $times(0, x, 0) \leftarrow$
(5) $times(s(x), y, z) \leftarrow times(x, y, u)\ plus(y, u, z)$

(6) $inf(0, s(x)) \leftarrow$
(7) $inf(s(x), s(y)) \leftarrow inf(x, y)$

$div(x_1, x_2, y_1, y_2)$ holds if y_1 and y_2 are respectively the quotient and the remainder of the division of x_1 by x_2.
times and *plus* respectively define the multiplication and the addition.
$inf(x, y)$ holds if x is less than y.

3.1 Notes about the folding

1. Let us consider the first clause c of the program (DIV)

$$c\ :\ div(x_1, x_2, y_1, y_2) \leftarrow\ times(y_1, x_2, z_1)\ plus(z_1, y_2, x_1)\ inf(y_2, x_2)$$

   The predicate *div* is defined by means of the predicates *times*, *plus* and *inf*, we have the objective to eliminate one or several of these predicates. For this reason we search a recursive definition of *div* by folding and unfolding transformations. Let us assume that after several unfolding steps we get the clause c'

$$c'\ :\ div(\bar{t}) \leftarrow \Delta\ times(t_1, t_2, t_3)\ plus(t_4, t_5, t_6)\ inf(t_7, t_8)\ \Theta$$

   where t_i $(1 \leq i \leq 8)$ are terms.
   The folding of c in c' is possible only if $times(t_1, t_2, t_3)\ plus(t_4, t_5, t_6)\ inf(t_7, t_8)$ is an instance of $times(y_1, x_2, z_1)\ plus(z_1, y_2, x_1)\ inf(y_2, x_2)$, we must have the equalities $t_2 = t_8$, $t_3 = t_4$ and $t_5 = t_7$.
   This note shows that the variables that have more than one occurrence in the body of c play an essential role for the success of a folding.
2. The possibility to execute a folding also depends on the definitions of the predicates *times*, *plus* and *inf*. Let us note that the unit clauses have generally no importance in the success of the folding, the unfolding with unit clauses products generally terminal cases. The variables that are shared in the body of c are x_2, y_2 and z_1. For example z_1 appears in the third argument of $times(y_1, x_2, z_1)$, for this reason we will consider in the clause (5) the third arguments of the atoms constructed with the symbol *times* ($times(s(x), y, z)$ and $times(x, y, u)$), namely the variables z and u that will define one part of a schema.

3.2 Recursion

When we recursively define a predicate we often write a clause in the following form

$$p(T_1, \ldots, T_k) \leftarrow \Delta\ p(t_1, \ldots, t_k)\ \Theta$$

and there generally exists a relation between the terms t_i and the terms T_i, here we distinguish the three following cases

1. t_i is a subterm of T_i, $t_i \ll T_i$.
2. T_i and t_i are equal to the same variable
3. t_i is a variable that does not occur in T_i

Let us illustrate these three cases by an example. The multiplication is defined by the two clauses (4) and (5) of (DIV)

(4) $times(0, x, 0) \leftarrow$
(5) $times(s(x), y, z) \leftarrow times(x, y, u) plus(u, y, z)$

We have a recursive definition of *times*,

In the clause (5) the arguments of the atoms $times(s(x), y, z)$ and $times(x, y, u)$ correspond to the three cases mentioned above.

3.3 Formalization

In this section we define the notions of linear predicates, of candidate clauses and of schema for candidate clauses.

Definition 1 (Recursive clauses). Let c be a clause in the following form $p_0(\bar{t}_0) \leftarrow p_1(\bar{t}_1) \dots p_n(\bar{t}_n)$

c is directly recursive if there exists i in $[1, n]$ such that $p_i = p_0$.

c is linear recursive if there exists an unique i in $[1, n]$ such that $p_i = p_0$.

Remark. In the following we abbreviate "directly recursive" in "recursive".

Definition 2 (Linear recursive predicate). A definition of a predicate is linear recursive if it contains a unique non-unit clause that is linear recursive.

Example 1. The definition of the predicate *times* (i_e the set of the clause *(4)* and *(5)*) defined in the program (DIV) is linear recursive.

Definition 3 (Schema of a linear recursive predicate). Let p be a linear recursive predicate and let c be the linear recursive clause that defines p (with arity n) $c : p(t_1, \dots, t_n) \leftarrow \Delta\, p(t'_1, \dots, t'_n)\ \Theta$. Let ζ_c be the mapping from $[1, n]$ in $T(F, V)^2$ defined by $\zeta_c(i) = (t_i, t'_i)$, the tuple $(\zeta_c(1), \dots, \zeta_c(n))$ is the schema of the linear recursive predicate p.

Example 2. The schema of the linear recursive *times* of the program (DIV) is $((s(x), x), (y, y), (z, u))$.

Our objective is to transform some non-recursive clauses into recursive ones, let us give some definitions about the non-recursive clauses that we call candidate clauses.

Definition 4 (Candidate clause). Let c be a clause in the following form

$c : p_0(\bar{t}_0) \leftarrow p_1(\overline{x_1}) \dots p_k(\overline{x_k})$,

c is a candidate clause if the following conditions hold :

- c is non-recursive (i_e $\forall i \in [1, k]\ p_i \neq p_0$).

- for all i in $[1, k]$ the definition of the predicates p_i are linear recursive.
- $\forall i \in [1, k]\ p_i(\overline{x}_i)$ is linear.

Let us note that the notions of linearity for the definition of predicate and for the atoms are different.

Example 3. The clause (1)
$div(x_1, x_2, y_1, y_2) \leftarrow times(y_1, x_2, z_1)\, plus(z_1, y_2, x_1)\, inf(y_2, x_2)$ of the program (DIV) is a candidate clause.

Definition 5 (Schema of a candidate clause). Let c a candidate clause in the following form $p_0(\overline{t}_0) \leftarrow p_1(\overline{x_1}) \ldots p_k(\overline{x_k})$.
For every $i \in [1, k]$, let be $V_i = \{v \in \mathcal{V}(p_i(\overline{x}_i))\ and\ \exists j \in [1, k] \setminus \{i\}\ v \in \mathcal{V}(p_j(\overline{x}_j))\}$.
For every $i \in [1, k]$ we define the mapping ψ_i from V_i to $T(F, V)^2$ by $\psi_i(x) = \zeta_{p_i}(j)$ where x a variable of $p_i(x_{i1}, \ldots, x_{ij}, \ldots, x_{in_i})$. The set $\{\psi_i, i \in [1, k]\}$ is the schema of the candidate clause c.

Example 4. $div(x_1, x_2, y_1, y_2) \leftarrow times(y_1, x_2, z_1)\, plus(z_1, y_2, x_1)\, inf(y_2, x_2)$ is the first clause of the program (DIV). The schemas of the definition of predicates $times$, $plus$ and inf are respectively
$\{((s(x), x), (y, y), (z, u))\}$, $\{((s(x), x), (y, y), (s(z), z))\}$ and $\{((s(x), x), (s(y), y))\}$.
In $times(y_1, x_2, z_1)$
$\psi_1(x_2) = \zeta_{times}(2) = (y, y)$
$\psi_1(z_1) = \zeta_{times}(3) = (z, u)$
in $plus(z_1, y_2, x_1)$
$\psi_2(z_1) = \zeta_{plus}(1) = (s(x), x)$
$\psi_2(y_2) = \zeta_{plus}(2) = (y, y)$
in $inf(y_2, x_2)$
$\psi_3(y_2) = \zeta_{inf}(1) = (s(x), x)$
$\psi_3(x_2) = \zeta_{inf}(2) = (s(y), y)$

Note 6. Below we sometimes represent the schemas of the candidate clauses by some arrays, the schema of the clause (1) of the previous example is represented by the array

$$\begin{bmatrix} & x_2 & y_2 & z_1 \\ 1\ times & (y, y) & & (z, u) \\ 2\ plus & & (y, y) & (s(x), x) \\ 3\ inf & (s(y), y) & (s(x), x) & \end{bmatrix}$$

The first column of the array is composed of places of the atoms in the body of the candidate clauses, the second column concerns the predicate symbols of these atoms; the other columns correspond to the variables that have more than one occurrence in the body of the candidate clause, at the intersection of the line p_i and the column x we find $\psi_i(x)$. Let (t, t') be a pair of terms we denote this pair by

- ι if $t = t'$.
- ω if t' a variable that has no occurrence in t.

The schema becomes

$$\begin{bmatrix} & x_2 & y_2 & z_1 \\ 1\ times & \iota & & \omega \\ 2\ plus & & \iota & (s(x),x) \\ 3\ inf & (s(y),y) & (s(x),x) & \end{bmatrix}$$

Definition 7 (Basic schema w.r.t. a variable). Let c be a candidate clause in the form $p_0(\overline{t_0}) \leftarrow p_1(\overline{x_1})\dots p_k(\overline{x_k})$ and $\{\psi_i, 1 \le i \le k\}$ its schema. Let x be a variable of c which has an occurrence in $p_i(\overline{t_i})$ and in $p_j(\overline{t_j})$ $(i \neq j)$. The set $\{\psi_i(x), \psi_j(x)\}$ is a basic schema of c w.r.t. the variable x.

Example 5. The basic schemas of the first clause of (DIV) are :

- w.r.t x_2, $\{\iota, (s(y), y)\}$
- w.r.t. y_2, $\{\iota, (s(x), x)\}$
- w.r.t. z_1, $\{\omega, (s(x), x)\}$

4 Results for the basic programs

In this section we define some basic programs and their corresponding schemas. We study for these basic programs the success or the failure of the folding.

Proposition 8. *Let P be a program composed of the clauses c_0, c_1 and c_2*

$$c_0 : p_0(U) \leftarrow p_1(x)\, p_2(x)$$

$$c_1 : p_1(T_1) \leftarrow p_1(x_1)$$
$$c_2 : p_2(T_2) \leftarrow p_2(x_2)$$

where U is a term, $x_1 \ll T_1$ and $x_2 \ll T_2$.

We assume that the pairs (T_1, x_1) and (T_2, x_2) are unifiable. by a substitution σ such that $x_1\sigma = x_2\sigma$ is a variable.

Let n_1 and n_2 be the numbers of unfolding of the atoms constructed with the predicate symbols p_1 and p_2. A folding is possible if and only if $n_1 = n_2$.

Proof. To prove this proposition it is sufficient to note the three following points.

1. The unfolding of $p_1(x)$ in c_0 produces the following clause c'

   $$c' : p_0(U)\theta \leftarrow p_1(x_1)\, p_2(T_1) \quad where\ \theta = \{(x/T_1)\}$$

   it is obvious that c_0 is not foldable in c' because $x_1 \ll T_1$.

2. Since by hypothesis (T_1, x_1) and (T_2, x_2) are unifiable, we have $T_1\sigma = T_2\sigma$ and $x_1\sigma = x_2\sigma = v$ where v is a variable, the unfolding of $p_2(T_1)$ in c' provides the clause c''

   $$c'' : p_0(U)\theta\sigma \leftarrow p_1(v)\, p_2(v)$$

   c_0 is obviously foldable in c''.

3. n unfolding of $p_1(x_1)$ in c' will provide some clauses in the following form

$$p_0(U)(\theta)^n \leftarrow p_1(x_1)\ p_2(T_1(\theta)^{n-1})$$

where $(\theta)^n$ denotes the composition of θ by itself n times, c_0 is not foldable in these clauses. □

Let us note that the basic schema of c_0 for the variable x is $\{\psi_1(x), \psi_2(x)\} = \{(T_1, t_1), (T_2, t_2)\}$.

Proposition 9. *Let P be the program composed of the clauses c_0, c_1 and c_2*

$$c_0 : p_0(U) \leftarrow p_1(x)\ p_2(x)$$

$$c_1 : p_1(T_1) \leftarrow p_1(t_1)$$
$$c_2 : p_2(y) \leftarrow p_2(y)$$

where U is a term and $t_1 \ll T_1$.

Let n_1 and n_2 be the numbers of unfolding of the atoms constructed with the predicates p_1 and p_2.

A folding is possible if and only if $n_1 = 0$.

The basic schema of the candidate clause c_0 for x is $\{\psi_1(x), \psi_2(x)\} = \{(T_1, t_1), \iota\}$.

Proposition 10. *Let P be a program composed of the clauses c_0, c_1 and c_2*

$$c_0 : p_0(U) \leftarrow p_1(x)\ p_2(x)$$

$$c_1 : p_1(T_1) \leftarrow p_1(t_1)$$
$$c_2 : p_2(T_2) \leftarrow p_2(z)$$

where U is a term, $t_1 \ll T_1$ and z a variable which has no occurrence in T_2. Let n_1 and n_2 be the numbers of unfolding of the atoms constructed with the symbols p_1 and p_2. A folding is possible if and only if $n_1 = 0$ and $n_2 = 0$.

Let us note that the basic schema of c_0 for x is $\{\psi_1(x), \psi_2(x)\} = \{(T_1, t_1), \omega\}$.

Proposition 11. *Let P be the program composed of the clauses c_0, c_1 and c_2*

$$c_0 : p_0(U) \leftarrow p_1(x)\ p_2(x)$$

$$c_1 : p_1(y) \leftarrow p_1(y)$$
$$c_2 : p_2(T_2) \leftarrow p_2(z)$$

where U is a term and z is a variable which does not occur in T_2.

Let n_1 and n_2 be the numbers of unfolding of the atoms constructed with the symbols p_1 and p_2. A folding is possible if and only if $n_2 = 0$.

Let us note that the basic schema of c_0 w.r.t. x is $\{\psi_1(x), \psi_2(x)\} = \{\iota, \omega\}$.
The table 1 recapitulates the results of the previous propositions 8, 9, 10 and 11.

Program	*Hypothesis*	*Schema*	*Conditions*
$p_0(U) \leftarrow p_1(x)\ p_2(x)$ $p_1(T_1) \leftarrow p_1(x_1)$ $p_2(T_2) \leftarrow p_2(x_2)$	$x_1 \ll T_1$ *et* $x_2 \ll T_2$ $(T_1, x_1)\sigma = (T_2, x_2)\sigma$ $x_1\sigma, x_2\sigma$ *variables*	$\{\psi_1(x), \psi_2(x)\} =$ $\{(T_1, x_1), (T_2, x_2)\}$	$n_1 = n_2$
$p_0(U) \leftarrow p_1(x)\ p_2(x)$ $p_1(T_1) \leftarrow p_1(t_1)$ $p_2(y) \leftarrow p_2(y)$	$t_1 \ll T_1$	$\{\psi_1(x), \psi_2(x)\} =$ $\{(T_1, t_1), \iota\}$	$n_1 = 0$
$p_0(U) \leftarrow p_1(x)\ p_2(x)$ $p_1(T_1) \leftarrow p_1(t_1)$ $p_2(T_2) \leftarrow p_2(z)$	$t_1 \ll T_1$ $z \notin \mathcal{V}(T_2)$	$\{\psi_1(x), \psi_2(x)\} =$ $\{(T_1, t_1), \omega\}$	$n_1 = 0\ \&\ n_2 = 0$
$p_0(U) \leftarrow p_1(x)\ p_2(x)$ $p_1(y) \leftarrow p_1(y)$ $p_2(T_2) \leftarrow p_2(z)$	$z \notin \mathcal{V}(T_2)$	$\{\psi_1(x), \psi_2(x)\} =$ $\{\iota, \omega\}$	$n_2 = 0$

Table 1. Results for the basic programs

Remark. Below we use the results about the basic programs for more general programs, for this reason we do not exclude the trivial folding of the initial clause c_0 in itself, (i.e. the sequence of unfolding can eventually be empty).

In the next section we describe a method for more general programs, this method is an immediate consequence of the results of this section, because the propositions 8, 9, 10 and 11 establish "if and only if" conditions.

5 Description of the method

5.1 Conditions associated with a candidate clause

We associate a condition of the table 1 with every basic schema of a candidate clause.

Definition 12 (Conditions associated with a candidate clause). Let $c = p_0(\overline{t_0}) \leftarrow p_1(\overline{x_1}) \ldots p_k(\overline{x_k})$ be a candidate clause and let v be a variable of c. For every basic schema $\{\psi_i(v), \psi_j(v)\}$ which verifies the same hypothesis as one basic schema of the table 1, we associate the corresponding condition of this basic schema, where n_1 and n_2 are replaced by n_i and n_j.

Let us show an example of a such association.

Example 6. The clause (1) of the program (DIV) is
(1) $div(x_1, x_2, y_1, y_2) \leftarrow\ times(y_1, x_2, z_1)\ plus(z_1, y_2, x_1) inf(y_2, x_2)$
The basic schema of (1) w.r.t. x_2 is $\{\psi_1(x_2), \psi_3(x_2)\} = \{\iota, (s(y), y)\}$ we have the same schema as the schema of the proposition 9, then we associate the condition $n_3 = 0$.

In the next section we expose a method that consists in using the basic schemas to deduce the possibility or the impossibility to fold. In the former case we give a sequence of unfolding steps which makes possible the folding.

5.2 Description of the method

Let c be a candidate clause

$$c : p_0(\bar{t_0}) \leftarrow p_1(\overline{x_1}), \ldots, p_k(\overline{x_k})$$

the method consists in the following steps :

1. Computation of the schema of c
2. From the schema of c we determine the basic schemas of c. Let l be the number of basic schemas of c.
3. With every basic schema of the previous step, we associate its condition, then we get l conditions $((cond_i)(1 \leq i \leq l)$.
   Let $\mathcal{S}$ be the following system of s variables $n_1, \ldots, n_s$

   $$\mathcal{S}\begin{cases} cond_i \ \ (1 \leq i \leq l) \\ n_1 + \ldots + n_s \geq 1 \end{cases}$$

   The system $\mathcal{S}$ is said to be associated with the candidate clause c.
   The inequality $n_1 + \ldots + n_s \geq 1$ means that we must unfold at least once (i.e we must not fold c in itself).
4. The next step consists in solving the system $\mathcal{S}$.
   (a) If the system has some solutions, we choose a solution that makes the sum $n_1 + \ldots + n_s$ minimal and we apply the corresponding sequence of unfolding.
   (b) If the system $\mathcal{S}$ has no solution we conclude that it is impossible to do a folding step, then we apply other strategies.

5.3 Examples of application

In this section we show some example of application of the method described above.

Let us begin with two examples where the folding is possible.

Example 7 Subsequence (first version). x is a contiguous subsequence of y if there exists two lists z_3 and z_2 such that $y = (z_3x)z_2$, it is specified by the following program :

(1) $subsequence(x, y) \leftarrow append(z_1, z_2, y)\ append(z_3, x, z_1)$
(2) $append(nil, x, x) \leftarrow$
(3) $append(cons(x_1, x), y, cons(x_1, z)) \leftarrow append(x, y, z)$

The first clause of this program is a candidate clause, its schema is

$$\begin{bmatrix} & z_1 \\ (1)\ append & (cons(x_1, x), x) \\ (2)\ append & (cons(x_1, z), z) \end{bmatrix}$$

The unique basic schema of c is $\{(cons(x_1, x), x), (cons(x_1, z), z)\}$, and its associated condition (or equation) is $n_1 = n_2$, the system $\mathcal{S}$ is

$$\begin{cases} n_1 = n_2 \\ n_1 + n_2 \geq 1 \end{cases}$$

A minimal solution of S is $(n_1, n_2) = (1, 1)$. By unfolding every atom of c once, then

by folding we get the following program :
(2)(3)
(4) $subsequence(nil, x) \leftarrow$
(5) $subsequence(cons(z, x), cons(z, y)) \leftarrow append(x, x_1, y)$
(6) $subsequence(x, cons(z, y)) \leftarrow subsequence(x, y)$

Example 8 Subsequence (Second version). Here is a quite different way to specify the contiguous subsequence. The list x is a contiguous subsequence of the list y if there exists two lists z_3 and z_1 such that $y = z_1(xz_3)$, we have the following program :

(1) $subsequence(x, y) \leftarrow append(z_1, z_2, y)\ append(x, z_3, z_2)$
(2) $append(nil, x, x) \leftarrow$
(3) $append(cons(x_1, x), y, cons(x_1, z)) \leftarrow append(x, y, z)$

The clause (1) is a candidate clause, its schema is

$$\begin{bmatrix} & z_2 \\ (1)\ append & \iota \\ (2)\ append & (cons(x_1, z), z) \end{bmatrix}$$

$\{\iota, (cons(x_1, z), z)\}$ is the unique basic schema of (1), the condition associated with this schema is $n_2 = 0$. The system to solve is then

$$\begin{cases} n_2 = 0 \\ n_1 + n_2 \geq 1 \end{cases}$$

$(n_1, n_2) = (1, 0)$ is the minimal solution of the system.

By unfolding the first atom of (1), then by folding we get the following program :

(2)(3)
(4) $subsequence(x, y) \leftarrow append(x, z, y)$
(5) $subsequence(x, cons(z, y)) \leftarrow subsequence(x, y)$

The previous examples show some cases when the folding is possible. Let us describe the technique when the folding is impossible, in this case we use a strategy of generalization.

5.4 A strategy of generalization based on the schemas

The strategy of generalization is well-known, it has been applied by Boyer and Moore ([2]) and Burstall and Darlington ([5]) for the functional program. Generalization generally consists in replacing some constants, some terms or several occurrences of the same variables by different variables [14].

Our approach consists in using the schemas to apply this technique in a natural way.

Let $c = p_0(\overline{t_0}) \leftarrow p_1(\overline{x_1}) \ldots p_k(\overline{x_k})$ be a candidate clause and S its associated system, we suppose that S has no solution.

$$\mathcal{S}\begin{cases} cond_i & (1 \leq i \leq l) \\ n_1 + \ldots + n_s \geq 1 \end{cases}$$

1. We select in the system $\mathcal{S}$ a condition $cond_m$ such that the following system $\mathcal{S}'$
$$\mathcal{S}'\begin{cases} cond_i & (1 \leq i \leq l)\ et\ i \neq m \\ n_1 + \ldots + n_s \geq 1 \end{cases}$$
has at least one solution.
2. Let $\{\psi_i(x), \psi_j(x)\}$ the basic schema of c w.r.t. the variable x whose condition is $cond_m$. The clause c has the following form
$p_0(\overline{t_0}) \leftarrow \Gamma\ p_i(\ldots, x, \ldots)\ p_j(\ldots, x, \ldots)$

   The strategy consists in generalizing the variable x in defining a new predicate q by a clause c'.
   (a) If $\psi_i(x) = (T_1, t_1)$ and $(\psi_j(x) = (T_2, t_2)$ or $\psi_j(x) = \iota)$
      i. If $x \in \overline{t_0} : c' \ : q(\overline{t_0}, x_1) \leftarrow \Gamma\ p_i(\ldots, x_1, \ldots)\ p_j(\ldots, x, \ldots)$
      ii. If $x \notin \overline{t_0} : c' \ : q(\overline{t_0}, x, x_1) \leftarrow \Gamma\ p_i(\ldots, x_1, \ldots)\ p_j(\ldots, x, \ldots)$
   (b) If $\psi_i(x) = \omega$ and $(\psi_j(x) = (T_1, t_1)$ or $\psi_j(x) = \iota)$
      i. If $x \in \overline{t_0} : c' \ : q(\overline{t_0}, x_1) \leftarrow \Gamma\ p_i(\ldots, x_1, \ldots)\ p_j(\ldots, x, \ldots)$
      ii. If $x \notin \overline{t_0} : c' \ : q(\overline{t_0}, x, x_1) \leftarrow \Gamma\ p_i(\ldots, x_1, \ldots)\ p_j(\ldots, x, \ldots)$
3. The last step is double.
   (a) We compute a recursive definition of the new predicate q, by unfolding according to the solution of $\mathcal{S}'$.
   After this sequence of unfolding we establish a relation between the old predicate p and the new predicate
   (b) We establish the relation between the old predicate p and the new predicate q by folding c' in c, this folding is obviously possible because c' is a generalization of c.

5.5 Example of application

Example 9 The queens problem. The queen problem consists in positioning n queens on a "chessboard" $n \times n$ so that no queen may capture any other.

We specify this problem by the following program ($QUEEN$) that is given in [10].

(1) $queen(l, r) \leftarrow perm(l, l_1)\ zip(l, l_1, r)\ safe(nil, r)$
(2) $perm(nil, nil) \leftarrow$
(3) $perm(cons(x, y), cons(u, v)) \leftarrow delete(u, cons(x, y), w)\ perm(w, v)$
(4) $zip(nil, nil, nil) \leftarrow$
(5) $zip(cons(x, y), cons(u, v), cons(c(x, u), w)) \leftarrow zip(y, v, w)$
(6) $safe(l, nil) \leftarrow$
(7) $safe(l, cons(v, r)) \leftarrow nodiag(l, v)\ safe(cons(v, l), r)$

the predicate $perm$ defines the permutation.
Given the two lists l and l_1, $zip(l, l_1, r)$ holds if r is the list of the pairs of the corresponding elements of the lists l and l_1.

$safe(nil, r)$ holds if the list of the pairs r is a solution of the problem, namely two queens are not on the same row, the same column or the same diagonal.

The functional symbol c is the constructor of pairs.

This specification is very inefficient because it consists in trying all the positions and then in selecting the solution.

The objective is to eliminate the predicate $perm$, then we search a recursive definition of the predicate $queen$.

The first clause of the program ($QUEEN$) is not a candidate clause because of the constant nil in the atom $safe(nil, r)$. For this reason we generalize the constant nil by defining the clause (8)

(8) $queen2(l, r, x) \leftarrow perm(l, l_1)\ zip(l, l_1, r)\ safe(x, r)$

The clause (8) is a candidate clause, its schema is

$$\begin{bmatrix} & l & l_1 & r \\ perm & \omega & (cons(u,v),v) & \\ zip & (cons(x,y),y) & (cons(u,v),v) & (cons(c(x,u),w),w) \\ safe & & & (cons(v,r),r) \end{bmatrix}$$

The system that is associated with (8) is

$$\mathcal{S} \begin{cases} (1)\ n_1 = 0 \ \&\ n_2 = 0 \\ (2)\ n_1 = n_2 \\ (3)\ n_2 = n_3 \\ n_1 + n_2 + n_3 \geq 1 \end{cases}$$

$\mathcal{S}$ has no solution, if we suppress the conditions (1) or (3) we get some solutions. We choose to suppress the first condition of $\mathcal{S}$, this corresponds to the generalization of the variable l. In the following we justify this choice. We define the predicate $queen3$ by :

(9) $queen3(l, r, x, l_1) \leftarrow perm(l_1, p)\ zip(l, p, r)\ safe(x, r)$

The schema of (9) is

$$\begin{bmatrix} & p & r \\ perm & (cons(u,v),v) & \\ zip & (cons(u,v),v) & (cons(c(x,u),w),w) \\ safe & & (cons(r,r),r) \end{bmatrix}$$

The system associated with (9) is $\mathcal{S}'$

$$\mathcal{S}' \begin{cases} n_1 = n_2 \\ n_2 = n_3 \\ n_1 + n_2 + n_3 \geq 1 \end{cases}$$

$(n_1, n_2, n_3) = (1, 1, 1)$ is a minimal solution of $\mathcal{S}'$. By unfolding every atom of (9) once we get

(10) $queen3(l,r,x,nil) \leftarrow zip(l,nil,r)\ safe(x,r)$
(13) $queen3(cons(x,y),cons(c(x,v_4),w),v_1,cons(v_2,v_3)) \leftarrow$
$delete(v_4,cons(v_2,v_3),v_6)$
$perm(v_6,v_5) zip(y,v_5,w)$
$nodiag(v_1,c(x,v_4))$
$safe(cons(c(x,v_4),v_1),w)$

The folding of (9) in (13) produces (14)

(14) $queen3(cons(v_7,y),cons(c(v_7,v_4),w),v_1,cons(v_2,v_3)) \leftarrow$
$delete(v_4,cons(v_2,v_3),v_6)$
$nodiag(v_1,c(v_7,v_4))$
$queen3(y,w,cons(c(v_7,v_4),v_1),v_6)$

By folding the clause (9) in the clause (1) we get the clause (15)

(15) $queen(v_1,v_2) \leftarrow queen3(v_1,v_2,nil,v_1)$

By unfolding the atoms $zip(l,nil,r)$ and $safe(x,r)$ in the clause (10) we get the unit clause (16)

(16) $queen3(nil,nil,nil,nil) \leftarrow$.
We get finally the program composed of the clauses (4), (5), (16), (14), (15) which is the same program as that one obtained by some strategies of tupling, composition and generalization in [10]. This program is more efficient that the initial one.

Final program :

(4) $zip(nil,nil,nil) \leftarrow$
(5) $zip(cons(x,y),cons(u,v),cons(c(x,u),w)) \leftarrow zip(y,v,w)$
(16) $queen3(nil,nil,nil,nil) \leftarrow$
(14) $queen3(cons(v_7,y),cons(c(v_7,v_4),w),v_1,cons(v_2,v_3)) \leftarrow$
$delete(v_4,cons(v_2,v_3),v_6)$
$nodiag(v_1,c(v_7,v_4))$
$queen3(y,w,cons(c(v_7,v_4),v_1),v_6)$
(15) $queen(v_1,v_2) \leftarrow queen3(v_1,v_2,nil,v_1)$

In the bodies of the clauses the variables which are common to several atoms can be viewed like links between these atoms.

When we have the choice of several generalizations, the experience shows that we must choose a generalization which does not destroy these links.

Let us go back over the choice of the variable to be generalized in the clause (8), we have had two possibilities, namely the variables l and r. The generalization of the variable r destroys the link between the atoms $zip(l,l_1,r)$ and $safe(x,r)$ while the generalization of the variable l does not destroy the link between $perm(l,l_1)$ and $zip(l,l_1,r)$ because of the variable l_1 which is also common to these two atoms. For this reason we have generalized l.

5.6 Comparison with the related works

In this section we compare our approach and the approach defined in [12]. The most important restriction in our approach is that the definitions of the program should contain only one linear recursive predicate, in [12] the class of programs, (the non-ascending programs) is more important. In [12] the strategy is based on the SDR-rule that is a partial function, then a SDR-rule is not always defined, in this case the strategy consists in performing a generalization, but it is not always possible because the generalization reduces the number of shared variables in the body of the clauses. Moreover the "loop absorption procedure" can generate a large number of clauses because it consists in performing unfolding steps to find the loop, on the contrary our strategy tries to minimize the number of the unfolding steps. Let us give the example of the "Prefix-Suffix" of a list ([12]).

(1) $presuf(ps,l) \leftarrow prefix(ps,l) suffix(ps,l)$
(2) $prefix(nil,l) \leftarrow$
(3) $prefix(cons(x,p),cons(x,l)) \leftarrow prefix(p,l)$
(4) $suffix(l,l) \leftarrow$
(5) $suffix(s,cons(x,l)) \leftarrow suffix(s,l)$

The objective of the transformation is to avoid a double visit of the list *ps* (i.e. to find a recursive definition of $presuf$).

The application of our strategy (generalization of the variable *ps*) produces the following final program :

(2) $prefix(nil,l) \leftarrow$
(3) $prefix(cons(x,p),cons(x,l)) \leftarrow prefix(p,l)$
(4) $suffix(l,l) \leftarrow$
(5) $suffix(s,cons(x,l)) \leftarrow suffix(s,l)$
(7) $presuf2(nil,,v_1,ps_2) \leftarrow suffix(ps_2,v_1)$
(9) $presuf2(cons(x,p),cons(x,v_1),cons(x,v_1)) \leftarrow prefix(p,v_1)$
(11) $presuf2(cons(v_2,p),cons(v_2,v_3),v_1) \leftarrow presuf2(p,v_1,v_3)$
(12) $presuf(ps,v_1) \leftarrow presuf2(ps,v_1,ps)$
This program is simpler than the one derived in [12].

6 Conclusion

We have presented a technique for the logic programs transformations using folding and unfolding. This technique allows us to compute the sequence of unfolding and also to detect if the folding is impossible, in the latter case this technique invents some new predicates in a natural way. This technique can be easily automated. It is applicable to a simple but important class of definite programs. Moreover this technique can be extended in two directions, on the one hand by studying some new cases for the basic programs, on the other hand by considering some predicates with more than one recursive clause.

Acknowledgment

I thank the anonymous referees for their useful comments.

References

1. K.R. Apt and M.H Van Emden. Contribution to the Theory of Logic Programming. *Journal of the Association for Computing Machinery*, 29(3):841–862, 1982.
2. R.S. Boyer and J.S. Moore. *A Computational Logic*. Academic Press, New York, 1979.
3. M. Bruynooghe, L. De Raedt, and D. De Schreye. Explanation Based Program Transformation. In *Proc. IJCAI Boston USA*, 1989.
4. M. Bruynooghe, D. De Schreye, and B. Krekels. Compiling control. *Journal of Logic Programming*, 6(2 & 3):135–162, January 1989.
5. R.M Burstall and J.A Darlington. Transformation System for Developing Recursive Programs. *Journal of the Association for Computing Machinery*, 24(1):44–67, 1977.
6. J. Darlington. An Experimental Program Transformation and Synthesis System. *Artificial Intelligence*, 16:1–46, 1981.
7. S.K. Debray. Unfold/Fold Transformations and Loop 0ptimization of Logic Programs. In *Proc. of the Sigplan'88 Conference on Programming Language Design and Implementation*, pages 297–307, Atlanta,Georgia, June 1988.
8. M.S. Feather. A Survey and Classification of some Program Transformation Techniques. In *Proc. TC2 IFIP Working Conference on Program Specification and Transformation, Bad-Tölz, F.R.G*, 1986.
9. J.W. Lloyd. *Foundations of Logic Programming*. Springer-Verlag, 1987.
10. A. Pettorossi and M. Proietti. The Automatic Construction of Logic Programs. In *IFIP WG2.1 Meeting*, january 1989. Preliminary Version.
11. A. Pettorossi and M. Proietti. Decidability Results and Characterization of Strategies for the Development of Logic Programs. In G. Levi and M. Martelli, editors, *6th International Conference on Logic Programming*, Lisbon (Portugal), 1989. MIT Press.
12. M. Proietti and A Pettorossi. The Synthesis of Eureka Predicates for Developing Logic Program. In N. Jones, editor, *3rd European Symposium on Programming*, volume 432 of *Lecture Notes in Computer Science*, pages 306–325, Copenhaguen, 1990. Springer-Verlag.
13. H. Tamaki and T. Sato. Unfold/Fold Transformation of Logic Programs. In *Proceedings of the 2nd International Logic Programming Conference*, Uppsala, 1984.
14. B. Wegbreit. Goal-Directed Program Transformation. *IEEE Transactions on Software Engineering*, SE-2(2):69–80, 1976.

FOLON: An Environment for Declarative Construction of Logic Programs

J. Henrard and B. Le Charlier

FOLON Research Project Institut d'Informatique
FUNDP Namur 5000 Namur, Belgium
Fax: +32 81 72 49 67 {jhe,ble}@info.fundp.ac.be

Abstract. Although very attractive from a theoretical standpoint, the "Program = Logic + Control" equation of logic programming is sometimes considered too idealistic by "real life" programmers. The lack of adequate tools to practically support a rigorous approach based on logic is advocated here to be a main cause of this discrepancy. An implemented environment based on a precise methodology is presented. It provides for the handling of specifications, the computer-aided construction and the prototyping of (pure) logic descriptions, and the derivation and optimization of Prolog procedures from those descriptions. The system and the methodology are outlined jointly. The system-aided construction of a complete example is presented afterwards.

1 Introduction

Logic Programming [19, 21] is recognized to be a powerful paradigm. It allows for a declarative and relational statement of the problems and of their solutions without paying attention to a particular execution mechanism. However this ideal is not fully achieved in practical logic languages and at least not in the main one: (standard) Prolog [5, 24, 25]. This is because Prolog uses an incomplete (depth-first) search strategy and several non logic features such as the cut, test predicates (**var**(X), **ground**(X), ...), omission of the occur-check, negation as failure, ...all introduced for efficiency reasons.

Many approaches are possible to try to overcome this drawback. A first approach consists of removing the impure features of Prolog and to build optimizing compilers based on abstract interpretation of pure programs (see for example [1, 20]). Another approach amounts to axiomatizing the impure features in order to reason in a non standard logic. This is for example the approach of Prolog II [16]. Better languages incorporating classical logic features more compatible with efficiency, such as typed logic, can also be investigated [18]. Aside from those theoretical attempts, a more pragmatical (and widely used) approach amounts to using Prolog as an operationally defined programming language with its own powerful mechanisms, independent from any logical concern. This can be satisfactory in practice but loses many advantages of logic programming such as the declarative reading of programs and multidirectionality. A last approach, originally advocated by Kowalski [19], is to separate as much as possible the logical and operational aspects of program construction. This is the well-known equation "Program = Logic + Control". A thorough attempt to provide a methodology adequate to this goal has been proposed in [12]. The objective is to use classical logic as much as possible during the construction process while catering for the use of Prolog as the implementation language. This is achieved through three main proposals: 1. A *specification schema* is proposed that neatly integrates declarative and operational aspects. 2. The notion of a *logic description* is introduced. Its correctness and construction process only rely on the logical part of the specification. 3. A set of *derivation techniques* is described. They allows to transform the logic description into a Prolog procedure correct with respect to the entire specification.

However applying the complete methodology can possibly appear too cumbersome for "real life" programmers. This drawback seemed to be solvable thanks to a programming environment supporting all automatable and clerical aspects of the methodology. Designing and implementing such an environment was one of the objectives of the FOLON research project started in 1988. This paper aims at presenting the system resulting from this research. The emphasis is on the support of the overall construction process from the specification to the final procedure. Other aspects such as the handling of types are described elsewhere [9]. The FOLON environment is implemented in *Prolog by BIM* with the help of *Carmen*, an interface generator, under *SunView*.

The rest of this paper is organized as follows. Section 2 contains a join overview of the system and of the supported methodology. In section 3, a (simple) example is fully developed. Finally, some conclusions are proposed in section 4 as well as some future improvements.

2 Overview of the system

We first present a simplified description of the FOLON environment. The reader is referred to [3, 6, 7, 8, 10, 13, 17] for further details. As the environment has been designed with the main goal of supporting the methodology described in [12], we also recall the aspects of it that are related to some component of the system.

2.1 Specification Handling

procedure $p(T_1, T_2, \ldots, T_n)$
Type: T_1 : $type_1$; T_2 : $type_2$; ...; T_n : $type_n$
Relation: Description of a relation p between the parameters $T_1, \ldots, T_n$.
Application conditions: – directionality
– behavior

Fig. 1. General form of a specification

Every procedure constructed with the help of the system has to be correct with respect to a specification. The specification schema used is shown in figure 1. This schema is basically the schema proposed in [12]. However parts related to "non pure" aspects such as side-effects are not considered. (See an example, paragraph 3.1).

Types are arbitrary sets of ground terms. They act as preconditions and postconditions on the parameters: when a procedure call $p(t_1, \ldots, t_n)$ is initiated, the tuple $<t_1, \ldots, t_n>$ of actual parameters must be instantiable to at least one tuple of ground terms $<d_1, \ldots, d_n>$ belonging to $type_1 \times \cdots \times type_n$. The same condition applies to the values of the parameters after the call.

Let p be the relation described in the *Relation* part. It means that for any *ground* tuple $<d_1,\ldots,d_n>\in type_1 \times \cdots \times type_n$, the procedure call $p(d_1,\ldots,d_n)$ succeeds if and only $<d_1,\ldots,d_n>\in p$ and fails if and only if $<d_1,\ldots,d_n>\notin p$. It also make sense for non ground calls in conjunction with the *Application conditions.*

Directionalities are application conditions of the form

$$\mathbf{in}(m_1,\ldots,m_n) : \mathbf{out}(M_1,\ldots,M_n);< Min, Max > .$$

The m_i and M_i respectively stand for the modes of the parameter T_i before (precondition) and after (postcondition) a call. Allowed modes are *ground, var* and *ngv* (neither *ground* or *var*) and any combination of them (for example *any* is equivalent to *ground* or *var* or *ngv*). *Min* and *Max* specify the minimum and maximum lengths of the sequence of computed answer substitutions returned by a procedure call respecting the **in** part of the directionality. Let $p(t_1,\ldots,t_n)$ be a call that respects the **in** part of at least one directionality. Let σ be a computed answer substitution for that call. Then, for all ground instances $<d_1,\ldots,d_n>$ of $<t_1,\ldots,t_n>\sigma$, such that $<d_1,\ldots,d_n>\in type_1 \times \cdots \times type_n$, $p(d_1,\ldots,d_n)$ must hold. Conversely, for each ground instance $<d_1,\ldots,d_n>$ of $<t_1,\ldots,t_n>$ such that $<d_1,\ldots,d_n>\in type_1 \times \cdots \times type_n$ and $p(d_1,\ldots,d_n)$ holds such a computed answer substitution σ will be produced. *No-sharing* constraints can be added to the **in** and **out** parts of directionalities and behaviors. A no-share is a couple (i,j) specifying that no variables are shared by parameters t_i and t_j. Possible sharing of variables is always assumed otherwise. This is an important point because logic programmers often implicitly assume that no-sharing occurs between the parameters at call time. This generally leads to procedures that are incorrect in the general case. *Behaviors* are more powerful application conditions that we describe in paragraph 2.4.

The FOLON environment allows the user to enter (add) a specification into the *specification database.* Modification and removal of a specification are also possible. Each specification is checked for consistency before being recorded in the specification database: we do not describe those checks completely, see [17]. Types are checked for their existence in the *type database* and directionalities are checked for consistency.

Specifications are used by the development process of the procedure, mainly during the construction of a logic description, the derivation of a logic procedure and the transformation of a procedure for optimizing purposes. At the present stage specifications are formal except for a (major) part: the relation description. So it is worthwhile to discuss the usefulness of our specification notion and what it means for a procedure to be correct with respect to it. The simplest way to understand the role of the relation part is to see it as an informal description of the relation formally described by the logic description to be constructed afterwards. Hence its role should be purely documentary and the "actual" (formal) specification should consist of the formal parts of the specification augmented with the logic description. Note however that some parts of the specification are of help to build the logic description itself. So, depending on the point of view, the LOGIST module (see below) can be seen either as an assistant to the elaboration of a formal specification or to the construction of a first pure logic procedure from a (partly) informal specification. The present FOLON environment could also be augmented with a logic description synthesis module. A major point is that all the rest of the system should remain unchanged. For example, the work of A. Bundy and al. [2] is fully compatible with our approach.

Another complementary work is the one of P. Flener and Y. Deville that is planned to be integrated to our environment in the future [14, 15].

2.2 Aided construction of the logic description

The next step is to construct the *logic description* corresponding to the specification. Such a logic description, denoted LD(p), has the form

$$p(X_1,\ldots,X_n) \Leftrightarrow F$$

where p is the procedure name, $X_1,\ldots,X_n$ are the parameters and F is a first-order formula (see [12] for details).

The construction of the logic description is the most creative part of the overall development process. Correctness of the logic description is defined as follows. Let $<d_1,\ldots,d_n>$ be a tuple of ground terms. Then $p(d_1,\ldots,d_n)$ is true in any Herbrand model of LD(p) if and only if $\langle d_1,\ldots,d_n\rangle \in p$ and $<d_1,\ldots,d_n> \in type_1 \times \cdots \times type_n$. Moreover $\neg p(d_1,\ldots,d_n)$ is true in any Herbrand model of LD(p) if and only if $\langle d_1,\ldots,d_n\rangle \notin p$ or $<d_1,\ldots,d_n> \notin type_1 \times \cdots \times type_n$. (Recall that p denotes the relation described in the *Relation* part of the specification!) Methods for constructing logic descriptions are proposed in [12].

At the present stage no tool exists in the system to prove formally the correctness of a logic description. It is the responsibility of the programmer to come up with such a correct description whatever this could mean. Possible meanings are

1. LD(p) is correct by definition[1];
2. LD(p) was constructed informally and is correct (by magic or whatever);
3. LD(p) was constructed thanks to a formal method not supported by FOLON.

However there is a component of the FOLON environment that helps the programmer to construct the logic description according to the schema guided approach described in [13]. This is more related to the second approach above although some formal aspects related to the other two points of view are present. The LOGIST component is composed of

1. a type database,
2. a set of logic description schemata,
3. a logic description editor.

The type database contains information about a set of *ground* types. Types are simply names whose meaning is unknown to LOGIST. They can be associated with well-founded relations, structural forms of terms and predicates able to decide if a term is minimal or not with respect to the well-founded relation. Subtyping relations can be defined allowing inheritance of well-founded relations. When LOGIST is used, the user is asked to choose a logic description schema for the new procedure. Schemata are parameterized on the information in the type database. For example, there is a schema based on structural induction. In order to instantiate it, the user has to specify an induction parameter and a well-founded relation. Then he is allowed to use the logic description editor to complete the logic description. An example is given at paragraph 3.2. Other schemata proposed by LOGIST are described in [13].

[1] Then some assumptions about F are needed to ensure existence and unicity of the defined relation.

2.3 Testing the logic description: the prototyper

As LOGIST does not formally ensure the correctness, a *prototyper* of logic description has been added to the FOLON environment. It allows to solve *ground queries* with the help of the user.

The prototyper behaves as follows. Actual parameters are substituted inside the logic description. Then the logic description is simplified by applying rules about the connectives $\wedge$, $\vee$, **not**, ... and built-in predicates (=, is, ...). This will directly solve the query for base cases. Otherwise the user is asked to give information about a subgoal. Ground subgoals are considered first. The user is asked for the truth value of one of them. He is free to answer that he does not know. Then another subgoal is considered. When non ground subgoals are considered the user is asked for their multiplicity, and deterministic ones are selected first. Furthermore the user is asked for a ground instantiation of the variables in the subgoal that makes it true. Simplification is then applied again and all steps are repeated until a truth value is obtained for the initial goal or no choice is left to the prototyper. In the later case a "don't know" answer is output. (See the example at paragraph 3.3.) In spite of its simplicity, the prototyper is useful to test the validity of the logic description construction process and especially to find counter examples. (See [10, 11] for more details.)

2.4 Deriving a Prolog procedure: the type analyzer[2]

The *type analyzer* is a major part of the system. It can be used either to derive a correct Prolog procedure from a specification and a logic description or to check a given Prolog procedure with respect to (the formal parts of) a specification.

Derivation of a correct Prolog procedure from a logic description involves two main steps. First the logic description is translated into a Prolog procedure whose completion[3] is the logic description again. This translation is purely syntactical and is automatized in the FOLON environment. The resulting procedure is defined up to a permutation of its clauses and of the subgoals in the body of the clauses. Not all of them are correct in general. The *find_permut* component of the type analyzer aims at finding correct permutations of the subgoals for each clause. This is achieved if each subgoal is correctly called with respect to the type, directionality and no-sharing parts of its specification [6]. In practice, *behaviors* are used. A behavior is a set of pre-post conditions, related to a logic procedure, involving combined type and mode information about the arguments of the procedure, possibly augmented with a set of no-share constraints. The combined type and mode information is provided by means of so-called *typed-terms* which are analogous to usual terms where variables are replaced by *indexed_types* of the form $T($i$) where T is a (possibly non ground) type and i is a natural number. The index i is used to express equality and no-sharing constraints. Non ground types are used to combine the type and mode information from specifications. Behaviors are more powerful (although less understandable) than separate information on (ground) types and modes. The possible usage of behaviors

[2] The name is explained by the fact that type analysis is the main method used in this module.

[3] The completion notion is defined in [12], it is a slight extension of Clark's completion [4].

in specifications stems from that. In any case all information about types, modes and sharing is translated into the behavior form before being used in the type analyzer. See [6, 7, 8] for more details.

When several permutations are correct for a clause, some of them can be more efficient or more amenable to an optimized version (see [12], chapter 10). Therefore all correct versions are generated by the system and the user is free to keep some of them for further manipulation by the optimization module (see paragraph 2.5). When no correct permutation is found, the *detail* tool can be used to find the causes of inconsistencies. This tool allows to display the abstract substitutions in each point of a clause assuming a given input abstract substitution. Abstract substitutions are of the form:

$$\langle \{X_1 \leftarrow tt_1, \ldots, X_n \leftarrow tt_n\}, \{nosh_1, \ldots, nosh_m\} \rangle$$

where the X_i are the variables in the clause, the tt_i are typed terms, and the $nosh_i$ are no-share constraints of the form ⟨$T(j),$T'(k)⟩ where $T(j) and $T'(k) are indexed types occurring in $tt_1, \ldots, tt_n$. Using *detail* allows to diagnose a failure of *find_permut*. (See paragraph 3.4.) Some changes can then be brought about to the clause, the logic description or the specification. Changes to the clause involve adding type checking literals to cut off inconsistent derivations. Going back to the logic description level, a new induction parameter or a new schema can be used, among other choices. Finally slight changes in the specification can often settle the problem without changing the clause. Directionalities can be weakened. For example, a directionality involving an input mode *any* can be split into two new directionalities involving *ground* and *var* respectively. Adding no-share constraints also allows for a more satisfactory analysis of types. More powerful changes to the specification are still obtainable by removing the usual type and directionality information and using behaviors instead. (See the example at paragraph 3.4). Lastly, *detail* can be used on its own to analyze the type consistency of Prolog procedures not constructed with the help of FOLON (see [9]).

When correct permutations of literals are found for all clauses, the procedure is guaranteed to be correct from a theoretical standpoint[4], i.e. all possible solutions are in the SLD-tree and only them. Practical correctness moreover requires that all solutions be reachable when the unfair depth first search strategy of Prolog is used. This requires an analysis based on the multiplicity of the procedures used by the subgoals and sometimes an additional termination proof (see [12] for more details). This aspect is not automated at the moment in our system[5] and the user is asked to choose a terminating permutation for each clause (if any) and a right permutation of the clauses (only the last clause is allowed to give infinitely many solutions).

2.5 Optimizing the procedure and running it

Once a fully correct procedure is obtained, some useful optimizations are often still possible. A set of optimizing transformations described in [12] is implemented in the FOLON environment. As there is no best (deterministic) way to apply those transformations, the current optimizer module is driven by the user. A panel of transformations is proposed by the system and the user is free to (repeatedly) choose one of

[4] Provided that the logic description is.

[5] Note that full automation is probably out of reach due to the undecidability of the halting problem.

them. The system then checks that the transformation is applicable before using it. Most of the checks are purely syntactical and therefore easily implementable. Some others involve semantic conditions such as a goal is *deterministic* or two goals are *incompatible*. Those conditions are undecidable in general although some interesting cases are solvable using type analysis, multiplicity of the procedures and general knowledge about the built-in operations (mostly unification). So when a transformation is selected by the user, an attempt is made by the system to also verify semantic conditions. If this attempt fails, the conditions in doubt are told to the user. He is then free to choose another transformation or to apply the initial one under his responsibility. The implemented transformations include elimination of common prefixes of clauses, replacing negations by cuts, partial evaluation, reduction of backtracking with cuts, forward and backward substitution, introduction of anonymous variables. In the end the final version is stored in the *procedure database*. It is compiled and can then be executed from the *execution window* of the environment.

2.6 Type handling

Type analysis is a main feature of our system. Our approach is hybrid and (currently) rather pragmatical. Different notions of types are used at the logical description level and at the Prolog procedure level. No complete description of the types[6] is used at any level. The types are only known via a collection of useful pieces of information or algorithms. The type analyzer [6] is parametrized on a set of primitive operations able for example to unify a type and a typed term or to test if the denotation of a typed term is a subset of a type. This approach is very flexible in theory as a type can be almost any set of (non ground) terms but it becomes cumbersome when many types are considered. An additional layer was therefore added to the system. It allows to automatically derive the primitive operations from a set of basic facts such as *type* T_1 *is included in type* T_2 or $f(T_1,\ldots,T_n)$ *is included in* T'.... A second layer able to automatically infer this information from formal type definitions is planned for the future [7]. Although technically different, our approach to using types for ensuring correctness has many similarities with Naish's one [22, 23].

3 A complete example: efface/3

In this section we explain how our environment works by means of an example. We take the procedure `efface/3` because although it looks very simple, it is not so easy to obtain a correct version that respects the specification for all the possible uses.

We also choose this example because it was already studied in detail in several books [5, 25] and especially in [12].

3.1 Entering the specification

We want to build a procedure to (informally speaking) remove, from a list L, its first element equal to X, giving list LEff. LEff should not be defined if X $\notin$ L. Moreover

[6] i.e. a formal notation defining the type denotation.

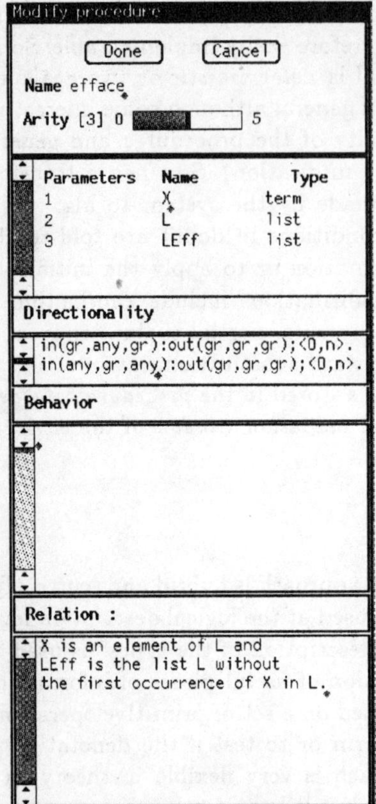

Fig. 2. The specification of **efface/3**

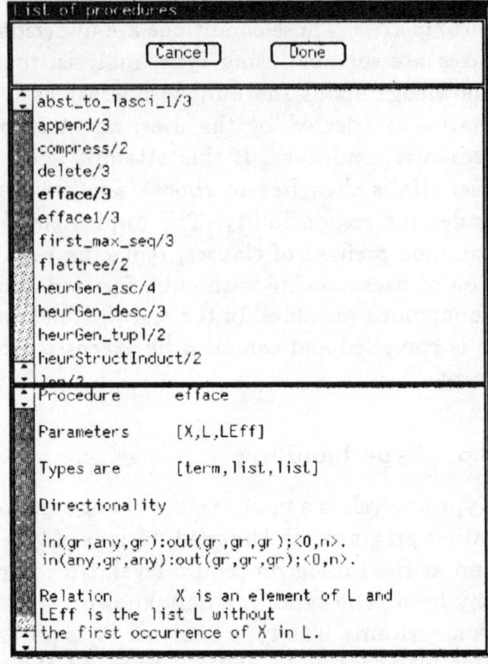

Fig. 3. The **select_procedure** window

we want the procedure to be as multidirectional as possible. Nevertheless some uses are unrealistic. For example, calling the procedure with X and L variable and LEff = [1, 3] should produce the following sequence of answers:

L = [X,1,3]; L = [1,X,3], X $\neq$ 1; L = [1,3,X], X $\neq$ 1,3;

which is not obtainable in standard Prolog. Looking around for possible directionalities we find that the two first arguments cannot be simultaneously free nor the two last ones. This results in the following specification:

efface(X, L, LEff)
  type X : term
    L, LEff : lists
  relation X is an element of L and LEff is the list L without the first occurrence of X in L.
  directionality
    in(gr, any, gr) : out(gr, gr, gr); $< 0, n >$
    in(any, gr, any) : out(gr, gr, gr); $< 0, n >$

It can be entered in the FOLON environment as depicted in figure 2.

3.2 Construction of the logic description

Design

Select procedure...

Current procedure is efface/3

Induction parameter...

Induction parameter : L

of type : list

Wf relation...

Well founded relation : sublist

Strategy structural induction

Create skeleton

done

Fig. 4. The **design** window

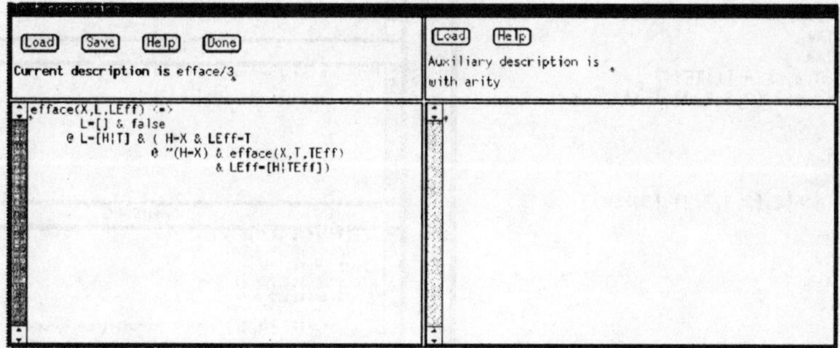

Fig. 5. The logic description of **efface/3**

The first step for the construction of the logic description is to select the procedure specification by means of the window shown in figure 3. A construction strategy is then selected through the panel of figure 4. We choose here the simplest one: structural induction.

If we use L as induction parameter, sublist as well-founded relation and structural induction as strategy we obtain the following skeleton (note that @ stands for the OR connective).

```
efface(X,L,LEff) <=>
    L=[] & directly_solve(L,X,LEff)
  @ L=[H|T] & decompose(L,FirstPart_L,Rem_L)
            & process(FirstPart_L,FirstPart_X,FirstPart_LEff)
            & efface(Rem_X,Rem_L,Rem_LEff)
            & compose(FirstPart_X,FirstPart_LEff,Rem_X,Rem_LEff,X,LEff)
```

We then use the logic description editor to instantiate the skeleton according to a (semi formal) structural induction reasoning. This result in the logic description of figure 5.

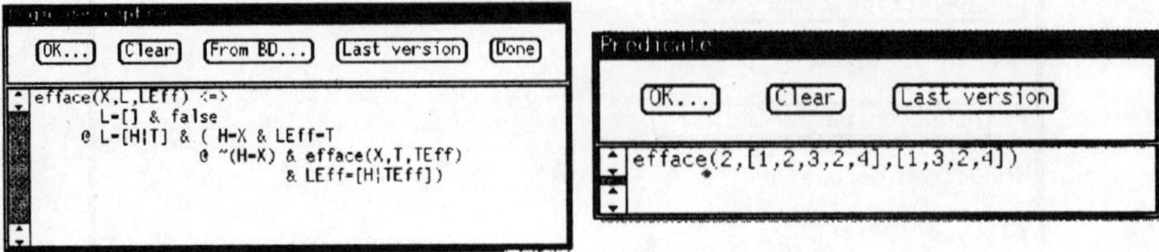

Fig. 6. the *logic_description* window

Fig. 7. the *predicate* window

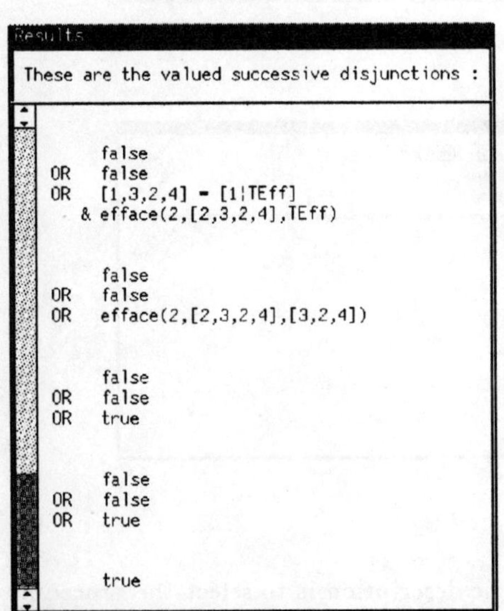

Fig. 8. The *prototype* window

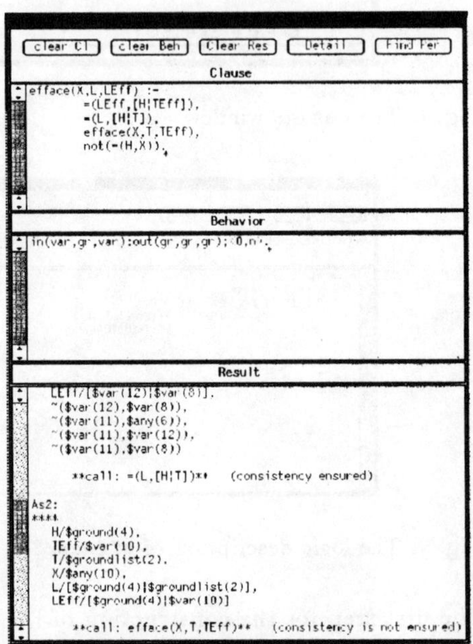

Fig. 9. The *detail* window

3.3 Prototyping

The user is prompted for the logic description he wants to interpret by means of the `logic_description` window, see figure 6, and for the query to be tested by means of the `predicate` window, see figure 7. The results obtained for the predicate `efface(2,[1,2,3,2,4],[1,3,2,4])` in the environment FOLON are given in figure 8.

3.4 Derivation of the Prolog procedure

The logic description is first translated by the synthesis tool into the two following clauses:

```
efface(X,L,LEff) :- =(L,[H|T]), =(H,X), =(LEff,T).
efface(X,L,LEff) :- =(L,[H|T]), not(=(H,X)),
                    efface(X,T,TEff), =(LEff,[H|TEff]).
```

The *find_permut* module is then called to find permutations of both clauses that are correct for both directionalities. No solution is found for the second clause. Reexecuting *find_permut* for each directionality separately reveals 3 solutions for directionality **in**(gr,any,gr) and 2 solutions for directionality **in**(any,gr,any). One can wonder why the permutation

```
efface(X,L,LEff) :- =(L, [H|T]), =(LEff,T),
                    efface(X,T,TEff), not(=(H,X)).
```

is not correct for the first directionality. This is solved with the help of the *detail* module which reveals that L can be bound to any term (not just a list) before the recursive call. The following call provides a counter example:

```
efface(a,[X|X],[b,a])
```

since the recursive call will be

```
efface(a,b,[a])
```

where b is not a list. Nevertheless the initial call will correctly fail, but it will not be the case for other problems (see [6, 9]). Note also that an optimizing compiler could exploit the type information that L is instantiable to a list. In such a case the recursive call is definitely wrong.

There are several ways to solve the problem. We only explain two of them. First, we can change the specification to suppress the constraint that L must be instantiable to a list at call time. This results in the following specification where types are weakened and directionalities are replaced by behaviors:

efface(X, L, LEff)
type X, L, LEff : terms
relation L and LEff are lists and X is an element of L and LEff is the list L without the first occurrence of X in L.
behavior
X/$grnd(1), L/$any(1), LEff/$grndlist(1) :: X/$grnd(1), L/$grndlist(1), LEff/$grndlist(2).
X/$any(1), L/$grndlist(1), LEff/$any(2) :: X/$grnd(1), L/$grndlist(1), LEff/$grndlist(2).

Note that the applicability domain of the procedure is broadened by this change.

On the contrary, the other approach consists in narrowing the applicability domain. We can argue that *any* is a too general mode and that it can be reduced to the combination of *ground* and *var*. This leads to the five following directionalities:

in(var,gr,gr) : out(gr,gr,gr); $< 0, 1 >$. in(gr,var,gr) : out(gr,gr,gr); $< 0, n >$.
in(gr,gr,var) : out(gr,gr,gr); $< 0, 1 >$. in(gr,gr,gr) : out(gr,gr,gr); $< 0, 1 >$.
in(var,gr,var) : out(gr,gr,gr); $< 0, n >$.

Unfortunately *find_permut* still fails to find a common permutation for all of them. However 3 permutations can be found for the four first directionalities. Using *detail* for the fifth directionality and the clause

```
efface(X,L,LEff) :- =(LEff,[H|TEff]), =(L,[H|T]),
                    efface(X,T,TEff), not(=(H,X)).
```

we find (see figure 9) that X can be bound to *any* term before the recursive call. Indeed, the initial call

```
efface(X,[a,b],X)
```

will induce the recursive call

```
efface([a|TEff], [b], TEff)
```

where [a|TEff] is not a variable. The problem disappears if a no-share constraint is added between X and LEff. Adding the (1,3) no-share constraint, *find_permut* reveals the following correct permutation

```
efface(X,L,LEff) :- =(LEff,[H|TEff]), =(L,[H|T]),
                    efface(X,T,TEff), not(=(H, X)).
```

3.5 Optimizing the procedure

Two main approaches are possible. The first consists of keeping a single procedure. Then the only possible optimization is putting unifications in the procedure head. This could easily be done by an intelligent compiler. The final procedure is then

```
efface(X,[X|T],T).
efface(X,[H|T],[H|TEff]) :- efface(X,T,TEff), not(H = X).
```

Another more lengthy approach consists of building separate optimized procedures for every directionality. Test predicates will then be used to direct the initial call to the adequate specialized version. Consider first the input directionality

in(ground,ground,var)

find_permut ensures that the following procedure is correct with respect to it:

```
efface(X,L,LEff) :- L =[H|T], H = X, LEff = T.
efface(X,L,LEff) :- L = [H|T], not(H = X),
                    LEff = [H|TEff], efface(X,T,TEff).
```

A first transformation allows to replace not(H = X) by a cut :

```
efface(X,L,LEff) :- L = [H|T], H = X, !, LEff = T.
efface(X,L,LEff) :- L = [H|T], LEff = [H|TEff],
                    efface(X,T,TEff).
```

then forward and backward substitution and the fact that LEff = T always gives one and only one solution leads to the following final version:

```
efface_1(X,[X|T],T) :- !.
efface_1(X,[H|T],[H|TEff]) :- efface_1(X,T,TEff).
```

Other optimizations applied to procedures correct for other directionalities lead to the following other ones:

in(ground,ground,ground) :

```
efface_2(X,[X|T],LEff) :- !, LEff = T.
efface_2(X,[H|T],[H|TEff]) :- efface_2(X,T,TEff).
```

in(var,ground,ground) and **in**(var,ground,var) :

```
efface_3(X,[X|T],T).
efface_3(X,[H|T],[H|TEff]) :- efface_3(X,T,TEff), not(X = H).
```

in(ground,var,ground) :

```
efface_4(X,[X|T],T).
efface_4(X,[H|T],[H|TEff]) :- not(X = H), efface_4(X,T,TEff).
```

So the optimized procedure will be

```
efface_o(_X,_L,_LEff) :- var(_X), !, efface_3(_X,_L,_LEff).
efface_o(_X,_L,_LEff) :- var(_L), !, efface_4(_X,_L,_LEff)
efface_o(_X,_L,_LEff) :- var(_LEff), !, efface_1(_X,_L,_LEff).
efface_o(_X,_L,_LEff) :- efface_2(_X,_L,_LEff).
```

Test Data			execution time in seconds for 10000 executions	
X	L	LEff	efface/3	efface_o/3
X	[1,...,30,2,4]	[1,3,4,...,30,2,4]	2.69	2.71
X	[1,...,30,2,4]	[1,...,30,4]	17.03	14.33
2	L	[1,3,4,...,30,2,4]	157.40	13.46
2	[1,...,30,2,4]	LEff	15.74	0.82
0	[1,...,30,2,4]	LEff	5.23	4.53
2	[1,...,30,2,4]	[1,3,4,...,30,2,4]	2.68	2.24
2	[1,...,30,2,4]	[1,...,30,4]	15.25	0.89
X	[1,...,30,2,4]	LEff	145.14	144.50

Table 1. Comparison of the execution times for efface/3 and efface_o/3

The comparison between the procedure that works for all directionalities (efface) and the procedure that checks the input mode (efface_o/3) is given in table 1.

4 Conclusion

We have presented in this paper an implemented environment that supports a methodology for logic program construction where the logic and control aspects are well separated. As it stands our system provides some evidence that the "Logic + Control" paradigm can be valuable for "real life" programming as the remaining weaknesses can clearly be overcome. A strong point of the system is that declarative construction of programs is fully supported. The programmer may concentrate on the specification and logic description parts which are necessarily creative ones. The derivation part is automatized to a great extent and relieves the programmer of much of the clerical task. But still this task is very error prone when multidirectionality is extensively used. Another strong point is that the system is fully open. For example, it is compatible with any (pure) logic program synthesis component and we plan to integrate one in the near future. Nevertheless FOLON is still an experimental environment and many components are improvable. In particular the handling of types should be made easier and safer. This is one of the main aspects we are working upon. Finally, it will be interesting to integrate the system with a Prolog compiler that will use the formal parts of the specifications (types, directionalities, multiplicity, no-sharing constraints) to optimize code generation.

5 Acknowledgements

Jean Burnay, Pierre De Boeck, Bruno Desart, Yves Deville and Jean-Pierre Hogne have contributed to the development of the FOLON environment. We take this opportunity to thank them as well as other former members of the FOLON project: Pierre Flener and Pascal Van Hentenryck for valuable discussions and comments.

The FOLON project is supported by the Belgian National Incentive Program for Fundamental Research in Artificial Intelligence under contract number AI/12.

References

1. M. Bruynooghe. A practical framework for the abstract interpretation of logic programs. *Journal of Logic Programming*, 10(2):91–124, 1991.
2. A. Bundy, A. Smaill, and G. Wiggins. The synthesis of logic programs from inductive proofs. In J.W. Lloyd, editor, *Computational Logic*, Esprit Basic Research Series, 1990.
3. J. Burnay. Logist. Research report, University of Namur, Belgium, 1989.
4. K.L. Clark. Negation as failure. In Gallaire and Minker, editors, *Logic and Databases*, pages 230–245. Plenum Press, New York, 1978.
5. W.F. Clocksin and C.S. Mellish. *Programming in Prolog*. Springer-Verlag, 1984.
6. P. De Boeck and B. Le Charlier. Static type analysis of Prolog procedures for ensuring correctness. In *Procceedings of PLILP'90*, volume 456 of *LNCS*, pages 222–237, Linköping, Sweden, 1990. Springer-Velag.
7. P. De Boeck and B. Le Charlier. Automatic construction of Prolog primitives for type checking analysis. In M. Billaud and al., editors, *JTASPEFL'91*, pages 165–172, Bordeaux, France, 1991. Bigre 74.
8. P. De Boeck and B. Le Charlier. Using static type analysis for constructing correct Prolog procedures. In *ICLP'91 Pre-Conference Workshop on Semantics-Based Analysis of Logic Programs*, INRIA Rocquencourt, France, 1991.

9. P. De Boeck and B. Le Charlier. Some lessons drawn from using static type analysis for ensuring the correctness of logic program. submitted for publication, 1992.
10. B. Desart. Prototypage d'algorithmes logiques. Master's thesis, University of Namur, Belgium, 1989.
11. B. Desart. Logic description interpretor: Integration into computer assistance for logic program construction. Research report, University of Namur, Belgium, 1990.
12. Y. Deville. *Logic Programming: Systematic Program Development.* Addison Wesley, 1990.
13. Y. Deville and J. Burnay. Generalization and program schemata: A step towards computer-aided construction of logic programs. In E.L. Lusk and R.A. Overbeek, editors, *Proceedings of NACLP'89*, pages 409–425, Cleveland, Ohio, 1989. The MIT Press.
14. P. Flener and Y. Deville. Synthesis of composition and discrimination operators for divide-and-conquer logic programs. In J.-M. Jacquet, editor, *Proceedings of the ICLP'91 Preconference Workshop on Logic Program Construction.* John Wiley, 1992.
15. P. Flener and Y. Deville. Towards stepwise, schema-guided synthesis of logic programs. In K.K. Lau and T. Clement, editors, *Proceedings of LOPSTR'91 Workshop.* Springer Verlag, 1992.
16. F. Giannesini, H. Kanoui, R. Pasero, and M. van Caneghem. *Prolog.* Wokingham: Addison-Wesley, 1986.
17. J. Henrard. Using the folon environment : A user guide. Research Report 13-92, University of Namur, Belgium, 1992.
18. P.M. Hill and J.W. Lloyd. The Gödel report (preliminary version). Technical Report TR-91-02, Computer Science Departement, University of Bristol, March 1991.
19. R.A. Kowalski. *Logic for Problem Solving.* Amsterdam: North-Holland, 1979.
20. B Le Charlier and P. Van Hentenryck. Experimental evaluation of a generic abstract interpretation algorithm for Prolog. In *Proceedings of ICCL'92*, San Franciso, April 1992.
21. J.W. Lloyd. *Foundations of Logic Programming.* Springer Series: Symbolic Computation–Artificial Intelligence. Springer-Velag, second, extended edition, 1987.
22. L. Naish. Specification = program + types. In K. Nori, editor, *Foundations of Software Technology and Theoretical Computer Science*, number 287 in LNCS. Springer-Verlag, 1987.
23. L. Naish. Verification of logic programs and imperative programs. In J.-M. Jacquet, editor, *Proceedings of the ICLP'91 Preconference Workshop on Logic Program Construction.* John Wiley, 1992.
24. R.A. O'Keefe. *The Craft of Prolog.* MIT Press, 1990.
25. L. Sterling and E. Shapiro. *The Art of Prolog: Advanced Programming Techniques.* MIT Press, 1986.

This article was processed using the LaTeX macro package with LLNCS style

A Complete Indexing Scheme for WAM-based Abstract Machines

Werner Hans*

RWTH Aachen, Lehrstuhl für Informatik II
Ahornstraße 55, W-5100 Aachen, Germany

Abstract. This paper introduces an indexing scheme for logic programming languages, complete in considering all parameters and nested terms. Nevertheless it does not lead to a code-size explosion, because the sets of valid clauses are not encoded by special control flow instructions. Instead, some kind of identifiers of the applicable clauses are stored in (clause) sets allowing the stepwise restriction of alternative clauses during the runtime analysis of the parameters.
We present the compilation scheme to integrate this approach in existing compilers. It shows the cooperation of the new instructions, the strict separation of the indexing code from the code executing the compiled clauses, and it demonstrates the easiness of integrating a complete indexer in compilers. The compilation scheme was originally developed for the stack-based narrowing machine of the functional logic language BABEL. We describe, however, the slightly modified indexing scheme for the usual WAM-architecture and assume Prolog as the language platform.

1 Introduction

Logic programming languages, such as Prolog, define predicates by several clauses describing the different conditions which must be fulfilled to apply the predicate. While evaluating the query (or parts of it) the described conditions are tested to determine the subset of applicable clauses. One request is their quick selection, because much time may be spent in this determination phase.

Indexing is an approach that

- improves the determination of the first applicable rule,
- separates the applicable rules from the non–applicable ones. This leads to an early reduction of the search space, being important for (or-)parallel implementations,
- offers the possibility of the detection of determinism, leading to less memory consumption, in particular of the runtime stack, because less choice point must be saved. [Hickey,Mudambi89] point out that indexing can affect the consumption of all memory areas.
- allows the fast detection of failure situations.

* The author is supported by the grant In 20/6-1 from the 'Deutsche Forschungsgemeinschaft'. e-mail: hans@zeus.informatik.rwth-aachen.de

– enables the lazy narrowing machine (in a functional + logic environment) to select the rules by viewing only the currently evaluated parameters. This mechanism delays (possibly infinite) computations which may be irrelevant for the decision.

[Kliger,Shapiro88] construct a decision tree at compile time taking all clauses of a predicate into consideration. They translate this tree to a header for the corresponding machine code of the predicate. At runtime the generated instructions control the flow which finally reaches the jump instruction pointing at the correct clause[2]. This is a fast and complete approach, but it consumes much program space. The decision tree may need program space exponential in the number of clauses and argument positions. Consequently they choose in [Kliger,Shapiro90] decision graphs rather than decision trees to encode the possible traces of each predicate. Although this eliminates many cases of exponential blow-up of codesize, it cannot prevent it. [Korsloot,Tick91] extend this algorithm to handle "don't know" nondeterminism. Now the control flow reaches try/trust blocks. Each of them consists of instructions, to jump to the first applicable clause as well as to choose available alternatives after failure(s). As the decision tree/graph may possess many branches at every level, this may result in many try/trust blocks at its leaves.

[Hickey,Mudambi89] use a similar approach, to determine the applicable clauses. For further improvements at runtime, they consider mode–information and encode each possible invocation (situation) by specialized machine code. But this leads to further code space consumption.

All these approaches need quite complex compilers. Some authors omit complete indexing and use instead simpler kinds of it. A well-known restriction is the first–argument–top–level–indexing[Aït-Kaci91]. This restriction considers that most of the programmers have in mind the depth–first–left–to–right evaluation order of Prolog (in particular during the unification) while they write programs. This specialized clauses support this simple indexing mechanism, frequently.

But looking at the recently developed functional + logic programming languages it becomes more attractive to consider complete indexing. An alternative approach is presented in [Chakravarty,Lock91]. The authors do not statically create a choice point, whenever a predicate with more than one clause is called. Instead, they dynamically create a choice point, only in cases, an unbound variable may get alternative bindings. To ensure the correctness of their approach, the programs must meet a nonambiguity requirement, that is usual in functional programming.

To decrease the size of the decision tree, they do a program transformation including clause– and parameter–reordering. For this transformed program they compute the indexing code similar to the pattern matcher in [Peyton,Jones87]. But their approach is illegal for programs being very sensible to clause– or parameter–reordering, as Prolog, BABEL.

The reason for the exponential blow-up is given by the kind of chains connecting the clauses. That chaining is done via special control flow instructions like try, retry, and trust, grouped to try/trust blocks. This is simple and clearly fast, but the compiled code may explode encoding such inflexible (unconditional) try/trust blocks. Additionally, the intermediate analysis results of several arguments are not stored,

[2] They present their ideas for FCP (Flat Concurrent Prolog).

but immediately used for branching. Therefore they are only implicit given by the paths from the root to the actual node in the decision tree. This must lead to space consuming decision trees.

Another interesting approach is taken in [Palmer,Naish91], who have proved that the generation of the decision tree is an NP-hard problem. They use so-called clause sets to store the applicable rules, which are computed dynamically. We choose their approach, too, because of its elegance and simplicity, but we focus on the compilation scheme.

This paper is organized as follows: The next section mentions the chosen indexing approach. It describes the extensions of the WAM and points out the new instructions. Section 3 deals with the compilation scheme and Section 4 gives a compilation example, demonstrating the simplicity of our scheme. In Section 5 the produced code is analyzed and some simple and impressive optimizations are presented. Section 6 mentions some restrictions that occur in real implementations and Section 7 concludes this paper presenting several runtime results and memory demands. In most of the sections we take Prolog as the source language and assume Prolog's evaluation strategy.

2 Indexing

Complete indexing divides the invocation of a predicate in a preceding analysis pass and the execution pass. During the analysis pass, the clauses are split into applicable and non–applicable ones. The applicable ones are stored in clause sets. Starting with the clause set containing the "identifiers" of all clauses, the non–applicable clauses are successively removed from it. This approach allows an independent analysis of each parameter as well as an easy examination of the components of nested terms. In terms of decision trees, this approach split the great decision tree in several less complex decision trees.

All (separate) restrictions are synthesized by the intersection of the superset[3] and the computed sets. The computed sets only consider restrictions got by a local analysis of each parameter, but the intersection of all sets delivers the desired set.

By applying Prolog's left-to-right evaluation strategy to the analysis, we only need one set for the set manipulation. This claims the new register *Alt* in the abstract machine, to hold the intermediate set.

The code of each procedure[4] is preceded by a special code for the analysis. It compares the current arguments with the formal ones and collects the different restrictions in Alt. This indexing part is eventually concluded by an instruction, which takes the evaluated clause set (*Alt*) and jumps to the first valid clause.

To profit from the analysis after failure, the choice point is extended with a new component *alt* storing the remaining clauses of the procedure. This component gets a "copy" of Alt when branching to the first clause. Its value is modified during backtracking. To capture this situation the indexing part is augmented by one further instruction, to jump to when a failure occurs. This instruction combines the actions of the usual WAM-instructions retry_me_else and trust_me.

[3] containing all defined clauses

[4] all clauses of a program with the same predicate symbol and the same arity.

In the following listing an informal description of each instruction is given:

switch_on_term X_i,(vlab,valt),(clab,calt),(flab,falt)[5]
dereferences[6] the content of the i-th argument register, inspects the dereferenced value, and jumps to the instruction labeled vlab, clab or flab, depending on the values type, i.e. whether it is a variable (unbound REF-cell), a constant- or a functor-cell, respectively. Additionally the current value in register Alt is intersected with one of the three sets valt, calt or falt with respect to the inspected data. The value of register X_i is replaced by the dereferenced value.

switch_on_constant X_i,(lab,alt),$\mathcal{A}$, $\mathcal{A} = \{(c_i, alt_i) \mid 1 \leq i \leq n\}$
expects a constant c in register X_i. If $\mathcal{A}$ contains a pair (c,alt′), Alt is intersected with alt′. Otherwise Alt is intersected with alt. In both cases the control continues at the instruction labeled lab.
The constants in the first position of all tuples in $\mathcal{A}$ are different in pairs.

switch_on_structure X_i,(lab,alt),$\mathcal{A}$ $\mathcal{A} = \{(f_i/n_i, lab_i, alt_i) \mid 1 \leq i \leq n\}$
compares the functor f/n pointed to by register X_i with the functors contained in $\mathcal{A}$. If $\mathcal{A}$ contains a triple (f/n,lab′,alt′) the *subterm* register S is set to the heap address following that functor cell. The mode is set to *read* mode and Alt and alt′ are intersected. The instruction labeled lab′ is executed next.
If $\mathcal{A}$ does not contain a valid triple, Alt is intersected with alt, and a jump to lab occurs.
The functor/arity–pairs in the first position of all triples in $\mathcal{A}$ are different in pairs[7].

try #arg
analyzes the current value of register Alt. If this register stores more than one alternative, the instruction creates a choice point similar to the WAM try_me_else instruction. The new component alt of the choice point is initialized with the current value of Alt. To determine the continuation point it accesses the label-list of the retry instruction, immediately following. If a is Alt's least element it branches to lab_a (see retry), and deletes this element a from alt. The continuation pointer of the choice point is initialized with the label of the following retry instruction.
Try needs its parameter #arg for the size alignment of the choice point.
If register Alt contains only one alternative no choice point must be created. Only the jump is performed.
If register Alt does not contain any alternative, a failure situation occurs.

retry (lab_1,...,lab_n)
is executed during backtracking to determine the next alternative. It is an amalgamation of the WAM-instructions retry_me_else and trust_me. If the component alt of the topmost choice point contains only one element "a", it behaves like trust_me and erases the choice point from the stack. It jumps further to lab_a.

---

[5] For simplicity we neglect the special consideration of lists.

[6] Dereferencing is done by following a possible reference chain until an unbound REF cell or a non-REF cell is reached.

[7] Conceptually it is possible to handle constants and functors in the same manner, but this division simplifies the compilation scheme given below.

Otherwise it deletes alt's least element "a" from alt and jumps to lab_a. But in both cases the computation environment must be restored. This includes the resetting of the heap, the unwinding of the trail, and the reloading of the argument registers.

In the indexing part the WAM instruction

unify_variable X_i,

is mentioned (which is executed only in read mode) as well as the unconditional *jump*.

To ensure the correct computation of the clause set, the correct initialization of register Alt is necessary. This is done by the instructions *call* and *execute*. They set Alt to $\mathbb{N}$, the set of all natural numbers[8].

3 The compilation scheme

The generation of the indexing part for each procedure consists of two parts. First of all, the necessary information for the static sets of the switch instructions has to be collected. Later, the compiler must be able to extract the currently interesting parts of the collection.

We start with the explanation of the auxiliaries (table 1).

$$\mathit{collect}\,(< \mathrm{p}(t_{i,1},\ldots,t_{i,n})\text{:-}\mathrm{body}_i \mid 1 \le i \le r >) := \bigcup_{1\le i\le r, 1\le j\le n} \{(i,j,t_{i,j})\}$$

$$\mathit{split}(\mathcal{A}, j) := \{(i,t) \mid (i,j,t) \in \mathcal{A}\}$$

$$\mathit{select}(\mathcal{A}, j) := \{ (i,t_j) \mid (i,f(t_1,\ldots,t_j,\ldots,t_n)) \in \mathcal{A}\}$$

$$\mathit{typesplit}\,(\emptyset) := \emptyset$$

$$\mathit{typesplit}\,((i,t)+\mathcal{A}) := \begin{cases} (\mathcal{A}_1, \mathcal{A}_2, \mathcal{A}_3 \cup \{(i,t)\}) & ; \text{if } t \in \mathrm{Var} \\ (\mathcal{A}_1 \cup \{(i,t)\}, \mathcal{A}_2, \mathcal{A}_3) & ; \text{if } t = c \\ (\mathcal{A}_1, \mathcal{A}_2 \cup \{(i,t)\}, \mathcal{A}_3) & ; \text{if } t = f(t_1,\ldots,t_n) \end{cases}$$

with $(\mathcal{A}_1, \mathcal{A}_2, \mathcal{A}_3) = \mathit{typesplit}(\mathcal{A})$.

$$\mathit{transform}(\emptyset) := \emptyset$$

$$\mathit{transform}((i,f(t_1,\ldots,t_n))+\mathcal{A}) :=$$

$$\begin{cases} (\mathcal{B} \setminus \{\mathcal{C}\} \cup \{\mathcal{C} \cup \{(i, f(t_1,\ldots,t_n))\}\} & ; \text{if } \exists \mathcal{C} \in \mathcal{B}, i', t'_j : (i', f(t'_1,\ldots,t'_n)) \in \mathcal{C} \\ \mathcal{B} \cup \{\{(i, f(t_1,\ldots,t_n))\}\} & ; \text{otherwise} \end{cases}$$

with $\mathcal{B} = \mathit{transform}(\mathcal{A})$.

$$\mathit{createalt}(\mathcal{A}) := \{i \mid (i,t) \in \mathcal{A}\}$$

Table 1. The auxiliaries

collect collects all necessary information for the generation of the indexing part. It extracts the information from the heads of the program clauses, grouped to procedures. The body of the clause is not viewed. At this point we remind that the origin of our scheme lies in BABEL. As BABEL possesses an explicit if_then_else,

---

[8] Clearly, it suffices to initialize Alt with the numbers of all rules or more restricted with the numbers of all the rules, which belongs to the called predicate.

neither the programmer must simulate this operation by two or more clauses[9], nor the compiler has to detect and group them. *collect* is called for each procedure. To simplify later manipulation this information is represented as a set of triples. Each triple (i,j,t) contains the number of the clause i, the argument position j, and the term t (formal parameter). The following *append* predicate

$$\text{append}([],X_1,X_1).$$
$$\text{append}([X_1\,|X_2],X_3,[X_1\,|X_4])\text{:-append}(X_2,X_3,X_4).$$

leads to $\{(1,1,[]),(1,2,X_1),(1,3,X_1),(2,1,[X_1\,|X_2]),(2,2,X_3),(2,3,[X_1\,|X_4])\}$.

The remainder of the indexing code generation uses only the delivered information, allowing the clause overlapping consideration of the program.

Called with the set computed by *collect*, *split* extracts all entries of it, which describe the terms at the desired argument position in the clauses. As the argument position is always known in the context, the argument position in the entries of the set is omitted. *Select* computes a set of tuples, where in each entry of the input set the nested term is replaced by its jth component. The context guarantees that all terms of the input set are nested structures.

Generating the indexing code for each argument position separately, the compiler calls *typesplit* to divide the given set[10] (of tuples) in accordance with the type of the term. An application results in three sets, one set contains all tuples with constants, the second one contains all structures, and the last one all tuples with variables.

Transform provides the information that is added as parameters to the instructions *switch_on_constant* and *switch_on_structure*. It modifies the given set being either a set of constants or a set of structures. This results in another set, each entry being a set itself and these sets contain all entries with the same constant or the same toplevel functor respective to the original set. We identify constants and structures of arity 0 in the formal description.

The function *createalt* creates the set of all possible alternatives by neglecting the terms of its input set.

Of these preparations we describe the compilation scheme (table 2). We simplify the management of labels by assuming a symbolic address space. We also assume that the i-th argument of a predicate is stored in the i-th register of the machine, denoted by X_i.

Proctrans compiles each procedure. If the procedure consists of only one clause the function *Ruletrans* is called immediately. The other case results in two parts of code: The indexing part containing mainly the switch-instructions is produced by several calls of *Switchtrans*. The other part containing the usual code for the clauses is built up by *Ruletrans*. It produces the machine code for each clause, that shall conclude with a *proceed* instruction or in the case of tail recursion with an *execute* instruction. This code contains no instruction for switch handling after failure. Because we focus on indexing no detailed description of *Ruletrans* is given.

The instructions *try* and *retry* conclude the indexing part. They direct the control flow to the first of all applicable clauses or, after failure, to the next valid one.

Each call of *Switchtrans* produces indexing code for one argument position. The behaviour of the code is comparable with the first two levels of Prolog's standard

---

[9] in pure Prolog

[10] this is the output of *split* (or *select*).

Proctrans(<p($t_{i,1},\ldots,t_{i,n}$):–body$_i$ | $1 \leq i \leq r$ >,l) :=

p/n: *Ruletrans*(p($t_{1,1},\ldots,t_{1,n}$):–body$_1$,l) if r=1

Switchtrans(1,*split*($\mathcal{A}$,1),l.0.1) if r>1

⋮

Switchtrans(n,*split*($\mathcal{A}$,n),l.0.n)

try n

retry (l.1,...,l.r)

l.1: *Ruletrans*(p($t_{1,1},\ldots,t_{1,n}$):–body$_1$,l.1)

⋮

l.r: *Ruletrans*(p($t_{r,1},\ldots,t_{r,n}$):–body$_r$,l.r)

with $\mathcal{A}$=*collect*(<p($t_{i,1},\ldots,t_{i,n}$):–body$_i$ | $1 \leq i \leq r$ >)

Switchtrans(i,$\mathcal{A}$,l) :=

switch_on_term X_i,(l.0,*createalt*($\mathcal{A}$)),(l.1,*createalt*($\mathcal{A}' \cup \mathcal{A}'''$)),
(l.2,*createalt*($\mathcal{A}'' \cup \mathcal{A}'''$))

l.1: *switch_on_constant* X_i,(l.0,*createalt*($\mathcal{A}'''$)),
$\{(c_j,\mathit{createalt}(\mathcal{A}'_j \cup \mathcal{A}'''))| \; 1 \leq j \leq k\}$

l.2: *switch_on_structure* X_i,(l.0,*createalt*($\mathcal{A}'''$)),
$\{(f_j/m_j,l.2.j,\mathit{createalt}(\mathcal{A}''_j \cup \mathcal{A}'''))| \; 1 \leq j \leq n\}$

l.2.1: *SwitchStructtrans*($\mathcal{A}''_1$,$\mathcal{A}'''$,m_1,l.2.1,l.0)

⋮

l.2.n: *SwitchStructtrans*($\mathcal{A}''_n$,$\mathcal{A}'''$,m_n,l.2.n,l.0)

l.0:

with ($\mathcal{A}',\mathcal{A}'',\mathcal{A}'''$)=*typesplit*($\mathcal{A}$)

$\{\mathcal{A}'_1,\ldots,\mathcal{A}'_k\}$=*transform*($\mathcal{A}'$), $(i'_j,c_j) \in \mathcal{A}'_j (1 \leq j \leq k)$,

$\{\mathcal{A}''_1,\ldots,\mathcal{A}''_n\}$=*transform*($\mathcal{A}''$), and $(i''_j,f_j(t_{j,1},\ldots,t_{j,m_j})) \in \mathcal{A}''_j (1 \leq j \leq n)$.

SwitchStructtrans($\mathcal{A}$,$\mathcal{A}'$,n,l,lab):=

unify_variable X_{new_1}

⋮

unify_variable X_{new_n}

Switchtrans(new_1,*select*($\mathcal{A}$,1)∪$\mathcal{A}'$,l.1)

⋮

Switchtrans(new_n,*select*($\mathcal{A}$,n)∪$\mathcal{A}'$,l.n)

jump lab

Table 2. The compilation scheme

indexing approach given in[Aït-Kaci91]. The first instruction *switch_on_term* realizes a conditional branch depending on the data in register X_i. The second instruction is executed if a constant is found. Its third parameter stores all given constant symbols together with the alternatives. *Switch_on_structure* will be enriched similar. Further code is generated by *SwitchStructtrans* for each valid functor.

SwitchStructtrans creates code to analyze the components of structures. Its parameters denote

– the set containing the tuples with identical functors of the same arity,
– the set of tuples with variables at the currently viewed argument position,
– the arity of the functor
– a symbol for the label generation, and
– the goal to create a jump to at the end of this code block.

Because the components of the structure must be saved[11], the components are loaded in free registers, indexed from new_1 till new_n, temporarily. Afterwards it calls *Switchtrans* recursively for each component. The code is eventually concluded by the *jump* instruction, that skips the code of other structures that may follow.

Note that the variables, visited so far, are passed to *SwitchStructtrans.* By this, recursive calls of *Switchtrans* will not forget the corresponding clause candidates.

4 Example

To get an impression of the code produced by this scheme, we present the code of the append predicate. At the first glance the presented code looks deterrent. But the optimizations, we are dealing with in the next section, show that many of the produced instructions are not needed anyway. The superfluous instructions are marked by the indexed plus signs in the first column. The different indices correspond to different degrees of optimizations.

	append:	*switch_on_term*	X_1,(l.13,{1,2}),(l.2,{1}),(l.3,{2})	1st arg.
$+_4$	l.2 :	*switch_on_constant*	X_1,(l.13,{}),{([],{1})}	
$+_4$	l.3 :	*switch_on_structure*	X_1,(l.13,{}),{(./2,l.4,{2})}	
$+_3$	l.4 :	*unify_variable*	X_4	[X_1|X_2]
$+_3$	l.5 :	*unify_variable*	X_5	
$+_2$	l.6 :	*switch_on_term*	X_4,(l.9,{2}),(l.7,{2}),(l.8,{2})	X_1
$+_1$	l.7 :	*switch_on_constant*	X_4,(l.9,{2}),{}	
$+_1$	l.8 :	*switch_on_structure*	X_4,(l.9,{2}),{}	
$+_2$	l.9 :	*switch_on_term*	X_5,(l.12,{2}),(l.10,{2}),(l.11,{2})	X_2
$+_1$	l.10 :	*switch_on_constant*	X_4,(l.12,{2}),{}	
$+_1$	l.11 :	*switch_on_structure*	X_4,(l.12,{2}),{}	
$+_3$	l.12 :	*jump*	l.13	
$+_2$	l.13 :	*switch_on_term*	X_2,(l.16,{1,2}),(l.14,{1,2}),(l.15,{1,2})	2nd arg.
$+_1$	l.14 :	*switch_on_constant*	X_2,(l.16,{1,2}),{}	
$+_1$	l.15 :	*switch_on_structure*	X_2,(l.16,{1,2}),{}	
	l.16 :	*switch_on_term*	X_3,(l.28,{1,2}),(l.17,{1}),(l.18,{1,2})	3rd arg.
$+_1$	l.17 :	*switch_on_constant*	X_3,(l.28,{1}),{}	
$+_4$	l.18 :	*switch_on_structure*	X_3,(l.28,{1}),{(./2,l.19,{1,2})}	
$+_3$	l.19 :	*unify_variable*	X_4	[X_1|X_4]
$+_3$	l.20 :	*unify_variable*	X_5	
$+_2$	l.21 :	*switch_on_term*	X_4,(l.24,{1,2}),(l.22,{1,2}),(l.23,{1,2})	X_1
$+_1$	l.22 :	*switch_on_constant*	X_4,(l.24,{1,2}),{}	

[11] the subterm register may be changed at runtime by other switch_on_structure commands.

```
+1 l.23: switch_on_structure  X4,(l.24,{1,2}),{}
+2 l.24: switch_on_term       X5,(l.27,{1,2}),(l.25,{1,2}),(l.26,{1,2}) X4
+1 l.25: switch_on_constant   X4,(l.27,{1,2}),{}
+1 l.26: switch_on_structure  X4,(l.27,{1,2}),{}
+3 l.27: jump                 l.28
   l.28: try                  3
   l.29: retry                (l.x1,l.x2)
   l.x1: Ruletrans(append([],X1,X1):-),...)
   l.x2: Ruletrans(append([X1|X2],X3,[X1|X4]):-append(X2,X3,X4)),...)
```

The symbolic labels are given in a more readable form and the last column of the table denotes the analyzed arguments or subterms of them.

5 Simple Optimization

When we consider the last example, we recognize that the code for the indexing analysis can grow very fast with the complexity of the formal parameters of the predicate (but within linear limits). This is undesirable, if the engine has to decide only between few alternatives. Such situations claim for optimizations to handle them in a better manner.

An observation shows that all switch_on_constant/structures with an empty third parameter are superfluous[12].($+_1$)

A second source for optimization is given if all formal parameters at a particular argument position are variables. Obviously all analysis is useless, because no restrictions will be possible. Such a situation can be treated by *Switchtrans* with a test $\mathcal{A}' = \mathcal{A}'' = \emptyset$. The same test removes code for testing variables in common subexpressions ($+_2$), too.

If we look at the indexing part of $[X_1|X_2]$, we can remove the three remaining lines l.4, l.5, and l.12. *SwitchStructtrans* generates this instructions. We can optimize this part of code generation by integrating a check, testing whether indexing code will be produced by the *Switchtrans* invocations. If no code is produced, the unify_variable and jump instructions can be suppressed, too. But we must augment *Switchtrans*: If *SwitchStructtrans* called for a functor f_j, produces no code, the label l.2.j has to be replaced by l.0 in the switch_on_structure instruction ($+_3$).

Adding some heuristics to the optimization, we can possibly do further reductions in code size. If we assume the completeness of the definitions of the predicates in a program, we can remove switch_on_constant and switch_on_structure[13] instructions, if their third parameter contains only one entry. If the assumption does not hold, the rejection of the wrong clauses is done in the usual manner by backtracking. Applied to the second example the lines marked by $+_4$ can be discarded and the indexing code shrinks from 29 to 4 lines.

All the optimizations can be integrated in the compiler in an easy manner.

---

[12] The deletion of instructions may require the correction of some labels.

[13] possibly together with the code produced by *SwitchStructtrans*.

6 Implementation

This section deals with the implementation aspects of our approach. Complete indexing had demanded extensions in both the compiler and the WAM. One important problem bases on the representation of the introduced sets, which are not sufficiently supported in usual programming environments, such as C. If we neglect the compilation time of programs, as we do, sets can simply be realized as linear lists in the compiler. The translation of the compilation scheme in a concrete programming language is straight forward and does not lead to any problems.

But we cannot neglect time in the WAM, because the indexing overhead competes with the original rejection mechanism. Therefore the sets are realized by fixed sized bitmaps, which are supported very well by nearly every hardware processor. This allows an easy and fast access and manipulation at runtime on the one hand, but this prohibits general sets on the other hand. The current implementation uses 32-bit bitmaps and thus they could store up to 32 elements. Procedures with more than 32 defined clauses have to be divided into groups containing 32 clauses at most. These groups are tied in the usual way by the WAM-like instructions *try_me_else*, *retry_me_else* and *trust_me*.

The representation by bitmaps allows an easy test of failure situations[14]. Therefore all switch instructions are extended by the simple 0 test that optimizes the analysis with a fast detection of failure situations.

It is also possible to implement dynamic bitmaps, which contain an entry storing the length of the bitmap[Palmer,Naish91]. But to keep costs of bitmap manipulation down, we choose the fixed representation. Dealing with predicates with many clauses, instructions dealing with dynamic bitmaps become more important. We think that the best way is given by having both kinds of instructions. Then the compiler can choose the best class of instructions.

7 Results

The runtime results are given for the abstract machine of the functional logic language BABEL, which is a slightly modified WAM. The main difference is found in the parameter passing mechanism. For a formal description of both the language BABEL and the abstract machine the curious reader may look at [Moreno,Rodríguez89] [Loogen,Winkler91].

The current implementation consists of a compiler translating BABEL programs into code for the abstract machine. The compiler is written in C, and supports all the optimizations mentioned so far. The code delivered by the compiler is executed by an emulator, written in C, too.

The different mechanisms of clause selection are compared in the tables 3 and 4. Table 3 compares the execution times[15] of the following examples, written in BABEL mostly in a functional way:

[14] One has to check the bitmaps to 0.

[15] All examples have been executed on a Sun-Sparc-Station 1+.

fib N : a recursive definition of the Fibonacci function applied to N

rev N : a naive definition of the function reversing a list of length N

quicksort N: a recursive quicksort algorithm applied to a list of length N

queens N : the problem of positioning N queens on a NxN chess-board, so that no queen threatens any other.

popul N : is a database program reporting the surface and population of N countries. It computes all pairs of countries with population densities differing at most 5%.

program	no indexing	complete indexing	ratio
fib 20	1500 msec	1570 msec	105%
rev 30	35 msec	31 msec	89%
quicksort 30	50 msec	49 msec	98%
queens 8	3810 msec	3730 msec	98%
popul 25	290 msec	100 msec	38%

Table 3. Runtimes with and without Indexing

program	no indexing	complete indexing	ratio
fib 20	21891– 10945= 10946	10946– 0 = 10946	50%
rev 30	496 – 465 = 31	0 – 0 = 0	0%
quicksort 30	641 – 484 = 157	0 – 0 = 0	0%
queens 8	28882– 28882= 0	7657 – 7657= 0	27%
popul 25	676 – 676 = 0	26 – 26 = 0	3.8%

Table 4. Behaviour of Choice Points with and without Indexing

The execution times of the first three examples describe the computation times till the first solution is found. Note that although each query has only one result the remaining parts of the computation tree, that are not cut by indexing, are not visited so far. The other two examples calculate all solutions whereby the whole computation tree is traversed.

Most of the examples show some speed up. Someone may be disappointed about the small speedups. This is due to the fact that the examples contain mostly predicates with only few clauses. A more thankful example is the last one. It shows which improvements complete indexing contains. Here we reach a speedup of 3.

Table 4 focuses on the behaviour of the choice points. The entries in the second and third column are given in the form "$a - b = c$". a denotes the number of choice points, that are created at runtime, b denotes the deleted ones, and c denotes the difference. The entries in the ratio column are related to a. We see that the extension to complete indexing decreases the number of choice points significant. Often this results in a strong reduction of space consumption. In particular the runtime stack shrinks more often after a successful predicate call, because fewer choice points prohibit the deletion of environments.

[Hickey,Mudambi89] give a detailed explanation that fewer choice points lead to less trailing and fewer demand of heap space. In the BABEL machine we also need fewer savings of data stack entries. This saves both runtime stack space and time for copy operations. Table 5 gives a comprehensive survey of the possible savings

program	no indexing	complete indexing	ratio
fib 20	963264 cells	963264 cells	100%
rev 30	15172 cells	924 cells	6.1%
quicksort 30	20132 cells	856 cells	4.3%
queens 8	3192 cells	1748 cells	55%
popul 25	388 cells	296 cells	76%

Table 5. Runtime Stack Space Consumption with and without Indexing

of stack space. We recognize that the savings differ extremely, but in the average we may expect the saving of 50%. A good candidate for complete indexing is the quicksort function saving more than 95% stack memory. The Fibonacci function, however, shows that complete indexing cannot guarantee memory savings.

8 Conclusion

We have presented an alternative approach of complete indexing. The formal specification has shown the simplicity of the evaluation of the necessary information and its translation into indexing code for the Warren Abstract Machine.

Because of the (small) overhead of analyzing the whole arguments of a predicate, we cannot expect the same speed-ups as we get by an extended pattern-matcher[16], which will need more program space for doing the same complex analysis. But even in the case of small programs with few clauses we recognize some runtime speed-ups[17] in comparison with a translation without indexing.

Another important point of view is the saving of memory as we have demonstrated in the last section. Especially in functional + logic environments the number of choice points should be reduced as far as possible, to be able for tail recursion optimization and utilization of determinism. Such saving will decrease the overhead of memory management and will indirectly improve the runtime behaviour.

References

[Aït-Kaci91] H. Aït-Kaci, *Warren's Abstract Machine: A Tutorial Reconstruction*, MIT Press, Logic Programming Series. Cambridge, MA, 1991

[16] as introduced in [Peyton,Jones87] for the functional environment
[17] in the BABEL environment

[Chakravarty,Lock91] M. M. T. Chakravarty and H. C. R. Lock, The Implementation of Lazy Narrowing, PLILP 91, *Lecture Notes in Computer Science*, 528, Springer Verlag, Aug. 1991

[Hickey,Mudambi89] T. Hickey and Sh. Mudambi, Global compilation of Prolog, *Journal on Logic Programming*, Vol. 7, 1989

[Kliger,Shapiro88] S. Kliger and E. Shapiro, A Decision Tree Compilation Algorithm for FCP(—,:,?), *Proceedings of the Fifth International Conference of Logic Programming and Symposium of Logic Programming*, MIT Press, 1988

[Kliger,Shapiro90] S. Kliger and E. Shapiro, From Decision Trees to Decision Graphs, *North American Conference on Logic Programming*, Austin, MIT Press, October 1990

[Korsloot,Tick91] M. Korsloot and E. Tick, Compilation Techniques for Nondeterminate Flat Concurrent Logic Programming Languages, *Logic Programming: Proceedings of the Eighth International Conference*, MIT Press, June 1991

[Loogen91] R. Loogen, From Reduction Machines to Narrowing Machines, In CCPSD, TAPSOFT 91, *Lecture Notes in Computer Science*, 494, Springer Verlag, 1991

[Loogen,Winkler91] R. Loogen and S. Winkler, Dynamic Detection of Determinism in Functional Logic Languages, PLILP 91, *Lecture Notes in Computer Science*, 528, Springer Verlag, 1991

[Moreno,Rodríguez89] J.J. Moreno-Navarro and M. Rodríguez-Artalejo, *Logic Programming with Functions and Predicates: The Language BABEL*, Technical Report DIA/89/3, Universidad Complutense, Madrid 1989

[Palmer,Naish91] D. Palmer and L. Naish, NUA-Prolog: An Extension to the WAM for Parallel Andorra, *Logic Programming: Proceedings of the Eighth International Conference*, MIT Press, June 1991

[Peyton,Jones87] S. L. Peyton Jones, *The Implementation of Functional Programming Languages*, Prentice Hall, 1987

[Warren83] D.H.D. Warren, *An Abstract PROLOG Instruction Set*, Technical Note 309, SRI International, Menlo Park, California, 1983

Fast Prolog with a VAM_{1p} based Prolog Compiler

Andreas Krall and Thomas Berger

Institut für Computersprachen
Technische Universität Wien
Argentinierstraße 8
A-1040 Wien
andi@mips.complang.tuwien.ac.at

Abstract. The VAM (Vienna Abstract Machine) is a Prolog machine developed at the TU Wien. In contrast to the standard implementation technique (Warren Abstract Machine) an inference in the VAM is performed by unifying the goal and head arguments in a single undivided step. The interpreter based VAM_{2p} implements unification by combining head and goal instructions during run time whereas the compiler based VAM_{1p} combines the instructions during compile time. This enables compilers based on the VAM_{1p} to make extensive optimizations like variable elimination, instruction elimination, extended clause indexing and fast last-call optimizations. This results in fast execution and small stack sizes. Our prototype compiler is implemented in Prolog and emits intermediate VAM_{1p} code. This intermediate code is translated to native code instructions for the MIPS R3000 processor. The native code instructions are reordered using a Prolog based instruction scheduler and assembled using the MIPS assembler. The resulting programs achieve 3.1 MLips on a DecStation 5000/200.

1 Introduction

Eight years ago, we began research in the area of implementation of logic programming languages. A small and portable interpreter [Ge84] and a compiler based on the WAM (Warren Abstract Machine [Warr83]) for a commercial Prolog System [Pich84] have been developed. With this experience the VIP research project (Vienna Integrated Prolog [Oppi85]) was started. Outcomes of this project are new interpreter and compiler implementation techniques [Kral86,Kral87] resulting in the VAM (Vienna Abstract Machine) [Kral88, KrNe90], database systems [KüLu88], a mulituser implementation of Prolog with a shared database [KrKN89], extensions for meta programming and constraints [Neum90], an instruction set design for a Prolog oriented RISC processor [Kral90] and a parallel logic programming language [KüPu91]. The latest outcome of this project concerning compiler techniques will be described in this paper.

In Chapter 2 we present the Vienna Abstract Machine. Using the introduction to the VAM_{2p} we describe the VAM_{1p} and its optimizations. Chapter 3 outlines the implementation of the prototype compiler in detail. Chapter 4 presents the results and compares them with related work. Chapter 5 describes future work currently under investigation.

2 The Vienna Abstract Machine

2.1 Introduction

The VAM has been developed as an alternative to the WAM at the TU Wien. The WAM divides the unification process into two steps. During the first step the arguments of the calling goal are copied into argument registers and during the second step the values in the argument registers are unified with the arguments of the head of the called predicate. The VAM eliminates the register interface by unifying goal and head arguments in one step. There are two variants of the VAM, the VAM_{1p} and the VAM_{2p}.

A complete description of the VAM_{2p} can be found in [KrNe90]. Here we give a short introduction to the VAM_{2p} to understand the VAM_{1p} and the compilation method. The VAM_{2p} (VAM with two instruction pointers) is well suited for an intermediate code interpreter implemented in C or in assembly language using direct threaded code [Bell73]. The goal instruction pointer points to the instructions of the calling goal, the head instruction pointer points to the instructions of the head of the called clause. During an inference the VAM_{2p} fetches one instruction from the goal, one instruction from the head, combines them and executes the combined instruction. Because information about the calling goal and the called head is available at the same time, more optimizations than in the WAM are possible. The VAM features cheap backtracking, needs less dereferencing and trailing, has smaller stack sizes and implements a faster cut.

The VAM_{1p} (VAM with one instruction pointer) uses one instruction pointer and is well suited for native code compilation. It combines instructions at compile time and supports additional optimizations like instruction elimination, resolving temporary variables during compile time, extended clause indexing, fast last-call optimization and loop optimization.

2.2 The VAM_{2p}

Like the WAM, the VAM_{2p} uses three stacks. Variables and choice points are allocated on the environment stack, structures and unbound variables are stored on the copy stack (sometimes called global stack or heap) and bindings of variables are marked on the trail. The intermediate code of the clauses is held in the code area. The machine registers are the goalptr and headptr (pointer to the code of the calling goal and of the called clause respectively), the goalframeptr and the headframeptr (frame pointer of the clause containing the calling goal and of the called clause respectively), the top of the environment stack, the top of the copy stack, the top of the trail and the pointer to the last choice point.

Values are stored together with a tag in one machine word. We distinguish atoms, integers, empty lists, lists, structures, free variables and references. Free variables are allocated on the copy stack to avoid the unsafe variables of the WAM. Structure copying is used for the representation of structures [Mell82]. Floating point numbers and arbitrary long integers are special structures.

Variables are classified into void, temporary and local variables. Void variables occur only once in a clause and need neither storage nor unification instructions. Different to the WAM temporary variables occur only in the head or in one subgoal, counting a group of builtin predicates as one goal. The builtin predicates following the head belong to the head. Temporary variables need storage only during one inference and can be held in registers. All other variables are local and are allocated on the environment stack. During an inference the variables of the head are held in registers. Prior to the call of the first subgoal the registers are saved in the stack frame. To avoid initialisation of variables we distinguish between their first occurence and further occurences.

unification instructions	
const(Constant)	integer or atom
nil	empty list
list	list (followed by its arguments)
struct(Functor)	structure (followed by its arguments)
void	void variable
fsttmp(Offset)	first occurence of temporary variable
nxttmp(Offset)	subsequent occurence of temporary variable
fstvar(Offset)	first occurence of local variable
nxtvar(Offset)	subsequent occurence of local variable

resolution instructions	
goal(Procedureptr)	subgoal (followed by arguments and call/lastcall)
nogoal	end of a fact
cut	cut
builtin(Index)	builtin predicate (followed by is arguments)
termination instructions	
call	termination of a goal
lastcall	termination of the last goal

Figure 1: VAM_{2p} instructions

The clauses are translated to the VAM_{2p} abstract machine code (see Fig. 1). This translation is simple due to the direct mapping between source code and VAM_{2p} code. During runtime a goal and a head instruction are fetched and the two instructions are combined. Unification instructions are combined with unification instructions and resolution instructions are combined with termination instructions. A different encoding is used for goal unification instructions and head unification instructions. To enable fast encoding the instruction combination is solved by adding the instruction codes and therefore the sum of two instruction codes must be unique. The following C statement is used for decoding:

```
switch (*headptr++ + *goalptr++)
```

An assembly language implementation can use direct threaded code [Bell73]. The implementation of a VAM_{2p} direct threaded code interpreter is described in [Pohl91]. Portability is achieved by macro expansion of low level virtual machine code into assembly language.

2.3 The VAM_{1p}

2.3.1 Introduction

The VAM_{1p} has been designed for native code compilation. The main difference to the VAM_{2p} is that instruction combination is done during compile time instead of run time. The representation of data, the stacks and stack frames (see fig. 2) are identical to the VAM_{2p}. The VAM_{1p} has one machine register less than the VAM_{2p}. The two instruction pointers goalptr and headptr are replaced by one instruction pointer called codeptr. Therefore the choice point (see fig. 3) is also smaller by one element since there is only one instruction pointer. The pointer to the alternative clauses now directly points to the code of the remaining matching clauses.

codeptr´	continuation code pointer
goalframeptr´	continuation frame pointer
variables	local variables
...	

Figure 2: stack frame

trailptr´	copy of top of trail
copyptr´	copy of top of copy stack
codeptr´	pointer to the alternative clauses
goalframeptr´	restart frame pointer
choicepntptr´	previous choice point

Figure 3: choice point

2.3.2 Optimizations

Due to instruction combination during compile time it is possible to eliminate instructions, to eliminate all temporary variables and to use an extended clause indexing, a fast last-call optimization and loop optimization.

All constants and functors are combined and evaluated to true or false. For a true result no code is emitted. All clauses which have an argument evaluated to false are removed from the list of alternatives. In general no code is emitted for a combination with a void variable. In a combination of a void variable with the first occurence of a local variable the next occurence of this variable is treated as the first occurence. If the local variable has only the first occurence in a subgoal, a `void_fstvar` instruction is generated.

Temporary variables are eliminated completely. The unification partner of the first occurence of a temporary variable is unified directly with the unification partners of the further occurences of the temporary variable. If the unification partners are constants no code is emitted at all. Flattened code is generated for structures. The paths for unifying and copying structures is split and different code is generated for each path. This makes it possible to reference each argument of a structure as offset from the top of the copy stack or as offset from the structure base pointer. If a temporary variable is contained in more than one structure combined unification or copying instructions are generated.

All necessary information for clause indexing is computed during compile time. Some alternatives are eliminated because of failing constant combinations. The remaining alternatives are indexed on the argument that contains the most constants or structures. For compatibility reasons with the VAM_{2p} a balanced binary tree is used for clause selection, but if assert and retract is not supported a perfect hashing scheme could be used instead.

The VAM_{1p} implements two versions of last-call optimization. The first variant (we call it post-optimization) is identical to the VAM_{2p}. If the determinacy of a clause can be determined during run time, the registers containing the head variables are stored in the callers stack frame. Head variables which resides in the stack frame due to the lack of registers are copied from the head (callee´s) stack frame to the goal (caller´s) stack frame.

If the determinacy of a clause can be detected during compile time, the caller´s and the callee´s stack frame are the same. Now all unifications between variables with the same offset can be eliminated. If not all head variables are held in registers reading and writing variables must be done in the right order. We call this variant of last-call optimization pre-optimization.

Loop optimization is done for a determinate recursive call of the last and only subgoal. The restriction to a single subgoal is due to the use of registers for value passing and possible aliasing of variables. Unification between structures is performed by unifying the arguments directly. So all accesses to the stack frame are eliminated.

2.3.3 The instruction set

The instruction set for the VAM_{1p} is divided into resolution instructions, general unification instructions, indexing instructions, structure unification instructions, structure copying instructions and optimization instructions. The complete instruction set summary is given in appendix A. In this appendix and in the following description a variable as an argument of an instruction is either a register or a frame pointer and the offset to that pointer.

The resolution instruction allocate_stackframe allocates the space for variables in a stack frame, adjust performs stack trimming. If last-call optimization is applicable the instruction store_continuation saves the continuation in the callers stack frame. Otherwise the continuation is copied from the callers to the callee´s frame (copy_continuation). read_continuation is used to continue the execution at the next subgoal. store_var saves the head variables residing in registers in the stack frame. If not all head variables can be held in registers copy_var copies the variables of the callee´s stack frame to the caller´s stack frame. This instructions is only used for last-call optimization. cut deletes the choicepoints and reduces the size of the stack frame. choicepoint creates a choice point.

The unification instructions are generated for all combinations of constants, structures and variables with variables. If a structure is combined with the first occurence of a variable (struct_firstvar) structure copying is started (like the write mode of the WAM). The parameter Size gives the size of the structure including all substructures. The parameter Register of the instruction struct_var is the register, which will hold the base pointer of the structure. The structure unifying instructions (like the read mode of the WAM) follow immediately, the parameter Adress_of_copymacros is the label of the structure copying instructions.

Depending on the type of the value contained in the variable the indexing instruction index_variable branches to one of the labels. The compare instructions (comp_xxx) implement the binary search tree. Future extensions of the VAM_{1p} will additionally support hashing. The xxx_undef instructions assign the value of type xxx to the unbound indexing variable. If more than one clause starts with the same structure struct_val restores the base pointer to the structure.

Structure unifying and copying instructions are equivalent to the unify instructions of the WAM in read mode and write mode. Due to the splitting of the path of copy and unify mode the offsets of the variables relative to the start of the structure or the top of copy stack are known during compile time.

The optimization instructions support the unification of structures optimized by temporary variable elimination or loop optimization. copy_undef initialises a cell on the copy stack to unbound. unify_copy copies a value from the source structure to the destination structure. unify_unify implements full unifcation between two arguments of structures. copy_ref let one argument of a structure reference the other. If Address_of_structpointer contains a structure, extract_struct stores the address of the start of the structure in the register. Otherwise it branches to Nostruct_label. constr_struct creates a structure. constr_or_extract_struct is the combination of the last two instructions.

3 The Implementation

3.1 Introduction

The PROLOG - VAM_{1p} compiler is implemented in Prolog. It needs two passes to translate a given Prolog source program into VAM_{1p} instructions. These are then expanded into instructions for the R3000 RISC processor from MIPS [Kane89] and reordered. In the last step, the generated code is assembled and linked with the run time environment (built-in-predicates, memory management).

3.2 Data representation

The old VAM_{2p} interpreter stored values in a machine word using the most significant bits as tag fields. The VAM_{1p} compiler uses the least significant bits as tag fields. This modification speeded up the produced code by about 10% compared to the old tag representation. Now pointers (lists, structures and references) use two tag bits, constants (integers and atoms) use 3 tag bits. Unbound variables are represented by a self reference. Integers use a tag value of zero to enable fast arithmetic and to use the builtin overflow checking of the processor. The pointer to the copy stack is offset by the list tag to get list pointers for free.

3.3 Pass one

Pass one performs the following actions:

- read the source program and translate each clause to VAM_{2p} like intermediate code
- build the atom table and replace the atoms in intermediate code by their table offsets
- variable classification
- compute the offsets of local variables

The source program is read using the built-in predicate `read/1`. Lexical and syntactical analysis are performed by this predicate. The internal representation of a clause after pass one is described by the following grammar:

```
Clause              -->  clause(Number, Varcount, Clausecode)
Clausecode          -->  [Head|Body] |
                         [Head]
Head                -->  Argumentlist
Body                -->  [goal(Number, Functor, Argumentlist)|Body] |
                         [builtin(Number, Functor, Argumentlist)|Body] |
                         []
Argumentlist        -->  [Argumentcode|Argumentlist] |
                         []
```

```
Argumentcode         --> nil |
                         const(C) |
                         list(Argumentcode,Argumentcode) |
                         struct(Functor,Argumentlist) |
                         void |
                         temp(Temporary) |
                         variable(Frameptr,Offset,Firstoccurence,Loop)
Functor              --> Name/Number
Name                 --> atom
Number               --> integer
Varcount             --> integer
```

The offsets of local variables are computed in the first pass of the compiler. To enable stack trimming, variables which have their last occurence in the last subgoal of the clause get the smaller offsets (near the continuation), those, which have their last occurence closer to the head get the relatively greater offsets.

All atoms are saved in an atom table. The offsets of all atoms in this table are computed in the first pass of the compiler. The intermediate code of an atom is `const(atom(offset))`.

3.4 Pass two

Actions of pass two:

- replace temporary variables by the intermediate code of the argument to be unified with
- assign registers to head variables (if possible)
- last-call optimization and loop optimization
- clause indexing
- generate code for handling temporary variables in structures
- emit VAM_{1p} code

Unifications with temporary variables are solved at compile time. The first occurence of a temporary variable is replaced by the intermediate code of the argument, with which it has to be unified. Clause indexing is performed for one argument of a calling subgoal. The indexed arguments and the starting labels of the called clauses are stored in an indexing structure. After the code for all possible unifications for the indexed subgoal is generated, the content of this indexing structure is used to generate the `index_variable` instruction and the compare and `xxx_undef` instructions. After each subgoal of a determinate clause the instruction `adjust/1` is generated to compute stacktrimming. Local variables, which occur in the head of a clause are held in registers. Before the body of the clause is called, they are saved in the stack frame (`store_var/2`). If there are not enough registers for all variables, some must be handled directly on the stack. If last-call optimization is possible, the variables are copied from the headframe to the goalframe before the computation proceeds with the called clause (`copy_var`).

If a temporary variable occurs in two or more structures or lists, which have to be unified with local variables, the content of this temporary variable is not known at compile time. Therefore we reorder the arguments. So we can compute the unify- (copy-) instructions for all structures or lists, which contain the same temporary variable, at the same time. The temporary variable is identified as an offset to the top of the copystack. In case of copy instructions an undefined cell is created on the actual position of the copystack for the temporary variable and all further occurences of this variable get a reference to this cell.

If loop optimization can be performed, instructions for the determinate case are generated in addition to the normal code. A code loop is generated which has a conditional branch to the nondeterminate case. As long as the looping argument is instantiated with a list or structure no stack frame operations have to be performed. When the looping argument is instantiated with a failing value the loop is exited and the program proceeds with the normal code.

3.5 Code generation and instruction scheduling

The second pass collects the VAM_{1p} instructions for one inference in a list. These instructions are then expanded to the MIPS R3000 instructions and collected in a list again. The R3000 processor is a pipelined RISC processor that requires that the result of a load is not used by the next instruction. Furthermore a branch is executed after the instruction following the branch. The first optimization is loop rotation which replaces the jump at the end of a loop by a conditional jump and increases the size of a basic block. Due to the single assignment nature of Prolog alias analysis is unnecessary. The only possible cause of an alias - the first occurence of a variable and immediate use of this variable - is detected by the compiler, which generates a simplified unification instruction in that case.

The scheduler is based on list scheduling [GiMu86, Warr90, ErKr92]. It determines the basic blocks and generates the dependence graph for a basic block. Instructions which have no predecessor in the dependence graph and which are not waiting for the result of a previous instruction can be used for scheduling. The heuristic used is to prefer the load instruction with the longest path to the end of the basic block. If no instruction is available a no operation instruction is scheduled. Branch instructions are scheduled as second last instruction. If this is not possible a no operation instruction is scheduled after a branch instruction. Because during backtracking all actions are undone the instruction in the delay of a branch to fail has no effect. In a second pass all no operation instructions in the delay slot of a branch to fail are replaced by the branch target. Scheduling can be suppressed by barriers which are included in the macros for VAM_{1p} instructions. Due to reduced dependences and better branch scheduling our Prolog based scheduler produces code that is up to 33% faster than the same code scheduled by the MIPS assembler.

4 Results

We executed a set of small benchmarks on a DecStation 5000/200 (25MHz MIPS R3000 processor). A description and the source code of the benchmarks can be found in [Beer89]. All benchmarks were executed as well with the SICStus Prolog 0.7 compiler and interpreter [CaWi89] as with the VAM_{2p} interpreter. We choose the SICStus Prolog interpreter/compiler as the basis for our comparison, because it is a portable and efficient system and is available cheap and easy for everybody. The SICStus compiler produces WAM code, which is interpreted by an emulator written in C. The VAM_{2p} interpreter is implemented in C, too. Timings were made by executing each benchmark between 100 and 10000 times. Figure 4 contains the execution time in milliseconds for the VAM_{2p} interpreter. The other values are scaled relative to the VAM_{2p} interpreter. The VAM_{1p} compiled code for the determinate append is 26 times faster than the VAM_{2p} interpreter, because only 8 instructions are generated by the compiler for the inner loop of append. Due to optimal reordering by the scheduler these instructions are executed in 8 cycles. This means a performance of 3.1 MLips. For the other more realistic benchmarks the compiled code is five to eight times faster than the interpreted code. The execution time for the interpreter and the compiler get closer, if a benchmark is predominated by input/output builtin predicates.

	interpreter			compiler	
	VAM2p	VAM2p	SICStus	SICStus	VAM1p
Test	ms	scaled	scaled	scaled	scaled
det. append	0.25	1	0.11	1.1	26.1
naive reverse	4.17	1	0.11	1.06	19.3
quicksort	6.00	1	0.12	1.1	7.23
8-queens	65.4	1	0.09	1.1	12.38
serialize	3.90	1	0.13	0.83	5.76
differentiate	1.14	1	0.17	0.99	6.32
query	41.7	1	0.19	0.89	7.58
bucket	247	1	0.15	0.88	5.02
permutation	4023	1	0.11	0.70	5.08

Figure 4: results, bigger values mean faster execution

The VAM1p compiler produces code compareable or faster to the compilers described in [Tayl89, RoDe92], which use global analysis. But global analysis favours small benchmarks with sufficiently bound goals. It is often impossible to get exact mode information, dereferencing and trailing information in real life applications due to metacall or builtin predicates like `read/1`.

The size of the code is about 7 to 10 times the size of the SICStus Prolog compiler, which produces interpreted byte code. This size is large but not so bad compared to the factor of 5 reported in [RoDe92] for other compilers. The large size results from flattening the structure unification code and from loop optimization. Furthermore for n calls to a procedure with m different clauses (m is general less or equal to 3), up to n*m unification instructions can be generated.

5 Further Work

Currently we are working on support for dynamic predicates (`assert`, `retract`) and on the reduction of the code size. We will reduce the code size further by mixing VAM_{1p} and VAM_{2p} code and by codesharing. If the call patterns in the calling subgoals of different clauses are the same, the same code can be shared by these clauses, if the continuation is saved before start of the unification and the local variables have the same offsets. Furthermore we investigate abstract interpretation and flow analysis for elimination of run time checks and code reduction [CoCo77, Mari89, Mell85, WaHD88]. Clause indexing will be extended with type information.

Acknowledgement

We express our thanks to Anton Ertl, Ulrich Neumerkel and Herbert Pohlai for their comments on earlier drafts of this paper. We would also like to thank the anonymous referees. Their reviews have been very helpful to us in preparing this version of the paper.

References

[Beer89] J. Beer, Concepts, *Design, and Performance Analysis of a Parallel Prolog Machine*, Springer, 1989

[Bell73] J.R. Bell, 'Threaded Code', *CACM 16(6)*, 1973.

[Berg91] T. Berger, *Implementierung eines Prologcompilers basierend auf der Vienna Abstract Machine*, M. Thesis, TU Wien, 1991.

[Bruy82] M. Bruynooghe, 'The Memory Management of PROLOG Implementations', *Logic Programming*, Clark & Tårnlund (ed.), Academic Press, 1982.

[CaWi90] M. Carlsson and J. Widén, *SICStus Prolog User's Manual*, SICS research report R88007C, 1990.

[CoCo77] P. Cousot and R. Cousot, 'Abstract Interpretation: A Unified Lattice Model for Static Analysis of Programs by Construction or Approximation of Fixpoints', *Forth Symp. Priciples of Programming Languages*, ACM, 1977

[ErKr92] A.M. Ertl and A. Krall, 'Instruction Scheduling for Complex Pipelines', *Int. Workshop on Compiler Construction*, LNCS, 1992

[Gelb84] M. Gelbmann, *Prolog Interpreter*, M. Thesis, TU Wien, 1984

[GiMu86] P.B. Gibbons and S.S. Muchnick, 'Efficient Instruction Scheduling for a pipelined architecture', in *Proceedings of the SIGPLAN '86 Symposium on Compiler Construction*, 1986

[Kane89] G. Kane, MIPS RISC Architecture, Prentice Hall, 1989.

[Kral86] A. Krall, *Comparing Implementation Techniques for Prolog*, VIP TR 1802/86/7, TU Wien, 1986.

[Kral87] A. Krall, 'Implementation of a High-Speed Prolog Interpreter', *ACM SIGPLAN 22(7), Conf. on Interpreters and Interpretative Techniques*, 1987.

[Kral88] A. Krall, *Analyse und Implementierung von Prologsystemen*, Ph.D. Thesis, TU Wien, 1988.

[Kral90] A. Krall, 'An Extended Prolog Instruction Set for RISC Processors', *Int. Workshop on VLSI for AI and Neural Networks*, Oxford, Plenum, 1991.

[KrKN89] A. Krall, E. Kühn and U. Neumerkel, 'Distributed Logic Programming', *EUUG Spring '89 Conference*, Brussels, 1989.

[KrNe90] A. Krall and U. Neumerkel, 'The Vienna Abstract Machine', *PLILP '90*, LNCS, Springer, 1990.

[KüLu88] E. Kühn and T. Ludwig, 'VIP-MDBS: A Logic Multidatabase System', *Int. Symposium on Databases in Parallel and Distributed Systems*, Austin Texas, 1988.

[KüPu91] E. Kühn and F. Puntigam, *The VPL Vienna Parallel Logic Language*, TR 185/91/1, TU Wien, 1991.

[Mari89] A. Marien et al., 'The impact of abstract interpretation: an experiment in code generation', *Sixth Int. Conf. on Logic Programming*, Lisbon, 1989.

[Mell82] C.S. Mellish, 'An Alternative to Structure Sharing in the Implementation of a Prolog Interpreter', *Logic Programming*, Clark & Tårnlund (ed.), Academic Press, 1982.

[Mell85] C.S. Mellish, 'Some Global Optimizations for a Prolog Compiler', *Journal of Logic Programming 2(1)*, 1985.

[Neum90] U. Neumerkel, 'Extensible Unification by Metastructures', *Meta90*, Leuven, 1990.

[Oppi85] M. Oppitz et al., VIP - A Prolog Programming Environment, VIP TR 1802/85/1, TU Wien, 1985.

[Pich84] C. Pichler, Prolog Übersetzer, M. Thesis, TU Wien, 1984.

[Pohl91] H. Pohlai, *Implementierung eines Prolog-Zwischencodeinterpreters basierend auf der Vienna Abstract Machine*, M. Thesis, TU Wien, 1991.

[RoDe92] P.V. Roy and A.M. Despain, 'High-performance Logic Programming with the Aquarius Prolog Compiler', *IEEE Computer*, 1992

[Tayl89] A. Taylor, 'Removal of Dereferencing and Trailing in Prolog Compilation', *Sixth Int. Conf. on Logic Programming*, Lisbon, 1989.

[Tayl90] A. Taylor, 'LIPS on a MIPS', *Seventh Int. Conf. on Logic Programming*, Jerusalem, 1990.

[Warr83] D.H.D. Warren, *An Abstract Prolog Instruction Set*, SRI International, Technical Note 309, 1983.

[Warr90] H.S. Warren, 'Instruction scheduling for the IBM RISC System/6000 processor', *IBM Journal of Research and Development*, 1(34), 1990

[WaHD88] R. Warren, M. Hermenegildo and S. Debray, 'On the Practicality of Global Flow Analysis of Logic Programs', *Fifth Int. Conf. and Symposium on Logic Programming*, Seattle, 1988.

Appendix A: VAM_{1p} instruction set summary

resolution instructions:

```
allocate_stackframe(Number_of_variables)
adjust(Number_of_variables)
store_continuation(Continuation_address)
read_continuation(Register)
copy_continuation()
call(Address_of_BIP)
goto(Adress)
store_var(Register, Variable)
copy_var(Offset_of_variable)
cut(Number_of_variables)
choicepoint(Address_of_alternative)
```

unification instructions:

```
const_firstvar(Constant, Variable)
const_var(Constant, Variable)
nil_firstvar(Variable)
nil_var(Variable)
list_firstvar(Variable, List_size)
list_var(Register, Size, Variable, Address_of_copymacros)
struct_firstvar(Variable, Struct_size)
struct_var(Register, Size, Variable, Address_of_copymacros)
firstvar_firstvar(Variable1, Variable2)
firstvar_var(Variable1, Variable2)
var_var(Variable1, Variable2)
void_firstvar(Variable)
```

indexing instructions:

```
index_variable(Variable,List,Nil,Const,Struct,Undef)
comp_const(Constant, Address_of_lt_const, Address_of_gt_const)
comp_struct(Constant, Address_of_lt_struct, Address_of_gt_struct)
const_undef(Constant)
nil_undef()
list_undef(Size)
struct_undef(Size)
list_val(Register, Variable)
struct_val(Register, Variable)
```

structure unifying instructions:

```
unify_const(Constant, Address_on_copystack)
unify_nil(Address_on_copystack)
unify_list(Register, Size, Address_on_copystack, Address_on_copystack)
unify_struct(Register, Size, Address_on_copystack, Address_on_copystack)
unify_functor(Functor, Address_on_copystack)
unify_firstvar(Variable, Address_on_copystack)
unify_var(Variable, Address_on_copystack)
```

structure copying instructions:

```
copy_const(Constant, Offset_in_struct)
copy_nil(Offset_in_struct)
copy_list(Offset_in_struct, Offset_of_listblock)
copy_struct(Offset_in_struct, Offset_of_structblock)
copy_functor(Functor, Offset_in_struct)
copy_firstvar(Variable, Offset_in_struct)
copy_var(Variable, Offset_in_struct)
```

optimization instructions:

```
copy_undef(Offset_in_struct)
unify_copy(Address_of_source, Offset_in_struct)
unify_unify(Address1, Address2)
copy_ref(Reference, Offset_in_struct)
extract_list(Register, Address_of_listpointer, Nolist_label)
extract_struct(Register, Address_of_structpointer, Nostruct_label)
constr_list(Offset_of_listpointer)
constr_struct(Offset_of_structpointer, Size)
constr_or_extract_list(Register, Address_of_listpointer, Copy_label)
constr_or_extract_struct(Register, Address_of_structpointer, Copy_label)
```

Appendix B: Abstract code for append

```
append([], L, L).
append([X|L1], L2, [X|L3]) :- append(L1, L2, L3)

append_3_2:          # the code for the unification is contained in the
                     # calling goal, therefore no code for append([],L,L)
append_3_2_last_1: # :- append(L1,L2,L3)
    index_variable(goalframeptr[0],
        append_3_xgoal_2,append_3_xgoal_3,_,_,append_3_xgoal_4)
    #   list_label          nil_label                undef_label
append_3_xgoal_4:
    choicepoint(append_3_2_last_2) # create choice point
    nil_undef                      # L1 = []
append_3_xgoal_3:
    var_var(goalframeptr[1],goalframeptr[2]) # L2 = L3
    read_continuation(R1)
    goto(R1)
append_3_2_last_2:                 # 2nd clause
    list_undef(2)
    goto(append_3_copy_5)
append_3_xgoal_2:
    adjust(3)
    list_val(R0)
    list_var(R1,2,goalframeptr[3],append_3_xgoal_10)
append_3_xgoal_8:                  # loop optimization, L1 bound, L3 bound
    unify_unify(R1+0,R0+0)         # unify first arguments
    extract_list(R0,R0+1,append_3_xgoal_9)
    constr_or_extract_list(R1,R1+1,append_3_xgoal_10)
    goto(append_3_xgoal_8)
append_3_xgoal_9:
    unify_firstvar(goalframeptr[1],R0+1)
    unify_firstvar(goalframeptr[3],R1+1)
append_3_copy_11:
    goto(append_3_2)               # recursive call
append_3_xgoal_11:
    unify_firstvar(goalframeptr[1],R0+1)
    copy_firstvar(goalframeptr[3],1)
    goto(append_3_2)               # recursive call
append_3_xgoal_10:                 # loop otimization, L1 bound, L3 free
    unify_copy(R1+0,0)
    extract_list(R0,R0+1,append_3_xgoal_11)
    constr_list(1)
    goto(append_3_xgoal_10)
append_3_copy_5:
    list_var(R0,2,goalframeptr[3],append_3_copy_12) # construct L1
    unify_firstvar(goalframeptr[3],R0+1)
    unify_copy(R0+0,0)
    copy_firstvar(goalframeptr[1],1)
    goto(append_3_copy_11)
append_3_copy_12:                  # construct both lists (L1 and L3)
    copy_undef(0)                  # free cell for X
    copy_firstvar(goalframeptr[3],1)
    copy_ref(0,2)                  # reference to X from L3
    copy_firstvar(goalframeptr[1],3)
    goto(append_3_copy_11)
```

Metastructures vs. Attributed Variables in the Context of Extensible Unification

Christian Holzbaur

Austrian Research Institute for Artificial Intelligence, and
Department of Medical Cybernetics and Artificial Intelligence
University of Vienna
Freyung 6, A-1010 Vienna, Austria
email: christian@ai.univie.ac.at

Abstract. We relate two mechanisms which aim at the extension of logic programming languages. The first mechanism directly extends syntactic unification through the introduction of a data type, whose (unification) semantics are specified through user-defined predicates. The second mechanism was utilized for the implementation of coroutining facilities, and was independently derived with optimal memory management for various Prolog extensions in mind. Experience from the application of both mechanisms to the realization of CLP languages, without leaving the logic programming context, enables us to reveal similarities and the potential with respect to this task. Constructive measures that narrow or close the gap between the two conceptual schemes are provided.

1 Introduction

As a serious user of two rather similar mechanisms — as far as their applications are concerned — we think that it is useful to expose this similarity in some detail. Both mechanisms provide means for the extension of logic programming languages.

Metastructures as introduced by Neumerkel (1990) aim at extensions to Prolog's builtin unification through user-defined behavior of metastructures during unification. A refined version of the concept of metastructures was used in (Holzbaur 1990) for the specification and implementation of a variety of instances of the general CLP scheme (Jaffar and Michaylov 1987).

More or less at the same time, the data type *attributed variable* was introduced by Hoitouze. Memory management issues as *early reset* and *variable shunting* by the garbage collector were addressed in (Hoitouze 1990). The behavior of attributed variables during unification was not mentioned. However, regarding applications, Hoitouze also proposed the use of attributed variables for the implementation of delayed computations, reversible modification of terms, variable typing, and others.

Earlier, Carlsson (1987) used a data type *suspension*, which was incorporated into SICStus Prolog (Carlsson and Widen 1990) for the implementation of coroutining facilities. As far as we can tell — as a third party — the data structures attributed variable and suspension are the same. The difference between Hoitouze's and Carlsson's exposition is that the former put some emphasis on the data type as such and on memory management. The latter used it as a low level primitive for the implementation of mechanisms that necessitated the specification of the behavior of the data type during unification.

In the following sections we will have a closer look on metastructures and attributed variables. In particular, we compare them with regard to their behavior during unification and their potential for the implementation of CLP languages.

2 Metastructures

Metastructures are ordinary, non-variable Prolog terms with the sole difference that they can be detected as members of this special sort. Metastructures are introduced by a declaration `:- meta_functor N/A`, where `N/A` denotes any functor. The behavior of metastructures during unifications can be specified precisely through a Prolog meta interpreter which makes unification explicit (Holzbaur 1990). The meta interpreter implements the unification table from (Neumerkel 1990) *and* makes some further conventions integral parts of the specification:

- Unifications between variables and metastructures just produce a binding as usual. If a metastructure is to be unified with an ordinary term, the reaction to this event is given by a user-supplied predicate `meta_term_unify/2`. Similarly, unifications between two metastructures are covered by the user-supplied predicate `meta_meta_unify/2`, the arguments being the two metastructures involved.
- Once extensible unification is put into force, we have a problem passing metastructures to the user-supplied predicates, without triggering further calls to them in a nonterminating fashion. Neumerkel solved the problem by the introduction of a builtin predicate `===/2`, which behaves as `=/2`, but treats metastructures as ordinary structures. In addition he has to rely on the programmers discipline: Nothing but variables may be used as formal arguments in the definition of the two user-supplied predicates. Access to the components of metastructures is via `===/2`. The disadvantages of this solution are that the user has to be very careful, and that indexing does not apply.
  Therefore, we specified the following mechanism: Calls to the two user-supplied predicates `meta_term_unify/2` and `meta_meta_unify/2` are made with syntactic unification in force. The encapsulation effect of this solution is at least as strong as the one with `===/2`, as the only means to get access to the 'internals' of a metastructure.
- The last part of the specification stemmed from a typical application of metastructures in the context of the implementation of CLP languages. It is covered in detail in the next section.

2.1 Metastructures and Reversible Modification

The implementations of many CLP instances require the functionality that is achieved with destructive updates in traditional, procedural realizations. In logic programming, this functionality is provided in a sound fashion by either copying or ***modifying by variable substitution***.

The latter option can be applied to metastructures through the convention that one particular argument of the structure is a free variable, which will eventually be bound to another metastructure, obeying the same convention. Therefore, sequences of modifications lead to metastructure chains. The current 'value' of a metastructure is to be found at the end of the chain. Traversing this chains could of course be left to the user, but it is so common a pattern, that is has been made part of our specification. The additional convention is that the user-supplied predicates **meta_term_unify/2** and **meta_meta_unify/2** are called with the *current* metastructures, and that the *first* argument of metastructures is used for modifying by variable substitution. In (Neumerkel 1990) this convention is also exploited by the garbage collector, which can therefore reclaim useless metastructures.

One step beyond, but in the same direction: To wait for the garbage collection to occur in order to reclaim space and to shorten metastructure chains (much like variable shunting) is a bad idea! Because of the need for traversal, access and modification operations are of $O(n^2)$[1]. After recognizing the metastructure traversal as being nothing but the *find* operation of the well known *union-find* algorithm, which is of $O(n)$ through *path compression* (Aho et al. 1983), path compression was applied for metastructure access (Holzbaur 1990). Although it is realized in a fashion transparent to the user, preserving logical soundness, we will also present a Prolog version of the *find* operation with and without path compression, because it nicely demonstrates the power of the logical variable:

The *find* operation

without path compression	with path compression

`find( Current, Last) :-`
`  arg( 1, Current, Next),`
`  ( var(Next) ->`
`     Last = Current`
`  ;`
 	
`     find( Next, Last)`
`  ).`
	`find( Current, Last) :-`
	`  arg( 1, Current, Next),`
	`  ( var(Next) ->`
	`     Last = Current`
	`  ;`
	`     setarg( 1, Current, Last),`
	`     find( Next, Last)`
	`  ).`

The first argument to the predicate **find/2** is the (meta)structure to be traversed, the second parameter will be unified with the last element of the (meta)structure chain. The predicate **setarg/3** is the SICStus Prolog (Carlsson and Widen 1990) primitive for reversible modification. The current implementation ensures that the value of a changed cell is only trailed by subsequent updates if an intermediate choice point is present.

3 Attributed Variables

Attributed variables are variables with an associated attribute, which is a term. Attributes are attached to variables, and attributes are referred to, through built-in predicates. As far as the rest of a given Prolog implementation is concerned,

[1] Each modification extends the chain by one element, which has to be skipped on the next access. $\sum_{i=1}^{n} i = \frac{n(n+1)}{2}$

attributed variables behave like variables — they can be considered as a subtype of type variable. The indexing mechanism treats variables and attributed variables the same way. Built-in predicates observe attributed variables as if they were ordinary variables. Special treatment for attributed variables applies:

- During memory management, as proposed in (Hoitouze 1990), i.e, early reset and variable shunting.
- During unification. Carlsson (1987) describes the data type ***suspension*** as:
  "A suspension is an unbound variable with a reference to a suspended goal, represented as a record on the heap. A suspended goal is ***woken*** when the suspension is unified with another term."

  Three observations:
  - The attribute associated with a suspension variable is supposed to be executed eventually — therefore the name ***suspension***.
  - The behavior of the suspension during unification is specified. In particular, an explicit WAM extension for the wakeup mechanism was presented.
  - From the remaining text of the reference cited above, we conclude that the suspension data type was not meant to be made available as such to the user.

Present versions of SICStus Prolog perform the proposed memory management of attributed variables alias suspensions, and implement the wakeup mechanism quoted. In order to be able to describe the problems we encountered with the original wakeup mechanism of SICStus Prolog, and the remedies, we sketch it here:

When a suspension — to be exact: the value part of a suspension — gets bound during unification to a term or to another suspension, the goal part of the bound suspension is prepended to the current continuation[2] of the execution state. At the next inference step, i.e., call or execute in WAM terminology, the woken goals will be run.

This mechanism is perfectly sufficient for the implementation of **freeze/2** and **dif/2** — no wonder, this was the intention behind the introduction of suspensions. In a wider context, however, the attribute of an attributed variable needs not to be executed. The narrow interpretation of attributed variables was the prime cause for the problems we encountered in more complex applications.

The Problem Description with the Help of an Example. From the point of view of the of the code which implements, say, a CLP($\Re$) solver via attributed variables, any number of binding and aliasing events may take place between two inference steps. Once the corresponding goals are woken, they are in the execution state of the WAM only. The association between the attributed variables and the attributes (goals) is lost, as the attributed variables are now ***transparent*** — we only see the objects bound to them.

This is a dilemma, because the bindings which changed the situation, temporarily invalidating invariants of the CLP($\Re$) implementation, conceptually took place at once (because there was no inference step in between).

[2] Scheme slang

Each executing woken goal has to find out for which bindings it is responsible, take a sort of 'repair' action, leaving the data structures in a partially repaired state, assuming that the remaining woken goals will repair the rest. This is not only cumbersome, but also a source of incompleteness. In a CLP($\Re$) implementation for example, we want to fix the linear equation system after a binding or aliasing event, which might turn some of the variables of the system into constants (numbers). Binding a variable potentially triggers actions of the nonlinear equation solver or the inequality solver. We want to postpone these actions until the invariants about the linear equation system (being in solved form) are true again. Making the first woken goal to repair everything at once does not work either, as some of the relevant data structures are in the execution state only, and therefore inaccessible.

The Solution. These problems can be avoided when the attributed variables are not bound immediately, but one by one, as part of the execution of the woken goals. This gives the (user)code a chance to look at the data structures *before* anything changes and, more important, conceptually there is always *one* and only one binding event taking place in isolation, and the (user)code has control over this event.

This treatment of attributed variables during unification leads to a situation that is equivalent to the one that was specified and implemented for metastructures.

4 Proposal for the Treatment of Attributed Variables during Unification

Carlsson's wakeup mechanism requires only minor changes, i.e., generalizations, to perform as proposed above. First we generalize suspensions in the sense that there is no need that the associated 'goal' will be executed eventually — this is why we prefer the name *attributed variable* instead of suspension. Next, the wakeup mechanism is supposed to work as follows:

- When an attributed variable is about to be bound during unification, the attributed variable and the value it should be bound to are recorded in some internal data structure, which could be allocated on the heap, or some special purpose area, which avoids the use of the general garbage collection mechanism for deallocation.
- If there is more than one such event between two inference steps, a list of attributed variable–value pairs is collected in some internal data structure.
- At the next inference step, the abstract machine takes measures to feed the attributed variable-value pairs to the two user-supplied predicates, in analogy to the specification for metastructures. The data structures for the representation of the list of variable-value pairs can be reclaimed at this point.

The memory management of attributed variables remains unchanged, except that we plan to repeat the incorporation of path compression on access and update of attributed variables.

4.1 Pragmatics

In this section we describe the user's point of view of a SICStus Prolog clone, providing extensible unification via attributed variables[3].

Source Transformation. If we want to get extensible unification through attributed variables, we have to transform terms with interpreted functors into terms with attributed variables with the interpreted functors as attributes. Static occurrences of interpreted functors can be dealt with through source transformations. Dynamically introduced interpreted terms would require changes in built-in predicates as `read/1`, `functor/3`, `=../2`.

Builtin Predicates. The following predicates provide for the introduction, detection, and manipulation of attributed variables.

`get_attribute(X,C)`
: If X is an attributed variable, unify the corresponding attribute with C, otherwise the predicate fails.

`attach_attribute(X,C)`
: Turn the free variable X into an attributed with attribute C, which must ***not*** be a variable. The restriction avoids unification events where the attribute(s) of the involved variable(s) are yet unspecified, i.e. unbound.

`detach_attribute(X)`
: Remove the attribute from an attributed variable, turning it into a free variable.

`update_attribute(X,C)`
: Change the attribute of the attributed variable X to C. Acts as if defined below, but might be more (memory) efficient.

```
update_attribute( X, C) :-
  detach_attribute( X),
  attach_attribute( X, C).
```

User-defined Predicates. The following two predicates have to be supplied by the user. They specify the behavior, i.e., the meaning of attributed variables during unification.

`verify_attribute(C,T)`
: This predicate is called when an attributed variable with attribute C is about to be unified with the non-variable term T.

`combine_attributes(C1,C2)`
: This predicate is called when two attributed variables with attributes *C1,C2* are about to be unified.

Note that the two predicates are are ***not*** called with the attributed variables involved, but with the corresponding attributes instead. The reasons are:

[3] The changes to the official SICStus distribution are available via anonymous ftp from ftp.ai.univie.ac.at, directory sicstus/clp

- As the/one attribute is the first argument to **verify_attribute/2** and **combine_attributes/2**, indexing applies. Note that attributed variables themselves look like variables to the indexing mechanism. To get the benefits of indexing is important, because in general the combination of n sorts of interpreted functors into a 'unified' unification theory and/or algorithm requires $2^n - 1$ clauses for **verify_attribute/2** in the worst case. The number is just the cardinality of the powerset of the set of basic sorts, excluding the empty set – therefore '−1'. Further, each pair of elements from the powerset has to be covered by clauses of **combine_attributes/2**, where the number of clauses is:

$$\binom{2^n - 1}{2} + 2^{n-1} = (2^n - 1)2^{n-1}$$

- If attributed variables were passed as arguments, the user's code would have to refer to the attributes through an extra call to **get_attribute/2**. Although this call is rather cheap, it *was* already performed by the underlying mechanism that feeds the attributed variable-value pairs to the two user supplied predicates, in order to decide which one applies. Also note that a pending unification between an attributed variable and a term might even reduce to a syntactic unification in the course of the execution of other pending unifications.

  Example 1. Assume that attributed variables are used to implement variables ranging over finite domains. Let $X \in 1..3, Y \in 3..10$. The goal **f(X,Y)=f(Y,2)** enqueues two unifications: $X = Y$ and $Y = 2$. Assuming a FIFO strategy, the first unification would bind X and Y to 3, the only element in the intersection of their domains. When the second pending unification is dequeued, it is already reduced to $3 = 2$, which fails of course, but more important, it does not refer to attributed variables any more.

- If the application wants to refer to the attributed variables themselves, they can be made part the attribute term. The implementation of **freeze/2** below utilizes this technique. Note that this does *not* lead to cyclic structures, as the connection between an attributed variable and it's attribute is invisible to the pure parts of a given Prolog implementation.

4.2 Comparison by Example

Example 2. In order to show that both metastructures and attributed variables are equally capable to serve for the implementation of **freeze/2**, and primarily to allow for the comparison of two solutions to the same task, we present two implementations of **freeze/2** side by side:

```
:- meta_functor( frozen/2).

freeze( frozen(_,Goal), Goal).

meta_term_unify( frozen(Value,Goal), Value) :-
  call( Goal).

meta_meta_unify( frozen(V,G1), frozen(V,G2)) :-
  V = frozen(_,(G1,G2)).
```

```
freeze( X, Goal) :-
  attach_attribute( V, frozen(V,Goal)),
  X = V.

verify_attribute( frozen(Var,Goal), Value) :-
  detach_attribute( Var),
  Var = Value,
  call(Goal).

combine_attributes( frozen(V1,G1), frozen(V2,G2)) :-
  detach_attribute( V1),
  detach_attribute( V2),
  V1 = V2,
  attach_attribute( V1, frozen(V1,(G1,G2))).
```

The first encoding of **freeze/2** with metastructures assumes the specification from (Holzbaur 1990) being in force. The second program builds on the semantics of the SICStus clone, as proposed in this paper.

5 Summary

The idea with extensible unification in the context of logic programming is that the user identifies the set of interpreted functors through the provision of a signature. The unification semantics of terms built from interpreted functors are specified in the form of predicates in the language whose unification part is to be extended. Extensible unification can be implemented via metastructures or with the data type attributed variable. The latter approach can be brought to congruence with the former as outlined above. An additional convention regarding the use of interpreted functors provides the functionality that is achieved with destructive updates in traditional, procedural realizations. Within the metastructure scheme the user performs modifications by *variable substitution*. On the implementation level the abovementioned convention allows for the efficient management of substitution chains. In total we get a sound declarative backtrackable 'update' mechanism with essentially $O(1)$ access time. Space requirements are directly related to the number of choice points in the execution path.

Attributed variables are available in a 'raw' version in an attractive, State of the Art Prolog implementation — SICStus. It would be irresponsible to ignore this potential, given that minor changes can produce the intended functionality. A slight aftertaste remains because of the explicit modification predicate for the attribute part of attributed variables and because of the need for the transformation of interpreted terms into attributed variables.

The combination of programmable unification and a sound update mechanism *within* declarative logical languages makes a perfect basis for the implementation of various CLP languages. The feasibility of the approach was demonstrated elsewhere through the realization of various CLP instances like 'forward checking' over finite domains, CLP($\Re$), CLP($\mathcal{Q}$) (Holzbaur 1990)[4].

Acknowledgements

Thanks to the anonymous referees for their helpful comments on this paper.
This work was supported by the Austrian Federal Ministry of Science and Research.

References

Aho A.V., Hopcroft J.E., Ullman J.D.: ***Data Structures and Algorithms***, Addison-Wesley, Reading, MA, 1983.

Carlsson M.: Freeze, Indexing, and Other Implementation Issues in the WAM, in Lassez J.L.(ed.), ***Logic Programming - Proceedings of the 4th International Conference - Volume 1***, MIT Press, Cambridge, MA, 1987.

Carlsson M., Widen J.: Sicstus Prolog Users Manual, Swedish Institute of Computer Science, SICS/R-88/88007C, 1990.

Holzbaur C.: Specification of Constraint Based Inference Mechanisms through Extended Unification, Dept. of Medical Cybernetics & Artificial Intelligence, University of Vienna, Dissertation, 1990.

Huitouze S.le: A new data structure for implementing extensions to Prolog, in Deransart P. and Maluszunski J.(eds.), ***Programming Language Implementation and Logic Programming***, Springer, Heidelberg, 136-150, 1990.

Jaffar J., Michaylov S.: Methodology and Implementation of a CLP System, in Lassez J.L.(ed.), ***Logic Programming - Proceedings of the 4th International Conference - Volume 1***, MIT Press, Cambridge, MA, 1987.

Neumerkel U.: Extensible Unification by Metastructures, ***Proc. META90***, 1990.

This article was processed using the LaTeX macro package with LLNCS style

[4] Implementations of CLP($\Re$) and CLP($\mathcal{Q}$), based on the SICStus clone mentioned earlier, can be obtained via anonymous ftp from ftp.ai.univie.ac.at, directory sicstus/clpr

Comparing the Galois Connection and Widening/Narrowing Approaches to Abstract Interpretation*

Patrick Cousot[1] and Radhia Cousot[2]

[1] LIENS, DMI, École Normale Supérieure, 45, rue d'Ulm, 75230 Paris cedex 05 (France)
cousot@dmi.ens.fr

[2] LIX, École Polytechnique, 91128 Palaiseau cedex (France)
radhia@polytechnique.fr

Abstract. The use of infinite abstract domains with widening and narrowing for accelerating the convergence of abstract interpretations is shown to be more powerful than the Galois connection approach restricted to finite lattices (or lattices satisfying the chain condition).

1 Introduction

A widely-held opinion is that finite lattices (or lattices satisfying the chain condition, i.e., such that all strictly increasing chains are finite) can be used instead of widenings and narrowings to ensure the termination of abstract interpretations of programs on infinite lattices. We show that, in general, this can only be to the detriment of precision and prove that the use of infinite abstract domains with widenings and narrowings is more powerful than the Galois connection approach for finite lattices (or lattices satisfying the chain condition). By way of example, various widenings are suggested for solving non-convergence problems left open in the literature.

2 Upper Approximation of the Collecting Semantics

Following [CC76, CC77a, CC79b], the abstract interpretation of a program can be formalized as the effective computation of an upper approximation A of the *collecting semantics* of the program.

This collecting semantics can often be specified as the least fixed point $\operatorname{lfp}_{\perp}(F)$ of a continuous[3] operator $F \in L \xrightarrow{\text{con}} L$ on a cpo $L(\sqsubseteq, \sqcup)$ greater than a *basis* $\perp$ satisfying $\perp \sqsubseteq F(\perp)$[4]. By Kleene fixpoint theorem (Prop. 1 in the appendix), $\operatorname{lfp}_{\perp}(F)$ is the least upper bound $\bigsqcup_{n \in \mathbb{N}} F^n(\perp)$ of the *iterates* $F^n(\perp)$ defined by $F^0(x) \stackrel{\text{def}}{=} x$ and $F^{n+1}(x) \stackrel{\text{def}}{=} F(F^n(x))$ for all $x \in L$.

This approximation A must be *sound* in the sense that $\operatorname{lfp}(F) \sqsubseteq A$[5].

* This work was supported in part by Esprit BRA action 3124 "Sémantique".

[3] Monotony is sufficient by considering transfinite iterations [CC79a].

[4] The basis $\perp$ is often the infimum $\perp$ of the cpo, in which case $\operatorname{lfp}_{\perp} F$ is written $\operatorname{lfp} F$.

[5] Although commonly satisfied, these hypotheses on the definition of the collecting semantics and the specification of the approximation are stronger than strictly necessary, see a discussion of various weaker hypotheses in [CC92b].

Example 1 (Imperative programs). **Assume that the collecting semantics of the following** PASCAL **program:**

```
program P;
   var I : integer ;
begin
   I := 1;
   while I <= 100 do
      begin
         { I ∈ [1, 100] }
         I := I + 1;
      end;
   { I = 101 }
end.
```

is the set of possible values of integer variable I **when starting execution of the loop body. It is the least fixed point** $\text{lfp}(F) = \text{lfp}_{\emptyset}(F) = \{i \in \mathbb{Z} \mid 1 \leq i \leq 100\}$ **of the continuous (and even additive) operator:**

$$F \in L \xrightarrow{\text{con}} L = \lambda X \cdot (\{1\} \cup \{i+1 \mid i \in X\}) \cap \{i \in \mathbb{Z} \mid i \leq 100\} \tag{1}$$

on the complete lattice $L = \wp(\mathbb{Z})(\subseteq, \emptyset, \mathbb{Z}, \cap, \cup)$ **where** $\mathbb{Z}$ **is the set of integers and** $\wp(S)$ **is the powerset of the set** S.

A sound upper approximation is the loop invariant $A = \{i \in \mathbb{Z} \mid i \geq 0\}$ **specifying that** I **is non-negative.** □

Example 2 (Logic programs). **Let** P **be a logic program (containing at least one constant),** B_P **be its Herbrand universe over a family** $\mathcal{F} = \bigcup_{n \in \mathbb{N}} \mathcal{F}^n$ **of** n**-ary functors** $f \in \mathcal{F}^n$ **and ground**(P) **be the set of all ground instances of clauses in** P. **The *immediate consequence operator* is** $T_P \in \wp(B_P) \xrightarrow{\text{con}} \wp(B_P)$ **such that:**

$$T_P = \lambda X \cdot \{A \mid A \leftarrow B_1, \ldots, B_n \in \text{ground}(P) \wedge \forall i = 1, \ldots, n : B_i \in X\} \ .$$

A *model* of P **is a set** $I \subseteq B_P$, **such that** $T_P(I) \subseteq I$. **The characterization theorem of van Emden and Kowalski [vEK76] shows that** P **has a least model** M_P **in the complete lattice** $\wp(B_P)(\subseteq, \emptyset, \cup)$ **such that** $M_P = \text{lfp}_{\emptyset} T_P = \bigcup_{n \in \mathbb{N}} {T_P}^n(\emptyset)$. □

Example 3 (Functional programs). **Following [CC92c], the *relational semantics* of the functional factorial program:**

```
f(n) ≡ if n = 0 then 1 else n * f(n − 1);
```

is $f \in \wp(\mathbb{N}_\perp \times \mathbb{N}_\perp)$, **where** $\mathbb{N}_\perp \stackrel{\text{def}}{=} \mathbb{N} \cup \{\perp\}$ **and** $\perp$ **represents non-termination, such that:** $f = \{\langle\perp, \perp\rangle\} \cup \{\langle n, \perp\rangle \mid n < 0\} \cup \{\langle n, n!\rangle \mid n \geq 0\}$. **It is the least fixpoint** $\text{lfp}_{\perp} F$ **of** $F \in \wp(\mathbb{N}_\perp \times \mathbb{N}_\perp) \xrightarrow{\text{con}} \wp(\mathbb{N}_\perp \times \mathbb{N}_\perp)$ **such that:**

$$F(f) = \{\langle\perp, \perp\rangle\} \cup \{\langle 0, 1\rangle\} \cup \{\langle n, n * \rho\rangle \mid \langle n-1, \rho\rangle \in f\}$$

where $\perp - \rho = \rho - \perp = \perp$ **and** $\perp * \rho = \rho * \perp = \perp$. **The semantic domain** $\wp(\mathbb{N}_\perp \times \mathbb{N}_\perp)(\sqsubseteq, \bot, \top, \sqcup)$ **is a complete lattice, where:**

$$\begin{aligned}
\bot &\stackrel{\text{def}}{=} \mathbb{N}_\perp \times \{\perp\} \\
\top &\stackrel{\text{def}}{=} \mathbb{N}_\perp \times \mathbb{N} \\
f \sqsubseteq f' &\stackrel{\text{def}}{=} (f \cap \top) \subseteq (f' \cap \top) \ \wedge \ (f \cap \bot) \supseteq (f' \cap \bot) \\
\sqcup_{i \in \Delta} f_i &\stackrel{\text{def}}{=} \cup_{i \in \Delta}(f_i \cap \top) \ \cup \ \cap_{i \in \Delta}(f_i \cap \bot) \ .
\end{aligned}$$

Observe that $f \sqsubseteq f'$ if and only if f' produces more output results in $\mathbb{N}$ that f for a given terminating or non-terminating argument in $\mathbb{N}_\perp$ and f' terminates more frequently than f. □

3 The Galois Connection Approach to Abstract Interpretation

Principle of the Approach. The Galois connection approach to abstract interpretation [CC76, CC77a] formalizes the idea that the equation $X = F(X)$ can be first simplified into $\overline{X} = \overline{F}(\overline{X})$, where $\overline{F} \in \overline{L} \overset{\text{mon}}{\longmapsto} \overline{L}$ and $\overline{L}(\overline{\sqsubseteq}, \overline{\sqcup})$ is a poset, and then solved iteratively starting from the basis $\overline{\perp}$. The technique consists in understanding $\overline{L}$ as a discrete approximation of L and in extending this notion of approximation, in various ways, to semantic domains such as products $L \times L$, powersets $\wp(L)$ and function spaces $L \longmapsto L$ [CC77b, CC79b].

Galois Connection. The correspondence between the semantic domain L and its abstract version $\overline{L}$ can be formalized by a Galois connection (also called *pair of adjoined functions*).

Definition. If L ($\sqsubseteq$) and $\overline{L}$ ($\overline{\sqsubseteq}$) are posets, then $\langle\alpha, \gamma\rangle$ is a *Galois connection*, written $L \underset{\alpha}{\overset{\gamma}{\leftrightarrows}} \overline{L}$, if and only if $\alpha \in L \longmapsto \overline{L}$ and $\gamma \in \overline{L} \longmapsto L$ are functions such that:

$$\forall x \in L, \overline{y} \in \overline{L} : (\alpha(x) \mathrel{\overline{\sqsubseteq}} \overline{y}) \iff (x \sqsubseteq \gamma(\overline{y})) \ . \tag{2}$$

$\alpha(x)$ is the ***abstraction*** of x, i.e., the most precise approximation of $x \in L$ in $\overline{L}$. $\gamma(\overline{y})$ is the ***concretization*** of $\overline{y}$, i.e., the most imprecise element of L which can be soundly approximated by $\overline{y} \in \overline{L}$.

Example 4 (Intervals). In [CC76], $\wp(\mathbb{Z})$ ordered by $\subseteq$ is approximated using the abstract lattice of intervals $\overline{L} = \{\perp\} \cup \{[\ell, u] \mid \ell \in \mathbb{Z} \cup \{-\infty\} \wedge u \in \mathbb{Z} \cup \{+\infty\} \wedge \ell \leq u\}$ ordered by $\overline{\sqsubseteq}$, such that:

$$\begin{aligned} \perp \ &\overline{\sqsubseteq}\ [\ell, u] \overset{\text{def}}{=} \text{true} \\ [\ell_0, u_0] \ &\overline{\sqsubseteq}\ [\ell_1, u_1] \overset{\text{def}}{=} \ell_1 \leq \ell_0 \leq u_0 \leq u_1 \ . \end{aligned} \tag{3}$$

This approximation is formalized by the Galois connection defined by:

$$\begin{aligned} \gamma(\perp) &= \emptyset & \alpha(\emptyset) &= \perp \\ \gamma([\ell, u]) &= \{x \in \mathbb{Z} \mid \ell \leq x \leq u\} & \alpha(X) &= [\min X, \max X] \ . \end{aligned}$$

For example the set $\{1, 2, 5\} \in \wp(\mathbb{Z})$ is soundly approximated by $[1, 5] \in \overline{L}$. □

Soundness and Precision. Here, the concrete and abstract notions of soundness and precision are formalized in the same way, by the respective partial orders $\sqsubseteq$ on L and $\overline{\sqsubseteq}$ on $\overline{L}$. $x \sqsubseteq y$ is interpreted as "y is a sound approximation of x", "x is a more precise concrete assertion than y" or "x logically implies y". The same way $\overline{x} \mathrel{\overline{\sqsubseteq}} \overline{y} \mathrel{\overline{\sqsubseteq}} \overline{z}$ means that $\overline{y}$ and $\overline{z}$ are sound approximations of $\overline{x}$ but $\overline{y}$ is more precise than $\overline{z}$. We may have $\overline{x} \mathrel{\overline{\sqsubseteq}} \overline{y}$ and $\overline{x} \mathrel{\overline{\sqsubseteq}} \overline{z}$ but neither $\overline{y} \mathrel{\overline{\sqsubseteq}} \overline{z}$ nor $\overline{z} \mathrel{\overline{\sqsubseteq}} \overline{y}$ in which case $\overline{y}$ and $\overline{z}$ are non-comparable sound approximations of $\overline{x}$. Equation (2) states that the concrete and abstract notions of soundness and precision coincide, up to an approximation, which consists in representing several concrete assertions $\{x \mid \alpha(x) = \overline{x}\}$ by the same abstract assertion $\overline{x}$.

Example 5 (Intervals, continued). For intervals considered in Ex. 4, the concrete approximation relation $\sqsubseteq$ is subset inclusion $\subseteq$ whereas the abstract approximation relation $\overline{\sqsubseteq}$ is defined by (3). For example, $\{1, 2, 5\} \subseteq \{i \in \mathbb{Z} \mid i \geq 1\}$ and $\{1, 2, 5\} \subseteq \{i \in \mathbb{Z} \mid i \leq 5\}$ since the assertion that the value of a variable can only be 1, 2 or 5 during execution is more precise than saying that it is strictly positive. These assertions are respectively abstracted by $[1, 5] \mathrel{\overline{\sqsubseteq}} [1, +\infty]$ and $[1, 5] \mathrel{\overline{\sqsubseteq}} [-\infty, 5]$ but these approximations are not comparable since $[1, +\infty] \mathrel{\overline{\not\sqsubseteq}} [-\infty, 5]$ and $[-\infty, 5] \mathrel{\overline{\not\sqsubseteq}} [1, +\infty]$. $[1, 5]$ is the best possible abstract approximation of the concrete assertion $\{1, 2, 5\}$. □

Extension to Function Spaces. The concrete approximation relation $\sqsubseteq \in \wp(L \times L)$ can be extended to the function space $L \longmapsto L$ pointwise, i.e., $F \sqsubseteq F' \stackrel{\text{def}}{=} \forall x \in L : F(x) \sqsubseteq F'(x)$. The intuition is that F is more precise than F' if and only if F always yields more precise results than F'.

Then, the approximation of L by $\overline{L}$ can be extended to the approximation of the function space $L \longmapsto L$ by $\overline{L} \longmapsto \overline{L}$ using the functional abstraction $\vec{\alpha}$ and concretization $\vec{\gamma}$ defined, as in [CC77b], by:

$$\begin{array}{ll} \vec{\alpha} \in (L \longmapsto L) \longmapsto (\overline{L} \longmapsto \overline{L}) & \vec{\gamma} \in (\overline{L} \longmapsto \overline{L}) \longmapsto (L \longmapsto L) \\ \vec{\alpha}(\varphi) \stackrel{\text{def}}{=} \alpha \circ \varphi \circ \gamma & \vec{\gamma}(\overline{\varphi}) \stackrel{\text{def}}{=} \gamma \circ \overline{\varphi} \circ \alpha \end{array} \tag{4}$$

such that, by Prop. 3 in the appendix:

$$(L \stackrel{\text{mon}}{\longmapsto} L) \xleftarrow[\vec{\alpha}]{\vec{\gamma}} (\overline{L} \stackrel{\text{mon}}{\longmapsto} \overline{L}) \ . \tag{5}$$

Intuitively, $\vec{\alpha}(F)$ is the abstract image of F up to the Galois connection $L \xleftarrow[\alpha]{\gamma} \overline{L}$. It follows, by Prop. 8 in the appendix, that if $L(\sqsubseteq, \sqcup)$ is a poset, $F \in L \stackrel{\text{con}}{\longmapsto} L$, and $\overline{\bot}$ is $\alpha(\bot)$, then $\text{lfp}_{\bot}(F) \sqsubseteq \gamma\left(\text{lfp}_{\overline{\bot}}(\vec{\alpha}(F))\right)$. Otherwise stated, the fixpoint operator lfp preserves the soundness of the approximation [CC77b].

Functional Abstraction. In practice $\vec{\alpha}(F)$ may not be easy to program. In this case we can use an upper approximation $\overline{F}$. More precisely, $\overline{F} \in (\overline{L} \longmapsto \overline{L})$ is an *abstraction* of $F \in (L \stackrel{\text{con}}{\longmapsto} L)$ if and only if $\vec{\alpha}(F) \mathrel{\overline{\sqsubseteq}} \overline{F}$ or, equivalently, $F \sqsubseteq \vec{\gamma}(\overline{F})$. Diagrammatically:

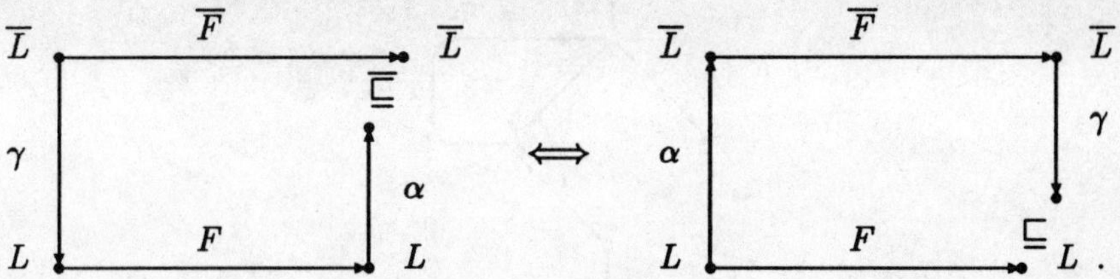

Intuitively, $\overline{F}(\overline{x})$ is an approximation of $F(x)$ when applied to an approximation $\overline{x}$ of x.

Definition. $\langle\overline{L}, \overline{\bot}, \overline{F}\rangle$ is an *abstract interpretation* of $\langle L, \bot, F\rangle$, written $\langle L, \bot, F\rangle \overset{\gamma}{\underset{\alpha}{\leftrightarrows}} \langle\overline{L}, \overline{\bot}, \overline{F}\rangle$, if and only if $L \overset{\gamma}{\underset{\alpha}{\leftrightarrows}} \overline{L}$, $\alpha(\bot) \mathrel{\overline{\sqsubseteq}} \overline{\bot}$ and $\vec{\alpha}(F) \mathrel{\overline{\sqsubseteq}} \overline{F}$[6].

If $\langle L, \bot, F\rangle \overset{\gamma}{\underset{\alpha}{\leftrightarrows}} \langle\overline{L}, \overline{\bot}, \overline{F}\rangle$ and $\overline{A}$ is an upper bound of the abstract iterates $\overline{F}^n(\overline{\bot})$, $n \in \mathbb{N}$, then $\text{lfp}_{\bot}(F) \sqsubseteq \gamma(\overline{A})$, as shown by Prop. 9 in the appendix[7]. Otherwise stated any upper bound of the abstract iterates is a sound approximation of the collecting semantics.

Example 6 (Intervals, continued). Given the interval abstraction of Ex. 4, the approximate equation $\overline{X} = \overline{F}(\overline{X})$ corresponding to (1) for program P is defined by:

$$\overline{F} \in \overline{L} \overset{\text{mon}}{\longmapsto} \overline{L} = \lambda X \cdot ([1, 1] \sqcup (X \oplus [1, 1])) \sqcap [-\infty, 100]$$

where $\bot \sqcup X = X \sqcup \bot = X$, $[\ell_0, u_0] \sqcup [\ell_1, u_1] = [\min(\ell_0, \ell_1), \max(u_0, u_1)]$, $\bot \sqcap X = X \sqcap \bot = \bot$, $[\ell_0, u_0] \sqcap [\ell_1, u_1] =$ if $\max(\ell_0, \ell_1) > \min(u_0, u_1)$ then $\bot$ else $[\max(\ell_0, \ell_1), \min(u_0, u_1)]$, $\bot \oplus X = X \oplus \bot = \bot$ and $[\ell_0, u_0] \oplus [\ell_1, u_1] = [\ell_0 + \ell_1, u_0 + u_1]$. It can be solved iteratively starting from the infimum $\bot$. The successive iterates are $\bot$, [1, 1], [1, 2], ..., [1, 100]. This sequence might be infinite and strictly increasing (e.g. for nonterminating programs). □

In practice, finite convergence of the abstract iterates $\overline{F}^n(\overline{\bot})$, $n \in \mathbb{N}$ must be ensured. This leads to hypotheses on $\overline{L}$ and $\overline{F}$ such as, e.g., $\overline{L}$ is finite or $\overline{F}^n(\overline{\bot})$, $n \in \mathbb{N}$ is an increasing chain and no strictly increasing chain in $\overline{L}$ can be infinite (i.e. $\overline{L}$ satisfies the so-called *ascending chain condition*). Observe that various hypotheses ensure that $\overline{F}^n(\overline{\bot})$, $n \in \mathbb{N}$ is an increasing chain. For example, $\overline{F}$ might be *extensive* (i.e., $\forall \overline{x} \in \overline{L} : \overline{x} \mathrel{\overline{\sqsubseteq}} \overline{F}(\overline{x})$) or $\overline{\bot}$ may be a *prefixpoint* of $\overline{F}$ (i.e., $\overline{\bot} \mathrel{\overline{\sqsubseteq}} \overline{F}(\overline{\bot})$) and $\overline{F} \in \overline{L} \overset{\text{mon}}{\longmapsto} \overline{L}$ may be monotone. For more details or equivalent approaches, see [CC79b], [Cou78, chapter 4] and [CC92a].

Example 7 (Descriptive types). In Prolog type analysis of Bruynooghe et al. [BJCD87, JB92], a set of ground terms is approximated by a *type graph* such as the following one (where a and b are constants of arity 0 and f is a binary functor):

---

[6] $\alpha(\bot) \mathrel{\overline{\sqsubseteq}} \overline{\bot}$ is equivalent to $\bot \sqsubseteq \gamma(\overline{\bot})$ and $\vec{\alpha}(F) \mathrel{\overline{\sqsubseteq}} \overline{F}$ is equivalent to $F \circ \gamma \sqsubseteq \gamma \circ \overline{F}$ or to $\alpha \circ F \mathrel{\overline{\sqsubseteq}} \overline{F} \circ \alpha$ (see Prop. 4 in the appendix), so that we can dispense with either α or γ, [CC92b].

[7] which is the case for $\overline{A} = \text{lfp}_{\overline{\bot}} \overline{F}$ whenever this least fixpoint exists.

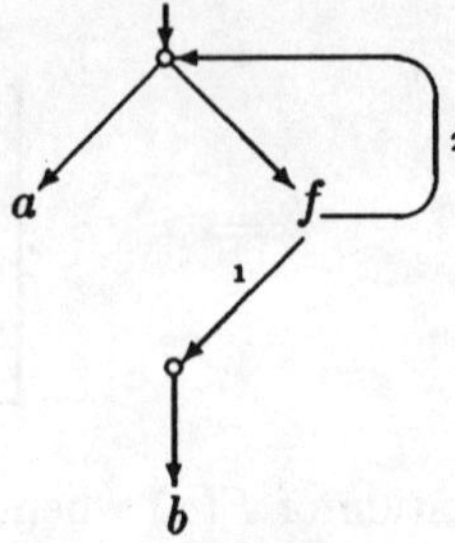

A type graph $G \in \mathcal{G}$ is a finite bipartite graph, consisting of:

1. A finite set N_t of type nodes (marked $\circ$ in diagrams),
2. A finite set N_f of functor nodes m, labeled with n-ary functors $f(m) \in \mathcal{F}^n$, and such that $N_t \cap N_f = \emptyset$,
3. A root $r \in N_t$ such that there is a path from r to any node of G,
4. A set $A \in \wp(N_t \times N_f) \cup \wp(N_f \times \mathbb{N} \times N_t)$ of arcs, such that:
   (a) All type nodes $k \in N_t$ have at least one outgoing arc and all outgoing arcs $\langle k, m\rangle$ go to functors nodes $m \in N_f$ with distinct labels $f(m)$,
   (b) All functors nodes $m \in N_f$ labeled with a functor $f(m) \in \mathcal{F}^n$ of arity $n \in \mathbb{N}$ have n outgoing arcs $\langle m, i, k^i\rangle$, $1 \leq i \leq n$ (so that there is no outgoing arc when $n = 0$).

We write $k : g(k^1, \ldots, k^n)$ for $\exists m \in N_f$: $\langle k, m\rangle \in A \wedge f(m) = g \in \mathcal{F}^n \wedge \forall i \in [1, n]$: $\langle m, i, k^i\rangle \in A$ and say that type nodes $k^1, \ldots, k^n$ are the *sons* of node k. A ground term $t \in B_P$ is said to *fold on type node k of type graph G*, if and only if:

1. $t = c \in \mathcal{F}^0$ and $k : c$,
2. $t = g(t_1, \ldots, t_n)$, $k : g(k^1, \ldots, k^n)$ and each ground term t_i, $1 \leq i \leq n$ folds on type node k^i of graph G.

The concretization function is defined by:

$$\gamma(G) = \{t \in B_P \mid t \text{ folds on the root of } G\}$$

For the type graph G above, we have $\gamma(G) = \{a, f(b, a), f(b, f(b, a)), f(b, f(b, f(b, a))), \ldots\}$.

Define the equivalence relation $G \equiv G'$ by $\gamma(G) = \gamma(G')$. The partial order relation $\sqsubseteq$ on $L = \mathcal{G}/_{\equiv}$ is defined by $G \sqsubseteq G'$ if and only if $\gamma(G) \subseteq \gamma(G')$. We have $G \sqsubseteq G'$ if and only if all paths in G exist in G', which can be checked by path-finding algorithms. □

Example 8 (Strictness analysis). In Mycroft's strictness analysis [Myc80], a relation $f \in \wp(\mathbb{N}_\perp \times \mathbb{N}_\perp)$ is approximated by a function $f^\sharp \in \{0, 1\} \xrightarrow{\text{mon}} \{0, 1\}$ such that $0 \sqsubseteq 1$ and $f^\sharp(0) = 0$ only if f is *strict*, that is: $\forall \rho \in \mathbb{N}_\perp$: $\langle \perp, \rho\rangle \in f \Longrightarrow \rho = \perp$. This approximation is formalized by the Galois connection defined by:

$$\begin{array}{ll} \gamma(\lambda\, x \cdot 0) = \mathbb{N}_\perp \times \{\perp\} & \alpha(f) = \lambda\, x \cdot 0 \quad \text{if } f = \mathbb{N}_\perp \times \{\perp\} \\ \gamma(\lambda\, x \cdot x) = \{\langle \perp, \perp\rangle\} \cup \mathbb{N} \times \mathbb{N}_\perp & \alpha(f) = \lambda\, x \cdot x \quad \text{if } \langle \perp, \rho\rangle \in f \Longrightarrow \rho = \perp \\ \gamma(\lambda\, x \cdot 1) = \mathbb{N}_\perp \times \mathbb{N}_\perp & \alpha(f) = \lambda\, x \cdot 1 \quad \text{otherwise .} \end{array}$$

This abstract interpretation can be lifted to higher-order functions using (4). □

4 The Widening/Narrowing Approach to Abstract Interpretation

Another method [CC76, CC77a] for enforcing termination of the abstract interpretation consists in using a *widening* $\nabla \in L \times L \longmapsto L$ such that:

$$\forall x, y \in L : x \sqsubseteq x \nabla y \quad (6)$$

$$\forall x, y \in L : y \sqsubseteq x \nabla y \quad (7)$$

for all increasing chains $x^0 \sqsubseteq x^1 \sqsubseteq \ldots$, the increasing chain defined by $y^0 = x^0, \ldots, y^{i+1} = y^i \nabla x^{i+1}, \ldots$ is not strictly increasing . (8)

It follows, as shown by Prop. 11 in the appendix, that the *upward iteration sequence with widening*:

$$\begin{aligned} \hat{X}^0 &= \bot \\ \hat{X}^{i+1} &= \hat{X}^i && \text{if } F(\hat{X}^i) \sqsubseteq \hat{X}^i \\ &= \hat{X}^i \nabla F(\hat{X}^i) && \text{otherwise} \end{aligned} \quad (9)$$

is ultimately stationary and its limit $\hat{A}$ is a sound upper approximation of $\text{lfp}_\bot(F)$[8]. Observe that if L is a join-semi-lattice (the least upper bound $x \sqcup y$ exists for all x, $y \in L$) satisfying the ascending chain condition, then $\sqcup$ is a widening.

This approximation can then be improved using a *narrowing* operator $\Delta \in L \times L \longmapsto L$ such that:

$$\forall x, y \in L : (y \sqsubseteq x) \implies (y \sqsubseteq (x \,\Delta\, y) \sqsubseteq x) \quad (10)$$

for all decreasing chains $x^0 \sqsupseteq x^1 \sqsupseteq \ldots$, the decreasing chain defined by $y^0 = x^0, \ldots, y^{i+1} = y^i \,\Delta\, x^{i+1}, \ldots$ is not strictly decreasing . (11)

It follows, as shown by Prop. 12 in the appendix, that the *downward abstract iteration sequence with narrowing*:

$$\begin{aligned} \check{X}^0 &= \hat{A} \\ \check{X}^{i+1} &= \check{X}^i \,\Delta\, F(\check{X}^i) \end{aligned} \quad (12)$$

is ultimately stationary and its limit $\check{A}$ as well as each term $\check{X}^i$ of this decreasing chain is a sound upper approximation of $\text{lfp}_\bot(F)$. Observe that if $F(\check{X}^i) = \check{X}^i$ then $\check{X}^{i+1} = \check{X}^i$ so that if the approximation $\hat{A}$ of $\text{lfp}_\bot F$ is a fixpoint of F then it cannot be improved by (12). Observe also that if L is a meet-semi-lattice (the greatest lower bound $x \sqcap y$ exists for all x, $y \in L$) satisfying the *descending chain condition* (no strictly decreasing chain in L can be infinite), then $\sqcap$ is a narrowing.

Example 9 (Widening and narrowing for intervals). The widening and narrowing introduced in [CC76] for the lattice of intervals $\overline{L} = \{\bot\} \cup \{[\ell, u] \mid \ell \in \mathbb{Z} \cup \{-\infty\} \wedge u \in \mathbb{Z} \cup \{+\infty\} \wedge \ell \leq u\}$ are defined as follows:

$$\begin{aligned} \bot \nabla X &= X \\ X \nabla \bot &= X \\ [\ell_0, u_0] \nabla [\ell_1, u_1] &= [\text{if } \ell_1 < \ell_0 \text{ then } -\infty \text{ else } \ell_0, \\ &\qquad \text{if } u_1 > u_0 \text{ then } +\infty \text{ else } u_0] \ . \end{aligned} \quad (13)$$

[8] Numerous variants are possible. For example, we might assume $x \sqsubseteq y$ in (6) and (7), and use $\hat{X}^{i+1} = \hat{X}^i \nabla (\hat{X}^i \sqcup F(\hat{X}^i))$ in (9), or use a different widening for each iterate (as in [Cou81]) or even have a widening which depends upon all previous iterates.

The widening (13) extrapolates unstable bounds to infinity. Observe that the widening (13) is not monotone. For example $[0, 1] \sqsubseteq [0, 2]$ but $[0, 1] \nabla [0, 2] = [0, +\infty] \not\sqsubseteq [0, 2] = [0, 2] \nabla [0, 2]$.

The narrowing introduced in [CC76] for the lattice of intervals $\overline{L} = \{\bot\} \cup \{[\ell, u] \mid \ell \in \mathbb{Z} \cup \{-\infty\} \wedge u \in \mathbb{Z} \cup \{+\infty\} \wedge \ell \leq u\}$ is defined by:

$$\begin{aligned} \bot \,\Delta\, X &= \bot \\ X \,\Delta\, \bot &= \bot \\ [\ell_0,\, u_0] \,\Delta\, [\ell_1,\, u_1] &= [\text{if } \ell_0 = -\infty \text{ then } \ell_1 \text{ else } \ell_0, \\ &\qquad \text{if } u_0 = +\infty \text{ then } u_1 \text{ else } u_0] \ . \end{aligned} \tag{14}$$

The narrowing (14) improves infinite bounds only.

Resolution of the equation:

$$X = \overline{F}(X) = ([1, 1] \sqcup (X \oplus [1, 1])) \sqcap [-\infty, 100]$$

considered in Ex. 6 starts with the following increasing iterates:

$$\begin{aligned} \hat{X}^0 &= \bot \\ \hat{X}^1 &= \hat{X}^0 \nabla \Big(([1, 1] \sqcup (\hat{X}^0 \oplus [1, 1])) \sqcap [-\infty, 100]\Big) \\ &= \bot \nabla \Big(([1, 1] \sqcup (\bot \oplus [1, 1])) \sqcap [-\infty, 100]\Big) \\ &= ([1, 1] \sqcup \bot) \sqcap [-\infty, 100] \\ &= [1, 1] \\ \hat{X}^2 &= \hat{X}^1 \nabla \Big(([1, 1] \sqcup (\hat{X}^1 \oplus [1, 1])) \sqcap [-\infty, 100]\Big) \\ &= [1, 1] \nabla \Big(([1, 1] \sqcup ([1, 1] \oplus [1, 1])) \sqcap [-\infty, 100]\Big) \\ &= [1, 1] \nabla (([1, 1] \sqcup [2, 2]) \sqcap [-\infty, 100]) \\ &= [1, 1] \nabla ([1, 2] \sqcap [-\infty, 100]) \\ &= [1, 1] \nabla [1, 2] \\ &= [1, +\infty] \\ \hat{X}^3 &= \hat{X}^2 \nabla \Big(([1, 1] \sqcup (\hat{X}^2 \oplus [1, 1])) \sqcap [-\infty, 100]\Big) \\ &= [1, +\infty] \nabla \Big(([1, 1] \sqcup ([1, +\infty] \oplus [1, 1])) \sqcap [-\infty, 100]\Big) \\ &= [1, +\infty] \nabla (([1, 1] \sqcup [2, +\infty]) \sqcap [-\infty, 100]) \\ &= [1, +\infty] \nabla ([1, +\infty] \sqcap [-\infty, 100]) \\ &= [1, +\infty] \nabla [1, 100] \\ &= [1, +\infty] \\ &\sqsubseteq \hat{X}^2 \ . \end{aligned}$$

Then the decreasing iterates are as follows:

$$\check{X}^0 = \hat{X}^2$$

$$
\begin{aligned}
\check{X}^1 &= \check{X}^0 \vartriangle \Big(([1, 1] \sqcup (\check{X}^0 \oplus [1, 1])) \sqcap [-\infty, 100] \Big) \\
&= [1, +\infty] \vartriangle \Big(([1, 1] \sqcup ([1, +\infty] \oplus [1, 1])) \sqcap [-\infty, 100] \Big) \\
&= [1, +\infty] \vartriangle (([1, 1] \sqcup [2, +\infty]) \sqcap [-\infty, 100]) \\
&= [1, +\infty] \vartriangle ([1, +\infty] \sqcap [-\infty, 100]) \\
&= [1, +\infty] \vartriangle [1, 100] \\
&= [1, 100] \\
\check{X}^2 &= \check{X}^1 \vartriangle \Big(([1, 1] \sqcup (\check{X}^1 \oplus [1, 1])) \sqcap [-\infty, 100] \Big) \\
&= [1, 100] \vartriangle \Big(([1, 1] \sqcup ([1, 100] \oplus [1, 1])) \sqcap [-\infty, 100] \Big) \\
&= [1, 100] \\
&= \check{X}^1 \ .
\end{aligned}
$$

In what follows, we will consider the fact that given two integer constants $n_1 \leq n_2$, the abstract interpreter SYNTOX [Bou90] will analyze the program:

```
program Pn1n2;
   var I : integer ;
begin
   I := n1;
   while I <= n2 do
      begin
         { I ∈ [n1, n2] }
         I := I + 1;
      end;
   { I = n2+1 }
end.
```

by solving a system of fixpoint equations equivalent to:

$$X = F(X) = ([n_1, n_1] \sqcup (X \oplus [1, 1])) \sqcap [-\infty, n_2]$$

and automatically discover the loop invariant:

$$\{ \mathtt{I} \in [n_1, n_2] \} \ . \qquad \square$$

Example 10 (Type graphs widening). [BJCD87] have defined the ***restriction*** of type graphs. It is a widening. For example:

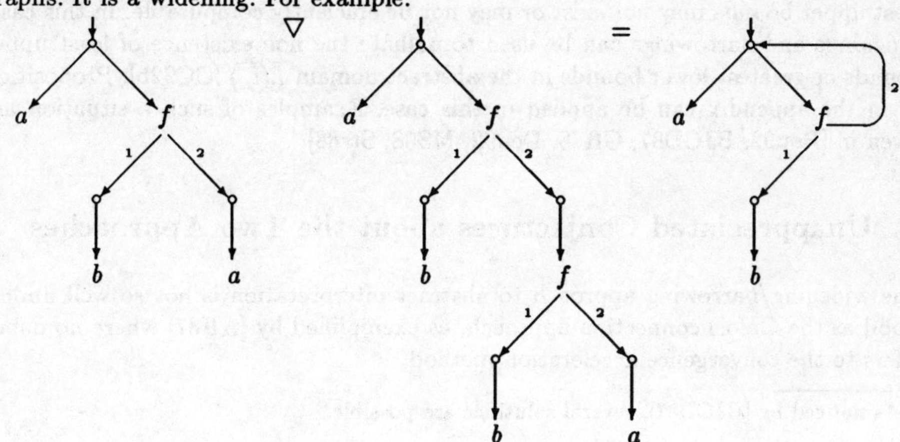

More precisely, the widening $G = G_1 \nabla G_2$ of two type graphs G_1 and G_2 is obtained by:

1. Initializing G with a copy of G_1 and G_2 where roots are merged (merging consists in joining type nodes without removing any arc),
2. and then, in repeatedly applying the following transformations to G:
   (a) type nodes k of G with distinct sons $k : g(k_1^1, \ldots, k_1^n)$ and $k : g(k_2^1, \ldots, k_2^n)$ with the same functor g have their sons k_1^i and k_2^i pairwise merged,
   (b) distinct type nodes $k_1 : g(k_1^1, \ldots, k_1^n)$ and $k_2 : g(k_2^1, \ldots, k_2^n)$ with the same functor g on an acyclic path from the root are merged[9].

All sons of a type node must have different functors, so that the breadth of a type graph is finite. No acyclic path starting from the root can contain the same functor twice, so that the depth of a widened type graph is finite. It follows that a strictly increasing chain of type graphs is finite. □

5 Combining the Galois Connection and Widening/-Narrowing Approaches to Abstract Interpretation

In practice both Galois connection and widening/narrowing approaches are used simultaneously [CC76, CC77a]. First a Galois connection is used to obtain approximate equations $\overline{X} = \overline{F}(\overline{X})$ on an abstract domain $\overline{L}$. The goal is to obtain computer representable properties of programs. These fixpoint equations are then solved iteratively. Widenings and narrowings are used when the domain $\overline{L}$ has infinite or very long strictly ascending chains or even when it is finite but very large. The goal is then to enforce or accelerate the convergence. For more details see [CC76, CC77a], consult [Cou81] to minimize the number of widenings within loops and chapter 4 of [Cou78] for dual problems.

The use of Galois connections corresponds to an ideal situation where concrete assertions have a unique best abstract interpretation [CC79b]. In practice this property is not always satisfied for reasons of efficient computer representation of abstract properties. Moreover the abstract domain need not be partially ordered since many equivalent abstract values can be used to represent the same abstract assertion or least upper bounds may not exist or may not be efficiently computable. In this case, widenings and narrowings can be used to palliate the non-existence of least upper bounds or greatest lower bounds in the abstract domain $\overline{L}(\overline{\sqsubseteq})$ [CC92b]. Proposition 13 in the appendix can be applied in this case. Examples of such a situation are given in [Bou92, BJCD87, CH78, Deu92, MS88, Str88].

6 Unappreciated Conjectures about the Two Approaches

The widening/narrowing approach to abstract interpretation is not so well understood as the Galois connection approach, as exemplified by [AH87] where no paper refers to the convergence acceleration method.

[9] As noticed by [BJCD87], several solutions are possible.

An often used argument for 'proving' the uselessness of the widening/narrowing approach is that given an infinite abstract domain together with specific widening and narrowing operators, it is possible to find a finite lattice which will give the same results. For example [KN87] claim that "One may wonder whether or not it is necessary to choose a finite domain for abstract interpretation, since apparently more information can be obtained from an interpretation over an infinite domain. The answer is that if uniform termination of the abstract interpretation is required, no more information can be obtained by choosing an infinite domain". In [HH90], a fixpoint approximation method is considered which consists in an upwards iteration using a safe approximation $\vec{\alpha}(F)$ of the function $F \in L \overset{\text{con}}{\longmapsto} L$ in a finite small lattice $\overline{L}$ such that $L \overset{\gamma}{\underset{\alpha}{\leftrightarrows}} \overline{L}$ and in which the problem of finding fixpoints is tractable, followed by a downwards iteration from $\gamma(\text{lfp}_{\alpha(\perp)}(\vec{\alpha}(F)))$ in L (or in a sequence of intermediate lattices larger than $\overline{L}$). [HH90] claim that "We have now shown the *equivalence* of step 1 of that process and the Cousot's notion of widening." For step 2, which consists in working in a larger lattice, [HH90] claim that "the refinement of the upper bound in intermediate lattice corresponds to narrowing".

7 Comparing the Two Approaches

To correct these overstatements, we show that, on the contrary and in general, no finite abstract domain (or domain satisfying the ascending chain condition) can be used instead of widening/narrowing operators on infinite domains to obtain the same results (or equivalent ones, up to the computer representation).

7.1 Finite Abstract Domains (or Domains Satisfying the Ascending Chain Condition) Cannot Do for Widenings and Narrowings

More precisely, we prove in this section that there exist infinite domains and widening/narrowing operators such that:

1. For each program there exists a finite lattice which can be used for this program to obtain results equivalent to those obtained using widening/narrowing operators;
2. No such a finite lattice will do for all programs;
3. For all programs, infinitely many abstract values are necessary;
4. For a particular program it is not possible to infer the set of needed abstract values by a simple inspection of the text of the program.

Let $\text{lfp}_{\perp}(F)$ where $F \in L \overset{\text{mon}}{\longmapsto} L$ be the collecting semantics of a given program P. Assume that $\langle L, \perp, F\rangle \overset{\gamma}{\underset{\alpha}{\leftrightarrows}} \langle \overline{L}, \overline{\perp}, \overline{F}\rangle$ is an abstract interpretation such that $\text{lfp}_{\perp}(\overline{F})$ is not computable iteratively in finitely many steps and $\overline{A}$ is an upper approximation of $\text{lfp}_{\perp}(\overline{F})$ effectively computed using the widening/narrowing approach. We have $\text{lfp}_{\perp}(F) \sqsubseteq \gamma\left(\text{lfp}_{\overline{\perp}}(\overline{F})\right)$ and $\text{lfp}_{\overline{\perp}}(\overline{F}) \sqsubseteq \overline{A}$, so that, by monotony and transitivity, $\text{lfp}_{\perp}(F) \sqsubseteq \gamma(\overline{A})$. We want to find a finite equivalent abstract interpretation $\langle L, \perp, F\rangle \overset{\gamma'}{\underset{\alpha'}{\leftrightarrows}} \langle \overline{\overline{L}}, \overline{\overline{\perp}}, \overline{\overline{F}}\rangle$ such that $\overline{\overline{L}}$ is finite and $\text{lfp}_{\overline{\overline{\perp}}}(\overline{\overline{F}})$ gives results equivalent to $\overline{A}$, i.e., $\gamma'\left(\text{lfp}_{\overline{\overline{\perp}}}(\overline{\overline{F}})\right) = \gamma(\overline{A})$.

We choose the finite lattice $\overline{\overline{L}}$ consisting of the elements $\overline{\overline{\bot}} \;\overline{\overline{\sqsubseteq}}\; \overline{A} \;\overline{\overline{\sqsubseteq}}\; \overline{\overline{\top}}$ and the operator $\overline{\overline{F}} \in \overline{\overline{L}} \overset{mon}{\longmapsto} \overline{\overline{L}}$ such that $\overline{\overline{F}}(\overline{\overline{\bot}}) = \overline{\overline{F}}(\overline{A}) = \overline{A}$ and $\overline{\overline{F}}(\overline{\overline{\top}}) = \overline{\overline{\top}}$. Define the Galois connection $\overline{L} \underset{\overline{\alpha}}{\overset{\overline{\gamma}}{\leftrightarrows}} \overline{\overline{L}}$ such that $\overline{\alpha}(X) =$ if $X = \bot$ then $\overline{\overline{\bot}}$ elsif $X \;\overline{\sqsubseteq}\; \overline{A}$ then $\overline{A}$ else $\overline{\overline{\top}}$ and $\overline{\gamma}(\overline{\overline{\bot}}) = \overline{\bot}$, $\overline{\gamma}(\overline{A}) = \overline{A}$, $\overline{\gamma}(\overline{\overline{\top}}) = \overline{\top}$, where $\overline{\top}$ is the supremum of L (which is added to $\overline{L}$ if no one exists). We have $L \underset{\overline{\alpha}\circ\alpha}{\overset{\gamma\circ\overline{\gamma}}{\leftrightarrows}} \overline{\overline{L}}$, $\overline{\alpha} \circ \alpha \circ F \circ \gamma \circ \overline{\gamma} \;\overline{\overline{\sqsubseteq}}\; \overline{\overline{F}}$ and $\mathrm{lfp}_{\overline{\overline{\bot}}}(\overline{\overline{F}}) = \overline{A}$. It follows that the effective computation of any upper approximation $\overline{A}$ of $\mathrm{lfp}_{\bot}(F)$ (obtained by widening/narrowing) can also be done by iteration of a fixpoint operator $\overline{\overline{F}}$ on a finite lattice $\overline{\overline{L}}$.

If equivalent results are required for the two approaches, we observe that $\overline{\overline{L}}$ must contain an element $\mathrm{lfp}_{\overline{\overline{\bot}}}(\overline{\overline{F}})$ such that $\gamma'(\mathrm{lfp}_{\overline{\overline{\bot}}}(\overline{\overline{F}})) = \gamma(\overline{A})$ for each program P. For the family of programs $\mathtt{P}n_1n_2$ defined in Ex. 9, this lattice $\overline{\overline{L}}$ would have to contain infinitely many different elements equivalent to $\gamma(\overline{A})$ where $\overline{A} = [n_1, n_2]$. It follows that in general, $\overline{\overline{L}}$ cannot be finite and must contain infinite strictly increasing chains.

Since the above proof is rather contrived, it could be argued that the finite subset of $\overline{L}$ which is needed for analyzing a given program can be directly derived from a simple inspection of its text. This is not possible in general since, as shown by the series of examples below, the invariant $\overline{A}$ which is found by the analysis does not necessarily appear in the program and, more generally, is not a simple function of the program text.

Example 11 (Interval analysis). Given an integer constant n, the abstract interpreter SYNTOX [Bou90] will analyze the program `Function91ofMcCarthy` below (known for $n = 100$) and automatically discover the invariant given as comment:

```
program Function91ofMcCarthy;
  var X, Y : integer;

  function F(X : integer) : integer;
  begin
    if X > n then
      F := X - 10
    else
      F := F(F(X + 11));
  end;
begin
  readln(X);
  Y := F(X);
  { Y ∈ [n - 9, maxint - 10] }
end.
```

Observe that the integer constants $(n - 9)$ and $(\mathrm{maxint} - 10)$ which are found as bounds for Y by the automatic interval analysis do not appear in the program. Even more convincing is the following example:

```
program Function91ofMcCarthy;
  var X, Y : integer;

  function F(X : integer) : integer;
  begin
```

```
    if X > 100 then
       F := X - 10
       { F ∈ [91, maxint - 10] }
    else
       F := F(F(F(F(X + 33))));
       { F ∈ [91, 93] }
    { F ∈ [91, maxint - 10] }
 end;

begin
   readln(X);
   Y := F(X);
   { Y ∈ [91, maxint - 10] }
end.
```

□

Example 12 (Rational congruence analysis). [Gra91a] considers the discovery of arithmetical congruences of the form $x \equiv p[q]$ where $p, q \in \mathbb{Q}$ are rational numbers automatically determined by the analysis and x denotes the value of a program variable. The non-extremal elements of the corresponding lattice $\overline{L} = \{\perp, \top\} \cup (\mathbb{Q} \times \mathbb{Q})$ are denoted $p + q\mathbb{Z}$ since $\gamma(p + q\mathbb{Z}) = \{x \in \mathbb{Q} \mid \exists k \in \mathbb{Z} : x = p + q.k\}$. This lattice does not satisfy the ascending chain condition since:

$$\frac{1}{2^0}\mathbb{Z} \sqsubset \frac{1}{2^1}\mathbb{Z} \sqsubset \frac{1}{2^2}\mathbb{Z} \sqsubset \ldots \sqsubset \frac{1}{2^n}\mathbb{Z} \sqsubset \ldots .$$

Using the widening/narrowing approach to abstract interpretation, the following loop invariant is derived in [Gra91b]:

```
program PC;
   var X : real;
begin
   X := 2.8542;
   while ... do begin
      { X ≡ 1/5000 [1/500] }
   X := X + 1/500;
   end;
end.
```

Observe that the constant 5000 which is derived from $2.8542 = \frac{14271}{5000}$ does not appear in the program text. □

Example 13 (Linear inequality analysis). The abstract interpretation introduced in [CH78] has been designed, using the widening/narrowing approach, to discover linear invariants such as:

```
program PL;
   var I, J : integer;
begin
   I := 2; J := 0;
   while ... do begin
      { 2J + 2 ≤ I ∧ 0 ≤ J }
```

```
        if ... then begin
            I := I + 4;
            { 2J+6 ≤ I  ∧  0 ≤ J }
        end else begin
            I := I + 2; J := J + 1;
            { 2J+2 ≤ I  ∧  1 ≤ J }
        end;
        { 2J+2 ≤ I  ∧  6 ≤ I+2J  ∧  0 ≤ J }
    end;
end.
```

Observe that the analysis discovers relations between variables that never appear within the same command. Incidentally, this fact can be used to prove automatically the termination of loops [Hal79]: a new counter is added to the program for each loop which is initialized to zero and incremented by one within the loop body. The analysis will relate its value to that of the other variables of the program. If the value of the counter is bounded on loop exit, then termination is automatically proved. □

7.2 Widenings and Narrowings Can Do for Finite Abstract Domains (or Domains Satisfying the Ascending Chain Condition)

To prove that the widening/narrowing approach is more general than the Galois connection approach, it remains to show that given an infinite domain L, it is always possible to find widening/narrowing operators giving results similar (in precision and speed of convergence) to the ones that could be obtained by approximations of the domain L based upon Galois connections $L \underset{\alpha}{\overset{\gamma}{\leftrightarrows}} \overline{L}$.

Assume that $L(\sqsubseteq, \sqcup)$ is a poset, $F \in L \overset{\text{con}}{\longmapsto} L$ is continuous, $\bot \in L$ is such that $\bot \sqsubseteq F(\bot)$, and $\text{lfp}_{\bot}(F) = \bigsqcup_{n \in \mathbb{N}} F^n(\bot)$ exists (see Prop. 1 in the appendix). Assume as well that $\overline{L}(\overline{\sqsubseteq}, \overline{\sqcup})$ is a poset satisfying the ascending chain condition and $\langle L, \bot, F\rangle \underset{\alpha}{\overset{\gamma}{\leftrightarrows}} \langle \overline{L}, \overline{\bot}, \overline{F}\rangle$. We can assume that $\gamma(\overline{\bot}) = \bot$ since otherwise more precision could be obtained by considering $\overline{L} \cup \{\overline{\bot}\}$ where $\overline{\bot} \notin \overline{L}$ is a new abstract element such that $\gamma(\overline{\bot}) = \bot$ and $\overline{\bot} \,\overline{\sqsubseteq}\, \overline{\bot}$. For simplicity, we can also assume that α is surjective since otherwise by choosing $\overline{L} = \{\alpha(x) \mid x \in L\}$ we could eliminate useless abstract values (these abstract value $\overline{x}$ are useless since they can be replaced by $\alpha \circ \gamma(\overline{x})$ without any loss of information). Consequently, by Prop. 7 in the appendix, $\forall \overline{x} \in \overline{L}$: $\alpha \circ \gamma(\overline{x}) = \overline{x}$. Finally we assume that $\overline{F} = \alpha \circ F \circ \gamma$ which, by Prop. 9 in the appendix, is the most precise $\overline{F}$ among those satisfying $\alpha \circ F \circ \gamma \,\overline{\sqsubseteq}\, \overline{F}$. By (24) and (25), $\overline{F}$ is monotone, hence it is continuous since $\overline{L}$ satisfies the ascending chain condition. Together with Prop. 8 in the appendix, this implies that the increasing chain $\overline{X}^0 = \overline{\bot}, \ldots, \overline{X}^{i+1} = \overline{F}(\overline{X}^i), \ldots$ converges in n steps to the limit $\overline{X}^n = \text{lfp}_{\overline{\bot}}(\overline{F})$, which is the result obtained by the Galois connection approach. The result of the analysis is sound since $\text{lfp}_{\bot}(F) \sqsubseteq \gamma(\overline{X}^n)$. Define the partial widening:

$$\begin{gathered} \nabla \in L \times L \mapsto L \\ x \nabla y = \gamma\big(\alpha(x) \,\overline{\sqcup}\, \alpha(y)\big) \ . \end{gathered} \tag{15}$$

According to (9), the widening approach consists in computing the iteration sequence $X^0 = \bot, \ldots, X^{i+1} =$ if $F(X^i) \sqsubseteq X^i$ then X^i else $X^i \nabla F(X^i), \ldots$ This sequence is well-defined and converges in m steps to $X^m = A$ which is the result obtained by the widening approach. We have $m = n$ and $A = \gamma(\text{lfp}_{\overline{\bot}}(\overline{F}))$ so that both approaches have the same cost and precision (up to $\langle\alpha, \gamma\rangle$ as far as the representation of abstract values is concerned). The proof is as follows:

Proof. First we must show that (15) defines a widening. Observe that if $x, y \in L$ then $\alpha(x) \mathrel{\overline{\sqsubseteq}} \alpha(x) \mathrel{\overline{\sqcup}} \alpha(y)$ by definition of upper bounds so that, by (22) and (25), $x \sqsubseteq \gamma \circ \alpha(x) \sqsubseteq \gamma(\alpha(x) \mathrel{\overline{\sqcup}} \alpha(y)) = x \mathbin{\nabla} y$ proving (6). The same way, (7) holds. Let $x^0 \sqsubseteq x^1 \sqsubseteq \ldots$ be an increasing chain such that $y^0 = x^0, \ldots, y^{i+1} = y^i \mathbin{\nabla} x^{i+1}, \ldots$ is well-defined. By (6) and (24), y^i, $i \in \mathbb{N}$ and x^i, $i \in \mathbb{N}$ hence $\alpha(y^i)$, $i \in \mathbb{N}$ and $\alpha(x^i)$, $i \in \mathbb{N}$ are increasing chains. Since $\overline{L}$ satisfies the ascending chain condition, there exists $\ell' \in \mathbb{N}$ such that $\alpha(y^{\ell'}) = \alpha(y^{\ell'+k})$ for $k \geq \ell'$ and $\ell'' \in \mathbb{N}$ such that $\alpha(x^{\ell''}) = \alpha(x^{\ell'+k})$ for $k \geq \ell''$. So let ℓ be the maximum of ℓ' and ℓ''. For all $k \geq \ell$, we have $\alpha(y^k) = \alpha(y^\ell)$ and $\alpha(x^k) = \alpha(x^\ell)$ so that, by (15), $y^{k+1} = y^k \mathbin{\nabla} x^k = \gamma(\alpha(y^k) \sqcup \alpha(x^k)) = \gamma(\alpha(y^\ell) \sqcup \alpha(x^\ell)) = y^\ell \mathbin{\nabla} x^\ell = y^{\ell+1}$, proving that $\forall k > \ell$: $y^k = y^{\ell+1}$, so that y^i, $i \in \mathbb{N}$ is eventually stable, as required by (8).

Since $\overline{L}$ is a poset, the least upper bound $\overline{\sqcup}$ may not exist in (15). Therefore, we must show that the iteration sequence X^i, $i \in \mathbb{N}$ is well-defined. More precisely, we prove that $\forall n \in \mathbb{N}$: X^n is well-defined such that $\alpha(X^n) \mathrel{\overline{\sqsubseteq}} \alpha(F(X^n))$. For the basis, we have $X^0 \sqsubseteq F(X^0)$ since $X^0 = \bot \sqsubseteq F(\bot)$ whence $\alpha(X^0) \mathrel{\overline{\sqsubseteq}} \alpha(F(X^0))$ by (24). If, by induction hypothesis, X^n is well-defined and such that $\alpha(X^n) \mathrel{\overline{\sqsubseteq}} \alpha(F(X^n))$, then $\alpha(X^n) \mathrel{\overline{\sqcup}} \alpha(F(X^n)) = \alpha(F(X^n))$ exists, whence, by (15), $X^n \mathbin{\nabla} F(X^n) = \gamma(\alpha(X^n) \mathrel{\overline{\sqcup}} \alpha(F(X^n))) = \gamma \circ \alpha(F(X^n))$ is well-defined. If $F(X^n) \sqsubseteq X^n$ then $X^{n+1} = X^n$ whence, by induction hypothesis, X^{n+1} is well-defined such that $\alpha(X^{n+1}) \mathrel{\overline{\sqsubseteq}} \alpha(F(X^{n+1}))$. Otherwise, we have shown that $X^{n+1} = X^n \mathbin{\nabla} F(X^n) = \gamma \circ \alpha(F(X^n))$ is well-defined. Moreover, by (22), induction hypothesis and (25), we have $X^n \sqsubseteq \gamma \circ \alpha(X^n) \sqsubseteq \gamma \circ \alpha(F(X^n)) = X^{n+1}$. From $X^n \sqsubseteq X^{n+1}$, we derive by (26) and continuity, hence monotony of F, (24), (25) that $\alpha(X^{n+1}) = \alpha \circ \gamma \circ \alpha(F(X^n)) = \alpha(F(X^n)) \mathrel{\overline{\sqsubseteq}} \alpha(F(X^{n+1}))$. By recurrence, we conclude that $\forall n \in \mathbb{N}$: X^n is well-defined such that $\alpha(X^n) \mathrel{\overline{\sqsubseteq}} \alpha(F(X^n))$.

We now prove, by recurrence, that $\forall k \in \mathbb{N}$: $\gamma(\overline{X}^k) = X^k$. For the basis, we have $\gamma(\overline{X}^0) = X^0$ since $\gamma(\overline{\bot}) = \bot$. For the induction step, assume $\gamma(\overline{X}^k) = X^k$ so that $\overline{X}^k = \alpha \circ \gamma(\overline{X}^k) = \alpha(X^k)$. If $F(X^k) \not\sqsubseteq X^k$ then $\gamma(\overline{X}^{k+1}) = \gamma(\overline{X}^k \mathrel{\overline{\sqcup}} \overline{X}^{k+1})$ [since $\overline{X}^k \mathrel{\overline{\sqsubseteq}} \overline{X}^{k+1}$] $= \gamma(\overline{X}^k \mathrel{\overline{\sqcup}} \overline{F}(\overline{X}^k))$ [since $\overline{X}^{k+1} = \overline{F}(\overline{X}^k)$] $= \gamma(\overline{X}^k \mathrel{\overline{\sqcup}} \alpha \circ F \circ \gamma(\overline{X}^k))$ [by definition of $\overline{F} = \alpha \circ F \circ \gamma$] $= \gamma(\alpha(X^k) \mathrel{\overline{\sqcup}} \alpha \circ F(X^k))$ [by induction hypothesis] $= X^k \mathbin{\nabla} F(X^k)$ [by (15)] $= X^{k+1}$ [by definition of X^{k+1} when $F(X^k) \not\sqsubseteq X^k$]. Otherwise $F(X^k) \sqsubseteq X^k$ in which case $\gamma(\overline{X}^{k+1}) = \gamma(\overline{F}(\overline{X}^k))$ [by definition of $\overline{X}^{k+1}$] $= \gamma \circ \alpha \circ F \circ \gamma(\overline{X}^k)$ [by definition of $\overline{F}$] $= \gamma \circ \alpha \circ F(X^k)$ [by induction hypothesis] $\sqsubseteq \gamma \circ \alpha(X^k)$ [by $F(X^k) \sqsubseteq X^k$, (24) and (25)] $= \gamma(\overline{X}^k)$ [since $\alpha(X^k) = \overline{X}^k$, by induction hypothesis] $= X^k$ [by induction hypothesis] $= X^{k+1}$ [by (9) when $F(X^k) \sqsubseteq X^k$]. Moreover $\overline{X}^k$, $k \in \mathbb{N}$ is an increasing chain so that $\overline{X}^k \mathrel{\overline{\sqsubseteq}} \overline{X}^{k+1}$ whence $X^k = \gamma(\overline{X}^k) \sqsubseteq \gamma(\overline{X}^{k+1})$ by (25). By antisymmetry, we have $\gamma(\overline{X}^{k+1}) = X^{k+1}$.

Observe that the chain X^k, $k \in \mathbb{N}$ is increasing but not strictly by (8), so that there exists $\ell \in \mathbb{N}$ such that $X^{\ell+1} = X^\ell$. By (9), we have $F(X^\ell) \sqsubseteq X^\ell$ or $X^{\ell+1} = X^\ell \mathbin{\nabla} F(X^\ell) = X^\ell$, whence $F(X^\ell) \sqsubseteq X^\ell$ by (7). So let m be the smallest ℓ such that

$F(X^\ell) \sqsubseteq X^\ell$. The chain $\overline{X}^k$, $k \in \mathbb{N}$ is increasing but not strictly since $\overline{L}$ satisfies the ascending chain condition so let n be the smallest natural such that $\overline{X}^{n+1} = \overline{F}(\overline{X}^n) = \overline{X}^n$.

We have $F(\gamma(\overline{X}^m)) \sqsubseteq \gamma(\overline{X}^m)$ which implies $\alpha(F(\gamma(\overline{X}^m))) \,\overline{\sqsubseteq}\, \overline{X}^m$ that is $\overline{F}(\overline{X}^m)$ $\overline{\sqsubseteq}\, \overline{X}^m$. Since the sequence $\langle \overline{X}^i, i \geq 0 \rangle$ is increasing, we have $\overline{X}^m \,\overline{\sqsubseteq}\, \overline{X}^{m+1} = \overline{F}(\overline{X}^m)$ so that $\overline{F}(\overline{X}^m) = \overline{X}^m$, by antisymmetry. It follows that $n \leq m$. Reciprocally, $\overline{F}(\overline{X}^n)$ $= \overline{X}^n$ so that $\alpha \circ F \circ \gamma(\overline{X}^n) = \overline{X}^n$ whence $F \circ \gamma(\overline{X}^n) \sqsubseteq \gamma(\overline{X}^n)$ by (2) that is $F(X^n)$ $\sqsubseteq X^n$ and therefore $m \leq n$. We conclude $m = n$ and $A = X^m = \gamma(\overline{X}^m) = \gamma(\overline{X}^n)$ $= \gamma(\mathrm{lfp}_{\overline{\bot}}(\overline{F}))$. □

8 Remarks on the Design of Widenings and Narrowings

The design of abstract domains using Galois connections is rather familiar since a great number of examples is available and because it can be presented using a number of equivalent and well understood mathematical objects such as upper closure operators, Moore families, topologies, complete join congruence relations, families of principal ideals (see [CC79b]). On the contrary, the design of widenings and narrowings is often thought off to be more difficult since it appears as an heuristic to cope with induction. The following remarks can help in the design of widenings and narrowings.

■ The rapprochement between the two approaches can be made by observing that whenever a Galois connection $L \underset{\alpha}{\overset{\gamma}{\leftrightarrows}} \overline{L}$ is available and $\overline{L}$ ($\overline{\sqsubseteq}$, $\overline{\sqcup}$) is a join-semi-lattice satisfying the ascending chain condition then a widening $\nabla \in \overline{\overline{L}} \times \overline{\overline{L}} \longmapsto \overline{\overline{L}}$ can be defined on any infinite abstract domain $\overline{\overline{L}}$ ($\overline{\overline{\sqsubseteq}}$) such that $L \underset{\overline{\alpha}}{\overset{\overline{\gamma}}{\leftrightarrows}} \overline{\overline{L}}$ by projection into $\overline{\overline{L}}$ of the least upper bound $\overline{\sqcup}$ defined on $\overline{L}$, as follows:

$$x \nabla y \;=\; \overline{\alpha}\Big(\overline{\gamma}(\alpha \circ \overline{\gamma}(x) \,\overline{\sqcup}\, \alpha \circ \overline{\gamma}(y))\Big) \;. \tag{16}$$

By Prop. 15 in the appendix, if $\overline{\alpha}$ is surjective then (16) defines a widening. In particular, when L is $\overline{\overline{L}}$ so that $\overline{\alpha}$ and $\overline{\gamma}$ are identity functions, we obtain the widening defined in (15). Similarly, if L ($\sqsubseteq$, $\sqcap$) is a meet-semi-lattice and $\overline{L}$ ($\overline{\sqsubseteq}$) is a poset satisfying the descending chain condition, then $\Delta \in L \times L \longmapsto L$ can be defined on L for speeding up the convergence by projection in $\overline{L}$, as follows:

$$x \,\Delta\, y \;=\; x \sqcap \gamma \circ \alpha(y) \;. \tag{17}$$

Proposition 16 in the appendix shows that Δ is a narrowing.

Example 14 (Rule of signs based widening and narrowing for interval analysis). Assume that L is the lattice of intervals and $\overline{L}$ is the lattice of signs $\{\overline{\bot}, 0, -, +, \overline{\top}\}$ [CC79b], such that $\overline{\bot} \,\overline{\sqsubseteq}\, 0 \,\overline{\sqsubseteq}\, - \,\overline{\sqsubseteq}\, \overline{\top}$, $0 \,\overline{\sqsubseteq}\, + \,\overline{\sqsubseteq}\, \overline{\top}$, and $\overline{\gamma}(\overline{\bot}) = \bot$, $\overline{\gamma}(0) = [0, 0]$, $\overline{\gamma}(-) = [-\infty, 0]$, $\overline{\gamma}(+) = [0, +\infty]$, $\overline{\gamma}(\overline{\top}) = [-\infty, +\infty]$. Then (15) becomes:

$$\bot \nabla X = X$$
$$X \nabla \bot = X$$

$$[\ell_0,\ u_0] \nabla [\ell_1,\ u_1] = \text{if } \ell_0 = u_0 = \ell_1 = u_1 = 0 \text{ then } [0,\ 0]$$
$$\text{elsif } (u_0 \leq 0) \wedge (u_1 \leq 0) \text{ then } [-\infty,\ 0]$$
$$\text{elsif } (0 \leq \ell_0) \wedge (0 \leq \ell_1) \text{ then } [0,\ +\infty]$$
$$\text{else } [-\infty,\ +\infty]\ .$$

Similarly, (17) becomes:

$$\bot \Delta X = \bot$$
$$X \Delta \bot = \bot$$
$$[\ell_0,\ u_0] \Delta [\ell_1,\ u_1] = [\text{if } \ell_0 \leq 0 \leq \ell_1 \text{ then } 0 \text{ else } \ell_0,$$
$$\text{if } u_1 \leq 0 \leq u_0 \text{ then } 0 \text{ else } u_0]\ .$$ □

Another example of application of (16) and (17) for boolean-based abstract interpretations of higher-order functional languages such as strictness analysis is given by [HH90]. However the restriction to a finite lattice $\overline{L}$ is unfortunate since expressiveness can be severely restricted without necessary speed up since only the length of strictly increasing and decreasing chains has to be taken into account. The use of (15) and (17) with finite lattices $\overline{L}$ should be understood as a last resort since the power of the widening/narrowing approach relies on the ability to extrapolate to infinitely many distinct abstract values for all programs but to a finite number only for any given program.

■ The results obtained using an infinite domain with a widening can be worse than those obtained using a finite domain corresponding to a coarser Galois connection. This is the case for example when using intervals with widening (13) which can give worse results than those obtained by application of the rule of signs [CC79b], as shown by the following:

Example 15 On loose widenings.

```
program S;
   var X : integer;
begin
   X := 1;
   while ... do begin
      { X1 }
      if ... then
         X := X + 1
      else
         X := 0;
     { X2 }
   end;
end.
```

The following system of approximate equations on intervals for program S:

$$X_1 = F_1(X_2) = [1,\ 1] \sqcup X_2$$
$$X_2 = F_2(X_1) = (X_1 \oplus [1,\ 1]) \sqcup [0,\ 0]$$

can be solved iteratively using widening (13), as follows:

$$\begin{aligned}
&\hat{X}_1^0 = \bot \\
&\hat{X}_2^0 = \bot \\
&\hat{X}_1^1 = \hat{X}_1^0 \mathbin{\nabla} F_1(\hat{X}_2^0) = [1,\ 1] \\
&\hat{X}_2^1 = F_2(\hat{X}_1^1) = [0,\ 2] \\
&\hat{X}_1^2 = \hat{X}_1^1 \mathbin{\nabla} F_1(\hat{X}_2^1) = [1,\ 1] \mathbin{\nabla} [0,\ 2] = [-\infty,\ +\infty] \\
&\hat{X}_2^2 = F_2(\hat{X}_1^2) = [-\infty,\ +\infty]\ .
\end{aligned}$$

The system of approximate equations on signs for program **S**:

$$\begin{aligned}
X_1 &= F_1(X_2) = + \sqcup X_2 \\
X_2 &= F_2(X_1) = (X_1 \oplus +) \sqcup 0
\end{aligned}$$

can be solved iteratively as follows:

$$\begin{aligned}
&\hat{X}_1^0 = \bot \\
&\hat{X}_2^0 = \bot \\
&\hat{X}_1^1 = F_1(\hat{X}_2^0) = + \\
&\hat{X}_2^1 = F_2(\hat{X}_1^1) = + \\
&\hat{X}_1^2 = F_1(\hat{X}_2^1) = + \\
&\hat{X}_2^2 = F_2(\hat{X}_1^2) = +
\end{aligned}$$

and this yields better results, that is $\mathtt{X} \in [0,\ +\infty]$. □

The remedy is very simple and consists in using a widening that does not lose more information than the Galois connection.

Example 16 On reducing the loss of information by widening. The widening (13) and narrowing (14) can be improved to give results always better than the rule of signs analysis, as follows:

$$\begin{aligned}
\bot \mathbin{\nabla} X &= X \qquad\qquad (18)\\
X \mathbin{\nabla} \bot &= X \\
[\ell_0,\ u_0] \mathbin{\nabla} [\ell_1,\ u_1] &= [\text{if } 0 \le \ell_1 < \ell_0 \text{ then } 0 \text{ elsif } \ell_1 < \ell_0 \text{ then } -\infty \text{ else } \ell_0, \\
&\qquad \text{if } \mathrm{u}_0 < \mathrm{u}_1 \le 0 \text{ then } 0 \text{ elsif } \mathrm{u}_0 < \mathrm{u}_1 \text{ then } +\infty \text{ else } \mathrm{u}_0] \\
\bot \mathbin{\Delta} X &= \bot \qquad\qquad (19)\\
X \mathbin{\Delta} \bot &= \bot \\
[\ell_0,\ u_0] \mathbin{\Delta} [\ell_1,\ u_1] &= [\text{if } (\ell_0 \le 0 \le \ell_1) \vee (\ell_0 = -\infty) \text{ then } \ell_1 \text{ else } \ell_0, \\
&\qquad \text{if } (\mathrm{u}_1 \le 0 \le \mathrm{u}_0) \vee (\mathrm{u}_0 = +\infty) \text{ then } \mathrm{u}_1 \text{ else } \mathrm{u}_0]\ .
\end{aligned}$$

The widening (18) extrapolates unstable bounds to zero or infinity whereas the narrowing (19) improves these bounds. Other bounds such as -1 and $+1$ or even declared bounds might also be taken into account in these definitions. The iterates are now:

$$\begin{aligned}
\hat{X}_1^0 &= \bot \\
\hat{X}_2^0 &= \bot \\
\hat{X}_1^1 &= \hat{X}_1^0 \nabla F_1(\hat{X}_2^0) = [1,\ 1] \\
\hat{X}_2^1 &= F_2(\hat{X}_1^1) = [0,\ 2] \\
\hat{X}_1^2 &= \hat{X}_1^1 \nabla F_1(\hat{X}_2^1) = [1,\ 1] \nabla [0,\ 2] = [0,\ +\infty] \\
\hat{X}_2^2 &= F_2(\hat{X}_1^2) = [0,\ +\infty]\ .
\end{aligned}$$

Another solution is to alternate the collection of bounds on one iteration and the extrapolation of the unstable ones by widening on the next iteration. □

■ A suggestion for designing widenings and narrowings consists in using least upper bounds/greatest lower bounds as long as the iterates follow finite chains in the lattice $\overline{L}$ and in extrapolating as soon as some iterate belongs to an infinite chain.

Example 17 (Widening for congruence analysis). Let us come back to the lattice $\overline{L} = \{\bot,\ \top\} \cup (\mathbb{Q} \times \mathbb{Q})$ considered in Ex. 12 for discovering arithmetical congruences of the form $x \equiv p[q]$. The widening proposed by [Gra91b] is:

$$p_0 + q_0\mathbb{Z} \nabla p_1 + q_1\mathbb{Z} = \text{if } 0 \neq |q_0| \neq |q_1| \neq 0 \text{ then } \overline{\top} \text{ else } p_0 + q_0\mathbb{Z} \sqcup p_1 + q_1\mathbb{Z} \tag{20}$$

where the least upper bound is defined by:

$$p_0 + q_0\mathbb{Z} \sqcup p_1 + q_1\mathbb{Z} = p_0 + \gcd(q_0,\ q_1,\ p_0 - p_1)\mathbb{Z}\ .$$

The idea is that extrapolation is necessary only when the modulus of the congruence class is not constant through consecutive iterates. □

■ The general idea of widenings is to eliminate unstable components through consecutive iterates (or through all previous iterates, which is equivalent, up to the choice of a different abstract domain which would allow for the accumulation of successive iterates in a single abstract value). Hence a very brute force widening would be:

$$x \nabla y = \text{if } y \sqsubseteq x \text{ then } x \text{ else } \overline{\top}\ .$$

Similarly, a naïve narrowing consists in immediately stopping the decreasing iteration sequence:

$$x \Delta y = x\ .$$

The above definitions prove that widenings and narrowings always exist, but this is not a convincing argument. Therefore the idea can always be softened by introducing a *extrapolation threshold* under which the least upper bound $\overline{\sqcup}$ or greatest lower bound $\overline{\sqcap}$ is used and above which extrapolation is enforced. A simple way to do this is to limit the number of exact iterations to some given positive integer n, as follows (abstract values are extended to pairs so as to memorize the number of iterations):

$$\begin{aligned}\langle x, i\rangle \,\overline{\nabla}\, \langle y, i+1\rangle &= \text{if } y \sqsubseteq x \text{ then } \langle x, i+1\rangle \\ &\quad\ \text{elsif } i \le n \text{ then } \langle x \sqcup y, i+1\rangle \\ &\quad\ \text{else } \langle x \nabla y, i+1\rangle \\ \langle x, i\rangle \,\overline{\Delta}\, \langle y, i+1\rangle &= \text{if } i \le n \text{ then } \langle x \sqcap y, i+1\rangle \\ &\quad\ \text{else } \langle x \Delta y, i+1\rangle\ .\end{aligned}$$

Example 18 (Widening for congruence analysis, continued). Following this idea of extrapolation threshold, [Gra91b] proposes to improve the widening (20) as follows:

$$\begin{aligned}p_0 + q_0\mathbb{Z} \nabla p_1 + q_1\mathbb{Z} &= \text{if } (0 \neq |q_0| \neq |q_1| \neq 0) \wedge (|q_0| < r) \\ &\quad\ \text{then } \overline{\top} \\ &\quad\ \text{else } p_0 + q_0\mathbb{Z} \sqcup p_1 + q_1\mathbb{Z}\ .\end{aligned}$$

The idea is that extrapolation is necessary only when the modulus is not constant and less than some fixed rational number $r > 0$, which, for example, can be chosen equal to 1 or to some modulus encountered during the first iterates. □

9 Using Widenings to Solve Convergence Problems Left Open in the Literature

Numerous program analysis methods can be found in the literature which can be easily generalized by expressing them as abstract interpretations. Non-convergence problems which are dodged by resorting to restricted classes of programs or to human interaction can be solved using widenings. We consider two examples.

9.1 Simple Sections

Balasundaram and Kennedy [BK89] use simple sections to provide a compact representation of commonly encountered array access shapes in Fortran programs. A *simple section* for program variables $x_1, \ldots, x_n$ is either $\emptyset$ (such that $\gamma(\emptyset) = \text{false}$) or a pair $\langle \ell, u\rangle$ representing the predicate:

$$\begin{aligned}\gamma(\langle \ell, u\rangle) = \quad & \bigwedge_{i=1}^{n} \ell_i \le x_i \le u_i \\ & \wedge \bigwedge_{i=1}^{n} \bigwedge_{j=1,\, j\neq i}^{n} \ell_{ij}^{+} \le x_i + x_j \le u_{ij}^{+} \\ & \wedge \bigwedge_{i=1}^{n} \bigwedge_{j=1,\, j\neq i}^{n} \ell_{ij}^{-} \le x_i - x_j \le u_{ij}^{-}\end{aligned}$$

where the ℓ_i, u_i, ℓ^+_{ij}, u^+_{ij}, ℓ^-_{ij}, u^-_{ij} belong to $\mathbb{Z}^\infty = \mathbb{Z} \cup \{-\infty, +\infty\}$.

Since Balasundaram and Kennedy consider only relationships between loop indices in Fortran programs that consist of a sequence of perfectly-nested DO-loops in which all subroutines calls are expanded inline, they can infer the loop invariants directly from the program text ([BK89], page 47). This solves the convergence problem but for a very particular class of programs only.

The simple sections analysis can be generalized to arbitrary programs using the framework of abstract interpretation. One obtains a slight extension of interval analysis [CC76] and a very restricted form of linear invariants [CH78]. To do this it is formally sufficient to specify the corresponding Galois connection (which is uniquely determined by the function γ above) as well as the widening operator:

$$\emptyset \nabla \langle \ell, u \rangle = \langle \ell, u \rangle$$
$$\langle \ell, u \rangle \nabla \emptyset = \langle \ell, u \rangle$$
$$\langle \ell, u \rangle \nabla \langle \ell', u' \rangle = \langle \ell'', u'' \rangle$$

where, x standing for one of the ℓ_i, ℓ^+_{ij}, ℓ^-_{ij}, x' for ℓ'_i, $\ell^{+\prime}_{ij}$, $\ell^{-\prime}_{ij}$ and x'' for the corresponding ℓ''_i, $\ell^{+\prime\prime}_{ij}$, $\ell^{-\prime\prime}_{ij}$, and similarly y, y', y'' standing for bounds in u, u' and u'', we have:

$$x'' = \text{if } x' < x \text{ then } -\infty \text{ else } x$$
$$y'' = \text{if } y' > y \text{ then } +\infty \text{ else } y$$

and the narrowing operator:

$$\emptyset \Delta \langle \ell, u \rangle = \emptyset$$
$$\langle \ell, u \rangle \Delta \emptyset = \emptyset$$
$$\langle \ell, u \rangle \Delta \langle \ell', u' \rangle = \langle \ell'', u'' \rangle$$

where:

$$x'' = \text{if } x = -\infty \text{ then } x' \text{ else } x$$
$$y'' = \text{if } y = +\infty \text{ then } y' \text{ else } y\ .$$

Again more precision can be obtained by widening or narrowing to -1, 0, 1 and bounds given by declarations of scalar variables of subrange type or arrays.

The step size of each loop index variable is ignored when computing simple sections. As noticed by [BK89], "this is an inadequacy in the simple section representation". A simple way to cope with this problem is to combine simple sections with arithmetical congruences [Gra89, Gra91b].

9.2 Deriving Constraints on the Sizes of Data Structures

van Gelder [vG90] proposes a method for deriving constraints among argument sizes in logic programs: the set of possible n-tuples of arguments of a logic procedure is approximated by the set of tuples of the sizes of these data structures which in turn is approximated by the polyhedron which is the convex hull of these points in $\mathbb{R}^n$

so as to obtain an invariant in form of a conjunction of inequalities proven to hold among the argument sizes. He shows that this invariant can be defined as a fixpoint of an operator associated with the logic program and observes that the iteration process to compute this fixpoint may not converge in finitely many steps. Therefore he proposes "an heuristic which often works" else resorts to human interaction, verifies experimentally that fixpoints are difficult to guess, therefore indicates in his "directions for further work" that "we need more ways to generate candidates for the fixpoint" and concludes that "there is still much work to be done in the automatic analysis of argument term size constraints".

Thinking in terms of abstract interpretation, a major step towards this goal was taken by [CC77a] who observed that post-fixpoints are upper approximations of the least fixpoint (as shown by Prop. 10 in the appendix) and that post-fixpoints are much easier to compute than fixpoints. Another major step towards this goal was taken by [CC76, CC77a] who used a widening/narrowing approach to enforce convergence of the iterates. As far as linear inequalities are concerned, one can choose the widening proposed in [CH78] and further improved in [Hal79] as follows:

If P_1 and P_2 are two polyhedra in $\mathbb{R}^n$, respectively defined by two sets of linear inequalities $S_1 = \{\beta_1, \beta_2, \ldots, \beta_n\}$ and $S_2 = \{\gamma_1, \gamma_2, \ldots, \gamma_m\}$ then

$$P_1 \nabla P_2 = S_1{}' \cup S_2' \tag{21}$$

where:

- $S_1{}'$ is the subset of S_1 consisting of all inequalities β_i which are satisfied by all points of P_2;
- $S_2{}'$ is the subset of S_2 such that: $\gamma_i \in S_2{}'$ if and only if there exists $\beta_j \in S_1$ such that $(S_1 - \{\beta_j\}) \cup \{\gamma_i\}$ defines the same polyhedron than P_1.

Observe that this widening also mitigates the non-existence of least upper bounds (the circle is the limit of inscribed polygons), see [CC92b].

Example 19 (Widening for linear inequality analysis). If $P_1 = \{\langle x, y\rangle \in \mathbb{R}^2 \mid 0 \leq x \leq 1 \wedge y = 0\}$ and $P_2 = \{\langle x, y\rangle \in \mathbb{R}^2 \mid x \leq 2 \wedge 0 \leq y \wedge y \leq x\}$ then $S_1 = \{0 \leq x, x \leq 1, y \leq 0, 0 \leq y\}$ and $S_2 = \{x \leq 2, 0 \leq y, y \leq x\}$. The extremal points of P_2 are $\langle 0, 0\rangle$, $\langle 2, 0\rangle$ and $\langle 2, 2\rangle$. They only satisfy the constraints $0 \leq x$ and $0 \leq y$ in S_1 so that $S_1' = \{0 \leq x, 0 \leq y\}$. The constraint $0 \leq x$ of S_1 can be replaced by $y \leq x$ without changing P_1. The constraint $0 \leq y$ appears in S_1 and S_2. The constraint $x \leq 2$ can replace no constraint in S_1 without changing P_1. It follows that $S_2' = \{0 \leq y, y \leq x\}$. We have $S_1' \cup S_2' = \{0 \leq x, 0 \leq y, y \leq x\}$ where the constraint $0 \leq x$ is redundant. Consequently, $P_1 \nabla P_2 = \{\langle x, y\rangle \in \mathcal{R}^2 \mid 0 \leq y \leq x\}$. □

A simple narrowing is obtained by limiting the length of the decreasing iteration sequence to some $k \geq 1$ (experience shows that $k > 1$ often brings no significant improvement).

Example 20 (Argument size analysis). The logic procedure below [vG90] might test for precedence in some partial order, thinking of s as successor:

$$\begin{array}{l} p(X, X) \\ p(X, s(Y)) \leftarrow p(X, Y) \ . \end{array}$$

Knowing that size(c) = 0 if c is a constant and that size$(s(Y)) = 1 + \text{size}(Y)$, the constraints among argument sizes of predicate p are upper approximations to the least solution of the fixpoint equation:

$$p = F(p) = \{\langle x, y\rangle \in \mathbb{R}^2 \mid x \geq 0 \wedge y \geq 0 \wedge ((x = y) \vee \langle x, y-1\rangle \in p)\}$$

which can be effectively computed by the following iteration sequence with widening (21):

$$\begin{aligned}
p^0 &= \emptyset \\
p^1 &= p^0 \nabla F(p^0) = \emptyset \nabla F(p^0) = F(p^0) = \{\langle x, y\rangle \in \mathbb{R}^2 \mid 0 \leq x = y\} \\
p^2 &= p^1 \nabla F(p^1) \\
&= \{\langle x, y\rangle \in \mathbb{R}^2 \mid 0 \leq x = y\} \nabla \{\langle x, y\rangle \in \mathbb{R}^2 \mid 0 \leq x \leq y \leq x+1\} \\
&= \{\langle x, y\rangle \in \mathbb{R}^2 \mid 0 \leq x \leq y\}
\end{aligned}$$

which is such that $F(p^2) = p^2$. □

Let us conclude with [vG90] that "the method may be applicable to other languages in which the sizes of data structures can be determined syntactically" and refer to chapter 7.3 of [Hal79] for examples illustrating this point of view.

10 Conclusion

The widening/narrowing approach [CC77a] to abstract interpretation, which is more powerful than the popular variations on the Galois connection approach [CC77a], deserves to be better understood since it can significantly improve the precision of the analyses as well as the speed of convergence including in the case of finite lattices which too large for the fixpoint finding problem to be tractable. Our practical experience is that the combination of the two approaches using infinite abstract domains is worthwhile.

Acknowledgments. We thank P. Granger and C. Hankin for their comments on a first version of this paper.

References

[AH87] S. Abramsky and C. Hankin, editors. *Abstract Interpretation of Declarative Languages.* Computers and their Applications. Ellis Horwood, Chichester, U.K., 1987.

[BJCD87] M. Bruynooghe, G. Janssens, A. Callebaut, and B. Demoen. Abstract interpretation: towards the global optimization of Prolog programs. In *Proceedings of the 1987 International Symposium on Logic Programming*, San Francisco, California, pages 192–204. IEEE Computer Society Press, Los Alamitos, California, August 31–September 4, 1987.

[BK89] V. Balasundaram and K. Kennedy. A technique for summarizing data access and its use in parallelism enhancing transformations. In *SIGPLAN'89 Conference on Programming Language Design and Implementation*, pages 41–53, Portland, Oregon, June 21–23, 1989.

[Bou90] F. Bourdoncle. Interprocedural abstract interpretation of block structured languages with nested procedures, aliasing and recursivity. In P. Deransart and Małuszyński, editors, *Proceedings of the International Workshop PLILP'90, Programming Language Implementation and Logic Programming*, Linköping, Sweden, Lecture Notes in Computer Science 456, pages 307–323. Springer-Verlag, Berlin, Germany, August 20–22, 1990.

[Bou92] F. Bourdoncle. Abstract interpretation by dynamic partitioning. *Journal of Functional Programming*, 1992. (to appear).

[CC76] P. Cousot and R. Cousot. Static determination of dynamic properties of programs. In *Proceedings of the 2nd International Symposium on Programming*, pages 106–130. Dunod, Paris, France, 1976.

[CC77a] P. Cousot and R. Cousot. Abstract interpretation: a unified lattice model for static analysis of programs by construction or approximation of fixpoints. In *Conference Record of the 4th ACM Symposium on Principles of Programming Languages*, pages 238–252, Los Angeles, California, 1977.

[CC77b] P. Cousot and R. Cousot. Static determination of dynamic properties of recursive procedures. In E.J. Neuhold, editor, *IFIP Conference on Formal Description of Programming Concepts*, St-Andrews, N.B., Canada, pages 237–277. North-Holland Pub. Co., Amsterdam, the Netherlands, 1977.

[CC79a] P. Cousot and R. Cousot. Constructive versions of Tarski's fixed point theorems. *Pacific Journal of Mathematics*, 82(1):43–57, 1979.

[CC79b] P. Cousot and R. Cousot. Systematic design of program analysis frameworks. In *Conference Record of the 6th ACM Symposium on Principles of Programming Languages*, pages 269–282, San Antonio, Texas, 1979.

[CC92a] P. Cousot and R. Cousot. Abstract interpretation and application to logic programs. *Journal of Logic Programming*, 13(2–3), 1992. (to appear).

[CC92b] P. Cousot and R. Cousot. Abstract interpretation frameworks. *Journal of Logic and Computation*, 1992. (to appear).

[CC92c] P. Cousot and R. Cousot. Inductive definitions, semantics and abstract interpretation. In *Conference Record of the 19th ACM Symposium on Principles of Programming Languages*, pages 83–94, Albuquerque, New Mexico, 1992.

[CH78] P. Cousot and N. Halbwachs. Automatic discovery of linear restraints among variables of a program. In *Conference Record of the 5th ACM Symposium on Principles of Programming Languages*, pages 84–97, Tucson, Arizona, 1978.

[Cou78] P. Cousot. *Méthodes itératives de construction et d'approximation de points fixes d'opérateurs monotones sur un treillis, analyse sémantique de programmes.* Thèse d'état ès sciences mathématiques, Université scientifique et médicale de Grenoble, Grenoble, France, 21 March 1978.

[Cou81] P. Cousot. Semantic foundations of program analysis. In S. S. Muchnick and N. D. Jones, editors, *Program Flow Analysis: Theory and Applications*, chapter 10, pages 303–342. Prentice-Hall, Inc., Englewood Cliffs, New Jersey, 1981.

[Deu92] A. Deutsch. A storeless model of aliasing and its abstraction using finite representations of right-regular equivalence relations. In *Proceedings of the 1992 International Conference on Computer Languages*, Oakland, California, pages 2–13. IEEE Computer Society Press, Los Alamitos, California, April 20–23, 1992.

[Gra89] P. Granger. Static analysis of arithmetical congruences. *International Journal of Computer Mathematics*, 30:165–190, 1989.

[Gra91a] P. Granger. *Analyses sémantiques de congruence.* Thèse de l'école Polytechnique en informatique, LIX, École Polytechnique, Palaiseau, France, 12 July 1991.

[Gra91b] P. Granger. Static analysis of linear congruence equalities among variables of a program. In S. Abramsky and T.S.E. Maibaum, editors, *TAPSOFT'91, Proceed-*

ings of the International Joint Conference on Theory and Practice of Software Development, Brighton, U.K., Volume 1 (CAAP'91), Lecture Notes in Computer Science 493, pages 169–192. Springer-Verlag, Berlin, Germany, 1991.

[Hal79] N. Halbwachs. *Détermination automatique de relations linéaires vérifiées par les variables d'un programme.* Thèse de 3ème cycle d'informatique, Université scientifique et médicale de Grenoble, Grenoble, France, 12 March 1979.

[HH90] C. Hankin and S. Hunt. Approximate fixed points in abstract interpretation. In B. Krieg-Brückner, editor, *Proceedings of the 4th European Symposium on Programming, ESOP '92*, pages 219–232. Springer-Verlag, Berlin, Germany, Rennes, France, February 26–28 1990.

[JB92] G. Janssens and M. Bruynooghe. On abstracting the procedural behaviour of logic programs. In A. Voronkov, editor, *Proceedings of the First Russian Conference on Logic Programming, Irkutsk, Russia, September 14–18, 1990 and of the Second Russian Conference on Logic Programming, St. Petersburg, Russia, September 11-16, 1991*, pages 240–262. Springer-Verlag, Berlin, Germany, 1992.

[KN87] R. B. Kieburtz and M. Napierala. Abstract semantics. In S. Abramsky and C. Hankin, editors, *Abstract Interpretation of Declarative Languages*, chapter 7, pages 143–180. Ellis Horwood, Chichester, U.K., 1987.

[MS88] K. Marriott and H. Søndergaard. On describing success patterns of logic programs. Technical Report 88/12, Department of Computer Science, University of Melbourne, Melbourne, Australia, 1988.

[Myc80] A. Mycroft. The theory and practice of transforming call-by-need into call-by-value. In B. Robinet, editor, *Proceedings of the Fourth International Symposium on Programming*, Paris, France, 22-24 April 1980Lecture Notes in Computer Science 83, pages 270–281. Springer-Verlag, Berlin, Germany, 1980.

[Str88] J. Stransky. *Analyse sémantique de structures de données dynamiques avec application au cas particulier de langages LISPiens.* Thèse de doctorat en science, Université de Paris-sud, Orsay, 28 June 1988.

[vEK76] M. H. van Emden and R. A. Kowalski. The semantics of predicate logic as a programming language. *Journal of the Association for Computing Machinary*, 23(4):733–742, October 1976.

[vG90] A. van Gelder. Deriving constraints among argument sizes in logic programs. In *Proceedings of the 9th ACM Symposium on Principles of Database Systems*, pages 47–60, Nashville, Tennesse, 1990.

Appendix

A *preorder* is a preordered set $L(\sqsubseteq)$ where $\sqsubseteq \in \wp(L \times L)$ is reflexive ($\forall x \in L : x \sqsubseteq x$) and transitive ($\forall x, y, z \in L$: $(x \sqsubseteq y \wedge y \sqsubseteq z) \Longrightarrow x \sqsubseteq z$). A *poset* is a preorder $L(\sqsubseteq)$ where $\sqsubseteq$ is antisymmetric ($\forall x, y \in L$: $(x \sqsubseteq y \wedge y \sqsubseteq x) \Longrightarrow x = y$). An *upper bound* u of $X \subseteq L$ is such that $\forall x \in X : x \sqsubseteq u$. The *least upper bound*, written $\sqcup X$ is an upper bound such that for all upper bounds u, $\sqcup X \sqsubseteq u$. When it exists, the least upper bound $\sqcup X$ is unique, by antisymmetry. A *strict* poset has an *infimum* $\perp$ such that $\forall x \in L : \perp \sqsubseteq x$. A *cpo* is a *complete* poset i.e., such that any $\mathbb{N}$-termed sequence $c_i \in L$, $i \in \mathbb{N}$, which is an *increasing chain* (i.e., $\forall i \in \mathbb{N} : c_i \sqsubseteq c_{i+1}$) has a least upper bound $\bigsqcup_{i \in \mathbb{N}} c_i$. A *complete lattice* is a poset such that every subset $X \subseteq L$ has a least upper bound $\sqcup X$ and a greatest lower bound $\sqcap X$. A map $F \in L \xrightarrow{\text{mon}} L$ is *monotone* i.e. $x \sqsubseteq y$ implies $F(x) \sqsubseteq F(y)$. It is *continuous* (written $F \in L \xrightarrow{\text{con}} L$)

if and only if $F(\bigsqcup_{i\in\mathbb{N}} c_i) = \bigsqcup_{i\in\mathbb{N}} F(c_i)$ for all increasing chains $c_i \in L$, $i \in \mathbb{N}$ such that the least upper bound $\bigsqcup_{i\in\mathbb{N}} c_i$ exists. Continuity implies monotony.

Proposition 1 (Kleene fixpoint theorem). *If $L(\sqsubseteq, \sqcup)$ is a poset, $F \in L \overset{\text{con}}{\longmapsto} L$ is continuous, and $\bot \in L$ is such that $\bot \sqsubseteq F(\bot)$*[10]*, then $F^n(\bot)$, $n \in \mathbb{N}$ is an increasing chain. If $\bigsqcup_{n\in\mathbb{N}} F^n(\bot)$ exists*[11]*, then it is the least fixpoint $\mathrm{lfp}_\bot(F)$ of F greater than or equal to $\bot$.*

Proposition 2 (Characteristic property of Galois connections). *If $L(\sqsubseteq)$ and $\overline{L}(\overline{\sqsubseteq})$ are posets, then (2) is equivalent to:*

$$\forall x \in L : x \sqsubseteq \gamma \circ \alpha(x) \text{ and} \tag{22}$$

$$\forall \overline{x} \in \overline{L} : \alpha \circ \gamma(\overline{x}) \overline{\sqsubseteq} \overline{x} \text{ and} \tag{23}$$

$$\alpha \in L \overset{\text{mon}}{\longmapsto} \overline{L} \quad \text{and} \tag{24}$$

$$\gamma \in \overline{L} \overset{\text{mon}}{\longmapsto} L\,. \tag{25}$$

Proposition 3 (Functional Galois connection). *If $L(\sqsubseteq)$ and $\overline{L}(\overline{\sqsubseteq})$ are posets, and $\alpha \in L \longmapsto \overline{L}$ and $\gamma \in \overline{L} \longmapsto L$ satisfy (2), then (4) implies (5).*

Proposition 4 (Function approximation). *If $L(\sqsubseteq)$ and $\overline{L}(\overline{\sqsubseteq})$ are posets, $F \in L \overset{\text{mon}}{\longmapsto} L$ and $\overline{F} \in \overline{L} \overset{\text{mon}}{\longmapsto} \overline{L}$ are monotone, then (2) and (4) imply that $\vec{\alpha}(F) \overline{\sqsubseteq} \overline{F}$ is equivalent to $F \circ \gamma \sqsubseteq \gamma \circ \overline{F}$, or to $\alpha \circ F \overline{\sqsubseteq} \overline{F} \circ \alpha$.*

Proposition 5 (Least upper bounds inducing). *If $L(\sqsubseteq, \sqcup)$ and $\overline{L}(\overline{\sqsubseteq}, \overline{\sqcup})$ are posets such that $L \underset{\alpha}{\overset{\gamma}{\leftrightarrows}} \overline{L}$ is a Galois connection, $X \subseteq L$, and $\sqcup X$ exists, then $\overline{\bigsqcup}_{x\in X} \alpha(x)$ exists and is equal to $\alpha(\sqcup X)$.*

Proposition 6 (Connection property). *If $L(\sqsubseteq)$ and $\overline{L}(\overline{\sqsubseteq})$ are posets such that $L \underset{\alpha}{\overset{\gamma}{\leftrightarrows}} \overline{L}$ is a Galois connection, then:*

$$\alpha \circ \gamma \circ \alpha = \alpha \tag{26}$$

$$\gamma \circ \alpha \circ \gamma = \gamma\,. \tag{27}$$

Proposition 7 (Galois surjection). *If $L(\sqsubseteq)$ and $\overline{L}(\overline{\sqsubseteq})$ are posets such that $L \underset{\alpha}{\overset{\gamma}{\leftrightarrows}} \overline{L}$ is a Galois connection, then α is surjective if and only if $\forall \overline{x} \in \overline{L}$: $\alpha \circ \gamma(\overline{x}) = \overline{x}$.*

Proposition 8 (Fixpoint abstraction). *If $L(\sqsubseteq, \sqcup)$ is a cpo, $\overline{L}(\overline{\sqsubseteq}, \overline{\sqcup})$ is a poset*[12]*, $L \underset{\alpha}{\overset{\gamma}{\leftrightarrows}} \overline{L}$ is a Galois connection, $F \in L \overset{\text{con}}{\longmapsto} L$ is continuous, $\bot \in L$ is such that $\bot \sqsubseteq F(\bot)$, and $\vec{\alpha}$ is defined by (4), then $\mathrm{lfp}_\bot(F) \sqsubseteq \gamma(\overline{A})$ where the least upper bound $\overline{A} = \overline{\bigsqcup}_{n\in\mathbb{N}} \vec{\alpha}(F)^n(\alpha(\bot))$ of the increasing chain $\vec{\alpha}(F)^n(\alpha(\bot))$, $n \in \mathbb{N}$ exists and is such than $\overline{A} \overline{\sqsubseteq} \vec{\alpha}(F)(\overline{A}) \overline{\sqsubseteq} \overline{x}$ whenever $\overline{\bot} \overline{\sqsubseteq} \overline{x} = \vec{\alpha}(F)(\overline{x})$. In particular, if $\vec{\alpha}(F) \in \overline{L} \overset{\text{con}}{\longmapsto} \overline{L}$, then $\overline{A} = \mathrm{lfp}_{\alpha(\bot)}(\vec{\alpha}(F))$, but this equality does not hold in general*[13]*.*

---

[10] If this is not true and L is a lattice, we can iterate with $\lambda X \cdot X \sqcup F(X)$ instead.

[11] This is the case when $L(\sqsubseteq, \sqcup)$ is a cpo.

[12] Not necessarily a cpo, see [CC92b] for even weaker hypotheses.

[13] But it does by considering transfinite iterates.

Proposition 9 (Fixpoint abstract approximation). *If $L(\sqsubseteq, \sqcup)$ is a cpo, $\overline{L}(\overline{\sqsubseteq}, \overline{\sqcup})$ is a poset, $L \underset{\alpha}{\overset{\gamma}{\leftrightarrows}} \overline{L}$ is a Galois connection, $F \in L \overset{\text{con}}{\longmapsto} L$ is continuous, $\bot \in L$ is such that $\bot \sqsubseteq F(\bot)$, $\vec{\alpha}$ is defined by (4), $\overline{F} \in \overline{L} \longmapsto \overline{L}$ is such that $\vec{\alpha}(F) \overline{\sqsubseteq} \overline{F}$ for the pointwise ordering $\overline{\sqsubseteq}$, $\overline{\bot} \in \overline{L}$ is such that $\alpha(\bot) \overline{\sqsubseteq} \overline{\bot}$, and $\overline{A} \in \overline{L}$ is such that $\forall n \in \mathbb{N}: \overline{F}^n(\overline{\bot}) \overline{\sqsubseteq} \overline{A}$, then,* $\text{lfp}_\bot(F) \sqsubseteq \gamma\left(\overline{\bigsqcup}_{n\in\mathbb{N}} \vec{\alpha}(F)^n(\alpha(\bot))\right) \sqsubseteq \gamma(\overline{A})$.

Proposition 10 (Approximation by postfixpoints). *If $L(\sqsubseteq, \sqcup)$ is a poset, $F \in L \overset{\text{con}}{\longmapsto} L$ is continuous, $\bot \in L$ is such that $\bot \sqsubseteq F(\bot)$, $\bigsqcup_{n\in\mathbb{N}} F^n(\bot)$ exists, and $A \in L$ is such that $\bot \sqsubseteq A$ and $F(A) \sqsubseteq A$, then* $\text{lfp}_\bot(F) \sqsubseteq A$.

Proposition 11 (Upward iteration sequence with widening). *If $L(\sqsubseteq, \sqcup)$ is a cpo, $F \in L \overset{\text{con}}{\longmapsto} L$ is continuous, $\bot \in L$ is such that $\bot \sqsubseteq F(\bot)$, $\nabla \in L \times L \longmapsto L$ satisfies (6), (7) and (8), then the upward iteration sequence with widening $\hat{X}^n$, $n \in \mathbb{N}$ defined by (9) is ultimately stationary and its limit $\hat{A}$ is such that* $\text{lfp}_\bot F \sqsubseteq \hat{A}$ *and $F(\hat{A}) \sqsubseteq \hat{A}$.*

Proposition 12 (Downward iteration sequence with narrowing). *If $L(\sqsubseteq, \sqcup)$ is a cpo, $F \in L \overset{\text{con}}{\longmapsto} L$ is continuous, $\bot \in L$ is such that $\bot \sqsubseteq F(\bot)$, $\Delta \in L \times L \longmapsto L$ satisfies (10) and (11), then the downward iteration sequence with narrowing $\check{X}^n$, $n \in \mathbb{N}$ defined by (12), where* $\text{lfp}_\bot F \sqsubseteq \hat{A}$ *and $F(\hat{A}) \sqsubseteq \hat{A}$, is ultimately stationary and all terms $\check{X}^n$, $n \in \mathbb{N}$ are such that* $\text{lfp}_\bot F \sqsubseteq F(\check{X}^n) \sqsubseteq \check{X}^n$.

Proposition 13 (Preordered upward iteration with widening). *If $L(\sqsubseteq, \sqcup)$ is a poset, $F \in L \overset{\text{con}}{\longmapsto} L$ is continuous, $\bot \in L$ is such that $\bot \sqsubseteq F(\bot)$, $\bigsqcup_{n\in\mathbb{N}} F^n(\bot)$ exists, $\overline{L}$ is a set, $\gamma \in \overline{L} \longmapsto L$, $\overline{\sqsubseteq}$ is the preorder defined by $x \overline{\sqsubseteq} y \overset{\text{def}}{=} \gamma(x) \sqsubseteq \gamma(y)$, $\overline{\bot} \in \overline{L}$ is such that $\bot \sqsubseteq \gamma(\overline{\bot})$, $\overline{F} \in \overline{L} \overset{\text{mon}}{\longmapsto} \overline{L}$ is such that $F \circ \gamma \sqsubseteq \gamma \circ \overline{F}$ and $\nabla \in \overline{L} \times \overline{L} \longmapsto \overline{L}$ satisfies (6), (7) and (8) (where $\sqsubseteq$, $\bot$ and F are respectively $\overline{\sqsubseteq}$, $\overline{\bot}$ and $\overline{F}$) then the upward iteration sequence with widening (9) is ultimately stationary with limit $\hat{A}$ such that* $\text{lfp}_\bot(F) \sqsubseteq \gamma(\hat{A})$ *and $\overline{F}(\hat{A}) \overline{\sqsubseteq} \hat{A}$.*

Proposition 14 (Preordered downward iteration with narrowing). *If $L(\sqsubseteq, \sqcup)$ is a poset, $F \in L \overset{\text{con}}{\longmapsto} L$ is continuous, $\bot \in L$ is such that $\bot \sqsubseteq F(\bot)$, $\bigsqcup_{n\in\mathbb{N}} F^n(\bot)$ exists, $\overline{L}$ is a set, $\gamma \in \overline{L} \longmapsto L$, $\overline{\sqsubseteq}$ is the preorder defined by $x \overline{\sqsubseteq} y \overset{\text{def}}{=} \gamma(x) \sqsubseteq \gamma(y)$, $\overline{\bot} \in \overline{L}$ is such that $\bot \sqsubseteq \gamma(\overline{\bot})$, $\overline{F} \in \overline{L} \overset{\text{mon}}{\longmapsto} \overline{L}$ is such that $F \circ \gamma \sqsubseteq \gamma \circ \overline{F}$ and $\Delta \in \overline{L} \times \overline{L} \longmapsto \overline{L}$ satisfies (10) and (11) where $\sqsubseteq$ is $\overline{\sqsubseteq}$, then the downward iteration sequence with narrowing $\check{X}^n$, $n \in \mathbb{N}$ defined by (12) where F is $\overline{F}$,* $\text{lfp}_\bot(F) \sqsubseteq \gamma(\hat{A})$ *and $\overline{F}(\hat{A}) \overline{\sqsubseteq} \hat{A}$, is ultimately stationary and all terms $\check{X}^n$, $n \in \mathbb{N}$ are such that* $\text{lfp}_\bot F \sqsubseteq \gamma(\check{X}^n)$ *and $\overline{F}(\check{X}^n) \overline{\sqsubseteq} \check{X}^n$.*

Proposition 15 (Widening inducing). *Let $L(\sqsubseteq)$ and $\overline{\overline{L}}(\overline{\overline{\sqsubseteq}})$ be posets and $\overline{L}(\overline{\sqsubseteq}, \overline{\sqcup})$ be a join-semi-lattice satisfying the ascending chain condition, such that $L \underset{\alpha}{\overset{\gamma}{\leftrightarrows}} \overline{L}$, $L \underset{\overline{\alpha}}{\overset{\overline{\gamma}}{\leftrightarrows}} \overline{\overline{L}}$ and $\overline{\alpha}$ is surjective. Then $\nabla \in \overline{\overline{L}} \times \overline{\overline{L}} \longmapsto \overline{\overline{L}}$ defined by (16) is a widening on $\overline{\overline{L}}$. (6) and (7) may not hold when $\overline{\alpha}$ is not surjective.*

Proposition 16 (Narrowing inducing). *if L $(\sqsubseteq, \sqcap)$ is a meet-semi-lattice and $\overline{L}$ $(\overline{\sqsubseteq})$ is a poset satisfying the descending chain condition then $\Delta \in L \times L \longmapsto L$ defined by (17) is a narrowing satisfying (10) and (11).*

This article was processed using the LaTeX macro package with LLNCS style

Derivation of Linear Size Relations by Abstract Interpretation

Kristof Verschaetse* and Danny De Schreye**

Department of Computer Science, K.U.Leuven,
Celestijnenlaan 200A, B-3001 Heverlee, Belgium.
e-mail : {kristof,dannyd}@cs.kuleuven.ac.be

Abstract. We propose an automated method for deriving *linear size relations*. Linear size relations are linear relations (the solutions of a system of linear equations) over the natural numbers. We associate one such relation to each predicate occurring in a given pure definite logic program. The linear size relation is a linear overestimation of the relation that exists between the sizes (with respect to some given norm) of the arguments of atoms in the least Herbrand model for the given predicate.
Size relations have been studied before and were often referred to as interargument relations. The main contribution of this paper is that our method for deriving the relations is presented as an application of abstract interpretation. Its abstract domain consists of affine subspaces or linear varieties, and the basic operations (procedure entry, procedure exit, etc.) are expressed in terms of operations from linear algebra. Applications of the technique are situated in e.g. automatic termination analysis and the specialisation of constraints in a constraint logic language.

1 Introduction

Recently, a lot of research has been devoted towards obtaining good estimations of the relationship between the sizes of the arguments of a predicate. Most of this research has been going on in the context of deriving automatic termination proofs for logic programs.

Ullman and Van Gelder [21] seem to have been the first to address the problem thoroughly. They define *interargument inequalities* of the form $p_i + c \geq p_j$, where p_i and p_j are *argument designators* denoting the *list-length* of the i-th and j-th argument of a predicate p. The constant c represents an integer offset. They present also a polynomial time algorithm for computing these inequalities.

Plümer [19] extends their results by allowing more general *linear norms* to measure the size of an argument and by taking more than two argument positions into account. His *linear predicate inequalities* are of the form $\sum_{i \in I} p_i + c \geq \sum_{j \in J} p_j$, where the offset $c \in \mathbb{Z} \cup \{\infty\}$ and I and J denote respectively a set of input and a set of output positions.

In [24] we proposed *linear interargument relations*, which are defined as a relation of natural numbers: $\{(p_1, \ldots, p_n) \in \mathbb{N}^n \mid c_0 + c_1 p_1 + \cdots + c_n p_n = 0\}$, with

* Partly supported by Esprit BRA Compulog and by RFO/AI/02 (Belgium).
** Supported by the Belgian National Fund for Scientific Research.

$c_0, c_1, \ldots, c_n \in \mathbb{Z}$. The relations are found by solving linear systems of equations. In contrast to the two previous approaches, coefficients can take any integer value, which of course extends the technique. However, the replacement of inequalities by equality, forms a restriction.

Another restriction is the fact that only one linear constraint $c_0 + c_1p_1 + \cdots + c_np_n = 0$ is allowed. Consider the following program.

Example 1.

$$p([], [], [0], [], [], []).$$
$$p([X|A], [X|B], [Y|C], [Y|D], [Z, Z|E], [Z|F]) \leftarrow p(A, B, C, D, E, F).$$

The predicate $p/6$ succeeds when called with its 6 arguments instantiated as ground lists, such that the first and second list are identical, the third list is obtained from the fourth list by adding a zero to the end, and the fifth list is obtained from the sixth list by repeating each element twice.

The corresponding linear interargument relation cannot be expressed by means of one linear constraint (without loosing too much precision). Instead, a conjunction of constraints is needed:

$$\{(p_1, p_2, p_3, p_4, p_5, p_6) \in \mathbb{N}^6 \mid p_1 = p_2, p_3 = p_4 + 1, p_5 = 2p_6\}.$$

The current paper deals with this type of interargument relation. We here refer to them as *linear size relations.* We present an automatic technique for deriving linear size relations. This technique is an application of *abstract interpretation.* The use of this generic tool for static analysis has the advantage that proving the correctness of our technique can be done by verifying that its abstract domain satisfies certain conditions and by proving the correctness of a small number of abstract operations. We will rely on the generic abstract interpretation framework of M. Bruynooghe [3] for the development of the application and we assume familiarity with it.

Applications of the technique are situated in various tools for static program analysis, such as the already mentioned automatic termination provers. Also in constraint logic programming, interesting applications seem feasible.

In the next section, we present some preliminaries on norms and size relations. In section three, we describe the abstract domain for the analysis. Section four contains our basic abstract operations. We conclude by pointing to related work in the field. Due to space restrictions, all proofs have been omitted. We refer to [23] and [25] for full details.

2 Preliminaries on Norms and Size Relations

In this section we briefly recall (see e.g. [24]) how the "size" of terms can be measured. Then, we describe what is meant by a *linear size relation.* The main idea is to transform a given program into an abstract version, in which only relevant information — namely so-called *size expressions* — is retained. Abstract programs are interpreted as defining relations between natural numbers. Hence, models of abstract programs are considered as sets of n-tuples of natural numbers. Such a model also forms a non-Herbrand model for the original program.

The extended Herbrand Universe, U_P^E, and the extended Herbrand Base, B_P^E, associated to a program P, were introduced in [11]. They are defined as follows. Let $Term_P$ and $Atom_P$ denote the sets of respectively all terms and all atoms that can be constructed from the alphabet underlying to P. The variant relation, denoted $\approx$, defines an equivalence. U_P^E and B_P^E are respectively the quotient sets $Term_P/\approx$ and $Atom_P/\approx$. For any term t (or atom A), we denote its class in U_P^E (B_P^E) as $\bar{t}$ ($\bar{A}$). However, in order to reduce notational complexity, we drop the bars when no real confusion is possible.

The "size" of a term is found by using *norms*.

Definition 1 (norm). A *norm* is a mapping $||.|| : U_P^E \to \mathbb{N}$.

Several examples of norms can be found in the literature. When dealing with lists, it is often appropriate to use *list-length*, which gives the depth of the rightmost branch in the tree representation of a list and 0 for any other term. A more general norm is *term-size*, which counts the number of function symbols in a term. Another frequently used norm is *term-depth*, which gives the maximum depth of (the tree representation of) a term. Of special interest are *semi-linear* norms (see [2]). Let us recall their definition.

Definition 2 (semi-linear norm; see [2]).
A norm $||.||$ is *semi-linear* if it can be defined recursively by means of the following schema:

$$\begin{array}{lll} ||V|| & = 0 & \text{if } V \text{ is a variable, and} \\ ||f(t_1,\ldots,t_n)|| & = c + \sum_{k\in I} ||t_k|| & \text{where } c \in \mathbb{N}, I \subseteq \{1,\ldots,n\} \\ & & \text{and } c, I \text{ depend only on } f/n. \end{array}$$

Examples of semi-linear norms are *list-length* and *term-size*. A notable exception is *term-depth*.

Concrete terms in a program are usually interpreted in the Herbrand universe. The idea is now to replace these terms by so-called *size expressions*, which are first order terms in the language $\mathcal{L}_{<0,1;+;\leq>}$, which consists of two constant symbols, the infix operator $+/2$ and the relational symbol $\leq/2$, in addition to the set of variables in the first order language of the given program. Terms in the language $\mathcal{L}_{<0,1;+;\leq>}$ are defined as usual. We use the shorthand form $3X + Y + 2$ to denote the term $X + Y + 1 + X + 1 + X$. The symbol $\mathcal{S}_{<0,1;+;\leq>}$ is used to represent the set of all terms in $\mathcal{L}_{<0,1;+;\leq>}$. Size expressions are interpreted in $\mathbb{N}_{+;\leq}$ where $+$ is the usual addition on natural numbers and $\leq$ is the usual order relation. The constants 0 and 1 are interpreted as the natural numbers 0 and 1.

Definition 3 (size expression).
Let $||.||$ be any semi-linear norm. A term t is mapped to the *size expression* $abs_{||.||}(t)$ by means of the function $abs_{||.||} : Term_P \to \mathcal{S}_{<0,1;+;\leq>}$, which is defined as:

$$\begin{array}{lll} abs_{||.||}(V) & = V & \text{if } V \text{ is a variable} \\ abs_{||.||}(f(t_1,\ldots,t_n)) & = c + abs_{||.||}(t_{i_1}) + \cdots + abs_{||.||}(t_{i_m}) & \text{otherwise,} \end{array}$$

where $c \in \mathbb{N}$, $I = \{i_1,\ldots,i_m\}$, c, I depend only on f/n and are the same as in the definition of $||.||$ (see definition 2).

Example 2.
Let $||.||_l$ denote *list-length*. Then $abs_{||.||_l}([X, f(Y)|T]) = T + 2$.
Let $||.||_t$ denote the *term-size* norm. Then $abs_{||.||_t}([X, f(Y)|T]) = X + Y + T + 3$.

In the same way as a size expression forms an abstract version of a concrete term, the abstract counterpart of an atom can be defined as well. Take an atom $p(t_1, \ldots, t_n)$, then $abs_{||.||}(p(t_1, \ldots, t_n))$ is defined as $p_{||.||}(abs_{||.||}(t_1), \ldots, abs_{||.||}(t_n))$ where $p_{||.||}/n$ is a fresh predicate symbol. Abstract literals, clauses, procedures and programs are defined in a straightforward way.

Example 3 (append/3).
Consider the well-known program defining append/3.

append$([], L, L)$.
append$([H|S], T, [H|U]) \leftarrow$ append(S, T, U).

Let $||.||_t$ denote the *term-size* norm. The abstract procedure for append/3 is

append$_{||.||_t}(0, L, L)$.
append$_{||.||_t}(H + S + 1, T, H + U + 1) \leftarrow$ append$_{||.||_t}(S, T, U)$.

For each predicate p/n, the corresponding abstract predicate $p_{||.||}/n$ defines a relation on $\mathbb{N}^n$. As an example, the predicate append$_{||.||_t}/3$ defines the relation $\{(x, y, z) \mid x + y = z\}$.

The semantics of the concrete and the abstract relations are linked by the following property. M_P denotes the least Herbrand model of P.

Proposition 4. *For all* $p(t_1, \ldots, t_n) \in M_P$: $(||t_1||, \ldots, ||t_n||) \in p_{||.||}$.

Abstract programs define relations between natural numbers. These relations must be seen as relations between the sizes of the arguments of all atoms in the least Herbrand model of the corresponding concrete programs. The least Herbrand model of the append/3 example contains all triples of ground lists such that the third list is found as the concatenation of the first and the second list. The abstract append$_{||.||_t}/3 = \{(x, y, z) \in \mathbb{N}^3 \mid x + y = z\}$ is a linear relation. However, in general the relation can be nonlinear (see [25] for an example). We will not try to compute such nonlinear relations explicitly; instead, we compute *linear size relations*, which form safe approximations (superrelations).

Definition 5 (linear size relation).
Given is a program P and a predicate p of arity n in P. The corresponding abstract predicate is denoted as $p_{||.||}$. A *linear size relation*, L_p, for p/n is a relation

$$\{(x_1, \ldots, x_n) \in \mathbb{N}^n \mid (x_1, \ldots, x_n) \text{ is a solution of a system of linear equations}\},$$

such that $p_{||.||} \subseteq L_p$.

There are two special linear size relations according to the above definition.

1. $L_p = \emptyset$ corresponds to all unsolvable systems of equations, and
2. $L_p = \mathbb{R}^n$ corresponds to the empty system of equations.

3 The Abstract Domain

A linear size relation is characterised by means of a system of linear equations. Although we are only interested in natural solutions, we will implicitly work with real[3] numbers. One linear equation corresponds to a hyperplane (i.e. an $(n-1)$-dimensional affine subspace) in the n-dimensional space. A system of linear equalities corresponds to the intersection of the hyperplanes that form part of the system. Obviously, different systems can have the same set of solutions. So, we need a canonical form, which is supplied by the so-called *row-echelon form.* Let us explain this in more details (see a.o. [13] and [20] for more details on linear algebra).

An *affine subspace* or *linear variety* corresponds to the solution set of a nonhomogeneous system of linear equations, which may conveniently be represented as $\bar{A} \cdot \bar{X} = \bar{c}$, where $\bar{A}$ is a $m \times n$ matrix of real numbers, $\bar{X}$ is a $n \times 1$ column vector of variables and $\bar{c}$ is a $m \times 1$ column vector of real numbers. Solving the system is done by considering the *augmented matrix* $\left[\bar{A}\,|\bar{c}\right]$ and reducing this matrix to the equivalent and canonical *row-echelon form.* This form is characterised by (a_{ij} occurs on the ith row and jth column in $\bar{A}$) (1) the first non-zero entry in a row (if any) is 1, (2) for any row i_0, let j_0 be the first column with a non-zero entry, then for all $i > i_0, j \leq j_0, a_{ij} = 0$, and (3) for any row i_0, let j_0 be the first non-zero entry, then for all $i < i_0$, $a_{ij_0} = 0$. The reduced row-echelon form is obtained by repeated application of one of three row operations (multiplication of a row by a non-zero scalar, addition of one row to another row, or permutation of two rows). Zero-rows are omitted. If row m of a reduced matrix $\bar{A}$ is zero ($a_{mj} = 0$ for all $j = 1, \ldots, n$), but $c_m \neq 0$, then the system is unsolvable, and we say that the corresponding affine subspace is empty.

The following operations on affine subspaces will turn out to be very useful.

Intersection: The intersection of two affine subspaces is again an affine subspace. In other words, the intersection of the sets of solutions of two systems of linear equations is the set of solutions of the combined system of equations. Hence, the intersection of $\bar{A}_1 \cdot \bar{X} = \bar{c}_1$ and $\bar{A}_2 \cdot \bar{X} = \bar{c}_2$, is obtained by reducing the augmented matrix

$$\left[\begin{array}{c|c} \bar{A}_1 & \bar{c}_1 \\ \bar{A}_2 & \bar{c}_2 \end{array}\right]$$

to row-echelon form. The intersection is empty if the corresponding system is unsolvable.

Disjunction: Unfortunately, the union of two affine subspaces is not an affine subspace anymore. Translated to geometry, the union of the intersections of hyperplanes cannot always be expressed as the intersection of a set of hyperplanes. Let $\bar{A}_1 \cdot \bar{X} = \bar{c}_1$ and $\bar{A}_2 \cdot \bar{X} = \bar{c}_2$ denote two systems of linear equations. Karr [15] gives a technique for computing the "most precise" system of equations such that its solution set contains the solution sets of the two given systems. Given the augmented matrices $\left[\bar{A}_1\,|\bar{c}_1\right]$ and $\left[\bar{A}_2\,|\bar{c}_2\right]$, his algorithm computes an augmented matrix $\left[\bar{A}\,|\bar{c}\right]$ such that every solution for the system $\bar{A}_1 \cdot \bar{X} = \bar{c}_1$ or $\bar{A}_2 \cdot \bar{X} = \bar{c}_2$ is also a solution for the system $\bar{A} \cdot \bar{X} = \bar{c}$.

[3] Rational numbers would do as well.

Example 4. Consider the following two systems of equations:

$$\left\{\begin{matrix} X=0 \\ Y=1 \end{matrix}\right\} \text{ and } \left\{\begin{matrix} X=1 \\ Y=0 \end{matrix}\right\},$$

or in matrix notation:

$$\begin{bmatrix} 1\,0 \\ 0\,1 \end{bmatrix} \cdot \begin{bmatrix} X \\ Y \end{bmatrix} = \begin{bmatrix} 0 \\ 1 \end{bmatrix} \text{ and } \begin{bmatrix} 1\,0 \\ 0\,1 \end{bmatrix} \cdot \begin{bmatrix} X \\ Y \end{bmatrix} = \begin{bmatrix} 1 \\ 0 \end{bmatrix}.$$

The augmented matrices are respectively:

$$\left[\begin{array}{c|c} 1\,0 & 0 \\ 0\,1 & 1 \end{array}\right] \text{ and } \left[\begin{array}{c|c} 1\,0 & 1 \\ 0\,1 & 0 \end{array}\right].$$

Given the two above matrices, the algorithm of Karr [15] computes $\left[\begin{array}{c|c} 1\,1 & 1 \end{array}\right]$. This matrix corresponds to the hyperplane $x+y=1$, which contains both $(1,0)$ and $(0,1)$, and is the least hyperplane doing so.

Restriction: Suppose that the system $\bar{A}\cdot\bar{X}=\bar{c}$ is in reduced row-echelon form ($\bar{A}$ is an $m\times n$-matrix). Frequently, we will need an operator mapping the system $\bar{A}\cdot\bar{X}=\bar{c}$ to another system $\bar{A}_r\cdot\bar{X}_r=\bar{c}_r$ ($\bar{A}_r$ is an $m'\times(n-k)$-matrix), such that

$$\exists x_1,\ldots,x_k\in\mathbb{R}:(x_1,\ldots,x_k,x_{k+1},\ldots,x_n) \text{ is a solution of } \bar{A}\cdot\bar{X}=\bar{c}$$
$$\Updownarrow$$
$$(x_{k+1},\ldots,x_n) \text{ is a solution of } \bar{A}_r\cdot\bar{X}_r=\bar{c}_r$$

We call this operation *restriction.* A simple technique to obtain the desired result is by considering the system[4]

$$\bar{A}\cdot\begin{bmatrix} X_1 \\ \vdots \\ X_k \\ X_{k+1} \\ \vdots \\ X_n \end{bmatrix}=\bar{c}.$$

Since this system is in row-echelon form, it can be written as

$$\begin{cases} a_{11}X_1 &= c_1 - a_{12}X_2 - \cdots - a_{1k}X_k - a_{1,k+1}X_{k+1} - \cdots - a_{1n}X_n \\ &\vdots \\ a_{kk}X_k &= c_k - a_{k,k+1}X_{k+1} - \cdots - a_{kn}X_n \\ a_{k+1,k+1}X_{k+1} &= c_{k+1} - a_{k+1,k+2}X_{k+2} - \cdots - a_{k+1,n}X_n \\ &\vdots \\ a_{n,n}X_n &= c_n \end{cases}$$

[4] In practice, the columns of $\bar{A}$ should be reordered, depending on which X_i are omitted.

with $a_{ii} \in \{0,1\}$ and $a_{ij} \in \mathbb{R}$ $(j > i)$. Observe that X_i $(i = k+1,\ldots,n)$ does not depend on any X_j $(j = 1,\ldots,k)$. So, omitting one of the equations with an X_j $(j = 1,\ldots,k)$ at the left-hand side does not alter the solution set for the variables $\{X_{k+1},\ldots,X_n\}$. Hence, the restriction of the system $\bar{A}\cdot\bar{X} = \bar{c}$ is found by first removing any row containing a first non-zero entry at position p $(1 \leq p \leq k)$, and then removing the first k columns.

Extension: The converse of restriction is *extension*. We want an operation mapping a system of linear equations $\bar{A}\cdot\bar{X} = \bar{c}$ to another system $\bar{A}_e\cdot\bar{X}_e = \bar{c}_e$ such that

$$(x_1,\ldots,x_k) \text{ is a solution of } \bar{A}\cdot\bar{X} = \bar{c}$$
$$\Updownarrow$$
$$\forall x_{k+1},\ldots,x_n \in \mathbb{R} : (x_1,\ldots,x_k,x_{k+1},\ldots,x_n) \text{ is a solution of } \bar{A}_e\cdot\bar{X}_e = \bar{c}_e$$

This operation comes down to adding $n-k$ columns of 0's to $\bar{A}$ and adding k rows consisting of a single 0 to $\bar{c}$.

We are now in a position to give the representation of an abstract substitution and to define its meaning.

Definition 6 (abstract substitution).
An abstract substitution β is syntactically represented by means of a system of linear equations, $\bar{A}\cdot\bar{X} = \bar{c}$, where:

- $\bar{A}$ is an $m \times n$ matrix in reduced row-echelon form,
- $\bar{X}$ is an $n \times 1$ column vector of the set of variables $\{X_1,\ldots,X_n\}$, which is called *the domain of the abstract substitution*,
- $\bar{c}$ is an $m \times 1$ column vector of real numbers.

In addition, we allow two extra syntactic constructs, $\bot$ and $\top$.

The semantics of an abstract substitution β is specified by means of the *concretisation function* γ.

Definition 7 (concretisation function).
We take a fixed semi-linear norm $||.||$. Let $\beta \equiv \bar{A}\cdot\bar{X} = \bar{c}$ be an abstract substitution and θ a concrete substitution $\{X_1 \leftarrow t_1,\ldots,X_n \leftarrow t_n\}$, with the same domain. For simplicity, we assume that a free variable X_i is represented as $X_i \leftarrow X_i$. Then $\theta \in \gamma(\beta)$, if and only if, for any substitution σ: $(||t_1\sigma||,\ldots,||t_n\sigma||)$ is a solution of $\bar{A}\cdot\bar{X} = \bar{c}$. In addition, $\gamma(\bot) = \emptyset$ and $\gamma(\top)$ is the set of all concrete substitutions with $\{X_1,\ldots,X_n\}$ as their domain.

We extend the meaning of γ to $\gamma(F\beta) = \{F\theta \mid \theta \in \gamma(\beta)\}$, where F is any formula. The presence of the substitutions σ in the definition of γ is to ensure that the abstract domain is closed under substitution, i.e. if $t' \in \gamma(t\beta)$, then for any σ, $t'\sigma \in \gamma(t\beta)$. This facilitates some of the subsequent operations.

One can easily define a partial order over the set of abstract substitutions. Intuitively, we say that one abstract substitution is smaller than another one, if the solution set of the latter system contains all solutions of the first system. Formally, given two abstract substitutions $\beta_1 \equiv \bar{A}_1\cdot\bar{X} = \bar{c}_1$ and $\beta_2 \equiv \bar{A}_2\cdot\bar{X} = \bar{c}_2$ (both abstract substitutions have the same domain), $\beta_1 \leq \beta_2$ if and only if

- $\beta_2 = \top$, or
- $\beta_1 = \bot$, or
- the intersection of $\bar{A}_1 \cdot \bar{X} = \bar{c}_1$ and $\bar{A}_2 \cdot \bar{X} = \bar{c}_2$ equals $\bar{A}_1 \cdot \bar{X} = \bar{c}_1$.

It is easy to verify that $\beta_1 \leq \beta_2$ if and only if $\gamma(\beta_1) \subseteq \gamma(\beta_2)$. Naturally, $\bot$ is minimal with respect to this order relation, while $\top$ is maximal.

Suppose β, β_1 and β_2 denote abstract substitutions on the same domain. The least upper bound of β_1 and β_2 is defined as follows.

- $\text{lub}(\beta, \top) = \text{lub}(\top, \beta) = \top$,
- $\text{lub}(\beta, \bot) = \text{lub}(\bot, \beta) = \beta$,
- $\text{lub}(\beta_1, \beta_2) = \beta$ with $\beta_1, \beta_2 \notin \{\top, \bot\}$, $\beta_1 \equiv \bar{A}_1 \cdot \bar{X} = \bar{c}_1$, $\beta_2 \equiv \bar{A}_2 \cdot \bar{X} = \bar{c}_2$, $\beta \equiv \bar{A} \cdot \bar{X} = \bar{c}$, and $\bar{A} \cdot \bar{X} = \bar{c}$ is the disjunction of $\bar{A}_1 \cdot \bar{X} = \bar{c}_1$ and $\bar{A}_2 \cdot \bar{X} = \bar{c}_2$.

The following property holds:

$$\gamma(\text{lub}(\beta_1, \beta_2)) \supseteq \gamma(\beta_1) \cup \gamma(\beta_2).$$

Similarly, a *greatest lower bound* (glb) is found by using intersection.

- $\text{glb}(\beta, \top) = \text{glb}(\top, \beta) = \beta$,
- $\text{glb}(\beta, \bot) = \text{glb}(\bot, \beta) = \bot$,
- $\text{glb}(\beta_1, \beta_2) = \beta$ with $\beta_1, \beta_2 \notin \{\top, \bot\}$, $\beta_1 \equiv \bar{A}_1 \cdot \bar{X} = \bar{c}_1$, $\beta_2 \equiv \bar{A}_2 \cdot \bar{X} = \bar{c}_2$, $\beta \equiv \bar{A} \cdot \bar{X} = \bar{c}$, and $\bar{A} \cdot \bar{X} = \bar{c}$ is the intersection of $\bar{A}_1 \cdot \bar{X} = \bar{c}_1$ and $\bar{A}_2 \cdot \bar{X} = \bar{c}_2$.

This finishes the description of the abstract domain. An important property is that it does not contain infinitely ascending chains.

Proposition 8. *There are no infinitely ascending chains of abstract substitutions $\beta_0 < \beta_1 < \beta_2 < \cdots$, where all β_i have the same domain and are defined as described in definition 6.*

4 The Abstract Operations

As stated in the introduction, we assume familiarity with the framework for abstract interpretation presented in [3]. In this section, we provide an automatic technique for computing linear size relations. This technique is presented as an instance of abstract interpretation. There are essentially two ways in which one can use abstract interpretation for this task. One can either apply abstract interpretation to the original program or to its corresponding abstract version. The difference only shows up during the abstract interpretation of the builtins, since we assume that all programs are written in normal form. We will discuss both approaches.

4.1 Initialisation

The initialisation operation adorns the root of the abstract And/Or-graph with an abstract call substitution. The concretisation function gives the corresponding set of concrete call substitutions that is considered. In many cases, we will start with

$\top$ as initial abstract call substitution, since we are usually interested in the relation that holds between the sizes of *all* possible success substitutions.

In the latter case, the abstract success substitutions that are obtained, are precisely linear size relations for the corresponding predicates. Linear size relations are declarative statements, since they are defined in terms of the least Herbrand model of a program. On the other hand, abstract substitutions are typically procedural information, since they are computed as the result of an abstract interpretation procedure, which simulates SLD-resolution. Due to completeness of SLD-resolution, the abstract success substitution safely approximates the (ground) correct answer substitution and therefore (by definition) produces correct linear size relations.

4.2 Procedure Entry

By only considering programs in *normal* form, we can assume that procedure headings and calls (except builtins) are in the form $p(X_1, \ldots, X_k)$, with all X_j $(1 \leq j \leq k)$ distinct variables. Consider a call $p(X_1, \ldots, X_k)$ and let $\{X_1, \ldots, X_n\}$ denote the set of all variables in the clause where $p(X_1, \ldots, X_k)$ occurs in $(k \leq n)$. Suppose the abstract substitution $\beta_{in} \equiv \bar{A} \cdot \bar{X} = \bar{c}$ (with $\bar{A}$ an $m \times n$ matrix) denotes a set of call substitutions for $p(X_1, \ldots, X_k)$.

The *procedure entry* operation is quite simple: it only involves a restriction of the domain, a renaming of the variables in the substitution, and an extension of the domain. Suppose that the following clause is used:

$$p(Y_1, \ldots, Y_k) \leftarrow B_1, \ldots, B_m,$$

and suppose further that $Y_{k+1}, \ldots, Y_l$ $(l \geq k)$ are the other variables occurring in this clause. The *procedure entry* operation is done in three steps.

1. An intermediate abstract substitution β_{in}^r is computed. Let $\beta_{in} \equiv \bar{A} \cdot \bar{X} = \bar{c}$ be as described above, then $\beta_{in}^r \equiv \bar{A}' \cdot \bar{X}' = \bar{c}'$ is obtained by applying the restriction operator (the domain of β_{in}^r, $\bar{X}'$, consists of the variables $X_1, \ldots, X_k$).
2. The domain of β_{in}^r is renamed; the resulting substitution is $\beta_{in}' \equiv \bar{A}' \cdot \bar{Y}' = \bar{c}'$, where $\bar{Y}'$ consists of the variables $Y_1, \ldots, Y_k$.
3. The abstract call substitution for the leftmost atom B_1 is computed by using the extension operator. Let $\beta_{in}^1 \equiv \bar{A}_1 \cdot \bar{Y}_1 = \bar{c}_1$ denote this abstract substitution. The extended domain $\bar{Y}_1$ consists of the variables $Y_1, \ldots, Y_k, \ldots, Y_l$.

Proposition 9 (correctness of the procedure entry operation).
The procedure entry *operation satisfies the correctness condition: if $\tau \in \gamma(\beta_{in})$ and if $p(X_1, \ldots, X_k)\tau$ and $p(Y_1, \ldots, Y_k)$ have most general unifier θ, then*

$$(p(Y_1, \ldots, Y_k) \leftarrow B_1, \ldots, B_m)\theta \in \gamma((p(Y_1, \ldots, Y_k) \leftarrow B_1, \ldots, B_m)\beta_{in}^1).$$

4.3 Procedure Exit

Consider again a call $p(X_1, \ldots, X_k)$ with abstract call substitution $\beta_{in} \equiv \bar{A} \cdot \bar{X} = \bar{c}$. Suppose $\{X_1, \ldots, X_n\}$ is the set of variables in the clause in which $p(X_1, \ldots, X_k)$

occurs ($k \leq n$). The domain of β_{in} is

$$\bar{X} = \begin{bmatrix} X_1 \\ \vdots \\ X_n \end{bmatrix}.$$

Suppose there are m clauses defining p/k:

$$p(Y_1^j, \ldots, Y_k^j) \leftarrow B_1^j, \ldots, B_{q_j}^j,$$

and let $\{Y_1^j, \ldots, Y_k^j, Y_{k+1}^j, \ldots, Y_{l_j}^j\}$ ($j = 1, \ldots, m$) denote the corresponding sets of variables in such a clause.

For each rightmost atom $B_{q_j}^j$, an abstract success substitution $\beta_{out}^j \equiv \bar{A}_j \cdot \bar{Y}_j = \bar{c}_j$ has already been computed. The domain of this abstract substitution is

$$\bar{Y}_j = \begin{bmatrix} Y_1^j \\ \vdots \\ Y_{l_j}^j \end{bmatrix}.$$

The *procedure exit* operation computes the abstract substitution $\beta_{out} \equiv \bar{A}_{out} \cdot \bar{X} = \bar{c}_{out}$. This computation is done in three steps.

1. For all $j = 1, \ldots, m$, β_{out}^j is restricted to the variables $\{Y_1^j, \ldots, Y_k^j\}$ by applying the restriction operator. So, we obtain $\bar{A}_j^r \cdot \bar{Y}_j' = \bar{c}_j^r$, where

$$\bar{Y}_j' = \begin{bmatrix} Y_1^j \\ \vdots \\ Y_k^j \end{bmatrix}.$$

2. Each abstract substitution $\bar{A}_j^r \cdot \bar{Y}_j' = \bar{c}_j^r$ is renamed to $\bar{A}_j^r \cdot \bar{X}' = \bar{c}_j^r$, with

$$\bar{X}' = \begin{bmatrix} X_1 \\ \vdots \\ X_k \end{bmatrix}.$$

   As a result one obtains m abstract substitutions over the same domain. By taking the least upper bound, one abstract substitution $\bar{A}' \cdot \bar{X}' = \bar{c}'$ is obtained.
3. Finally, $\bar{A}' \cdot \bar{X}' = \bar{c}'$ is extended into $\beta_{out} \equiv \bar{A}_{out} \cdot \bar{X} = \bar{c}_{out}$. This is done by first extending $\bar{A}' \cdot \bar{X}' = \bar{c}'$, such that an intermediate abstract substitution $\beta' \equiv \bar{A}_e \cdot \bar{X} = \bar{c}_e$ is obtained. By taking $glb(\beta_{in}, \beta')$, one finally obtains β_{out}.

Proposition 10 (correctness of procedure exit).
*Suppose $p(X_1, \ldots, X_k)$ occurs in a clause $H \leftarrow B_1, \ldots, p(X_1, \ldots, X_k), \ldots, B_q$. Take $\tau_j \in \gamma(\beta_j^{out})$ and suppose there exist substitutions τ_{in} and θ such that $\tau_{in} \in \gamma(\beta_{in})$ and $p(X_1, \ldots, X_k)\tau_{in}\theta = p(Y_1^j, \ldots, Y_k^j)\tau_j$, and θ does not contain variables that occur in $(H \leftarrow B_1, \ldots, p(X_1, \ldots, X_k), \ldots, B_q)\tau_{in}$ but not in $p(X_1, \ldots, X_k)\tau_{in}$, then $(H \leftarrow B_1, \ldots, p(X_1, \ldots, X_k), \ldots, B_q)\tau_{in}\theta$
$\in \gamma((H \leftarrow B_1, \ldots, p(X_1, \ldots, X_k), \ldots, B_q)\beta_{out})$.*

4.4 Abstract Interpretation of a builtin

Suppose $\{X_1, \ldots, X_n\}$ denotes the set of variables in the clause where a builtin occurs in. This set of variables corresponds to the $n \times 1$ column matrix

$$\bar{X} = \begin{bmatrix} X_1 \\ \vdots \\ X_n \end{bmatrix}.$$

Suppose the builtin is called with abstract call substitution $\beta_{in} \equiv \bar{A} \cdot \bar{X} = \bar{c}$. We make a distinction between two cases.

- Abstract interpretation of $X_i = X_j$. $(1 \leq i < j \leq n)$
  This corresponds to a simple linear equation. The resulting abstract success substitution β_{out} is found by adding the equation $X_i = X_j$ to the system $\bar{A} \cdot \bar{X} = \bar{c}$ and reducing this system to row-echelon form.
- Abstract interpretation of $X_{i_0} = c_0 + c_1 X_{i_1} + \cdots + c_k X_{i_k}$, with $c_j \in \mathbb{N}$ and $1 \leq i_j \leq n$ for all $j = 0, \ldots, k$, and $i_0 \notin \{i_1, \ldots, i_k\}$. The resulting abstract success substitution β_{out} is again found by adding the equation to the system and reducing the resulting system to row-echelon form.
  The above case holds when we apply abstract interpretation immediately to an abstract program. In the case where abstract interpretation is applied to the original program, one should first compute the size expression that corresponds to a builtin $X_{i_0} = f(X_{i_1}, \ldots, X_{i_k})$. This size expression can always be expressed in the form $X_{i_0} = c_0 + c_1 X_{i_1} + \cdots + c_k X_{i_k}$, with $c_j \in \mathbb{N}$.

Proposition 11 (correctness of abstract interpretation of a builtin). *Let P be the builtin, and suppose that P occurs in a clause*

$$H \leftarrow B_1, \ldots, P, \ldots, B_q.$$

Take $\tau_{in} \in \gamma(\beta_{in})$ and suppose that executing $P\tau_{in}$ yields θ, then

$$(H \leftarrow B_1, \ldots, P, \ldots, B_q)\tau_{in}\theta \in \gamma((H \leftarrow B_1, \ldots, P, \ldots, B_q)\beta_{out}).$$

As a (simple) example, consider the well-known `rev/3` program (with accumulating parameter). The program in normal form is:

Example 5.

$$\texttt{rev}(A, B, C) \leftarrow A = [], B = C.$$
$$\texttt{rev}(A, B, C) \leftarrow A = [E|F], D = [E|C], \texttt{rev}(F, B, D).$$

We use the *term-size* norm to measure the size of a term. The program is normally called with its third argument (the accumulating parameter) instantiated to the empty list. This corresponds to an initialisation of the abstract interpretation procedure with the abstract call `rev(X,Y,Z)` β_0, where $\beta_0 \equiv (Z = 0)$, or

$$\beta_0 \equiv [0\,0\,1] \cdot \begin{bmatrix} X \\ Y \\ Z \end{bmatrix} = [0].$$

Applying the complete procedure described above yields a final abstract success substitution:

$$\beta_{19} \equiv \begin{bmatrix} 1 & -1 & 0 \\ 0 & 0 & 1 \end{bmatrix} \cdot \begin{bmatrix} X \\ Y \\ Z \end{bmatrix} = \begin{bmatrix} 0 \\ 0 \end{bmatrix}.$$

This substitution states that every computed answer substitution θ for rev(x, y, z), with $||z|| = 0$, satisfies the linear equation $||x\theta|| = ||y\theta||$.

Due to space restrictions we are unable to give a complete tracing of the computation for the rev/3 example nor for any other non-trivial example. We refer to [23]. Still the technique has been implemented and successfully tested on a large class of examples. For instance, we found that it produces accurate results for a variety of sorting algorithms, including e.g. permutation sort, quick sort, merge sort, insertion sort, bubble sort and heap sort.

5 Discussion and Related Work

Linear size relations are computed using abstract interpretation. The use of a generic tool for static analysis looks very appealing, especially when compared with previous ad hoc approaches. Of course, other frameworks for abstract interpretation could be used as well. Especially, the bottom-up approach of Barbuti et al. (e.g. [1]) seems an interesting alternative for this application. Also, the recent frameworks for abstract interpretation in the context of constraint logic programming seem interesting candidates ([5], [12]). The power of the approach hides in the abstract domain, in which relations between natural numbers are approximated by affine relations.

The idea of detecting the affine relationships that hold between the values of program variables (in imperative programs) goes back to M. Karr [15]. He proposed an efficient algorithm for computing the upper bound of two affine subspaces and introduced the elegant notation that we used for our abstract domain.

Affine relationships are conjunctions of equalities of the form $c_0 + c_1X_1 + \ldots + c_nX_n = 0$. It is possible to generalise this, by considering conjunctions of linear inequalities of the form $c_1X_1 + \ldots + c_nX_n \leq c_0$. These are called *closed convex polyhedrons.* An automated technique for discovering these relations was proposed by P. Cousot and N. Halbwachs [6], also in the context of imperative programs

To our knowledge, these ideas were partially reinvented by researchers active in the field of logic programming. J. Ullman and A. Van Gelder [21] were the first to propose *interargument inequalities* of the (restricted) form $p_i + c \geq p_j$, where p_i and p_j denote the size of two terms, and c is a constant. This idea was extended by L. Plümer [19] to so-called *linear predicate inequalities* of the form: $\sum_{i \in I} p_i + c \geq \sum_{j \in J} p_j$. Finally, fully linear *equalities* were proposed in [24]. The above approaches were all directed towards automated techniques for proving termination of logic programs. In another context, namely estimating the complexity of a program, a further generalisation was proposed in [9] and [10]. There, the restriction of linearity is omitted, and general inequalities are allowed, which relate the size of one output argument to a function of the sizes of the input arguments. The functions are computed as the solutions of difference equations. This idea of transforming a program into a set of difference equations formed actually the starting point for our ***abstract programs.***

A restriction of our approach is that we consider only equalities. Consider the (abstract) relation given below.

$$p(0,0).$$
$$p(X+2, Y+3) \leftarrow p(X, Y).$$
$$p(Z+3, T+2) \leftarrow p(Z, T).$$

Applying our technique gives the linear size relation $\{(x, y) \mid x, y \in \mathbb{R}\} = \mathbb{R}^2$. No precise linear relation is found. It seems feasible to implement the ideas of [6], and hence work with inequalities. Recently, A. Van Gelder ([22]) has reported on similar work. He considers *feasible argument sizes*, which are seen as sets of points (n-tuples of positive real numbers) in n-dimensional space. They are approximated by computing *interargument constraints* in the form of a polyhedral convex set, which is found as the fixpoint of a transformation. However, no general method for obtaining the fixpoint is given.

Besides the application that was described above, several instances of the framework for abstract interpretation were proposed before. A simple application concerning mode inference was given in [3]. A more powerful abstract domain is introduced in [14]. The combined use of mode and type information ensures that a lot more of information can be inferred at compile time. Another, even more complex abstract domain is described in [17]. In this application, information about possible sharing of term substructures is taken into consideration. A recent application, dealing with freeness and sharing of program variables, is given in [18].

The main use of all these approaches is optimal code generation, while our main interest is the analysis of the termination behaviour of a program. This is described in [7], [8] and [23]. Proving termination of a program with respect to a set of queries depends heavily on the linear size relations. We refer to [7] for more details.

Notice however, that the use of linear size relations is not restricted to termination analysis alone. We already mentioned [9], were general size relations are used to obtain an estimate of the computational complexity of a program. Also, in the work described in [16], if size relations are available, a preprocessing step adds an extra argument to the predicates (which represents the size of another argument). By doing so, the technique can be applied to more programs, which can then be compiled in such a way that more parallelism is gained. Applications in constraint logic programming also seem promising. The technique can be used to automatically generate or specialise constraints concerning the length of lists or other data structures, which can improve the execution of a program (see [4]).

Acknowledgements

The authors wish to thank Patrick Cousot for some valuable pointers to previous work and Maurice Bruynooghe for comments on a draft version of the paper.

References

1. R. Barbuti, R. Giacobazzi, and G. Levi. A general framework for semantics based bottom-up abstract interpretation of logic programs. Technical Report 20/89, Dipartimento di Informatica, Universita di Pisa, 1989. To appear in ACM transactions on programming languages and systems.
2. A. Bossi, N. Cocco, and M. Fabris. Norms on terms and their use in proving universal termination of a logic program. Technical Report 4/29, CNR, Department of Mathematics, University of Padova, March 1991.
3. M. Bruynooghe. A practical framework for the abstract interpretation of logic programs. *Journal Logic Programming*, 10(2):91–124, 1991.
4. M. Bruynooghe, V. Dumortier, and G. Janssens. Improving the efficiency of constraint logic programming languages by deriving specialized versions. In *Proceedings PDK'91*, Lecture Notes in Artificial Intelligence 567, pages 309–317, Kaiserslautern, July 1991. Springer-Verlag.
5. Ph. Codognet and G. Filé. Computations, abstractions and constraints in logic programs. Technical Report 13, Department of Mathematics, University of Padova, Italy, November 1991.
6. P. Cousot and N. Halbwachs. Automatic discovery of linear restraints among variables of a program. In *Proceedings 5th ACM symposium on principles of programming languages*, pages 84–96, 1978.
7. D. De Schreye and K. Verschaetse. Termination analysis of definite logic programs with respect to call patterns. Technical Report CW 138, Department Computer Science, K.U.Leuven, January 1992.
8. D. De Schreye, K. Verschaetse, and M. Bruynooghe. A framework for analysing the termination of definite logic programs with respect to call patterns. In *Proceedings FGCS'92*, Tokyo, June 1992.
9. S.K. Debray and N.-W. Lin. Automatic complexity analysis of logic programs. In *Proceedings ICLP'91*, pages 599–613, June 1991.
10. S.K. Debray, N.-W. Lin, and M. Hermenegildo. Task granularity analysis in logic programs. In *Proceedings ACM SIGPLAN'90 conference on programming language design and implementation*, pages 174–188, June 1990.
11. M. Falaschi, G. Levi, M. Martelli, and C. Palamidessi. Declarative modeling of the operational behaviour of logic languages. *Theoretical Computer Science*, 69(3):289–318, 1989.
12. R. Giacobazzi, S.K. Debray, and G. Levi. A generalized semantics for constraint logic programs. In *Proceedings FGCS'92*, Tokyo, June 1992.
13. P.E. Gill, W. Murray, and M. H. Wright. *Numerical linear algebra and optimization, Volume 1*. Addison-Wesley, 1991.
14. G. Janssens and M. Bruynooghe. Deriving descriptions of possible values of program variables by means of abstract interpretation. Technical Report CW 107, Department of Computer Science, K.U.Leuven, March 1990. To appear in Journal of Logic Programming, in print.
15. M. Karr. Affine relationships among variables of a program. *Acta Informatica*, 6:133–151, 1976.
16. H. Millroth. *Reforming compilation of logic programs*. PhD thesis, UPMAIL Computing Science Department, Uppsala University, 1990.
17. A. Mulkers. *Deriving Live Data Structures in Logic Programs by means of Abstract Interpretation*. PhD thesis, Department of Computer Science, K.U.Leuven, 1991.

18. K. Muthukumar and M. Hermenegildo. Combined determination of sharing and freeness of program variables through abstract interpretation. In *Proceedings ICLP'91*, pages 49–63, Paris, June 1991. MIT Press.
19. L. Plümer. *Termination proofs for logic programs.* Lecture Notes in Artificial Intelligence 446. Springer-Verlag, 1990.
20. A. Schrijver. *Theory of linear and integer programming.* Wiley & Sons, 1986.
21. J.D. Ullman and A. Van Gelder. Efficient tests for top-down termination of logical rules. *Journal ACM*, 35(2):345–373, April 1988.
22. A. Van Gelder. Deriving constraints among argument sizes in logic programs. In *Proceedings 9th symposium on principles of database systems*, pages 47–60. Acm Press, April 1990.
23. K. Verschaetse. *Static Termination Analysis for Definite Horn Clause Programs.* PhD thesis, Department Computer Science, K.U.Leuven, June 1992.
24. K. Verschaetse and D. De Schreye. Deriving termination proofs for logic programs, using abstract procedures. In *Proceedings ICLP'91*, pages 301–315, Paris, June 1991. MIT Press.
25. K. Verschaetse and D. De Schreye. Automatic derivation of linear size relations. Technical Report CW 139, Department Computer Science, K.U.Leuven, January 1992.

This article was processed using the LaTeX macro package with LLNCS style

Generic Abstract Interpretation Algorithms For Prolog: Two Optimization Techniques and Their Experimental Evaluation*

Vincent Englebert[1], Baudouin Le Charlier[1], Didier Roland[1], Pascal Van Hentenryck[2]

[1] University of Namur, 21 rue Grandgagnage, B-5000 Namur (Belgium)
[2] Brown University, Box 1910, Providence, RI 02912 (USA)

Abstract. The efficient implementation of generic abstract interpretation algorithms for Prolog is reconsidered after [12, 14]. Two new optimization techniques are proposed and applied to the original algorithm of [12]: dependency on clause prefixes and caching of operations. The first improvement avoids reevaluating a clause prefix when no abstract value which it depends on has been updated. The second improvement consists of caching all operations on substitutions and reusing the results whenever possible. The algorithm together with the two optimization techniques have been implemented in C (about 8000 lines of code each), tested on a large number of Prolog programs, and compared with the original implementation on an abstract domain containing modes, patterns and sharing. In conjunction with refinments of the domain algorithms, they produce an average reduction of more than 58 % in computation time. Extensive experimental results on the programs are given, including computation times, hit ratios for the caches, the number of operations performed, and the time distribution. As a main result, the improved algorithms exhibit the same efficiency as the specific tools of [26, 8], despite the fact that our abstract domain is more sophisticated and accurate. The abstract operations also take 90% of the computation time indicating that the room left for improvement is very limited. Results on a simpler domain are also given and show that even extremely basic domains can benefit from the optimizations. The general-purpose character of the optimizations is also discussed.

1 Introduction

Abstract interpretation [5] of Prolog has attracted many researchers in recent years. The motivation behind those works stems from the need for optimization in Prolog compilers (given the very high level of these languages) and the large potential for optimization since the semantic features of logic languages make them more amenable to optimization. Mellish [18] was probably the first to define an abstract interpretation framework for Prolog motivated by early analysis tools for Prolog programs. Subsequently, many frameworks have been developed [10, 18, 22, 28, 15, 16, 1, 2] and a variety of abstract domains have been proposed to cater for various program analysis tools involving modes (e.g. [6, 17]), types (e.g. [4]), occur-check (e.g. [23]), garbage collection (e.g. [19]), static detection of parallelism (e.g. [21]), and program specialization [27] to name a few.

* This work was done when V. Englebert and D. Roland were visiting Brown University.

Our research has been devoted to demonstrate the practicality of this area of research. Our starting point was the design of a generic abstract interpretation algorithm and its complexity analysis [12]. The algorithm, initially motivated by [3], is a top-down algorithm focusing on relevant parts of the least fixpoint necessary to answer the user query. It is polynomial in the worst-case and linear in the sizes of the abstract domain and of the Prolog program in many interesting cases. The algorithm, together with its instantiation to a sophisticated abstract domain (derived from [4]) containing modes, patterns, sharing, and aliasing, has been implemented in Pascal and run on a large number of programs. The experimental results have shown the practical value of the algorithm and have indicated that abstract interpretation can be competitive with specialized algorithms such as those reported in [26, 8].

In this paper, we reconsider the problem of implementing efficiently generic abstract interpretation algorithms for Prolog. We propose two new optimization techniques to the original algorithm: dependency on clause prefixes and caching of operations. The first improvement avoids reevaluating a clause prefix when no abstract value it depends on has been updated. As a consequence, it generalizes the dependency graph proposed in [12] and avoids reevaluating clauses and part of clauses unnecessarily. A conceptually similar optimization has in fact been proposed independently by Bruynooghe [2] and implemented by Janssens [9] although the implementations are rather different. No algorithm and experimental evaluation on large programs was given however. The second improvement consists of caching all operations on substitutions and reusing the results whenever possible. Garbage collection is performed automatically on substitutions which are no longer in use when necessary. This improvement subsumes (in some sense) the first improvement because most of the computation time is consumed by the abstract operations. Therefore executing clause prefixes using cached operations only requires a negligible amount of time. Caching also allows the sharing of results between independent computations albeit at a higher cost in memory. Moreover, in case of finite abstract domains, it implies that the number of operations performed by the algorithm is bounded by the number of program points times the number of times their associated operations can be executed (in the worst case the square of the abstract domain size). The two optimization techniques are in fact general-purpose and can be used for other languages and approaches as well.

The algorithms (the original algorithm together with each improvement) have been implemented in C (about 8000 lines of code each). They have been tested on a large number of Prolog programs and compared with the original implementation. In conjunction with refinments of the abstract operations implementation, they produce an average reduction of more than 50 % in computation time. Extensive experimental results on the programs are given, including computation times, hit ratios for the caches, the number of operations, and the time distribution. As a main result, the improved algorithms exhibit the same efficiency as the specific tools of Warren, Debray, and Hermenegildo [26, 8], despite the fact that our abstract domain (including patterns and sharing) is more sophisticated and accurate. The abstract operations also take 90% of the computation time indicating that the room left for improvement is very limited. Results on a simpler domain are also given and show that even extremely basic domains can benefit from the optimizations.

The rest of the paper is organized in the following way. Section 2 gives an overview of the original abstract interpretation algorithm. Section 3 presents the clause prefix improvement while Section 4 presents the caching improvement. Section 5 is devoted to the experimental results of the algorithms. Section 6 discusses how to apply the optimizations to other contexts. Section 7 contains some discussion and directions for further work.

2 Preliminaries

```
procedure solve(in βin,p; out sat,dp)
begin
   sat := ∅;
   dp := ∅;
   solve_call(βin,p,∅,sat,dp)
end

procedure solve_call(in βin,p,suspended; inout sat,dp)
begin
   if (βin,p) ∉ (dom(dp) ∪ suspended) then
   begin
      if (βin,p) ∉ dom(sat) then
         sat := EXTEND(βin,p,sat);
      repeat
         βout := ⊥;
         EXT_DP(βin,p,dp);
         for i := 1 to m with c1,...,cm clauses-of p do
         begin
            solve_clause(βin,p,ci,suspended ∪ {(βin,p)},βaux,sat,dp);
            βout := UNION(βout,βaux)
         end;
         (sat,modified) := ADJUST(βin,p,βout,sat);
         REMOVE_DP(modified,dp)
      until (βin,p) ∈ dom(dp)
   end
end

procedure solve_clause(in βin,p,c,suspended; out βout; inout sat,dp)
begin
   βext := EXTC(c,βin);
   for i := 1 to m with b1,...,bm body-of c do
   begin
      βaux := RESTRG(bi,βext);
      switch (bi) of
      case Xj = Xk:
         βint := AI_VAR(βaux)
      case Xj = f(...):
         βint := AI_FUNC(βaux,f)
      case q(...):
         solve_call(βaux,q,suspended,sat,dp);
         βint := sat(βaux,q);
         if (βin,p) ∈ dom(dp) then
            ADD_DP(βin,p,βaux,q,dp)
      end;
      βext := EXTG(bi,βext,βint)
   end;
   βout := RESTRC(c,βext)
end
```

Fig. 1. The Generic Abstract Interpretation Algorithm

This section recalls, very informally, our original algorithm and its basic notions. See [11, 12, 14] for accurate description or the technical version of this paper. Our original generic abstract interpretation algorithm is defined on normalized logic programs. The use of normalized logic programs, suggested first in [3], greatly simplifies the semantics, the algorithm, and its implementation. The normalized version of the classical list concatenation program as generated by our implementation is as follows:

```
append( X1 , X2 , X3 ) :- X1 = [], X3 = X2.
append( X1 , X2 , X3 ) :- X1 = [ X4 | X5 ], X3 = [ X4 | X6 ],
    append( X5 , X2 , X6 ).
```

The advantage of normalized programs comes from the fact that an (input or output) substitution for a goal p/n is always expressed in terms of variables $X_1, \ldots, X_n$. The algorithm uses a number of operations on substitutions, i.e. UNION$\{\beta_1, \ldots, \beta_n\}$, AI_VAR($\beta$), AI_FUNC($\beta, f$), EXTC($c,\beta$), RESTRC($c,\beta$), RESTRG($g,\beta$), and EXTG($g,\beta,\beta'$). These operations are used respectively to collect the results of a set of clauses, perform the unification of two variables (in the program text), and the unification of a variable and a functor (in the program text), to enter and exit a clause, and to call and return from a goal.

The algorithm computes a set of abstract tuples. An abstract tuple $(\beta_{in}, p, \beta_{out})$ indicates that β_{out} is the substitution resulting from the application of p on β_{in}. In the following, we use *sat*, possibly subscripted or superscripted, to represent sets of abstract tuples and denote by $sat(\beta_{in}, p)$ the unique substitution β_{out} such that $(\beta_{in}, p, \beta_{out}) \in sat$.

In addition to the above operations, the algorithm uses of two operations to manipulate sets of abstract tuples: EXTEND(β, p, sat) and ADJUST(β, p, β', sat). The first operation extends a set of abstract tuples with a new abstract tuple while the second one adjusts the value of an abstract tuple (i.e. $sat(\beta, p)$).

To improve efficiency, our algorithm also includes a specific data structure, a dependency graph, to maintain goal dependencies. A dependency graph dp contains elements of the $\langle(\beta, p), lt\rangle$ where lt is a set $\{(\alpha_1, q_1), \ldots, (\alpha_n, q_n)\}$ $(n \geq 0)$. We denote by $dp(\beta, p)$ the set lt such that $\langle(\beta, p), lt\rangle \in dp$ if it exists. We also denote by $dom(dp)$ the set of all (β, p) such that $\langle(\beta, p), lt\rangle \in dp$. The basic intuition here is that $dp(\beta, p)$ represents at some point the set of pairs which (β, p) depends directly upon.

The algorithm uses the dependency graph through three operations: EXT_DP(β, p, dp), ADD_DP(β, p, α, q, dp), and REMOVE_DP($modified, dp$). The first operation introduces a new element in the dependency graph with no dependencies, the second operation inserts a dependency of (β, p) on (α, q) while the last operation removes from the dependency graph dp all nodes depending (transitively) on the elements in *modified*. The algorithm makes sure that the elements (β, p) that need to be reconsidered are such that $(\beta, p) \notin dom(dp)$.

We are now in position to present the basic algorithm which is depicted in Figure 1. It consists of three procedures: `solve`, `solve_goal`, and `solve_clause`.

3 Clause Prefix Dependency

We now turn to the optimization techniques of the original algorithm. We start with the clause prefix improvement. To motivate this improvement, consider the execution of the above algorithm on the append/3 program as depicted in Figure 2. All operations which are executed more than once are marked redundant and we have removed (for space reasons) the third iteration which is essentially the same as the second one. The algorithm here uses an abstract domain using a pattern component (to store information about functors), a mode component, a same value component and a possible sharing component. See [20, 14] for accurate description of this domain. The first iteration considers both clauses. Only the first clause produces a result since the second clause calls itself recursively with the same

```
TRY CLAUSE 1
   EXIT EXTC (Var(1),Var(2),Gro(3)) ps: (1,1)(2,2)
   CALL AI-FUN (Var(1),Var(2),Gro(3)) ps: (1,1)(2,2)
   EXIT AI-FUN (Gro(1):[],Var(2),Gro(3)) ps: (2,2)
   CALL AI-VAR (Gro(1):[],Var(2),Gro(3)) ps: (2,2)
   EXIT AI-VAR (Gro(1):[],Gro(2),Gro(2))
   EXIT RESTRC (Gro(1):[],Gro(2),Gro(2))
   EXIT UNION (Gro(1):[],Gro(2),Gro(2))
EXIT CLAUSE 1
TRY CLAUSE 2
   EXIT EXTC (Var(1),Var(2),Gro(3),Var(4),Var(5),Var(6)) ps: (1,1)(2,2)(4,4)(5,5)(6,6)
   CALL AI-FUN (Var(1),Var(2),Gro(3),Var(4),Var(5),Var(6)) ps: (1,1)(2,2)(4,4)(5,5)(6,6)
   EXIT AI-FUN (Ngv(1):.(Var(2),Var(3)),Var(4),Gro(5),Var(2),Var(3),Var(6)) ps: (2,2)(3,3)(4,4)(6,6)
   CALL AI-FUN (Ngv(1):.(Var(2),Var(3)),Var(4),Gro(5),Var(2),Var(3),Var(6)) ps: (2,2)(3,3)(4,4)(6,6)
   EXIT AI-FUN (Ngv(1):.(Gro(2),Var(3)),Var(4),Gro(5):.(Gro(2),Gro(6)),Gro(2),Var(3),Gro(6)) ps: (3,3)(4,4)
   CALL PRO-GOAL append(Var(1),Var(2),Gro(3)) ps: (1,1)(2,2)
   EXIT PRO-GOAL append bottom
   EXIT EXTG bottom
   EXIT RESTRC bottom
   EXIT UNION (Gro(1):[],Gro(2),Gro(2))
EXIT CLAUSE 2 ADJUST
TRY CLAUSE 1
   EXIT EXTC **REDUNDANT** (Var(1),Var(2),Gro(3)) ps: (1,1)(2,2)
   CALL AI-FUN (Var(1),Var(2),Gro(3)) ps: (1,1)(2,2)
   EXIT AI-FUN **REDUNDANT** (Gro(1):[],Var(2),Gro(3)) ps: (2,2)
   CALL AI-VAR (Gro(1):[],Var(2),Gro(3)) ps: (2,2)
   EXIT AI-VAR **REDUNDANT** (Gro(1):[],Gro(2),Gro(2))
   EXIT RESTRC **REDUNDANT** (Gro(1):[],Gro(2),Gro(2))
   EXIT UNION **REDUNDANT** (Gro(1):[],Gro(2),Gro(2))
EXIT CLAUSE 1
TRY CLAUSE 2
   EXIT EXTC **REDUNDANT** (Var(1),Var(2),Gro(3),Var(4),Var(5),Var(6)) ps: (1,1)(2,2)(4,4)(5,5)(6,6)
   CALL AI-FUN (Var(1),Var(2),Gro(3),Var(4),Var(5),Var(6)) ps: (1,1)(2,2)(4,4)(5,5)(6,6)
   EXIT AI-FUN **REDUNDANT** (Ngv(1):.(Var(2),Var(3)),Var(4),Gro(5),Var(2),Var(3),Var(6))
       ps: (2,2)(3,3)(4,4)(6,6)
   CALL AI-FUN (Ngv(1):.(Var(2),Var(3)),Var(4),Gro(5),Var(2),Var(3),Var(6)) ps: (2,2)(3,3)(4,4)(6,6)
   EXIT AI-FUN **REDUNDANT** (Ngv(1):.(Gro(2),Var(3)),Var(4),Gro(5):.(Gro(2),Gro(6)),Gro(2),Var(3),Gro(6))
       ps: (3,3)(4,4)
   ** RESTRG REDUNDANT **
   CALL PRO-GOAL append(Var(1),Var(2),Gro(3)) ps: (1,1)(2,2)
   EXIT PRO-GOAL append(Gro(1):[],Gro(2),Gro(2))
   EXIT EXTG (Gro(1):.(Gro(2),Gro(3):[]),Gro(4),Gro(5):.(Gro(2),Gro(4)),Gro(2),Gro(3):[],Gro(4))
   EXIT RESTRC (Gro(1):.(Gro(2),Gro(3):[]),Gro(4),Gro(5):.(Gro(2),Gro(4)))
   EXIT UNION (Gro(1),Gro(2),Gro(3))
EXIT CLAUSE 2 ADJUST
```

Fig. 2. The Original Algorithm on append/3

abstract substitution. The current approximation is the result of the first clause. The second iteration considers once again both clauses and updates the approximation to its final value. The third iteration does not produce any change to *sat* and hence the algorithm terminates. The key points to notice here are as follows: (1) the first clause should not be considered more than once as it does not depend recursively on the call; (2) the second clause should only be reconsidered from the point where new information may be produced, i.e. `CALL PRO-GOAL`. Note that the optimization is also possible even if there are several procedure calls in a clause.

The algorithm with the clause prefix improvement produces exactly the expected result as depicted in Figure 3. Only the second clause is considered for the second and third iteration and reexecution starts only with the recursive call. The `EXIT PREFIX` line simply shows the substitution at this stage of the clause. All the operations performed by the algorithm are now strictly necessary.

More generally, the clause prefix improvement amounts to reconsidering only those clauses whose an element they depend upon has been updated. Moreover execution in a clause restarts from the first goal whose an element it depend upon has been updated. The improvement thus avoids reconsidering any prefix of clause which is known to give exactly the same result as its previous execution.

We now formalize the extension. The key idea behind the clause prefix improvement is to extend the dependency graph to clauses and clause prefixes. Since only procedure calls can produce different results from one execution to another, we only consider clause

```
TRY clause 1
   EXIT EXTC (Var(1),Var(2),Gro(3)) ps: (1,1)(2,2)
   CALL AI-FUN (Var(1),Var(2),Gro(3)) ps: (1,1)(2,2)
   EXIT AI-FUN (Gro(1):[],Var(2),Gro(3)) ps: (2,2)
   CALL AI-VAR (Gro(1):[],Var(2),Gro(3)) ps: (2,2)
   EXIT AI-VAR (Gro(1):[],Gro(2),Gro(2))
   EXIT RESTRC (Gro(1):[],Gro(2),Gro(2))
   EXIT UNION (Gro(1):[],Gro(2),Gro(2))
EXIT CLAUSE 1
TRY CLAUSE 2
   EXIT EXTC (Var(1),Var(2),Gro(3),Var(4),Var(5),Var(6)) ps: (1,1)(2,2)(4,4)(5,5)(6,6)
   CALL AI-FUN (Var(1),Var(2),Gro(3),Var(4),Var(5),Var(6)) ps: (1,1)(2,2)(4,4)(5,5)(6,6)
   EXIT AI-FUN (Ngv(1):.(Var(2),Var(3)),Var(4),Gro(5),Var(2),Var(3),Var(6)) ps: (2,2)(3,3)(4,4)(6,6)
   CALL AI-FUN (Ngv(1):.(Var(2),Var(3)),Var(4),Gro(5),Var(2),Var(3),Var(6)) ps: (2,2)(3,3)(4,4)(6,6)
   EXIT AI-FUN (Ngv(1):.(Gro(2),Var(3)),Var(4),Gro(5):.(Gro(2),Gro(6)),Gro(2),Var(3),Gro(6)) ps: (3,3)(4,4)
   CALL PRO-GOAL append (Var(1),Var(2),Gro(3)) ps: (1,1)(2,2)
   EXIT PRO-GOAL append bottom
   EXIT EXTG bottom
   EXIT RESTRC bottom
   EXIT UNION (Gro(1):[],Gro(2),Gro(2))
EXIT CLAUSE 2 ADJUST
TRY CLAUSE 2
   EXIT PREFIX (Ngv(1):.(Gro(2),Var(3)),Var(4),Gro(5):.(Gro(2),Gro(6)),Gro(2),Var(3),Gro(6)) ps: (3,3)(4,4)
   CALL PRO-GOAL append (Var(1),Var(2),Gro(3)) ps: (1,1)(2,2)
   EXIT PRO-GOAL append (Gro(1):[],Gro(2),Gro(2))
   EXIT EXTG (Gro(1):.(Gro(2),Gro(3):[]),Gro(4),Gro(5):.(Gro(2),Gro(4)),Gro(2),Gro(3):[],Gro(4))
   EXIT RESTRC (Gro(1):.(Gro(2),Gro(3):[]),Gro(4),Gro(5):.(Gro(2),Gro(4)))
   EXIT UNION (Gro(1),Gro(2),Gro(3))
EXIT CLAUSE 2 ADJUST
TRY CLAUSE 2
   EXIT PREFIX (Ngv(1):.(Gro(2),Var(3)),Var(4),Gro(5):.(Gro(2),Gro(6)),Gro(2),Var(3),Gro(6)) ps: (3,3)(4,4)
   CALL PRO-GOAL append (Var(1),Var(2),Gro(3)) ps: (1,1)(2,2)
   EXIT PRO-GOAL append (Gro(1),Gro(2),Gro(3))
   EXIT EXTG (Gro(1):.(Gro(2),Gro(3)),Gro(4),Gro(5):.(Gro(2),Gro(6)),Gro(2),Gro(3),Gro(6))
   EXIT RESTRC (Gro(1):.(Gro(2),Gro(3)),Gro(4),Gro(5):.(Gro(2),Gro(6)))
   EXIT UNION (Gro(1),Gro(2),Gro(3))
EXIT CLAUSE 2
```

Fig. 3. The Clause Prefix Algorithm on append/3

prefixes ending at procedure calls.

Definition 1. Let c be a normalized clause and $g_1, \ldots, g_m$ the successive procedure calls in the body of c. Prefix i of clause c, say $c[i]$, is simply clause c truncated after procedure call $g[i]$ ($1 \leq \mathrm{i} \leq \mathrm{m}$). The position (an integer) of the last goal of $c[i]$ in clause c will be denoted by $last(c[i])$. To ease the presentation, we take the convention that prefix 0, say $c[0]$, will be the entire clause and $last(c[0])$ $(= 1)$ is the position of the first goal in c.

Definition 2. A dependency graph is a set of tuples of the form $\langle(\beta, e), lt\rangle$ where e is a goal, a clause or a clause prefix and lt is a set $\{(\alpha_1, q_1), \ldots, (\alpha_n, q_n)\}$ $(n \geq 0)$ such that, for each (β, e), there exists at most one lt such that $\langle(\beta, e), lt\rangle \in dp$.

All the definitions given previously can be generalized in a straightforward way to deal with clauses and clause prefixes. We now define some new operations and notations. Operation G_ADD_DP $(\beta, p, c, i, \alpha, q, dp)$ is a generalization of ADD_DP which takes into account clauses and clause prefixes. Informally speaking, this operation updates the dependency graph for a call (β, p), the clause c in which the goal appears, and all the relevant clause prefixes. We denote by $nbproc(c)$ the number of procedure calls in a clause c. The operation is defined as follows.

procedure G_ADD_DP(in $\beta, p, c, i, \alpha, q$; **inout** dp)
begin
   ADD_DP $(\beta, p, \alpha, q, dp)$;
   ADD_DP $(\beta, c, \alpha, q, dp)$;
   for $k := i$ **to** $nbproc(c)$ do
      ADD_DP $(\beta, c[k], \alpha, q, dp)$
end

```
procedure solve_call(in βin,p, suspended; inout sat,dp)
begin
  if (βin,p) ∉ (dom(dp) ∪ suspended) then
  begin
    if (βin,p) ∉ dom(sat) then
      sat := G_EXTEND(βin,p,sat);
    repeat
      βout := ⊥;
      SC := MODIFIED_CLAUSES(βin,p);
      G_EXT_DP(βin,p,dp);
      forall c ∈ SC do
      begin
        solve_clause(βin,p,c,suspended ∪ {(βin,p)},βaux,sat,dp);
        βout := UNION(βout,βaux)
      end;
      (sat,modified) := ADJUST(βin,p,βout,sat);
      REMOVE_DP(modified,dp)
    until (βin,p) ∈ dom(dp)
  end
end

procedure solve_clause(in βin,p, c, suspended; out βout; inout sat,dp)
begin
  (f,βext) := FIRST_PREFIX(βin,c);
  for i := f to m with b1,...,bm body-of c do
  begin
    βaux := RESTRG(bi,βext);
    switch (bi) of
    case Xj = Xk:
      βint := AI_VAR(βaux)
    case Xj = f(...):
      βint := AI_FUNC(βaux,f)
    case q(...):
      logclause(βin, c[i]) := βext;
      solve_call(βaux,q, suspended,sat,dp);
      βint := sat(βaux,q);
      if (βin,p) ∈ dom(dp) then G_ADD_DP(βin,p,c,i,βaux,q,dp)
    end;
    βext := EXTG(bi,βext,βint)
  end;
  βout := RESTRC(c,βext)
end
```

Fig. 4. The Algorithm with the Clause Prefix Improvement

Operation G_EXT_DP is a replacement of operation EXT_DP to update the dependency graph for clauses and clause prefixes as well. The operation is defined as follows.

```
procedure G_EXT_DP(in β, p; inout dp)
begin
  EXT_DP(β,p,dp);
  for i := 1 to m with c1,...,cm clauses-of p do
  begin
    EXT_DP(β,ci,p);
    for j := 0 to nbproc(ci) do
      EXT_DP(β,c[j],p);
  end
end
```

Note, at this point, that the above definitions are conceptual. At the implementation level, the dependency set is replaced by pointers from abstract tuples to other abstract tuples together with additional information to distinguish between goal, clause, and prefix dependencies. In addition, we maintained all information on which clauses and prefixes to execute together with the abstract tuples.

During reexecution of a goal, only the clauses whose an element they depend upon has been updated need to be reconsidered. The set of these clauses is defined by

$$\texttt{MODIFIED\_CLAUSES}(\beta, p) \;=\; \{\; c \mid (\beta, c) \notin dom(dp) \text{ and } c \text{ is a clause of } p \;\}.$$

To avoid unnecessary UNION operations, two solutions are possible. One solution amounts to computing only the UNION of the reexecuted clauses. This requires UNION to be "accumulative" (which is the case in the domains discussed here) and cannot be used in all circumstances (e.g. when the algorithm is applied to a greatest fixpoint computation). The second solution is general and amounts to memoizing the successive values of the variable β_{out}. Both solutions have been implemented and the difference in efficiency is negligible. Only the first solution is presented here for simplicity.

Similarly, during execution of a clause, only the prefixes whose a goal they depend upon has been updated need to be reconsidered. The index of the first such prefix can be defined as

$$\texttt{FP}(\beta, c) \;=\; min\{i \mid (\beta, c[i]) \notin dom(dp)\; (0 \leq i \leq nbproc(c))\}.$$

To avoid unnecessary computation, the successive values of the local variable β_{ext} need to be saved. We use $logclause(\beta, c[i])$ to represent the value of β_{ext} before the execution of $last(c[i])$ $(1 \leq i \leq nbproc(c))$.

Operation G_EXTEND generalizes operation EXTEND to initialize the above data structures properly.

procedure G_EXTEND(in β, p,inout sat)
begin
    EXTEND(β,p,sat);
    logclause(β,c[0]) := EXTC(c,β);
end

Finally, to simplify the algorithm, we use the function FIRST_PREFIX(β,c) defined as

FIRST_PREFIX(β,c) = (last(c[FP(β,c)]),logclause(β,c[FP(β,c)]))

We are now in position to define the algorithm with the clause prefix improvement. The new versions of procedures `solve_call` and `solve_clause` are shown in Figure 4.

Procedure `solve_call` is modified to execute a clause only when the clause does not belong to $dom(dp)$, i.e. some elements it depends upon have been updated. It also contains the generalized versions of EXTEND and EXT_DP.

Procedure `solve_clause` is modified to find the first prefix which has been updated together with its associated substitution. It executes all the atoms in the prefix. When a procedure call is encountered, the current value of β_{ext} is stored in the log. In addition, the call to ADD_DP has been replaced by a call to G_ADD_DP which inserts not only the dependencies on goals but also on clauses and clause prefixes.

To be even more precise, we must add that our implementation also stores in the log the intermediate values of variable β_{aux}. β_{aux} needs to be stored to avoid the RESTRG operation for the first goal of the first prefix to reexecute. This allows us to gain 2 to 3 % in execution time.

4 Caching of Operations

The second improvement we propose is based on the recognition that the operations on substitutions are in fact the most time-consuming operations and should be avoided whenever possible. The improvement is extremely simple conceptually and amounts to caching the results of all operations on substitutions. Each time an operation is executed, the program first looks up to find out if the operation has been encountered already and makes use of the result whenever possible. The optimization subsumes the improvement presented in the previous section in the sense that it avoids computing all the operations for redundant clauses and clause prefixes. (Practically it does not really subsume the first improvement in the sense that it is still necessary to reconsider these clauses although at a negligible cost.) In addition, the caching enables to share results between clauses since substitutions are represented in a canonical way. An immediate consequence in case of finite abstract domains is that the number of operations performed by the algorithm is bounded by the number of program points times the number of times their associated operations can be executed (in the worst case the square of the abstract domain size). (Of course, this is only true when all substitutions can fit in memory simultaneously. Otherwise, garbage collection will automatically recover those substitutions which are not strictly necessary (i.e. those in not appearing in *sat*).)

The execution of `caching` on the `append/3` avoids all redundant operations marked in Figure 2. In this particular case, no further improvement is brought by the caching improvement. However, in other programs, other results will also be shared.

The implementation of the caching algorithm requires two main components (1) a memory manager for the substitutions; (2) a number of hashtables, one for each operation, to store the results of the operations. In addition, all abstract operations are modified to work with pointers to substitutions and to guarantee that the inputs are not modified. The memory manager is responsible for allocating and deallocating the substitutions. It is accessed by a number of functions to create new substitutions and to copy, to modify, and to free them. Allocation of a substitution occurs mainly as the result of applying an abstract operation. When allocated, a substitution is stored in a hashtable and subsequent requests for the same substitution will reuse it. Hence, when asked for allocation of a new substitution, the manager uses the hashtable to find out if the substitution already exists, in which case it returns a pointer to the existing substitution. Note that testing if an entry in the hashtable is equal to the substitution is extremely fast since the substitutions are represented in a unique way. "Syntactic" equality (instead of the abstract operation) can be used. The hash function is domain-specific and, in the above domain, it includes all the fields (modes, same value, patterns, sharing) although the sharing does not increase the cache ratio. Experimental results have shown that the function produces less than 20 % of collisions (but better functions could certainly improve this ratio). Garbage collection is performed by associating a counter with each substitution and releasing the substitution when it is no longer referenced.

Each operation (e.g. `EXTG`, `AI_FUNC`) is also modified to store its results into a hashtable (after the operation is performed) and to look up in the hashtable (before the operation is performed). The hash function is much simpler here and is performed directly on substitution pointers (instead of on the actual substitutions as is the case for the memory manager). Similarly only pointers to substitutions need to be stored since they identify uniquely a substitution. Almost all operations are worth caching. In addition, operations to compare substitutions, i.e. `COMPARE` and `SMALLER`, are also cached although they are internal to other abstract operations. Operation `ADJUST` is not cached due to the fact that some of its internal operations are already cached. The first task of `ADJUST` is to find out if the new result is greater or non comparable to the current result. This comparison is cached and if the result is smaller or equal, nothing else needs to be done. Otherwise the set of abstract tuples is updated but no saving can occur. The system also caches operation EXTEND because of the special role held in the implementation by this operation. In fact, this operation is responsible for testing membership to *dom*(*sat*), to extend the set of abstract tuples if necessary and, in all cases, to return a pointer to the correct element in the set of abstract tuples. This of course implies a search in the set of abstract tuples (represented as Hasse diagrams). All other operations are expressed then in terms of this pointer (including operation ADJUST). Hence, by caching operation EXTEND, we make sure that the search is avoided most of the time (only the first time is not cached).

5 Experimental Evaluation

In this section, we report our experimental results on the optimization techniques. For space reasons, only parts of the results and few tables are presented here. See the technical version of this paper for the complete results. In the following, we denote respectively by Pascal, Original, Prefix and Caching (Pa,Or,Pr,Ca for short) the original algorithm coded in Pascal, the original algorithm coded in C with a number of optimization techniques on the domain implementation, the algorithm with the clause prefix improvement, and the algorithm with the caching improvement. The optimization techniques of Original over Pascal include a lazy computation of the transitive closure of the sharing component (i.e. call by need) and a data-driven implementation (instead of a straightforward top-down implementation) of various operations on substitutions (in particular the unification operation). The programs used are the same as those described in [14].

5.1 Computation Times

Two versions of the algorithms have been implemented, one with the sharing represented by characters (i.e. bytes) favouring speed and another with the sharing represented by bits favouring memory. Table 1 depicts the results with the sharing represented by characters (i.e. bytes). The first four columns present the computation times in seconds while the last five columns present the improvement in percentage (i.e. P1-P2 denotes (P1-P2)/P1). As

Program	Pa	Or	Pr	Ca	Pa-Or	Pa-Pr	Or-Pr	Pa-Ca	Or-Ca
Append	0.06	0.02	0.01	0.01					
Kalah	17.82	9.20	6.33	5.59	48.37	64.48	31.20	68.63	39.24
Queens	0.37	0.22	0.15	0.16	40.54	59.46	31.82	56.76	27.27
Press1	65.91	37.89	28.82	25.62	42.51	56.27	23.94	61.13	32.38
Press2	19.52	11.53	8.65	8.36	40.93	55.69	24.98	57.17	27.49
Peep	11.34	7.14	5.79	6.29	37.04	48.94	18.91	44.53	11.90
CS	16.02	7.93	5.70	5.92	50.50	64.42	28.12	63.05	25.35
Disj	12.26	6.75	3.03	3.25	44.94	75.29	55.11	73.49	51.85
PG	1.79	1.11	0.86	0.76	37.99	51.96	22.52	57.54	31.53
Read	50.41	30.26	24.42	25.37	39.97	51.56	19.30	49.67	16.16
Gabriel	4.88	2.89	1.95	2.06	40.78	60.04	32.53	57.79	28.72
Plan	1.26	0.71	0.59	0.60	43.65	53.17	16.90	52.38	15.49
QSort	0.56	0.34	0.22	0.23	39.29	60.71	35.29	58.93	32.35
Mean					42.21	58.49	28.38	58.42	28.31

Table 1. Computation Times of the Algorithms and Percentages: Character Version

far as the character version is concerned, Caching produces an improvement of 58.42% compared to the original version in Pascal. Caching also produces an improvement of 28.31%

compared to the original version in C. Programs Read and Peep are those producing the least improvement (44.53% and 49.67%) while Disj and Kalah produce the best improvement (73.49% and 68.63%). All the times are below 10 seconds except Press1 and Read which require respectively 25.62 and 25.37 seconds. Prefix is marginally faster than Caching. It produces an average improvement of 58.49% over the original implementation and 28.38% over the improved implementation in C. All programs are still under 28 seconds and Prefix loses around 3 seconds on one of the largest programs.

As far as the bit version is concerned, Caching produces an improvement of 44.15% over the Pascal implementation (Booleans are not coded as bits by the Pascal compiler) and 31.82% over the improved C implementation. All programs still run below 12 seconds except Press1 and Read which take respectively 34.68 and 35.82 seconds. Prefix is slower with an average improvement of 41.70% over the Pascal implementation and an average of 28.75% over the improved C implementation.

The results seem to indicate that the more costly the abstract operations, the more attractive caching will be. On our domain, the character implementation of sharing (which is the fastest) produces a gain of 0.07 % in favor of Prefix while the bit implementation produces a gain of 2.45 % in favor of caching. We discuss this result later in the paper in light of other results.

The above results compare well with the specialized algorithms of [26, 8], which were written in Prolog. On Peep, Read and PG, their best programs achieve respectively 22.52, 60.18 and 3.25 on a SUN 3/50. This means that our algorithm is respectively 3.89, 2.46, 4.27 times faster on a SPARC-I (Sun 4/60)(which is around 2-4 times faster). Moreover our algorithms execute on a more sophisticated and accurate domain than the one used in [26, 8]. In particular, our domain also includes a more sophisticated sharing and pattern components than those in [26, 8].

5.2 Number of Abstract Operations

Operation	Or	Pr	Ca	Ca eval	% Or-Pr	% Or-Ca	% Or-Ca eval
COMPARE	7294	5994	3493	1736	17.82	52.11	76.20
SMALLER	24840	20390	13329	8428	17.91	46.34	66.07
EXTEND	3416	2370	3416	987	30.62	0.00	71.11
AI_TEST	934	565	934	462	39.51	0.00	50.54
AI_IS	513	303	513	240	40.94	0.00	53.22
AI_VAR	896	615	896	566	31.36	0.00	36.83
AI_FUNC	13916	9086	13916	8208	34.71	0.00	41.06
EXTG	4982	3879	4982	3334	22.14	0.00	33.08
RESTRG	4982	2942	4982	2442	40.95	0.00	50.98
EXTC	5170	3388	5170	3388	34.47	0.00	34.47
RESTRC	5170	4325	5170	2704	16.34	0.00	47.70
UNION	9068	8468	9068	5349	6.62	0.00	41.01

Table 2. Number of Abstract Operations on all Programs for all Algorithms

To avoid considering the specificities of our implementation, we now give a more abstract view of the efficiency of the algorithms: the number of operations on abstract substitutions performed by the various algorithms. The results are summarized in Table 2.

Table 2 contains, for each abstract operation on all benchmark programs, the number of calls in algorithms Original, Prefix and Caching. CA eval also gives the number of calls in Caching which are really evaluated (all the others being cached). Finally, it gives the percentage of operations saved for each of the improvements. Besides the traditional operations such as RESTRG and EXTG, results are also given for COMPARE (i.e. comparing two substitutions and returning equal, smaller, greater, or not comparable), SMALLER (i.e. testing if a substitution is smaller than another substitution), AI_TEST (i.e. the built-in arithmetic comparisons) and AI_IS (i.e. the function is of Prolog). Note also that operation EXTG is only performed for procedure calls and is integrated into operations AI_FUNC and AI_VAR for built-ins.

The ratio OR-PR indicates that the percentage of calls saved for each of the operations by Prefix over the original algorithm. Half of the operations have a ratio of over 30% reaching peaks of about 39% and 41% for AI_TEST and AI_IS. The time consuming operations AI_VAR, AI_FUNC and EXTG dealing with unification achieve improvements of about 31, 34, and 22%.

The ratio OR-CA eval indicates the percentage of executed calls saved by Caching. These ratios are much higher than in the case of Prefix including peaks of 76 and 71% for COMPARE and EXTEND and 36, 41, and 33% on the unification operations. This seems to indicate and to confirm the results of our previous section that, the more costly the abstract operations, the more attractive will be Caching. When only unification instructions are concerned (i.e. AI_VAR, AI_FUNC, EXTG) are considered, Caching produces a 7% improvement over Prefix and a 36% improvement over Original. Given the overhead for handling the caches, this fits nicely with the results observed for computation times.

The ratio OR-CA gives the number of calls to the operations spared by Caching. Caching basically calls the same operations as Original (but many of them are trivially performed through caching) except in the case where some operations are called inside operations. This is true for SMALLER and COMPARE where the number of calls is substantially reduced.

The lowest improvement occurs for EXTG which was to be expected since this is the instruction executed just after a goal. Each time the output of an abstract tuple has been updated EXTG has to be evaluated. On the other hand, EXTEND has the highest improvement which is not surprising since this is the operation performed first when an abstract tuple is considered. The most important differences between Caching and Prefix appear in operations UNION and RESTRC, no difference occurring in EXTC. The last result is easily explained since different clauses have very often a different number of variables in their normalized versions. The former result is explained by the fact that Prefix has in fact little to offer for the above operations. For instance, RESTRC is only avoided when the whole clause is not reconsidered.

5.3 Time Distribution

In this section, we investigate the distribution of the computation time in various categories, including the abstract time (the time spent in the abstract operation), the control time (the total time - the abstract time), and the cache time (the time taken in managing the caches).

For caching, the results indicate that about 90% of the time is spent in the abstract operations. PG and CS are the most demanding in terms of abstract time, which is easily explained as they manipulate large substitutions and make relatively few iterations (especially CS). The results also indicate that the cache time takes a significant part of the control time, including 10% on Press2. However, assuming a no-cost implementation of the control part, only about 10 % can be saved on the computation times. This indicates that the room left for improvement is rather limited.

For Original, the results indicate that the control time is very low, only reaching 9 and 8 % for Queens and Plan but being lower than 3% in most cases. Comparing those results with Caching, we observe that the control time in Caching has grown significantly due to the cache time (the rest of the control time being theoretically the same between Caching and Original).

For Prefix, the results indicate, as expected, that the control times are almost always smaller to those of Caching and greater than those of Original. Also the control times are much closer to Original than to Caching,

Results concerning the distribution of the abstract time among the abstract operations for Caching clearly indicates that the most time-consuming operations are AI_FUNC and EXTG confirming some of the results of the previous section. For Caching, operations AI_FUNC and EXTG take more than 80% of the time except for Queens (75%). Operation UNION seems to be the next most demanding operation, but far behind the above two operations.

For Original, the results indicate once again that the most time-consuming operations are AI_FUNC and EXTG. The results are also almost similar to those of Caching. Other operations have somewhat different ratios due to the fact that the unification takes most of the time.

5.4 Results on a Simpler Domain

In this section, we report some experimental results on a simpler domain, i.e. the mode domain of [20] which is a reformulation of the domain of [2]. The domain could be viewed as a simplification of the domain discussed so far where the pattern information has been omitted and the sharing has been simplified to an equivalence relation. As a result, the algorithms are in fact significantly different. They are much simpler but the loss of accuracy is significant. Nevertheless the efficiency results illustrate the potential of the improvements even in unfavorable conditions.

For the bit version, Prefix reduces the computation by 28% compared to Original while Caching produces a 26% improvement. The improvements still remain significant, given that the improvements of Prefix and Caching on the sophisticated domain were respectively 28% and 31%. For the character version, there is now a much larger difference in efficiency between Prefix and caching. Prefix now brings around 29% improvement while Caching only improves Original by 6%. Note also that the computation times are significantly reduced compared to the sophisticated domain, all times being less than 8 seconds.

These results indicate the potential of the improvements even on small and simple domains. It also gives us a first confirmation that the simpler the abstract domain, the more interesting Prefix becomes.

6 Generality of the two Optimization Techniques

Although the results of this paper only deal with (side-effect free) Prolog program analysis, the two proposed techniques are in fact general-purpose. They can be used in any abstract interpretation algorithm based on a fixpoint semantics. Therefore they can be useful for the analysis of procedural, functional and parallel languages as well.

The generality of the caching technique is obvious. Note however that this technique should not be taken as a panacea. Its value depends on several factors: (1) the control time of the algorithm should be negligible with respect to the time spent by the abstract operations; (2) percentage of recomputed abstract operation calls must be sufficiently high; (3) the overhead due to the caching technique must be significantly lower than the gain due to non recomputing abstract operations.

Note also that it is not always obvious to choose the right operations to cache. In this paper, caching all "top level" abstract operations (plus a number of comparison operations) seemed to be an obvious choice. However it does not produce any improvement for some operations. For instance, EXTC is never recomputed for clear reasons. Further research will be devoted to compare the present results with other granularity levels for caching, i.e. auxiliary operations acting on components of abstract substitutions.

The prefix optimization may seem to be rather specific to Prolog at first glance since it is based on the clause and procedure concepts. However the principle can be extended to many situations, especially if the abstract interpretation algorithm is designed manually (and not automatically). Suppose that the abstract semantics is defined by an arbitrary algorithm T computing some functional transformation. We show in [13] that the algorithm of [12] can be generalized to compute the least fixpoint of such a transformation. This algorithm can then be optimized by inserting some "recovery points" inside algorithm T. Each time algorithm T is called with a previously encountered input, its execution will be restarted at the last recovery point whose information does not depend on the changes having occurred since the previous call. More clever and specific improvements can be obtained by analyzing the internal structure of algorithm T. Independent parts can be identified and recomputed only if some value they depend upon has been improved. Finally automatization of the method is conceivable. Assuming that the abstract semantics be expressed in a very high level language (e.g. denotational style), a preliminary data flow analysis of the definition could provide a way to decompose the code of the transformation into several independent parts similar to the clauses of a Prolog procedure. Providing mathematical properties of some operations to the pre-analyzer could be necessary.

7 Discussion

It is not fully clear which of the two optimization techniques is most valuable in practice. The clause prefix improvement has the advantage of simplicity and memory consumption. The `Caching` algorithm can be reused more easily in other contexts but it also requires more memory. Attempts to combine both improvements turned out to be unsuccessful, the combined algorithm being always worse than at least one of the two algorithms. It is our belief that `Caching` is more attractive for sophisticated domains and `Prefix` for simpler domains. Future research and experimentation on other domains will help us answering this question and identify what were the peculiarities of our domains.

Acknowledgements

Saumya Debray and Leon Sterling provided us with some of the programs used in the experiments. This research was partly supported by the Belgian National Incentive-Program for fundamental Research in Artificial Intelligence (Baudouin Le Charlier) and by the National Science Foundation under grant number CCR-9108032 and the Office of Naval Research under grant N00014-91-J-4052 ARPA order 8225. (Pascal Van Hentenryck).

References

1. R. Barbuti, R. Giacobazzi, and G. Levi. A General Framework for Semantics-based Bottom-up Abstract Interpretation of Logic Programs. (To Appear).
2. M. Bruynooghe. A Practical Framework for the Abstract Interpretation of Logic Programs. *Journal of Logic Programming*, 10:91–124, 1991.
3. M. Bruynooghe and al. Abstract Interpretation: Towards the Global Optimization of Prolog Programs. In *Proc. 1987 Symposium on Logic Programming*, pages 192–204, San Francisco, CA, August 1987.
4. M Bruynooghe and G Janssens. An Instance of Abstract Interpretation: Integrating Type and Mode Inferencing. In *Proc. of the Fifth International Conference on Logic Programming*, pages 669–683, Seattle, WA, August 1988.
5. P Cousot and R. Cousot. Abstract Interpretation: A unified Lattice Model for Static Analysis of Programs by Construction or Approximation of Fixpoints. In *Conf. Record of Fourth ACM Symposium on POPL*, pages 238–252, Los Angeles, CA, 1977.
6. S. Debray and P. Mishra. Denotational and operational semantics for prolog. *Journal of Logic Programming*, 5(1):61–91, 1988.
7. M. Dincbas, H. Simonis, and P. Van Hentenryck. Solving Large Combinatorial Problems in Logic Programming. *Journal of Logic Programming*, 8(1-2):75–93, 1990.

8. M. Hermenegildo, R. Warren, and S. Debray. Global Flow Analysis as a Practical Compilation Tool. *Journal of Logic Programming*, 1991. (To appear).
9. G Janssens. *Deriving Run Time Properties Of Logic Programs By Means of Abstract Interpretation.* PhD thesis, Katholieke Universiteit Leuven, Department Computerwetenschappen, Leuven (Belgium), 1990.
10. N.D. Jones and H. Sondergaard. *A Semantics-Based Framework for the Abstract Interpretation of Prolog*, volume Abstract Interpretation of Declarative Languages, pages 123–142. Ellis Horwood, 1987.
11. B. Le Charlier, K. Musumbu, and P. Van Hentenryck. Efficient and Accurate Algorithms for the Abstract Interpretation of Prolog Programs. Research Paper RP-90/9, University of Namur, August 1990.
12. B. Le Charlier, K. Musumbu, and P. Van Hentenryck. A Generic Abstract Interpretation Algorithm and its Complexity Analysis (Extended Abstract). In *Eighth International Conference on Logic Programming (ICLP-91)*, Paris (France), June 1991.
13. B. Le Charlier and P. Van Hentenryck. A Universal Top-Down Algorithm for Fixpoint Computation and its Correctness Proof. Technical report, 1992. Forthcoming.
14. B. Le Charlier and P. Van Hentenryck. Experimental Evaluation of a Generic Abstract Interpretation Algorithm for Prolog. In *Fourth IEEE International Conference on Computer Languages (ICCL'92)*, San Fransisco, CA, April 1992.
15. K. Marriott and H. Sondergaard. Bottom-up Abstract Interpretation of Logic Programs. In *Proc. of Fifth International Conference on Logic Programming*, pages 733–748, Seattle, WA, August 1988.
16. K. Marriott and H. Sondergaard. Notes for a Tutorial on Abstract Interpretation of Logic Programs. North American Conference on Logic Programming, Cleveland, Ohio, 1989.
17. C. Mellish. The Automatic Generation of Mode Declarations for Prolog Programs. Technical Report DAI Report 163, Department of Artificial Intelligence, University of Edinburgh, 1981.
18. C. Mellish. *Abstract Interpretation of Prolog Programs*, volume Abstract Interpretation of Declarative Languages, pages 181–198. Ellis Horwood, 1987.
19. A. Mulkers, W. Winsborough, and M. Bruynooghe. Analysis of Shared Data Structures for Compile-Time Garbage Collection in Logic Programs. In *Seventh International Conference on Logic Programming (ICLP-90)*, Jerusalem, Israel, June 1990.
20. K. Musumbu. *Interpretation Abstraite de Programmes Prolog.* PhD thesis, University of Namur (Belgium), September 1990.
21. K. Muthukumar and M. Hermenegildo. Determination of Variable Dependence Information Through Abstract Interpretation. In *Proceedings of the North-American Conference on Logic Programming (NACLP-89)*, Cleveland, Ohio, October 1989.
22. U. Nilsson. *A Systematic Approach to Abstract Interpretation of Logic Programs.* PhD thesis, Department of Computer and Information Science, Linkoeping University, Linkoeping (Sweden), December 1989.
23. H. Sondergaard. An Application of Abstract Interpretation of Logic Programs: Occur Check Reduction. In *Proc. of ESOP'86*, pages 327–338, Sarrbruecken (FRG), 1986.
24. L. Sterling and E. Shapiro. *The Art of Prolog: Advanced Programming Techniques.* MIT Press, Cambridge, Ma, 1986.
25. P. Van Hentenryck. *Constraint Satisfaction in Logic Programming.* Logic Programming Series, The MIT Press, Cambridge, MA, 1989.
26. R. Warren, M. Hermedegildo, and S. Debray. On the Practicality of Global Flow Analysis of Logic Programs. In *Proc. of the Fifth International Conference on Logic Programming*, pages 684–699, Seattle, WA, August 1988.
27. W. Winsborough. Multiple Specialization using Minimal-Function Graph Semantics. To appear in the Journal of Logic Programming, August 1990.
28. W.H. Winsborough. A minimal function graph semantics for logic programs. Technical Report TR-711, Computer-Science Department, University of Wisconsin at Madison, August 1987.

A Bottom-Up Interpreter for a Higher-Order Logic Programming Language

Alain Hui Bon Hoa *

INRIA Rocquencourt, Domaine de Voluceau, 78153 Le Chesnay Cedex
Ecole Normale Supérieure, 45 rue d'Ulm, 75005 Paris

Abstract. Higher-order logic is known to be a good basis for meta-programming languages. Dale Miller's L_λ is such a higher-order logic programming language, for which an interpreter extending the SLD-resolution used in Prolog has been provided.
No alternative to SLD-resolution is known however, and in particular no Bottom-Up strategy has been developed. Such a strategy would be interesting in domains such as natural language, databases, or software engineering. We present here a restriction of L_λ, which we call l_λ, providing λ-abstraction, quantification and function variables, and for which we prove it possible to define a very simple semi-naïve Bottom-Up interpreter.

1 Introduction

Many authors have pointed out how higher-order logic could provide the basis for a meta-programming language, able to represent and deal with such concepts as programs, formulas and proofs. This is made possible by λ-abstraction and function variables. Amy Felty and Dale Miller use such a higher-order logic to specify tactics and tacticals in theorem provers [Fel88]. It may also be applied to program transformation as was proved in [HL78] and realized by Dale Miller and Gopalan Nadathur [MN87].

Now, different arguments contest the necessity of higher-order logic languages:

- Higher-order features actually provide writing facilities but λ-expressions and function variables can be encoded into Prolog, and thus does not increase its expressivity [War82]. We agree on this point but claim that quantification actually extends the language: given the formula $\forall x\ (P(x) : -\forall y\ Q(xy))$, no simple Prolog code can be given, expressing that x cannot depend on y (i.e. be instantiated by a term containing y).
- Higher-order unification is not decidable and even in a successful case, no most general unifier (m.g.u.) may be found [Hue75]. This is true in general, but we use terms which Dale Miller proved not only to allow a simple, decidable unification, but also to lead to some kind of m.g.u. when the unification is successful.

Such a higher-order logic is contained in Dale Miller's programming language L_λ, relying on (a fragment of) Higher-Order Hereditary Harrop Formulas [Mil91].

* This work was partially supported by a grant from a European Software Factory (ESF) project.

As was shown in [MNPS91], this fragment of logic supports goal-directed proofs. An interpreter could then be designed for L_λ, which integrates its higher-order features into a computational procedure extending the SLD-resolution used in Prolog. This provides us with a nice programming language (with decidable unification), which contains a large fragment of higher-order logic.

Now, one most interesting feature of logic programming languages based on first-order Horn Clauses is their suitability to a wide number of applications: syntactic analysis can be performed with Definite Clause Grammars [PW83], requests in databases (using Datalog) or in software engineering [RS90] may be expressed in a formalism resembling Horn Clauses. The higher-order logic proposed by L_λ also bodes well for these domains: in computational linguistics, it is capable of unifying both syntactical and semantical analyses [MN86], and of accounting for filler-gap dependencies [PM90]. In software engineering, it may be used to search within a library [RW91, Rou].
In addition to their flexibility, Horn Clauses offer a variety of strategies to evaluate programs (Top-Down with or without tabulation, Bottom-Up or mixed strategies), each possibly suitable to a particular kind of application. This encourages us to explore additional strategies for L_λ, for which, to our knowledge, only SLD-resolution has been developed yet. In particular, no Bottom-Up procedure is known for L_λ. This kind of evaluation may be preferable in some applications, for completeness or computational reasons.

Thus, in an effort to extend Prolog applications, we undertook the definition of a Bottom-Up strategy for L_λ. In this paper, we consider a fragment of L_λ, providing λ-abstraction, quantification and function variables, which we call l_λ. In this restricted language, terms are untyped, and clause bodies do not admit implication, as they do in L_λ. We show that it is possible to describe a very simple Bottom-Up interpreter for l_λ which is similar to the one used for first-order Horn Clauses, except that it makes use of higher-order unification (which is of course also decidable for l_λ). In particular, quantification over higher-order variables may induce scope constraints between them, which are handled by mixed quantifier prefixes in SLD-resolution. We show that, in the case of a Bottom-Up strategy, no quantifier prefix needs to be kept during the resolution: the scope constraints always appear under a very limited form, and may be easily synthesized each time they are needed (i.e., for each unification).

This paper is organized as follows: in the next section, we briefly present the language l_λ, the scope constraints involved in the resolution of programs in l_λ, and the interpreter deduced from Dale Miller's for L_λ. Glossing over Top-Down resolution, we concentrate in section 3 on a Bottom-Up approach, in which these scope constraints are weakened and may be easily treated. We thus obtain a very simple, sound, and complete Bottom-Up interpreter, where the complications induced by higher-order (mainly quantification over function variables) are handled by unification.

In this presentation, we will adopt the usual conventions: D will stand for a general definite clause, G for a goal, and A, B, C for atomic formulas.

2 l_λ, a Higher-Order Logic Programming Language

We present here rather informally the kind of logic programs authorized in l_λ, and the problems which may be encountered. We then sketch a Top-Down interpreter for l_λ deduced from the one designed for L_λ. More details on this part may be found in [Mil91]. The reader familiar with L_λ, or the λ-Prolog family of languages, may skip to the next section.

l_λ appears as an untyped restriction of L_λ, in which implication in clause bodies is not admitted. Thus it contains the usual Horn Clauses, extended with function variables, λ-expressions and universal quantification. The interpreter presented in this section may be conceived as an extension of Prolog SLD-resolution to higher-order features and will therefore also be alluded to as a SLD interpreter.

2.1 Extended Horn Clauses

We extend the usual Horn Clauses in three ways:

- λ-*expressions*, which means we can use λ-abstraction to represent functions and that the interpreter cansynthesize λ-functions.
- *function variables*, which means we can use free variables to represent functions, and have them instantiated either by defined functions or by synthesized ones.
- *universal quantifications*, which have different interpretations according to where in the clauses they are quantified:

  Consider for instance the following logic program:

  $$query?\ :-\ \forall x\ P(f(x))$$
  $$\forall y\ (P(y)\ :-\ Q(y))$$

  In this example, the variable x is quantified in the body of the clause. It is then said to be *essentially universal*: the goal requires we prove $P(f(x))$ for all x, and thus it cannot be instantiated during the resolution, behaving just like a new constant. For the same reason, variables bound by a λ-abstraction, which can neither be instantiated, will also be said essentially universal.

  Conversely, a variable quantified in the head of a clause or outside the clause (like y) will be said *essentially existential*. This variable may be instantiated during the resolution to prove a goal, as $f(x)$ in this case.

The following condition (#) is set on terms to guarantee good properties of the unification (decidability, unique m.g.u.): for each application $(xt_1t_2\dots t_n)$ where x is an essentially existential variable, the t_i's are required to be distinct essentially universal variables, quantified under the scope of x.

The definite clauses authorized in l_λ have the following form:

$$\forall\vec{x}\ (\forall\vec{x}_A\ A\ :-\ \forall\vec{x}_1\ B_1\ \wedge\forall\vec{x}_2\ (\forall\vec{x}_{21}B_{21}\dots))$$

where

- $\vec{x}$ represents a set of essentially existential variables which may appear in any term of the quantified formulas A, $B_1, \ldots$

- $\vec{x}_A$ are also essentially existential variables, but which appear only in A.

- the $\vec{x}_i$ are essentially universal variables which may appear in each of the formulas quantified by $\forall \vec{x}_i$.

In usual Horn Clauses, the logical variables correspond to the essentially existential variables. No notion corresponding to essentially universal variables is available. In l_λ, the presence of both essentially universal and essentially existential variables induce some problems which we highlight on the following example:

Example 1. Let us consider the following program:

$$\forall x \forall l \forall k \forall m\, (append\ (cons\ x\ l)\ k\ (cons\ x\ m)\ :-\ append\ l\ k\ m)$$
$$\forall k'\, (append\ nil\ k'\ k')$$

and the goal formula query? $:-\ \forall y\ (append\ (cons\ a\ nil)\ y\ Z)$.
Notice that the unknown Z is implicitly quantified by $\exists Z\ \forall y$, which means Z cannot depend on y.

Then a SLD-like resolution would roughly proceed this way:

- *We replace the essentially universal variable y by a new constant $\tilde{y}$ and prove the goal*

$$(append\ (cons\ a\ nil)\ \tilde{y}\ Z)$$

- *We unify this formula with the head of the first clause, obtaining the substitution*

$$\begin{cases} x \rightarrow a \\ l \rightarrow nil \\ k \rightarrow \tilde{y} \\ Z \rightarrow cons\ a\ m \end{cases}$$

and the new goal: $(append\ nil\ \tilde{y}\ m)$.

- *Unifying this new goal with the head of the second clause , we get the final substitution*

$$\begin{cases} x \rightarrow a \\ l \rightarrow nil \\ k \rightarrow \tilde{y} \\ k' \rightarrow \tilde{y} \\ m \rightarrow \tilde{y} \\ Z \rightarrow cons\ a\ \tilde{y} \end{cases}$$

This would lead to a solution for the initial goal (contrary to the intuition), if we had not first specified that Z could not be instantiated by a term containing y. Therefore the resolution leads to no solution, which was the correct and expected answer.

If we had considered instead the goal formula

$$query? \ :- \ \forall y \ (append \ (cons \ a \ nil) \ y \ (Hy)),$$

where H is a functional variable, the same resolution would have lead to two solutions:

$$H \rightarrow \lambda u \bullet cons \ a \ \tilde{y}$$
$$and \ H \rightarrow \lambda u \bullet cons \ a \ u$$

Again, the condition on H eliminates the first solution and we get the expected higher-order answer: $H \rightarrow \lambda u \bullet cons \ a \ u$.

This example shows that a correct resolution of our programs needs to retain

- which variables are essentially existential and which are essentially universal.
- their order of appearance during the resolution, so that we can define for each essentially existential variable the appropriate essentially universal variables its substitution terms may contain (notion of scope of a variable).

2.2 A Top-Down Interpreter

Here is a formalization of the method used in the previous example. This interpreter is deduced from the one for L_λ due to Dale Miller [Mil91]: the proving strategy extends the SLD-resolution used in Prolog, and the scope constraints are encoded in quantifier prefixes.

We consider the simple meta-logic containing the logical constants $\wedge$, $\top$ (for true), $\bot$ (for false), $\underline{\forall}$ and $\underline{\exists}$. These meta-level quantifications are used to denote essential quantifications , and are underlined so that they should not be confused with the syntactic symbols in the object-level formulas.
An atomic proposition of this meta-logic is either a constant $\top$ or $\bot$, a sequent judgement $\mathcal{P} \Rightarrow G$, or an equality judgement $t = s$. The sequent judgement intuitively stands for "prove the goal G from the program $\mathcal{P}$" and the equality judgement for "unify the two terms s and t".
The formulas used in the interpreter are the closed formulas of the meta-logic, which means that each variable appearing is bound either (a) at the object-level by a λ-abstraction or a quantification or (b) at the meta-level by a meta-logical quantifier. The scope constraints are encoded as shown in the following example:

> $\underline{\exists x_1 \forall x_2 \forall x_3 \exists x_4}$ F retains that, in the meta-level formula F, x_1 and x_4 are essentially existential variables while x_2 and x_3 are essentially universal ones; moreover x_4 is in the *scope* of x_2 and x_3 (i.e. its substitution terms may contain x_2 and x_3) while x_1 is not.

The interpreter then appears as rules over this meta-logic:

AND A sequent of the form $\mathcal{P} \Rightarrow G_1 \wedge G_2$ is replaced with the conjunction of sequents

$$(\mathcal{P} \Rightarrow G_1) \ \wedge \ (\mathcal{P} \Rightarrow G_2)$$

GENERIC A sequent of the form $(\mathcal{P} \Rightarrow \forall x\, G)$ is replaced with the sequent

$$\underline{\forall \tilde{x}}\ (\mathcal{P} \Rightarrow G[x \mapsto \tilde{x}])$$

where $\tilde{x}$ is a new symbol.

BACKCHAIN A sequent of the form $\mathcal{P} \Rightarrow A$ is replaced with the sequent

$$\underline{\exists \vec{x} \exists \vec{x}_B}\ ((A = B)\ \wedge\ (\mathcal{P} \Rightarrow G))$$

if the program contains the clause $\forall \vec{x}(\forall \vec{x}_B B\ :-\ G)$

The resolution is initialized with $\underline{Q_0}\ (\mathcal{P} \Rightarrow G)$ where $\underline{Q_0}$ contains the constants of the program $\mathcal{P}$ followed by the unknown variables in G, the initial goal. Quantified equality judgements are treated by higher-order unification. A search branch leads to a failure when the unification fails, in which case the corresponding equality judgement is replaced by $\perp$. The resolution ends when there is only a logical constant left, $\top$ meaning a success and $\perp$ a failure.

Provided the correctness of the unification algorithm, this interpreter can be proved sound and complete [Mil91].
In the following we will keep the same notation x, even when it should be replaced by the new symbol $\tilde{x}$.

2.3 Unification in l_λ

Though general higher-order unification was proved undecidable [Hue75], in the case of L_λ and thus of l_λ, the condition (#) required on the terms leads to a correct and decidable algorithm [Mil], which provides some kind of m.g.u. in case of success of the unification.

This operation is used in the BACKCHAINing step of the resolution, and evaluates the equality judgement by setting the computation $unify\ (\underline{Q_A \exists \vec{x} \exists \vec{x}_B}\ ,\ A = B)$, where $\underline{Q}_A$ is the meta-level quantifier prefix of $\mathcal{P} \Rightarrow A$ and $\vec{x}$ and $\vec{x}_B$ the essentially existential variables of the clause $\forall \vec{x}(\forall \vec{x}_B B\ :-\ G)$.

We sketch its mechanisms on an example:

Example 2. Consider the following unification:

$$\underline{\forall m \exists x \forall y \forall z \forall w \exists u \exists v} \quad f(xy)z = f(\lambda a \bullet u)v$$

as the functional symbols are essentially universal and identical, we compare their arguments

$$\underline{\forall m \exists x \forall y \forall z \forall w \exists u \exists v} \quad \begin{cases} xy = \lambda a \bullet u \\ z = v \end{cases}$$

λ- abstraction is treated by using the extensionality property $M = \lambda x \bullet Mx$

$$\underline{\forall m \exists x \forall y \forall z \forall w \exists u \exists v \forall a} \begin{cases} xya = u \\ v = z \end{cases}$$

we then reveal the dependencies of $\underline{\exists u}$ *over essentially universal variables by* raising *it up to* x

$$\underline{\forall m \exists x \exists u' \forall y \forall z \forall w \exists v \forall a} \begin{cases} xya = u'yzw \\ v = z \end{cases} \qquad u \mapsto u'yzw$$

the irrelevant argument variables are then suppressed by pruning *over* z *and* w

$$\underline{\forall m \exists x \exists u'' \forall y \forall z \forall w \exists v \forall a} \begin{cases} xya = u''y \\ v = z \end{cases} \qquad \begin{cases} u \mapsto u'yzw \\ u' \mapsto \lambda yzw \bullet u''y \end{cases}$$

we finally get the solution:

$$\underline{\forall m \exists u'' \forall y \forall z \forall w \forall a} \qquad \begin{cases} u \mapsto u''y \\ x \mapsto \lambda ya \bullet u''y \\ v \mapsto z \end{cases}$$

This unification thus leads to a meta-level quantifier prefix $\underline{Q}$ and a substitution σ, which represents a m.g.u. in the sense that each closed substitution θ respecting the scope constraints encoded by $\underline{Q_A \exists \vec{x} \exists \vec{x}_B}$ and such that $\theta(s) = \theta(t)$ is of the form $\theta = \sigma \circ \phi$, where ϕ respects $\underline{Q}$.

2.4 An Overview of SLD

We have so far obtained a higher-order programming language with an interpreter using a SLD-resolution similar to that used in PROLOG The unification is decidable and leads to a m.g.u. in case of success. The constraints between variables are captured by meta-level quantifier prefixes which are lists memorizing the essential quantifications of the variables, ordered so that a variable is contained in the scope of the variables on its left in the list. These quantifier prefixes present no real problem for implementations, since it was proved that they could be encoded by simple integers [NJ91].

However it is known that SLD-resolution has termination problems: the depth-first strategy it uses may be trapped in an infinite computation path in the search tree, and thus fail to find an existing solution. The breadth-first strategy is a theoretical solution to this problem, but suffers from infinite paths of the search tree, and thus of storage difficulties. More realistic solutions to incompleteness have been proposed for first-order Horn Clauses, notably using the tabulation technique [TS86]: this technique relies on the context-free property of the subgoals to re-use them to detect loops, as well as to avoid redundant evaluations of a goal. This technique hardly extends to l_λ, where scope constraints have to be memorized (in quantifier prefixes) during the resolution. These constraints are inherited, and behave like traces of previous computations, which make the resolution highly contextual. These problems of completeness and context-free are solved in the Bottom-Up interpreter we present in the next section.

3 A Bottom-Up Interpreter

3.1 Some Motivations

No alternative to this SLD-interpreter has been considered. In particular, to our knowledge, no real attempt at a Bottom-Up interpreter has been made. Yet we believe this kind of strategy may have its interest in some cases, as for first-order Horn Clauses:

- Bottom-Up proceeds by iteratively deriving sets of facts, as when using the "immediate consequence operator" defined for least fixed point semantics in [vEK76]. So, for a given goal, after a finite number of iterations, we obtain all the answers to this goal. Bottom-Up is then operationally complete. A naïve Bottom-Up strategy also suffers from infinite paths, but this may be partly addressed by a tabulation technique (see next item).
- Bottom-Up, at the opposite of Top-Down strategies, favors context-free features: derived facts are considered as new axioms, and may be re-used without knowing their origin. As a consequence, loops may be detected and redundant proofs avoided.

These properties are interesting for applications in natural language, where complete parsers may appear as a solution to the ambiguity of sentences. Foremost, Bottom-Up appears as a more natural way to perform semantical interpretation [Per90]. It also authorizes semantical interpretation and syntactical analysis to be more tightly coupled. In the domain of databases, in addition to being complete, a Bottom-Up strategy also presents the advantage of being an efficient way of processing queries [BR88].

3.2 The Bottom-Up Approach

We show that a very simple interpreter, very close to what could be written for Horn clauses and relying on the deduction rule:

$$\frac{(p\ :-\ q \wedge r)\ \ r}{(p\ :-\ q)}$$

can be applied to our language l_λ; the higher-order unification algorithm takes care of all the constraints over the variables.

The key to this simplicity is the following: Bottom-Up reasoning proceeds by iteratively computing sets of facts, each as "immediate consequence" of the previous one, starting from the axioms of the program and using the deduction principle given above. As there is no need in Bottom-Up to memorize the origin of a fact (while, in Top-Down, subgoals keep related to the goal which called them), the scope constraints are simplified, and, in particular, we will show that they may be reduced to such a point that no quantifier prefix needs to be memorized during the resolution (more precisely, it only contains essentially existential variables, and may be directly deduced from the considered fact). It is needed for each unification, and is then simply synthesized. This very simple form makes it very easy to re-use the same fact to prove different goals.

We try to give an intuition of the Bottom-Up mechanism on the following example, applying it to the same program as in example 1:

Example 3. Let $\mathcal{P}$ be the program

$$\forall x \forall l \forall k \forall m\, (append\ (cons\ x\ l)\ k\ (cons\ x\ m)\ :-\ append\ l\ k\ m)$$
$$\forall k'\, (append\ nil\ k'\ k')$$

and G the goal query? $:- \forall y\, (append\ (cons\ a\ nil)\ y\ (Hy))$.

A Bottom-Up resolution would proceed this way:

Starting from the axiom, we chain it with the other clause, obtaining the derived fact:

$$\forall x \forall k'\, (append\ (cons\ x\ nil)\ k'\ (cons\ x\ k'))$$

We chain this new fact with the desired goal by the unification:
$Unify\ (\underline{\exists H \forall y \exists x \exists k'}\ ,$
$append\ (cons\ a\ nil)\ y\ (Hy) = append\ (cons\ x\ nil)\ k'\ (cons\ x\ k'))$

which identifies x to a and k' to y (which is correct as to the scope constraint) and gives:

$$H \rightarrow \lambda u \bullet cons\ a\ u$$

3.3 An Extended Study

The Basic Case We first consider the case of a clause of the following form:

$$\forall \vec{x}\ (\forall \vec{x}_D\ D\ :-\ \forall \vec{y} A) \qquad \text{with } A \text{ atomic.}$$

where

$\vec{x}$ represent a set of essentially existential variables shared by the quantified formulas D, A
$\vec{x}_D$ are also essentially existential variables, but appear only in D.
$\vec{y}$ are essentially universal variables appearing only in A.

Now if we consider a chaining step with the axiom $\forall \vec{u}\ \ B$. (the $\vec{u}$ are thus essentially existential), we have to realize the unification $Unify\ (\underline{\exists \vec{x} \exists \vec{x}_D \forall \vec{y} \exists \vec{u}}\ ,\ A = B)$, for which we can make the following remarks on the scopes:

- the $\vec{x}_D$ do not enter in the process since they do not figure in the terms to be unified. They may even be removed from the quantifier prefix in the unification, which we will do henceforth.
- the $\vec{x}$ are in the scope of no y. So they cannot be substituted by any term containing some of the $\vec{y}$.
- a variable from $\vec{u}$ may be substituted by a term containing some of the $\vec{y}$, but, if so, it cannot appear in any substitution term of one of the $\vec{x}$.

- a variable from $\vec{u}$ may be raised up to a essentially existential variable u'. u' is then in the scope of no essentially universal y any more, and thus may appear in some substitution term of one of the $\vec{x}$.

The result of the unification is therefore a pair $< \underline{Q}\ , \sigma >$ such that:

- $\underline{Q}$ has the form $\underline{\exists\vec{x}'\exists\vec{u}'\exists\vec{x}_D\forall\vec{y}\exists\vec{u}''\forall\vec{v}}$, where
  $\vec{x}'$ is $\vec{x}$, where the substituted variables have been suppressed
  $\vec{u}'$ are the unsubstituted variables raised from $\vec{u}$
  $\vec{u}''$ are the other ones
  $\vec{v}$ are the essentially universal variables possibly created by the treatment of a lambda case (see ex. 2)
- The image by σ of a variable from $\vec{x}$ does not contain any variable from $\vec{y}$ nor a variable under the scope of one of the $\vec{y}$. Moreover, as the unification only manipulates variables occurring in the terms A and B, it cannot contain any other essentially universal variables.

The chaining step thus produces the derived fact $\sigma(D)$, with the scope constraints encoded in $\underline{Q}$. The previous remark about σ shows that $\sigma(D)$ does not contain any variable from $\vec{y}$ nor $\vec{u}''$, but only variables from $\vec{x}'$, $\vec{u}'$, and $\vec{x}_D$. As a further chaining step involving $\sigma(D)$ will only make use of the variables present in the term, we can afford losing the information concerning $\vec{y}$, $\vec{u}''$ and $\vec{v}$. All the information required in $\underline{Q}$ is then that the variables in $\sigma(D)$ are essentially existential.
This shows that:

1. $\sigma(D)$ eventually has the structure of an axiom of l_λ, and thus the Bottom-Up mechanism is safe.
2. all the information needed about $\sigma(D)$ (i.e. its scope constraints) is contained in the term. We may get rid of the $\underline{Q}$ computed by the unification. In other words, no quantifier prefix needs to be memorized with the derived fact.

Omitting the quantifiers corresponding to essentially existential variables, as is usually done in λ-Prolog, we thus obtain the following computation principle for Bottom-Up, presented as a sequent:

$$\frac{(D\ :-\ \forall\vec{y}\ A)\ \ B}{\sigma(D)}\ \text{if}\ \ Unify\ (\underline{\exists\vec{x}\forall\vec{y}\exists\vec{u}}\ ,\ A = B)\ =\ (\underline{Q}, \sigma)$$

This rule is just that for first-order Horn Clauses, except that the unification is higher-order: the mixed prefix is simply synthesized by putting first the essentially existential variables $\vec{x}$ of the goal A, then the $\vec{y}$, and at the end the (essentially existential) variables $\vec{u}$ of the axiom.

Generalisation

1. We consider now the following more general clause

$$\forall\vec{x}\ (\forall\vec{x}_D\ D\ :-\ \forall\vec{y}_1\ A_1\ \wedge\ \forall\vec{y}_2\ A_2)$$

where the $\vec{y}_1$ appear only in A_1 and the $\vec{y}_2$ in A_2.
Once again, we remark on the scopes of the variables that:

– the essentially universal variables $\vec{y}_i$ only appear in the corresponding A_i.
– the only variables which may be changed in this clause during the unification of a A_i are the ones in $\vec{x}$ (they are the only essentially existential variables occurring in the D_i). If so, their substitution terms contain no essentially universal variables from the $\vec{y}_i$.

Therefore, proving A_1 and proving A_2 may be considered as two separate procedures, whose only interaction concerns the variables in $\vec{x}$. For each essentially existential variable x, a unification over the substitution terms provided by each search branch handles this interaction. This results in the following proof strategy:
We can, for instance, first chain A_2 with an axiom to obtain:

$$\underline{\exists \vec{x}' \exists \vec{u}'} \;\; (\forall \vec{x}_D \; \sigma_2(D) \; : - \; \forall \vec{y}_1 \; \sigma_2(A_1))$$

and then prove:

$$\underline{\exists \vec{x}' \exists \vec{u}' \forall \vec{y}_1} \;\; (\sigma_2(A_1))$$

This may be presented under the form of a sequent, as in the basic case:

$$\frac{(D \; : - \; \forall \vec{y}_1 \; A_1 \wedge \forall \vec{y}_2 \; A_2) \;\; B}{\sigma_2(D) \; : - \forall \vec{y}_1 \sigma_2(A_1)} \text{ if } \mathit{Unify} \; (\underline{\exists \vec{x} \forall \vec{y}_2 \exists \vec{u}} \;, \; A_2 = B) \; = \; (\underline{Q_2}, \sigma_2)$$

Remark. A parallel strategy may be adopted: proving simultaneously A_1 and A_2, we obtain two substitutions σ_1 and σ_2. Since the only variables shared by A_1 and A_2 are the $\vec{x}$ which are in the scope of no essentially universal variables, we can deduce

$$\underline{\exists \vec{x}'' \exists \vec{u}'' \exists \vec{v}''} \;\; (\sigma(G)) \; \textit{where } \sigma = mgu(\sigma_1, \sigma_2)$$

Once again, all the variables appearing in $\sigma(G)$ are essentially existential, and we may simply memorize the term $\sigma(G)$.

2. The previous case may be easily extended by iteration to that of any conjunction in the body of the clause, as in:

$$D \; : - \; \forall \vec{y}_1 \; A_1 \wedge \ldots \wedge \forall \vec{y}_n \; A_n$$

This extension relies on the tautology:

$$D \Leftarrow (\forall y_1 \; A_1 \wedge \forall y_2 \; A_2) \equiv (D \Leftarrow \forall y_1 \; A_1) \Leftarrow \forall y_2 \; A_2$$

The rule may be presented under the form of the following sequent:

$$\frac{(D \; : - \; \forall \vec{y}_1 \; A_1 \wedge \ldots \wedge \forall \vec{y}_n \; A_n) \qquad B}{\sigma_n(D) \; : - \; \forall \vec{y}_1 \sigma_n(A_1) \wedge \ldots \wedge \forall \vec{y}_{n-1} \sigma_n(A_{n-1})}$$

$$\text{if } \mathit{Unify} \; (\underline{\exists \vec{x} \forall \vec{y}_n \exists \vec{u}} \;, \; A_n = B) \; = \; (\underline{Q_n}, \sigma_n)$$

3. In the most general case of the form:

$$\forall \vec{x}\ (\forall \vec{x}_D\ D\ :-\ \forall \vec{y}\ (\forall \vec{y}_1\ G_1\ \wedge\ \forall \vec{y}_2\ G_2))$$

As G_1 and G_2 may be treated separately and the essentially universal variables $\vec{y}$ cannot appear in the substitution terms for the $\vec{x}$, we may distribute $\forall \vec{y}$ and replace this problem by that of:

$$\forall \vec{x}\ (\forall \vec{x}_D\ D\ :-\ \forall \vec{y} \forall \vec{y}_1\ G_1\ \wedge\ \forall \vec{y} \forall \vec{y}_2\ G_2)$$

This is only expressing the logical equivalence:

$$\forall y\ (G_1\ \wedge\ G_2)\ \Leftrightarrow\ (\forall y\ G_1)\ \wedge\ (\forall y\ G_2)$$

We may iterate this transformation until we have a conjunction of universally quantified atoms, where the previous case applies.

3.4 A Simple Interpreter

Relying on our previous remarks, we may now describe a Bottom-Up interpreter, which is exactly the same as for Horn clauses except:

- an initial compilation must distribute the quantifications to obtain clauses of the form:

$$\forall \vec{x}\ (\forall \vec{x}_D\ D\ :-\ \forall \vec{y}_1\ A_1\ \wedge \ldots \wedge \forall \vec{y}_n\ A_n)$$

  where the A_i are atomic formulas.
- the unification is higher-order, and the quantifier prefix needed may be easily synthesized from the terms to unify, by appending the scope constraints of the clause ($\exists \vec{u}$) to that of the goal to prove ($\exists \vec{x} \forall \vec{y}$).

The interpreter may then be written with a unique rule, very close to the *modus ponens* of natural deduction: (we neglect to mention the essentially existential variable of a clause, as is done in Prolog)

$$\frac{(D\ :-\ \forall \vec{y}_1\ A_1 \wedge \ldots \wedge \forall \vec{y}_n\ A_n) \qquad B}{\sigma_n(D)\ :-\ \forall \vec{y}_1 \sigma_n(A_1) \wedge \ldots \wedge \forall \vec{y}_{n-1} \sigma_n(A_{n-1})}$$

$$\text{if } Unify\ (\underline{\exists \vec{x} \forall \vec{y}_n \exists \vec{u}}\ ,\ A_n = B)\ =\ (\underline{Q_n}, \sigma_n)$$

Contrary to Top-Down strategies, scope constraints appear here in a very simple form: they may be easily synthesized when needed for unification, and the derived facts are sufficiently context-free (they only contain essentially existential variables) to avoid redundant evaluations when used to prove different goals.

Theorem 1. *The interpreter described above is sound and complete.*

The proof uses the natural deduction rules and is straightforward.

4 Conclusions

We have thus shown that a very simple Bottom-Up interpreter may be applied to our higher-order language l_λ. In this interpreter, the scope constraints do not have to be memorized during the resolution, as in the SLD approach, but may be synthesized only when necessary. As a result of these simple scope constraints, derived facts may be re-used to prove different goals, leading to a "semi-naïve" Bottom-Up evaluation, as defined in [BR86].

To the best of our knowledge, no interpreter based on the fixed point semantics principle had been given for such a higher-order language, and it is somehow satisfying to find it rather simple although the language was partly designed based on Top-Down properties (i.e. uniform proofs [Mil91]).

We believe exploring such a strategy for a higher-order logic language is of interest since:

- although it may be less efficient than SLD-resolution, it guarantees the completeness of the evaluation.
- it allows quite a context-free approach, whereas context-free in Top-Down strategies, as OLDT [TS86], is made difficult for higher-order languages because the need for quantifier prefixes makes the resolution highly contextual.

Moreover, for one or another of the previous reasons, this Bottom-Up strategy is appealing to fields such as natural language, where higher-order logic represents a nice mean of solving some problems (semantical interpretation, filler-gap dependencies [PS87]). For instance, although implication in clause bodies is not permitted in l_λ, this part of higher-order logic is already enough to describe simple semantic interpretation rules for a fragment of English [Per90]. The program obtained happens to loop when using a SLD-resolution, but this problem vanishes in the Bottom-Up procedure. We therefore believe this kind of strategy for l_λ represents a first interesting step towards efficient appropriate applications of higher-order logic.

Although Bottom-Up tends to compute many useless facts, its performance may be improved by making use of more sophisticated algorithms such as Earley Deduction [Ear70] (or Magic Templates [Ram88] which may be considered as a Bottom-Up implementation of the Earley method), which mixes strategies: a Top-Down predictive (i.e. not necessarily sound but complete) resolution is performed, defining relevant and restricted domains on which a Bottom-Up resolution is then performed. As a result, simplicity and context-free features remain, while decreasing the number of Bottom-Up explorations. In l_λ, the predictive phase could easily be performed by a unification "discarding" the quantifications (making the Top-Down phase, and particularly unification, quite simple). Such an implementation taking advantage of both strategies is in progress.
Another issue of such a strategy is to use its context-free features in implementations using the *Dynamic Programming* method. This implementation method exploits the analogy between logic programs and parsing [PW83] to apply techniques developed for context-free parsing to evaluate logic programs. These techniques are therefore

designed to be complete. They rely on context-free properties of the computation, and provide declarative and (more) complete compilers for definite clause programs whatever the chosen strategy is [Lan88]. Thanks to the context-free features of forward chaining strategies, Dynamic Programming could be efficiently applied to l_λ, leading to a declarative and operationally (more) complete interpreter for this higher-order language.

5 Further Work

Much of the work concerns handling all the features of L_λ, and particularly the possibility of an implication in the clause bodies. This feature gives quantification a much more expressive power by permitting relative quantification, the most usual form of quantification.

In Dale Miller's Top-Down interpreter, implication is treated by the deduction rule:

$$\frac{\Gamma \vdash (D \Rightarrow G)}{\Gamma \cup \{D\} \vdash G}$$

Implication is really a problem for Bottom-Up strategies since its natural treatment requires assuming some clause D and then prove G to prove $D \Rightarrow G$. An arbitrary choice of D would induce a fatal increase of the computations. The solution may appear from a prediction phase, somehow extending the Earley deduction method.

6 Acknowledgements

I am grateful to Dale Miller and the conference reviewers for their comments and suggestions on an earlier draft of this paper. Thanks to Ian Jacobs for helping me to improve my English style.

References

[BR86] F. Bancilhon and R. Ramakrishnan. An amateur's introduction to recursive query processing strategies. In *SIGMOD, invited paper*, 1986.

[BR88] F. Bancilhon and R. Ramakrishnan. *Performance Evaluation of Data Intensive Logic Programs.* Morgan Kaufman, 1988.

[Ear70] Jay Earley. An efficient context-free parsing algorithm. *Communications A.C.M.*, 13(2):92–102, February 1970.

[Fel88] Amy Felty. Specifying theorem provers in a higher-order logic programming language. In E. Lusk and R. Overbeek, editors, 9th *International Conference on Automated Deduction.* Springer Verlag, May 1988.

[HL78] Gérard Huet and Bernard Lang. Proving and applying program transformations expressed with second-order logic. *Acta Informatica*, 11:31–55, 78.

[Hue75] Gérard Huet. A unification algorithm for typed λ-calculus. *Theoretical Computer Science*, 1:27–57, 1975.

[Lan88] Bernard Lang. Complete evaluation of Horn Clauses: an automata theoretic approach. Research Report 813, INRIA, November 1988.

[Mil] Dale Miller. Unification under a mixed prefix. to appear in the Journal of Symbolic Computation.

[Mil91] Dale Miller. A logic programming language with lambda-abstraction, function variables, and simple unification. *Journal of Logic and Computation*, 1:497–536, 1991.

[MN86] Dale Miller and Gopalan Nadathur. Some uses of higher-order logic in computational linguistics. In *Proceedings of the* 24th *Annual Meeting of the Association for Computational Linguistics*, 1986.

[MN87] Dale Miller and Gopalan Nadathur. A logic programming approach to manipulating formulas and programs. In *Proceedings of the* 4th *Symposium on Logic Programming*, pages 379–388. IEEE Press, 1987.

[MNPS91] Dale Miller, Gopalan Nadathur, Frank Pfenning, and Andre Scedrov. Uniform proofs as a foundation for logic programming. *Annals of Pure and Applied Logic*, 51:125–157, 1991.

[NJ91] Gopalan Nadathur and Bharat Jarayaman. Implementation techniques for scoping constructs in logic programming. In Koichi Furukawa, editor, *Proceedings of the Eighth International Conference on Logic Programming*, pages 871–886, 1991.

[Per90] Fernando C. N. Pereira. Semantic interpretation as higher-order deduction. In Springer-Verlag, editor, *Lecture Notes in Artificial Intelligence*, pages 78–96, 1990.

[PM90] Remo Pareschi and Dale Miller. Extending definite clause grammars with scoping constructs. In *Proceedings of the* 7th *International Conference on Logic Programming*, pages 373–389, 1990.

[PS87] Fernando C.N. Pereira and Stuart M. Shieber. *Prolog and Natural-Language Analysis*, volume 10 of *Lecture Notes*, pages 178–185. CSLI, 1987.

[PW83] F.C.N. Pereira and D.H.D. Warren. Parsing as deduction. In *Proceedings of the 21st Annual Meeting of the Association for Computationnal Linguistic*, pages 137–144, Cambridge (Massachussetts), 1983.

[Ram88] Raghu Ramakrishnan. Magic templates: A spellbounding approach to manipulating formulas and programs. In *Proceedings of the* 5th *International Conference/Symposium on Logic Programming*, pages 140–159, 1988.

[Rou] François Rouaix. Personal communication.

[RS90] Anthony Rich and Marvin Solomon. A logic–based approach to system modelling. Extended Abstract, 1990.

[RW91] Eugene J. Rollins and Jeannette M. Wing. Specifications as search keys for software libraries. In Koichi Furukawa, editor, *Proceedings of the* 8th *International Conference on Logic Programming*, pages 173–187, 1991.

[TS86] H. Tamaki and T. Sato. OLD–resolution with tabulation. In E. Shapiro, editor, *Proc. of Third Int. Conf. on Logic Programming*, pages 84–98, London, 1986. Springer–Verlag.

[vEK76] M. van Emden and R. Kowalski. The semantics of predicate logic as a programming language. *Journal of the ACM*, 23(4), 1976.

[War82] D. H. Warren. Higher-order extensions to Prolog: Are they needed? *Machine Intelligence*, 10:441–454, 1982.

This article was processed using the LaTeX macro package with LLNCS style

CAMEL: An Extension of the Categorical Abstract Machine to Compile Functional / Logic Programs

Andy Mück
Universität München
Leopoldstraße 11B
W-8000 München 40
E-mail: mueck@informatik.uni-muenchen.de
Fax: ++49 89 21 80 52 46

Abstract: In this paper we present a clean implementation technique for functional / logic (or algebraic) programming languages. First we define an intermediate language to which a functional / logic program is compiled. In order to implement this intermediate language, we extend the Categorical Abstract Machine (CAM) by an additional data structure to handle logical variables and by a few instructions covering unification and backtracking. Finally, we show how the intermediate language is compiled into the instruction set of our Categorical Abstract Machine extension.

1 Introduction

Functional / logic programming languages are languages combining both, functional programming style and logic programming style. This means that functional programming is enriched by the possibility to solve equations between functional expressions and logic programming is extended in the sense that there is no need to flatten complex expressions as is necessary in Prolog [Han90 a].
A functional / logic program consists of a signature Σ, a set of rewrite rules A (over Σ) and a set of equations E (over Σ) to be solved. Like SLD-resolution serves as operational semantics for Prolog, narrowing is the underlying operational semantics of functional / logic languages. Narrowing unifies a subterm in E with a left-hand side of a rule in A resulting in a substitution σ and then rewrites the subterm with the right-hand side of the rule and applies σ to E.
In the past few years, several abstract machines were developed in order to compile functional / logic programming languages [i.e. Han 90 b, Bos 89, Loc 91 a, Loo 91 a, Kuc 90]. Most of these machines are extensions of the Warren Abstract Machine (WAM) [War 83, Ait 90] which has become established as "the de facto standard for implementing Prolog" ([Ait 90]). Since WAM is a highly optimized machine, a high degree of efficiency is guaranteed if it is used as a starting point to implement narrowing. On the other hand, WAM extensions inherit the complexity of WAM´s instruction set (about 40 instructions in the pure WAM) and the complicated way these instructions transform the machine state. This fact, of course, exerts an influence on a correctness proof of the WAM and, in the same way, to WAM extensions. Apart from a verification of a simplified WAM by D. Rusinof [Rus 89], there was no correctness proof of this machine since E. Boerger [Boe 91] recently came up with a formal derivation of WAM by stepwise refining dynamic Prolog algebras.
Our intention now is to develop an abstract machine for functional / logic programming languages for which verification should easily be possible [Mue 92]. Instead of starting with implementation techniques known from Prolog and extending them for functional programming, we begin by taking a look at the functional world. Here several (verified) abstract machines exist, i.e. secd-machine [Lan 64], Functional Abstract Machine (FAM) [Car 86], Categorical Abstract Machine (CAM) [Cou 86, Cou 90] and so on.
Out of this collection we choose CAM as a starting point since it provides an acceptable com-

promise between abstractness and efficiency. CAM is then enriched by logical programming features, i.e. a stack of logical variables (called heap), unification instructions and a backtracking mechanism. To achieve a stepwise compilation of functional / logic programs into the instruction set of our CAM extension called CAMEL (CAM Extension for Functional / Logic Programming), we introduce an intermediate language to which a functional / logic program is compiled in a first step by partially evaluating the rules of the program [Mue 90]. In a second step, the program in the intermediate language is compiled to CAMEL instructions. CAMEL itself turns out to be a straightforward extension of CAM. We will also see that the compilation of the intermediate language (to CAMEL code) can easily be derived from a compiler for a functional language (to CAM instructions).
After giving some basic definitions and notations in section 2 of this paper, we define in section 3 the intermediate language to which a functional / logic program is compiled in a first step. In section 4 we start with a short review of CAM and then we describe the extensions mentioned above. In section 5 we give a compiler from the intermediate language to the instruction set of CAMEL. Finally, we conclude with a view to further research.

2 Basic Definitions

Let Σ =(S,C,F) be a *signature* with a set S of *sorts*, a set C of *constructor symbols* and a set F of *function symbols* together with an arity for each $c \in C$ and $f \in F$. The set of all *finite and well-formed Σ-terms $T_\Sigma(X)$* with variables in X is defined as follows:

i) each $x \in X$ is a Σ-term
ii) if $t_1,...,t_n$ are Σ-terms of appropriate sorts then for each $g{:}s_1 \times ... \times s_n \rightarrow s \in C \cup F$ $g(t_1,...,t_n)$ is a Σ-term. g is called the function symbol at the *root* of the term.

Terms only built of variables and symbols of C are called *constructor terms* which are denoted by $T_C(X)$. The notation of constructor terms is necessary to define the *leftmost innermost redex* [Fri 85] of a term. This is the leftmost innermost subterm $f(t_1,...,t_n)$ of a term t where $f \in F$ and $t_i \in T_C(X)$ for all i. A subterm of a term t at an occurrence u is denoted by $t|_u$.
Let p and t be terms and u an occurrence of p. Then $p[u \leftarrow t]$ denotes the term which is obtained by replacing the subterm of p at the occurrence u with t. A term t is called *linear*, if no variable in t occurs more than once.
A *functional / logic program* P consists of a signature Σ, a set of rules A and a set of Σ-equations E to be solved. The rules are of the form

$f(t_1,...,t_n) \rightarrow r$, where $f \in F$, $t_i \in T_C(X)$ for all i, $r \in T_\Sigma(X)$ and $f(t_1,..,t_n)$ is linear and the variables occurring in r are a subset of those occurring in $f(t_1,...,t_n)$.
In the context of this paper we restrict function symbols and constructor symbols to be of arity 0, 1 or 2 and the set of equations E to be a singleton. These restrictions only serve to avoid technical details.

The following *narrowing calculus* is a slight variation of the one given in [Hus 85]. It serves to solve an equation e with respect to the rules of a functional / logic program P=(Σ,A,E).

$$\frac{q_1=q_2 \text{ with } \sigma}{\emptyset \text{ with } \tau\circ\sigma} \qquad \tau=mgu(q_1,q_2)$$

$$\frac{e \text{ with } \sigma}{\tau(e[u \leftarrow r]) \text{ with } \tau\circ\sigma}$$ if $p \rightarrow r$ is a new variant of a rule in A, the variable sets of p and e are disjoint, $\tau=mgu(p,e|_u)$, $e|_u$ is not a variable.

A narrowing computation starts with an equation e (of the form $q_1=q_2$) and the empty substitution ε. If q_1 and q_2 are unifiable with a most general unifier (mgu) [Rob 65] τ, then τ is returned as a result. Otherwise one searches for a rule p→r and for a non-variable occurrence u in e, such that p and $e|_u$ can be unified with an mgu τ. Now, computation continues recursively with the equation τ(e[u←r]). In this paper as a narrowing strategy we take leftmost innermost narrowing [Fri 85]. Leftmost innermost narrowing applies a rule to the leftmost innermost redex of an equation e.

Whenever we speak of lists we use the following SML-like notation:

x::l	means appending an element x to a list l.
l1@l2	means concatenation of two lists.
hd(l)	denotes the head of a list l and *tl(l)* its tail.
[x_1 , ... , x_n]	denotes a list with entries x_1 , ... , x_n.
nil or *[ ]*	denote the empty list.
l[i]	returns the i-th element of a list l starting from the head of the list. That is: *l[1] = hd(l)*.
update(l,i,e)	updates the list l at the i-th position with an element e.

3 The Intermediate Language

In this section we give syntax and semantics of the intermediate language a functional / logic program is compiled to. We do not give the compiler explicitly in this paper. The reader is referred to [Mue 90] where code generation by partial evaluation of the rules of a functional / logic program is explained for a target language similar to the following intermediate language.

Having in mind that the intermediate language will be compiled into the instruction set of an extension of CAM the language should be similar to a functional programming language. Furthermore, since it should cover logical features too, it must contain a built-in unification function and a choice operator for explicitly expressing the choice between several alternatives.

We only consider first order functional / logic programs because higher order unification is undecidable in the general case. Because of this, our intermediate language is restricted to be first order.

3.1 Syntax of the Intermediate Language

In the following let f,g,.. be function symbols, c,d,.. be symbols for constants and x,y,.. be variables. The syntax of the intermediate language is given as follows (keywords are written in bold letters):

```
Program ::= Decl ; .. ; Decl ; Term
Decl ::= fun f Pattern = MatchExpression
MatchExpression ::=   Expression |
                      if Condition then MatchExpression else MatchExpression |
                      choice ( UnifExpression ; ... ; UnifExpression )
UnifExpression ::= ( Expression , Term ) => MatchExpression
Expression ::= x | c | f Expression | ( Expression , Expression ) | πi Expression   i=(1,2)
Term ::= ∃x | c | f Term | ( Term , Term )
Condition ::= isa ( {f | c} , Expression )
Pattern ::= () | ( x ) | ( Pattern , Pattern )
```

Remark: This intermediate language extends a usual functional language like SML by the notation of **terms and explicit unification.** Terms are necessary since a functional / logic language may contain so called **logical variables.** These are variables which might be unbound or bound to different values within the same closure (see section 4 and 5). Terms are expressions which contain logical variables instead of functional variables. Unification expressions of the form (ex,t) => mex are used to make unification explicit. The semantics of a unification expression is as follows: first, the expression ex is evaluated (to a term) and unified with t. Then the match expression mex is evaluated under the substitution obtained by unification. **isa(f,e)** decides whether the evaluation of an expression e starts with a function (or constructor) symbol f.

Example: The following rules of a functional / logic program which decides whether a list of natural numbers is sorted

```
issorted (empty) → true,
issorted (cons (x,empty)) → true,
issorted (cons (x,cons(y,s))) → and (le (x,y),issorted (cons(y,s)))
```

compile (by partial evaluation, see [Mue 90]) to

```
fun issorted(p) =
if isa (empty,p)
then true
else  if isa (cons,p)
      then  if isa (empty, π2 p )
            then true
            else if isa (cons , π2 p )
                 then and ( le (π1 p , π1( π2 p ) ) , issorted (cons (π1(π2 p) , π2( π2 p ) ) ) )
                 else choice ( (π2 p , empty ) => true , (* now, π2 p must be a logical variable *)
                               (π2 p , cons(∃y,∃s) ) =>
                               and (le(π1 p, π1 ( π2 p ) ),issorted (cons (π1(π2 p),π2(π2 p ) ) ) ) )
      else  choice (  ( p , empty ) => true, (*now, p must be a logical variable *)
                      ( p , cons (∃x,empty) => true,
                      ( p , cons (∃x,cons(∃y,∃s)) =>
                      and (le (π1 p , π1 ( π2 p ) ) , issorted (cons (π1(π2 p) , π2( π2 p ) ) ) ) ) );
```

Remark: The compilation in the example above is optimized in the sense that one first tries to detect determined cases by matching. A choice point is created only if matching is not possible (compare [Loo 91 b]). A straightforward code generation without optimization would result in

```
fun issorted(p) =
choice ( ( p, empty ) => true,
         ( p , cons (∃x,empty) => true,
         ( p , cons (∃x,cons(∃y,∃s)) =>
         and (le (π1 p , π1 ( π2 p ) ) , issorted (cons (π1(π2 p) , π2( π2 p ) ) ) ) ) );
```

3.2 Semantics of the Intermediate Language

In the following we give the semantics of the above intermediate language. Suppose we have:

SUBST: Logical Variables → Term
GOAL: Term x SUBST
RES: (Term x (SUBST + failure)) Set
VAL: Variables → Term
ENV: function symbol → GOAL → RES

The semantics of a program is given by a function mapping programs to results. After creating an environment we apply the term *t* together with the identity substitution to the environment:

P: Program → RES
P [df_1 ;..; df_n ; t] = ($\mathbf{D_2}$ [df_n] ($\mathbf{D_2}$ [df_{n-1}] (..($\mathbf{D_2}$ [df_1] e_0)..))) g (t,σ_{id}) , *if root* (tl_{occ})=*g*
where e_0 *is the empty environment and* σ_{id} *is the identity substitution*

The semantic function $\mathbf{D_2}$ takes a declaration and an environment and returns a new environment which is an update of the old one by the semantics of the function declaration:

$\mathbf{D_2}$: Decl → ENV → ENV
$\mathbf{D_2}$ [fun g p = mex] e = e [$\mathbf{D_1}$ [fun g p = mex] e / g]

The function $\mathbf{D_1}$ maps a function declaration *fun g p = mex* and an environment to a mapping *f* from goals to results. *f(t,s)* is recursively defined by the semantics of the match expression *mex* under the old environment updated by the function f itself for the function symbol *g*.

$\mathbf{D_1}$: Decl → ENV → GOAL → RES
$\mathbf{D_1}$ [fun g p = mex] e = (let f = λ(t,σ) . **ME** [mex] e[f / g] s_0[q / p] (t,σ) in f)
where s_0 *is the empty valuation and* tl_{occ} = *g (q)*

The semantics of a match expression is given by the semantic function **ME** which maps a match expression, an environment, a valuation and a goal to results.

ME: MatchExpression → ENV → VAL → GOAL → RES

If the match expression is the compilation of a right hand side of a rule **ME** inserts the right hand side into the term at the leftmost innermost occurrence *occ* and applies the substitution to the new term. If the new term contains a leftmost innermost redex the new goal is applied to the environment. Otherwise the left and right hand sides of the new term are unified and a result, which might be failure, is returned:

ME [exp] e s (t,σ) = e g (t_{new},σ), *if root* ($t_{new}/_{occ}$)=*g*
ME [exp] e s (t,σ) = { (t,σ) }, *otherwise*
where $t_{new} = \sigma$ *(t[occ ← E[exp] s])*

If the match expression is a conditional expression, the path according to the evaluation of the condition is computed:

ME [if cond then mex1 else mex2] e s (t,σ) = **ME** [mex1] e s (t,σ), *if C[cond] s = true*
ME [if cond then mex1 else mex2] e s (t,σ) = **ME** [mex2] e s (t,σ), *otherwise*

The result of a choice expression is the union of the results of the single unification expressions:

ME [choice(u_1,..,u_n)] e s (t,σ) = **U** [u_1] e s (t,σ) ∪ .. ∪ **U** [u_n] e s (t,σ)

To define the semantics of a unification expression *(ex,t) => me* we first have to unify the evaluation of *ex* and the term *t*. Suppose unification results in a substitution τ, τ is composed with the substitution in the goal as well as with the valuation of the formal parameters. The later composition is necessary because before unification a formal parameter may have been bound to an uninstantiated logical variable which may by unification be instantiated with a value. The match expression me must now be evaluated with the new valuation for this formal parameter.

U: UnifExpression → ENV→ VAL→ GOAL → RES

U [(ex,t) => me] e s (t,σ) = **ME** [me] e τos (t,τoσ) *if* τ = *unify(E [ex] s, t)*
U [(ex,t) => me] e s (t,σ) = { **failure** } *if unification fails*

The semantics of expressions and conditional expressions is given by the following functions:

E: Expression ⟶ VAL ⟶ Term
E [x] s = s(x)
E [π_i(ex)] s = Π_i (s(x)) *where* $\Pi_i\,(f\,(t_1,...,t_n)) = t_i$
E [f (ex$_1$,...,ex$_n$)] s = f (E[ex$_1$] s ,..., E[ex$_n$] s)

C: Condition ⟶VAL ⟶ BOOL
C [isa (f,ex)] s = (f=root (s(ex))) *where root(t) yields the topmost function symbol of t*

4 Extending CAM to CAMEL

Following, we extend the Categorical Abstract Machine (CAM) [Cou 86, Cou 90] in order to implement the intermediate language given in section 3. We start with a short review of CAM.

4.1 The Categorical Abstract Machine (CAM)

We describe CAM in its original form developed by G. Cousineau, P.-L. Curien, M. Mauny and A. Suarez in [Cou 86] and [Cou 90]. Since CAM executes categorical combinators directly as machine instructions it is a clean and comprehensible abstract machine. Because of environment sharing and closure optimization CAM is more efficient than the secd-machine [Lan 64]. Due to these reasons CAM seems to be best suited to our needs.
CAM consists of 3 data areas:

i) **value area** containing values. A value is either a dummy value denoted by Ω, a constant, a pair of values (v,w) or a closure <v,C> consisting of a value v and machine code C.
ii) a list of values called **stack**
iii) **code area** which contains a list of machine instructions.

CAM State Transitions:

old state			new state		
Value	Stack	Code	Value	Stack	Code
v	S	**id**::C	v	S	C
(v,w)	S	**fst**::C	v	S	C
(v,w)	S	**snd**::C	w	S	C
v	S	**push**::C	v	v::S	C
v	w::S	**swap**::C	w	v::S	C
w	v::S	**cons**::C	(v,w)	S	C
v	S	**cur**(C)::C1	<v,C>	S	C1
(<v,C>,w)	S	**app**::C1	(v,w)	<Ω,C1>::S	C
v	S	**quote**(c)::C	c	S	C
v	<Ω,C>::S	nil	v	S	C
(v,w)	S	**op**::C	v op w	S	C
(v,false)	S	**branch**(C1,C2)::nil	v	S	C2
(v,true)	S	**branch**(C1,C2)::nil	v	S	C1
where op is any binary operation (addition etc.)			*operating on values.*		

Compiling a Functional Language to CAM Instructions:
To illustrate how a functional language is compiled to CAM code, we give a compiler for the following language.

prog ::=	def;...;def;expr	*program*
def ::=	fun var pattern = expr	*function definition*
expr ::=	c I	*constant*
	var I	*variable*
	$expr_1$ $expr_2$ I	*application*
	$expr_1$ op $expr_2$ I	*binary operation*
	($expr_1$, $expr_2$) I	*pair*
	if expr then $expr_1$ else $expr_2$ I	*conditional expression*
pattern::=	var I	*variable pattern*
	() I	*empty pattern*
	(p_1 , p_2)	*pair pattern*

We give a compiler for this functional language by the following function compile which maps a functional program to a list of CAM instructions.

<u>compile</u> (def_1;...;def_n;ex) = <u>comP</u> (def_1;...;def_n;ex , ())

To compile function definitions, annotated patterns according to [Cousineau 90] are introduced. An annotated pattern is a pattern $P_{f=code}$. The annotation *f=code* indicates that the variable f is associated with the CAM program *code.*

<u>comP</u> (fun f p = ex ;def_2;...;def_n;ex , P) = <u>comP</u> (def_2;...;def_n;ex ,P1)
where $P1 = (P_{f = cur(\,comE\,(ex\,,\,(P1,p)\,)\,)})$
Note that the definition of P1 covers a non-terminating compilation process for f if f is a recursive function definition. At this point the compilation function <u>comE</u> should lazily be evaluated.
<u>comP</u>(ex , P) = <u>comE</u>(ex , P)
<u>comE</u>(x , (x,P)) = locate(x,P),
where *locate(x,(x)) = nil*
locate(x,$(P)_{x=code}$) = code
locate(x,(P,Q)) = [***fst*** *] @ locate(x,P), if x is located in P*
locate(x,(P,Q)) = [***snd*** *] @ locate(x,Q), if x is located in Q*
<u>comE</u>(c , P) = [**quote(c)**]
<u>comE</u>(ex_1 ex_2 , (P,Q)) = [**push**] @ <u>comE</u>(ex_1,(P,Q))@[**swap**]@ <u>comE</u>(ex_2,(P,Q)) @ [**cons , app**]
<u>comE</u>((ex_1 , ex_2) , P) = [**push**] @ <u>comE</u>(ex_1,(P,Q)) @ [**swap**] @ <u>comE</u>(ex_2,(P,Q)) @ [**cons**]
<u>comE</u>((ex_1 op ex_2) , P) = [**push**] @ <u>comE</u>(ex_1,P) @ [**swap**] @ <u>comE</u>(ex_2,P) @ [**op**]
<u>comE</u>(if c then ex_1 else ex_2 , P) = [**push**] @ <u>comE</u>(c,P) @ [**cons, branch(** <u>comE</u>(ex_1,P), <u>comE</u>(ex_2,P) **)**]

For any further details on CAM the reader is referred to [Cou 90].

4.2 Extending CAM to CAMEL or "Rollin´ the Cigarette"

In order to implement our intermediate language we now extend CAM by

i) a data structure to handle logical variables (called heap)
ii) an instruction to perform unification
iii) a few additional instructions and a choice point closure to handle backtracking

ad i): whenever a function is called in an eager functional language the formal parameters are bound to the value of the actual parameters. In our intermediate language however, a formal parameter may also be bound to an uninstantiated logical variable. A straightforward approach to treat logical variables as special expressions in the value area only, fails because unification may bind this logical variable to another value. As long as the logical variable does not occur more than once in a term this treatment would not cause any problems. But, analogously to multiple occurrences of an expression in the pure functional world, multiple occurrence of a logical variable means that the variable´s machine code occurs exactly as often as the variable itself. If the logical variable is now bound to another value, we would have to substitute the value´s code instead of the encoding of the variable in the rest of the machine program. Therefore, with every call of a function as well as in the initial term to be reduced, we reserve a list of empty heap cells (called *logical variable list*) for all logical variables occurring in the function (term resp.). To achieve sharing variables occurring more than once, these variables are represented only once in this list. When a logical variable is now bound to a value by unification, the value it is bound to is stored in the according heap cell. Note that an empty heap cell corresponds to an unbound logical variable. Since every call of a function creates a logical variable list, the heap is a list of logical variable lists together with a natural number (heap pointer) indicating which logical variable list is valid for the current incarnation of a function. We get

heap = ((entry list) list) * nat,
where entry is either an empty cell (denoted by ⊥) or a value

Speaking in terms of the narrowing calculus given in section 2, a single list of the heap represents the substitution calculated by one narrowing step. So, the whole heap represents the composition of all substitutions calculated by the single narrowing steps.
Suppose the logical variable ∃x is represented in the n-th position of the current variable list. We encode a logical variable ∃x by a get instruction which either puts a reference log_var(n,a) into the value area if the n-th variable in the current variable list (indicated by the heap pointer a) is uninstantiated or copies the value at the n-th position in the variable list into the value area, otherwise. For details see section 5.

ad ii): For the purpose of unification we simply introduce a unify instruction which unifies two values (represented as a pair value) in the value area. Note that unify creates a side effect in the heap. Whenever an unbound logical variable log_var(n,m) is unified with a value v, the n-th cell in the m-th variable list on the heap is altered to contain v.

ad iii): To compile a choice statement of several unification expressions we introduce the cp instruction. cp is analogously to cur and branch a compound instruction which contains a list of machine code as argument. This list consists of the compiled code for each unification expression in a choice statement. cp creates a choice point saving the current machine state at the bottom of the stack.

CAMEL State Transitions: Having shown the main extensions of CAM we now explain the state transitions of CAMEL:

First we give those state transitions which are identical to those of pure CAM:

	old state				new state			
	heap	value	stack	code	heap	value	stack	code
1	h	v	S	id::C	h	v	S	C
2	h	v	S	quote(con)::C	h	"con"	S	C
3	h	v	S	push::C	h	v	v::S	C

4	h	v	w::S	swap::C	h	w	v::S	C
5	h	w	v::S	cons::C	h	(v,w)	S	C
6	h	(v,false)	S	branch(C1,C2)::nil	h	v	S	C2
7	h	(v,true)	S	branch(C1,C2)::nil	h	v	S	C1

As stated earlier, the heap pointer is necessary to indicate which logical variable list in the heap is the actual one. The heap must not be popped when a function call is finished because unification may bind variables of earlier function calls to values in the last list of the heap. Because of that, the logical variable list according to a function call is not necessarily the last list in the heap. We use the heap pointer to refer to the actual variable list of a function call. To save the current value of the heap pointer when a new call is executed, CAM closures are extended to store this value, too. Whenever a closure is created by a **cur** instruction (compare rule 9) the value of the heap pointer is saved in this closure. Execution of an **app** instruction (compare rule 10) passes the saved value to the dummy-closure on the stack. When execution of a function has finished (compare rule 8) the heap pointer is restored. Except for the treatment of the heap pointer, the following state transitions are identical to those of CAM:

	old state				new state			
	heap	value	stack	code	heap	value	stack	code
8	(l,n)	v	closure(Ω,i,C)::S	nil	(l,i)	v	S	C
9	(l,n)	v	S	cur(C)::C1	(l,n)	closure(v,n,C)	S	C1
10	h	(closure(v,i,C),w)	S	app::C1	h	(v,w)	closure(Ω,i,C1)::S	C

The state transitions for the instructions **fst** and **snd** are almost identical to the corresponding CAM transitions. They only differ when the first (second resp.) value is a reference to heap cell. In this case we have to look up in the heap whether the cell is empty. If it is empty, the reference remains in the value area. Otherwise the value stored in the cell is copied into the value area.

	old state				new state			
	heap	value	stack	code	heap	value	stack	code
11	(l,n)	(v,w)	S	fst::C	(l,n) *where u = (l[m])[i], if v = log_var(i,m) and* $(l[m])[i] <> \bot$ *u = v, otherwise*	u	S	C
12	(l,n)	(v,w)	S	snd::C	(l,n) *where u = (l[m])[i], if w = log_var(i,m)and* $(l[m])[i] <> \bot$ *u = w, otherwise*	u	S	C

As the **cp** instruction encodes a choice between several alternatives, it is a compound instruction which contains the code for each alternative as parameter. Execution of this instruction (see rules 13,14) puts the code of the first alternative to the code area and creates a choice point at the bottom of the stack. As a choice point saves the current machine state it contains the current heap, the value, the stack and a **cp** instruction with the code of the remaining alternatives as parameter. If the code area is empty and if there is no closure at the top of the stack, the choice point at the bottom of the stack serves to restore the machine state in order to compute the next alternative (see rule 15).

	old state			new state			
	heap	value	stack	code	heap	value	stack	code
13	h	v	S	cp(C1::Cl)::nil	h	v	S @ [choice(h,v,S,cp(Cl))]	C1
14	h	v	S	cp(nil)::nil	h	v	S	nil
15	h	v	S @[choice(g,w,T,cp(Cl))]	nil	g	w	T	cp(Cl)
					if S <> closure(n, v, C) :: S1			

The instruction **pop** simply pops the stack and the instruction **isa** decides whether a value representing a term starts with a special function symbol. Both, the function symbol and the value are represented by a pair value in the value area.

	old state				new state			
	heap	value	stack	code	heap	value	stack	code
16	h	v	w::S	pop::C	h	v	S	C
17	h	pair(v,"f")	S	isa::C	h	b	S	C
					where b =((v="f") or (v=pair("f",w)))			

We now explain the most important new instructions which operate on the heap. These are the instructions **put, get** and **set. put**(n) simply creates a new list of n empty heap cells (denoted by ⊥) on the heap. **get**(i) checks in the current logical variable list of the heap (indicated by the heap pointer) whether the i-th cell in this list is empty. If it is empty, a reference to this heap cell is created in the value area. If it is not empty, the value stored in the cell is copied into the value area. The **set** instruction sets the heap pointer to the last list on the heap.

	old state				new state			
	heap	value	stack	code	heap	value	stack	code
18	(l,m)	v	S	put(n)::C	(l@vl ,m)	v	S	C
					vl = [⊥,...,⊥] and length vl = n			
19	(l,m)	v	S	get(i)::C	(l,m)	w	S	C
					where w = (l[m])[i], if (l[m])[i]<>⊥			
					where w = log_var(i,m), otherwise			
20	(l,m)	v	S	set::C	(l,n)	v	S	C
					where n = length(l)			

In the following we show the state transitions of the unification instructions **subst** and **uni**. The **subst** instruction updates an empty heap cell value. Both, the reference to the heap cell as well as the value itself are represented as a pair value in the value area. The instruction **uni** unifies two values represented as a pair in the value area. To describe unification on machine level we use the function **unify** which is specified in detail below. Whenever unification fails, a **failure value** is created in the value area. If the value area contains a failure value, the rest of the machine code is ignored. Please note that as soon as the code area is empty, the machine state saved in a (possible) choice point at the bottom of the stack is restored and computation continues for the next alternative.

	old state				new state			
	heap	value	stack	code	heap	value	stack	code
21	(l,n)	(log_var(i,m),v)	S	subst::C	(l1,n)	v	S	C
					where l1 = update(l[m],i,v)			
22	(l,n)	(v,log_var(i,m))	S	subst::C	(l1,n)	v	S	C
					where l1 = update(l[m],i,v)			
23	h	(v,w)	S	uni::C	h1	u	S	C
					where (h1,u) = unify(l,v,w)			
24	h	failure	S	c::C	h	failure	S	C for all instructions c

Remark: Note that after a successful execution of the uni-instruction the heap represents a result substitution for the initial term. Since this heap might be replaced by another one saved in a choice point, the current heap must be used to display the result substitution.

Following we specify in an SML-like language the function **unify**. unify takes a list of logical variable list and two values as arguments and computes a pair consisting of a new list and a value. If one of the two value arguments is a reference to a (necessarily) empty heap cell in the variable list the value is written into the empty cell. If both values are equal constants, nothing happens. If both values are pairs they are unified sequentially. If none of the previous cases holds, failure is returned in the value part of the result.

```
fun  unify(l,log_var(i,n),t) =
               if (l[n])[i]=⊥
               then (update(l,n,update(l[n],i,t)),t)
               else unif(l,(l[n])[i],t) |
     unify(l,t,log_var(i,n)) =
               if (l[n])[i]=⊥
               then (update(l,n,update(l[n],i,t)),t)
               else unif(l,(l[n])[i],t) |
     unify(l,c,c) = (l,c) (* where c is a constructor symbol *) |
     unify(l,(s1,t1),(s2,t2)) =
               let val (l1,s) = unif(l,s1,t1)
               in  let val (l2,t) = unif(l1,s2,t2)
                   in if s=failure or t= failure
                   then failure
                   else (l2,pair(s,t))
     unify(l,s,t) = (l,failure);
```

5 Compilation of the Intermediate Language

In this section we show how the intermediate language is compiled into the instruction set of CAMEL. The main difference to the compilation of a functional language lies in the treatment of terms and especially logical variables. Since unbound logical variables are at machine level represented in the heap and not in the value area we cannot use the pattern attribute of the compilation functions to synthesize the code for logical variables. In order to compile those syntactical units which may contain logical variables (these are terms, match expressions and unification expressions), we need an additional attribute which contains the list of logical variables occurring in such units. Therefore the compilation functions comM, comU and comT contain this additional attribute.

compile ($decl_1$;...;$decl_n$;eq) = comP ($decl_1$;...;$decl_n$;eq , ())
where () is the empty pattern.

comP (fun f p = mex ;$decl_2$;...;$decl_n$; eq , P) = comP ($decl_2$;...;$decl_n$;eq , P1)
where $P1 = P_{f\,=\,cur\,(\,put(m)\,,\,set\,,\,comM\,(mex,[y1,...,ym]\,,\,(P1,p)\,)}$
and $[y_1,...,y_m]$ *is the of list different logical variables occurring in mex.*

When compiling a term t we first create a new list of empty cells on the heap. The length of this list is determined by the number of different logical variables occurring in t. Then, the heap pointer is set to refer to this list. Following, code for the term t is created.

comP(t , P) = **[put (n) , set]** @ comT(t , $[x_1,...,x_n]$, P)
where $[x_1,...,x_n]$ is the list different logical variables occurring in the term t=s.

If a match expression simply consists of an expression the expression is compiled. Compilation of a conditional expression is straightforward like compilation of conditional expressions in the CAM compilation schema. Compilation of a choice of several alternatives creates a cp instruction containing the code of each single alternative as parameter. Note that comM contains an additional attribute which consists of the list of logical variables occurring in the match expression to be compiled.

comM(exp , l , P) = comE(exp , P)
comM(if cond the mex_1 else mex_2 , l , P) = **[push]** @ comC(cond , P) @ **[cons , branch(**comM(mex_1 , l , P) , comM(mex_2 , l P) **]**
comM(choice($[u_1,...,u_n]$) , l , P) = **cp(**comU(u_1 , l , P),...,comU(u_n , l , P))

Compilation of a unification expression returns code which creates a pair value consisting of the evaluation of the expression ex and the term t in the value area. Note that the expression ex always evaluates to a logical variable (see example of section 3 and [Mue 90]). For that reason this logical variable is substituted with the evaluation of t by a subst instruction. Due to technical reasons, the stack must be popped before executing the code for the match expression mex.

comU((ex,t) => mex , l , P) = **[push , push]** @ comE(ex,P) @ **[swap]** @ comT(t,l,P) @ **[cons , subst , swap , pop]** @ comM(mex,l,P)

Terms are compiled almost in the same way as expressions in the CAM compilation scheme. The only difference is that logical variables are compiled to a get(i) instruction. Thereby i is determined by the position of the logical variable in the list of logical variables which is an additional attribute for this compilation schema. In the following, let con be a constant, c be a constructor symbol and f be a function symbol.

comT($\exists x$, [$\exists x_1,...,\exists x_{i-1},\exists x,\exists x_{i+1},...,\exists x_n$] , P) = **[get(i)]**
comT(con , l , P) =**[quote(con)]**
comT(f t , l , P) = **[push]** @ locate(f,P) @ code @ **[swap]** @ comT(t,l,P) @ **[cons , app]**
where locate(x,(x)) = nil
locate(x,$(P)_{x=code}$) = code
locate(x,(P,Q)) = [fst] @ locate(x,P), if x is located in P
locate(x,(P,Q)) = [snd] @ locate(x,Q), if x is located in Q
comT(c t , l , P) = **[push]** @ **[quote(c)]** @ **[swap]** @ comT(t,l,P) @ **[cons]**
comT((t_1 , t_2) , l , P) = **[push]** @ comT(t_1,l,P) @ **[swap]** @ comT(t_2 , l , P) @ **[cons]**

The pure functional part of the intermediate language is compiled like a functional program in the CAM compilation schema. It is even more simpler since we do not have higher order functions in our intermediate language.

comE(x , ,P) = locate(x,P)
comE(con , P) = **[quote(con)]**
comE(f ex , P) = **[push]** @ locate(f,P) @ code @ **[swap]** @ comE(ex,P) @ **[cons , app]**
comE(c ex , P) = **[push]** @ **[quote(c)]** @ **[swap]** @ comE(ex,P) @ **[cons]**
comE((ex_1 , ex_2) , P) = **[push]** @ comE(ex_1) @ **[swap]** @ comE(ex_2) @ **[cons]**
comE(π_1 ex , P) = comE(ex,P) @ **[snd , fst]**
comE(π_2 ex , P) = comE(ex,P) @ **[snd , snd]**

comC(isa(f,ex) , P) = **[push]** @ comE(ex,P) @ **[swap , quote(f) , cons , isa]**

Example: We give the first few instructions of CAMEL code for the following intermediate language program for concatenation of lists together with the term append(s,s):

```
fun append (p,q) =
if isa (empty,p) then q
else   if isa (cons,p) then cons ( π1 p , append ( π2 p , q) )
         else choice ( (p,empty) => q ,
                              (p,cons (∃x,∃s)) => cons ( π1p , append ( π2 p , q) ) );
append(s,s);
```

Encoding the equation append(s,s) returns:

```
[ put 1, set, push, cur ( [ put 2 , set , APPEND ]), ]
```

The code for the function definition (APPEND) is as follows:

```
APPEND = [ push, push, snd, fst, swap, quote "empty", cons, isa, cons, branch(C1,C2) ]
where C1 = [ snd, snd ]
where C2 = [ push, push, snd, fst, swap, quote "cons", cons, isa, cons, branch (C3,C4) ]
where C3 = [ push, quote "cons", swap, push, snd, fst, snd, fst, swap, push, fst, cur (...), ... ]
where C4 = [ cp ( [ push, push, snd, fst, swap, quote "empty", cons, subst, swap, pop, snd, snd ],
                        [ push, push, snd, fst, swap, push, quote "cons",swap,push,...] ) ]
```

Execution of this CAMEL program is left as an exercise to the reader.

6 Conclusions

Apart from several WAM-extensions to compile functional / logic programs, [Loc 91 b] describes a method for systematically designing an abstract narrowing machine. He starts with an intermediate language in form of an enriched non-deterministic λ-calculus [Pat 90]. Then he formally develops an abstract narrowing machine which is based on graph reduction. This systematic design allows him to give a detailed operational description and realization of the machine concepts.
Alternatively, we presented an implementation for functional / logic programs starting from an environment machine (namely CAM) known from the compilation of functional languages. We have described a compiler for the given intermediate language and the state transitions for each instruction of the target language.
The advantage of CAMEL over WAM-extensions is its clear operational semantics which can easily be described with a few state transitions, most of which are straightforward extensions of CAM transitions. The same holds for the compiler from the intermediate language to CAMEL instructions. This compiler only extends the CAM compiler by a compilation schema to handle logical variables, unification and backtracking. As both, the compiler and the state transitions of CAMEL, are straightforward extensions of the concepts known from CAM, verification of both is easily possible. For a proof, the reader is referred to [Mue 92].
In order to achieve the efficiency of WAM-based approaches without losing comprehensibility, we plan stepwise refinements of CAMEL. We think that such refinements will lead to a verified machine which is similar to a WAM-extension for functional /logic programming.

Finally I would like to thank H. Hußmann, P. Padawitz, V. Pollara, B. Reus, Th. Streicher and M. Wirsing for useful suggestions. Thanks also to M. Hanus, H. Lock and R. Loogen for their helpful comments on the intermediate language.
Without the help of Tatjana, the paper would not have been ready in time.

References:

[Ait 90] H. Ait Kaci: The WAM: A (Real) Tutorial, DEC Research Centre, Paris, PRL Research Report 5, 1990

[Boe 90] Egon Börger, Dean Rosenzweig: From Prolog Algebras Towards WAM - A Mathematical Study of Implementation, Proc. 4th Workshop on Computer Science Logic, Springer LNCS, 1991

[Bos 89] P.G. Bosco et al: An Extension of WAM for K-LEAF: A WAM-based Compilation of Conditional Narrowing, Proc. Int. Conf.. on Logic Programming, pp. 318-336, MIT Press, 1989

[Car 86] L. Cardelli: The Amber machine, Proc. Combinators and Functional Programming, LNCS 242, 1986

[Cou 86] G. Cousineau et al: The Categorical Abstract Machine, Proc. Functional Programming Languages and Computer Architectures, Nancy, France, pp. 50-64, Springer LNCS 201, 1986

[Cou 90] G. Cousineau: The Categorical Abstract Machine, in G. Huet (ed.): Logical Foundations of Functional Programming, Addison Wesley, 1990

[Fri 85] L. Fribourg: Handling Function Definition through Innermost Superposition and Rewriting, Proc. RTA 85, pp. 325-344, Springer LNCS, 1985

[Han 90 a] M. Hanus: Logic programs with equational type specifications, Proc. ALP 90, Nancy, France, pp. 70-85, Springer LNCS 463, 1990

[Han 90 b] M. Hanus: Compiling Logic Programs with Equality, Proc. PLILP 90, Linköping, Sweden, pp. 387-401, Springer LNCS 456, 1990

[Hus 85] H. Hussmann: Unification in Conditional Equational Theories, Research Report MIP 8502, Universität Passau, 1985

[Kuc 90] H. Kuchen et al: Graph-based Implementation of a Functional Logic Language, Proc. ESOP 90, pp. 271-290, Springer LNCS 432, 1990

[Lan 64] P.J. Landin: The mechanical evaluation of expressions, Computer Journal 6, pp. 308-320, 1964

[Loc 91 a] H.C.R. Lock, M.M.T. Chakravarty: The Implementation of Lazy Narrowing, Proc. PLILP 91, Passau, Germany, pp. 111-122, Springer LNCS 528, 1991

[Loc 91 b] H.C.R.Lock:A Systematic Method For Designing Abstract Narrowing Machines, Workshop on Declarative Programming, Sasbachwalden, Workshops in Computing, Springer Verlag 1991

[Loo 91 a] R. Loogen: From Reduction Machines to Narrowing Machines, Proc. TAPSOFT 91, Brighton, UK, pp. 438-457, Springer LNCS 494, 1991

[Loo 91 b] R. Loogen, S. Winkler: Dynamic Detection of Determinism in Functional Logic Languages, Proc. PLILP 91, Passau, Germany, pp. 335-346, Springer LNCS 528, 1991

[Mue 90] A. Mück: Compilation of Narrowing, Proc, PLILP 90, Linköping, Sweden, pp. 16-29, Springer LNCS 456, 1990

[Mue 92] A. Mück: A Verified Implementation of a Functional Logic Language, University of Munich, forthcoming report, 1992

[Pat 90] R. Paterson: A non-deterministic λ-calculus, Imperial College London, 1990

[Rob 65] J.A. Robinson: A Machine Oriented Logic Based on the Resolution Principle, JACM, Vol. 12, No. 1, pp. 23-41, 1965

[Rus 89] D.M. Rusinoff: A Verified Prolog Compiler for the Warren Abstract Machine, MCC Technical Report, ACT-ST-292-89, Austin, Texas, USA, 1989

[War 83] D.H.D. Warren: An Abstract Prolog Instruction Set, SRI International, Technical Note 309, 1983

On the Interaction of Lazy Evaluation and Backtracking

Werner Hans, Rita Loogen and Stephan Winkler*

RWTH Aachen, Lehrstuhl für Informatik II
Ahornstraße 55, W-5100 Aachen, Germany

Abstract. We investigate the interaction of lazy evaluation and backtracking in the framework of functional logic languages, whose operational semantics is based on lazy narrowing. Technically, it is no problem to realize a lazy narrowing strategy by adapting the well-known techniques, which have been developed for functional languages, to the more general evaluation mechanism of functional logic languages. But, unfortunately, it turns out, that the use of a lazy strategy has some severe disadvantages. In particular, it may lead to nontermination in combination with backtracking, where an innermost strategy will determine a solution. The use of demandedness information for function arguments allows us to define a mixture between an eager and a lazy evaluation strategy, which partially helps to cope with these problems. The runtimes obtained for various example programs with respect to the different strategies, substantiate that the mixed strategy is a reasonable compromise between an eager and a lazy strategy for functional logic languages.

1 Introduction

Lazy evaluation is the evaluation mechanism of modern functional languages as e.g. Miranda [17] and Haskell [9]. It delays the evaluation of function arguments, until their values are definitely needed to determine the result of the function application. Thus, lazy evaluation avoids superfluous computations. Furthermore, it enables the use of possibly infinite data structures.

Backtracking is used in the implementation of logic languages to handle the rule selection nondeterminism. In general, it realizes a depth first search of the computation tree of a query.

In the framework of purely functional or purely logic languages the two mechanisms do not come into contact, as there is no need for arbitrary backtracking in functional languages and there are no nested predicate applications in logic languages.

During the last decade, there has however been an increasing interest in the integration of the functional and logic programming paradigms within a uniform language framework [1], [5]. Coarsely, one can distinguish two main research directions within this area. On the one hand, Horn clause logic languages have been enhanced with equality and functions (see e.g. [7], [8]), where one essentially assumes an innermost evaluation strategy for nested function applications. On the

* The authors are supported by the grant In 20/6-1 from the 'Deutsche Forschungsgemeinschaft'. (e-mail address for correspondence: rita@informatik.rwth-aachen.de)

other hand, functional languages have been augmented with logical capabilities (see e.g. [2], [13]. The resulting languages are usually characterized as functional logic languages [16], which retain functional syntax but use narrowing instead of reduction as operational semantics. Narrowing is a generalization of reduction, which is obtained by using unification instead of pattern matching for parameter passing. Functional logic languages usually focus on a lazy evaluation strategy. This is the context, where lazy evaluation meets backtracking.

The aim of our paper is to show that it is in principle no problem to incorporate a lazy evaluation strategy into a narrowing implementation based on an abstract machine, whose backtracking mechanism has been borrowed from the well-known Warren Abstract Machine (WAM) [18], by using the techniques which have been developed for functional languages [6], [15]. But, unfortunately, the combination of lazy evaluation and backtracking has some negative effects. The delayed evaluation of arguments causes backtracking to initiate the re-evaluation of arguments before switching to another rule for the function symbol of the application. This implies on the one hand that arguments may be repeatedly evaluated for several function rules. On the other hand, the evaluation of a function application will not terminate, whenever an argument yields infinitely many solutions which do not match with the pattern of the currently selected function rule.

This risk of nontermination is not present in implementations that combine an eager (innermost) evaluation strategy and backtracking. With an innermost evaluation strategy all rules of a function are tried before backtracking on the arguments. Because there are only finitely many rules for each function symbol, nontermination may not occur during rule selection.

Multiple re-evaluations of locally deterministic arguments can simply be avoided by refining the backtracking mechanism. The nontermination problem is however more obstinate. It is only possible to avoid divergence during rule selection by evaluating arguments before the execution of function calls, which is however not safe, if the program admits nonterminating derivation sequences. For this reason, we will consider demandedness (strictness) information for function arguments to guarantee safeness and to get rid of the problems. The demandedness information allows us to define a mixture of an eager and a lazy evaluation strategy, which allows the eager evaluation of demanded arguments. It will however turn out, that this approach avoids the nontermination problems only for a subclass of programs, which will be syntactically characterized. An example program, for which nontermination due to backtracking can only be avoided by the eager evaluation of a non-demanded function argument, shows that it is impossible to find a strategy that is safe and avoids the nontermination problems of lazy narrowing plus backtracking, in general. The mixed strategy shows acceptable runtimes in comparison with an eager and a lazy strategy.

The paper is organized as follows. In Sect. 2, we present a very simple subset of a functional logic language. Section 3 describes our lazy narrowing implementation. In Sect. 4, the disadvantages of the lazy narrowing implementation are discussed. Section 5 shows in how far demandedness information helps to cope with the nontermination problems. Section 6 compares the runtimes of the innermost, the lazy and the mixed strategy for several example programs. Section 7 contains a discussion of related work and the conclusions.

2 A Sample Functional Logic Language

Our sample language Mini-BABEL is a first order subset of the functional logic language BABEL [13], which will be sufficient to discuss the interaction of lazy evaluation and backtracking in the framework of a functional logic language. BABEL, itself, is a higher order polymorphically typed functional logic language based on a constructor discipline. Its operational semantics is lazy narrowing.

2.1 Syntactic Domains

Let $\langle S, DC, FS\rangle$ be a first order signature with the set S of base types, the alphabet $DC = \bigcup_{(w,s)\in S^*\times S} DC^{(w,s)}$ of typed *constructors* and the alphabet $FS = \bigcup_{(w,s)\in S^*\times S} FS^{(w,s)}$ of typed *function symbols*.

In the following, letters $c, d, e \ldots$ are used for constructors and letters $f, g, h \ldots$ for function symbols. In our example programs, we usually assume that S contains the type *nat* and that DC contains the constructors $0 \in DC^{(\varepsilon,nat)}$ and $s \in DC^{(nat,nat)}$. The following syntactic domains are distinguished:

- *Variables* $X, Y, Z \ldots \in Var = \bigcup_{s\in S} Var^s$
- *Terms* $s, t \ldots \in Term = \bigcup_{s\in S} Term^s$:
  $t ::= X$ % Variable
  $\mid c(t_1, \ldots, t_n)$ % $c \in DC^{(s_1\ldots s_n,s)}$, $t_i \in Term^{s_i}, n \geq 0$
- *Expressions* $M, N \ldots \in Exp = \bigcup_{s\in S} Exp^s$:
  $M ::= X$ % Variable
  $\mid \varphi(M_1, \ldots, M_n)$ % $\varphi \in DC^{(s_1\ldots s_n,s)} \cup FS^{(s_1\ldots s_n,s)}$, $M_i \in Exp^{s_i}, n \geq 0$

2.2 Mini-BABEL Programs

A *Mini-BABEL program* consists of a finite set of defining rules for the function symbols in FS. Let $f \in FS^{(s_1\ldots s_n,s)}$. Each *defining rule for* f must have the form:

$$f(t_1, \ldots, t_n) := M.$$

and satisfy the following conditions:

1. *Term Pattern and Well Typedness*: $t_i \in Term^{s_i}$ $(1 \leq i \leq n)$ and $M \in Exp^s$.
2. *Left Linearity*: $f(t_1, \ldots, t_n)$ does not contain multiple variable occurrences.
3. *Local Determinism*: Variables occurring in M must also occur in $f(t_1, \ldots, t_n)$.
4. *Nonambiguity*: Given any two (variable disjoint variants) of rules for the same function symbol f:

   $$f(t_1, \ldots, t_n) := M. \text{ and } f(s_1, \ldots, s_n) := N.$$

   such that $f(t_1, \ldots, t_n)$ and $f(s_1, \ldots, s_n)$ have a unifier σ, then $M\sigma$ and $N\sigma$ must be identical. ($M\sigma$ denotes the expression M where all variables X have been replaced by $\sigma(X)$.)

f is *totally defined*, if for all $\tilde{t}_j \in Term^{s_j}$ $(1 \leq j \leq n)$ there exists (a variable disjoint variant of) a defining rule $f(t_1, \ldots, t_n) := M$ for f such that $f(\tilde{t}_1, \ldots, \tilde{t}_n)$ and $f(t_1, \ldots, t_n)$ are unifiable.

2.3 Narrowing Semantics

The operational semantics of BABEL is based on the following *narrowing rule*, which describes how to apply a BABEL rule to an expression through unification:

> Let $f(M_1, \ldots, M_n)$ be an expression and $f(t_1, \ldots, t_n) := R.$ be some variant of a program rule, which shares no variables with the expression.
> If $\theta \cup \sigma : Var \rightarrow Exp$ is a most general unifier with $t_i\theta = M_i\sigma$ for $1 \leq i \leq n$, then:
> $$f(M_1, \ldots, M_n) \rightsquigarrow_\sigma R\theta.$$

Contextual narrowing is defined by the rule:

> If $M_i \rightsquigarrow_\sigma N_i$ for some $i \in \{1, \ldots, n\}$ and $\phi \in DC \cup FS$, then
> $$\phi(M_1, \ldots, M_i, \ldots, M_n) \rightsquigarrow_\sigma \phi(M_1\sigma, \ldots, N_i, \ldots, M_n\sigma)$$

The execution of several computation steps is given by the transitive, reflexive closure of the narrowing relation with composition of the substitutions: $\rightsquigarrow_\sigma^*$.
Narrowing of a Mini-BABEL expression M may lead to the following outcomes:

- *Success:* $M \rightsquigarrow_\sigma^* t$ with $t \in Term$,
- *Failure:* $M \rightsquigarrow_\sigma^* N$, N is not further narrowable and $N \notin Term$,
- *Nontermination.*

2.4 Narrowing Strategies

The narrowing relation has two sources of nondeterminism. On the one hand, an expression may contain several narrowable subexpressions (*redex nondeterminism*). On the other hand, a function application containing free (logical) variables may be narrowable using different program rules (*rule nondeterminism*).

In an implementation, rule nondeterminism is usually handled by backtracking, i.e. the first applicable rule is chosen and the alternative rules and the state of the computation are retained in a so-called choice point. Whenever a failure occurs, the last choice point is inspected in order to reset the computation and to try the next alternative rule. Backtracking describes a a depth first search of the computation tree, which is of course incomplete, because it may fail to determine all possible narrowing results in the presence of infinite computations paths. Nevertheless, this technique is chosen in most implementations due to efficiency reasons.

The redex nondeterminism is usually handled by imposing a redex selection strategy. One distinguishes between innermost (eager) and outermost (lazy) strategies.

An innermost strategy restricts the application of the narrowing rule to innermost redexes (reducible expressions), i.e. to applications of a function symbol to terms, only. It is complete for confluent and terminating rewrite systems when all function symbols are totally defined [7]. As Mini-BABEL programs in general enable infinite derivations and partially defined functions, an innermost strategy is not adequate. Nevertheless, we will consider this strategy to the end of comparison.

In principle, an outermost or lazy strategy allows only the evaluation of outermost function applications. In order to guarantee completeness, it is however necessary to admit the evaluation of certain inner expressions. Sometimes it cannot be decided, whether a program rule can be applied to an outermost function application, because the unification of the rule's left hand side and the function application is successful, except for function applications in the arguments of the application meeting constructor terms in the left hand side of the rule. Such rules are called *pending rules* in [13]. They demand the evaluation of inner expressions of a function application.

Example. The rule "$f(0, s(Y)) := \ldots$" is pending for the application $f(0, g(X))$. Applicability of the rule can only be decided after the evaluation of the inner function application $g(X)$. $\triangleleft$

For this reason, a lazy strategy allows the evaluation of inner expressions, which are demanded by pending program rules. Contextual narrowing must be restricted to these cases. In [13] soundness and completeness results have been proved, which relate the narrowing semantics with a lazy selection strategy to a declarative semantics for first order BABEL.

3 Implementation of Functional Logic Languages

In this section we shortly describe the structure and the behaviour of the stack narrowing machine that has been introduced in [11]. The narrowing machine has been designed as the extension of a reduction machine for purely functional languages by mechanisms for performing unification and backtracking. The backtracking mechanism has been borrowed from Warren's Prolog Engine [18].

3.1 Structure of the Narrowing Machine

The store of the narrowing machine is illustrated in Fig. 1. Its central component is the environment stack which contains environments and argument blocks for the control of forward computations and choice points for the control of backward computations, i.e. backtracking.

Terms, i.e. structured terms and variables, and arguments, whose evaluation is postponed in case of a lazy evaluation strategy, are represented in the graph. Consequently, we distinguish between *constructor nodes*, unbound and bound *variable nodes*, and *suspension nodes* (see Fig. 1).

Suspension nodes need some further explanation. The code address ca is the address, at which the code for the evaluation of the delayed or suspended argument starts, *lvars* are the bindings of local variables, to which some instructions in the code may refer. The third component *res* is only necessary for the organization of backtracking. It equals '?' as long as the suspension node has not been evaluated. Due to the possibility of backtracking, the suspension node must not be overwritten by the result after its evaluation, as it is practice in implementations of functional languages. Instead the result address is noted in the suspension node, which behaves then just as an indirection node. When the computation fails and the state of the machine is reset to a state, where the suspension node had not been evaluated yet, the result component of the suspension node is reset to '?'.

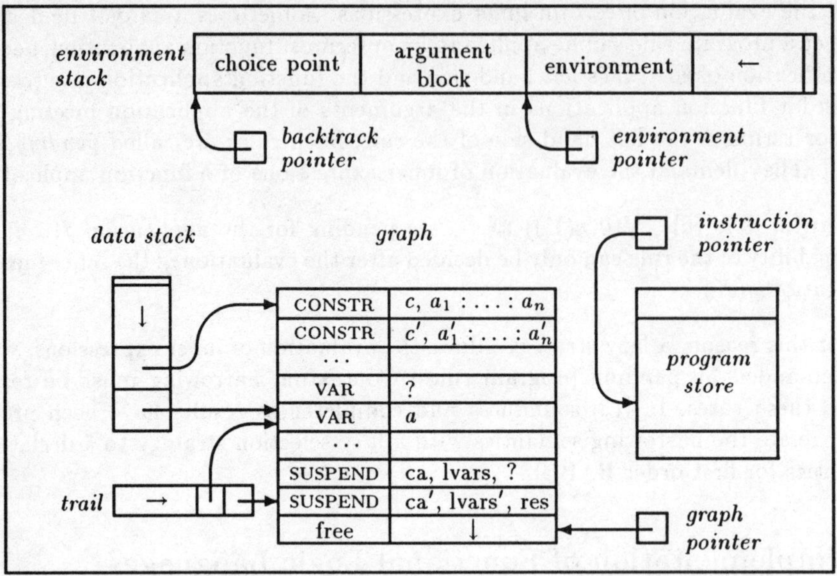

Fig. 1. Structure of the Narrowing Machine

The organization of delayed computations via suspension nodes is adopted from functional languages. Suspension nodes are a generalization of *closures*, which have been introduced in [10] for the representation of functions. The closure concept has been adapted for the representation of arbitrary unevaluated expressions in [6]. The extension of the concept for functional logic languages has been introduced in [4].

The graph is organized as a global stack. It grows during forward computations and is reset on backtracking to the value of the graph pointer, which has been saved in the choice point.

The trail is used to keep note of bound variable nodes and updated suspension nodes in order to enable their reconstruction on backtracking. Resetting the trail means unbinding the variables and resetting the result component of the suspension nodes whose addresses have been noted in the trail.

3.2 Behaviour of the Narrowing Machine

In order to evaluate a function application, the addresses of the graph representations of the arguments are written on top of the data stack and a function call is executed. An *environment* and an *argument block* are allocated on top of the environment stack. The environment block contains locations for the local variables of the function rules, the saved pointer to the previously active environment, and the return address of the function call, i.e. the program address at which the computation has to be continued after a successful termination. The arguments on the data stack are moved into the argument block.

Let f be a function symbol with arity n. Then:

$$
\begin{array}{ll}
\multicolumn{2}{l}{\textit{proctrans}(\langle f(t_{i1},\ldots,t_{in}) := M_i. \mid 1 \le i \le r, r \ge 2\rangle)} \\
:= & \text{TRY\_ME\_ELSE } \textit{rule}_2 \\
 & \textit{ruletrans } (f(t_{11},\ldots,t_{1n}) := M_1.) \\
\textit{rule}_2\text{:} & \text{RETRY\_ME\_ELSE } \textit{rule}_3 \\
 & \textit{ruletrans } (f(t_{21},\ldots,t_{2n}) := M_2.) \\
\textit{rule}_3\text{:} & \vdots \\
 & \vdots \\
\textit{rule}_r\text{:} & \text{TRUST\_ME\_ELSE\_FAIL} \\
 & \textit{ruletrans } (f(t_{r1},\ldots,t_{rn}) := M_r.)
\end{array}
$$

$$
\begin{array}{l}
\textit{ruletrans}(f(t_1,\ldots,t_n) := M.) \\
\quad := \text{LOAD } 1 \\
\quad\;\;\; \textit{matchtrans}(t_1) \\
\quad\;\;\; \vdots \\
\quad\;\;\; \text{LOAD } n \\
\quad\;\;\; \textit{matchtrans}(t_n) \\
\quad\;\;\; \text{POP\_ARGS} \\
\quad\;\;\; \textit{exptrans } (M) \\
\quad\;\;\; \text{RETURN}
\end{array}
$$

Fig. 2. Compilation of Procedures and Rules

If the function symbol is defined by more than one rule, the defining rules are tested in their textual ordering. The machine code that is generated for such a function symbol is given in Fig. 2. First, the instruction 'TRY_ME_ELSE $rule_2$' creates a *choice point* on top of the argument block. The choice point contains the information that is necessary for restoring the current state of the machine on backtracking, i.e. among other things the current depth of the data stack, the length of the trail, the pointer to the previous choice point and especially the backtrack address, which indicates the code address of the next alternative rule, $rule_2$. Note that backtracking will either be initiated by a failing unification or a user's request for an alternative solution, after a solution has been determined.

After the creation of the choice point, the first function rule is applied to evaluate the application. The translation of a function rule consists of code for the unification of the arguments of the function application with the terms on the left hand side of the rule and code for the evaluation of the right hand side after a successful unification (see Fig. 2). The unification of an argument and the formal parameter term of the function rule is done by traversing the parameter term top down left to right and performing local comparisons using the instructions MATCHVAR and MATCHCONSTR (see compilation scheme *matchtrans* in Fig. 3). The evaluation of arguments, which are represented as suspension nodes, is started by the instruction INITIATE, whenever these must be unified with constructor terms. If no failure occurs during the unification phase, the POP_ARGS-instruction removes the argument block from the stack, unless a choice point is on top of the stack. Then, the rule's right hand side is evaluated. Finally, the RETURN instruction successfully terminates the function call, by giving the control back to the previously active environment and by setting the instruction pointer to the return address stored in the environment.

If the unification of the parameter terms and arguments is not successful, backtracking is initiated which uses the information given in the top level choice point to reset the components of the machine and to jump to the backtrack address. If there are still more alternative rules for the function, the RETRY_ME_ELSE $rule_i$ instruc-

$matchtrans(X_i)$
$:=$ MATCHVAR i
$matchtrans(c(t_1, ..., t_n))$
$:=$ INITIATE
MATCHCONSTR (c, n)
$matchtrans(t_1)$
$\vdots$
$matchtrans(t_n)$

$exptrans(X_i)$
$:=$ LOAD i
INITIATE
$exptrans(c(M_1, ..., M_n))$
$:= argtrans(M_1)$
$\vdots$
$argtrans(M_n)$
NODE (c, n)
$exptrans(f(M_1, ..., M_n))$
$:= argtrans(M_1)$
$\vdots$
$argtrans(M_n)$
CALL (f, n)

$delaytrans(X_i)$
$:=$ LOAD i
$delaytrans(c(M_1, ..., M_n))$
$:= delaytrans(M_1)$
$\vdots$
$delaytrans(M_n)$
NODE (c, n)
$delaytrans(f(M_1, ..., M_n))$
$:=$ SUSPEND l
JUMP l'
l: $exptrans(f(M_1, ..., M_n))$
UPDATE
l': ...

$$argtrans(M) := \begin{cases} exptrans(M) & \text{in case of an "eager" evaluation strategy} \\ delaytrans(M) & \text{in case of a "lazy" evaluation strategy} \end{cases}$$

Fig. 3. Code for Unification and Compilation of Expressions

tion updates the backtrack address within the choice point. If the next alternative rule is the last defining rule for the function symbol, the choice point is removed from the environment stack by the TRUST_ME_ELSE_FAIL instruction (see Fig. 2). The latter has the effect that backtracking will subsequently reset the computation to the topmost choice point below the current environment, which belongs to a function application whose evaluation terminated successfully, but for which there are still alternative function rules which have not been tried yet. If there is no more choice point on the environment stack, a failure will cause the overall computation to fail.

The narrowing machine is capable of realizing an innermost and a lazy strategy. Which strategy is chosen to execute a program, depends on the compilation of argument expressions. In case of an innermost strategy, arguments are translated by the *exptrans*-scheme. This implies that expressions are evaluated to normal form and INITIATE instructions can be omitted. In case of a lazy evaluation strategy, arguments are translated by the *delaytrans*-scheme, which generates suspension nodes for the representation of function calls using the instruction SUSPEND. Furthermore, code for the evaluation of the suspension is generated using the *exptrans*-scheme. This code is concluded by the instruction UPDATE, which writes the result of the evaluation into the suspension node and gives control back to the calling environment. A lazy evaluation strategy evaluates expressions to head normal form, i.e. until the top level constructor of the result is determined. In order to force the complete evaluation of the goal expression, a special mechanism must be incorporated into the machine.

This gives an impression of the principal behaviour of the narrowing machine. For simplicity, we have not considered any optimization techniques as e.g. tail recursive function calls and the dynamic detection of determinism. The interested reader is referred to [11] and [12] for further details.

4 Disadvantages of Lazy Narrowing

The lazy narrowing implementation described in the last section has several disadvantages which are due to the interaction of lazy evaluation and backtracking. As argument evaluations are initiated during unification, the environments and choice points of the arguments are allocated on top of the environment and choice point of the function call. Thus, a failing unification causes backtracking on the argument evaluations and all alternative evaluations of arguments are tried for a fixed function rule, before the next alternative function rule is selected. To put it clearly, arguments may be completely re-evaluated for each function rule.

Example. Consider the following definition of the function symbols *even* and *odd*:

$$\begin{array}{ll} even(0) & := s(0). \\ even(s(s(X))) & := even(X). \quad odd(X) := even(even(X)). \\ even(s(0)) & := 0. \end{array}$$

During the lazy execution of the expression $odd(s(s(0)))$ the argument expression $even(s(s(0)))$ will be evaluated three times, once for each defining rule of *even*. ◁

Multiple argument evaluations are caused by the resetting of suspension nodes on backtracking. But this resetting is only necessary, if the evaluation of the suspension node depends on logical variables, which are also reset. Suspension nodes can only depend on logical variables, which existed already when the node was generated, i.e. the graph address of which is less than the graph address of the suspension node. This immediately leads to the following

> **Refinement of the Backtracking Mechanism:**
> Reset suspension nodes on backtracking, only if a variable, the address of which is less than the address of the suspension node and which has been noted in the trail before the suspension node, is reset.

This refinement applies only to suspension nodes, the evaluation of which is locally deterministic. If a suspension node is not reset, the graph cannot be reset on backtracking, too, because the result of the suspension node must be kept.

Thus, the problem of superfluous argument re-evaluations can be avoided by a careful treatment of suspension nodes on backtracking. A more severe problem is however the divergence of lazy function calls, if an argument evaluation yields infinitely many alternative solutions which do not match the pattern of the selected function rule.

Example. The program rules

$$\begin{array}{ll} one(0) & := s(0). \\ one(s(N)) & := one(N). \end{array}$$

define the unary function *one*, that maps all constructor terms built from the nullary constructor 0 and the unary constructor s to the constructor term $s(0)$.

Note that there are infinitely many narrowing derivations starting from the expression $one(X)$, where X is a logical variable:

$$\forall\, i \in \mathbb{N}: \; one(X) \rightsquigarrow^*_{\{X/\underbrace{s(\ldots s(0)\ldots)}_{i \text{ times}}\}} s(0).$$

Each derivation yields the result $s(0)$, while the variable X is bound to a term of the form $s(\ldots s(0)\ldots)$. An innermost evaluation of the expression $one(one(X))$ has the same outcomes.
A lazy evaluation of the same expression with backtracking will however fail to terminate. This is due to the fact, that the system tries to apply the first rule of the *one*-function with the argument not evaluated yet. The evaluation of the argument yields the result $s(0)$ binding the logical variable X to 0. As the unification of 0 and $s(0)$ fails, backtracking is initiated that leads to the re-evaluation of the argument. As there are infinitely many alternative evaluations of the argument yielding the same result, the whole computation will not terminate. ◁

Note that the nontermination problems are not restricted to the case of circumstantial definitions of constant functions.

Example. Consider the following definitions of the arithmetic operations for addition and multiplication:

$$\begin{array}{llll} add(0,Y) & := Y. & mult(0,Y) & := 0. \\ add(s(X),Y) & := add(X,s(Y)). & mult(s(X),Y) & := add(Y, mult(X,Y)). \end{array}$$

With these definitions, the lazy narrowing evaluation of the expression

$$mult(add(X,s(0)), s(s(0)))$$

will not terminate.
Replacing the second rule for *add* by "$add(s(X),Y) := s(add(X,Y))$." would avoid the nontermination, but in general the tail recursive version is preferred as it is more efficient. ◁

Simply changing the order of backtracking is in general not possible, because the evaluation of arguments may depend on logical variables which have been bound to pattern of the selected function rule. The only way to avoid the nontermination problem, is to evaluate arguments before function calls (i.e. using an innermost evaluation strategy). The innermost evaluation strategy should of course only be used for demanded arguments of function calls, i.e. for arguments that are necessary to determine the result of the application. In the following section, we will define a notion of demandedness, which implies strictness of functions. Strictness is a semantic property of functions. Let $\mathcal{A}_i = \langle A_i, \leq_i \rangle$ be complete partial orders with least elements $\perp_i$ $(0 \leq i \leq n, n \in \mathbb{N})$. A function $f : A_1 \times \ldots \times A_n \rightarrow A_0$ is called *strict in its ith argument*, if for all $a_j \in A_j$ $(1 \leq j \leq n)$:

$$f(a_1, \ldots, a_{i-1}, \perp_i, a_{i+1}, \ldots, a_n) = \perp_0,$$

i.e. whenever the ith argument is not defined, the application of f is not defined.

In the context of purely functional languages, it is safe to evaluate strict arguments before evaluating the function application. Thus, the use of an innermost evaluation strategy for the strict arguments of functions is a well-known optimization technique for the implementation of purely functional languages [15]. A straightforward adaptation of the strictness analysis methods, which have been developed for purely functional languages, to BABEL is however only possible, if a pattern matching compiler is used to transform the programs. But such a compiler does not always preserve the semantics of programs. Therefore, we will develop an analysis method, that directly works on function symbols defined by several rules.

5 Incorporation of Demandedness Information

For simplicity, we will assume that Mini-BABEL programs are transformed into equivalent programs with flat left hand side, i.e. the term pattern of the left hand side of rules are variables or constructors applied to variables. Such a transformation is always possible by the introduction of auxiliary function symbols [14].

For a given program with flat left hand sides, we will now try to find out, which arguments are demanded by the functions defined in the program. For each $f \in FS$ we will compute a set $\mathcal{D}(f) \subseteq \mathbb{N}$, which will contain the argument positions, which are needed for the evaluation of an application of f.

Let $f \in FS$. The demandedness of f's arguments depends on the structure of the defining rules for f. A single rule demands the evaluation of an argument, if the corresponding term pattern of the rule's left hand side (lhs) is non-variable or if the evaluation of the argument is demanded by the rule's right hand side (rhs). The latter is the case, when the argument variable occurs in a demanded argument position of another function symbol or if the right hand side is identical to the argument variable. Whenever the right hand side of a rule is a constructor application, no arguments are demanded by it. We will say that f demands an argument when this argument is demanded by all defining rules of f. Formally, the sets of demanded arguments of the function symbols defined in a program are specified by the following recursive equation system.

Let $\mathcal{P} = \langle\langle f^j(t^j_{i1}, \ldots, t^j_{in_j}) := M^j_i \mid 1 \leq i \leq r_j\rangle \mid 1 \leq j \leq m\rangle$ be a Mini-BABEL program which defines the function symbols f^j. The sets $\mathcal{D}(f^j) \subseteq \mathbb{N}$ of *demanded arguments of* f^j are determined by the least fixpoint of the following system of recursive set equations:

$$\langle \mathcal{D}(f^j) = \bigcap_{i=1}^{r_j} \overbrace{(\underbrace{\{k \mid t^j_{ik} \notin Var\}}_{\text{demanded by lhs}} \cup \underbrace{\{k \mid t^j_{ik} \in Var \wedge t^j_{ik} \in DVar(M^j_i)\}}_{\text{demanded by rhs}})}^{\text{demanded arguments of rule } i} \mid 1 \leq j \leq m\rangle$$

where

$$\begin{array}{lll} DVar(X) & := \{X\} & \% \ X \in Var \\ DVar(c(M_1, \ldots, M_n)) & := \emptyset & \% \ c \in DC \\ DVar(f(M_1, \ldots, M_n)) & := \bigcup_{l \in \mathcal{D}(f)} DVar(M_l) & \% \ f \in FS. \end{array}$$

Note that this least fixpoint is well-defined in the complete partial order $\langle \mathcal{P}(\mathbb{N}), \subseteq\rangle$, where $\mathcal{P}(\mathbb{N})$ denotes the powerset of $\mathbb{N}$. It can be computed following the well-known theorem of Knaster-Tarski by iteratively computing approximations of the sets $\mathcal{D}(f^j)$ $(1 \leq j \leq m)$, starting with $\emptyset$ for each set, until a stagnation occurs.

Example. For the example programs of the previous section, we get the following demandedness information: $\mathcal{D}(one) = \mathcal{D}(add) = \mathcal{D}(mult) = \{1\}$. ◁

Demandedness implies strictness with respect to the declarative semantics of BABEL defined in [13], i.e. demandedness is a computable approximation of strictness information and the demandedness analysis corresponds to a strictness analysis.

The demandedness information makes it possible to switch from a purely lazy evaluation strategy to a mixture of the eager and the lazy strategy by using the innermost evaluation strategy for demanded arguments and the lazy strategy for non-demanded arguments, as it is usually done in the context of functional languages. This means for the compilation of Mini-BABEL that we modify the *argtrans*-scheme in the following way:

$$argtrans(M) := \begin{cases} exptrans(M) & \text{if } M \text{ is a demanded argument} \\ & \text{of a function application} \\ delaytrans(M) & \text{otherwise} \end{cases}$$

The mixed strategy has several advantages with respect to the purely lazy strategy. It is more efficient, because the (time and space) overhead of producing suspension nodes for the representation of demanded arguments is saved. This is confirmed by the implementation results given in the next section. Its advantage with respect to an innermost strategy is that it does not evaluate unnecessary subexpressions. Furthermore, it solves the nontermination problems for a large class of programs, in particular for the examples of the previous section.

The following example shows that it is however not possible to define a *safe* evaluation strategy for arbitrary programs, that avoids the nontermination problems caused by the interaction of lazy evaluation and backtracking.

Example. Let $DC^{(\varepsilon,bool)} := \{tt, ff\}$. Consider the following program rules:

$$\begin{array}{ll} cond(tt, X) := s(X). & one\_zero(s(X)) := zero\_zero(X). \\ cond(ff, X) := s(0). & zero\_zero(0) \quad := 0. \end{array}$$

The demandedness analysis yields $\mathcal{D}(cond) = \mathcal{D}(one\_zero) = \mathcal{D}(zero\_zero) = \{1\}$. Thus the mixed strategy evaluates all argument expressions eagerly, except for the second argument of *cond*. But the only possibility to avoid the nontermination caused by the delayed evaluation of the first argument of *cond* in the expression $one\_zero(cond(B, one(X)))$ is to evaluate this argument before evaluating the application of *cond*. Only the innermost evaluation strategy yields the result 0 binding X to 0 and B to ff. ◁

This example reveals that strictness information is not sufficient to solve the nontermination problems in general. The following lemma contains a syntactic characterization of a program class, for which the mixed strategy is safe and avoids the nontermination problems.

Lemma. Let $\mathcal{P} = \langle\langle f^j(t^j_{i1}, \ldots, t^j_{in_j}) := M^j_i \mid 1 \le i \le r_j\rangle \mid 1 \le j \le m\rangle$ be a Mini-BABEL program.
If for each $j \in \{1, \ldots, m\}$, f^j is totally defined and for each non-demanded argument position of f^j, $k \in \{1, \ldots, n_j\} \backslash \mathcal{D}(f^j)$: $\{t^j_{1k}, \ldots, t^j_{r_jk}\} \subseteq Var$, then the mixed strategy guarantees that divergence cannot occur during rule selection. ◁

Proof. As function symbols are totally defined, there will be always a rule that is applicable. Additionally, no argument evaluation is ever initiated during the unification phase, as demanded arguments are evaluated before function calls and non-demanded arguments always meet variable parameters. □

The consistency of our demandedness notion and the semantic strictness notion is due to the fact that the standard semantics of BABEL does not distinguish between non-definedness caused by nontermination and non-definedness caused by partially defined functions, usually called finite failure. For deterministic computations and in purely functional languages the identification of the two non-definedness situations makes no problems. Occurrence of either means the non-definedness of the result of the overall computation. In the context of functional logic languages, the replacement of finite failure and nontermination may however lead to the incompleteness of the evaluation mechanism. A finite failure may cause the inspection of alternative computation paths, while nontermination leads to the nontermination of the overall computation, at least in a sequential system.

The evaluation of demanded arguments of functions is only safe, if function symbols are totally defined. For partially specified functions the demandedness notion must be refined in such a way that it corresponds to strictness with respect to a denotational semantics which distinguishes finite failure from divergence. The discussion of this refinement is however out of the scope of this paper.

6 Implementation Results

The runtimes given in this section have been measured using an implementation of full BABEL, which consists of a compiler frontend that translates BABEL programs into code for the abstract narrowing machine, and an interpreter for the abstract machine code, written in C. The implementation supports natural numbers and the usual arithmetic operations as primitives. All examples have been executed on a SPARC station 1+ (Sun-4/65).

The following table shows the runtimes that are saved by the refined backtracking mechanism for the functional quicksort algorithm. As this algorithm is deterministic, updated suspension nodes need not be reset on backtracking and thus useless recomputations of argument expressions can be avoided.

Example Program	Runtimes without	Runtimes with
	refined backtracking	
quicksort([5,..,1])	0.42 sec	0.089 sec
quicksort([6,..,1])	2.33 sec	0.121 sec
quicksort([7,..,1])	13.41 sec	0.158 sec
quicksort([8,..,1])	79.37 sec	0.201 sec

Currently, the compiler allows the programmer to specify for each function the demanded arguments. Thus, it is possible to compare the various evaluation strategies. The execution times of the innermost, the lazy and the mixed evaluation strategy are compared in the following table for some example programs: *fib_nat* denotes the recursive definition of the fibonacci function for natural numbers; ***fib_list*** selects elements from the infinite list of fibonacci numbers; *queens n* is the problem of finding all possibilities to place n queens on an $n \times n$ chessboard in such a way that they cannot beat each other, and *solitaire* is a simple game program.

Example Program	Evaluation Strategies innermost	mixed	lazy
fib_nat 15	0.191 sec	0.191 sec	0.254 sec
fib_nat 20	2.048 sec	2.048 sec	2.818 sec
fib_list 15	∞	5.00 msec	5.68 msec
fib_list 20	∞	6.40 msec	7.30 msec
queens 8	9.244 sec	9.906 sec	10.342 sec
solitaire	826 sec	847 sec	856 sec

On the one hand, the runtimes show the overhead of delayed evaluations, when the suspensions are almost always evaluated. The mixed strategy saves time by the eager evaluation of demanded arguments. On the other hand, lazy evaluation admits a different style of programming using infinite data structures, as indicated by the *fib_list*-example.

Note that the order, in which solutions are produced for nondeterministic programs, varies from strategy to strategy, because the backtracking behaviour is altered by the different argument evaluation strategies, as discussed in the previous sections.

7 Related Work and Conclusions

The lazy narrowing implementation described in [3] does not take notice of the nontermination problems caused by the interaction of lazy evaluation and backtracking. For the first time, these problems have been noted and discussed in [14]. In order to avoid them, a program transformation to so-called uniform programs has been proposed. The demandedness analysis presented in Sect. 5 can be seen as a continuation and improvement of the approach of uniform programs. The purely syntactic notion of demanded arguments introduced in [14] has been extended to a more semantics based notion, which has the advantages that demandedness is invariant with respect to equivalent program transformations, and that the special nontermination problems of lazy narrowing are avoided more often.

In [4] the pattern matching compiler described in [15] is used to translate programs into an intermediate form, which allows a deterministic selection of rules for non-variable arguments. This method also sometimes avoids the nontermination problems. But the example, for which the nontermination can only be avoided by the innermost evaluation of a non-demanded argument, will also not terminate.

To sum up, the interaction of lazy evaluation and backtracking has several disadvantageous effects, which can be avoided by postponing the resetting of suspension nodes during backtracking as long as possible and by incorporating demandedness information of function arguments into the evaluation strategy. Unfortunately, the nontermination caused by the backtracking strategy and the nontermination caused by the evaluation of non-demanded arguments cannot both be avoided for arbitrary programs by a uniform strategy. Nevertheless, we believe that the strategy based on the demandedness information is a reasonable compromise between an innermost and a lazy strategy that will meet the requirements of most real-life programs.

Acknowledgements

We are grateful to Michael Hanus and Andreas Mück for helpful comments on a previous version of this paper.

References

1. M. Bellia, G. Levi: *The Relation between Logic and Functional Languages*, Journal of Logic Progr., Vol. 3, 1986, 217–236.
2. P. G. Bosco, E. Giovannetti: *IDEAL: An Ideal Deductive Applicative Language*, IEEE Symp. on Logic Progr. 1986, IEEE Comp. Soc. Press, 89-94.
3. P. G. Bosco, C. Cecchi, C. Moiso: *An extension of WAM for K-LEAF: A WAM-based compilation of conditional narrowing*, Conf. on Logic Progr. 1989, MIT Press 1989, 318–333.
4. M. M. T. Chakravarty, H. C. R. Lock: *The Implementation of Lazy Implementation*, Symp. on Progr. Language Impl. and Logic Progr. (PLILP) 1991, LNCS 528, Springer Verlag 1991, 123–134.
5. D. DeGroot, G. Lindstrom (eds.): *Logic Programming: Functions, Relations, Equations*, Prentice Hall 1986.
6. J. Fairbairn, St. Wray: *TIM: A Simple, Lazy Abstract Machine to Execute Supercombinators*, Conf. on Func. Progr. Languages and Computer Arch. 1987, LNCS 274, Springer Verlag 1987, 34–45.
7. L. Fribourg: *SLOG: A Logic Programming Language Interpreter Based on Clausal Superposition and Rewriting*, IEEE Symp. on Logic Progr. 1985, IEEE Computer Society Press 1985, 172–184.
8. M. Hanus: *Compiling Logic Programs with Equality*, Workshop on Progr. Language Impl. and Logic Progr. (PLILP) 1990, LNCS 456, Springer Verlag 1990, 387–401.
9. P. Hudak, P. Wadler: *Report on the Functional Programming Language Haskell*, SIGPLAN Notices, Vol. 27, No. 5, May 1992.
10. P. J. Landin: *The Mechanical Evaluation of Expressions*, Computer Journal, 6, 4, 1964.
11. R. Loogen: *From Reduction Machines to Narrowing Machines*, TAPSOFT 1991, LNCS 494, Springer Verlag 1991, 438–457.
12. R. Loogen, St. Winkler: *Dynamic Detection of Determinism in Functional Logic Languages*, Symp. on Progr. Language Impl. and Logic Progr. (PLILP) 1991, LNCS 528, Springer Verlag 1991, 335–346.
13. J. J. Moreno-Navarro, M. Rodríguez-Artalejo: *Logic Programming with Functions and Predicates: The Language BABEL*, Journal of Logic Progr., Vol. 12, North Holland 1992, 191–223.
14. J. J. Moreno-Navarro, H. Kuchen, R. Loogen, M. Rodríguez-Artalejo: *Lazy Narrowing in a Graph Machine*, Conf. on Algebraic and Logic Progr. 1990, LNCS 463, Springer Verlag 1990, 298–317.
15. S. Peyton Jones: *The Implementation of Functional Programming Languages*, Prentice Hall 1987.
16. U. S. Reddy: *Narrowing as the Operational Semantics of Functional Languages*, IEEE Symp. on Logic Progr., IEEE Computer Society Press 1985, 138–151.
17. D. Turner: *Miranda: A non-strict functional language with polymorphic types*, Conf. on Func. Progr. Lang. and Computer Arch. 1985, LNCS 201, Springer Verlag 1985, 1–16.
18. D. H. D. Warren: *An Abstract Prolog Instruction Set*, Technical Note 309, SRI International, Menlo Park, California, October 1983.

Interprocedural Dynamic Slicing[1]

Mariam Kamkar (Email: mak@ida.liu.se)
Nahid Shahmehri (Email: nsh@ida.liu.se)
Peter Fritzson (Email: paf@ida.liu.se)

Department of Computer and Information Science, Linköping University,
S-581 83 Linköping, Sweden. Phone: (+46) 13-281000

Abstract. This paper presents the first algorithm for *interprocedural dynamic slicing*. Previous methods for dynamic slicing only considered languages without procedures and procedure calls. This method generates summary information for each procedure call and represents a program as a summary graph of dynamic dependencies. A slice on this graph consists of nodes for all procedure calls of the program that affect the value of a given variable. The size of the information saved by this method is considerably smaller than what is needed by previous methods for dynamic slicing [AH90], since it only depends on the size of the *program's execution tree*, i.e. the number of executed procedure calls, which is much smaller than the size of a trace of all executed statements. In addition, work space for the temporary graph is needed, proportional to the maximum sum of the sizes of simultaneously active procedures. A program slice can be produced from the interprocedural slice on the graph if a suitable definition of control dependency is used when the summary graph is constructed. The interprocedural dynamic slicing introduced in this paper is being used to improve the bug localization properties of the Generalized Algorithmic Debugging Technique [FGKS91], a method for declarative semi-automatic debugging.

1 Introduction

This paper concerns the problem of *interprocedural dynamic slicing*, where a particular execution of a program is of interest when analyzing dependencies. Thus, the effects of only those call statements which are executed are considered. The interprocedural dynamic slicing presented in this paper is an efficient method regarding run-time and space consumption since it uses a combination of information from compile time and run-time analysis to keep the overhead of the application system low. We are currently using the information produced by interprocedural dynamic slicing to further improve the bug localization properties of a declarative debugger.

To solve the interprocedural dynamic slicing problem, two dynamic dependence graphs are introduced. The first one is the program execution graph called the *dynamic dependence summary graph* or simply the *summary graph*. It represents the data and control dependencies between all procedure activations during an execution of the program.The second one represents the data and control dependencies inside a procedure for one execution of the procedure. This graph is called the *temporary dependence graph* since it has a short life and only exists temporarily to contribute dependence information to the relevant parts of the summary graph.

---

1. This work is supported by NUTEK, the Swedish National Board for Technical Development.

This paper introduces the notion of *execution slice* as a subgraph of the *summary graph* which captures a subset of the program behavior during an execution, while the term *program slice* still refers to an appropriate portion of the source program.

2 Background and Motivation

Program slicing was originally defined by Weiser in [Wei84]. He presented a program slice as the set of all statements in a program which directly or indirectly may affect the value of a specified variable (or a set of variables) at some program point.

This notion of program slicing is referred to as *static* program slicing, since it is valid for all possible executions of a program. Dynamic program slicing [KL90], in contrast, considers only a particular execution of a program. A program slice in this case contains all executed statements relevant to the computation of the value of a specified variable at an execution point. The main application of dynamic program slicing is hence in program debugging and testing.

The definition of dynamic slices is generally based on the notion of an *execution trace* of a program. The algorithms to find dynamic slices, in spite of differences in details, perform the following four steps. Figure 1 illustrates the relationships between these steps.

Steps in Computing Dynamic Slices

1. Produce an execution trace *T* of program *P*.
2. Determine the data and control dependencies between elements in *T*.
3. Define a subtrace *T'* on *T*, in a way that it contains those elements of *T* which affect the value of a specified variable at an execution point. We call *T'* a *(trace) execution slice*.
4. Perform the mapping from *T'* to the program *P*. The result will be *P'*, a dynamic program slice containing those statements in the program *P* which affect the value of the specified variable at the execution point. The type of the execution slice and the mapping can lead to a *partially equivalent program* or just a *set of program statements* (see below).

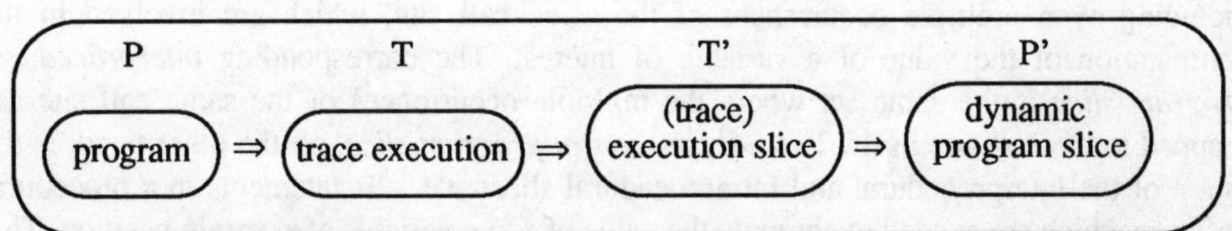

Figure 1: The transformation of a program to an execution slice and its corresponding program slice.

A partially equivalent program: A slice of a program with respect to a program point *p* and a variable *v* is a program which is partially equivalent to the original one, in the sense that it computes the same sequence of values for *v* at *p*. This slice is executable and its behavior at the program point *p* is the same as the original program with respect to the variable *v* [Lyl84] [Wei84] [LG89] [KL90].

A set of statements: A slice of a program with respect to a program point *p* and a variable *v* is a set of all statements of the program that may affect the value of *v* at *p*. This set is not necessarily executable [HRB90] [AH90] [Ven91].

Venkatesh [Ven91] provides formal semantics and comparisons of different forms of slicing. He also briefly discusses the problem of non-termination of certain types of slices. However, as mentioned in Section 3.1 in this paper, the problem of non-termination in this context is due to the definition of control dependency in the current literature. If instead *termination-preserving control dependency* (see Section 3.1) is used, a slice will be a terminating program. However, proving this conjecture is outside the scope of this paper.

As this paper only concerns the dynamic case of program slicing, we henceforth use "dynamic program slice" and "program slice" synonymously.

As an example consider the program *sumofoddnrs* in Figure 2a which computes the square of the integer *n* through summation of the *n* first odd numbers starting at *1*. An execution of this program for the input value *n=1* is shown in Figure 2b. The value of variable *sum* at execution point *9* is data dependent [FOW87] on the value of *sum* computed at execution point *5*. This value (the value of *sum* at execution point *5*) in turn is control dependent [FOW87] on instruction *4* at execution point *4*. Due to the use of traditional *control dependency* when producing the execution slice (see Figure 2c), this dynamic program slice (Figure 2d) is a nonterminating program which does not produce the same sequence of values for variable *sum* as the original program does. If *termination-preserving control dependency* (Section 3.1) also had been used in producing the dynamic slice, it would have become a somewhat larger but terminating program.

The four steps mentioned above perform dynamic program slicing as a source to source transformation. It first transfers a program to an *execution slice* and then, in step 4, to a *program slice*.

Performing step 4 and hence having the program slice is mostly desirable when the user of a debugging system is a human who wants to work on a portion of the source program.

3 Interprocedural Dynamic Slicing

We consider a program as a set of procedures and functions. We refer to a call statement or a function application as a *call site*. Our attention is on programs which halt, so infinite or nonterminating execution of procedures or functions is excluded.

An interprocedural *execution slice* is defined to be the *set of all executed call sites*, including even multiple occurrences of the same call site, which are involved in the computation of the value of a variable of interest. The corresponding *interprocedural program slice* is the same set where the multiple occurrences of the same call site are mapped to the call site itself. The *full procedural program slice,* on the other hand, is the union of the interprocedural and intraprocedural slices, i.e. all statements in a procedural program which are needed to compute the value of some variable at a certain position. This includes both call-statements and other statements.

In the following, first the terminology used in this paper is explained through a few definitions. Then a graph representation of dependencies between call sites, a *dynamic dependence summary graph,* is introduced. Finally an *execution slice* and an *interprocedural program slice* are defined on the summary graph and the source program respectively.

For the sake of simplicity in the remainder of this paper the term procedure is used to denote both procedure and function when the difference is not essential.

```
Instruction Program
number      text
------------------------------------
        program sumofoddnrs;
        var n, sum, i: integer;
        begin
1           sum:= 0;
2           i:= 1;
3           read(n);
4           while n>0 do begin
5               sum := sum + i;
6               i :=i + 2;
7               n := n -1;
            end;
8           write(sum);
        end.
```

(a): P

Execution point	Instruction number	Instruction text
1	1	sum:= 0;
2	2	i:= 1;
3	3	read(n);
4	4	while n>0 do begin
5	5	sum := sum + i;
6	6	i :=i + 2;
7	7	n := n -1;
8	4	while n>0 do begin
9	8	write(sum);

(b): T

Execution point	Instruction number	Instruction text
1	1	sum:= 0
2	2	i:=1;
3	3	read(n);
4	4	while n > 0 do begin
5	5	sum := sum + i;
9	8	write(sum);

(c): T'

```
Instruction Program
number      text
------------------------------------
        program sumofoddnrs;
        var n, sum, i: integer;
        begin
1           sum:= 0;
2           i:=1;
3           read(n);
4           while n > 0 do begin
5               sum := sum + i;
            end;
8           write(sum);
        end.
```

(d): P'

Figure 2: (a) The source program, P for an example program which sums the n first odd numbers starting at 1. (b) The trace execution T of the program P. (c) An execution slice T' of T with respect to variable sum at execution point 9. (d) The dynamic program slice P' of the source program P. Note: If termination-preserving control dependency (Section 3.1) had been used when computing the execution slice in (c), the program slice in (d) would have been a terminating program.

3.1 Definitions

Definition: An *input variable* to a procedure is a variable which can pass a value into the procedure whereas an *output variable* does the opposite and an *input/output variable* refers to either of those or both. A formal parameter or a global variable of a procedure are examples of input/output variables.

Definition: Let *Params(p)* be the set of all input/output variables of procedure *p*. Then *In_Params(p)* is the set of input variables of *Params(p)* whose values may be used at *p* and *Out_Params(p)* is the set of output variables of *Params(p)* whose values may be changed at *p*. A variable can belong to both *In_Params(p)* and *Out_Params(p)*.

Definition: A procedure is defined as consisting of a *procedure header* and a *procedure body*. In the presence of global variables the procedure header can be extended to contain even these variables as additional formal parameters. Different executions of a procedure may provide different procedure headers regarding in- and out-parameter values. We refer to such a header as a *procedure activation*:

procedure activation= $<in_p, p, out_p>$, where:

p is a *procedure name*,

$in_p = \{(x,vx) \mid x \in In\_Params(p)$ and vx is the value of x before execution of $p\}$

and

$out_p = \{(x,vx) \mid x \in Out\_Params(p)$ and vx is the value of x after execution of $p\}$

In the case of a function variable, this pair is shown as *(-:vf)*, where *vf* denotes the value returned by the function variable.

Definition: A *program execution tree / program activation tree* is a structure which contains information about an execution of a program on a certain input [ASU86]. Each node of the execution tree represents an activation of a procedure. An execution tree of the program *sumofoddnrs* in Figure 3 for input $n=1$ is shown in Figure 4, excluding the dotted arrows.

Definition I: *Data dependency*. The value of variable x defined at statement s_1 is data dependent on the value of variable y defined at statement s_2 if there is a definition_use chain for y between s_2 and s_1.

Definition II: Control dependency, using the definition from [FOW87]: Let G be a control flow graph. Let X and Y be nodes in G. Y is *control dependent* on X *iff* (1): there exists a directed path P from X to Y with any Z in P (excluding X and Y) post-dominated by Y and (2): X is not post-dominated by Y.

Informally, this means that the value of a variable y defined at statement s_1 is control dependent on some predicate X whose value immediately controls the execution of s_1. This is the same notion found in most of the current literature [FOW87], [HRB90], [AH90], [KL90]. The predicate X can appear in if-statements, while-statements, etc. of terminating programs.

Control dependency does not include all dependencies which are needed to preserve the termination properties of programs. Korel, [KL90], extends his dynamic slice in order to achieve terminating programs. Below we give a definition of control dependency which includes such dependencies.

Definition III: Termination-preserving control dependency: Let G be a control flow graph. Let X, Y and W be nodes in G. W is *termination-preserving control dependent* on X *iff* (1) it fulfills definition II of *control dependency* above, or (2) if there exists some X (and some *Y:s* which do not post-dominate X) according to definition II above, then W postdominates X. Note that X is usually a predicate node in some conditional control structure.

The notion of *termination-preserving control dependency* includes termination properties of programs. Given a terminating program, the termination of this program is dependent on the proper termination of all its loops and recursive calls. For example, control will never reach the statement after a while-loop if its predicate is not evaluated to False (if there is no direct goto to this statement). Thus, the statement after the while-loop is *termination-preserving control dependent* on the predicate of the while-loop. If this notion had been used in producing the execution slice in Figure 2c according to the description at the end of Section 4.1.1, then the dynamic program slice of Figure 2d would have been a terminating program.

3.2 Dynamic Dependence Summary Graph

The *dynamic dependence summary graph* (or simply *summary graph)* of a program is the execution tree of that program decorated with the actual *dependence information* for all input/output variables of its procedure activations. As an example consider the program in Figure 3 which is a new version of the program in Figure 2a. An execution of this program for the test case *n=1* yields the execution tree in Figure 4, which is decorated with the dependence information as edges between input/output variables of procedure activations.

```
program sumofoddnrs;
var n, sum, i: integer;
procedure add(in out a: integer; in b:integer);
begin a:=a + b; end;
procedure increment2(in out c: integer);
begin add(c, 2) end;
procedure decrement1(in out d: integer);
begin add(d, -1) end;
procedure summation(in out s, i, n: integer);
begin
    add(s, i);
    increment2(i);
    decrement1(n)
end;
begin (* main *)
    sum:= 0;
    i:=1;
    read(n);
    while n > 0 do
         summation(sum, i, n);
    write(sum);
end.
```

Figure 3: The example program sumofoddnrs decomposed into procedures.

We define a summary graph *SummaryG* as a directed graph with a set of vertices *V* and a set of edges *E* as follows:

SummaryG = $<V, E>$ where
$V = \{s \mid s$ is a *procedure activation*: $<in_p, p, out_p>\}$
$E = E_1 \cup E_2$:

- E_1: a set of *activation* edges $p_1 \rightarrow p_2$ between two vertices. Such an edge shows that p_2 is activated from the body of p_1 during program execution. Procedures

p_1 and p_2 are in a *parent-child* relation.

- E_2: a set of *dependency* edges *(y,vy)* ← *(x,vx)* between input/output variables of vertices. Such an edge shows that the computation of *vx*, the value of *x*, is dependent on *vy*, the value of *y*. An edge represents either a control dependency or a data dependency. We distinguish two kinds of dependency edges:
  - *Internal dependency*, when an edge connects two input/output variables belonging to the same vertex.
  - *External dependency*, when an edge is between two input/output variables belonging to vertices that are either in *parent-child* relation or have the same parent.

Section 4 describes how a summary graph is constructed at run-time, while using some of the static information about the program obtained at compile time.

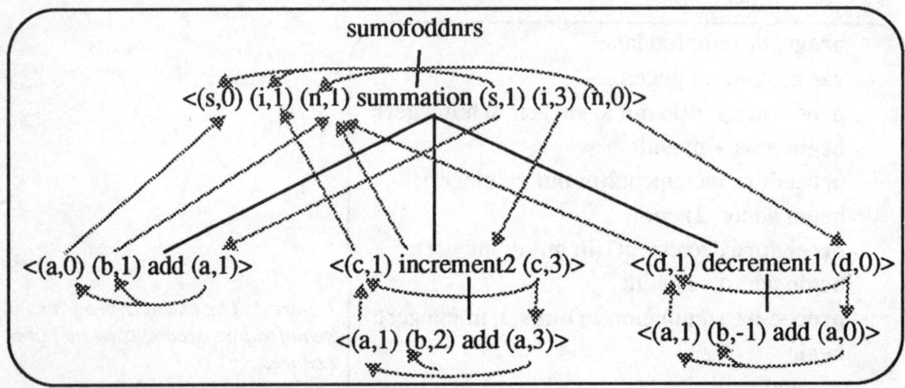

Figure 4: The summary graph containing the execution tree and the dependence information of an execution of sumofoddnrs for the test case n=1.

3.3 Interprocedural Execution Slice

Once the summary graph of a program has been constructed, the computation of an execution slice on an input/output variable is straightforward.

We define a *slice criterion C* to be a pair of a vertex *s* representing a procedure activation $<in_p, p, out_p>$ and an input/output variable instance *var= (x,vx)* which belongs to in_p, out_p or both:

$C = <s, var>$

An execution slice on the summary graph with respect to the slicing criterion *C* is a subgraph containing all vertices with a variable instance *var'=(y,vy)* such that there is a transitive dependency between *var=(x,vx)* observed at the vertex of slicing criterion *C* and *var'=(y,vy)*. In the following we use the term variable to also denote variable instance. The *interprocedural program slice* consists of all procedure activations which have affected the computation of the value *vx* of *x*, whereas the *full procedural slice* consists of all affecting statements.

Execution Slice(C=<s, var>) is a subgraph g = <V', E'> where

V' = {*s'* | *s'* is a vertex in the *summary graph* with an input/output variable *var'* reachable from *var* through some edges.}

$E' = E'_1 \cup E'_2$:

- E'_1: $\{e_1 \mid e_1$ is an activation edge in the *summary graph* between *s and s'*$\}$
- E'_2: $\{e_2 \mid e_2$ is a dependency edge in the *summary graph* between *var and var'*$\}$

Figure 5 below shows an execution slice of the summary graph of Figure 4, with the slice criterion:

C = <s, var> where s=<(s,0) (i,1) (n,1) summation (s,1) (i,3) (n,0)>, and var=(n,0)
The slice is computed with respect to output variable *n* at the end of the execution of procedure *summation.*

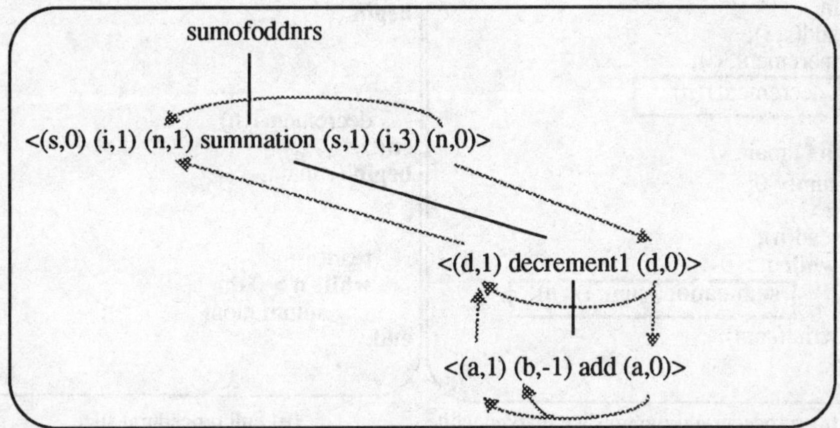

Figure 5: An execution slice on the summary graph of Figure 4 with respect to output variable n at the end of the execution of the procedure summation.

3.4 Mapping from Execution Slice to Program Slice

The execution slice on a summary graph contains multiple occurrences of nodes for all procedure calls and function applications which are executed during a program execution and have affected the value of a variable of interest. If the connection between call sites in the source program and their execution in the execution tree has been saved during execution of the program, then a dynamic program slice, when required, can be simply obtained from the corresponding execution slice. In this case, a mapping function *M* can map a vertex in the execution slice to a call site in the source program. Note that a vertex in the execution slice belongs to the execution tree at the same time.

$M(s) = cs$ where
s is a vertex in the execution slice and
cs is a call site in the source program.
and
$program\ slice\ (C) = \cup_{s \in execution\ slice(C)} M(s)$ where *C* is the slicing criterion.

Thus, the interprocedural program slice will be the set of all procedure calls and function applications in the program which affect the computation of the variable of interest. Figure 6a is the result of mapping from the execution slice in Figure 5 to the source program in Figure 3.

```
program sumofoddnrs;
var n, sum, i: integer;
procedure add(in out a: integer;
              in b:integer);
begin a:=a + b; end;
procedure increment2(in out c: integer);
begin add(c, 2) end;
procedure decrement1(in out d: integer);
begin  add(d, -2)  end;
procedure summation
          (in out s, i, n: integer);
begin
   add(s, i);
   increment2(i);
   decrement1(n)
end;
begin (* main *)
   sum:= 0;
   i:=1;
   read(n);
   while n > 0 do
       summation( sum, i,  n);
   write(sum);
end.
```

(a) Interprocedural program slice marked white

```
program sumofoddnrs;
var n          : integer;
procedure add(in out a: integer;
              in b:integer);
begin a:=a + b; end;


procedure decrement1(in out d: integer);
begin add(d, -1) end;
procedure summation
          (in out      n: integer);
begin



   decrement1(n)
end;
begin (* main *)


   read(n);
   while n > 0 do
       summation(         n);
end.
```

(b) Full procedural slice

Figure 6: The dynamic program slice resulting from mapping the execution slice in Figure 5 to the source program in Figure 3.Construction of the Summary Graph.

4 Construction of the Summary Graph

This section describes the construction of the summary graph introduced in the previous section. The method collects and summarizes the dependence information within each procedure activation. The summarized information is then transferred to the corresponding vertex of the summary graph.

4.1 Collection of Dependence Information

A procedure may be *statically* represented by a *control flow graph* [ASU86]. The control flow graph consists of a number of *basic blocks* as its nodes and a number of control flow edges.

Here we use a *Combined Compile time and Run-time Analysis* to compute a *"reasonable"* amount of information at compile time and leave the rest to run-time. A similar example of such an approach may be found in [Choi89].

We use the combined approach to gather information about dependencies between input/output variables of procedures. The information which is collected for each procedure, at compile time, consists of the data dependence information within basic blocks and the control dependence information between basic blocks. The computation of inter-block data dependencies and call block information is delayed until run-time. The next two sections describe compile-time computations and the application of static information in run-time computations.

Aliases also introduce dependencies between variables. We use Bannings method [Ban78] to compute possible parameter aliases. For such aliases, the program is instrumented with tracing code as in [Choi89], to determine actual alias information. Aliased variables are grouped in pairs in the temporary dependence graph. We do not yet handle pointer aliases.

4.1.1 Compile time computations

Basic blocks in a procedure have the useful property that their static and dynamic data dependencies are the same. For each basic block we determine its input/output variables, in a structure called a *block instance*:

block instance = <in_b, *b*, out_b>, where:

b is a *block name* for a basic block or a call block,

in_b: <*in-data*$_b$, *in-control*$_b$> where

- *in-data*$_b$ = {(*x*,*vx*) | *x* is a variable whose value, *vx*, is referenced in *b*; *vx* is the value of *x* before execution of *b*}
- *in-control*$_b$= {(*x*,*vx*) | *x* is a variable whose value *vx* affects the execution of block *b*}

out_b = {(*x*,*vx*) | *x* is a variable whose value is modified in *b*; *vx* is the value of *x* after execution of *b*.}

The dependencies between variables of a basic block *b* can be summarized in the form of (internal) dependence edges between variable instances belonging to in_b or out_b in its block instance.

Figure 7 illustrates a basic block *b* of four assignment statements, a data dependence graph representing data dependencies between variables inside the block, the summarized version of the data dependence graph and finally the block instance of the basic block together with dependencies between its input/output variables.

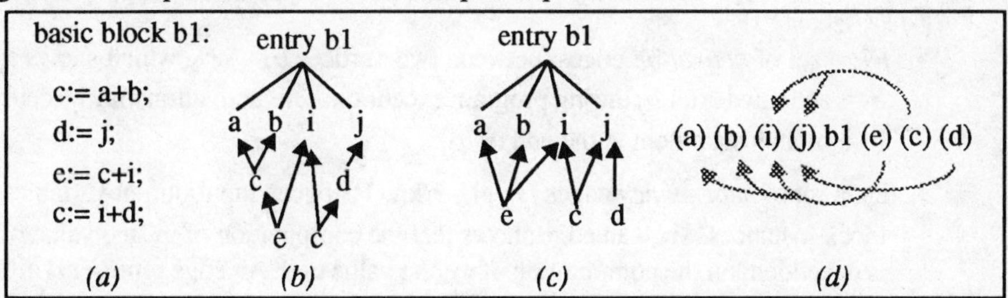

Figure 7: (a) basic block b1, (b) data dependence graph of b1, (c) summarized data dependence graph, (d) the internal dependencies of the block instance: <in_{b1}, b1, out_{b1}>.

The control dependence information between basic blocks of a procedure is saved in terms of the control variables. These control variables are assigned to the control edges in the control flow graph of a procedure, see Figure 8. Control variables are referenced in predicates which decide whether a block is executed or not. For example, consider the basic blocks in Figure 8. The value of variable *i* in *b1* is the basis for the decision of whether block *b2* is going to be executed or not. Thus, variable *i* is the control variable for the block *b2* (but not for *b4*). If the predicate is complex, for example containing function calls, then an auxiliary variable can be introduced as control variable and assigned the value of the predicate. When a terminating program should be the result of a program slice, then the notion of termination-preserving control dependency should be used to include statements in the execution slice which influence predicates that conditionally control loops or recursion.

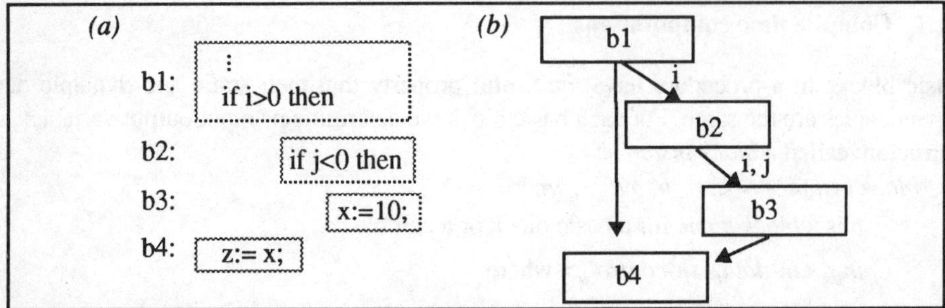

Figure 8: (a) Dividing a sequence of statements into basic blocks. (b) The control flow between the basic blocks, b1 .. b4, is shown in this figure. The control variables here are: i for b2 and i, j for b3.

4.1.2 Run-time Computations

The goal of the run-time computations is to find the dependencies between input/output variables of procedure activations. It uses the compile time information and collects enough run-time information to conclude about input/output variable dependencies. Then the collected run-time information is thrown away, since we have the required variable dependencies. To solve the problem in this way, we introduce a new kind of graph called a *temporary dependence graph*, or simply a *temporary graph*. Such a graph, *TempG*, may be defined as a directed graph with a set of vertices *V* and a set of edges *E*:

TempG = <*V*, *E*> where

V = {*s* | *s* is a *block instance*: <in_b, *b*, out_b>}

$E = E_1 \cup E_2$:

- *E1*: a set of *activation* edges, between two vertices $b_1 \rightarrow b_2$, which shows that b_2 is activated after b_1 during program execution. This activation may be caused by a branch statement at the end of b_1.
- E_2: a set of *dependency* edges $(y,vy) \leftarrow (x,vx)$ between input/output variables in block instances. Such an edge shows that the computation of *vx*, the value of *x*, is dependent on the computation of *vy*, the value of *y*. An edge represents either a control dependency or a data dependency. We distinguish two kinds of dependency edges:
  - *Internal dependency*, when an edge connects two variables belonging to the same vertex.

- *External dependency*, when an edge is between two variables belonging to different vertices, not necessarily in a *parent-child* relation between vertices.

The construction of a temporary graph for a procedure p_2 starts when the procedure is activated by another procedure p_1. When the execution of p_2 is terminated, the summary of the dependence information on the temporary graph of p_2 is transferred to the corresponding vertex of the summary graph and to the temporary graph of procedure p_1. The temporary graph for p_2 may now be deleted. Note that the construction of the dependence information during run-time is a bottom-up process.

The algorithm *ComputeAndSummarizeDependencies* describes the process of constructing the temporary graph together with constructing some parts of the summary graph. An intuitive explanation of the algorithm via an example follows below.

Algorithm *ComputeAndSummarizeDependencies*(p, returned-info)
Step1: Create a vertex for **procedure activation p** on the summary graph: **SummaryG**
Step2: (* Creation of a temporary graph, **TempG**, for the procedure activation **p**. *)
Create and initialize an **entry block instance** for **p** as the root of **TempG**,
For each block **b** in **p** in the execution order of blocks **do begin:**
  Before the execution of **b do begin**
    case block type **of**
    basic block: Add a new **block instance & internal dependencies** to **TempG**
      by using available information from compile-time analysis
    call block: use information obtained from
      ComputeAndSummarizeDependencies(q, return-info)
      when q is the procedure called by the call block, and add a new
      block instance & internal dependencies to **TempG**.
    end (* case *);
    If this block is activated due to the value of some **control variables, then**
      also take into account control variables and their dependencies.
  end;
  After the execution of **b do**
    Create **external dependency edges** between the new block instance and
    the previous block instances in **TempG**
end (* For *);
Determine the dependencies between the **entry** block instance and other
block instances of **TempG**
Step3: Transfer the dependence information from **TempG** to **SummaryG** for the
relevant vertices.
Step4: Summarize the TempG dependencies for in/out variables of entry block to
returned-info.
Step5: **Delete TempG** and **Return** with returned-info.
end Algorithm;

The construction of the temporary graph develops gradually during a trace execution of the procedures of the program. As an example consider procedure *p* which consists of four basic blocks *b1*, *b2*, *b4*, *b5* and a call block *b3* calling procedure *q*. The procedure *q* has only one basic block *b1*. Assume that an execution of this procedure goes through the blocks *b1*, *b3*, *b4* and *b5*.

Figure 10, parts I to V, illustrates the process of constructing a temporary graph for procedure *p*. Initially during the building of the temporary graph for procedure *p*, an entry block instance *<in, p, out>* is created (see Figure 10-I). Then, when execution reaches a block, a block instance with its internal dependencies can be created immediately if the required information is available. For a basic block such as *b1* of *p*, this information has been computed in advance at compile time. Thus the block instance *<in, b1, out>* and its internal dependencies can be created immediately (see Figure 10-II).

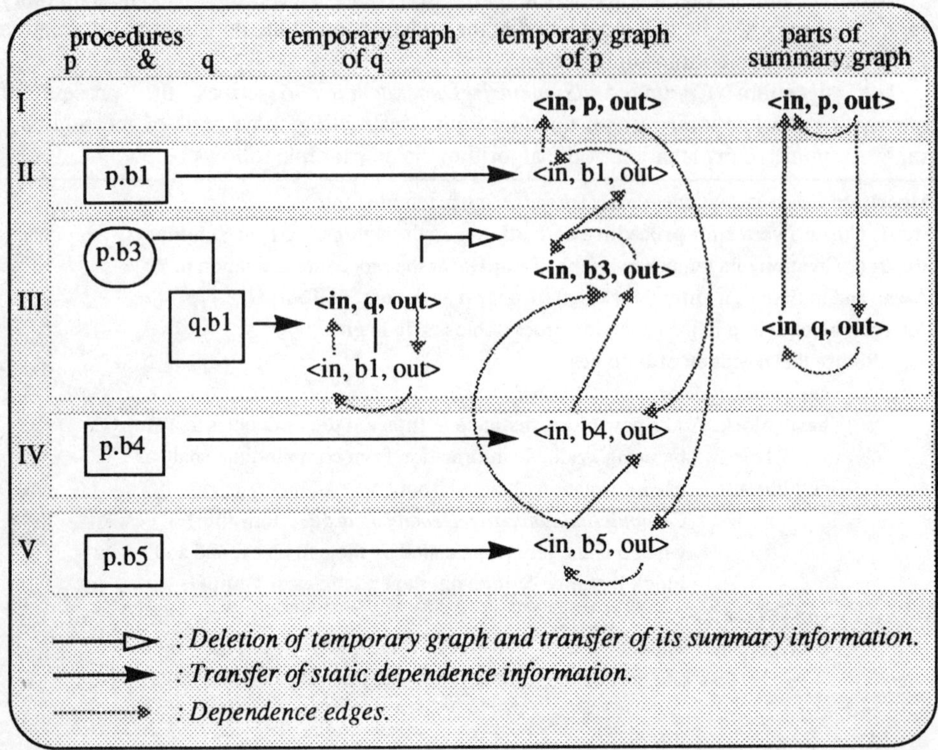

Figure 9: An example of building the temporary graph for procedure p. (I) The entry block of temporary graph p and the procedure activation of procedure p in the summary graph. (II) The block instance of basic block b1 and its internal dependencies created from compile-time information. The external dependencies of b1 are shown, too. (III) The creation of a block instance and its internal dependencies for the call block b3 with help of the temporary graph of procedure q. The procedure activation of q and its internal dependencies are created in the summary graph, too. (IV) The block instance for basic block b4 and its external dependencies. (V) The block instance of b5 and its internal dependencies together with its external dependencies.

The construction of the temporary graph will be suspended when execution reaches a call block such as block b3. The information needed to create a block instance is not easy to compute at compile time. In this case another temporary graph which contains information about the called procedure can produce the exact dependence information for the calling block instance. The call block b3 calls procedure q. In this case the process of building a temporary graph is started for procedure q, which has only one basic block. Thus the temporary graph for this procedure can be constructed without waiting for completion of other subgraphs, see Figure 10-III.

When a temporary graph has been completed, its information can be summarized and transferred to the temporary graph of the calling procedure and to the summary graph as well. Then there will be no need to keep the completed temporary graph any more. In Figure 10-III the temporary graph of procedure *q* is completed. Its information has been transferred to the summary graph and the temporary graph of procedure *p*. The summary graph retrieves this information for the procedure activation < *in, q, out*>, in the form of dependency edges from *out* variables to *in* variables. The temporary graph of *p* makes use of this information to create the vertex <*in, b3, out*> and its internal dependency edges. Since the temporary graph for *q* will not be used any more, it can be deleted.

The process of constructing the temporary graph of procedure *p* will be continued as before. The external dependency edges between block instance of *b3* and its predecessors will be inserted. The other blocks *b4* and *b5* are all basic blocks, so the block instance and internal dependencies for *b4* and *b5* can be created immediately and processed as *b1*. Here *out* variables in the entry block have received their values from *out* variables in blocks *b3* and *b5*. This is represented by two external edges from entry block in Figure 10-I to the block instances of *b3* and *b5* in the parts IV and V of the same figure.

Now when the temporary graph of *p* has been completed, its information will be summarized within the summary graph. The external dependencies between *in*/*out* variables of <*in, p, out*> and <*in, q, out*> in the summary graph can be found by following transitive dependencies in the temporary graph *p* between the corresponding vertices, i.e. the entry block and the block *b3*. The temporary graph *p* also transfers information to the previous temporary graph of the procedure calling *p*, whose construction has been delayed due to this particular execution of *p* (this is not shown in Figure 10). Finally the temporary graph of *p* can be deleted.

5 Applications

The interprocedural dynamic slicing introduced in this paper is being used in a semi-automated debugging system, GADT (Generalized Algorithmic Debugging Technique/ Tool) [FGKS91] to improve the bug localization process. This is done by using the exact dependence information provided by the dynamic slicing to avoid searching irrelevant parts of the execution tree during bug localization. Other potential applications could be in data-flow testing, see [Har89].

6 Conclusions and Current Status

We have presented the (to our knowledge) first algorithm for interprocedural dynamic slicing. Previous algorithms only handle small languages without procedures [AH90]. This algorithm is considerably more memory-efficient than previous dynamic slicing algorithms, since it only needs to save summary trace information at procedure calls - not at every statement as most previous algorithms. Thus it may be the first dynamic slicing method that can be applied to realistic programs. We have also informally defined the notion of *termination-preserving control dependency*, which if used leads to terminating program slices, in contrast to certain types of slices based on control dependency described in most current literature.

We are currently implementing the interprocedural slicing algorithm for Pascal. The most important parts of the prototype just recently became operational. We have also hand-simulated the algorithm on several program examples and as an application have used the obtained dynamic slicing information together with the Generalized Algorithmic Debugging Tool (GADT) as a replacement for the imprecise static slicing currently used by GADT.

References

[AH90] Hiralal Agrawal and Joseph R. Horgan. Dynamic Program Slicing. In *Proceedings of the ACM SIGPLAN'90 Conference on Programming Language Design and Implementation*, pages 246–256, New York, June 90.

[ASU86] Alfred V. Aho, Ravi Sethi, and Jeffry D. Ullman. *Compilers: Principles, Techniques and Tools*. Addison-Wesley, 1986.

[Bann78] J.P.Banning. A Method for Detemining the Side Effects of Procedure Calls. PhD thesis, Stanford, 1978.

[Choi89] Jongdeok Choi. Parallel Program Debugging with Flowback Analysis. TR#871, Computer Sciences Department, University of Wisconsin , Madison, August 1989.

[FGKS91] Peter Fritzson, Tibor Gyimothy, Mariam Kamkar, and Nahid Shahmehri. Generalized Algorithmic Debugging and Testing. In *Proceedings of the ACM SIGPLAN'91*, pages 317–326, Toronto, Ontario, Canada, June 1991. Also as report LiTH-IDA-R-90-42.

[FOW87] Jeanne Ferrante, Karl J. Ottenstein, and Joe D. Warren. The Program Dependence Graph and its Use in Optimization. *ACM Transactions on Programming Languages and Systems*, 9(3):319–349, July 1987.

[Har89]Mary J. Harrold. *An Approach to Incremental Testing*. PhD thesis, TR-89-1, Dept. of Computer Science, University of Pittsburgh, 1989.

[HRB90] Susan Horwitz, Thomas Reps, and David Binkley. Interprocedural Slicing using Dependence Graphs. *ACM Transactions on Programming Languages and Systems*, 12(1):26–61, January 1990.

[KL90] Bogdan Korel and Janusz Laski. Dynamic Slicing of Computer Programs. *The Journal of Systems and Software*, 1990.

[LG89] James R. Lyle and Keith B. Gallagher. A Program Decomposition Scheme with Applications to Software Modification and Testing. In *Proceedings of the 22nd Hawaii International Conference on System Sciences*, pages 479–485, Hawaii, January 1989.

[Lyl84] James R. Lyle. *Evaluating Variations on Program Slicing for Debugging*. PhD thesis, University of Maryland, December 1984.

[Ven91] G. A. Venkatesh. The Semantic Approach to Program Slicing. In *Proceedings of the ACM SIGPLAN'91*, pages 107–119, Toronto, Ontario, Canada, June 1991.

[Wei84] Mark Weiser. Program Slicing. *IEEE Transactions on Software Engineering*, Se–10(4):352–357, July 1984.

Algorithmic Debugging for Lazy Functional Languages

Henrik Nilsson and Peter Fritzson

Programming Environments Laboratory
Department of Computer and Information Science
Linköping University, S-581 83 Linköping, Sweden[1]
E-mail: henni@ida.liu.se, paf@ida.liu.se

Abstract. Lazy functional languages have non-strict semantics and are purely declarative, i.e. they support the notion of referential transparency and are devoid of side effects. Traditional debugging techniques are, however, not suited for lazy functional languages since computations generally do not take place in the order one might expect. Since *algorithmic debugging* allows the user to concentrate on the declarative aspects of program semantics, and will semi-automatically find functions containing bugs, we propose to use this technique for debugging lazy functional programs. In this paper we present an algorithmic debugger for a lazy functional language and some experience in using it. Because of the non-strict semantics of lazy functional languages, arguments to functions are in general partially evaluated expressions. The user is, however, usually more concerned with the values that these expressions represent. We address this problem by providing the user with a *strictified* view of the execution trace whenever possible.

1 Introduction

Debugging has always been a costly part of software development, and several attempts have been made to provide automatic computer support for this task [10]. The algorithmic debugging technique, introduced by Shapiro [12], was the first attempt to lay a theoretical framework for program debugging and to take this framework as a basis for a partly automatic debugger. In this system, the programmer supplies a partial specification of the program by answering questions during the debugging process.

In previous research [11, 4], we have presented the first generalization of the algorithmic debugging method to a class of imperative languages (GADT - Generalized Algorithmic Debugging Technique) and improved its bug finding properties by integrating the method with program slicing.

The aim of the research presented here is to investigate whether or not algorithmic debugging is a relevant technique for debugging programs written in lazy functional languages and, if possible, to implement a useful debugger for such languages. Traditional debugging techniques (e.g. breakpoints, tracing, variable watching etc.) are not particularly well suited for the class of lazy functional languages [2] since computations in a program generally do not take place in the order one might expect from reading the source code.

However, algorithmic debugging allows a user to concentrate on the declarative semantics of an application program, rather than its operational aspects such as evaluation order. During debugging, the user only has to decide whether or not a particular function

1. This work is supported by the Swedish Board for Technical Development, NUTEK.

applied to some particular arguments yields a correct result. Given correct answers from the user, the debugger will determine what function that contains the bug. Thus, the user need not worry about why and when a function is invoked, which suggests that algorithmic debugging might be a suitable basis for a debugging tool for lazy functional languages.

Algorithmic debugging is a two phase process: an execution trace tree is built at the procedure/function level during the first (trace) phase which is then traversed during the second (debugging) phase. Each node in the tree corresponds to an invocation of a procedure or function and holds a record of supplied arguments and returned results.

A problem with algorithmic debugging for lazy functional languages is that, because of the non-strict semantics, arguments to functions and their results are in general partially evaluated expressions. Presenting these directly, would place an unreasonably large burden on the user who has to deduce whether the behaviour of a particular function invocation is correct or not. It is, therefore, desirable to use information regarding which expressions that have been evaluated and to what they evaluated (which is exactly what has been collected by the debugger during the trace phase) in order that questions put to the user can be simplified by substituting values for expressions. Note that it is not possible to simply evaluate unevaluated expressions as they are encountered during the debugging phase, since they may represent infinite structures or non-terminating computations.

To test these ideas in practice, support for algorithmic debugging was added to an existing compiler for a small lazy functional language and an algorithmic debugger was implemented. The language, called Freja [8], is essentially a subset of Miranda [13]. It is based on graph reduction and implemented using a G-machine approach [1, 6, 9]. In comparison with some other compilers for lazy functional languages, this compiler is rather basic; in particular, it does not do any strictness analysis and it does not perform fully-lazy lambda-lifting. Both the compiler for the functional language and the algorithmic debugger are implemented in C and currently run on Sun SPARC stations.

We are only aware of two other debuggers for lazy functional languages. One is part of a programming environment for rapid prototyping developed at Technische Hochschule Darmstadt [5]. This debugger, however, seems to be conventional in the sense that it is based on setting breakpoints and single stepping, and it does not address the problem of unevaluated function arguments and results. The other is an algorithmic debugger, inspired by our work, that very recently has been developed at the University of Melbourne [7].

The rest of this paper is organized as follows. In Sect. 2 the principles behind algorithmic debugging are explained. Section 3 describes how algorithmic debugging may be adapted for lazy functional programs and the idea of *strictification* is developed. In Sect. 4, we give some details on our implementation and in Sect. 5 we report some experience in using the debugger. Section 6 discusses various aspects of our approach and in Sect. 7 we consider whether or not it would be possible to avoid construction of the entire execution trace tree. Finally, in Sect. 8, some conclusions are given.

2 Basic Algorithmic Debugging

In this section we describe the basic principles of algorithmic debugging. To simplify the presentation and provide a background to our work, we use a debugger based on the original algorithmic program debugging method by Shapiro [12].

Algorithmic debugging is based on the notion of an *externally visible bug symptom*, i.e. an execution of a program did not produce the expected result. This must have a cause; either the topmost procedure did something wrong, or some procedure invoked from the topmost one produced some erroneous result. By inspecting the invocations performed from the topmost procedure, it is possible to determine what is the case: if all invocations yielded correct results, then the topmost procedure must be at fault. Otherwise, one of the invocations exhibits some visible bug symptom, and we may thus apply the above reasoning over again, tracing the source of the bug down the execution trace tree. Since the debugger cannot know what is a bug symptom and what is correct behaviour, at least not initially, there must be an *oracle*, i.e. the user, ready to supply it with this information.

Algorithmic debugging guarantees that the procedure or function containing the bug eventually will be found, provided that the user answers the questions about the program behaviour correctly. If there are more than one bug in a program, only one of them will be found. However, algorithmic debugging may be applied again, once this bug is removed, in order to find the next bug.

In more detail, algorithmic debugging proceeds as follows. The debugger first executes the program and builds an execution trace tree at the procedure level. A node in the tree is constructed for each procedure invocation and essential trace information, such as the procedure name and the values of all input and output parameters, are recorded. If any further procedure calls are made during the current invocation, these become children of the current node. New children are inserted from left to right, in the same order as the corresponding procedures are invoked.

Once the execution has completed, the algorithmic debugger starts searching for the bug by traversing the execution tree in a preorder manner. For each node, the debugger interacts with the user by asking whether or not the behaviour of the procedure invocation corresponding to the node is correct. The user may reply yes or no to this[1]. If a positive answer is given, the search continues from the next branch to the right of the current one, otherwise the search continues from the leftmost child of the current node (if it has any). The search ends at a node exhibiting incorrect behaviour when one of the following holds:

- No further procedure calls were made during the procedure invocation corresponding to this node; i.e. this node has no children.
- All procedure calls performed during the procedure invocation corresponding to this node fulfil the user's expectations.

Finally, the debugger reports the name of the offending procedure. The user's answers are remembered so that the same question does not have to be asked twice.

Figure 1 shows an example of algorithmic debugging. The bug is in the function `insert`. Since the user answers no to the first two questions, the debugger moves down to the leftmost child of `sort([1,3])`. According to the user, the behaviour recorded in this node is correct, so the next branch to the right is investigated next. The behaviour of that node is wrong, but its only child behaved correctly. The bug must therefore be in the body of the procedure that is associated with this node, i.e. in `insert`.

---

1. Shapiro's original method [12] could only handle yes/no answers. A capability of handling assertions about the intended behaviour of a procedure was presented later by Drabent, Nadjm-Tehrani and Maluszynski [3], and is also present in the design of GADT.

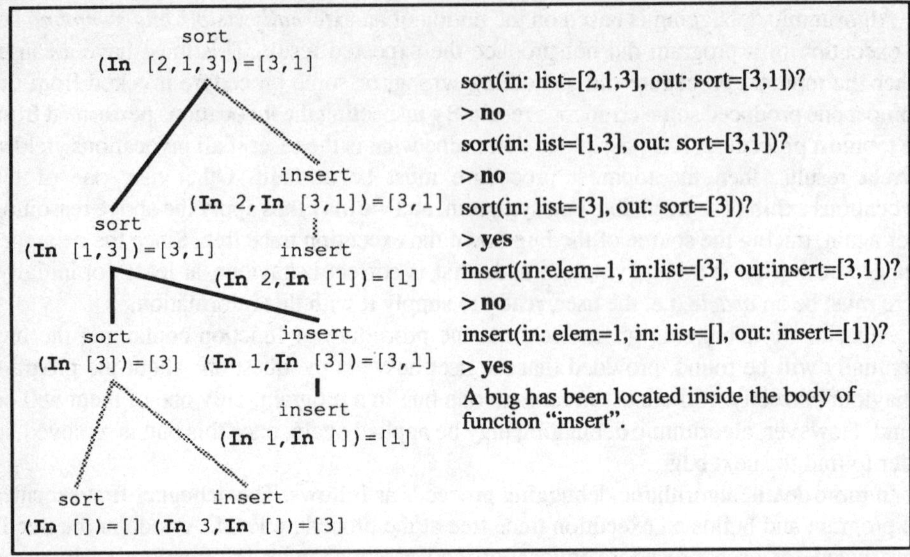
sort
(In [2,1,3])=[3,1]
sort(in: list=[2,1,3], out: sort=[3,1])?
> no
sort(in: list=[1,3], out: sort=[3,1])?
insert
> no
(In 2,In [3,1])=[3,1]
sort(in: list=[3], out: sort=[3])?
sort
> yes
(In [1,3])=[3,1]
insert
(In 2,In [1])=[1]
insert(in:elem=1, in:list=[3], out:insert=[3,1])?
> no
sort
insert
insert(in: elem=1, in: list=[], out: insert=[1])?
(In [3])=[3]
(In 1,In [3])=[3,1]
> yes
A bug has been located inside the body of function "insert".
insert
(In 1,In [])=[1]
sort
insert
(In [])=[]
(In 3,In [])=[3]

Fig. 1. The execution tree of an erroneous sort program and the ensuing user interaction.

Note that, in order to be able to give a correct answer, the user must be given the "full picture" for each question, i.e. the computation must depend only on its input parameters and there must be no effects of the computation besides what is indicated by the output parameters. Procedures that fulfil this criterion are said to be *side-effect-free*. It is possible to achieve side-effect-freeness in programs written in imperative languages by program transformations [11].

3 Algorithmic Debugging for Lazy Functional Languages

3.1 Basic Algorithmic Debugging

Algorithmic debugging may readily be used for lazy functional languages since functions *are* side-effect-free: they can only return results to their callers; there are no updateable variables. We do have to regard the execution environment of a function as belonging to its input parameters, though, since a function may contain references to *free variables* [9]. Nodes in the execution trace tree will thus correspond to function applications and basic algorithmic debugging (as outlined in Sect. 2) can be applied without modification. This is how the first version of our debugger was implemented.

However, while gaining experience in using the debugger, the fact that arguments to functions in general are partially evaluated expressions soon proved to be a major problem for the user. He is usually concerned with the values that these expressions represent; details of the inner workings of the underlying evaluation machinery is often of little or no interest. Furthermore, the questions that the debugger asked were frequently very large and difficult to interpret.

This problem might have been especially apparent in our case since our compiler does not do strictness analysis (something any good compiler would have to do). However, strictness analysis is not perfect and there will always be occasions when unevaluated expressions are passed as parameters (otherwise we would not need the lazy semantics in the first place).

This suggests that we should replace unevaluated expressions by the values they represent whenever possible, in order to give the user an impression of strict evaluation, which is probably his usual mental model of the evaluation anyway. We will refer to the process of giving an impression of strict evaluation (where possible to do so) as *strictification* from now on.

In theory, it should be possible to achieve "perfect" strictification since the debugger holds a complete record of everything that was evaluated during the execution. Our debugger does not get quite there, though, due to the way the way the graph reducer works (see 4.3). Also, strictification is not as straight forward as it first might appear and we have to exercise care when doing it, as we shall see in the next section.

3.2 Why Simple-Minded Strictification Does Not Work

Suppose that strictification was implemented in the obvious way, i.e. before asking whether a function application yielded a correct result or not, any unevaluated expressions[1] that occur in the arguments or in the result of the application are replaced by the results of evaluating the expressions in case they are known to the debugger (i.e. were needed at some point during the execution). This of course has to be done recursively in case the results themselves contain any unevaluated subexpressions. The user will then see a version of the function application which is as strict as possible given a particular execution trace. Unfortunately, the debugging algorithm is no longer guaranteed to find the bug, as illustrated below (the function `add` is incorrect).

```
double x = add x x;
add x y = x * y;
```

Now, assuming that `double` at some point is applied to `(1+2)` and that strictification is not performed, the user would eventually be asked if it is correct that `(double (1+2))` evaluates to `(add (1+2) (1+2))`. This in fact is correct, keeping in mind that the *intended* behaviour of `add` is to sum its arguments. Assuming that the user answers yes, he would then be asked if `(add (1+2) (1+2))` should evaluate to `9`. Obviously, this is wrong, and given an answer indicating this the debugger would correctly conclude that the bug is inside the function `add`.

However, had strictification as described above been done, the user would instead have been asked whether or not `(double 3)` should evaluate to `9`. Presumably he would answer no, which would lead the debugger to the erroneous conclusion that the bug is located inside `double` (since this node in the execution tree does not have any children).

The problem is that questions are asked in an order given by the lazy execution tree, but that the questions themselves are shown as if we had had strict semantics. The structure of

1. An expression is of course itself an application of a function to some arguments.

a strict execution tree is of course completely different from the structure of the corresponding lazy one (but note that there is no guarantee that strict evaluation will terminate just because lazy evaluation does so) and this must be reflected by the order in which questions are asked. It takes more than simply performing substitution to give a correct impression of strict evaluation.

3.3 Correct Strictification

A correct way of doing strictification can be derived from the following two observations:

- Performing a substitution of a result for an expression in one of the arguments of a function application, corresponds to evaluation of the expression in question *before* entering the function. Thus, a new node should in principle be inserted in the execution tree to the left of the node corresponding to the function application.
- Performing a substitution of a result for an expression in the result of a function application, corresponds to evaluation of the expression in question *inside* the invocation of the function. Thus, the node corresponding to the function application should in principle be given a new child (inserting it to the right of its siblings will do).

These transformations should be applied recursively; that is to say, the new nodes must themselves be strictified. However, there is no need to actually perform these transformations on the execution tree; it is sufficient to ask the questions during the debugging phase in such an order as if the transformation had been performed

Thus, before a substitution is performed in an argument of a function application, we have to *ask* whether the expression we are substituting for should really evaluate to that which we are going to replace it by. This has to be done recursively which might lead to further questions being asked.

On the other hand, substitutions in the result of an application should be performed without asking at this stage. Questions should instead be asked if the user indicates incorrect behaviour and it is found that all real children of the application did behave as expected.

3.4 Algorithmic Debugging with Strictification

The algorithm for algorithmic debugging with strictification is given in pseudo code below. The implemented debugger, in addition to yes and no answers, also supports "maybe" answers and a kind of simple assertions, details of which are omitted from the pseudo code for reasons of simplicity. These features are instead outlined informally.

Also missing from the pseudo code are checks for preventing attempts to strictify nodes in the execution tree that already are being strictified. This can be achieved by keeping nodes currently under strictification in a list. Then, before strictification of a new node is started, it is checked whether it is already present in the list or not. If it is, it can safely be ignored. Similar arrangements must be provided for the evaluation procedures below.

Two abstract data types are assumed: `exec_tree` and `expr`. An execution tree node consists of a function application and its result (both of type `expr`) and zero, one or more children. These are accessed by means of the functions `App`, `Res` and `Children`. A function `Tree` that returns the execution tree corresponding to a function application is also supposed to exist. This function can of course only be used if the application was evaluated during the execution, which is checked by the function `Has_Been_Evaluated`.

An expression is either an application of a function to some arguments; a constructed data object (e.g. a tuple) having zero, one or more fields; or some atomic object such as an integer. The functions `Args` and `Fields` are used to access the arguments of an application and the fields of a constructed object respectively.

There is also an oracle that can be queried about the status of a function application. Initially, the status is "unknown". This is changed to "correct" whenever the user answers that an application behaved correctly. Thus the same question need not be asked twice. The remaining function and procedure names should hopefully be self-explanatory.

```
(* Locates the bug in the execution tree. *)
PROCEDURE Strictify_And_Debug(tree: exec_tree)
VAR
   strictified_app, ev_res: expr;
BEGIN
   IF Status_Is_Unknown(App(tree)) THEN
      strictified_app :=
         Make_App(Fun_Name(App(tree)),
                  MAP Evaluate_And_Debug Args(App(tree)));
      ev_res := Evaluate(Res(tree));
      Pretty_Print(strictified_app); PRINT "=>";
      Pretty_Print(ev_res); PRINT "? "
      IF User_Answer = "YES" THEN
         Set_Status_To_Correct(App(tree));
      ELSE
         FOR ALL c IN Children(tree) DO
            Strictify_And_Debug(c);
         ENDFOR;
         Evaluate_And_Debug(Res(tree));
         (* If we get here, no bug in children. *)
         PRINT "Bug located in function ";
         PRINT Fun_Name(App(Tree)); PRINT ".\n";
         EXIT; (* Exit immediately when bug found. *)
      ENDIF;
   ENDIF;
   (* If we get here, the behaviour was correct *)
END;

FUNCTION Evaluate_And_Debug(e: expr): expr
BEGIN
   IF Is_App(e) THEN          (* Function application *)
      IF (Has_Been_Evaluated(e)) THEN
         Strictify_And_Debug(Tree(e));
         RETURN Evaluate(Res(Tree(e)));
      ELSE
         RETURN Make_App(Fun_Name(e),
```

```
                                MAP Evaluate_And_Debug Args(e));
         ENDIF;
      ELSEIF Is_Constr(e) THEN (* Tuple, CONS-cell... *)
         RETURN Make_Constr(Constr_Name(e),
                               MAP Evaluate_And_Debug Fields(e));
      ELSE                      (* Integer, character...*)
         RETURN e;              (* Already fully evaluated. *)
      ENDIF;
   END;

   FUNCTION Evaluate(e: expr): expr
   BEGIN
      IF Is_App(e) THEN         (* Function application *)
         IF (Has_Been_Evaluated(e)) THEN
            RETURN Evaluate(Res(Tree(e)));
         ELSE
           RETURN Make_App(Fun_Name(e),MAP Evaluate Args(e));
         ENDIF;
      ELSEIF Is_Constr(e) THEN (* Tuple, CONS-cell... *)
         RETURN Make_Constr(Constr_Name(e),
                                MAP Evaluate Fields(e));
      ELSE                      (* Integer, character...*)
         RETURN e;              (* Already fully evaluated. *)
      ENDIF;
   END;
```

There are of course cases when the user might be unwilling to supply a definite yes or no answer to a question, either because he really does not know the answer, or because the question seems to be large and complicated. Thus, there is an option to answer "*maybe* this is correct, I don't know". This effectively lets the user postpone answering the question and get on with the debugging in the hope that a bug is positively identified before he is faced with this question again.

Initially, a "maybe" answer is treated as "no". Thus the children of the current node will be searched. If no bug is found, the algorithm will eventually get back to the node that the user was unsure about, knowing that all its children behaved correctly. At this point, the user is again asked about the node. If he this time indicates that the result is correct, debugging will proceed as usual, the only difference being that the user has had to answer more questions than otherwise would have been the case. If the answer is that the result is incorrect, then there must be a bug in the applied function. However, if the users insists on answering "maybe", the algorithm is forced to conclude that there might be a bug in the function applied. This is reported to the user and the algorithm then continues as if the result was correct, since it is still possible that a more definite bug will be found.

The assertion facility gives a user a possibility to suppress questions regarding a particular function (thus asserting its correctness). This has occasionally proved to be a convenient feature, but obviously it is very primitive as far as assertions go.

3.5 Algorithmic Debugging of a Small Program

The following Freja program, that is supposed to calculate the first five prime numbers, contains a bug in the function `not_div_x` defined locally in `sieve`, (the operator equal (==) should be replaced with the operator not equal (~=)).

```
shownums [] = [];
shownums (x:xs) = shownum x ++ " " ++ shownums xs;

filter p [] = [];
filter p (x:xs) = x : filter p xs, if p x
                = filter p xs, otherwise;

from n = n : from (n + 1);

take 0 xs = [];
take (n + 1) [] = [];
take (n + 1) (x:xs) = x : take n xs;
sieve (x : xs) = x : sieve (filter not_div_x xs)
            where
               not_div_x y = (y mod x == 0);
            ;

primes = sieve (from 2);
main = shownums (take 5 primes);
```

The interaction between the user and the debugger, when the above program is executed, is shown below, with bold-face indicating the user's input and responses. The questions have been numbered for easy reference. The user may answer "y" for "yes", "n" for "no" and "m" for "maybe" to the questions. He may also issue commands that control various printing options and give assertions; "h" for "help" gives a list of all available options. Note that missing arguments in applications (i.e. instances of partial applications) are indicated with an underscore ("_") and that an ellipsis ("...") is used to represent tails of long lists and tails that are not evaluated. Also, note that any variables used by a function that are part of its environment, are shown to the user in a `where`-clause (see for example question 8). The notation `foo.fie` indicates that function `fie` is declared locally in function `foo`.

```
2 4 8 16 32

1) Did the program behave correctly?
(y/n/m/h)? n

2) main => "2 4 8 16 3..."
(y/n/m/h)? n

3) primes => [2,4,8,16,32,...]
(y/n/m/h)? n

4) (from 2) => [2,3,...]
(y/n/m/h)? y
```

```
5) (sieve [2,3,...]) => [2,4,8,16,32,...]
(y/n/m/h)? n

6) (from 3) => [3,...]
(y/n/m/h)? uet
(from 3) => [3:(from ($plus 3 1))]
(y/n/m/h)? y

7) (filter (sieve.not_div_x _ where x=2)
           [3:(from ($plus 3 1))]) =>
[4,6,8,10,12,14,16,18,20,22,...]
(y/n/m/h)? n

8) (sieve.not_div_x 3 where x=2) => False
(y/n/m/h)? n

Bug located in function sieve.not_div_x
```

Clearly, the numbers 2, 4, 8, 16 and 32 are not the first five prime numbers, so the answer to question 1 has to be no. The same holds for questions 2 and 3 as well. The application in question 4 reduces to a list of numbers starting with 2 and 3 which seems to be correct. However, `sieve` applied to this list should evaluate to a list of prime numbers which obviously is not the case in question 5. The answer to this question is therefore again no.

To be able to answer question 6, the user first requests unevaluated tails of lists to be shown (the command `uet`). Since `(from 3)` reduces to a list starting with 3 and having `(from 4)` as its tail, this reduction is correct.

The expression in question 7 should filter out everything divisible by 2 from the list of natural numbers starting from 3. Apparently, however, we are left with all even numbers from 4 and upwards, so this is wrong. Finally, in question 8, the offending function is found. Since 3 is not divisible by 2 the expression ought to have yielded `true`.

For comparison, an unstrictified version of question 2 is given below. It is not too hard to infer the answer to this question, but it is clearly not as straight forward as above. The result of the reduction is a list whose head is the first prime number (2) and whose tail is an expression that according to its specification *should* evaluate to the remaining prime numbers. Therefore, the answer to the unstrictified version of the question is yes, whereas the answer to the strictified question is no since the tail *in fact* evaluates to something erroneous.

```
main =>
['2':
 ($append
     [' ']
     (shownums
        (take 4 (sieve (filter
                            (sieve.not_div_x _ where x=2)
                            (from ($plus 2 1))))))))]
(y/n/m/h)? y
```

4 Implementation

4.1 Modifications of the Compiler

As noted in 3.1, free variables must somehow be dealt with. Being a G-machine implementation [1, 6, 9], Freja is based on graph reduction using supercombinators[1]. A source program containing functions with free variables is transformed into supercombinator form by lambda-lifting[2]. Since only basic lambda-lifting is performed (i.e. free variables are taken out as extra parameters rather than maximal free expressions, which is the case when doing fully-lazy lambda-lifting), followed by η-reduction and removal of redundant supercombinators [9], there is a one-to-one mapping between the functions in the source program and the supercombinators in the object program.

Therefore, by implementing the algorithmic debugging on the supercombinator form of a program, no extra work is needed to take out free variables; this is already done as a part of the basic compilation process. To support algorithmic debugging, the compiler only has to add some extra debugging information to each supercombinator definition and insert calls to tracing routines in the object code so that an execution tree may be built at run time. Note that this has to be done for system supplied supercombinators as well, even though we know they are correct, since we need a complete trace tree in order to perform strictification.

The extra information that is needed consists of the name of the function corresponding to the supercombinator, the arity of the supercombinator, and the number of free variables that have been taken out as extra parameters as well as the names of these variables. The information is needed in order that questions from the algorithmic debugger may be phrased in terms of the original source program rather than in terms of the transformed program, which would be very inconvenient for the user.

Calls to two different tracing routines are inserted in the code of a supercombinator, one call at the beginning and one just before each possible exit point. The routine that is called first creates a node in the trace tree and records the values of all parameters (including the abstracted free variables), the second routine records the result of the supercombinator application. Thus one node in the trace tree will be created whenever a supercombinator reduction is initiated, which happens exactly when the corresponding function is applied to enough arguments, i.e. at least as many arguments as the arity of the function.

In case of a program error (which terminates execution immediately), a call to a special routine is made that first fixes any tree nodes for which no results as yet have been recorded and then immediately invokes the algorithmic debugger. Nodes are fixed by inserting a special result, "error", which is semantically equivalent to non-termination or $\perp$. If a program goes into an infinite loop, the user may force termination by pressing CTRL-C. The tree is then fixed in the same manner as if a program error had occurred.

The Freja compiler consists of some 10000 lines of C-code (not counting blank lines and comments). In this respect the modifications needed for supporting algorithmic debugging were fairly minor, a rough estimate is that about 400 lines had to be modified or added.

1. A supercombinator is basically a function without free variables.
2. Lambda-lifting is the process of converting free variables to additional function arguments.

4.2 The Algorithmic Debugger

The algorithmic debugger itself is implemented in about 3000 lines of C. The debugger is linked with the compiled Freja program that is going to be debugged, forming a single executable. When it is run, the Freja program is first executed and the trace tree is built. Then the debugger is invoked and algorithmic debugging begins.

The debugger consists of two main parts: routines for building the tree and routines for performing the actual debugging. The tree is constructed by making calls to the two trace routines as described above. Arguments to supercombinators and returned results are all pieces of graph located on the functional program's own private heap. In order to preserve them for the execution tree, they have to be copied off the heap. We cannot simply keep a pointer to them, not even if garbage collection is turned off, since applications are physically overwritten as the last step of a graph reduction. If we did keep pointers, we would end up with (automatic) "simple-minded strictification" (see 3.2). The copying algorithm must be able to handle circular graphs; otherwise, the debugger might end up in an infinite loop.

To facilitate equality testing on graphs, equal graphs are mapped into the same storage using a hashing algorithm, i.e. before any graph node is built, it is checked whether an equal graph node already exists. Thus pointer comparison can be used to test for graph equality within the debugger and the pointers themselves can be used for further hashing when indexing the execution trace tree in order to make the strictification efficiently.

4.3 Why Perfect Strictification Is Not Achieved

Since the results of all applications that have been evaluated during the program execution have been recorded by the algorithmic debugger, it should theoretically be possible to do a perfect strictification. Unfortunately, this is quite difficult to do in practice.

Consider an unevaluated application `(foo (1+2))` (that would evaluate to `7` say). Suppose further that the value of `(foo (1+2))` is indeed needed later on, but that the subexpression `(1+2)` is shared with some other expression, the value of which is needed before the value of `(foo (1+2))` is needed. Then the debugger would record that the result of `(foo 3)` is `7`, but it would not know anything about the result of `(foo (1+2))`. Therefore, it is not possible to substitute `7` for this application during the strictification.

In an attempt to somewhat compensate for this imperfectness of the strictification, the debugger explicitly evaluates some system function applications in a few special cases when it is safe to do so. Clearly, better strictification would be preferable.

4.4 The Graphic User Interface

The graphic user interface (see Fig. 2) to our lazy language algorithmic debugger provides a better overview of the debugging process by showing both source code and other useful information in separate windows. Most of the user interface has been re-used from the GADT system [11].

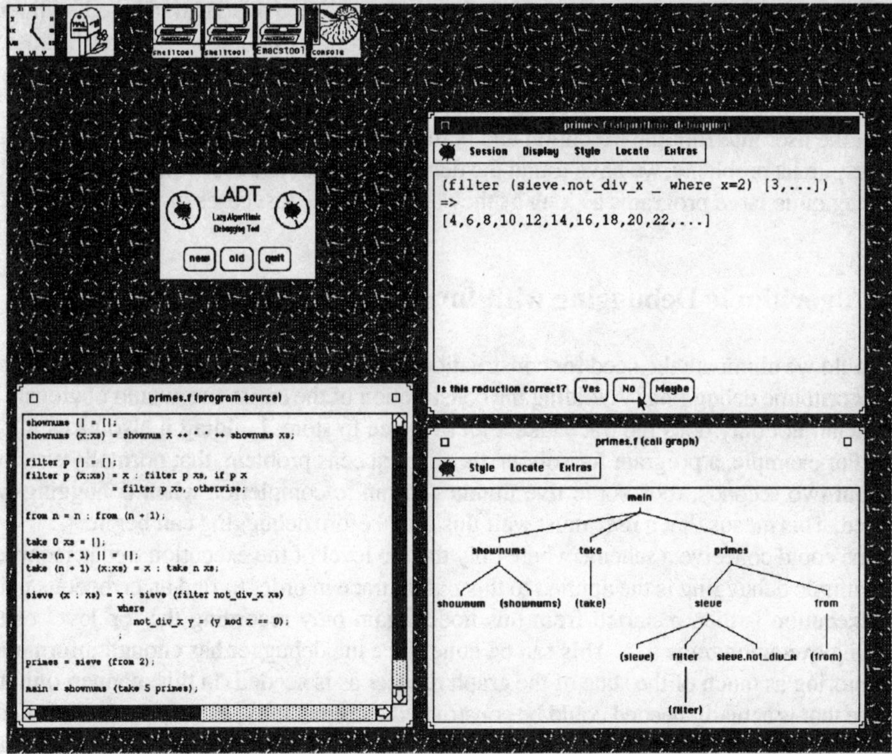

Fig. 2. The graphic user interface when debugging the prime number example.

5 Experience in Using the Debugger

The debugger has so far been used to successfully debug a number of toy programs, including programs calculating Fibonacci numbers and solving the eight queens problem, as well as a somewhat larger program to evaluate arithmetic expressions (around 250 lines of code). We intend to test it on even larger examples (e.g. a SLR(1) parser generator) in the near future.

The number of questions that on average has to be answered in order to find a bug of course varies drastically with the size and type of the program. Finding a bug in the expression evaluator seemed to require some 50 to 60 questions to be answered on average. There is clearly room for further improvements here.

6 Evaluation of the Debugger

One problem with the current implementation of the debugger is that perfect strictification is not achieved. This means that the user sometimes will have to deal with unevaluated expressions when there should not have been any need for him to do so. We think that combining with static strictness analysis would sometimes make the problem less apparent. Still, strictification is better than just using static strictness analysis.

The biggest problem, however, is probably the large space overhead induced by having to store the complete trace tree. The fact that large, partially evaluated structures frequently occurs does not improve the matter. Again, strictness analysis would help to some extent.

As mentioned in Sect. 4.1, debugging non-terminating programs can be dealt with by letting the user interrupt the execution and perform searching on the trace produced so far.

Despite its problems, we have found the debugger useful, and it should even be possible to debug quite large programs as long as they are applied to test cases of reasonable size.

7 Algorithmic Debugging with Incremental Trace Construction

Could we eliminate the need for construction of a complete execution trace tree and still use algorithmic debugging? Avoiding the construction of the entire tree would obviously be beneficial: not only does the trace take a lot of space to store; building it also takes a long time. For example, a program for solving the eight queens problem, that normally executes in about two seconds, took some five minutes to run to completion when debugging was enabled. This means that a user must wait this long before debugging can begin.

One could conceive a scheme where only the top level of the execution tree is recorded. Algorithmic debugging is the applied to this partial trace in order to find an erroneous node. The execution is then restarted from this node, again only recording the top level of the resulting execution trace tree. This can be done since the debugger has enough information for restoring as much of the state of the graph reducer as is needed. In this manner, only the subtree that is actually needed could be constructed incrementally, at the price of repeatedly re-executing (parts of) the application program. This would be cheaper spacewise, and may be cheaper timewise, than building the entire trace.

However, not having the entire trace at our disposal means that we have to sacrifice strictification and rely entirely on static strictness analysis. But strictness analysis is in principle less precise than strictification, so again the user would have to deal with hard-to-understand un-evaluated expressions.

Possibly then, one could imagine an ad hoc facility whereby the user could ask the debugger to evaluate unevaluated expressions as he sees fit. This might of course lead to non-termination, but the user could abort execution if he suspects this and one could attempt to trap heap and stack overflows and similar events. Note that it is easy to device examples that use up all available memory resources of the graph reducer without producing anything printable, so it is not in general possible to circumvent the problem by only printing an initial part of the result of an attempted evaluation.

It would probably be awkward to implement a debugger as described above, and it is not clear to us whether it would be really practical, but the approach might be worth further investigation.

8 Conclusions

An algorithmic debugger has been implemented for a lazy functional language and has been found to be useful in debugging some program examples. A process called strictification is performed on the execution trace to give the user an impression of strict evaluation. This makes the debugging process independent of the complexity of lazy evaluation order and also helps the user to focus on the high-level declarative semantics of the application program. A problem is that perfect strictification is not achieved in the current implementation; another problem is the large space and time overhead caused by building the entire execution tree.

References

[1] Lennart Augustsson. A compiler for Lazy ML, in *Proceedings 1984 ACM Conference on LISP and Functional Programming*, pp. 218–227, August 1984.

[2] Lennart Augustsson. Personal communication on the lack of suitable debugging tools for lazy functional languages, November 1991.

[3] Wlodek Drabent, Simin Nadjm-Tehrani, Jan Maluszynski. The Use of Assertions in Algorithmic Debugging, in *Proceedings of the FGCS Conference*, pp. 573–581, Tokyo, Japan, 1988.

[4] Peter Fritzson, Tibor Gyimothy, Mariam Kamkar, and Nahid Shahmehri. Generalized Algorithmic Debugging and Testing, in *Proceedings of the ACM SIGPLAN'91*, pp. 317–326, Toronto, Ontario, Canada, June 1991.

[5] Wolfgang Henhapl, Stefan Kaes, Gregor Snelting. *Utilizing Fifth Generation Technology in Software Development Tools*, report PI-R3/91, Technische Hochschule Darmstadt, March 1991.

[6] Thomas Johnsson. Efficient Compilation of Lazy Evaluation, in *Proceedings of the ACM SIGPLAN 1984 Symposium on Compiler Construction, SIGPLAN Notices* **19**(6), pp. 58-69, June 1984.

[7] Lee Naish. *Declarative debugging of lazy functional programs*, report 92/6, Department of Computer Science, University of Melbourne, Australia, 1992.

[8] Henrik Nilsson. *Freja: a small, non-strict, purely functional language*, MSc dissertation, Department of Computer Science and Applied Mathematics, Aston University, Birmingham, England, 1991.

[9] Simon L. Peyton Jones. *The Implementation of Functional Programming Languages*, Prentice Hall, 1987.

[10] Rudolph E. Seviora. Knowledge-Based Program Debugging Systems, in *IEEE Software* **4**(3), pp. 20–32, May 1987.

[11] Nahid Shahmehri. *Generalized Algorithmic Debugging*, PhD thesis, Department of Computer and Information Science, Linköping University, Linköping, Sweden, December 1991.

[12] E. Y. Shapiro. *Algorithmic Program Debugging*, MIT Press, May 1982.

[13] David A. Turner. Miranda: a non-strict functional language with polymorphic types,, in *Proceedings of the IFIP International Conference on Functional Programming Languages and Computer Architecture*, Nancy, Springer Lecture Notes in Computer Science, LNCS 201, 1985.

A general trace query mechanism based on Prolog

Mireille Ducassé

European Computer-Industry Research Centre
Arabellastrasse 17, D-8000 Munich 81, Germany
tel: +49 89/926 99 142, fax: +49 89/926 99 170
email: Mireille.Ducasse@ecrc.de

Abstract. We present a general trace query language which is a solution to the ever growing command sets of other tracers. It provides all the required generality while being very simple and efficient. We model a program execution into a trace which is a stream of events. Execution events have a uniform representation, and can be analysed by Prolog programs. With this approach and thanks to the expressive power of Prolog, two high-level primitives plus Prolog are enough to provide a general trace query language. With a few optimizations this language can work on large executions without any loss of performance, if compared to traditional tracers. This paper describes the trace query mechanism from its high level specification down to some implementation details. The proposed model of trace query depends only on the sequentiality of the execution, and the principles behind the design of the optimizations do not depend on the traced language.

1 Introduction

While debugging, programmers develop hypotheseses about the errors they are seeking. These hypotheses are often related to details of executions and require a tracer to be verified. However, current tracers are poorly adapted to this task. The command language of tracers is usually restricted to a fixed set of hard-coded commands, and the functionality is reduced a priori. Therefore tracers' commands are not expressive enough, and programmers cannot formulate what they want to verify in a precise enough way. In order to avoid this drawback tracers should be *programmable*.

Existing programmable tracers have tried to model the *debugging process* and offer a set of primitives to perform basic debugging actions (see for example Dispel [15] and Kraut [3]). However, the debugging process is a difficult task, and its basic tasks are not yet well understood (see for example the cognitive studies of Carver [6] and Vessey [27]). In fact, existing programmable tracers are based on a large number of complicated constructs which are difficult to use. Worse, there is no guarantee that these constructs cover the whole debugging process.

In Opium, our programmable debugger for Prolog, we model the *debugging data* instead of the debugging process. An execution is modeled into a trace which is a stream of events. Execution events have a uniform representation, and can be analysed by programs. The only mandatory primitives are those which retrieve information about execution events. The generality of the debugging process is provided by a general purpose programming language, namely Prolog. With this approach and thanks to the expressive power of Prolog, *two* high-level primitives plus Prolog are enough to provide a general trace query language which is more simple and more powerful than hard-coded sets of tracing commands.

Other systems consider execution traces as data (see for example Omega [25] and Yoda [19]). They, however, require that an actual trace database is created. This is much too costly in the highly dynamic context of trace analysis where new execution traces are generated and discarded with a high frequency. The performances of these systems prevent their use for large executions. In Opium the trace analysis can be used on the fly (with no trace database), and optimizations have been introduced. In particular we propose a "pre-filtering" primitive which can optimize part of the search for execution events.

Opium is fully implemented. The proposed primitives have been used to develop high level debugging strategies and the pre-filtering primitive can process executions with *several million* events with satisfactory response times. The actual formats of trace and source information depend on the traced language (in this case Prolog), and so does the actual design of the pre-filtering primitive. However, the proposed model of trace query depends only on the sequentiality of the execution, and the principles behind the design of the pre-filtering primitive do not depend on Prolog. Opium can also use a trace database but this raises different problems which are addressed in [12, ch. 5].

This paper describes the trace query mechanism from its high level specification down to some implementation details. In the following we first describe our trace query model. We illustrate how common tracing commands can be implemented by simple trace queries. We then give some examples of more powerful queries which cannot be specified with usual tools. The modeling of Prolog execution used in Opium is introduced, and trace query optimizations are detailed. The actual primitives used to implement the trace query mechanisms of Opium are listed. Some details of the two-process implementation of Opium are explained.

2 A trace query model

The execution under examination is modeled into a trace which is a *stream* of events. Execution events have a uniform representation, and can be analysed by programs. There are thus two execution contexts, one where the *traced* program is executed and one where the *analysis* programs are executed. When we talk about "execution events" we refer to the traced execution.

Our trace query model consists of virtually receiving all the execution events and analysing them on the fly to show only interesting information. This model, specified in the following in Prolog, actually runs under Opium, with satisfactory response time for small executions (several hundred execution events). The model explains the basic ideas of Opium which the optimizations presented afterwards make practicable for larger programs.

2.1 A trace query language

At a conceptual level, only two tracing primitives are necessary to retrieve trace information on the fly. A trace can be considered as a history of execution events, and our two primitives can be matched on the notions of today (current event) and tomorrow (next event). The primitive which retrieves the next event is required to parse the forthcoming events. The need for the primitive which retrieves the current event is less obvious. Let us illustrate it with the day metaphor. For example, if we want to check whether the first day of next month is a Monday, we need to know what the current month is. Hence we have to retrieve information related to today (current event). Some of the examples below illustrate further the need for the `current/1` primitive. A specification of the two primitives is:

current(Event) retrieves the trace information related to the current execution event. If the execution is finished the current event is the last event of the execution.

next(Event) retrieves the trace information related to the very next execution event. If the retrieval starts from the last event of the execution the predicate fails and the current event remains the last execution event. The primitive is furthermore backtrackable: if it succeeds and a subsequent part of the trace query fails, the query execution can backtrack on `next/1`.

These specifications and the following examples do not suppose any special representation of the execution events. Let us assume that an event representation contains all the interesting information. How events are actually modeled in Opium is discussed in section 3.

The previous primitives together with Prolog make a powerful trace query language. In the following we first show how the usual hard-coded tracing commands can be generalized by simple trace queries. We then show more sophisticated queries which in general are impossible to specify with the usual tracers. The generality of these examples shows the versatility required from a debugger. A debugger *cannot* provide a fixed set of debugging actions covering all the possibilities illustrated here, which are only a subset of what it is possible to program with our query language. A trace query language is the solution to the ever growing command sets of other tracers. It provides all the required generality while being very simple.

2.2 Common trace queries

We illustrate here how common tracing commands can be implemented by simple trace queries and we show that these queries are more general than any fixed set of tracing commands. To describe the examples, we use a Prolog-like syntax. The predicate arguments starting with upper case letters are variables. The only difference with the Prolog syntax is that user definable predicates start with upper case letters while primitive predicates start with lower case letters. We give queries which are actually Prolog top level goals to show how precise the trace queries can be. However, any complex query can be abstracted by defining a new command:

```
NEW_COMMAND :- <complex query>.
```

The usual tracing functionalities are, of course, also provided coded in Opium. Furthermore, in Opium, commands have abbreviations. Users therefore do not have to type as much as might be feared.

Tracing the very next event. This is a basic action in a tracer. The information related to this event has to be retrieved and displayed, as done in the following goal:

```
?- next(Event), DISPLAY(Event).
```

In usual tracers retrieving events and displaying them are not separated. This separation, however, has many advantages. For example, it is straightforward to implement display procedures dedicated to a special application. The rest of this section will illustrate various possibilities deriving from this separation.

Exhaustive trace. A special command is sometimes provided to have an exhaustive trace, but this is not necessary. One can play with the backtracking possibilities of Prolog. The following goal can be read as "*repeatedly get the next event and display it until there are no more events to be retrieved* (ie the execution is finished)".

```
?- next(Event), DISPLAY(Event), fail.
```

The request will, of course, ultimately fail, but before that all the execution events will be traced.

Conditional breakpoints. Breakpoints are the basis of traditional tracers. More sophisticated tools provide their users with a set of possible conditions and actions attached to breakpoints. In Opium, thanks to the power of Prolog, any condition on the retrieved event can be inserted between the retrieval and the display. The following goal can be read as "*repeatedly get the next event until the CONDITION on Event is true, then display the Event which passed the checking*".

```
?- next(Event), CONDITION(Event), DISPLAY(Event).
```

As an `Event` representation contains information about variable values and related source code, CONDITIONs can relate to these types of information. The CONDITIONs often check equality on limited aspects of the Events, in which case the unification of Prolog can be used directly inside `next/1`.

DISPLAYing is just one example of possible actions. A more general query is:

```
?- next(Event), CONDITION(Event), ACTION(Event).
```

This is equivalent to the most general existing conditional breakpoint mechanisms. A still more general query is:

```
?- next(Event), CONDITIONAL_ACTION(Event).
```

where conditions and actions can be mixed in any way. The latter query cannot be specified in all its generality with existing conditional breakpoint mechanisms.

Much can be achieved with the previous scheme; however it is not general enough. Conditions often refer to both the initial event (starting point of the search) and the retrieved event. For example, a common tracing command looks for the end of execution of the current goal. It requires being able to find what the current goal is. In the following query the initial event is retrieved and used to check the retrieved events.

```
?- current(Event0), next(Event), COND(Event0,Event), DISPLAY(Event).
```

It is impossible to determine all the possible queries where the initial event could be involved. Hence in order to have a general diagnosis tool, `current` is of major importance. It is, unfortunately, usually absent from tracers.

Note that once the user has typed in the whole query and has seen the first event which satisfies the CONDITION, if he wants to see the next related event he can simply rely on the Prolog backtracking mechanism at top level and ask for the next solution (by typing ";").

2.3 More powerful trace queries

With our model, more sophisticated trace queries can be specified than with usual tracers. Verifying hypotheses on a bug can be automated. Thanks to Prolog backtracking, sets of events are straightforward to gather. The model can even be pushed as far as trace analysis.

Verifying hypotheses. Displaying the retrieved trace events can become unnecessary. As emphasized in the introduction, users develop hypotheses about possible errors which they want to verify. For example, users may want to know whether a particular behaviour occurs. In such a case it is not even useful to display the related event(s), a `yes/no` answer is sufficient. The following goal will check whether there is an event which satisfies CONDITION:

```
?- current(Event0), next(Event), CONDITION(Event0, Event).
```

If so the tracer will be positioned on the first event which satisfies the condition, otherwise the goal will fail. If the user decides that he wants to see the event after all, then he can simply type:

```
?- current(Event), DISPLAY(Event).
```

Note again the importance of the `current/1` primitive to be able to display or re-display the current event.

Sets of events. With our model there is no need for hooks to tell the tracer at which place to prompt the user. Indeed, Prolog can be used in a natural way to stop tracing where the user desires. For example the following goal can be read as *"repeatedly print the forthcoming events which fulfil CONDITION until one of them fulfils the stop condition (or the trace is exhausted)"*.

```
?- next(Event), CONDITION(Event), DISPLAY(Event), STOP_AT(Event).
```

If the execution is finished before the stop condition is satisfied the query simply fails. Note that this query is very powerful; to express it with something other than a failure-driven loop would require a number of nested loops with many "breaks" in them. This would certainly prevent users from using such a query on the fly.

A degenerate form of this query is to ask for all the events which fulfil a condition (the `STOP_AT` predicate is simply replaced by `fail`) :

```
?- next(Event), CONDITION(Event), DISPLAY(Event), fail.
```

Trace analysis. The previous examples, although they cover more than traditional tracing and conditional breakpoints, do not cover all possible debugging tasks. One could, for example collect, a set of events and analyse them afterwards:

```
?- bagof(Event, (next(Event),COND(Event)), Events), ANALYSE(Events).
```

The trace analysis capabilities of Opium have been used to build abstract views of executions and bug symptom analyses [10, 14, 11].

3 Modeling Prolog executions

This section briefly argues that the "extracted model" (ie the basic execution events) should be distinguished from the "stories" told to users. It then describes the representation of selected execution events used in Opium.

3.1 Selecting execution events

The execution events shown by a trace build a model of the execution under examination. There has been much discussion about which execution model is *the* best model, see for example [1, 13, 23, 26]. However, in our view there cannot exist one best model which would fulfil all needs and satisfy all users. There are only models adapted to different people and different situations. Accordingly, we believe that the "extracted model" (ie the basic execution events) should be distinguished from the "stories" told to users (for examples of stories see [4]).

The extracted model should be as close as possible to the actual implementation of Prolog, so that the trace can be faithful to procedural details and so that it is cheap to extract. It should also contain as many details as it is possible to extract cheaply because reconstructing events is very costly [16]. Then the analysis module, built for example on top of the mechanism described in the current paper, should provide whatever views are required by users.

For example, the model of Byrd [5] shows the events in an order which is different from the order in which they actually occur in the execution. Backtracking in a subgoal of a goal g is traced as if backtracking was occurring first on g. We find this misleading, but even if some users like this story it should not be the extracted model because it is too costly to produce. This point of view should be reconstructed by the analysis module, and only upon explicit request.

Therefore, in our view, which model is actually extracted is *independent* of what programmers need. What is important is to be able to provide different views afterwards. The abstract views we developed [10] are an illustration of this approach.

We use an extracted model close to the "four port" model of Byrd [5]. The main difference is that the events are traced in chronological order. The actual ports have no influence on the mechanisms described in this paper and there is no need to go into much detail. Briefly, the four ports are four different types of events related to goals: "call", "exit", "fail" and "redo". A goal is invoked ("call"), its proof can either succeed ("exit") or fail ("fail"). In case of a failure alternate clauses of the same predicate may be tried ("redo").

3.2 Representation of selected execution events

Execution events of models related to Byrd's "four ports" are traditionally bound to goals. The execution can then be easily represented as a history of events of the same format. In Opium the current execution event is represented by a record in which related information is *copied*, so that trace queries can manipulate it without corrupting the traced execution.

The record contains three types of information: *control flow*, *data*, and *source connection*. The control flow attributes consist of time stamp, goal invocation number, execution depth, event type (port), and executed predicate. The data part gives the instantiation of predicate arguments at the time the event occurs. The source connection part gives the clause from which the current goal is called.

The event record is illustrated by the figure below. The identifiers in parentheses

Time stamp (`Chrono`)	`2741`
Invocation number (`Call`)	`5`
Execution depth (`Depth`)	`3`
Event type (`Port`)	`fail`
Executed predicate (`Pred`)	`nqueens: range/3`
Argument values (`ArgList`)	`(2, 4, Ns)`
Calling clause (`Clause`)	`nqueens:range/3.1`

are the actual names used in Opium. The displayed record is related to an event of the execution of the famous Nqueens program. It shows that the goal `range(2,4,Ns)` has been called in module `nqueens`. It was the 5th goal to be invoked, and it has only 2 ancestors (the execution depth is `3`). Its execution failed at time `2741`. The clause from which this goal was called is the first clause of `range/3` in module `nqueens`.

The record contains more information than trace lines usually display. This information is to be used mainly by debugging programs, and the more information they have the more efficient they are. In this record, the event type, the executed predicate and the argument values are mandatory pieces of information. Without them a user cannot understand a trace. The time stamp, the invocation number and the execution depth are not so important from a user point of view, but they are very useful for computerized analysis. They are very cheap to compute and they provide information which enables a quick retrieval of useful events. For example they enable the user to easily specify (and efficiently execute) queries such as "*skip the details of the execution of the current goal. If there were more than N events skipped, re-execute the goal and trace a level deeper.*" There could be more of these subsidiary attributes if they prove useful for scanning execution traces. The requirement is, however, that the computation of their values does not require too much time in the first place.

4 Optimizing trace queries

The `current` and `next` primitives together with Prolog make a simple, powerful and precise trace query language. Unfortunately, systematically processing all the information at every event is impracticable for large executions, especially when the data of the program are large. We propose some optimizations which improve the response time while keeping close to the model. Firstly we provide a priori filtering so that the executions of stable modules do not need to be analysed. Secondly, we separate the retrieval of a new event and its processing. Thirdly, the `next` primitive is refined to achieve pre-filtering of the trace according to attributes which are cheap to compute.

A priori filtering. While debugging big programs, not all the program modules need to be analysed at the same time. Libraries and stable modules seldom require debugging. There are ways in Opium to set predicates *skipped* (their trace will look like the trace of facts) or *untraceable* (they do not even appear in the trace). These facilities are static as opposed to the dynamic filtering provided by the previous scheme, but they are an important feature of a practical tracer.

Separating retrieval and processing of execution events. In practice there is no need to copy in the event record all the information related to an event every time a new event is retrieved. The trace queries usually check only a small part of the information related to events. Hence, instead of implementing `next(Event)` we implement `next/0` which moves one step further and keeps pointers to the state of the traced execution. Then `current(Event)` explicitly retrieves only the portions of the event information which are required:

```
next(Event) :- next, current(Event).
```

The control flow attributes of an event record can be represented by integers. They are cheap to copy in the record whereas the data and clause parts are not. Debugging strategies working only on control flow information should not be penalized by the cost of data computation. For this reason `current(Event)` has been split into 3 different primitives:

```
current((ControlFlow, Data, Source)) :-
    curr_line(ControlFlow),
    curr_arg(Data),
    curr_clause(Source).
```

The corresponding parts of an event is then only copied into the event record if a trace query explicitly request their values.

Pre-filtered retrieval. The previous optimizations already speed up the trace query mechanisms. But there are still too many changes of context. Events are retrieved in the traced execution context and checked in the tracing context. We introduce a pre-filtering primitive which enables users to a priori constrain the search for events. The pre-filtering checkings are then processed in the same context as the traced execution.

As the control flow attributes of an event record can be represented by integers, they can be cheaply checked with a low-level language such as C. On the other hand the argument values and calling clause do not have a fixed structure and they are possibly large pieces of information. It is difficult to check them with a low-level language, whereas Prolog with its unification and flexibility makes it very easy to analyse them. Therefore the pre-filtering primitive optimizes the search for execution events when requirements are imposed on control flow attributes.

Each time a new event is reached, Opium copies the values of the control flow attributes into the event record and checks whether they match their requirements. The filtering on control flow features is achieved in C and is efficient. The data and source filtering is done at Prolog level; this is not as efficient but the filtering programs are elegant. Furthermore, data and source information, which are not addressed by the pre-filtering primitives, are always associated with control flow information. Indeed, in Prolog, variables are local to a predicate, and a calling clause is always related to a goal. Hence a query which sets constraints on data or source must also set constraints on some control flow attributes. The pre-filtering primitive can be used on the latter and the overall efficiency is still reasonable.

The pre-filtering primitive is `get(Chrono,Call,Depth,Port,Pred)`, which works on the five control flow attributes listed earlier. It is designed to allow complex matching which goes beyond simple unification. Besides exact values, users can also specify a list of possible values, an interval, or a negated value against which the matching is performed. For example the following request asks Opium to display the next event whose time stamp is less than `350`, whose execution depth is `3`, whose port is different from `redo`, whose predicate is either `foo` arity 2 or `bar` arity 2 and whose second argument is an empty list:

```
?- get(< 350, _, 3, ~redo, [foo/2, bar/2]),
   curr_arg([_, []]),
   print_line.
```

Note that the `next/0` primitive is actually defined as:

```
next :- get(_,_,_,_,_).
```

5 The actual trace query primitives

Here is the list of Opium's primitives which implement the functionalities discussed so far, together with the standard `abort_trace` and `no_trace` primitives. All "on the fly" tracing facilities of Opium are built on top of them.

- `get(Chrono, Call, Depth, Port, Pred)` moves through the execution until the first event which matches the specified attribute values.
- `curr_line(Chrono, Call, Depth, Port, Pred)` retrieves the value of the control flow attributes of the current event.
- `cur_arg(ArgList)` retrieves the value of the arguments in the current event. ArgList is a *copy* of the actual arguments, hence unification can be used without side-effects in the traced execution.
- `curr_clause(Clause)` retrieves the clause which has spawned the current goal.
- `set_predflag(Predicate, Flag)` sets predicates traceable/untraceable, or skipped/unskipped for a priori filtering.
- `remote_call_once(Goal)` (resp. `remote_call_all(Goal)`) returns the first (resp. all) solution(s) of Goal, which is executed using the traced program's database.
- `abort_trace` aborts the traced execution and as a consequence aborts the tracing session too.
- `no_trace` stops tracing. The traced execution is resumed, without extracting any further trace information.

6 A two-process implementation

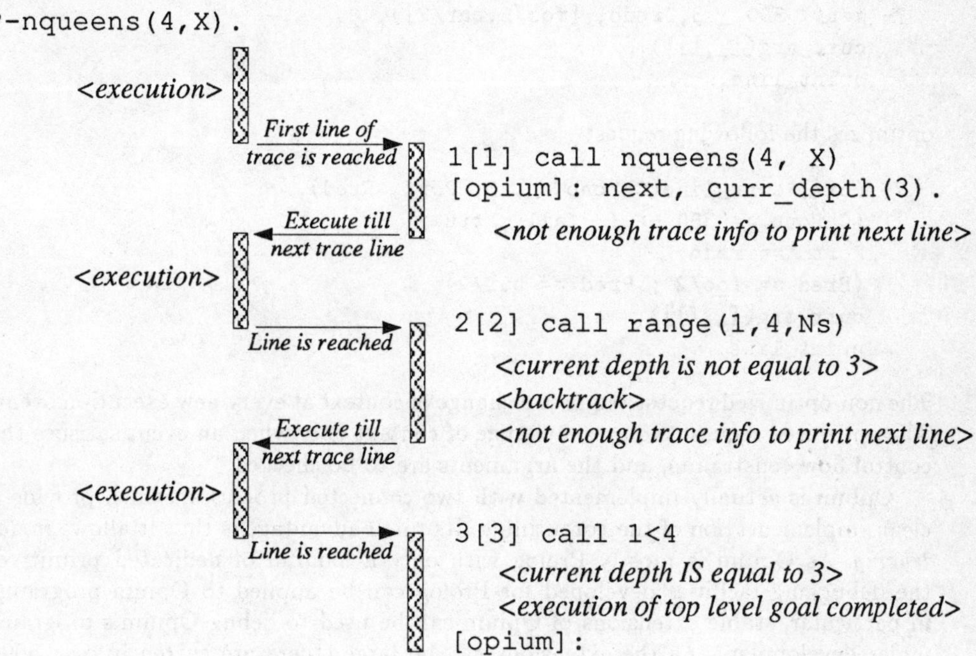

Fig. 1. Simplified coroutining between traced and tracing executions

Prolog tracers are usually implemented as a subroutine of the main execution. However, some coroutining between the traced and tracing executions is required to enable a synchronous tracing process.

This is illustrated by Figure 1, where the programmer has asked the traced process to execute the Nqueens program for a 4x4 board. When the execution reaches the first interesting event it sends its information to the Opium process which displays it and then prompts the programmer for a tracing command. The programmer enters a goal which tells the debugger that the execution of `nqueens(4,X)` should be traced until an event at depth "3" is reached. At that moment not enough of the traced execution has been performed, so Opium cannot trace further and has to return control to the traced execution. However, the tracing goal has not yet been achieved and its execution has to be delayed until the traced execution sends more information. When the traced process reaches another interesting event it sends it to Opium, which displays it and checks that the current depth is not equal to "3". Opium's execution backtracks and tries to display the next event. Again there is not enough information, the tracing goal is delayed and the traced execution is resumed. When the next event is reached it is sent to Opium which displays it. The current depth is equal to the requested value and the execution of the tracing goal is completed. The programmer is then prompted for another trace query.

The `get` primitive reduces the changes of context but does not suppress the need for coroutining. Indeed, it cannot usually optimize whole queries but only parts of them. For example, the previously introduced query

```
?- get(< 350,_,3,~redo, [foo/2,bar/2]),
   curr_arg([_,[]]),
   print_line.
```

optimizes the following request

```
?- next, curr_line(Chrono, _, 3, Port, Pred),
   (Chrono >= 350 -> !, fail ; true),
   Port \== redo,
   (Pred == foo/2 ; Pred == bar/2),
   curr_arg([_,[]]),
   print_line.
```

The non-optimized request requires a change of context at every new execution event. The optimized request requires a change of context only when an event satisfies the control flow constraints, and the arguments are to be checked.

Opium is actually implemented with two connected processes, which provide a clean implementation of the coroutining. Its main advantage is that it allows *meta-tracing*. As Opium is mostly Prolog with only a handful of dedicated primitives the debugging facilities developed for Prolog can be applied to Opium programs; in particular, stable extensions of Opium can be used to debug Opium's programs under development. As the extensions can be large (there are currently over 5000 lines of debugging programs) it is necessary to be able to debug them. As a matter of fact a first implementation of Opium used coroutining inside the same process and we badly missed the debugging facilities.

The coprocessing is made practicable by the `get` primitive. The pre-filtering queries are sent to the traced process and executed there locally. Hence there are relatively few information transfers between the two processes. Some details about the synchronization of the two processes can be found in [12, ch. 4].

7 Performance and implementation details

Opium is implemented inside Sepia, ECRC's Prolog system [21], reusing the "extraction module" of Sepia's debugger [1]. The two processes are connected by pipes, communicating with `write` and `read` Prolog primitives. Signals are sent using the interrupt-handler of Sepia. Opium runs on Sun3 and Sun4 under Unix [2].

The pre-filtering primitive `get/5` which optimizes queries on control flow information can parse several million execution events with reasonable response times. It takes only 1.5 of the time required by the standard debugger of Sepia to check for a normal breakpoint. As the standard debugger of Sepia is fast [22], pre-filtering of execution events offers a response time equivalent to the response time of equivalent functionalities hard coded in other Prolog debuggers. Therefore, the flexibility and preciseness of Opium do not slow down the tracing process if the pre-filtering primitive is used where possible. The time taken by other queries depends on their complexity. Moreover, if it takes a lot of time for a query to discard irrelevant information, it would probably take the user even more time to perform the same analysis "by hand".

Considering the gain in functionality, the implementation of Opium's kernel is relatively simple. The described primitives are implemented in about 1000 lines of well documented C, and 1000 lines of well documented Prolog. Over 5000 lines of debugging programs have already been written on top of the kernel.

8 Related work

The main advantage of Opium over other practicable programmable tracers is that its primitives model the trace data and do not try to model the debugging process. As a result the definition of Opium's primitives is very simple, and can be given in a single page. For comparison the descriptions of the Dispel language designed by Johnson [15] or the language of Lazzerini and Lopriore [17] take approximatively 10 pages each. Furthermore programmable tracers in general offer mechanisms such as the path rules of Kraut designed by Bruegge and Hibbard [3] which state general conditional breakpoints. For these conditional breakpoints the notion of "current event", which enables users to state general conditions, does not in general exist, except in Dalek designed by Olsson et al. [24]. Our trace query language is more powerful than conditional breakpoints when used dynamically. However, conditional breakpoints can be used to specify static assertions. Kraut can build an automaton to test a large set of conditions in a reasonably efficient way. This has not been done in Opium so far.

---

[1] both Opium and Sepia are available for academic sites

[2] UNIX is a registered trademark of AT&T. Sun3 and Sun4 are trademarks of Sun Microsystems, Inc.

As far as we know, Opium is the only programmable debugger on top of which actual debugging programs have been written. In our view this sustains the claim that trace analysis is a better paradigm than conditional breakpoints for debugging. Opium is also the only programmable debugger which offers meta-debugging. Dalek [24] seems a powerful system, for example it offers interesting extraction control, but it only offers limited meta-tracing hooks. We cannot agree with its authors who argue that debugging the debugging programs does not require sophisticated tools. Our experience writing over 5000 lines of debugging programs shows exactly the opposite.

Some programmable debuggers are based on a full programming language. For example, UPS designed by Bovey et al. [2], Cola designed by Dencker [9] and Dalek [24] offer C-like interpreters. However, a procedural language like C does not seem appropriate here. Only a few primitives need to be efficient. What is important is the prototyping power of the debugging language so that users can easily enter trace queries on the fly to adjust their diagnosis process. Prolog, with its expressive power, is better suited to this than procedural languages. Failure driven loops and unification help to express queries which otherwise would require very complicated control structures. The IL system of Cohen and Carpenter [8] provides regular expressions to specify debugging commands, which is more satisfactory than procedural languages but does not offer the power of a full programming language.

Opium does not need to wait for an execution to finish in order to analyse it as do the systems which need an actual trace database: the OMEGA environment [25], the YODA debugger [18], the IL system [8] and the Traceview system of Malony et al. [20]. Traceview can handle traces of several languages. This cannot be easily provided by Opium because of optimizations which require the implementation of part of the analysis module in the traced session. We believe, however, that to be able to efficiently trace synchronously is an important feature of a debugger. In the four systems previously cited *all* events are first stored in some sort of database whereas in Opium users can control the tracing process while the execution is processed. Secondly, *all* the information related to an event has to be computed, whereas in Opium the costly parts are computed only if needed.

Some meta-interpreters written in Prolog produce abstract traces (see for example [7]) but they are "subroutines" of the main execution and therefore cannot offer sophisticated synchronous trace as discussed in section 6.

9 Concluding remarks

We have presented a trace query model in which two primitives provide execution traces as programming data; the latter can then be processed by Prolog programs. With some optimizations, which we described, this model can work on very large executions without any loss of performance (if compared to traditional tracers). The unique functionalities offered by our model are

- a general and efficient trace query language, and
- meta-debugging capabilities.

The trace query language is based on Prolog and shows that Prolog is an accurate basis for this. Our trace query language gives more power than a fixed set of commands and is more simple to use. Opium is a debugging environment and contains more than the mechanism described here; a broader description is given in [12].

Acknowledgements. Anna-Maria Emde contributed many ideas and has engineered Opium into its pre-release state. Diomidis Spinellis implemented the first version of the coprocessing. Jean-Marc Andreoli, Alexander Herold, Jacques Noyé, Joachim Schimpf, André Véron, and Mark Wallace gave fruitful comments on previous and current drafts of this paper. Steven Prestwich helped with the English.

References

1. P. Boizumault. Un modèle de trace pour Prolog. In M. Dincbas, editor, *4e Seminaire de Programmation en Logique*, pages 61–71, CNET lannion, April 1984.
2. J.D. Bovey, M.T. Russel, and O. Folkestadt. Direct manipulation tools for Unix workstations. In *Proceedings of the EUUG Autumn'88*, pages 311–319, October 1988.
3. B. Bruegge and P. Hibbard. Generalized path expressions: A high-level debugging mechanism. *The Journal of Systems and Software*, 3:265–276, 1983.
4. A. Bundy, H. Pain, P. Brna, and L. Lynch. A proposed Prolog story. D.A.I. Research Paper 283, Department of Artificial Intelligence, University of Edinburgh, 1986.
5. L. Byrd. Understanding the control flow of Prolog programs. In *Logic Programming Workshop*, Debrecen, 1980.
6. D.L. Carver. Programmer variations in software debugging approaches. *International Journal of Man-Machine Studies*, 31:315–322, 1989.
7. A. Casson. Event abstraction debuggers for layered systems in Prolog. In *Proceedings of the UK Logic Programming Conference.* Association for Logic Programming- UK Branch, March 1990.
8. J. Cohen and N. Carpenter. A language for inquiring about the run-time behaviour of programs. *Software-Practice and Experience*, 7:445–460, 1977.
9. P. Dencker. *Debugger chapter of the Alsys Ada System user's manual.* Alsys Gmbh, May 1991.
10. M. Ducassé. Abstract views of Prolog executions in Opium. In V. Saraswat and K. Ueda, editors, *Proceedings of the International Logic Programming Symposium*, pages 18–32, San Diego, October 1991. ALP, MIT Press.
11. M. Ducassé. Analysis of failing Prolog executions. In *Proceedings of the ICLP'91 Preconference Workshop on Logic Programming Environments*, Paris, June 1991. Proceedings published as Technical Report LIFO N 91-61, University of Orléans, France.
12. M. Ducassé. *An extendable trace analyser to support automated debugging.* PhD thesis, University of Rennes, France, June 1992. Numéro d'ordre 758. European Doctorate. In English.
13. M. Eisenstadt. A powerful Prolog trace package. In *Proceedings of the 6th ECAI*, September 1984.
14. A.-M. Emde and M. Ducassé. Automated debugging of non-terminating Prolog programs. In S. Bourgault and M. Dincbas, editors, *Actes du Séminaire de programmation en Logique*, pages 89–103. CNET, Lannion, May 1990.
15. M.S. Johnson. Dispel: A run-time debugging language. *Computer languages*, 6:79–94, 1981.

16. A.J. Kusalik and G.M. Oster. Towards a generalized graphical interface for Logic Programming development. Technical report, University of Saskatchewan, 1992. (Forthcoming).
17. B. Lazzerini and L. Lopriore. Abstraction mechanisms for event control in program debugging. *IEEE Transactions on Software Engineering*, 15(7):890–901, July 1989.
18. C.H. LeDoux. *A knowledge-based system for debugging concurrent software.* PhD thesis, University of California, Los Angeles, 1985.
19. C.H. LeDoux and D.S. Parker. Saving traces for Ada debugging. In *Proceedings of the ADA International Conference*, pages 97–108, 1985.
20. A. Malony, D. Hammerslag, and D. Jablonowski. Traceview: A trace visualization tool. *IEEE Software*, pages 19–28, September 1991.
21. M. Meier, A. Aggoun, D. Chan, P. Dufresne, R. Enders, D. Henry de Villeneuve, A. Herold, P. Kay, B. Perez, E. van Rossum, and J. Schimpf. SEPIA - an extendible Prolog system. In *Proceedings of the IFIP '89*, 1989.
22. M. Meier and J. Schimpf. Sepia system evaluation. Internal Report IR-LP-13-35, ECRC, August 1991.
23. S. Moroshita and M. Numao. Prolog computation model BPM and its debugger PROEDIT2. In *Proceedings of the 5th Logic Programming Conference*, pages 147–158, Tokyo, June 1986. Springer Verlag.
24. R.A. Olsson, R.H. Crawford, and W.W. Ho. A dataflow approach to event-based debugging. *Software-Practice and Experience*, 21(2):209–229, February 1991.
25. M.L. Powell and M.A. Linton. A database model of debugging. In M.S. Johnson, editor, *ACM SIGSOFT/SIGPLAN Software Engineering Symposium on high-level debugging*, pages 67–70. ACM, March 1983.
26. A. Schleiermacher and J.F.H. Winkler. The implementation of ProTest a Prolog-Debugger for a refined box model. *Software-Practice and Experience*, 1990.
27. I. Vessey. Toward a theory of computer program bugs: an empirical test. *International Journal of Man-Machine Studies*, 30(1):23–46, January 1989.

This article was processed using the LaTeX macro package with LLNCS style

Fully Declarative Logic Programming

Jan A. Plaza

University of Miami
Department of Mathematics and Computer Science
P.O. Box 249 085
Coral Gables, Florida 33124
U.S.A.
janplaza@math.miami.edu

Abstract. In this paper we present a theoretical basis for implementation of a fully declarative logic programming language which allows use of quantifiers and negation in the statement bodies. We formulate SLPG – a resolution system extending SLD-resolution, but alternative to SLDNF. SLPG computes over an open universe of terms. It is complete for the full class of positive programs (with statements $A \leftarrow B$ where B involves $\top, \bot, \wedge, \vee, \forall, \exists, =$), and also for a class of programs involving negative information in the form of guards (i.e. inequations between terms.) By augmenting SLPG with a mechanism of constructive negation we obtain SLPGCN-resolution which is complete for broader classes of programs involving negation $\neg$ (without assuming any notion of stratification.)

1 Introduction

A major concern in programming is the *correctness* of program P with respect to intended specification $S; \alpha$. This can be formulated as

> $S \vdash \alpha(I, O)$ iff given program P and input I, the computational mechanism returns output O.

(In the specification we distinguish two parts: a defining part S and a goal part α. For instance, for a program that finds the last element of a list, S contains definitions explaining what is meant by the "last element", and α is the formula saying that O is the last element in I.) However, proving correctness is a difficult task, and it is never undertaken for big programs. As a result, all big programs contain mistakes and their actual behavior differs from what was intended. In this situation R. A. Kowalski and A. Colmerauer proposed creating languages of a very high level, for which proofs of correctness of programs become very simple or even obvious. Their revolutionary ideas underlying *logic programming* include the following:

1. Write specifications, not programs, using a fragment of the language of first-order classical logic, representing possible inputs, outputs and all the intermediate data by means of logical terms.

* This research has been partly supported from the NSF grant CCR-8702307

2. Take the specification itself as a program.
3. Use a resolution system as a computational mechanism. (Linear resolution can be efficient.) Substitutions calculated by the resolution will be considered as output.
4. The (desired) correctness of a program with respect to the specification is automatic; programming turns into *declarative programming*:

   Procedural meaning of $P \equiv$ declarative meaning of P.

   More specifically, this is expressed as *soundness and completeness:*

   Given (program) P and a formula $\alpha(I, x)$, resolution computes $x{=}O$ iff (specification) P proves $\alpha(I, O)$.

To make this idea work one has to choose the resolution system and the fragment of first-order logic in such a way that the equivalence from point 4 becomes true. This is partly done in Prolog — the first logic programming language. Further theoretical work suggested however that one should not insist the program and its specification be identical. K. L. Clark proposed that, as a specification for a program P, we may admit a certain completion of P, which can be obtained from P in an automatic way.

Example 1. The empty list can be represented by a constant []. The list consisting of an element *e* followed by a list *rest* can be represented as a term [*e* | *rest*]. So, the list of three elements 1, 5, 3, in that order, is represented as [1 | [5 | [3 | []]]], which will be also abbreviated as [1, 5, 3]. One can write the following specification S for a program that finds last element of the input list:

$$last([x \mid rest], y) \equiv (x{=}y \wedge rest{=}[\,]) \vee last(rest, y)$$
$$last([\,], y) \equiv \bot$$

This can be automatically turned into the following Prolog program P:

```
last([X|Rest],Y) :- (X=Y, Rest=[]) ; last(Rest,Y).
last([],Y) :- false.
```

where variable names are capitalized, conjunction $\wedge$ is denoted by a comma, disjunction $\vee$ is denoted by a semicolon, false constant $\bot$ is denoted by `false`, and where equivalence $\equiv$ has been turned deliberately into reversed implication denoted by the symbol `:-` . Given `last([1,5,3],Z)` as a goal, Prolog computes the substitution `Z=3`. In fact, S is equivalent to Clark's completion *Comp*(P), and we have $S \vdash last([1,5,3], z)(3/z)$.

Declarativeness of logic programming can be expressed by means of formal conditions of soundness and completeness. Using the notion of program completion they can be formulated as follows:

> *Resolution* with program P and a query A computes substitution θ iff *Completion*(P) $\vdash A\theta$.

Achieving soundness and completeness can make true the dream of easy and correct programming. The first results of this sort, for SLD-resolution, definite programs P and definite queries A, were proved by K. L. Clark [2]:

[2] The version above is a reformulation of the original version; Clark used the *Comp* only in his theorems for SLDNF-resolution, but not for SLD-resolution

Soundness: If SLD-resolution with program P and query A computes substitution θ then $Comp(P) \vdash A\theta$.

Completeness: If $Comp(P) \vdash A\theta$ then SLD-resolution with program P and query A computes substitution θ' more general than θ.

Definite programs, for which these theorems hold, do not admit negations in bodies of clauses. Therefore a question arises: Can one incorporate negation $\neg$ into the syntax of logic programs while still keeping declarativeness (i.e. soundness and completeness) ? A partial answer to this problem was provided again by K. L. Clark who, with the same notion of completion, proved soundness of SLDNF-resolution for normal programs and normal goals:

If SLDNF-resolution with program P and a query L computes θ then $Comp(P) \vdash L\theta$.

Unfortunately counter-examples exist, both at the propositional and the first-order level, showing that the converse theorem (i.e. completeness) doesn't hold.

This paper is written to address the following problem.

Problem: Can one extend the syntax of logic programs (allowing statements $A \leftarrow B$ with B containing $\top, \bot, \wedge, \vee, \forall, \exists, =, \neq, \neg$), and also extend SLD-resolution to handle such programs, still keeping declarativeness (i.e. soundness and completeness) ?

In our answer, we intend to specify four components:

- The fragment of the language of first-order logic used to write programs.
- Resolution and additional computational mechanisms (handling $\neg$, $=$, etc.)
- The completion of the program (possibly different from Clark's.)
- The consequence operation used in the intended soundness and completeness theorem (possibly different from $\vdash$ of classical logic.)

In the full version of the paper we will show *why* SLDNF-resolution is not satisfactory for first-order languages. If completeness is sought, another resolution system is needed. We formulate SLPG-resolution, capable of handling positive programs with guards. (Guards are formulas built from inequations between terms.) SLPG is an extension of SLD-resolution. We prove that SLPG is complete for the full class of positive programs (with $\top, \bot, \wedge, \vee, \forall, \exists, =$), and also for another class in which some negative information (in the form of guards) is allowed in statement bodies. Then by augmenting SLPG with mechanisms based on the idea of constructive negation, we define SLPGCN-resolution which allows more uses of negation $\neg$. Answers computed by SLPGCN coincide with those computed by SLDNF if only the SLDNF-computation returns an answer. We prove completeness of SLPGCN for two broad classes of programs involving negation. However the entire class of programs with negation is not covered, and we found examples suggesting that in this case, incompleteness is not the fault of resolution, but it is an inherent property of the class of normal programs. Independently of that, fully declarative logic programming can be achieved for the classes of programs mentioned earlier.

Resolution systems specified in the paper can be efficiently implemented, and this issue is briefly discussed in the corresponding sections.

The problem of soundness and completeness for programs with extended syntax, has been studied from the early days of logic programming. In References we list some of the research papers related to this topic. A big part of that work is devoted to obtaining completeness with Clark's notion of program completion for some artificially restricted classes of programs and goals (allowed, admissible, hierarchical, stratified, locally stratified, etc.) Other attempts, in which many-valued logics were used, resulted only in soundness theorems. In our considerations we obtain soundness and completeness for classes of programs which are not restricted in such ways. The language we consider enjoys a bigger expressive power than those of [Chan '88] and [Przymusinski '89]. Unlike the languages of [Clark '78], [Lloyd and Topor '84] our language is fully declarative and admits programs which are not stratified, not hierarchical, etc. The SLPGCN-resolution described in this paper is essentially different from the deduction process of Extended Negation as Failure in [Lugiez '89] based on disunification of [Comon '88] and [Maher '88]: the system proposed by Lugiez assumes the domain closure axiom and computes over the Herbrand universe of terms, while SLPGCN-resolution computes over an open universe of terms called an ω-Herbrand universe. The concepts related to the ω-Herbrand universe has been discussed in [Plaza '92]); the methods of constructive negation which we use in this paper generalize those of [Plaza '91].

Because of space limitations proofs are not given in this version of the paper. The proofs can be found in the author's doctoral dissertation [Plaza '90] they will also appear in a professional journal.

2 Syntax of positive programs with guards

In this presentation we start from a class of programs which admit only very restricted uses of negation. Programs allowing the full use of negation will be considered in Section 5.

Throughout this paper symbol $\neq$ is used only as an abbreviation: $t_1{\neq}t_2$ abbreviates $\neg t_1{=}t_2$. By a *guard* we understand any first-order formula containing no predicates except $=$. Recall that a formula is *positive* if it is built from atomic formulas, including $\top, \bot$, by means of $\wedge, \vee, \forall, \exists$. By a *positive formula with guards* we mean any formula $B(S_1/p_1, \ldots, S_n/p_n)$ where $B(p_1, \ldots, p_n)$ is a positive formula with predicate variables $p_1, \ldots, p_n$ and with no occurrences of $=$, and where $S_1, \ldots, S_n$ are guards. So, any positive formula with guards results from inserting (possibly negative) guards into a positive formula. By $\leftarrow$ we denote a reversed implication: $A \leftarrow B$ is the same as $B \rightarrow A$. By $var(B)$ we denote the set of free variables of B. By a *positive statement with guards* we understand any formula $A \leftarrow B$ such that: A is an atomic formula other than $\top, \bot$ or $t'{=}t''$, and B is arbitrary positive formula with guards such that $var(B) \subseteq var(A)$. Notice that a definite clause $p(x) \leftarrow q(x, y)$ is not considered a positive statement with guards. It becomes such if we rewrite it as $p(x) \leftarrow \exists_y q(x, y)$. A *positive program with guards* is any finite set of positive statements with guards; a *positive goal with guards* is any formula $\leftarrow B$ where B is a positive formula with guards. The *hierarchy of positive programs with guards* is defined by imposing restrictions on formulas $B(p_1, \ldots, p_n)$ and on the guards $S_1, \ldots, S_n$

in statement bodies. If $B(p_1, \ldots, p_n)$ is built exclusively by means of $\wedge, \vee, \exists$, and if $S_1, \ldots, S_n$ are arbitrary guards, then the statement $A \leftarrow B(S_1/p_1, \ldots, S_n/p_n)$ is called a *positive existential statement with arbitrary guards* or a *$+\Sigma_1$-statement with Δ_ω-guards.* If $B(p_1, \ldots, p_n)$ is arbitrary positive formula, and if also $S_1, \ldots, S_n$ are positive, then the resulting statement is called a *positive statement with positive guards* or a *$+\Delta_\omega$-statement with $+\Delta_\omega$-guards.* Other levels of the hierarchy can be defined in a similar way.

Any positive programs with guards can be used in our programming language, we will see however that $+\Sigma_1$-programs with Δ_ω-guards and $+\Delta_\omega$-programs with $+\Delta_\omega$-guards are of special importance.

Much research in the theory of logic programming has been devoted to analyzing completeness issues for SLDNF-resolution for normal programs (i.e. programs with negative literals in clauses bodies.) We argue that before such a task is undertaken, it is necessary to investigate $+\Delta_\omega$-programs with $+\Delta_\omega$-guards. Notice that existential quantifiers are implicitly present in bodies of clauses: $A(x) \leftarrow B(x, y)$ is interpreted as: $A(x) \leftarrow \exists_y B(x, y)$. If one allows normal programs, then $\neg$ together with $\exists$ gives rise to implicit universal quantifiers. This can be fully justified only if we decide how to interpret normal clauses. The interpretation with constructive negation (which is weaker than the interpretation based on Clark's completion) seems to be appropriate. Consider the following normal program:

$$p \leftarrow \neg q(x)$$
$$q(x) \leftarrow \neg r(x, y)$$
$$r(x, y) \leftarrow \neg s(x, y, z)$$

Using constructive negation the program is interpreted as the following program in an extended language:

$$p \leftarrow \exists_x \overline{q}(x) \qquad \overline{p} \leftarrow \forall_x q(x)$$
$$q(x) \leftarrow \exists_y \overline{r}(x, y) \qquad \overline{q}(x) \leftarrow \forall_y r(x, y)$$
$$r(x, y) \leftarrow \exists_z \overline{s}(x, y, z) \qquad \overline{r}(x, y) \leftarrow \forall_z s(x, y, z)$$

and the following formulas follow:

$$p \leftarrow \exists_x \forall_y \exists_z s(x, y, z) \qquad \overline{p} \leftarrow \forall_x \exists_y \forall_z \overline{s}(x, y, z).$$

(One can check that the first of these formulas follows also from Clark's completion of P.) One can see that in this way arbitrary strings of quantifiers can be built. Of course using $\wedge$ is allowed in clauses bodies. Also an implicit $\vee$ can be constructed by introducing several clauses with the same head and with bodies corresponding to intended disjuncts. Thus, once we admit negation in clauses bodies, we program in fact with statements $A \leftarrow B$, where B is an arbitrary quantified formula. Before completeness for such general programs is considered, one should be able to prove completeness for the simpler case of $+\Delta_\omega$-programs with $+\Delta_\omega$-guards.

The second class of programs, $+\Sigma_1$-programs with Δ_ω-guards, is a natural extension of the class of definite programs, which is of basic importance for programming practice. In Prolog one often uses clauses such as: $p(x, y) \leftarrow x \neq y \wedge B(x, y)$ calling $x \neq y$ a guard. Using guards is a way of incorporating negative information into an otherwise positive clause body. Guards have also some technical applications. Consider the following program P:

$$p(x, x) \leftarrow B_1(x),$$
$$p(x, y) \leftarrow B_2(x, y).$$

A goal $p(t,t)$ can be resolved with either clause. Sometimes it is important to deal with generalized programs in which clauses are mutually exclusive, i.e. with programs in which a goal can be resolved without immediate failure with at most one clause. This is the case in concurrent, committed choice languages (with no backtracking) such as FGHC of [Ueda '87]. To achieve such a situation we would like to rewrite P as:

$$p(x,x) \leftarrow B_1(x) \vee B_2(x,x),$$
$$p(x,y) \leftarrow x{\neq}y \wedge B_2(x,y).$$

Another example:

$$q(f(x)) \leftarrow B_3(x),$$
$$q(x) \leftarrow B_4(x)$$

could be transformed to:

$$q(f(x)) \leftarrow B_3(x) \vee B_4(f(x)),$$
$$q(x) \leftarrow \forall_y(x{\neq}f(y)) \wedge B_4(x).$$

Guards such as $\forall_y(x \neq f(y))$ go beyond the syntax of Prolog. Notice that $x \neq y$ means $\neg(x{=}y)$ and it is a *negative* literal; $\forall_y(x{\neq}f(y))$ is not a literal at all. Therefore in examples above, $p(x,y) \leftarrow x{\neq}y \wedge B_2(x,y)$ is not a definite clause, and $q(x) \leftarrow \forall_y(x{\neq}f(y)) \wedge B_4(x)$ is not a clause at all. Conditions such as $x{\neq}y$ or $\forall_y(x{\neq}f(y))$ are not handled by SLD-resolution but they deserve a place in logic programming. This is why we wish to consider the class of $+\Sigma_1$-programs with Δ_ω-guards.

Now, as we will need to define answers returned by the system when a program and a query are given, it is important to generalize the notion of substitution. We will use substitutions guarded by conditions involving inequations. For instance,

$$\{c/x_1,\ f(x_5)/x_2,\ x_4/x_3\}\ \text{WHERE}\ (x_5{\neq}x_4 \wedge \forall_y x_5{\neq}f(y))$$

will mean that while considering valuations in a universe of terms, x_1, x_2, x_3 can be replaced respectively by elements $c, f(e), e'$ where $e \neq e'$ and e is not a term having f as its main functor. In general, by a ***guarded substitution*** we understand any expression (θ WHERE S) such that θ is a substitution and S is a guard. We define the result $B(\theta$ WHERE $S)$ of applying guarded substitution (θ WHERE S) to formula B as $B\theta \vee \neg S$. In the full version of the paper we will introduce with details *canonical* substitutions which are guarded by a conjunction of conditions of the form $x{\neq}t$ or $\forall y\ x{\neq}f(y)$. Such guarded substitutions are easy to interpret for the programmer/user, and in fact the answers returned by the system will be always in canonical form.

3 Declarative semantics and fix-point semantics

The universe of terms over which the program computes will be different from the conventional Herbrand universe. Let $\mathcal{L}$ be a first-order language and let $\mathcal{L}^{\mathcal{K}}$ result by adding a countable set $\mathcal{K} = \{k_i \mid i < \omega\}$ of new individual constants to the alphabet of $\mathcal{L}$. By the *ω-Herbrand universe* $U^\omega_{\mathcal{L}}$ for $\mathcal{L}$ we understand the set of all ground terms of the language $\mathcal{L}^{\mathcal{K}}$. Such an universe has contains infinitely elements which cannot be named in $\mathcal{L}$ and therefore it can be can be called "open" as opposed to the conventional Herbrand universe which is "closed". By an *ω-Herbrand interpretation* for language $\mathcal{L}$ we understand any interpretation I based on $U^\omega_\mathcal{L}$ in which every function symbol f of $\mathcal{L}$ is interpreted in a natural way: $f^I(t_1,\ldots,t_n) = f(t_1,\ldots,t_n)$, where $t_1,\ldots,t_n$ are terms of $\mathcal{L}^\mathcal{K}$. We will use symbol $U^\omega_\mathcal{L}$ to denote not only the set of all ground terms of $\mathcal{L}$ but also to denote the ω-Herbrand interpretation based on $U^\omega_\mathcal{L}$ in which all predicates except $=$ are interpreted as $\emptyset$. We define $\Gamma \models^\omega_\mathcal{L} \alpha$ to mean: for any ω-Herbrand interpretation I for $\mathcal{L}$, $I \models \Gamma$ implies $I \models \alpha$.

Now we introduce notation which allows us to think of terms and substitutions as of subsets of (a power of) an ω-Herbrand universe. If t is a term, we define

$$[\![t]\!] = \{t[\nu] \in U^\omega_\mathcal{L} \mid \nu : Var \longrightarrow U^\omega_\mathcal{L}\}$$

where Var is the set of variables of our language $\mathcal{L}$. For instance: $[\![f(c_1, g(c_2))]\!] = \{f(c_1, g(c_2))\}$, $[\![x]\!] = U^\omega_\mathcal{L}$, $[\![g(x)]\!] = \{g(e) \mid e \in U^\omega_\mathcal{L}\}$.
We assume that $Var = \{x_i \mid i < \omega\}$. If $\theta = \{t_i/x_i \mid i < \omega\}$ is a substitution, we identify it with $\tilde{\theta} = \langle t_0, t_1, t_2, \ldots\rangle$ and interpret all the terms t_i in that sequence:

$$[\![\theta]\!] = \{\tilde{\theta}[\nu] \in (U^\omega_\mathcal{L})^\omega \mid \nu : \mathrm{Var} \longrightarrow U^\omega_\mathcal{L}\}.$$

For a guarded substitution (θ WHERE S) the interpretation is similar but the class of valuations ν is restricted by S – we define:

$$[\![\theta \text{ WHERE } S]\!] = \{\tilde{\theta}[\nu] \in (U^\omega_\mathcal{L})^\omega \mid U^\omega_\mathcal{L} \models S[\nu]\}.$$

In the next section we will define SLPG-resolution which is capable of handling positive programs with guards. Given such a program P and a query $\leftarrow B$ the resolution is expected to return a family $(\theta_i$ WHERE $S_i) : i \in I$ of (canonical) computed answers. Their union $\bigcup_{i\in I}[\![\theta_i \text{ WHERE } S_i]\!]$ will be denoted by $SLPG(P, B)$ and called an *SLPG-answer set.* This set conveys the *procedural semantics* of the program and the goal.

Now let us recall some classical notions introduced by Clark.

Clark's transformation P^C of program P is constructed in the following way: Transform every statement: $p(\boldsymbol{t}) \leftarrow B$ in P to: $p(\boldsymbol{x}) \leftarrow \exists \boldsymbol{y}((\boldsymbol{x} = \boldsymbol{t}) \wedge B)$, where all the variables in the sequence $\boldsymbol{x}$ are distinct, and where $\boldsymbol{y}$ is the sequence of all free variables that occur in $(\boldsymbol{x} = \boldsymbol{t}) \wedge B$ but do not occur in $p(\boldsymbol{x})$. Then for every predicate p, list all statements defining this predicate: $p(\boldsymbol{x}) \leftarrow B_1$, ... , $p(\boldsymbol{x}) \leftarrow B_n$, and form $p(\boldsymbol{x}) \leftarrow B_1 \vee \ldots \vee B_n$. If there are no statements defining p, form $p(\boldsymbol{x}) \leftarrow \bot$. Program P^C consists of the formulas obtained in this way.

Clark's completion[3] of program P is defined as: $Comp(P) = \{(p(\boldsymbol{x}) \equiv B) \mid (p(\boldsymbol{x}) \leftarrow B) \in P^C\}$.

The declarative semantics of a program P will be conveyed by the ω-Herbrand consequence ($\models^\omega_\mathcal{L}$) of P or $Comp(P)$.

In proofs of completeness theorems for SLD-resolution the key role is played by an operator T_P on the lattice of Herbrand interpretations. We adapt this operator to the situation of ω-Herbrand interpretations defining $T^\omega_P : 2^{B^\omega_\mathcal{L}} \longrightarrow 2^{B^\omega_\mathcal{L}}$ as:

$$T^\omega_P(I) = \{A[\nu] \in B^\omega_\mathcal{L} \mid (A \leftarrow B) \in P \text{ and } I \models B[\nu]\}$$

The *fixed point semantics* of a program P will be conveyed by the least fixed point $lfp(T^\omega_P)$ of this operator.

[3] Unlike in the original definition we do not assume that $Comp(P)$ contains any axioms of equality.

Theorem 1 (on soundness and completeness of SLPG-resolution).
Let P be a positive program with guards and let $\leftarrow B$ be a positive goal with guards in a first-order language $\mathcal{L}$ with a finite alphabet. Consider the following conditions:

1. $SLPG(P, B) \supseteq [\![\theta \text{ WHERE } S]\!]$
2. $P \models^{\omega}_{\mathcal{L}} B(\theta \text{ WHERE } S)$
3. $Comp(P) \models^{\omega}_{\mathcal{L}} B(\theta \text{ WHERE } S)$
4. $lfp(T^{\omega}_{P}) \models B(\theta \text{ WHERE } S)$

The following implications hold.

Soundness: Condition 1 implies each of 2, 3 and 4.

Completeness: If P is a $+\Sigma_1$-program with Δ_ω-guards and B is a $+\Sigma_1$-formula with Δ_ω-guards, or if P is a $+\Delta_\omega$-program with $+\Delta_\omega$-guards and B is a $+\Delta_\omega$-formula with $+\Delta_\omega$-guards then each of conditions 2, 3 and 4 implies 1.

The soundness part of the theorem says that answers returned by SLPG are always correct with respect to the semantics; the completeness part says that the answers which are correct with respect to the semantics can be computed by SLPG. Due to this theorem the programmer can construct a program thinking about its meaning in declarative semantics (points 2, 3) or in fixed-point semantics (point 4) and be assured that the procedural behavior of the program will be as expected (point 1.)

4 The procedure of SLPG-resolution

If a first-order language $\mathcal{L}$ has a finite alphabet, one can axiomatize the formal theory of equality determined by $U^{\omega}_{\mathcal{L}}$. The decision procedure for this theory is related to the algorithm which is mentioned in the following theorem. This algorithm will be used later to generate computed answer substitutions in our resolution system.

Theorem 2 (on computing substitutions).
Let $\mathcal{L}$ be a first-order language with a finite alphabet. There exists an algorithm which takes as input a positive formula with guards $B(\boldsymbol{x})$ in $\mathcal{L}$, and returns as output either the statement: "$U^{\omega}_{\mathcal{L}} \not\models \exists_{\boldsymbol{x}} B(\boldsymbol{x})$" if it is correct, or otherwise returns a finite sequence $(\theta_i \text{ WHERE } S_i) : i \leq k$ of finite (canonical) guarded substitutions, such that:

$$U^{\omega}_{\mathcal{L}} \models B(\boldsymbol{x})(\theta \text{ WHERE } S) \quad \textit{iff} \quad [\![\theta \text{ WHERE } S]\!] \subseteq \bigcup_{i \leq k} [\![\theta_i \text{ WHERE } S_i]\!].$$

The next two definitions embody the description of SLPG-resolution i.e. SL-resolution for Positive programs with Guards. They assume that we first turn program P into an equivalent program P^C which for every predicate p in its language contains exactly one statement defining p, and that this statement is of the form $p(\boldsymbol{x}) \leftarrow B$. Such an operation is known as Clark's transformation.

Definition 3. Let $\leftarrow B'$ and $\leftarrow B''$ be positive goals with guards, and let $p(\boldsymbol{x}) \leftarrow B(\boldsymbol{x})$ be a positive statement with guards. The goal $\leftarrow B''$ is said to be *SLPG-derived* from $\leftarrow B'$ and $p(\boldsymbol{x}) \leftarrow B(\boldsymbol{x})$ if there is an occurrence of an atomic formula $p(\boldsymbol{t})$ in B', called the *selected atom*, and B'' is $B'[B(\boldsymbol{t})/p(\boldsymbol{t})]$.

Definition 4. Let P be a positive program with guards, and let $\leftarrow B$ be a positive goal with guards.

An *SLPG-derivation* for $P; \leftarrow B$ consists of a (finite or infinite) sequence $G_0, G_1, \ldots$ of positive goals with guards, and a sequence $C_1, C_2, \ldots$ of variants of statements of (Clark's transformation) P^C, such that G_0 is $\leftarrow B$ and each G_{i+1} is SLPG-derived from G_i and C_{i+1}.

An *SLPG-refutation* of $P; \leftarrow B$ (or a *successful SLPG-derivation*) is a finite SLPG-derivation that has as the last goal $\leftarrow B'(\boldsymbol{x})$, such that $U^{\omega}_{\mathcal{L}} \models \exists_{\boldsymbol{x}} B'(\boldsymbol{x})$. Then any guarded substitution (θ' WHERE S') such that $U^{\omega}_{\mathcal{L}} \models B'(\theta'$ WHERE $S')$, is called an *SLPG-computed answer* for $P; \leftarrow B$.

Example 2.

1. Consider program P with a single statement $p(x, y) \leftarrow x{\neq}y$. If the goal G is $\leftarrow p(f(x), f(f(y)))$, in SLPG we can derive in one step $\leftarrow f(x){\neq}f(f(y))$. We have $U^{\omega}_{\mathcal{L}} \models f(x){\neq}f(f(y))(\{x/x, y/y\}$ WHERE $x{\neq}f(y))$ guarded substitution $(\{x/x, y/y\}$ WHERE $x{\neq}f(y))$ is the SLPG-computed answer for $P; G$ (in this case the algorithm from Theorem 2 returns only one guarded substitution.) We also have: $Comp(P) \models^{\omega}_{\mathcal{L}} p(f(x), f(f(y)))(\{x/x, y/y\}$ WHERE $x{\neq}f(y))$, as expected due to the soundness and completeness theorem.
2. Consider the following program P:
$$q(x) \leftarrow \forall_y r(x, y)$$
$$r(x, y) \leftarrow x{\neq}y \vee \exists_z y{=}f(z).$$
If the goal G is $\leftarrow q(x)$, in first step we derive $\leftarrow \forall_y r(x, y)$, in the second step we derive $\leftarrow \forall_y (x{\neq}y \vee \exists_z y{=}f(z))$. We have $U^{\omega}_{\mathcal{L}} \models \forall_y (x{\neq}y \vee \exists_z y{=}f(z))(f(v)/x)$, the substitution $\{f(v)/x\}$ is the SLPG-computed answer for $P; G$ (in this case the algorithm from Theorem 2 returns only one substitution, with a trivial guard.) We also have: $Comp(P) \models^{\omega}_{\mathcal{L}} q(x)(f(v)/x)$, as expected due to the soundness and completeness theorem.

SLPG is an example of a resolution system that works on formulas from the inside, without decomposing them into clauses. In conventional resolution systems one first turns formulas into prenex normal form, Skolemizes, and then applies the resolution rule. [Fitting '90] has shown that Skolemization can be incorporated into special decomposition rules, so that the preparatory step of transforming the formula to prenex form is not necessary. As one uses decomposition rules and the resolution rule, one Skolemizes on the way. SLPG-resolution, presented in this section, uses a similar idea. However, as we consider not arbitrary sets of formulas, but just positive programs with guards, even decomposition rules are not necessary. We delay decomposition till the very last step, in which we use our algorithm computing answer substitutions.

In the implementation of our language the first step will be to transform P into P^C, then to use SLPG-resolution with the answer generating algorithm from Theorem 2. The main concern in such an implementation will be the efficiency (i.e. time complexity) of the answer generating algorithm. To address this issue we need to mention that SLPG can be shown to be an extension of SLD-resolution. SLPG in contrast to SLD works not only for definite programs but for arbitrary positive programs with guards. It is possible to implement SLPG with its algorithm computing answer substitutions so that for definite programs it is as efficient as SLD. Of course processing programs going beyond the syntax of definite clauses and involving complex guards will be more time-consuming. It should be left to the programmer to decide whether to write with some effort a very efficient definite program, or whether to write effortlessly in a broader language, obtaining a program that needs more time for its execution.

5 Programs with negation and SLPGCN-resolution

In this section we consider programs involving arbitrary formulas (with negation) in statements bodies.

By a *program* we understand any finite collection of statements of the form $A \leftarrow B$ where A is an atomic formula other than $\top, \bot, t'{=}t''$, and B is arbitrary first-order formula such that $var(B) \subseteq var(A)$. By a *goal* we understand any first-order formula $\leftarrow B$.

Programs, as defined above will be handled by SLPGCN-resolution which results by augmenting SLPG-resolution with deMorgan transformation and a mechanism of constructive negation.

By deMorgan laws any formula can be transformed into an equivalent formula with negations occurring only at the atomic level. For instance:

$$\exists_{x_1}\neg(p(x_1) \vee \forall_{x_2}\neg q(x_1,x_2)) \equiv \exists_{x_1}(\neg p(x_1) \wedge \exists_{x_2} q(x_1,x_2)).$$

For the remaining part of our considerations let us fix an algorithm that performs such a task, and if the input formula is B, denote the output formula by B^{deM}.

The idea of constructive negation, which is used in the next definition, comes from a Prolog programming trick: instead of using a negative literal $\neg p$, define in a positive way a new predicate $\overline{p}$ with the same properties as $\neg p$. This idea is different from the idea of constructive negation as failure in [Chan '88] and [Przymusinski '89].

Definition 5. let $\mathcal{L}'$ be an extension of a language $\mathcal{L}$ obtained by adding for each predicate symbol p, except $=$, a new predicate symbol $\overline{p}$ of the same arity. For any program P and any goal $\leftarrow B$ in $\mathcal{L}$ we define the *constructive version* P^+ of P. P^+ is obtained in the following way. Form

$$P' = \{A \leftarrow B^{deM} \mid (A \leftarrow B) \in P^C\}$$
$$P'' = \{\neg A \leftarrow (\neg B)^{deM} \mid (A \leftarrow B) \in P^C\}$$

where P^C is Clark's transformation of P; then replace every negative literal $\neg p(t)$ in $P' \cup P''$ by $\overline{p}(t)$. Similarly, the *constructive version* $(\leftarrow B)^+$ of a goal $\leftarrow B$ is obtained by replacing every negative literal $\neg p(t)$ in $\leftarrow B^{deM}$ by $\overline{p}(t)$.

Notice that P^+ is always a positive program with guards, so it can be processed by SLPG-resolution.

Definition 6. Let P be a program and let $\leftarrow B$ be a goal. We define the *SLPGCN-answer set* for $P; \leftarrow B$ as: $SLPGCN(P,B) = SLPG(P^+, B^+)$.

To implement SLPGCN-resolution it will be enough to augment SLPG with modules which transform given program P first to deMorgan form P^{deM} and then to constructive version P^+.

By Theorem 1 we immediately obtain completeness of SLPGCN for programs P such that P^+ is a positive program with positive guards, or a positive existential program with arbitrary guards. More direct characterization of classes of programs for which SLPGCN is complete is given in the next theorem.

Theorem 7 (on soundness and completeness of SLPGCN-resolution). *Let P be a program and let $\leftarrow B$ be a goal in a first-order language $\mathcal{L}$ with a finite alphabet. Consider the following conditions:*

1. $SLPGCN(P, B) \supseteq [\![\theta \text{ WHERE } S]\!]$
2. $P^+ \models^{\omega}_{\mathcal{L}} B^+(\theta \text{ WHERE } S)$
3. $Comp(P^+) \models^{\omega}_{\mathcal{L}} B^+(\theta \text{ WHERE } S)$
4. $lfp(T^{\omega}_{P^+}) \models B^+(\theta \text{ WHERE } S)$

The following implications hold.

Soundness: Condition 1 implies each of 2, 3 and 4.

Completeness: If P is a program consisting of statements of the form $p(\boldsymbol{x}) \leftarrow B'$, where B' is a first-order formula without $=$, and B is a first order formula without $=$, or if P is a program consisting of statements $p(\boldsymbol{x}) \leftarrow B'$ where B' is a first-order formula without quantifiers, and B is a first-order formula without quantifiers, then each of conditions 2, 3 and 4 implies 1.

6 Conclusion

We presented a system of SLPGCN-resolution. SLPGCN is an extension of SLDNF-resolution, in the following sense: for a normal program, if SLDNF returns an answer then SLPGCN returns an equivalent answer. However SLPGCN often returns an answer, while SLDNF does not. For programs with negation which are both normal and belong to the classes specified in Theorem 7, SLPGCN is complete while SLDNF is not. Also Theorem 7 implies that SLPGCN is sound and complete for the full class of propositional logic programs with negation (cf. [Plaza '91].) Notice also that in our completeness theorems we do not need assumption that programs are stratified, hierarchical, allowed, etc., which are always used in the case of SLDNF resolution. SLPGCN and ENF proposed by [Lugiez '89] can be considered counterparts computing – respectively – over an open and closed universes of terms.

We believe that SLPGCN-resolution is an optimal alternative to SLDNF and also SLSC-resolution, and that it constitutes a solid theoretical base on which more expressive and fully declarative logic programming can be based.

As a continuation of this research the author will undertake experimental implementation of a fully declarative logic programming language based on SLPGCN.

Acknowledgments

Warmest thanks to Professor Helena Rasiowa and to Professor Melvin Fitting – my advisors during my doctoral research.

References

[Apt, Blair and Walker '88] K.R. Apt, H. A. Blair and A. Walker, Towards a Theory of

Declarative Knowledge, in [Minker '88], pp. 89-148.

[Apt and van Emden '82] K.R. Apt and M.H. van Emden, Contributions to the Theory of Logic Programming, *Journal of the ACM* Vol. 29, No. 3, July 1982, pp. 841-862.

[Chan '88] D. Chan, Constructive Negation Based on the Completed Database, in [Kowalski and Bowen '88], vol. 1, pp. 111-125.

[Clark '78] K.L. Clark, Negation as Failure, in [Gallaire and Minker '78], pp. 193-322.

[Clark '79] K.L. Clark, Predicate Logic as a Computational Formalism, *Research Report DOC 79/59*, Dept. of Computing, Imperial College, London, 1979.

[Comon '88] H. Comon, *Unification et Disunification: Theorie et Applications*, Doctoral Dissertation, I.N.P. de Grenoble, France, 1988.

[Fitting '90] M. Fitting, *First-order Logic and Automated Theorem Proving*, Springer Verlag, New York 1990.

[Gallaire and Minker '78] H. Gallaire and J. Minker (eds.), *Logic and Databases*, Plenum Press, New York, 1978.

[Jaffar, Lassez and Lloyd '83] J. Jaffar, J.-L. Lassez and J.W. Lloyd, Completeness of the Negation as Failure Rule, *IJCAI-83*, Karlsruhe, 1983, pp. 500-506.

[Kowalski '74] R.A. Kowalski, Predicate Logic as a Programming Language, *Information Processing '74*, Stockholm, North Holland, 1974, pp. 569-574.

[Kowalski '79] R. A. Kowalski, Algorithm = Logic + Control, *Communications of the ACM* 22, 7, July 1979, pp. 424-436.

[Kowalski and Bowen '88] R.A. Kowalski and K.A. Bowen (eds.), *Logic Programming, Proceedings of the Fifth International Conference and Symposium*, MIT Press, 1988.

[Kunen '87] K. Kunen, Negation in Logic Programming, *Journal of Logic Programming* 1987, No. 4, pp. 289-308.

[Levi and Martelli '89] G. Levi and M. Martelli (eds.), *Logic Programming, Proceedings of the Sixth International Conference*, MIT Press, 1989.

[Lifschitz '88] V. Lifschitz, On the Declarative Semantics of Logic Programs with Negation, in [Minker '88], pp. 177-192.

[Lloyd '87] J.W. Lloyd, *Foundations of Logic Programming*, Second extended edition, Springer Verlag, 1987.

[Lloyd and Topor '88] J.W. Lloyd and R.W. Topor, Making Prolog More Expressive, *Journal of Logic Programming 3*, 1984.

[Lugiez '89] D. Lugiez, A Deduction Procedure for First Order Programs, in [Levi and Martelli '89], pp. 585-599.

[Lusk and Overbeek '89] E.L. Lusk and R.A. Overbeek (eds.), *Logic Programming, Proceedings of the North American Conference 1989*, MIT Press, 1989.

[Maher '88] M.J. Maher, *Complete Axiomatization of the Algebras of Finite, Rational and Infinite Trees*, research report, IBM - T.J. Watson Research Center, Yorktown Heights, NY.

[Minker '88] J. Minker (ed.), *Foundations of Deductive Databases and Logic Programming*, Morgan Kaufmann, 1988.

[Plaza '90] J.A. Plaza, *Fully Declarative Programming with Logic*, Ph.D. Dissertation, City University of New York, 1990.

[Plaza '91] J.A. Plaza, Completeness for Propositional Logic Programs with Negation, in [Ras and Zemankova '91], pp. 600-609.

[Plaza '92] J.A. Plaza, Operators on Lattices of ω-Herbrand Interpretations, in [Taitslin and Nerode '92].

[Przymusinski '88] T.C. Przymusinski, On the Declarative Semantics of Deductive Databases and Logic Programs, in [Minker '88], pp. 193-216.

[Przymusi nski '89] T.C. Przymusinski, On Constructive Negation in Logic Programming, in [Lusk and Overbeek '89], addendum.

[Przymusinski '92] T.C. Przymusinski, On the Declarative and Procedural Semantics of Logic Programs, *Journal of Logic Programming,* to appear.

[Ras and Zemankova '91] Z.W. Ras and M. Zemankova (eds.), *Methodologies for Intelligent Systems, Proceedings of the* 6th *International Symposium*, Lecture Notes in AI 542, Springer Verlag, Berlin - New York, 1991.

[Shapiro '87] E.Y. Shapiro (ed.), *Concurrent Prolog: Collected Papers*, MIT Press, Cambridge MA, 1987.

[Shepherdson '88] J.C. Shepherdson, Negation in Logic Programming, in [Minker '88], pp. 19-88.

[Taitslin and Nerode '92] M.A. Taitslin and A. Nerode (eds.), *Proceedings of the Symposium on Logical Foundations of Computer Science - Logic at Tver '92*, Lecture Notes in Computer Science, Springer Verlag, 1992, to appear.

[Ueda '87] K. Ueda, Guarded Horn Clauses, in [Shapiro '87], vol.1, pp. 140-156.

[Van Gelder, Ross and Schlipf '91] A. Van Gelder, K.A. Ross, and J.S. Schlipf, The Well-founded Semantics for General Logic Programs, *Journal of the ACM*, Vol. 38, No. 3, July 1991, pp. 620-650.

This article was processed using the LaTeX macro package with LLNCS style

Our LIPS Are Sealed: Interfacing Functional and Logic Programming Systems

Gary Lindstrom[1]*, Jan Małuszyński[2] and Takeshi Ogi[3]

[1] Computer Science Department, University of Utah, Salt Lake City, UT 84112 USA; lindstrom@cs.utah.edu
[2] Department of Computer and Information Science, Linköping University, S-581 83 Linköping, Sweden; jmz@ida.liu.se
[3] Kyocera Corp., 2-14-9 Tamagawa-dai, Setagaya-ku, Tokyo, Japan.

Abstract. We report on a technique for interfacing an untyped logic language to a statically polymorphically typed functional language (FL). Our key insight is that polymorphic types can be interpreted as "need to know" specifications on function arguments. This leads to a criterion for liberally yet safely invoking the FL to reduce application terms as required during unification in the logic language. This method, called P-unification, enriches the capabilities of each language while retaining the integrity of their individual semantics and implementation technologies. The results presented suggest that a Horn clause logic programming (HCLP) systems can utilize unmodified implementations of FL's to (i) manipulate untyped or dynamically typed data, even though the FL is statically typed; (ii) act lazily, even though the FL is strict, and (iii) build structures containing HCLP terms alien to the FL, such as unbound variables.

1 Motivation

There have been countless attempts to combine the best features of functional programming (FP), e.g. functional notation, higher order objects, lazy evaluation, etc., with those of logic programming (LP), e.g. "don't know" nondeterminism, computation on non-ground data, constraint-based search, etc. Most of these approaches are described as "amalgamation," i.e. homogenization into a new language. At best, this semantic stew emerges as a purée; at worst, a goulash. In any case, the contributing languages surrender their semantic integrity, and combining their implementation technologies becomes problematic.

We address this problem from a different perspective, in keeping with the trend toward "open systems." Our approach is based on an experiment employing the Standard ML of New Jersey (SMLNJ) FP language (FPL) system as a reduction server to an LP language (LPL) client, written in Common Lisp [Ogi90].

This work builds on the approach presented in [BM88] to integrating a logic language with an external functional language. The declarative semantics of this

* This material is based upon work supported by the National Science Foundation under Grants CCR-8920971 and ASC-9016131.

integration is defined in terms of an equational logic. The operational semantics suggested there is based on an extended unification method, called *S-unification*. S-unification is inherently incomplete since it combines term unification with function application, restricted to ground arguments. We present here an extended form of S-unification, taking into account polymorphic type information. This allows us to relax the ground argument requirement in many cases.

2 Language Requirements

We assume that the FPL is (i) purely functional *in effect* (i.e. semantically benign use of imperative features is permitted); (ii) statically polymorphically typed; (iii) applicative-order (strict, non-lazy, call-by-value), and (iv) equipped with constructor-based user defined types. The LPL is not assumed to be statically typed, since many of today's LPL's, including most versions of PROLOG, are untyped. However, we assume that the type signatures of all accessible FPL data objects (including function identifiers) are known to the LPL.

Our polymorphic type domain is represented:

$$\begin{aligned} \mathsf{T} &::= \mathsf{Tvar} \mid (\mathsf{T}_1, \ldots, \mathsf{T}_n)\ \mathsf{Dtype} \\ \mathsf{Tvar} &::= \alpha \mid \beta \mid \ldots \\ \mathsf{Dtype} &::= \mathsf{Identifier} \end{aligned}$$

All schemes are implicitly closed (via outermost $\forall\alpha$ ...). This includes the core of STANDARD ML since:

1. Primitive data types int, bool, string etc. are subsumed by $(\mathsf{T}_1, \ldots, \mathsf{T}_n)$ Dtype, with $n = 0$ and parentheses omitted.
2. Function data types $\mathsf{T}_1 \rightarrow \mathsf{T}_2$ are subsumed by $(\mathsf{T}_1, \mathsf{T}_2)$ func.
3. Tuple types are subsumed by $(\mathsf{T}_1, \ldots, \mathsf{T}_n)$ cross.

Note that substitution on Tvar's creates a partial order on T, whereby $\mathsf{T}_1 \sqsubseteq \mathsf{T}_2$ iff there exists a substitution Θ such that $\mathsf{T}_1\Theta = \mathsf{T}_2$. Traditional surface representations will be used henceforth, e.g. int, $\alpha \times \beta$, α list, α list $\rightarrow \alpha$, etc.

3 LPL Terms

Our term language TL is a first-order LPL term language extended by a binary functor apply, with the interpretation that apply(fn, arg) means "rewrite this term by evaluating fn arg in the FPL."

$$\begin{aligned} \mathsf{Term} ::= &\ \mathsf{Var} \mid \mathsf{Constant} \mid \mathsf{Functor}(\mathsf{Term}_1, \ldots, \mathsf{Term}_n) \qquad (n \geq 1) \\ &\mid \mathsf{apply}(\mathsf{Term}_1, \mathsf{Term}_2) \end{aligned}$$

Var denotes logical variables, and Constant denotes atomic symbols (e.g. integers). The syntax $\mathsf{Functor}(\mathsf{Term}_1, \ldots, \mathsf{Term}_n)$ is reserved for *constructions* (i.e. constructor applications), where the constructor may be (i) known to both languages (e.g. cons(...)), or (ii) unknown in the FPL (e.g. foo(...)). We consider parentheses to be optional for nullary constructors, i.e. f and f( ) are synonyms. The construction tuple($Term_1$, ..., $Term_n$), for $n \geq 2$, represents functor-less tuples. Once again, more congenial surface representations will often be used henceforth, e.g. [1, 2] (rather than cons(1, cons(2, nil))), [true, false | X] (rather than cons(true, cons(false, X))), (1, true) (rather than tuple(1, true)), and 1+2 (rather than apply(plus, tuple(1, 2))).

4 Datatypes: Common, Alien, and Mixed

Some types in T represent values that are meaningful to both the FPL and LPL. These values include common primitive types (int, bool, ...), and certain constructions, e.g. tuples and lists. The surface representation of these values will generally need conversion as they pass between languages (e.g. the FPL value (v_1, ..., v_n) will need to be converted to the LPL term tuple(v_1, ..., v_n) — see Sec. 3), but we assume that no semantically significant mapping issues arise.

There are, in addition, data values that each language can manipulate but must regard as semantically "alien." For example, the LPL must appeal to the FPL for interpretation of non-constructor functions, while the FPL cannot be expected to make sense of logical variables, ill-typed expressions, or insufficiently instantiated constructions such as [1 | X] $\equiv$ cons(1, X), where X is an unbound variable. Hence the data under manipulation will in general be, from the perspective of each language, a mixture of common, private and alien objects.

5 A "Need to Know" Strategy For Term Reduction

Clearly one cannot expect the FPL to reduce terms such as apply(plus, tuple(1, true)). Yet one might hope that apply(head, [1, X]) could yield 1, and even that apply(tail, [1, X]) could yield [X]. How might such a "liberalized" sense of function application be safely obtained? By observing that *variables in function domain types indicate "hands off" treatment.* Thus length: α list $\rightarrow$ int means that list elements: (i) are not inspected by length; (ii) need not be evaluated; (iii) can be objects "alien" to the FPL, and (iv) need not even be typable, static FPL typing notwithstanding!

Note this type scheme interpretation significantly extends the interpretation customarily observed in SML, which construes the polymorphic type α list $\rightarrow$ int to be the union of all its monomorphic instances (int list $\rightarrow$ int, bool list $\rightarrow$ int, int list list $\rightarrow$ int, etc.).

Our strategy is embodied in a mechanism for enlisting the FPL as a reduction server as needed by the LPL during unification. Our approach is thus (yet another) version of *extended unification* [DV87], which we term *P-unification.* A term apply(fn, arg) is reduced *lazily*, i.e. as needed during unification, but only when (i) fn has become a function, and (ii) arg has become acceptably instantiated to the degree dictated by the domain type of fn. The following examples illustrate the desired effect (resulting substitutions omitted).[4]

[4] The fact that unifying [P, Q] and apply(apply(map, add1), [13, Y]) *suspends* rather than *succeeds* with {P := 14, Q := apply(add1, Y)} is a consequence of our FPL strictness assumption.

U	V	*P-unify*(U, V)
X	apply(length, Y)	*succeeds*
1	apply(length, [ ])	*fails*
2	apply(length, [R, S])	*succeeds*
3	apply(length, [R, S | T])	*suspends*
[P, Q]	apply(apply(map, add1), [13, Y])	*suspends*
[2, 0]	apply(apply(map, length), [[13, Y], [ ]])	*succeeds*

We will define P-unification in three increasingly precise presentations. In each case, the method will be described operationally by means of prioritized, symmetric rules for eliminating *term disagreement pairs*. We omit the occur check in each case to simplify the presentation. In the presence of apply terms the occur check becomes more elaborate, since e.g. the terms X and apply(+, tuple(X, 0)), where + is the addition function, are unifiable. In this paper we focus on the problem of using types for interfacing functional and logic programming systems. A proper treatment of the occur check problem would follow the approach of S-unification [BM88, Bon91].

P-unification Formulation 1:

1. {v, x}, where v is an unbound variable, and x is arbitrary: Bind v to x, and remove this pair from the disagreement set.
2. {$f_1(t_{1,1}, \ldots, t_{1,n1})$, $f_2(t_{2,1}, \ldots, t_{2,n2})$}, where f_1 and f_2 are constructors: If $f_1 \neq f_2$, or $n1 \neq n2$, fail; otherwise, remove this pair from the disagreement set and add the pairs {$t_{1,i}$, $t_{2,i}$} for $i = 1, \ldots, n1$ (subsumes tuples and non-function constants).
3. {x, y}, where x = apply(fn, arg):
   (a) If the FPL can be invoked without type error to reduce x, do so and reconsider this pair.
   (b) If x might be instantiated to meet condition (a), defer consideration of this pair until that possibility is resolved affirmatively or negatively.
   (c) Otherwise, fail.

   The apply rule is the focus of this work, and will be made more precise in the following sections.

Failure arises in 3(c) because no instantiation of arguments could permit reduction of the apply term, even in the "liberalized" sense being defined here. Hence a fundamental typing error has been detected, and the apply term is meaningless in both languages.

Because of the concept of deferred pairs, a non-failed P-unification results generally in a set of bindings and a set of deferred pairs, which may or may not be processed at later unification steps, depending on subsequently produced variable bindings. A formal presentation of this idea in the context of S-unification can be found in [Boy91], where sufficient conditions for the absence of deferred pairs upon non-failed termination of a program are given and in [KK91] where an implementation of this concept is described.

Note that constructions receive special treatment with respect to other function applications. In particular, they: (i) enjoy a special syntax $f(t_1, \ldots, t_n)$; (ii) can (if f is known to the FPL) be either applied by the FPL or be selected directly upon by the LPL during unification, and (iii) have an LPL meaning even if they do not conform to the FPL's static typing. Hence we contrast X+Y and cons(X, Y), in the case that X becomes 1 and Y becomes true. That is, cons(1, true), while malformed as an FPL object, can continue to serve as a valid construction in the (untyped) LPL, while 1+true is meaningless in both languages.

6 Reduction Desiderata

How should an apply(fn, arg) term be reduced during P-unification? We claim the following properties are desirable:

1. **Safety:** No reduction service request should cause an FPL type error.
2. **Laziness:** Subterms in apply(fn, arg) terms should be reduced only if their values are needed (i) by an FPL reduction, or for successful completion of a P-unification step. Thus we aspire *not* to apply acker in apply(head, [1, apply(acker, (100, 99))]), since under a lazy evaluation regime we need not evaluate the elements of a list to which head is applied.
3. **Maximality:** FPL evaluation requests should include a maximal composition of function applications, consistent with our laziness criterion. For example, the nested reduction add1(add1(add1(add1(13)))) should be evaluated in one service request, rather than in four.

In fact, laziness and maximality are somewhat opposing criteria. We will achieve a pragmatically attractive middle ground by means of (i) *sealed envelopes*, (ii) *maximal consensus types*, and (iii) *minimal term "truncations"* bearing these types.

7 Sealed Envelopes

Our type-based "need to know" strategy lets us encapsulate data objects alien to the FPL in carriers that hide the identity of these objects along with their type idiosyncrasies. This is accomplished through:

1. Augmenting T to include a *nullary type constructor* union, which will be attributed to subterms whose type is not germane to an FPL reduction request.
2. A *term constructor* seal(Term) of type $\alpha \rightarrow$ union. A seal application constitutes a static typing boundary. We denote the TL term language augmented with seal as the augmented term language ATL.
3. An *FPL datatype definition* datatype union = seal of int.
4. An *LPL* $\leftrightarrow$ *FPL* interface convention:
   (a) On output to the FPL, seal(x) is translated to seal(χ), where χ = loc x, the address of the expression x in the LPL address space.
   (b) On input from the FPL, seal(i) is translated to deref(i), the expression at address i.[5]

To illustrate, consider t = head [1, true]. This is not acceptable to the FPL, due to its heterogeneous list [1, true]. However, if t is reformulated as head [seal(loc 1), seal(loc true)], then the FPL can be invoked to return seal(loc 1), which yields 1 upon dereferencing.

[5] If addresses are unstable, as with compacting garbage collection, then symbolic names can be used.

8 Attributing Types to TL Terms

P-unification, as outlined in Sec. 5, presumes testability of an apply term for error-free FPL reducibility. Our formal realization of this criterion is based on a notion of type attribution for TL terms, which permits (i) a maximal type notion for TL terms, guaranteeing reduction safety, and (ii) a type-driven reduction scheme meeting the laziness and maximality criteria of Sec. 6.

We begin by adapting the Hindley-Milner type attribution method [Mil78] to apply to ATL terms. This done by:

1. Directly attributing types to literals (e.g. 13 : int, and nil : α list) and to FPL symbols (e.g. length : α list $\rightarrow$ int, and map : $\alpha \rightarrow \beta \rightarrow \alpha$ list $\rightarrow \beta$ list).
2. Interpreting apply(fn, arg) as having type β, where the type of fn is constrained to $\alpha \rightarrow \beta$, and the type of arg is constrained to α.
3. Interpreting constructions f(t_1, ..., t_n), where f has an FPL-type, as apply(f, tuple(t_1, ..., t_n)), if $n \geq 2$, and apply(f, t_1) if $n = 1$.
4. Viewing as untypable:
   (a) Unbound variables, and
   (b) Constructions foo(a, 13), where foo is an LPL-only constructor. Note this implies untypability of LPL-only symbols, e.g. a in [1, a].
5. Interpreting seal(t) to have type union, as per Sec. 7, independent of whether t is typable.

Theorem 1. *If $t \in$ ATL has a type, then t is attributed a most general type, i.e. all other attributable types can be obtained by substitutions on this most general type.*

Proof. If t has a type, then all its subterms must be typable, except possibly those within seal(...) occurrences. Let us substitute seal(true) in t for each occurrence of seal(...), and call the new term t'. Clearly, the set of types attributable to t and to t' are the same. But t' is now isomorphic to an ordinary FPL term, which has a principal Hindley-Milner type. Moreover, our extended method reduces to the Hindley-Milner method on t'. Hence our method must yield a principal type for t', and that must be the principal type of t. □

We denote the principal type of $t \in$ ATL, if it exists, by $\tau(t)$. Let t be a TL term. A *truncation* $t1 \in$ ATL of t is constructed from t by the introduction of zero or more unnested seal constructions. Hence a truncation of $t \in$ TL may be viewed as a copy of t in which selected subtrees (including all descendant nodes) are logically deleted.

Let *trunc*(t) be the set of all truncations of t. A subterm occurrence s in $t1 \in$ *trunc*(t) is *sealed* if s is immediately surrounded by a seal construction, or appears within a sealed subterm occurrence. If $t1, t2 \in$ *trunc*(t), we say $t1 \sqsubseteq t2$ if every sealed subterm occurrence in $t2$ is sealed in $t1$. Observe that $\sqsubseteq$ is a partial order on *trunc*(t), and forms a (finite) lattice, with $\bot =$ seal(t), and $\top = t$. To compute *glb*($t1, t2$), we form $t1 \cup t2$, and remove nested seal applications; for *lub* we form $t1 \cup t2$ and retain only deepest seal applications.

We now change the ordering on our type domain T to deal more effectively with the effects of truncation. The primitive type union is repositioned such that (i) $\alpha \sqsubseteq$

union $\sqsubseteq ty$ for all $ty \neq \alpha$ (or any other type variable), and (ii) the same ordering holds recursively under type constructors, e.g. α list $\sqsubseteq$ union list $\sqsubseteq$ int list, etc.

If $t \in$ TL possesses no subterms with principal type α then we say it is *α-free.* Henceforth we will assume all TL terms are α-free.

Theorem 2. *Let $t \in$ TL be α-free. Then τ is monotonic on trunc(t), wherever it is defined. That is, if t1 and t2 are both typable truncations of t, with $t1 \sqsubseteq t2$, then $\tau(t1) \sqsubseteq \tau(t2)$.*

Proof. Let $t1$ and $t2$ be two typable truncations of a TL term with $t1 \sqsubseteq t2$. The typability of a truncation t is equivalent to the existence of a most general unifier (mgu) Θ solving a set of equations $eq(t)$ on type variables $dom(\Theta)$ associated with the nodes of t that are either unsealed or directly sealed (i.e. occurrences of seal(...)).

Since $t1$ and $t2$ are typable, $\Theta_1 = mgu(eq(t1))$ and $\Theta_2 = mgu(eq(t2))$ both exist. Let $v(t)$ be the type variable associated with the overall term t. Since $t1$ and $t2$ are truncations of the same TL term, $v(t1)$ is $v(t2)$. Hence $\tau(t1) = v(t1)\Theta_1$, and $\tau(t2) = v(t2)\Theta_2 = v(t1)\Theta_2$.

Let $tr(t)$ denote the equations in $eq(t)$ of the form $\mathsf{T}_i =$ union arising from directly sealed subterms in t, and $e(t)$ denote $eq(t) - tr(t)$. Then $eq(t1) = e(t1) \cup tr(t1)$, and $eq(t2) = e(t1) \cup e'$, where $e' = (e(t2) - e(t1)) \cup tr(t2)$. Note that $mgu(eq(t1)) = mgu(mgu(e(t1)) \cup mgu(tr(t1))) = mgu(mgu(e(t1)) \cup tr(t1))$, and $mgu(eq(t2)) = mgu(mgu(e(t1)) \cup mgu(e'))$.

Since $mgu(eq(t2))$ exists, so must $mgu(e')$. By α-freeness, all type variables in $dom(e')$ must be bound to values union or greater. We say two mgu's Θ and Θ' obey $\Theta \sqsubseteq \Theta'$ iff $dom(\Theta) \subseteq dom(\Theta')$, and $\forall v \in dom(\Theta), v\Theta \sqsubseteq v\Theta'$. We have $dom(tr(t1)) \subseteq dom(e')$, so $mgu(tr(t1)) \sqsubseteq mgu(e')$; hence $mgu(eq(t1)) \sqsubseteq mgu(eq(t2))$, and $\tau(t1) \sqsubseteq \tau(t2)$[6] □

A word of explanation is appropriate concerning our exclusion of ATL terms possessing subterms of principal type α. Such subterms must denote "fully polymorphic" FPL values, which are anomalous. Expressions denoting such objects include: (i) head nil; (ii) f 13 where fun f x = f x, and (iii) f 13 where fun f x = raise exception1. In short, α-typed expressions can never deliver values, due to inescapable divergence or exception.

9 Maximal Types of TL Terms

Let us define $t1 \in trunc(t)$ to be *FPL-safe* if $t1$, as outputted under the seal interface protocol described in Sec. 7, is typable by the FPL.

Theorem 3. *Every typable truncation of a* TL *term is FPL-safe.*

[6] What happens if a TL term is not α-free? Consider $t =$ apply(head,nil), with Hindley-Milner principal type α, and $trunc(t) = \{t, \text{seal}(t)\}$. The maximal typable truncation of t is t itself with type α, but its maximal type is union. Hence τ is not monotonic on $trunc(t)$.

Proof. Follows by an argument similar to that for Theorem 1. Note that at least one typable truncation always exists for any $t \in \mathsf{TL}$, since at worst we can seal t in its entirety. □

Theorem 4. *If $t1$ and $t2$ are two typable truncations of a term t, then $t1 \sqcup t2$ is typable.*

Proof. Our proof uses the notation introduced in the proof of Theorem 2. To prove typability of $t1 \sqcup t2$ it suffices to prove existence of $mgu(eq(t1 \sqcup t2))$. Denote by $e(t1, t2)$ the intersection of the sets $e(t1)$ and $e(t2)$, and by $e'(t2)$ the set $e(t2) - e(t1, t2)$. Hence $eq(t1 \sqcup t2) = e(t1) \cup e'(t2) \cup tr(t1 \sqcup t2)$ and we seek to prove existence of its mgu.

Clearly the set $e(t1)$ has a unifier since $t1$ is typable. The set $e'(t2)$ has a unifier since it is a subset of $e(t2)$. The set $tr(t1 \sqcup t2)$ includes the equations arising from the directly sealed subterms of $t1 \sqcup t2$. The set $e'(t2) \cup (tr(t1 \sqcup t2) - tr(t1))$ is a subset of $eq(t2)$ and has a unifier. The remaining equations in $tr(t1 \sqcup t2)$ share no variables with this set. Thus $e'(t2) \cup tr(t1 \sqcup t2)$ also has a unifier. Now $mgu(e(t1) \cup e'(t2) \cup tr(t1 \sqcup t2))$ can be computed as $mgu(\tau 1, \tau 2)$, where $\tau 1 = mgu(e(t1))$ and $\tau 2 = mgu(e'(t2) \cup tr(t1 \sqcup t2))$.

We now show existence of $mgu(\tau 1, \tau 2)$. Consider the set V of variables of $e(t1)$ denoting the types of the directly sealed subterms of $t1$. Since the type equations in $e(t1)$ include no occurrence of union $\tau 1$ binds these variables at most to type variables (or leaves them unbound). Otherwise they could not be bound to union and $t1$ would not be typable. On the other hand, $\tau 2$ binds every variable of V to a type not including the variables of V, since these variables characterize types of the disjoint subterms of $t1 \sqcup t2$ truncated by the boundary of $t1$.

Two cases should be considered.

Case 1: No variables of V are bound by $\tau 1$ to a common type variable. In this case $mgu(\tau 1, \tau 2)$ exists and is obtained by binding the variable $\tau 1(x)$ to the type $\tau 2(x)$ for every $x \in V$.

Case 2: Some variables x and y in V are bound by $\tau 1$ to a common type variable.

- *Case 2a:* Both x and y occur either in (1) $tr(t1) - eq(t2)$ or in (2) $tr(t1) \cap eq(t2)$. If (1) applies, $\tau 2(x) = \tau 2(y) = \mathsf{union}$. If (2) applies, then by the assumption of typability of $t2$ terms $\tau 2(x)$ and $\tau 2(y)$ must be unifiable, since $e'(t2)$ is a subset of the unifiable set $eq(t2)$. From these observations one can conclude existence of $mgu(\tau 1, \tau 2)$.
- *Case 2b:* One of the variables x, y, say x, occurs in $tr(t1) - eq(t2)$ while the other occurs in (2) $tr(t1) \cap eq(t2)$. In that case there exists a variable z in $tr(t2) \cap eq(t1)$ which is bound by $\tau 1$ to the same variable as x. This is because y is both in $eq(t1)$ and $eq(t2)$ while x is not in $eq(t2)$. As they are bound to the same variable they must "communicate" over the boundary of $t2$ in $t1$. The mgu of $e(t2)$ binds z to a variable since it is bound to union by the mgu of $eq(t2)$. It also must bind z and y to a common variable since $\tau 1$ does that. Hence $e'(t2)$ which is a subset of $e(t2)$ can only bind y to a variable. Consequently $\tau 2(x) = \tau 2(y) = \mathsf{union}$ which allows us to conclude the existence of $mgu(\tau 1, \tau 2)$.

Given that *Case 1* and *Case 2* are exhaustive, we see that the set $e(t1) \cup e(t2)$ has an mgu. □

The maximal typable truncation of a term is the lub of its typable truncations. Hence every term has a unique maximal type, yielded by its maximal typable truncation. This permits us to extend τ to be total on TL, by defining $\tau(t)$ to be the type of the maximal Hindley-Milner typable truncation of t.

Note that the maximal type of t may be assumed by more than one of its truncations. Consider for example t = head [1, true]. The maximal type of t is union, obtained from both $t1$ = seal(head [1, true]) and $t2$ = head [seal(1), seal(true)]. However, $t1 \sqsubset t2$, so $t2$ corresponds to a greater amount of FPL reduction. Indeed, maximal typable (FPL-safe) truncations indicate maximal FPL reductions. This leads to:

P-unification Formulation 2: When reducing t = apply(fn, arg) in Step 3 of Formulation 1:

- Compute the maximum typable truncation $t1$ of t.
- If $t1$ = seal(...), suspend.
- Otherwise, reduce $t1$ and continue.

Unification of two TL terms fails when (i) both of their types are of the form $\delta \longrightarrow \rho$ (since we decline to unify functions for soundness reasons), or (ii) their types are not compatible, as explained in Sec. 11.

This strategy is *safe* (by Theorem 3) but sacrifices *laziness* (consider the example apply(head, [1, apply(acker, (100, 99))]) given earlier). We assert informally that it is also *maximal*.

10 Implementing Type Attribution

Truncation enumeration and typability testing can be merged into a simple, acceptably efficient algorithm succinctly expressible in PROLOG (see Fig. 1). Let $R(t)$ denote our PROLOG representation of TL term t. $R(t)$ = `e(T, S)`, where:

1. `T` is a Prolog term representing a type attributed to t, i.e. `int`, `bool`, `union`, etc., `cross(T1, ..., Tn)`, `list(T1)`, `arrow(T1, T2)`, or `_` (an unbound variable, for untyped terms).
2. `S` is a Prolog term representing the syntax of t:

t	`S`
V ∈ Var	`var(V)`
f(t_1, ..., t_n) (*f an LPL-only constructor*)	`f(`t_1`, ..., `t_n`)` (*subsumes constants and tuples*)
apply(t_1, t_2) (*includes FPL-constructions; see Sec. 8*)	`apply(`$R(t_1)$`, `$R(t_2)$`)`

Hence: nil ⇔ `e(_, nil)`; foo(1, true) ⇔ `e(_, foo(1, true))`; apply(add1, X) ⇔ `e(_, apply(e(_, add1), e(_, var(X))))`, etc.

```
type(e(R, apply(F, A))) :-
    F = e(arrow(D, R), _), A = e(D, _), type(F), type(A).
type(e(cross(T1, T2), tuple(E1, E2))) :-
    E1 = e(T1, _), E2 = e(T2, _), type(E1), type(E2).
type(e(list(T1), cons(E1, E2))) :-
    E1 = e(T1, _), E2 = e(list(T1), _), type(E1), type(E2).
type(e(list(_), nil)).
type(e(int, S)) :- integer(S).
type(e(bool, true)).
type(e(bool, false)).
type(e(arrow(list(T), T), head)).
type(e(arrow(int, arrow(int, int)), plus)).
type(e(arrow(arrow(T1, T2), arrow(list(T1), list(T2))), map)).
type(e(arrow(X, X), ident)).
...
type(e(union, _)).
```

Fig. 1. Type attribution in Prolog via type/1 predicate.

Note that in the algorithm of Fig. 1:

1. Typing of subterm occurrences is attempted in a top-down, left-right order.
2. Clause `type(e(union, _)).` implicitly seals a given subterm, as last resort.
3. Sealed subterms are unnested.
4. Type union is the only attribution to variables and LPL-only constructions.
5. All typable truncations are enumerated, with principal types, in topologically sorted order (maximal first).
6. Backtracking is somewhat "intelligent," in that attributing union to a subterm will "short circuit" type attribution search on subterms that must agree in type. For example, once union is attributed to true (by implicitly sealing it) in [true, apply(acker, tuple(100, 99))], attribution of union to the apply term will ensue without attempting any type attribution of tuple(100, 99).

11 P-unification Formulation 3

We can now precisely define our P-unification algorithm. Given the preliminary algorithm in Sec. 5, we need only refine the case where x = apply(fn, arg), and y is either a construction or an apply term. Let $L = R$([x, y]). First, we solve `type(e(T, ` L`))`, obtaining τ_{max}, the maximal type of L.

- *Case 1:* τ_{max} = `list(arrow(_, _))`: *Fail.*
- *Case 2:* τ_{max} = `list(union)`:
  - *Case 2a:* Only one truncation of L has this type, viz. [seal(x), seal(y)]: *Suspend.*
  - *Case 2b:* More than one truncation of L is attributed type `list(union)`. *Let t1 be a minimal typable truncation of L greater than* [seal(x), seal(y)].

Reduce x *and* y *using their respective truncations in* $t1$, *and reconsider this pair.*

- *Case 3:* **list(union)** $\sqsubset$ τ_{max}: *Let* t *be a minimal truncation of* L *with type* τ_{max}. *Reduce* x *and* y *using their respective truncations in* t, *and reconsider this pair.*

This *"max type / min truncation"* reduction strategy is our key to achieving both *maximality* and *laziness.* The favorable enumeration order of typable truncations provided by the algorithm in Fig. 1 means that we can abort the solution of **type(e(T,** L**))** as soon as the *second* distinct binding for **T** results (and select the truncation constructed immediately prior). This strategy encourages laziness, as the following examples indicate.

- τ_{max} = **list(union)**: Let $L = R$([apply(head, [X]), apply(head, [Y])]). L's maximal typable truncation L is t_{max} = [apply(head, [seal(X)]), apply(head, [seal(Y)])], and the minimal truncation with this type is t_{min} = [seal(apply(head, [X])), seal(apply(head, [Y]))]. Two other typable truncations lie between t_{max} and t_{min}, viz. t_1 = [apply(head, [seal(X)]), seal(apply(head, [Y]))] and t_2 = [seal(apply(head, [X])), apply(head, [seal(Y)])]. Unfortunately, t_1 and t_2 are incomparable, and $t_1 \sqcap t_2 = t_{min}$, which indicates no reduction of the two terms. Selecting *either* t_1 or t_2 will cause some reduction to take place, and constitute progress toward success or failure of the unification step (successful, in this case). Which truncation to choose is imponderable, so an arbitrary selection must be made. Of course, a more aggressive (less lazy) implementation may opt for reduction as indicated by t_{max}, which is always unique (and outputted first by our algorithm).
- τ_{max} $\sqsubset$ **list(union)**: Now let L = [apply(head, [false]), apply(first, tuple(true, apply(acker, tuple(100, 99))))], where τ(first) $= \alpha \times \beta \rightarrow \alpha$. The maximal typable truncation t_{max} of L is L itself, with type **list(bool)**. However, another typable truncation of t exists with the same type: t_1 = [apply(head, [false]), apply(first, tuple(true, seal(apply(acker, tuple(100, 99)))))]. We elect to reduce according to t_1 in the spirit of laziness, thereby avoiding evaluation of acker(100, 99).

One may ask: what are sufficient grounds for turning suspension (*Case 2a*) into failure? *When the maximal typable truncations of all ground instances of* L *seal both arguments of its list.* An effective test for this is easily implemented:

- Solve **susp(e(T,** L**))**, where procedure **susp/1** renames **type/1**, with added clause **susp(e(X, var(X))).** positioned just before **susp(e(union, _)).**
- If there is only one typable truncation of L with type greater than union (necessarily, with both of its list elements sealed), *fail.* Otherwise, *suspend.*

Note the trick in clause **susp(e(X, var(X))).** of pressing a variable **X** into service as its own (unbound) type denotation. This verifies that a potential type consensus exists for all uses of **X**. Hence we will detect that (i) {1+X, 13} and {1+X, 3-X} should *suspend*, but (ii) {1+X, true}, {1+true, 13}, and {apply(length, X), 1+X} should *fail*.

12 Type Retention, Polymorphism, and Lazy Copying

Our type attribution method for TL terms has another important monotonicity property:

Theorem 5. *Let t and t' be typable* TL *terms, with $t\Theta = t'$ for some substitution Θ. Then $\tau(t) \sqsubseteq \tau(t')$.*

Proof. Let t'' be t' with a seal(...) surrounding each occurrence in t of a variable bound by Θ. Clearly, t'' is typable, and has the same type as t. Since $t'' \sqsubseteq t'$, by Theorem 2 $\tau(t'') \sqsubseteq \tau(t')$, hence $\tau(t) \sqsubseteq \tau(t')$. □

Since type attribution is monotonic on variable instantiation, could we retain prior attributions of a term t to give us a "head start" on subsequent typings? The answer is *yes* in principle, but several complications arise.

1. A term representation for types must be designed that permits type attributions to be "raised" by variable binding. This not true of the representation used in Fig. 1, since union $\sqsubseteq$ int, but `union` may not be instantiated to become `int`. Such a representation is illustrated below:

Type	Term Representation
union	`union(_)`
int	`union(int)`
α list	`union(list(_))`
union list	`union(list(union(_)))`
int list	`union(list(union(int)))`
α list list	`union(list(union(list(_))))`

2. The type attribution code of Fig. 1 can be amended to use the representation shown above. However, care must be taken that sealed subterms are given *fixed* union attributions, lest [1, true] be attributed type bool list. This can result from the `union(_)` attribution of seal(1) being raised by unification with the type of true to `union(bool)`. A suitable defense is to use `type(e(union(fixed), _)).` as our "sealing" rule. In contrast, `susp(e(union(X), var(X))).` gives exactly the right "optimistic" typing effect. However, in both cases the `union(_)` argument bindings must be undone, if the type attributions are to be permanently retained.
3. The most severe impediment to retaining type attributions is the unfortunate collision of the "cultures" underlying polymorphism and lazy copying. Consider, for example,[7] goal G = `type(e(T, tuple(X, X)))`, where `X` has been bound in a prior unification step to `e(list(T1), nil)`. The sharing of `X`'s binding in G will cause the code in Fig. 1 to bind `T` to `cross(list(T1), list(T1))`, which incorrectly attributes only one degree of polymorphism to G. The correct binding is `cross(list(T1), list(T2))`. The implication is that we must copy the type attribution of every bound variable on each dereference — a very disheartening prospect indeed.

[7] For clarity, we revert in this example to our prior type representation.

For these reasons, we advocate the simplicity and space economy of building transient type attributed `e(T,` $R(t)$`)` representations of TL terms only as needed during P-unification. Since this would be done by direct traversal, type variables would be created anew (i.e. "polymorphically") for each subterm encounter, independent of whether or not that term's representation is physically shared (example: `buildexp([], e(_,nil)).`).

Note that this construction would only be undertaken when unification cannot proceed without reducing an apply term. Hence ordinary LPL proceeds unimpeded (indeed, more efficiently than if type attributions were permanently associated with every term).

13 What About Equality?

The only primitive polymorphic (actually, overloaded) operator in SML is equality. Types required to admit equality are indicated by special type variables, denoted $'\alpha$. Consequently, functions which apply equality to their arguments indicate this fact in their type signatures, e.g. mkset = $'\alpha$ list $\rightarrow$ $'\alpha$ list which removes duplicates from a list. We can easily distinguish types with equality in our domain by incorporating all $'\omega$ type variables, and ensuring that $'\omega$ variables in function argument types do not unify with function types or types containing union's. The effect of this on P-unification is suggested by the following examples:
(i) P-unifying 3 with length(mkset [X, Y, Z]) *suspends*;
(ii) P-unifying 3 with length(mkset, [1, 2, 1]) *fails*.

14 Related Work

In addition to the S-unification work mentioned earlier, the freeze / thaw notions in sequential implementations such as MU-PROLOG, and representative approaches to narrowing, are relevant. Barklund and Millroth [BM87] discuss dealing with alien ("hairy") data structures in PROLOG; their techniques bear some similarity with our sealed envelopes. A sound treatment of dynamic typing in an extension of SML is described in [ACPP89]. Our type union is very similar to their type dynamic; however, we also consider partially instantiated and lazily evaluated expressions. In contrast, their treatment includes a typecase expression permitting dynamic type testing within the source language. The work most vitally related to ours is that of Phil Wadler [Wad89], who derives theorems about functions working simply from their type signatures.

The issue of types in logic programming has been studied by many authors (see [Red88] and [Pfe90] for recent surveys). The approaches can be classified as *prescriptive* (e.g. [Han89]), where type declarations restrict the success set of the program, and *descriptive*, where types (declared as e.g. in [MO85] or inferred as in e.g. [Mis84]) describe properties of the success set of the program. (A recent paper [LR91] reconstructs the Mycroft-O'Keefe type system as a prescriptive one.) Types of the predicates of a logic program are in the focus of attention of both categories. Introduction of types is often motivated by their potential for early detection of errors and by their usefulness for program analysis and optimization. Our work has different motivations and objectives. We assume that the external functional procedures used in our logic programs are typed. We do not care whether these types have been inferred or declared by the user. We leave as the topic of future work the question how to use them for inferring types of the predicates. Thus our predicates are not typed. Our main objective is the use of the types of the functional procedures for interfacing them with our logic programs. Types provide the only source of information about the external procedures which are otherwise considered black boxes. As shown in the paper this information may often be sufficient to know that an external procedure can safely be invoked with non-ground arguments. This allows for improvement of the operational semantics of logic programs with external procedures described in [BM88]: some error denotations under S-unification can be avoided by using instead our P-unification.

Our language allows for the use of higher-order functional procedures but the syntax of terms is restricted to applicative terms and λ-abstraction is not allowed in our logic programs. Higher-order features are commonly supported by functional programming languages and can be used from logic programs by the interface based on P-unification. In this way we avoid full higher-order unification which is required for clean integration of higher-order features in logic programming, as exemplified by λ-Prolog [NM88]. However, as pointed out in [Mil90] many interesting λ-Prolog programs can be executed with a restricted kind of higher-order unification. In contrast to λ-Prolog our functional procedures are external and the only information about their behavior is given by their type signatures. This causes inherent incompleteness of P-unification, which may result in unresolved deferred disagreement pairs.

15 Conclusions

In this paper we seek to develop a systematic approach to interfacing logic programming systems to functional programming systems based on polymorphic typing. This interface coordinates these systems, but does not integrate them, in contrast to the previous work on amalgamating LP and FP languages. A key objective is to explore the possible role of polymorphic types as a basis for ensuring the safety of such an interface.

A critical issue in our approach is efficiency. In full generality the cost of dynamic typing and runtime handling of delays may be prohibitive. Static analysis of types and modes may ameliorate runtime overhead; this topic and related avenues for efficient compilation merit further study. A promising starting point lies in Bonnier's approach to static typing of logic programs with polymorphically typed external procedures [Bon92], and Boye's approach to delay analysis [Boy91] based on modes and dependency relations.[8]

References

[ACPP89] Martín Abadi, Luca Cardelli, Benjamin C. Pierce, and Gordon D. Plotkin. Dynamic typing in a statically typed language. Technical Report 47, DEC Systems

[8] The insights of Staffan Bonnier, Charles Clark, and Laurie Hannon have been very helpful in the preparation of this paper.

Research Center, June 10, 1989.

[BM87] Jonas Barklund and Hakan Millroth. Integrating complex data structures in Prolog. In *Symposium on Logic Programming*, pages 415–425, San Francisco, August 1987. IEEE Computer Society.

[BM88] Steffan Bonnier and Jan Małuszyński. Towards a clean amalgamation of logic programs with external procedures. In Robert A. Kowalski and Kenneth A. Bowen, editors, *Logic Programming: Proceedings of the Fifth International Conference and Symposium*, pages 311–326, Seattle, 1988. MIT Press.

[Bon91] Staffan Bonnier. Unification in incompletely specified theories: a case study. In A. Tarlecki, editor, *Mathematical Foundations of Computer Science 1991*, pages 84–92. Springer-Verlag, 1991. LNCS 520.

[Bon92] Staffan Bonnier. *A Formal Basis for Horn Clause Logic with External Polymorphic Functions.* PhD thesis, Linköping University, 1992. Linköping Studies in Science and Technology, Dissertation No. 276.

[Boy91] Johan Boye. S-SLD-Resolution: An operational semantics for logic programs with external procedures. In Jan Maluszynski and Martin Wirsing, editors, *Proc. PLILP'91*, pages 383–394. Springer-Verlag, 1991. LNCS 528.

[DV87] M. Dincbas and P. Van Hentenryck. Extended unification algorithms for the integration of functional programming into logic programming. *Journal of Logic Programming*, 4(3):199–227, 1987.

[Han89] Michael Hanus. Horn clause programs with polymorphic types: Semantics and resolution. In *Proc. of TAPSOFT'89*, pages 225–240, 1989. Springer LNCS 352.

[KK91] A. Kågedal and F. Kluzniak. Enriching Prolog with S-Unification. In *Proc. of Phoenix Seminar on Declarative Programming.* Springer-Verlag, 1991.

[LR91] T.K. Lakshman and U.S. Reddy. Typed Prolog: A semantic reconstruction of the Mycroft-O'Keefe type system. In *Proc. of ILPS*, pages 202–217. MIT Press, San Diego, 1991.

[Mil78] R. Milner. A theory of type polymorphism. *J. of Comp. and Sys. Sci.*, 17(3):348–375, 1978.

[Mil90] Dale Miller. A logic programming language with lambda-abstraction function variables, and simple unification. Technical Report MS-CIS 90-54, University of Pennsylvania, Philadelphia, 1990.

[Mis84] Prateek Mishra. Towards a theory of types. In *Symp. on Logic Programming*, pages 289–298, Atlantic City, 1984. IEEE.

[MO85] Alan Mycroft and Richard A. O'Keefe. A polymorphic type system for Prolog. *Artificial Intelligence*, 23(3), August 1985.

[NM88] Gopalan Nadathur and Dale A. Miller. An overview of λProlog. In Robert A. Kowalski and Kenneth A. Bowen, editors, *Logic Programming Proceedings of the Fifth International Conference and Symposium.* IEEE Computer Society, MIT Press, August 1988.

[Ogi90] Takeshi Ogi. Using types to interface functional and logic programming. MS thesis, University of Utah, May 1990.

[Pfe90] Frank Pfenning. Types in Logic Programming. Tutorial Notes, Symposium on Logic Programming, Jerusalem, June 1990.

[Red88] Uday Reddy. Notions of polymorphism for predicate logic programs. In Robert Kowalski and Kenneth Bowen, editors, *Proc. 5th Int. Conf. and Symp. on Logic Programming*, Seattle, 1988. MIT Press.

[Wad89] Phil Wadler. Theorems for free! In David MacQueen, editor, *Proc. Symposium on Functional Languages and Computer Architecture*, London, September 11-13 1989. Springer-Verlag.

Analyses of Inconsistency for Incremental Equational Logic Programming*

María Alpuente[1], Moreno Falaschi[2] and Ferdinando Manzo[2]

[1] Departamento de Sistemas Informáticos y Computación,
Universidad Politécnica de Valencia,
Camino de Vera s/n, Apdo. 22012, 46020 Valencia, Spain.

[2] Dipartimento di Informatica,
Università di Pisa,
Corso Italia 40, 56125 Pisa, Italy

Abstract. The problem of unifying pairs of terms with respect to an equational theory $\mathcal{E}$ (as well as detecting the inconsistency of a system of equations) is in general undecidable. We propose a static analysis which allows to detect inconsistent sets of equations. The method consists of building an *abstract narrower* for equational theories and executing the sets of equations to be detected for inconsistency in the approximated narrower. The accuracy of this method is enhanced by some simple loop-checking technique. We show that our method can also be actively used for pruning the search tree of an incremental equational constraint solver. Our method results to well relate and integrate with other methods in the literature.

Keywords: Abstract interpretation, Equational logic programming, term rewriting systems, universal unification.

1 Introduction

Equational Logic Programming [17,21] is a relevant extension of the logic programming paradigm where logic programs are augmented by Horn equational theories. The operational semantics of an equational logic language is some special form of equational resolution (such as SLDE-resolution [14,17,21]), which is in turn based upon equational unification [10,14,31]. Equational unification ($\mathcal{E}$-*unification* [14,17]) is the problem of unifying a pair of terms with respect to an equational theory $\mathcal{E}$. There is in general no single most general $\mathcal{E}$-*unifier* of two terms. A complete set of $\mathcal{E}$-*unifiers* of a pair of terms may even be infinite. The set of $\mathcal{E}$-*unifiers* of a pair of terms is semidecidable, even for unconditional and canonical equational theories. The inconsistency of a system of equations is also undecidable. A number of $\mathcal{E}$-*unification* procedures have been developed [10,14,17,19,22]. Conditional narrowing, e.g., has been shown to be complete for equational theories satisfying different restrictions [17,19,22,26].

* This work has been partially supported by CICYT under grant TIC-92-0793

The definition of any equational logic language must necessarily address the problem of the completeness and termination of $\mathcal{E}$-unification. In order to overcome the latter problem, lazy strategies relying on delayed unification have been defined [2,6,17]. In [6,17] only a partial unifier of the equations is computed and the unsolved equations are added as residuum to the goal clause to be solved later. In [2] unificands are reduced before they are submitted to the unification algorithm. Equations which are not ready for evaluation are postponed until they can be decided. Verified ground equations are then discarded.

Several methods to improve the termination of *$\mathcal{E}$-unification* algorithms have been reported [1,7,29]. These algorithms are guided by a graph of terms to detect and remove some loops of the search tree which do not lead to any solution. The improved algorithms are still complete but termination is only guaranteed for theories which satisfy a given condition.

The ability to detect unsatisfiability, i.e. inconsistency of a set of equations, is also very important to prune useless paths from the search tree and save a lot of unnecessary computation. The standard methods to recognize failure are based on the idea that two terms headed by different irreducible symbols can never be equal [2,13]. [12] introduces another decidable notion to detect unsatisfiability which is based on an analysis of joinability of the outermost function symbols of each equation.

In this paper we define an algorithm for detecting statically when a set of equations is inconsistent with respect to an equational theory. The algorithm is based on the idea that rewrite rules can be abstracted and an approximated narrowing can be performed. We make use of a simple technique of loop detection to build a graph of functional dependences and improve our method. We discuss the relation of our method with a similar mechanism to detect inconsistencies defined in [12]. The algorithm can obviously be used to prune useless paths in the search tree for a given set of equations. It may as well be used for constraint languages like CLP($\mathcal{H}/\mathcal{E}$) [3] which integrates equational and logic programming as instance of the CLP scheme [21,20]. In this language equations are treated as constraints and are incrementally added to the "store" to be checked for satisfiability. This test can be very costly (not to mention termination is not guaranteed) and, as pointed out in [16], partial but efficient constraint solvers turn out to be valuable. Our algorithm always terminates and says that the set of equations is unsatisfiable or returns a (complete) set of (partial) $\mathcal{E}$-unifiers which can be effectively used to prune the search tree incrementally. The set of answers has the property that each concrete solution is an instance of one of these answers. It is conceivable a lazy procedure for CLP($\mathcal{H}/\mathcal{E}$) which does not prove the satisfiability of a set of equations E but just checks that E is not "inconsistent" by means of our algorithm and then uses the collected set of answers for pruning the search tree of the constraint solver incrementally. A final guided execution of the "full" narrower may find the concrete solutions and possibly detect the inconsistency not detected by this lazy procedure. This methodology is similar to that followed by [16]. In the framework of CLP [16] introduces a relaxation function which associates with each constraint c another constraint (that is implied by c) for which satisfiability can be easily tested. The inconsistency of the relaxed constraint implies the inconsistency of c. [16] mainly considers constraints over finite domains, the case of equational theories is not considered.

We formalize the idea of approximated narrowing as constraint solver in the framework of abstract interpretation [8,9]. The solver is specially tailored to be incremental. We prove that our analysis of inconsistency always terminates and it is correct, i.e. if it terminates with failure the constraint is inconsistent. Clearly, since the problem is undecidable the analysis may sometimes fail to detect unsatisfiability. Interesting to note we abstract term rewriting systems and obtain a form of compiled simplified "program" which always terminates and in which we can execute a compiled query efficiently. Differently to the standard approach to abstract interpretation [25] where all the work of abstraction is left to the procedure which computes the abstract most general unifier of two terms.

The structure of the paper is as follows. After introducing some preliminary notions in Section 2 we present the concrete basic narrowing in Section 3. Then Section 4 recalls the concept of abstract transition system [8]. In Section 5 we define an algorithm to detect inconsistent equations. Section 6 shows an incremental equational analyzer which incrementally builts the search tree as long as new constraints are added. In Section 7 we present some optimizations for our analyzer and make a comparison with some related work [2,12,13,17] which is shown to well integrate with our method. In the full paper [4] we give the proofs of the theorems which have been omitted for reason of space and present the (extension and) formalization in our framework of other methods in the literature like [2,12,13].

2 Preliminaries

By Σ, Π and V (possibly subscripted) we denote denumerable (disjoint) collections of function symbols, predicate symbols and variable symbols with their signatures. $\tau(\Sigma \cup V)$ and $\tau(\Sigma)$ denote the sets of terms and ground terms built on Σ and V, respectively. $\tau(\Sigma)$ is usually called the Herbrand Universe ($\mathcal{H}$) over Σ. A (Π, Σ)-atom is an element $p(t_1, \ldots, t_n)$ where $p \in \Pi$ is n-ary and $t_i \in \tau(\Sigma \cup V)$, $i = 1, \ldots, n$. A (Π_C, Σ)-constraint is a (possibly empty) finite set of (Π_C, Σ)-atoms, with $\Pi_C \subseteq \Pi$. Throughout the paper we assume $\Pi_C = \{=\}$.

Let us briefly recall some basic notions about equations, conditional rewrite systems and universal unification. For full definitions refer to [23]. Terms are viewed as labelled trees in the usual way. Occurrences are represented by sequences, possibly empty, of naturals. $O(t)$ denotes the set of occurrences of a term t. $\bar{O}(t)$ denotes the set of nonvariable occurrences of a term t. t/u is the subterm at the occurrence u of t. $t[u \leftarrow r]$ is the term t with the subterm at the occurrence u replaced with r. $t[u]$ denotes the label in t at occurrence $u \in \bar{O}(t)$. These notions extend to equations in a natural way.

A Σ-equation s=t is a pair of terms $s, t \in \tau(\Sigma \cup V)$. The equational representation of a substitution $\theta = \{x_1/t_1, \ldots, x_n/t_n\}$ is the set of equations, $\widehat{\theta} = \{x_1 = t_1, \ldots, x_n = t_n\}$. The empty substitution is denoted by ϵ. $Var(e)$ is the set of distinct variables occurring in the expression e.

The notions of application, composition and relative generality are defined in the usual way [5]. We consider the usual preorder on substitutions $\leq$: $\theta \leq \sigma$ iff $\exists \gamma .\, \sigma = \theta\gamma$. We denote by $mgu(c)$ the most general unifier of a set of equations c.

A Horn equational Σ-theory $\mathcal{E}$ consists of a finite set of equational Horn clauses of the form $e \leftarrow e_1, \ldots, e_n$, $n \geq 0$, where e, e_i, $i = 1, \ldots, n$, are Σ-equations. Σ-equations and Σ-theories will often be called equations and theories, respectively.

A Term Rewriting System (TRS for short) is a pair $(\Sigma, \mathcal{R})$ where $\mathcal{R}$ is a finite set of (conditional) reduction (or rewrite) rule schemes of the form $(\lambda \rightarrow \rho \Leftarrow \tilde{e})$, $\lambda, \rho \in \tau(\Sigma \cup V)$, $\lambda \notin V$ and $Var(\rho) \subseteq Var(\lambda)$. The condition $\tilde{e}$ is a possibly empty conjuction $e_1, \ldots, e_n$, $n \geq 0$, of equations. When the condition in every rule in $\mathcal{R}$ is empty the system is said to be unconditional. Otherwise it is said to be conditional. Often we will write just $\mathcal{R}$ instead of $(\Sigma, \mathcal{R})$.

A Horn equational theory $\mathcal{E}$ which satisfies the conditions above can be viewed as a term rewriting system $\mathcal{R}$ where the rules are the heads (implicitely oriented from left to right) and the conditions are the respective bodies. We implicitely assume that these conditions hold for all theories we consider in this paper. The equational theory $\mathcal{E}$ is said to be canonical if the binary one-step rewriting relation $\rightarrow_{\mathcal{R}}$ defined by $\mathcal{R}$ is noetherian and confluent [23].

For TRS $\mathcal{R}$ and a syntactic object s, $r \ll_s \mathcal{R}$ denotes that r is a renaming of a rule in $\mathcal{R}$ such that $vars(r) \cap vars(s) = \emptyset$ (standardized apart). The instantiated left-hand side $\lambda\sigma$ of a reduction rule $(\lambda \rightarrow \rho \Leftarrow \tilde{e})$ is called a *redex* (*red*ucible *ex*pression) with *contractum* $\rho\sigma$.

Two terms s and t are *joinable*, $s \downarrow_{\mathcal{R}} t$ if there exists a term w such that $s \rightarrow^*_{\mathcal{R}} w$ and $t \rightarrow^*_{\mathcal{R}} w$. When no confusion can arise, we omit the subscript $\mathcal{R}$.

Given two terms s and t, we say that they are *$\mathcal{E}$-unifiable* iff $\exists$ a substitution σ such that $\mathcal{E} \models s\sigma = t\sigma$. The substitution σ is called an *$\mathcal{E}$-unifier* of s and t.

For an equational theory, the notion of most general unifier generalizes to complete sets of minimal (incomparable) *$\mathcal{E}$-unifiers*. Minimal complete sets of *$\mathcal{E}$-unifiers* do not always exist. A *$\mathcal{E}$-unification* procedure is complete if it generates a complete set of *$\mathcal{E}$-unifiers* for all input equations. *$\mathcal{E}$-unification* is semidecidable.

Let $\mathcal{E}$ be a Horn equational theory. A function symbol $f \in \Sigma$ is called irreducible iff there is no clause $(l = r \leftarrow e_1, e_2, \ldots, e_n) \in \mathcal{E}$ such that f occurs as the outermost function symbol in l or l is a variable; otherwise it is a defined function symbol. In theories where the above distinction is made, the signature Σ is partitioned as $\Sigma = C \biguplus F$, where C is the set of irreducible function symbols and F is the set of definite function symbols.

3 Basic Narrowing

Given a conditional TRS $\mathcal{R}$, an equational goal clause g conditionally narrows into a goal clause g' if there exists an equation $e \in g$, $u \in \bar{O}(e)$, a (standardized apart) variant $(\lambda \rightarrow \rho \Leftarrow \tilde{e}) \ll_g \mathcal{R}$ and a substitution σ such that $\sigma = mgu(e/u, \lambda)$ and $g' = (g \sim \{e\} \cup \{e[u \leftarrow \rho]\} \cup \tilde{e})\sigma$

Basic (conditional) narrowing is a restricted form of (conditional) narrowing where only terms at *basic* occurrences are considered to be narrowed. Informally, a basic occurrence is a nonvariable occurrence of the original goal or one that was introduced into the goal by the nonvariable part of the right hand side or the condition of a rule applied in a preceeding narrowing step. The idea behind the concept of *basic* is to avoid narrowing steps on subterms that are introduced by instantiation. Basic Conditional Narrowing (BCN) is a complete $\mathcal{E}$-*unification* algorithm for level-canonical Horn equational theories [26].

Let $\mathcal{R}$ be a level-canonical TRS. We formulate a Basic Conditional Narrowing calculus according to the partition of equational (sub-)goals into a *skeleton* and an *environment* part, as in [17]. The *skeleton* part is a multiset of equations g (the empty multiset is denoted *true*) and the *environment* part is a substitution θ. Due to this representation, the basic redexes in $g\theta$ are all in g whereas the non-basic redexes are all in θ. To solve g, the algorithm starts with the subgoal $\langle g, \epsilon\rangle$ and tries to derive subgoals until a terminal goal $\langle true, \phi\rangle$ is reached. Each substitution ϕ in a terminal goal is an $\mathcal{E}$-*unifier* of g. By abuse of notation, it is often called solution. The calculus BCN is defined by the following two rules:

BCN unification rule:

$$\frac{\sigma = mgu(g\theta)}{\langle g, \theta\rangle \quad \rightarrow_{BCN} \quad \langle true, \theta\sigma\rangle}$$

BCN narrowing rule:

$$\frac{e \in g \ \wedge \ u \in \bar{O}(e) \ \wedge \ (\lambda \rightarrow \rho \Leftarrow \tilde{e}) \ll_{\langle g,\theta\rangle} \mathcal{R} \ \wedge \ \sigma = mgu((e/u)\theta, \lambda)}{\langle g, \theta\rangle \quad \rightarrow_{BCN} \quad \langle (g \sim \{e\}) \cup \{e[u \leftarrow \rho]\} \cup \tilde{e}, \theta\sigma\rangle}$$

In the following section we recall a general method to approximate transition systems [8]. We then show how to use this method for approximating term rewriting systems and narrowers.

4 Approximating Transition Systems

4.1 Abstract Interpretation

Abstract interpretation [9] formalizes the concept of a semantic based analysis of programs. The computations are performed with respect to descriptions (i.e. approximations) of data rather than the data itself. Thus, an analysis is a computation performed with respect to a *non-standard interpretation* of data and operators in the program. The *standard interpretation* gives the usual behavior of the program.

We follow the approach of [8]. Thus we define the "approximation relation" in terms of a "concretization function" which maps elements in a non-standard domain to those elements in the standard domain which they describe. The approximation relation is then lifted from the "base" domains to relations and tuples.

Definition 1. [8] A *description* $Desc = \langle D, \gamma, E\rangle$ consists of a *description domain* (a poset) D, a *data domain* (a poset) E, and a monotonic *concretization function* $\gamma : D \rightarrow \wp E$. When $E = Eqn$, $E = Sub$ or $E = State$ the description is called a *equation description*, a *substitution description* or a *state description* respectively.

We say that d γ-approximates e, written $d \propto_\gamma e$, iff $e \in \gamma(d)$. The approximation relation is lifted to relations and cross products as follows:

- Let $\langle D_1, \gamma_1, E_1\rangle$ and $\langle D_2, \gamma_2, E_2\rangle$ be descriptions, and $F \subseteq D_1 \times D_2$ and $F' \subseteq E_1 \times E_2$ be relations. Then $F \propto F'$ iff $\forall d \in D_1. \forall e \in E_1.\ d \propto_{\gamma_1} e \wedge \langle e, e'\rangle \in F' \Rightarrow \exists \langle d, d'\rangle \in F \wedge d' \propto_{\gamma_2} e'$.
- Let $\langle D_1, \gamma_1, E_1\rangle$ and $\langle D_2, \gamma_2, E_2\rangle$ be descriptions, and $(d_1, d_2) : D_1 \times D_2$ and $(e_1, e_2) : E_1 \times E_2$. Then $(d_1, d_2) \propto (e_1, e_2)$ iff $d_1 \propto_{\gamma_1} e_1 \wedge d_2 \propto_{\gamma_2} e_2$.

When clear from the context we say that d approximates e and write $d \propto e$. By an abuse of notation we will sometimes let *Desc* denote both the description and the description domain.

Given an equation and a substitution description, we can define the concept of "abstract transition system". We have chosen the approach of abstracting transition systems, similarly to [8], for two reasons. The method results to be quite simple and general since standard formal operational semantics for narrowing are often given in terms of transition systems. Besides, the abstract algorithm requires the collection of all intermediate states for proving the inconsistency of a set of equations.

4.2 Abstract Transition System

Given an equation description and a substitution description, an associated state description is constructed as follows:

Definition 2. Let $Eqn_{\mathcal{A}}$ be an equation description, $Sub_{\mathcal{A}}$ a substitution description. Define the *abstract state domain*, $State_{\mathcal{A}}$ induced by $Eqn_{\mathcal{A}}$ and $Sub_{\mathcal{A}}$, to be $State_{\mathcal{A}} = \{\langle g, \kappa\rangle : g \in Eqn^n_{\mathcal{A}}, n \geq 0, \kappa \in Sub_{\mathcal{A}}\}$. Associated with $State_{\mathcal{A}}$ are extraction functions $sub : State_{\mathcal{A}} \rightarrow Sub_{\mathcal{A}}$ and $eqn : State_{\mathcal{A}} \rightarrow \{g : g \in Eqn^n_{\mathcal{A}}, n \geq 0\}$ defined by $eqn(t) = g$, if $t = \langle g, \kappa\rangle$ and $sub(t) = \kappa$, if $t = \langle g, \kappa\rangle$

Abstract states describe states which are equivalent modulo variable renaming. This is because the operational behavior preserves this type of equivalence, and so it is not necessary to distinguish between such states. Furthermore, to ensure termination of analyses we do not distinguish between abstract states which describe the same set of states.

Definition 3. [8]induced state description
Let $State_{\mathcal{A}}$ be an abstract state domain induced from an equation description $Eqn_{\mathcal{A}}$ and a substitution description $Sub_{\mathcal{A}}$. Let $t \in State_{\mathcal{A}}$, $s \in State$ and ρ be a renaming. Then $t \propto_\rho s$ iff:

1. $sub(t) \propto \rho(sub(s))$; and
2. $eqn(t) \propto \rho(eqn(s))$.

We write $t \propto s$ iff $\exists \rho. t \propto_\rho s$. Define $\gamma : State_{\mathcal{A}} \rightarrow \wp\, State$ by $\gamma(t) = \{s \mid t \propto s\}$, and let $\simeq$ be the equivalence relation on elements of $State_{\mathcal{A}}$ induced by γ; that is $t_1 \simeq t_2$ iff $\gamma(t_1) = \gamma(t_2)$. We let $State_{\mathcal{A}}/\simeq$ denote the equivalence classes of $State_{\mathcal{A}}$ and *rep* be a function returning a representative of an equivalence class. The induced state description for $Eqn_{\mathcal{A}}$ and $Sub_{\mathcal{A}}$ is $\langle State_{\mathcal{A}}/\simeq, \gamma \circ rep, State\rangle$.

Let us now define an abstract transition system. The definition is parametric with respect to a generic TRS and the set of abstract states.

Definition 4. abstract transition system
Let T be a TRS, s a state and $State_{\mathcal{A}}$ an induced state description. Let $\mathcal{N}_{\mathcal{A}}^{T} \subseteq State_{\mathcal{A}} \times State_{\mathcal{A}}$ be a relation (depending on T). An abstract transition system for $\mathcal{N}_{\mathcal{A}}^{T}$, s and $State_{\mathcal{A}}$ is a transition graph $\mathcal{G}$ with elements of $State_{\mathcal{A}}$ as nodes which is defined in terms of the abstract reduction relation $\mathcal{N}_{\mathcal{A}}^{T}$. The graph $\mathcal{G}$ must satisfy:

- The source of $\mathcal{G}$ is an approximation of s.
- Let $\hat{t} \in State_{\mathcal{A}}/\simeq$ denote the equivalence class of $t \in State_{\mathcal{A}}$. There is an edge from $\hat{t}$ to $\hat{t}'$ iff there is an abstract reduction from t to t' such that $\langle t, t'\rangle \in \mathcal{N}_{\mathcal{A}}^{T}$.

5 Analysis of inconsistency

In this section we present an abstract algorithm to prove that a set of equations is inconsistent with respect to a (level-canonical) Horn equational theory. We define the descriptions for terms, equations and term rewriting systems. We need first some technical definitions. Notice that we do not distinguish between equivalence classes and representatives. Moreover, by abuse of notation, we denote in the same way a preorder and the corresponding ordering induced on the equivalence classes of the equivalence relation associated with the preorder.

By $\mathcal{T} = (\tau(\Sigma \cup V), \leq)$ we denote the standard domain of (equivalence classes of) terms ordered by the standard partial order $\leq$ induced by the preorder on terms given by the relation of being "more general". Let $\perp$ be an irreducible symbol, where $\perp \notin \Sigma$. Roughly speaking, the special symbol $\perp$ introduced in the abstract domains represents any concrete term. Let $\mathcal{T}^{\perp} = (\tau(\Sigma \cup V \cup \{\perp\}), \preceq)$ be the domain of (equivalence classes of) terms over the signature augmented by $\perp$, where the partial order $\preceq$ extends $\leq$ as follows: (a) $\forall t \in \mathcal{T}^{\perp}. \perp \preceq t$ and $t \preceq t$ and (b) $\forall s_1, \ldots, s_n, s_1', \ldots, s_n' \in \mathcal{T}^{\perp}, \forall f/n \in \Sigma.\ s_1 \preceq s_1' \wedge \ldots \wedge s_n \preceq s_n' \Rightarrow f(s_1, \ldots, s_n) \preceq f(s_1', \ldots, s_n')$ and (c) $\forall t, t' \in \mathcal{T}^{\perp}. t \preceq t'$ if $t \leq t'$.
This order can be extended to equations: $s = s' \preceq t = t'$ iff $s \preceq t$ and $s' \preceq t'$ and to sets of equations S, S': $S \preceq S'$ iff $\forall e' \in S'. \exists e \in S$ such that $e \preceq e'$. $S \sqsubseteq S'$ iff $(S \preceq S')$ and $(S' \preceq S)$ implies $S \subseteq S'$. We can extend in the same way the order $\leq$ in $\mathcal{T} = (\tau(\Sigma \cup V), \leq)$ to sets of equations.

Define $[t] = t'$, where the n-tuple of occurrences of $\perp$ in t is replaced by an n-tuple of distinct new variables in t'. This definition extends naturally to equations, sets of equations and substitutions.

Definition 5. upward
Let $(X, \leq)$ be a poset and let $Y \subseteq X$. Define $upw(Y) = \{x \in X \mid \exists y \in Y . y \leq x\}$.

Definition 6. Let $\mathcal{T} = (\tau(\Sigma \cup V), \leq)$ and $\mathcal{T}^{\perp} = (\tau(\Sigma \cup V \cup \{\perp\}), \preceq)$. The *term description* is $\langle \mathcal{T}^{\perp}, \gamma, \mathcal{T}\rangle$ where $\gamma : \mathcal{T}^{\perp} \rightarrow \wp\mathcal{T}$ is defined by: $\gamma(t) = upw(\{[t]\})$

Definition 7. Let $E^{\perp}$ be the set of finite sets of equations over $\tau(\Sigma \cup V \cup \{\perp\})$ and E the set of sets of equations over $\tau(\Sigma \cup V)$. The *equation description* is $\langle (E^{\perp}, \sqsubseteq), \gamma, (E, \sqsubseteq) \rangle$, where $\gamma : E^{\perp} \to \wp E$ is defined by: $\gamma(e) = \{S \mid upw([e]) \subseteq S\}$.

Definition 8. Let $Sub^{\perp}$ be the set of substitutions over $\tau(\Sigma \cup V \cup \{\perp\})$ and Sub be the set of substitutions over $\tau(\Sigma \cup V)$. The *substitution description* is $\langle (Sub^{\perp}, \preceq), \gamma, (Sub, \leq) \rangle$, where $\gamma : Sub^{\perp} \to \wp\, Sub$ is defined by: $\gamma(\theta) = upw(\{[\theta]\})$.

The behaviour of the symbol $\perp$ resembles that of an "anonymous" variable in Prolog. Thus the unification algorithm has to be modified accordingly. When an equation of the form $\perp = t$ is found it is considered implicitely satisfied and thus immediately discarded.

Definition 9. abstract most general unifier ($mgu_{\mathcal{A}}$)
Let E be a finite set of equations over $\tau(\Sigma \cup V \cup \{\perp\})$. Then $mgu_{\mathcal{A}}(E)$ is the idempotent substitution whose equational representation is computed by the following modification of the unification algorithm [24]. We use the notation $t \not\equiv t'$ to denote that t and t' are not syntactically identical. Start from the set E. Choose nondeterministically from E an equation of a form below and perform the associated action.

1) $f(s_1, \ldots, s_n) = f(t_1, \ldots, t_n)$: replace by the equations $s_1 = t_1, \ldots, s_n = t_n$;
2) $f(s_1, \ldots, s_n) = g(t_1, \ldots, t_n)$ where $f \not\equiv g$: halt with failure;
3) $x = x$, or $t = \perp$, or $\perp = t$: discard the equation;
4) $t = x$ where t is not a variable: replace by the equation $x = t$;
5) $x = t$ where $x \not\equiv t$, $t \not\equiv \perp$ and x has another occurrence in the set of equations: if x appears in t then halt with failure, otherwise apply the substitution $\{x/t\}$ to all the other equations.

The graph $\mathcal{G}_{\mathcal{R}}$ of functional dependencies is constructed to perform a simple loop check over the function symbols involved in the term rewriting system $\mathcal{R}$ as formalized by the following definition.

Definition 10. Graph of functional dependencies
Let $(C \uplus F, \mathcal{R})$ be a term rewriting system. The following transformation defines the directed graph $\mathcal{G}_{\mathcal{R}}$ of functional dependencies induced by $\mathcal{R}$. To build $\mathcal{G}_{\mathcal{R}}$, the algorithm starts with $\langle \mathcal{R}, \emptyset \rangle$ and applies the inference rule as long as the terminal configuration $\langle \emptyset, \mathcal{G}_{\mathcal{R}} \rangle$ has not been reached. The symbol $\cup$ stands for set union.

$$\frac{r = (f(t_1, \ldots, t_n) \to \rho \Leftarrow \tilde{e}) \in \mathcal{R}}{\begin{array}{lll} \langle \mathcal{R}, \mathcal{G}_{\mathcal{R}} \rangle & \longmapsto & \langle \mathcal{R} \sim \{r\}, \mathcal{G}_{\mathcal{R}} \cup \{f \stackrel{dep}{\to} h \mid u \in \bar{O}(\rho) \ \wedge \ \rho[u] = h \in F\} \cup \\ & & \{f \stackrel{dep}{\to} h \mid e \in \tilde{e} \ \wedge \ u \in \bar{O}(e) \ \wedge \ e[u] = h \in F\} \rangle \end{array}}$$

Roughly speaking, for each rule $(f(t_1, \ldots, t_n) \to \rho \Leftarrow \tilde{e})$ in $\mathcal{R}$ and for each function symbol h occurring in ρ or $\tilde{e}$ we add an arc $f \stackrel{dep}{\to} h$ to $\mathcal{G}_{\mathcal{R}}$. Note that we do not need to consider rules where ρ is a variable since we are only concerned with basic derivations. The termination of the calculus is ensured since the number of reduction rules in $\mathcal{R}$ is finite and a rule is dropped at each step. Clearly if there is an infinite basic narrowing derivation for a given goal then there is a cycle in the graph of functional dependencies. This graph can be useful to prove the termination of basic narrowing derivations for simple cases as stated by the following:

Proposition 11. *Let $\mathcal{R}$ be a term rewriting system, $\mathcal{G}_{\mathcal{R}}$ be the corresponding graph of functional dependencies and g_0 be an equational goal. Let $\mathcal{D}$ be the set of defined function symbols occurring in g_0. If the paths in $\mathcal{G}_{\mathcal{R}}$ starting from each $f \in \mathcal{D}$ contain no cycles then any basic narrowing derivation issuing from g_0 terminates.*

The following definition represents the core of our algorithm. A term rewriting system is abstracted by simplifying the right hand side and the body of each rule. This definition is given inductively on the structure of terms. Irreducible symbols are kept, while terms whose main functor is a defined symbol are drastically simplified by replacing them by $\perp$. Notice that we do not perform this approximation when for the function symbol f which we consider there is no path with a cycle in $\mathcal{G}_{\mathcal{R}}$. In this case we can be more accurate and retain the subterm originating in f.

Definition 12. *Abstract term rewriting system*
Let $(C \biguplus F, \mathcal{R})$ be a TRS. Let $\mathcal{G}_{\mathcal{R}}$ be the corresponding graph of functional dependencies. We define the abstraction of $\mathcal{R}$ as follows:
$\mathcal{R}_{\mathcal{A}} = \{\lambda \to cx(\rho) \Leftarrow cx(\tilde{e}) \mid \lambda \to \rho \Leftarrow \tilde{e} \in \mathcal{R}\}$, where cx is defined inductively

$$cx(s) = \begin{cases} X & \text{if } s = X \in V \\ c(cx(t_1), \ldots, cx(t_m)) & \text{if } s = c(t_1, \ldots, t_m), c \in C \\ f(cx(t_1), \ldots, cx(t_k)) & \text{if } s = f(t_1, \ldots, t_k), f \in F \text{ and the paths in } \mathcal{G}_{\mathcal{R}} \\ & \text{starting from } f \text{ contain no cycles} \\ cx(l) = cx(r) & \text{if } s = (l = r) \\ cx(e_1), \ldots, cx(e_n) & \text{if } s = e_1, \ldots, e_n \\ \perp & \text{otherwise} \end{cases}$$

Notice that a corresponding concretization function for abstract term rewriting systems can be easily defined.

Definition 13. Let $\mathcal{R}_{\mathcal{A}}$ be an abstract *TRS*, and $State_{\mathcal{A}}^{\perp}$ the abstract state associated to the equation description $E^{\perp}$ and the substitution description $Sub^{\perp}$. *Abstract (basic) narrowing* is a relation $\mathcal{B}^{\mathcal{R}_{\mathcal{A}}} \subseteq State_{\mathcal{A}}^{\perp} \times State_{\mathcal{A}}^{\perp}$, defined as follows.
Let $t, t' \in State_{\mathcal{A}}$. $\langle t, t' \rangle \in \mathcal{B}^{\mathcal{R}_{\mathcal{A}}}$ (we also say that there is an abstract (basic) narrowing reduction from t to t') iff:

1) $\exists \lambda \to \rho \Leftarrow \tilde{e} \ll_t \mathcal{R}_{\mathcal{A}}$ such that $t = \langle g, \kappa \rangle$ and $t' = \langle g', \kappa' \rangle$ where $g' = (g \sim \{e\}) \cup \{e[u \leftarrow \rho]\} \cup \tilde{e}$, $e \in g$, $u \in \bar{O}(e)$, $\sigma = mgu_{\mathcal{A}}((e/u)\kappa, \lambda)$ and $\kappa' = \kappa\sigma$; or,
2) $t = \langle g, \kappa \rangle$, $\sigma = mgu_{\mathcal{A}}(g\kappa)$ and $t' = \langle true, \kappa\sigma \rangle$; or,

3) $t = t'$ and ($\perp$ occurs in t or $eqn(t) = true$).

The following lemma essentially states that abstract (basic) narrowing reduction approximates (basic) narrowing reduction.

Lemma 14. *Let $t \propto_\rho s$. If there is a (basic) narrowing reduction from s to s', then there is an abstract (basic) narrowing reduction from t to some t' such that $t' \propto s'$.*

We give an example that illustrates the definitions above.

Example 1. Let us consider the following TRS $\mathcal{R}$ and its abstraction $\mathcal{R}_\mathcal{A}$.

$$\begin{array}{llll}
\mathcal{R} = \{ & & \mathcal{R}_\mathcal{A} = \{ & \\
r1) & h(0) \rightarrow s(0). & r1_\mathcal{A}) & h(0) \rightarrow s(0). \\
r2) & h(f(X)) \rightarrow X \Leftarrow g(X) = X. & r2_\mathcal{A}) & h(f(X)) \rightarrow X \Leftarrow g(X) = X. \\
r3) & f(0) \rightarrow c(0). & r3_\mathcal{A}) & f(0) \rightarrow c(0). \\
r4) & f(c(X)) \rightarrow c(f(X)). & r4_\mathcal{A}) & f(c(X)) \rightarrow c(\perp). \\
r5) & g(0) \rightarrow 0.\} & r5_\mathcal{A}) & g(0) \rightarrow 0.\}
\end{array}$$

There is an abstract narrowing reduction that approximates each basic narrowing reduction from a given goal. The correspondence is most clearly seen in a diagram. Figures 1 and 2 depict the search tree of basic narrowing and abstract basic narrowing for the (unsatisfiable) equation $h(f(Z)) = s(0)$.

Let us notice that the unsatisfiability of the equation cannot be determined either using methods based on loop-checking [7], unification rules [6,13], operator joinability [12] or eager normalization [2,12]. The following proposition and theorem show that our analysis terminates and is correct.

Proposition 15. *(Termination of the analysis) Let $\mathcal{E}$ be a level-canonical Horn equational theory. Let $\mathcal{R}_\mathcal{A}$ be the associated abstract TRS. The abstract transition system for $\mathcal{B}^{\mathcal{R}_\mathcal{A}}$, state s and $State_\mathcal{A}^\perp$ has a finite number of nodes.*

Definition 16. An abstract transition system for $\mathcal{B}^{\mathcal{R}_\mathcal{A}}$, s and $State_\mathcal{A}^\perp$ is *finitely failed* iff it does not contain leaves of the form $\langle true, \kappa \rangle$.

Theorem 17. *(Correctness of the analysis) Let $\mathcal{E}$ be a level-canonical Horn equational theory and $\mathcal{R}_\mathcal{A}$ the associated abstract TRS. If the abstract transition system for $\mathcal{B}^{\mathcal{R}_\mathcal{A}}$, state s and $State_\mathcal{A}^\perp$ is finitely failed then s is inconsistent in $\mathcal{E}$.*

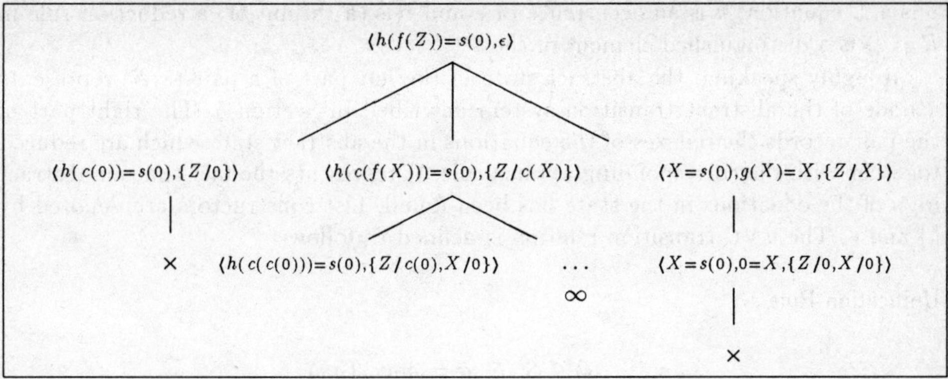

Fig. 1. *Basic Narrowing*

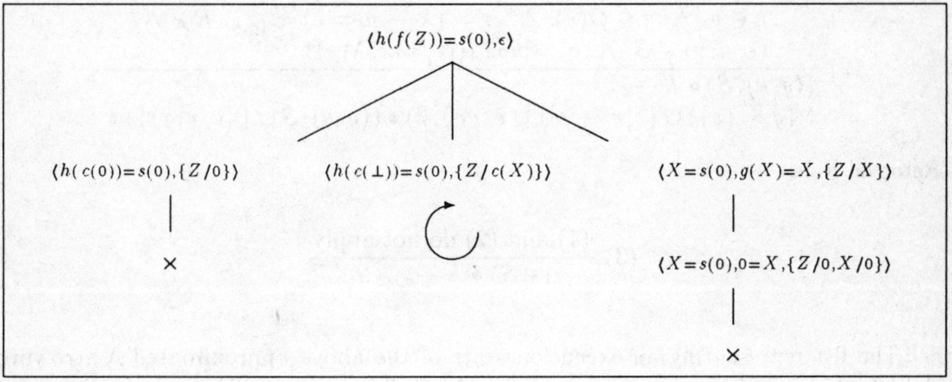

Fig. 2. *Abstract Basic Narrowing*

6 Incremental Equational Analyzer

In this section we describe an incremental algorithm for analizing the unsatisfiability of sets of equations. In this context, incrementality [3,15] means that the problem resulting from adding a new set of equations (constraints) does not require the repetition of all the work already done. The kernel of this algorithm is a calculus which is based on abstract narrowing reduction as described in Section 5. The calculus explores with a depth-first strategy the nodes of the abstract transition system for the accumulated constraint which is incrementally built as long as new equations are added. Since the number of nodes to be visited is finite, a depth-first strategy is fair, i.e. every node of the abstract transition system will be eventually visited.

Definition 18. *approximated $\mathcal{N}$arrowing $\mathcal{C}$alculus ($a\mathcal{NC}$)*
Let $(\Sigma, \mathcal{R}_{\mathcal{A}})$ be an abstract TRS. An $a\mathcal{NC}$-state is a list of pairs $(s, \mathcal{S})$, where $s = \langle g, \kappa \rangle \in State_{\mathcal{A}}^{\perp}$ and $\mathcal{S}$ is a set. The elements of the set are triples $\langle e, u, r \rangle$, where

e is a Σ-equation, u is an occurrence of e and r is (a variant of) a reduction rule in $\mathcal{R}_{\mathcal{A}}$. $\langle\rangle$ is a distinguished element of the set.

Roughly speaking, the abstract state in the left part of a pair $(s, \mathcal{S})$ represents a node of the abstract transition system described in Section 5. The right part of the pair records the redexes of the equations in the abstract state which are reduced together with the corresponding applied rule. $\langle\rangle$ represents the fact that an abstract mgu of the equations in the state has been found. List constructors are denoted by $[\,]$ and $\bullet$. The $a\mathcal{NC}$ transition relation is defined as follows:

Unification Rule

$$(1)\ \frac{\langle\rangle \notin \mathcal{S} \ \wedge\ \sigma = mgu_{\mathcal{A}}(g\kappa)}{(\langle g, \kappa\rangle, \mathcal{S}) \bullet L \rightarrow_{a\mathcal{NC}} (\langle true, \kappa\sigma\rangle, \emptyset) \bullet (\langle g, \kappa\rangle, \mathcal{S} \cup \{\langle\rangle\}) \bullet L}$$

Narrowing Rule

$$(2)\ \frac{\begin{array}{l} e \in g \ \wedge\ u \in \bar{O}(e) \ \wedge\ r = (\lambda \rightarrow \rho \Leftarrow \tilde{e}) \ll_{\langle g,\kappa\rangle} \mathcal{R}_{\mathcal{A}} \ \wedge \\ \langle e, u, r\rangle \notin \mathcal{S} \ \wedge\ \sigma = mgu_{\mathcal{A}}((e/u)\kappa, \lambda) \end{array}}{\begin{array}{l} (\langle g, \kappa\rangle, \mathcal{S}) \bullet L \rightarrow_{a\mathcal{NC}} \\ (\langle (g \sim \{e\}) \cup \{e[u \leftarrow \rho]\} \cup \tilde{e}, \kappa\sigma\rangle, \emptyset) \bullet (\langle g, \kappa\rangle, \mathcal{S} \cup \{\langle e, u, r\rangle\}) \bullet L \end{array}}$$

Removal Rule

$$(3)\ \frac{\text{(1) and (2) do not apply}}{(s, \mathcal{S}) \bullet L \rightarrow_{a\mathcal{NC}} L}$$

The list representing an execution state of the above $a$pproximated $\mathcal{N}$arrowing $\mathcal{C}$alculus is treated as a stack to emulate a depth-first strategy. These derivations can be represented as a finite tree. Leaves which have been already visited are simply removed. The calculus can be slightly improved if *failed* nodes are recognized and removed from the list. A *failed* node is any node $\langle g, \kappa\rangle$ such that one equation $e \in g$ is not (abstractly) unifiable and no abstract narrowing step can be applied to any of the occurrences in e. Our analysis can only detect inconsistency if no leaf of the tree has the form $\langle true, \kappa\rangle$.

Definition 19. *Behaviour of the $a\mathcal{NC}$ calculus*
Define the (set valued) function $\mathcal{N}_a$: $L' \in \mathcal{N}_a(L)$ if $L \rightarrow^*_{a\mathcal{NC}} (\langle true, \kappa\rangle, \emptyset) \bullet L'$

This list L' in the definition above can be thought of as the representation of the execution state of the $a\mathcal{NC}$ calculus when the analysis fails to detect the unsatisfiability of c. We can now define an *incremental Equational Analyzer (iEA)*:

Definition 20. An *iEA*-state is a pair $\langle c, L\rangle$, where c is a constraint and L is an $a\mathcal{NC}$-state. The empty *iEA*-state is $\langle\emptyset, [\,]\rangle$.

Definition 21. (*iEA transition relation* $\overset{\tilde{c}}{\hookrightarrow}_{iEA}$)

$$\frac{L' \in \mathcal{N}_a(merge(L, \tilde{c}))}{\langle c, L\rangle \quad \overset{\tilde{c}}{\hookrightarrow}_{iEA} \quad \langle c \cup \tilde{c}, L'\rangle}$$

where

$$merge([\,], \tilde{c}) = [(\langle \tilde{c}, \epsilon\rangle, \emptyset)] \; merge([(\langle g, \epsilon\rangle, \emptyset)], \tilde{c}) = [(\langle g \cup \tilde{c}, \epsilon\rangle, \emptyset)]$$
$$merge((\langle g, \kappa\rangle, \mathcal{S}) \bullet L, \tilde{c}) = (\langle g \cup \tilde{c}, \kappa\rangle, \mathcal{S} \sim \{\langle\rangle\}) \bullet merge(L, \tilde{c}) \quad \text{if } L \neq [\,].$$

Theorem 22. (correctness of *iEA*) *Let c be a constraint and L be a list representing the execution state of the calculus a$\mathcal{NC}$ when the (incremental) analysis of inconsistency fails to detect the unsatisfiability of c. Let $\tilde{c}$ be a new constraint. If a transition $\langle c, L\rangle \overset{\tilde{c}}{\hookrightarrow}_{iEA} \langle c \cup \tilde{c}, L'\rangle$ cannot be proven then the constraint $c \cup \tilde{c}$ is unsatisfiable.*

7 Optimizations and related work

In equational logic programming different strategies to detect equational unsatisfiability have been proposed. The distinction between defined and irreducible function symbols has been proven to be extremely useful for recognizing failures. Two terms whose outermost functors are different irreducible symbols can never be equal (*failure rule*); if two terms have the same irreducible outermost symbol then they are equal iff their respective arguments are equal (*decomposition rule*). If the conditional TRS is decreasing [22,26] then term rewriting can be combined with the rules of failure and decomposition to simplify equations.

The analysis of unsatisfiability based on the notion of *operator joinability* [12] can be formalized in the framework presented in this paper [4]. Terms (and TRS) are abstracted by the (outermost) function symbols. Let us call $\mathcal{R}_\mathcal{A}$ the corresponding abstract TRS. An equation like $f(\tilde{t}) = h(\tilde{s})$ is unsatisfiable if f and h are not joinable in $\mathcal{R}_\mathcal{A}$, i.e. $f \not\downarrow_{\mathcal{R}_\mathcal{A}} h$. It is clear that this method is able to recognize unsatisfiability of equations in cases where the syntactic transformations above cannot and vice versa. Let us consider a simple example. Let $\mathcal{R} = \{f(0) \rightarrow 0, f(c(X)) \rightarrow c(f(X)), h(g(Y)) \rightarrow h(Y)\}$ be a TRS and let us consider the unsatisfiable equation $f(Z) = h(W)$. Both f and h are defined, hence no syntactic transformation can be applied. However, the analysis of joinability do recognize the inconsistency as f and h are not joinable in $\mathcal{R}_\mathcal{A} = \{f \rightarrow 0, f \rightarrow c, h \rightarrow h\}$. Note that the inconsistency of the equation $c(c(z)) = c(g(w))$ can only be detected by applying both the failure and decomposition rules. Orthogonally, the inconsistency of the equation $f(0) = c(0)$ can be proven by applying term rewriting first. Note that the test of joinability cannot decide the unsatisfiability of this equation. All these methods are thus complementary since they do not subsume one another.

The analysis of inconsistency based on approximated narrowing seems to be particularly suitable for CLP($\mathcal{H}/\mathcal{E}$) [3] since constraints monotonically grow and the analysis can be made incrementally as long as a new set of equations is added. Example 1 shows that our method is able to recognize inconsistencies in cases where the other methods would fail. The contrary is also true in general. Hence, standard methods to detect unsatisfiability should be preferably combined with our analysis. All the above mentioned methods always terminate and reduce the search tree without affecting the completeness of the calculus.

Informally, let $\rightarrow_{Simpl}$ be the set of rules consisting of term rewriting, trivial equations removal, variable substitution, term decomposition and failure rule [17]. The set $\rightarrow_{Simpl}$ of transformations should be applied as much as possible both for eager detection of inconsistency and for incrementally simplifying the constraints. Since unification rules compute a (partial) $\mathcal{E}$-unifier θ of a constraint, incrementality is enhanced if constraints are represented as pairs $(\widehat{\theta}, c)$. An iEA-state is now a pair $\langle(\widehat{\theta}, c), L\rangle$, where θ is a substitution, c is a constraint and L is an $a\mathcal{NC}$-state. An empty iEA-state is $\langle(\emptyset, \emptyset), []\rangle$. The transition relation $\overset{\tilde{c}}{\hookrightarrow}_{iEA}$ can be reformulated as follows.

$$\frac{(\widehat{\theta}, c \cup \tilde{c}\theta) \rightarrow_{Simpl} (\widehat{\theta'}, c') \ \wedge \ L' \in \mathcal{N}_a(merge(L, \tilde{c} \cup \widehat{\theta'}))}{\langle(\widehat{\theta}, c), L\rangle \ \overset{\tilde{c}}{\hookrightarrow}_{iEA} \ \langle(\widehat{\theta'}, c'), L'\rangle}$$

We notice that the concrete narrower can use the result computed by the abstract narrower in the way that we informally suggest. Let $\mathcal{E}$ be an equational theory and c a set of equations consistent in $\mathcal{E}$. Let $\{\sigma_1, \ldots, \sigma_k\}$ be the collection of all the abstract substitutions (answer set) in the leaves $\langle true, \sigma_j\rangle$, $j = 1, \ldots, k$ of the abstract narrowing tree for c. Then, for each $\mathcal{E}$-unifier θ of c, there exists i such that $\forall X \in Var(c)$, $X\sigma_i \preceq X\theta$. Thus if we collect the set of answers we can prune all paths which contain a substitution which is not an instance of any element in the answer set. The formal definition of this method is a current matter of research.

References

1. G. Aguzzi and M.C. Verri. On the termination of a unification procedure. In A. Bertoni, C. Böhm, and P. Miglioli, editors, *Proc. of the Third Italian Conference on Theoretical Computer Science*, pages 59–70, 1989.
2. H. Aït-Kaci, P. Lincoln, and R. Nasr. Le Fun: Logic, equations, and Functions. In *Proc. Second IEEE Symp. on Logic In Computer Science*, pages 17–23. IEEE Computer Society Press, 1987.
3. M. Alpuente and M. Falaschi. Narrowing as an Incremental Constraint Satisfaction Algorithm. In J. Maluszyński and M. Wirsing, editors, *Proc. of PLILP'91*, volume 528 of *Lecture Notes in Computer Science*, pages 111–122. Springer-Verlag, Berlin, 1991.
4. M. Alpuente, M. Falaschi, and F. Manzo. Analyses of Inconsistency for Lazy Equational CLP. Technical report, Dipartimento di Informatica, Università di Pisa, 1992.
5. K. R. Apt. Introduction to Logic Programming. In J. van Leeuwen, editor, *Handbook of Theoretical Computer Science*, volume B: Formal Models and Semantics. Elsevier, Amsterdam and The MIT Press, Cambridge, Mass., 1990.
6. H.J. Bürckert. Lazy E-unification - a method to delay alternative solutions. Technical report, Université de Nancy, France, 1987.
7. J. Chabin and P. Réty. Narrowing directed by a graph of terms. In G. Goos and J. Hartmanis, editors, *Proc. of RTA'91*, volume 488 of *Lecture Notes in Computer Science*, pages 112–123. Springer-Verlag, Berlin, 1991.
8. M. Codish, M. Falaschi, and K. Marriott. Suspension Analysis for Concurrent Logic Programs. In K. Furukawa, editor, *Proc. Eighth Int'l Conf. on Logic Programming*, pages 331– 345. The MIT Press, Cambridge, Mass., 1991.

9. P. Cousot and R. Cousot. Abstract Interpretation: A Unified Lattice Model for Static Analysis of Programs by Construction or Approximation of Fixpoints. In *Proc. Fourth ACM Symp. Principles of Programming Languages*, pages 238–252, 1977.
10. M. Dincbas and P. van Hentenryck. Extended Unification Algorithms for the Integration of Functional Programming into Logic Programming. *Journal of Logic Programming*, 4:197–227, 1987.
11. N. Dershowitz and G. Sivakumar. Solving Goals in Equational Languages. In S. Kaplan and J. Joaunnaud, editors, *Proc. First Int'l Workshop on Conditional Term Rewriting*, volume 308 of *Lecture Notes in Computer Science*, pages 45–55. Springer-Verlag, Berlin, 1987.
12. L. Fribourg. Slog: a logic programming language interpreter based on clausal superposition and rewriting. In *Proc. Second IEEE Int'l Symp. on Logic Programming*, pages 172–185. IEEE, 1985.
13. J.H. Gallier and S. Raatz. Extending SLD-resolution to equational Horn clauses using E-unification. *Journal of Logic Programming*, 6:3–43, 1989.
14. P. Van Hentenryck. Incremental Constraint Satisfaction in logic programming. In D. H. D. Warren and P. Szeredi, editors, *Proc. Seventh Int'l Conf. on Logic Programming*, pages 189–202. The MIT Press, Cambridge, Mass., 1990.
15. P. Van Hentenryck and Y. Deville. Operational Semantics of Constraint Logic Programming over Finite Domains. In J. Maluszyński and M. Wirsing, editors, *Proc. of PLILP'91*, volume 528 of *Lecture Notes in Computer Science*, pages 395–406. Springer-Verlag, Berlin, 1991.
16. S. Hölldobler. *Foundations of Equational Logic Programming*, volume 353 of *Lecture Notes in Artificial Intelligence*. Springer-Verlag, Berlin, 1989.
17. H. Hussman. Unification in conditional-equational theories. Technical report, Fakultät für Mathematik und Informatik, Universität Passau, 1986.
18. J. Jaffar and J.-L. Lassez. Constraint Logic Programming. In *Proc. Fourteenth Annual ACM Symp. on Principles of Programming Languages*, pages 111–119. ACM, 1987.
19. J. Jaffar, J.-L. Lassez, and M.J. Maher. A logic programming language scheme. In D. de Groot and G. Lindstrom, editors, *Logic Programming, Functions, Relations and Equations*, pages 441–468. Prentice Hall, Englewood Cliffs, NJ, 1986.
20. S. Kaplan. Fair conditional term rewriting systems: unification, termination and confluence. In H.-J. Kreowski, editor, *Recent Trends in Data Type Specification*, volume 116 of *Informatik-Fachberichte*, pages 136–155. Springer-Verlag, Berlin, 1986.
21. J.W. Klop. Term rewriting systems. In S. Abramsky, D. Gabbay, and T. Maibaum, editors, *Handbook of Logic in Computer Science*, I. Oxford University Press, 1991.
22. J.-L. Lassez, M. J. Maher, and K. Marriott. Unification Revisited. In J. Minker, editor, *Foundations of Deductive Databases and Logic Programming*, pages 587–625. Morgan Kaufmann, Los Altos, Ca., 1988.
23. K. Marriott and H. Søndergaard. Semantics-based Dataflow Analysis of Logic Programs. In G. Ritter, editor, *Information Processing 89*. North-Holland, 1989.
24. A. Middeldorp and E. Hamoen. Counterexamples to completeness results for basic narrowing. To appear in Proc. Third Int'l Conf. on Algebraic and Logic Programming, 1992.
25. P. Réty, C. Kirchner, H. Kirchner, and P. Lescanne. NARROWER: A new algorithm for unification and its applications to logic programming. In *Proc. of RTA'85*, volume 202 of *Lecture Notes in Computer Science*, pages 141–157. Springer-Verlag, Berlin, 1985.
26. J.H. Siekmann. Unification Theory. *Journal of Symbolic Computation*, 7:207–274, 1989.

I/O Trees and Interactive Lazy Functional Programming

Samuel A. Rebelsky*

Department of Computer Science, University of Chicago
Chicago IL 60637, USA

Abstract. Computer programs interact with users, and programmers must describe this interaction when they write programs. Programming languages usually allow programmers to describe this interaction with primitive *read* and *write* functions. The situation is not so simple in the realm of lazy functional languages. Because read and write are not referentially transparent, programmers cannot use them in lazy functional languages.
This paper shows that lazy programs can interact with users by generating *I/O Trees*—structures that describe possible interactions between user and program. I/O trees encode a program's dynamic behavior in static structure. This paper presents the fundamental structure and interpretation of I/O trees, describes extensions to I/O trees, and suggests ways programmers can write programs that generate I/O trees.

1 Introduction

In the early days of computing, users only interacted with computer programs in a batch-oriented manner—users presented a large batch of input to a program and sometime later received a large batch of output. Fortunately, those days are gone. Most modern programs interact more directly with users, writing prompts and reading responses. Interactive programs have many key properties, including: *integration*, which dovetails data development and program execution, and *incremental computation*, which relieves users from waiting a long time for responses [Not84]. Features of programming languages can simplify or complicate development of interactive programs.

Lazy functional languages (LFLs)—such as Haskell [HPW+92], Gofer [Jon91], or Equational Logic Programming (ELP) [O'D85]—provide many features that make it easier to develop interactive programs. These languages usually allow one to integrate not only program execution and data development, but also program development. In addition, LFLs encourage small functions, which support incremental computation.

LFLs have many other beneficial features. LFLs make it easy to describe and manipulate dynamic data structures. Laziness allows programmers to create potentially-infinite recursive data structures. Finally, the core of most LFLs is small, which means that implementations can be small and highly optimized.

These advantages are not without potential drawbacks, or what may appear to be drawbacks for a programmer used to a more imperative style of programming. In

* Partially supported by NSF grant #CCR 9016905

particular, a lazy language requires that functions be *referentially transparent*—given the same arguments, a function should always return the same value. Unfortunately, the functions one often associates with interactive programs—such as printing a prompt or reading a response—are not referentially transparent. We certainly would not want *read* to return the same value each time it's called!

This is not to say that lazy functional programs neither read nor write data—programs acts as maps from terms to terms, and therefore *inspect* expressions (input terms) and *generate* corresponding values (output terms). But this I/O is implicit, not explicit. In particular, it does not allow programmers to directly read input and write output. (Throughout this paper, *inspect* and *generate* indicate the implicit term input and output operations a program executes in a *dialogue* with the user or front-end, and *read* and *write* indicate the steps of an *interaction* with the user.)

Modern functional languages provide various solutions to the problem of providing explicit read/write I/O. One can treat programs as maps from lazy streams of characters (the input) to lazy streams of characters (the output) [Tho90]. Similarly, one can treat each program as a map from a stream of responses to a stream of requests [HS88]. That is, a program generates a request (such as *read*) as part of the output stream and inspects the result from a corresponding position on the input stream. Functional languages may also provide explicit I/O with continuation-based I/O transactions [HS88]. These transactions take continuations as arguments, and call the appropriate continuation on the value returned by the I/O operation or on a description of the reason the operation failed. These solutions require modifying or extending the core of the language. In the stream-based solutions, programs are no longer simply maps from terms to terms. In the continuation-based solution, one has to add new functions to the core of the language or simulate these functions.

This paper suggests another method for providing explicit read and write operations for LFLs. Unlike previous solutions, this solution does not require lazy functional programs to do anything but inspect input terms and generate output terms. In particular, programs that wish to interact with users will generate *I/O trees*, expressions that describe possible user-computer interactions.

1.1 Equational Logic Programming

This paper will examine I/O trees in the context of Equational Logic Programming (ELP) [O'D85]. ELP is a declarative programming language in which every program is a set of equations. An ELP program transforms an input question (a term) into an output answer (the term's normal form) that can be proven correct with the equations given. Current implementations [Str88, SS90, Bai92], treat the equations as directed rewrite rules and compile them to code that lazily matches patterns and rewrites intermediate terms. These implementations restrict the program rules in such a way that they guarantee unique answers and produce programs that match patterns in time linear in the size of the pattern matched.

ELP has many useful characteristics. In particular, ELP provides simple and straightforward logical criteria that can be used to judge the correctness of program transformations and other modifications [O'D85, She92]. A primary requirement is that a modified program must maintain lazy behavior—that is, a program should only inspect as much of a term as is necessary to produce its normal form.

1.2 Term-based I/O

Terms (expressions) form the natural input and output for ELP programs. Yet ELP programs operate within a Unix[1] environment in which programs use pipes to communicate, so ELP programs must coerce terms into streams for input and output. This coercion can defeat any internal lazy behavior, primarily when independent ELP programs communicate. In particular, any attempt to represent a term with linear text requires a predefined traversal order of the term, and it is unlikely that this traversal order will precisely mimic the inspection order a program uses.

Consider the following two ELP function definitions, *intlist*, which generates an infinite list of integers, and *firstn*, which returns the first *n* elements of a list:

intlist(N) = [N:intlist(N+1)]
firstn([],N) = []
firstn([H:T],N) = if(N=0, [], [H:firstn(T,N−1)])

If the two definitions are compiled into one compound program, the compound program can compute a result given *firstn(intlist(5),7)* as input. On the other hand, if each definition is compiled into a separate program, and the two are joined with pipes (and terms are converted to terms using the standard preorder, depth-first, left-right traversal), then the pair of programs will run forever on input *firstn(intlist(5),7)*. The *intlist* program will pass the outer *firstn* symbol, but will evaluate the inner *intlist(5)* expression. The *firstn* program must then inspect the infinite list *intlist* produces before it can inspect the second argument to *firstn*, even though it only needs a small portion of that list.

To handle problems like this we have recently extended ELP's run-time library with *tours* [Reb91], a system of "pipes for terms." Using *tours*, every ELP program acts as a lazy term-transformer that converts input terms into output terms according to the rules in the program, as in Fig. 1. If one compiles *firstn* and *intlist* separately and joins them with a tour connection, then the joined programs and the compound program will exhibit the same behavior on the input given above.

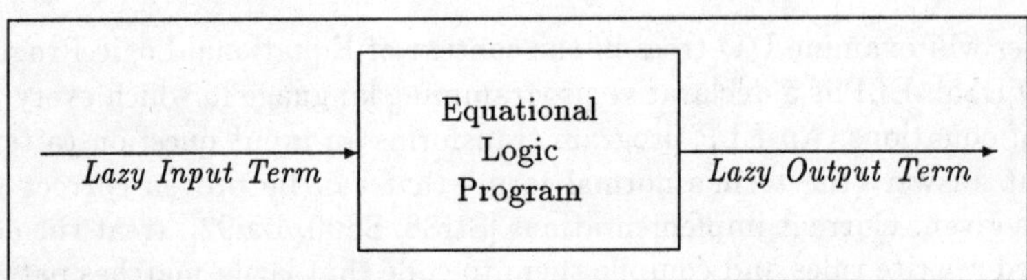

Fig. 1. Connecting ELP programs

Users interact with ELP programs by connecting front ends that govern the action of the program. Front ends provide an input term for the first in a series of

[1] Unix is a registered trademark of AT&T Bell Laboratories.

ELP programs and read an output from the last in the series, as in Fig. 2. A typical front end might read user input, convert it to term form, send the term to an ELP program, read the output term from an ELP program, and print the output term, as in:

function term-based-front-end
  read the characters the user types
  parse the characters into a term
  lazily provide that term to an ELP program
  read and print the output term from the ELP program
end term-based-front-end

The front end need not force the user to define the complete input term before providing it to the ELP program; a graphical interface might allow the user to simultaneously build an input term and explore an output term [RS90]. There need not be a direct relationship between input from the user and the input to the ELP program, or output to the user and output from the ELP program; for example, the front end can use portions of the user input to determine how to traverse the term that the ELP program generates.

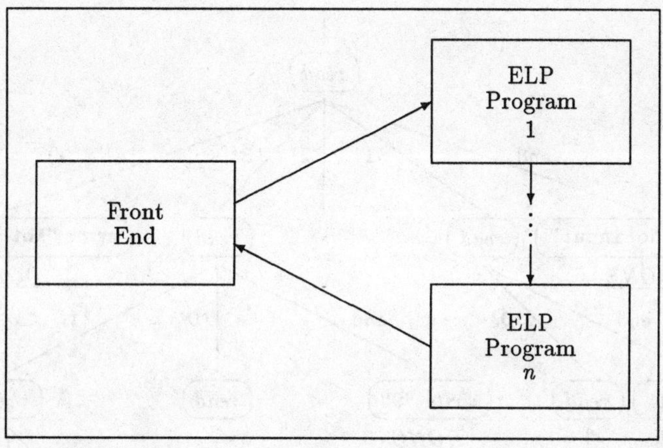

Fig. 2. Front ends for ELP programs

2 I/O Trees

Many features of ELP hinder explicit I/O: ELP does not have a predictable evaluation order (ELP is lazy, but this says nothing about the order in which needed arguments are evaluated); ELP does not allow operations with side effects; and ELP provides no facilities for referring to input, output, or any form of environment. We do not wish to make extensive modifications to ELP. It is still possible to provide explicit read and write operations for ELP. As in Haskell's I/O system [HPW+92, HS88], ELP programs can specify and sequence I/O operations through the output term they generate.

ELP programs can obtain explicit I/O through *I/O trees*, which represent the possible dialogues between user and program as a potentially infinite tree of operations. That is, an ELP program that explicitly reads and writes data will inspect a standard input term— such as *main*—and produce an I/O tree with nodes that specify the operations to execute. An interactive session between user and program specifies a single traversal of the program's I/O tree. The simplest I/O trees are built from:

- *write* nodes, which specify data to output, as well as the sequence of operations that follow;
- *read* nodes, which give a choice of further actions that depend on the next character read; and
- *DONE* leaves, which mark the end of the dialogue.

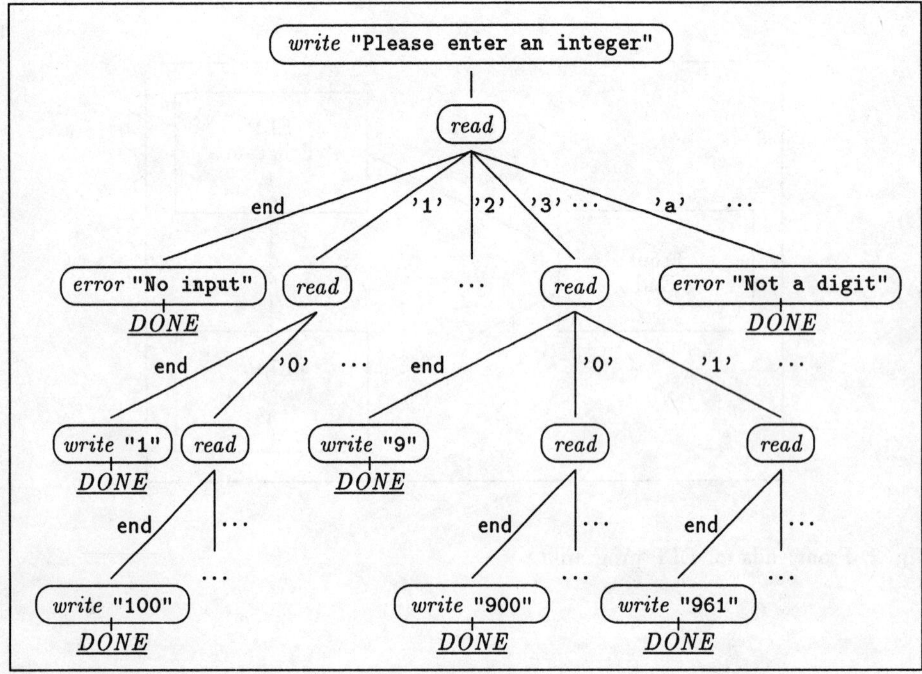

Fig. 3. A sample I/O tree

Consider a program that prints a prompt, reads in an integer, and prints the square of the integer that the program read. Such a program might generate the I/O tree in Fig. 3. Inspecting this tree, one sees that the program prints `Please enter` an `integer`, reads digits until it reaches the special symbol end, writes a result, and stops. Suppose a user typed 30. Following the branch labeled `'3'`, the branch labeled `'0'`, and the branch labeled end, the final value printed will be `900`.

Notkin claims that interactive programs should allow users to change input [Not84]. I/O trees make this easy; if the user changes part of the input, the front end need only back up and follow a different path in the tree. In the example above, if the user changes the '0' to '1' simply back up and follow the branch labeled `'1'` to determine the result is `961`.

One normally thinks of I/O as a two-way dialogue between a real or virtual front-end and a program—input from the user is part of the term a program inspects, and output to the user is part of the term a program generates. For example, in Haskell a output to a user is included as `AppendChan` terms in the stream of requests a program generates, and user input is part of the stream of responses the program inspects. With I/O trees, this is no longer the case—user input and output are *both* part of the term the program generates. I/O trees encode dynamic behavior (the sequence of reads and writes) into static structure. The front end reproduces dynamic behavior from this structure. Although I/O trees may be infinite, they are generated lazily, and only a finite portion is inspected during a single dialogue.

To run an I/O tree program, one attaches a front end. This front-end provides the appropriate input the program can use to generate the I/O tree, and then uses the user's input to determine traversal of the tree, as in the example above. Such a front end might look something like the following:

```
function iotree-front-end
    lazily provide term main and get term t
    while inspect-symbol(t) is not DONE
        switch inspect-symbol(t)
            Read     read a character c the user types
                     t := nthchild(t, ord(c))
            Write    print-term(nthchild(t,1))
                     t := nthchild(t, 1)
            default  print "Error in term: "
                     print-term(t)
end iotree-front-end
```

We have not changed the operation or meaning of the ELP program; we have changed the way the front end uses the term the program generates. Given an ELP program that reads and writes data using I/O trees, one can attach an I/O tree front-end to obtain the I/O behavior the programmer specified. One can also attach a standard term to term front-end to debug portions of the program or to examine an overview of the I/O tree.

3 Practical Considerations

The discussion of I/O trees in Sect. 2 ignores many practical issues, including how one writes I/O trees; how I/O trees provide for more general operations, such as writing to a file or checking the status of an input channel; and how programmers, compilers, and front ends deal with the large nodes I/O trees require. Section 3.1

shows how one might write programs that generate I/O trees and Sect. 4 provides a small interactive I/O trees program. Section 3.2 presents some basic extensions to I/O trees. Section 3.3 discusses some problems with the *read* node and suggests possible solutions.

3.1 Writing I/O Tree Programs

Let us now look at how one might write programs that use I/O trees. Clearly, one cannot simply list all possible sequences of actions, so an I/O tree program attempts to provide a finite description for an interaction that consists of a potentially infinite sequence of reads and writes. One way to generate I/O trees is with continuation-based operations that build the appropriate portion of an I/O tree for reading a certain type of object, such as a word or an integer, and then call the continuation on that object. One such function is *readIntegerC*, which takes two arguments—a success function that maps integers to I/O trees and an error function that maps strings to I/O trees—and generates enough of the I/O tree to read an integer. The following program uses *readIntegerC* to generate the tree in Fig. 3.

```
main() = write("Please Enter an integer",
               readIntegerC(λI.printIntFunc(square,I,DONE,
                                            error("Program failed",DONE)),
                            λE.error(E,DONE)));

printIntFunc(Func, Val,Rest,Error) = write(int2string(Func(Val)), Rest)
          where Val is an integer;
printIntFunc(Func,error,Rest,Error) = Error;
```

Without the definition of *readIntegerC*, it may be unclear how this program produces an I/O tree. Recall that *readIntegerC* is responsible for building enough structure to read an integer, such as the *read* nodes in Fig. 3. Appendix A.1 contains a definition for *readIntegerC* that produces the expected tree. Given arguments *ICont* and *ECont*, *readIntegerC* produces the tree in Fig. 4. When these continuations are evaluated, the tree is further expanded, as in Fig. 3.

3.2 Extending I/O Trees

The definition of I/O trees from Sect. 2 is clearly too primitive. As defined, I/O trees only allow input from one predefined channel and output to another predefined channel. One often needs to work both with files and with multiple channels. Extended I/O trees therefore provide equivalents to the lazy message stream requests given in the Haskell report [HPW+92], although the I/O tree versions do not differentiate between files and channels. In addition, I/O trees require explicit *open* and *close* nodes. Finally, because the extended operations can fail (e.g., the program may write to an unopen file), many of the new nodes must also include *error* edges to be followed if the operation fails.

3.3 Representing Large Nodes

ELP requires one to list all the arguments to a function, so programmers may find it hard to use symbols with large arity, such as *read*. The utility functions *basicRead*,

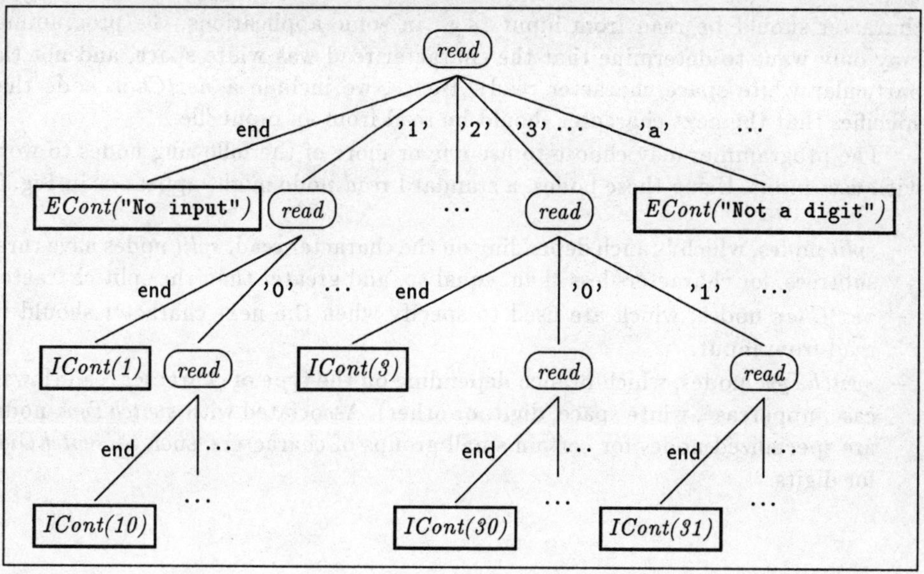

Fig. 4. The tree produced by *readIntegerC*

changeSubTrees, and *setSubTree*—given in Appendix A.1—make it somewhat easier to generate *read* nodes. *basicRead* creates a read tree with identical subtrees. *changeSubTrees* and *setSubTree* allow the programmer to change subtrees.

These functions do not solve all representational problems. First, it is neither convenient nor efficient to build a term and then change many of its subterms. Second, the current compiler and optimizers behave badly with nodes of large arity. In fact, the current register optimizer cannot deal with as many term registers as *read* requires. Third, *suspensions* of unused structure are costly to store.

One can solve this problem by simulating each *read* node with a binary tree. The front-end follows a series of branches in this simulation tree when it reads a character, rather than the single branch it followed with the standard *read* node. Such a tree requires about log(*arity*) extra traversal steps, but no extra inspection (since the shape of the simulation is predefined, the front-end can determine the path to take without checking for the types of nodes it traverses).

In practice, a programmer often only wants a function to operate on certain characters (e.g., *readIntegerC* from Sect. 3.1 and Appendix A.1 is primarily concerned with digits). Since we already simulate *read* nodes with a decision tree, we allow programmers to explicitly represent the decisions made using *switch* nodes. This solution has some advantages: there is less inspection if the programmer only uses a few characters, the programmer can easily work with sets of characters, and the tree may require fewer suspensions. This solution also has some disadvantages. In particular, the front end must now inspect every node when traversing the tree (since the shape of the simulation is no longer predefined).

Once we allow *switch* nodes, it becomes necessary to specify when the next character should be read from input (e.g., in some applications, the programmer may only want to determine that the character read was white space, and not the particular white space character read). Hence, we include a *nextChar* node that specifies that the next character should be read from an input file.

The programmer may choose to use one or more of the following nodes to work with user input. Using these nodes, a standard *read* node might appear as in Fig. 5.

- *split* nodes, which branch depending on the character read. *split* nodes have three subtrees, for characters less than, equal to, and greater than the split character.
- *nextChar* nodes, which are used to specify when the next character should be read from input.
- *switchType* nodes, which branch depending on the type of character read (lowercase, uppercase, white space, digit, or other). Associated with *switchType* nodes are specialized nodes for certain small groups of characters, such as *switchDigit* for digits.

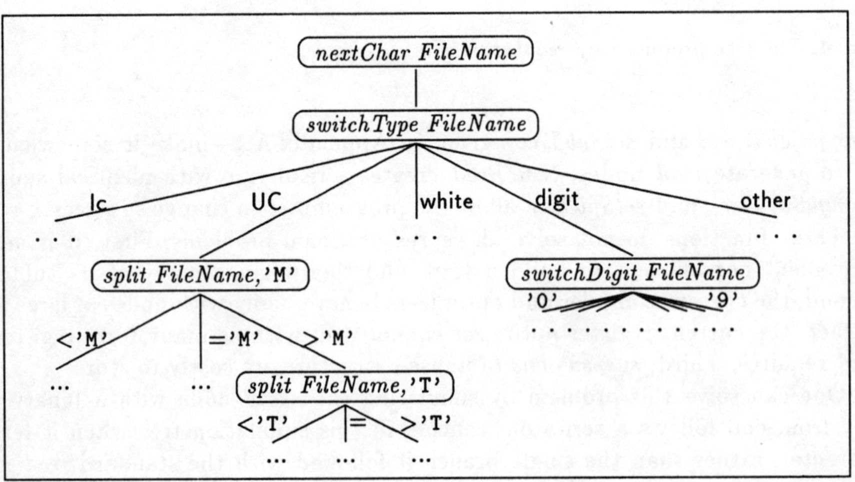

Fig. 5. Simulating a *read* node

Utility Functions for Simulated Nodes. Programmers can access simulated *read* nodes indirectly, with *basicRead* and *setSubTree*, or directly, with the nodes given in the previous section. Direct access to these operations makes it easier to write many functions. Using these operations, the *readDigitsC* procedure used by *readIntegerC* can now immediately generate errors on nondigits without having to build the full decision tree to determine the precise letter typed. This new version of *readDigitsC* appears in Appendix A.2.

We have also found that *splitRange*— a function that takes a lower and upper bound on a character to read, and a continuation to call on that character—makes it easier to build many trees. *splitRange* is defined and used in Appendix A.2.

4 An Example: The Animals Game

Consider the animals game, a simple program that traverses and modifies decision trees. Using ELP and I/O trees, one can separate the animal trees programs into two portions: tree manipulation and user interaction. Tree manipulation can be defined without reference to user interaction, and the user interaction can be specified by using the manipulation functions with functions that generate an I/O tree.

4.1 Manipulating the Animals Tree

Because the program will continually traverse and modify decision trees, each decision tree is represented as a pair containing the portion of the tree not yet traversed, and the portion already traversed. Internal nodes in the main tree are questions, and leaves are animals. Nodes in the saved tree are represented by *savedNo* and *savedYes*, which describe the portion of the tree saved.

The function *basicTree* produces a basic decision tree.

```
basicTree() = pair(question("Does it fly?", animal("Duck"), animal("Squirrel")),
                   nullTree);
```

The function *traverse* steps down one level in the tree according to a user response.

```
traverse(pair(question(Q,YesTree,NoTree),Saved), Answer) =
   if(isYes(Answer),pair(YesTree,savedNo(Q,NoTree,Saved)),
   if(isNo(Answer),pair(NoTree,savedYes(Q,YesTree,Saved)),
     pair(question(Q,YesTree,NoTree,Saved)) ));
```

The function *rebuildTree* rebuilds a traversed tree.

```
rebuildTree(pair(Restored,nullTree)) = pair(Restored,nullTree);
rebuildTree(pair(YesTree, savedNo(Q,NoTree,Saved))) =
   rebuildTree(pair(question(Q,YesTree,NoTree), Saved));
rebuildTree(pair(NoTree, savedYes(Q,YesTree,Saved))) =
   rebuildTree(pair(question(Q,YesTree,NoTree), Saved));
```

The function *newTree* creates a new tree.

```
newTree(Ani,Saved,NewAni,Q,Resp) =
   if(isYes(Resp), question(Q,animal(Ani),animal(NewAni)),
                   question(Q,animal(NewAni),animal(Ani)));
```

4.2 An Interface to the Animals Game

Given these basic functions for manipulating decision trees, one can write an interface for the animals game as follows. First, print a prompt and call *startGame* on the basic tree to start the game.

```
main() = write*(stdout, "Welcome to the animals game.\n",
            startGame(basicTree()));
```

To start a game, print an introductory prompt, and call *playGame* to play the game. To restart a game, first check if the user wants to stop. If not, rebuild the tree and continue.

```
startGame(Tree) =
   write*(stdout, "Think of an animal, and I'll try to guess it.\n",
   playGame(Tree));

restartGame(Tree) =
   write*(stdout, "Play again?",
   readWordC*(stdin, λA.
     if(isYes(A),
        startGame(rebuildTree(Tree)),
        write*(stdout,"Thanks for playing",DONE))));
```

To play one step in the game, check whether the current node is an internal question or an animal leaf. If it's a question, ask the question and follow the appropriate branch. If it's a leaf, guess the animal at the leaf, get a user response, and either restart or build a new subtree.

```
playGame(T@pair(question(Q,Y,N),Saved)) =
   write*(stdout,Q,
   readWordC*(stdin,λA.
   playGame(traverse(T,A))));
playGame(T@pair(animal(Ani),Saved)) =
   write*(stdout, "Is it"++article(Ani)++Ani,
   readWordC*(stdin,λA.
     if(isYes(A),
        write*(stdout,"I won!\n", restartGame(T)),
        write*(stdout,"I lost.\n", handleLoss(Ani,Saved)))));
```

If the program fails to guess the animal, read in the name of the new animal and a question to use in building the new tree. Using this information, build the new subtree and restart.

```
handleLoss(Ani,Saved) =
   write*(stdout, "What animal were you thinking of?",
   readWordC*(stdin, λNewAni.
   write*(stdout, "What question separates"++Ani++"and"++NewAni++"?",
   readLineC*(stdin, λNewQ.
   write*(stdout, "The answer for"++NewAni++"is?",
   readWordC*(stdin, λAns.
   restartGame(rebuildTree(newTree(Ani,Saved,NewAni,NewQ,Ans))) ))))));
```

If the program encounters any type of error, stop the game by building a tree with the *error* and *DONE* constructors.

write(OutFile,Text,Next) = write(OutFile,Text,Next,errFun);*
readWordC(InFile,LCont) = readWordC(InFile,LCont,errFun);*
readLineC(InFile,LCont) = readLineC(InFile,LCont,errFun);*
errFun(E) = error(E,error(`"Quitting animals.\n"`*,DONE));*

5 Related Work

As mentioned in Sect. 1, there are many ways to provide explicit read/write I/O for lazy functional languages. Two major methods of providing read/write I/O for LFLs are continuation-based I/O and stream-based I/O [HS88].

In the continuation-based solution, the language provides certain predefined transactions (I/O operations) that take continuations to call when the operation fails or succeeds. For example, to call function `foo` on the contents of a file named `name`, one would write:

```
readFile name (\msg -> (printError msg))
              (\contents -> (foo contents))
```

The basic operations used for generating I/O trees, such as *readIntegerC*, are similar to transactions in that they take continuations as arguments and apply continuations to the result of an I/O operation. The I/O tree generators differ from transactions in two primary ways. First, the generators are external to the language definition, and do not have to perform I/O. They do not implement I/O but generate a structure the front end uses. This separation allows us to keep the core of the language small. It also allows one to add new I/O tree generators or constructors without modifying the core of the language (to add a new constructor, simply modify the front end). Second, the I/O tree generators operate on smaller objects. In Haskell, the read transactions return a complete lazy stream, which means the programmer must keep track of the stream throughout the program. It is often more convenient to work with words, numbers, and similar sized objects. Smaller generators allow the program of Sect. 4 to call *readWordC* to get the user's responses without explicitly passing an environment, while other solutions require functions to pass and split the input stream.

There are two views of stream-based functional I/O. In one, a program is treated as a lazy map from an input stream to an output stream [Tho90]. The other view, used in Haskell, is that programs produce a stream of I/O requests (e.g. "read this file," "write this file") and read a stream of responses (e.g. "you read this lazy stream of characters," "the write succeeded"). Naïve use of either may lead to programs that print a few prompts before reading any input, or that read input before printing the appropriate prompt. [Dwe88] describes many problems one may encounter using stream I/O and suggests a programming style that avoids them.

I/O trees are also similar to stream-based I/O. As with Haskell's request streams, I/O trees specify I/O operations by producing a structure that describes the operations that need to be done. Unlike Haskell's request streams, I/O trees do not require the programmer to manipulate both the response and request streams (Haskell programs may need to carry around the remainder of the response stream as well as all input streams derived from the response stream). I/O trees are also more restrictive in the ways in which programmers can refer to I/O operations, but these restrictions lead to clearer sequencing.

6 Conclusion

When a programming language lacks a feature, one can add the feature by changing the language to allow new operations. Instead of modifying ELP to allow for read/write operations, we kept a firm stand on ELP's description and behavior, yet were able to provide read and write operations by developing a simple interface programs can use to describe interaction between ELP programs and users.

There are many advantages to this I/O tree solution. I/O trees provide an abstract description of the behavior of a program. One can easily use that description to interact with the user. I/O trees can also be analyzed without reference to a general environment, such as the response list that programs that use Haskell's streams need to manipulate and pass. Finally, we found it easy to write interactive programs by writing programs that produce I/O trees.

Acknowledgements

Thanks to Stephen Bailey, Michael J. O'Donnell, and David Sherman for their comments on I/O trees and various drafts of this paper.

References

[Bai92] Stephen W. Bailey. *Ielp User Guide.* University of Chicago, February 1992. Part of the ielp distribution. Available via anonymous ftp from cs.uchicago.edu.

[Dwe88] Andrew Dwelly. Synchronizing the I/O behavior of functional programs with feedback. *Information Processing Letters*, 28:45–51, 1988.

[HPW+92] Paul Hudak (editor), Simon Peyton Jones (editor), Phil Wadler (editor), Brian Boutel, Jon Fairbairn, Joseph Fasel, María M. Guzmán, Kevin Hammond, John Hughes, Thomas Johnsson, Dick Keiburtz, Rishiyur Nikhil, Will Partain, and John Peterson. Report on the programming language Haskell, a non-strict, purely functional language, version 1.2. *ACM SIGPLAN Notices*, 27(5), May 1992.

[HS88] Paul Hudak and Raman S. Sundaresh. On the expressiveness of purely functional I/O systems. Technical Report YALEU/DCS/RR665, Yale University, December 1988.

[Jon91] Mark P. Jones. *An Introduction to Gofer*, 1991. Available via anonymous ftp.

[Not84] David Notkin. *Interactive Structure Oriented Computing.* PhD thesis, Carnegie-Mellon University, 1984.

[O'D85] Michael J. O'Donnell. *Equational Logic As a Programming Language.* The MIT Press, Cambridge, MA, 1985.

[Reb91] Samuel A. Rebelsky. An introduction to Tours, a protocol for demand-driven communication of terms. Technical Report CS91-28, University of Chicago Department of Computer Science, November 1991.

[RS90] Samuel A. Rebelsky and David J. Sherman. Developing an interactive interface for equational logic programs. Technical Report 90-05, University of Chicago Department of Computer Science, February 1990.

[SS90] Linda Sellie and David J. Sherman. Preliminary notes on version 4.1 of the equational compiler. Technical Report 90-013, University of Chicago Department of Computer Science, 1990.

[She92] David J. Sherman. EM code semantics, analysis, and optimization. Technical Report Rapport 92-04, Greco de Programmation du CNRS, 1992.

[Str88] Robert I. Strandh. *Compiling Equational Programs into Efficient Machine Code.* PhD thesis, Johns Hopkins University, Baltimore, Maryland, 1988.

[Tho90] Simon Thompson. Interactive functional programs, a method and a formal semantics. In David A. Turner, editor, *Research Topics in Functional Programming.* Addison-Wesley, 1990.

A I/O Tree Manipulation and Generation

The discussion in Sects. 2, 3, and 5 suggests that I/O trees can be created with generation functions, such as *readIntegerC*, *basicRead*, and *setSubTree*. Section A.1 contains code for some basic I/O generators. Section A.2 contains code for the extended I/O generators that use filenames and include error functions.

A.1 A Continuation-based I/O Tree Generator

readIntegerC takes two arguments, a success function that maps integers to I/O trees and an error function that maps strings to I/O trees, and builds a portion of an I/O tree that reads an integer. *readIntegerC* calls many helper functions, both directly and indirectly. *readDigitsC* reads a list of digit characters (`'0'` through `'9'`). *convertDigits* converts a list of characters into a list of integers. *convertDigit* converts a single digit to the corresponding integer. *buildInt* converts a list of integers into a single integer. *basicRead* creates a generic *read* node with identical children. Finally *setSubTree* modifies the subtrees of a tree created by *basicRead.* These functions are all defined using the basic I/O trees of Sect. 2.

```
readIntegerC(ICont,ECont) =
   readDigitsC(λL.ICont(buildInt(convertDigits(L))),ECont);

readDigitsC(LCont,ECont) =
   changeSubTrees(basicRead(ECont("Not a character")),
                  [ change(' ',LCont([])),
                    change('0', readDigitsC(λL.LCont([0:L]))),
                    change('1', readDigitsC(λL.LCont([1:L]))),
                       ⋮
                    change('9', readDigitsC(λL.LCont([9:L]))) ]);
convertDigits([]) = [];
convertDigits([Ch:Chars]) = [convertDigit(Ch):convertDigits(Chars)];

convertDigit(Ch) = ord(Ch) - ord('0');

buildInt([]) = error; buildInt(error) = error; buildInt([X;error]) = error;
buildInt([X]) = X;
buildInt([X:[Y:Z]]) = buildInt([10*X+Y:Z]) where X,Y,Z are integers;

basicRead(Tree) = read(Tree, Tree, ..., Tree);

changeSubTrees(Tree,[]) = Tree;
changeSubTrees(Tree, [change(Char,NewTree) : Changes]) =
   changeSubTrees(setSubTree(Tree,Char,NewTree), Changes);
```

```
setSubTree(read(T0,T1,...,T255),'\0',NewTree) = read(NewTree,T1,...,T255);
setSubTree(read(T0,T1,...,T255),'\1',NewTree) = read(T0,NewTree,...,T255);
  .
  .
  .
setSubTree(read(T0,T1,...,T255),'\255',NewTree) = read(T0,T1,...,NewTree);
```

A.2 Extended Versions of the I/O Tree Generators

As mentioned in Sect. 3.2, both the nodes that in I/O trees and the functions that generate I/O trees should be more extensive. In particular, they should allow for multiple types of input. Each of *readDigitsC*, *readWordC*, and *readCharC* reads a type of object from an input file, and calls a continuation on the object read or on a failure description.

In Sect. A.1, the continuation-based functions were built from *basicRead* and *setSubTree*. Using the extended model of I/O trees, they can be defined somewhat more directly, although many use the utility function *splitRange*.

```
readDigitsC(FileName,LCont,ECont) =
   nextChar(FileName,
          switchType(FileName,
                   ECont("Not a digit"),
                   ECont("Not a digit"),
                   LCont([]),
                   switchDigit(FileName,
                            readDigitsC(FileName, λL.LCont(['0':L])),
                            readDigitsC(FileName, λL.LCont(['1':L])),
                              .
                              .
                              .
                            readDigitsC(FileName, λL.LCont(['9':L])) ),
                   ECont("Not a digit") ));

readWordC(InFile,LCont,ECont) =
   nextChar(FileName,
          switchType(FileName,
                   splitRange(InFile,'a','z',
                            λC.readWordC(InFile,λL.LCont([C:L])),ECont)
                   splitRange(InFile,'A','Z',
                            λC.readWordC(InFile,λL.LCont([C:L])),ECont),
                   LCont([]),
                   splitRange(InFile,'0','9',
                            λC.readWordC(InFile,λL.LCont([C:L])),ECont),
                   ECont("Not a legal character.\n") ))

readCharC(InFile,CCont,ECont) =
   nextChar(InFile, splitRange(InFile,minChar(),maxChar(),CCont,ECont))

splitRange(InFile,LB,UB,CCont,ECont) =
   if((UB<LB),ECont("Illegal Character"),
     split(InFile,(LB+UB)/2,
          splitRange(InFile,LB,(LB+UB)/2-1,CCont,ECont),
          CCont(char((LB+UB)/2)),
          splitRange(InFile,(LB+UB)/2+1,UB,CCont,ECont)))
```

This article was processed using the LaTeX macro package with LLNCS style

UCG-E: An Equational Logic Programming System

Lutz H. Hamel
BKS Software GmbH, Guerickestr. 27, 1000 Berlin 10, Germany

UCG-E is an equational logic programming system inspired by O'Donnell's system (O'Donnell, 1985) and Hatcher's UCG system (Hatcher, 1991) and was designed to allow the integration of logic systems into imperative style programming environments. Equational logic systems are interesting, since they may be implemented very efficiently with term rewriting systems (Herman, 1991). Backtracking, a major source of inefficiencies in other logic programming systems, is unnecessary in equational logic if the confluency of the underlying rewriting system is guaranteed. O'Donnell has identified four restrictions to the form of the equational axioms which assure the confluency of a system. Since the restrictions are purely syntactical, no runtime checks need to be performed to see whether a transformation is legal or not.

The UCG-E system takes an equational specification and translates it into C code. The generated code consists of a lookup table and a set of C function definitions. Each specification has two parts: First, a *declaration section* containing the alphabet and variable declarations; second, an equational or *rule section.*

Each equation in the rule section has the form `M:=N` and represents a directed rewrite rule `M`→`N`, where the term `N` replaces the term matched by `M`. Currently the system enforces two restrictions on the form of the rewrite rules. Let `Q` be a well-formed term and `V(Q)` be the set of variables in term `Q`, then

(1) The term `M` must be linear.

(2) `V(N)` $\subseteq$ `V(M)`.

The first restriction insures that if a rule matches an input term the variables in `M` are uniquely instantiated. The second restriction insures that instead of having to do a global unification of the variables we may copy the values of the variables from the left hand side to the right hand side during rewriting if necessary. As it turns out, these are two of the four restrictions which O'Donnell identified. The other two restrictions are currently not checked for, but have to be enforced by the programmer through disciplined programming.

Three features distinguish the UCG-E system from other equational logic systems:

User Defined Attributes -

UCG-E allows the user to define and attach attributes to terms (especially, attributes of C-basic and C-typedef types).

Term Generating Functions -

A term generating function is built for each symbol in the alphabet. The user may call these functions from the C environment to build terms labeled by symbols from the alphabet. In addition of generating a term these functions make the new term known to the term rewriting mechanism which attempts to apply any of the given rules to this newly generated term.

User Action Functions -

The user action functions allow the use of side effects in the rewrite rules. These side effects could take on the form of I/O or any other action which lies outside the realm of efficient equational processing. User action functions are distinguished symbols in the alphabet definition of the specification and may only appear on the right hand side of the rewrite rules.

Since the UCG-E system does allow side effects to be used in its rewriting rules, the rewrite sequence is as much part of the solution as is the final answer and therefore a deterministic selection of the rewrite sequence is important. UCG-E selects rules based on the order in which they appear in the specification rather than selecting them non-deterministically.

The programming and debugging of equational specifications is greatly facilitated by the integrated interactive debugger. The debugger allows the user to single-step rewrite sequences one rule at a time and to browse current state information.

As an illustration of a typical specification we show a program which appends an item to a list of items; in this case the items are integers.

```
%nullary nil;
%nullary item [int i]; /* 'item' has 'i' as attribute */
%binary  cons;
%binary  append;

%var TERM head;
%var TERM tail;
%var int int_val;
%%
append(item(int_val), nil)  := cons(item(int_val), nil);

append(item(int_val), cons(head, tail)) :=
       cons(head, append(item(int_val), tail));
```

References

Hatcher, 1991.

Hatcher, P., "The Equational Specification of Efficient Compiler Code Generation," *Comp. Lang.* **16(1)** pp. 81-95 Pergamon Press, (1991).

Herman, 1991.

Herman, M., Kirchner, C., and Kirchner, H., "Implementations of Term Rewriting Systems," *The Computer Journal* **34** pp. 20-33 (January 1991).

O'Donnell, 1985.

O'Donnell, M., *Equational Logic as a Programming Language,* The MIT Press, Cambridge, Massachusetts (1985).

A Relational Programming System with Inferred Representations

Dave Cattrall and Colin Runciman

University of York, York, YO1 5DD, England

1 Introduction

Relational programming was originally proposed by MacLennan [4, 5, 6]. He advocated a language based on binary relations and operators for combining and manipulating relations. Such operators form a *relational algebra* — a set of combining forms for relations which generalise a language like FP from functions to relations.

MacLennan designed a relational language and built an interpreter for it [1] but his implementation was achieved at the expense of an explicit compromise to relational abstraction. He split relational programming into two worlds — an intensional world (relations represented by many-to-one functions) and an extensional world (relations represented by association lists). The relational operators were similarly segregated into two groups — one applicable to intensional, the other to extensional relations. This representation divide considerably inhibited the freedom of programmer expression.

The Drusilla system removes this *representation bottleneck* by automatically selecting representations for relations and allowing operators to be applicable to relations of any representation. This permits more freedom of expression and the resulting form of relational programming has aspects of both functional and logic programming. A full description of this system is given in [3]

2 The Language

The Drusilla language is applicative, declarative and hence referentially transparent. It is also purely relational — the central notion is that *all the world is a binary relation*. Consequently there is no explicit divide between program code and data structure since both alike are represented by relations.

The basic values are numbers, strings and the unit value. Any set can be represented as a relation between the elements of the set and the unit value. The data structures available are relations and n-tuples.

Drusilla has many functional language aspects. Programs can be statically typed using Milner polymorphism. Higher-order relations — ones which contain relations as domain or range elements — are common since relations are used both for computation and data structuring. Drusilla has a lazy reduction semantics.

Drusilla has many logical aspects. Relations can be used to reason about the relationships between entities. Prolog uses a calculus and new relationships are deduced from existing ones by logical inference. By contrast, Drusilla uses an algebra and new relationships are constructed from existing ones by algebraic operations. Relations can be glued together directly without the need for information to be communicated by logical variables. Control in a Drusilla expression is determined by the operators used to construct that expression. Consequently extra-logical operators such as the cut are superfluous.

3 The Implementation

An interpreter for Drusilla has been written in Miranda[1] using implementation techniques more sophisticated than MacLennan's.

Three representations are available for relations — two intensional (set-valued functions and Boolean-valued characteristic functions) and one extensional (association lists). Set-valued functions permit handling of non-determinism since they model many-to-many relations.

Each relational operator is given a number of definitions, each of which is applicable to a particular combination of representations. All these definitions, however, are for the same operator symbol. By *overloading* operators in this way we remove MacLennan's intensional/extensional operator division.

The heart of the implementation is a *typed representation inference system*. This is a generalisation of Milner polymorphic type inference that not only ensures a program is type correct but also automatically selects representations for relations. This removes MacLennan's fixed representation scheme.

A typed representation inference rule is a normal type inference rule augmented with representation information. Each operator has its own set of typed representation inference rules. Each rule in the set gives the type and representation for the resulting relation when that operator is applied to relation(s) of particular type and representation. Typed representation information generated for an expression indicates the appropriate definition for each occurrence of a relational operator.

Representation possibilities can be further improved by use of a symbolic manipulation technique. This uses relational equivalences as rewrite rules. The rules are combined intelligently to form a number of methods. These methods are used to rewrite expressions to forms that can be represented. This is based on Bundy's [2] meta-level inference technique.

References

1. Brown, J., Mitton, S. Relational Programming: Design and Implementation of a Prototype Interpreter M.S. thesis, Naval Postgraduate School, Monterey, California (1985)
2. Bundy, A., Welham, B. Using Meta-level Inference for Selective Application of Rewrite Rule Sets in Algebraic Manipulation Artificial Intelligence **16** (1981)
3. Cattrall, D., Runciman, C. A Relational Programming Language with Functional and logical Aspects internal report, University of York, York, England (1992)
4. MacLennan, B. Introduction to Relational Programming ACM FPCA (1981)
5. MacLennan, B. Overview of Relational Programming ACM SIGPLAN Notices (1983) **18, 3**
6. MacLennan, B. Four Relational Programs ACM SIGPLAN Notices (1988) **23, 1**

This article was processed using the LaTeX macro package with LLNCS style

[1] Miranda is a trademark of research software

An Implementation of Action Semantics (Summary)

Hermano Moura*

University of Glasgow
Department of Computing Science
Glasgow G12 8QQ, Scotland
moura@dcs.glasgow.ac.uk

Abstract. Action semantics is a formalism for the definition of programming languages. We present an interpreter for actions, which are the meanings of programs in action semantics. The interpreter shows a clear picture of an action's behaviour. We also describe how an interpreter for a language $\mathcal{L}$ can automatically be derived from its action semantic definition.

Action Semantics. The structure of an action semantic definition is similar to a denotational semantic one: a compositional translation from syntactic entities to semantic entities using semantic functions [2, 4]. However action semantics uses *actions* as semantic entities (instead of higher order functions). An action is an entity that can be performed, using and giving information. Action notation is the formal language used in action semantics. It has a set of carefully designed primitive actions and action combinators that operate on well known computational entities like transients, bindings, storage, abstractions, etc. Some examples: the action "give 5" just gives the integer 5; the action "bind "x" to 10" binds the identifier "x" to 10; the compound action "give 5 and bind "x" to 10", when performed, will be equivalent to the performance of both subactions, in any order. The "then" combinator in "give 5 then give the integer" is similar to functional composition: it propagates the transient 5, given by the performance of the left subaction, into the right subaction. The data term "the integer" yields 5. In general, "the S" yields the received transient provided that it is of sort S. Action notation has a well defined operational semantics [2].

The Action Notation Interpreter. The action notation interpreter (ANI), which was implemented using STANDARD ML (SML), includes the action notation abstract syntax and an interpreting function that takes an action and interprets it giving an interpretation output. The interpretation output is basically a triple representing transients, bindings and storage produced by the action. The interpretation output for "give 5 and bind "x" to 10", for example, is the transient 5, binding ("x", 10) and an unchanged storage.

Internally, we define a *state* to consist of the action being interpreted, together with the transients, bindings and storage received by the action. (The *initial state* is formed by the action to be interpreted, no transients, no bindings and an empty

* Supported by CNPq, Brazil. On leave from Caixa Econômica Federal, Brazil.

storage). The interpretation of a primitive action gives a *step* containing the transients, bindings and storage resulting from the action interpretation, as well as an outcome status indicating the completion or failure of the action. A compound action is interpreted by interpreting its subactions and combining the outcome steps into one single step. This process is guided by the semantics of the combinator involved. Data terms such as "the integer" are evaluated using the received transients, bindings and storage (this evaluation has no side effects).

The Actioneer Generator. Although ANI was designed to interpret arbitrary actions, it is very useful to interpret actions that are denotations of programs (*program actions*). To achieve this, we use ANI in conjunction with the *actioneer generator*. Consider a language $\mathcal{L}$. The abstract syntax of $\mathcal{L}$, defined in terms of an SML data type, must be provided by the user. The actioneer generator is used to generate a program, the *actioneer for* $\mathcal{L}$, from $\mathcal{L}$'s action semantic definition. Thus, the program action for an $\mathcal{L}$-program is produced by the application of the actioneer for $\mathcal{L}$ to the program's parse tree. This is done according to $\mathcal{L}$'s semantic definition.

Suppose we want to build an interpreter for $\mathcal{L}$. Initially we use a parser generator to build a parser for $\mathcal{L}$. This parser must produce an SML data type as the representation of a parse tree. Then, we obtain an actioneer for $\mathcal{L}$ by application of the actioneer generator to $\mathcal{L}$'s semantic definition. Parsing the source program gives its abstract syntax tree representation. Applying the semantic function for $\mathcal{L}$-programs, present in the actioneer, to this tree, gives the program action, which can then be interpreted by ANI.

Conclusion. To achieve a better understanding of action notation and to obtain executable action semantic definitions were the main initial motivations for this work. Almost all action notation was implemented, as well as many of the standard data operations present in action notation (such as sum of integers, union of sets, head of a list, etc). A collection of useful functions, such as a pretty printer for action trees, is available. Also, ANI is completely integrated to the action semantics directed compiler generator, ACTRESS, presently being developed at Glasgow [1]. The correctness of the interpreter, although not proved, should be based on Mosses' definitive operational semantics given in [2]. Finally, ANI seems to be a good friend to introduce to new action people! For a more complete description see Moura [3].

References

1. D. F. Brown, H. Moura, and D. A. Watt. ACTRESS: an action semantics directed compiler generator. In *Compiler Construction '92*. Springer-Verlag, October 1992. To appear.
2. P. D. Mosses. *Action Semantics*. Cambridge University Press, 1992.
3. H. Moura. An implementation of action semantics. Research report, Glasgow University, Computing Science Department, Glasgow, Scotland, 1992. In preparation.
4. D. A. Watt. *Programming Language Syntax and Semantics*. Prentice Hall International Series in Computer Science. Prentice Hall, 1991.

This article was processed using the LaTeX macro package with LLNCS style

BinProlog: a Continuation Passing Style Prolog Engine

Paul Tarau[1]

Université de Moncton, Moncton N.B., Canada, E1A 3E9,
Email: tarau@info.umoncton.ca

Abstract. BinProlog is an efficient, compact and portable Prolog system, based on a source-level transformation to *continuation passing binary clauses*, a completely side-effect free compiler written in Prolog and a simplified WAM, optimized for execution of binary logic programs. We give a short description of the compiler and the engine, some performance data, and we point out some of the reasons why BinProlog compares so well with systems based on the full WAM in terms of absolute performance.

The BinProlog system consists of a compiler written in Prolog and a small C-emulator (40K executable) giving 215 KLIPS on a Sparcstation 2. BinProlog 1.24 (Sparc, Sun-3 and DOS-extended 386 versions) and some related papers are available by ftp from 139.103.16.2. It supports incremental development and it can create very small (7K) stand-alone applications. RISC philosophy has been consistently followed at each level of the design and the implementation of BinProlog. Rarely used or unessential features of the full WAM have been avoided through source-level transformations while carefully optimizing a small set of key instructions.

The one-pass compiler works on a clause-by-clause basis. It is side-effect free (no asserts and retracts) and very small (20K Prolog code). The compiler uses R.A. O'Keefe and D.H.D Warren's public domain read, write, and DCG-expander. A simple preprocessor converts each clause into its binary equivalent. A clause like `c(A) :- a(A),e(A,B),b(B)` becomes `c(A,Cont) :- a(A,e(A,B,b(B,Cont)))` where `Cont` is a new variable representing the *continuation* that is recursively passed between calls (see [2]). Efficient WAM-support deals with metavariables resulting from the transformation in the case of unit clauses (for example the clause `a(X)` becomes `a(X,Cont):-Cont`). An interesting feature is the use of logical variables as dictionaries, for variable classification and life-time analysis. Instead of putting this information in an explicit dictionary, variables are instantiated to a structure containing the information and a new variable. This ensures that information is propagated to each occurrence of the logic variable, without an explicit look-up operation.

The BinProlog engine is a variant of the WAM, specialized for efficient execution of *binary programs.* As a result of binarization we can give up WAM's environments (the AND-stack) and put on the heap the *continuation*, recursively embedded in the last arguments of our binary programs. We use a simplified OR-stack for nondeterministic predicates. An activation record contains the argument registers, the top of the heap and trail and the address of the next clause (see [3]).

As performance data shows, simplicity of implementation and a small and clean run-time system are enough to compensate for the more intensive heap-consumption, to be competitive in absolute terms with well-engineered standard WAM implementations like Sicstus Prolog 2.1. The following table shows some benchmarks executed on a Sparcstation IPC (no garbage collection time is included).

Benchmark program	Sicstus 2.1 Emulated	BinProlog 1.24 Emulated	Sicstus 2.1 Native
NREV	117 klips	125 klips	374 klips
CNREV	93 klips	125 klips	296 klips
CHAT-Parser	1.849 sec	1.980 sec	0.810 sec
FINDALL-PERMS(7)	1.410 sec	0.760 sec	1.300 sec
BFIRST-META	1.230 sec	0.420 sec	1.070 sec
BOOTSTRAP	24.000 sec	25.050 sec	10.720 sec

NREV is the well-known naive reverse benchmark, CNREV is obtained from CNREV by replacing the list constructor with another binary functor, BFIRST-META is a naive breadth-first prolog meta-interpreter, and BOOTSTRAP is our compiler compiling itself. The differences between CNREV and NREV (25%) in the case of Sicstus give an idea of the potential speed-up for BinProlog if we implement specialized list instructions and tags. The unusually good performances compared to Sicstus 2.1 in the case of FINDALL-PERMS(7) (an all-permutations program) and BFIRST-META come from our heap-based *findall/3 and findall/4* builtins based on a novel *heap lifting* technique.

Basically, the heap is split in a small lower half and a larger upper half. The goal is executed in the upper half of the heap. We push a copy of the answer to an open ended list located in the lower half starting from the initial position of the top of the heap H. The list grows with each new answer. After finding an answer we force backtracking. At the end, H is set to point just after the last answer in the lower half of the heap. A cons-cell containing the end of the list and the list itself is returned. At user-level, for findall/3 we give the list of answers and close its end with the empty list, while in findall/4 it is closed with a free variable that is unified with an existing list. A stack ensures correctness for embedded uses of findall.

Optimization of binary programs by partial evaluation and argument reordering (see [1]), combined with global analysis can further speed-up the BinProlog engine. The small size of the system makes it an ideal starting point for a hardware Prolog chip and for large scale parallel implementations where code is distributed on each processor.

Acknowledgements. We are grateful for support by NSERC (grant OGP0107411) and the FESR of the Université de Moncton.

References

1. Demoen, B. On the transformation of a prolog program to a more efficient binary program. Technical Report 130, K.U.Leuven, Dec. 1990.
2. Tarau, P., Boyer, M.: Elementary Logic Programs, *Proceedings of PLILP 90*, LNCS 456 (1990) 159–173.
3. Tarau, P.: A simplified abstract machine for the execution of binary metaprograms *Proceedings of LPC 91*, (1991) 119–128, ICOT, Tokyo.

LaToKi: A Language Toolkit for Bottom-Up Evaluation of Functional Programs

Peter Thiemann

Wilhelm Schickard Institut, Universität Tübingen, Sand 13, D-W7400 Tübingen, Germany

Abstract. LaToKi is a toolkit for experimentation with different implementations of recursion in strict functional programs. Its main emphasis is on the bottom-up evaluation of structural recursive defined programs. We have developed a technique that allows the evaluation of a wide subclass of structural recursive functions using a constant amount of control memory.

1 Introduction

The purpose of LaToKi is to provide an environment to compare different evaluation strategies for strict functional programs. We felt that such a toolkit was needed when we tried to compare the usual runtime stack implementation and its improvements (elimination of tail recursion and tail recursion mod constructors) with our bottom-up implementation for structural recursive functions.

Structural recursion arises naturally with inductively defined data types. Suppose we have a finite set Σ of data constructors with arities. Let T_Σ denote the set of all ground terms over Σ.

Definition. A function f defined by $f(x_1, \ldots, x_n) = e$ is *structural recursive defined* (srd) if there is a *recursion argument* $x_r \in T_\Sigma$ and inside of e there is a case distinction **case** x_r **of** $\ldots \sigma_j(z_1, \ldots, z_k) : e_j \ldots$ on x_r's top symbol (*e.g.* σ_j) in such a way that all recursive calls of f occur inside of some e_j and the rth argument of f in a recursive call is one of $z_1, \ldots, z_k$, *i.e.*, an immediate subterm of x_r.

The definition (as well as the evaluation scheme described below) can be generalized to mutual structural recursive functions and to functions with finite course-of-value recursion. See [3] for more information.

2 Bottom-up Evaluation

Evaluation of srd functions is done with visits to the nodes of the recursion argument. Visits are a well-known concept from evaluators for attribute grammars. A traversal of the derivation tree of the underlying grammar is a sequence of visits to its nodes. In our approach the recursion argument plays the rôle of the derivation tree. The tree traversal is compiled to iterative code. It works by reversing the tree pointers (similar to the Schorr-Waite garbage collection algorithm) and by saving a continuation address in the tag field for the identification of the data constructor. The information in the tag field can be recovered after the visit since it is implicit in the continuation address. Thus the state of the traversal (the node which is just visited, what action to perform next, the way back to the root of the tree) can be captured in two registers and in some part of the recursion argument. The first approach to bottom-up evaluation — an interpretative approach without continuation addresses — is found in [1], a condensed description of our current technique is [4], more details and an introduction are found in [2].

3 Structure of the system

LaToKi is written in Edinburgh SML. It consists of three parts. The first is a front end covering syntax analysis and language dependent semantic analysis. Currently, there is a front end for ModAs/6000 (developed from the language of [1]) and for an experimental language whose only data type is tree. Front ends are planned for a functional subset of SML and for a language based on order-sorted algebra.

The second part works on a common abstract syntax. It does language independent analyses and compiles to the abstract iterative machine AIM (cf. [4]). Here, the compiler examines each function definition and chooses the appropriate implementation strategy. We thank Jochen Spranger for its implementation.

The third part is a native code generator. Currently, we have a prototype code generator for the RS/6000. An optimizing version of it is under development. We also plan a version for SPARC processors. Recently, many groups are compiling functional languages into C. This was not possible here, since we need explicit access to return addresses for efficiency reasons.

4 Performance

Each of the implementation strategies mentioned above has its advantages. The current code generator only implements bottom-up evaluation (srd) and the usual runtime stack method (rec). In the table below we give some measurements for sample code (without optimization and garbage collection). We have applied the functions **append** and **nreverse** to lists of various lengths with both evaluation techniques.

nreverse	elapsed time		user time	
length	rec	srd	rec	srd
1000	1.1	0.9	1.10	0.95
2000	4.6	3.8	4.50	3.63

append	elapsed time		user time	
length	rec	srd	rec	srd
10^5	0.3	0.2	0.29	0.23
10^6	84.8	2.3	5.71	2.31

References

1. Herbert Klaeren and Klaus Indermark. Efficient implementation of an algebraic specification language. In M. Wirsing and J. A. Bergstra, editors, *Algebraic Methods: Theory, Tools, and Applications*, pages 69–90. Springer, 1987. LNCS 394.
2. Peter Thiemann. Efficient implementation of structural recursive programs. Technical Report WSI-91-12, Universität Tübingen, 1991.
3. Peter Thiemann. Konzepte zur effizienten Implementierung strukturell rekursiver Programme. Dissertation, Fakultät für Informatik, Universität Tübingen, 1991.
4. Peter Thiemann. Optimizing structural recursion in functional programs. In *Proceedings International Conference on Computer Languages 1992*, pages 76–85, April 1992.

This article was processed using the LaTeX macro package with LLNCS style

Implementing Higher-Order Functions in an Algebraic Specification Language with Narrowing

Bernhard Reus

Institut für Informatik, Universität München, Leopoldstraße 11B, D-8000 München 40, Germany

Abstract. The presented HO-RAP system combines λ-calculus with Horn clause specifications interpreted by rewriting and narrowing techniques. Therefore, higher-order programming becomes available for the prototyper together with logic programming features introduced via narrowing. Still unification is first-order and accordingly not satisfactory with regard to functional equality.

Motivation Functional and logic programming are standard techniques for interpreting algebraic specifications. But most functional/logical languages are lacking higher-order functions as a built-in concept. However, higher-order functions may be extremely useful in parameterising (and therefore saving) code. Typical examples are general tree or list traversals. The HO-RAP system offers higher-order functions in conditional equations and, moreover, λ-expressions, narrowing and term-rewriting. It is based on the (first-order) RAP system [3] that is of particular interest because its computing engine consists of a conditional narrowing algorithm that is sped up by several optimizations [4] and provides a simple syntax and good debugging facilities.

Implementation The higher-order terms are internally coded by *apply*-s, e.g. the term $add(zero, succ(zero))$ becomes $apply2(zero, apply1(succ, zero))$, which is, however, hidden from the user. This "trick" is not new, of course; it has been discussed e.g. by [7] and [2]. Warren once noticed that the higher-order approach is therefore uninteresting from a theoretical point of view. But in practice in a strongly typed environment many differently typed *apply*-s are needed which in turn produce a large amount of useless syntax the user should be liberated from.

For λ-expressions α- and β conversion are built-in, the first is implemented via DeBruijn indices. Both conversion rules can certainly not be used for narrowing. Terms are always rewritten into α-β-normal form before the user-defined conditional equations are applied. Therefore, the termination problems described in [5] are avoided. Typical examples for the use of λ-expressions are functional programming languages or logical frameworks.

The theoretical foundations for the first-order representation of higher-order functions can be found e.g. in [7]. Since extensionality is not a computational rule, it will not be reflected by the system. For problems with extensionality and initial approach in a more general setting see also [1].

Some optimizations of the narrowing procedure, described in [4] are not sensible any more when working with *apply* functions. Accordingly, in HO-RAP some of these had to be modified [8]. As a major problem the equality of functions comes up quite naturally when considering higher-order objects. Since higher-order unification is rather complicated and semidecidable, we still use first-order unification with the consequence, that the equality of functions is an intensional one defined by the Horn formulae of the program. Following the ideas of [6] some special purpose unification algorithms that are slightly stronger than the simple first-order one, are planned to be integrated into the system.

Experiments Some small examples have already been tested in HO-RAP. Logical quantifiers with induction have been specified where predicates are functions with codomain *Bool* and the universal quantifier is given by a higher-order function. Other examples are program transformations or specification of program languages and denotational semantics.

Conclusion HO-RAP provides an SML-like prototyping environment - ignoring the fact that it lacks a polymorphic type system - with pattern-matching, higher-order functions and functional abstraction, plus the possibility of logic variables. With additional features like polymorphic types, a convenient module system and more than first-order-unification such a system could be a quite comfortable prototyping tool. Moreover, the experiment proved that extending a first-order system by higher-order functions is a quite manageable task even if we had to pay the price of an about 50-60% loss of speed.

References

1. E. Astesiano, M. Cerioli: *On the existence of initial models for partial (higher-order) conditional specifications.* In: J. Diaz, F. Orejas (eds.): TAPSOFT '89, Vol. 1, Lecture Notes in Computer Science 351, Springer, Berlin, 1989, 74 - 88.
2. M. Hanus: *Compiling Logic Programs with Equality.* In Proc. PLILP 90, Linköping, Sweden, Lecture Notes in Computer Science 456, Springer, Berlin, 1990, 387 - 401.
3. H. Hußmann: *Rapid Prototyping for Algebraic Specifications - RAP - System User's Manual.* Universität Passau, MIP - 8504, Research Report, Passau, 1985.
4. H. Hußmann: *Unification in Conditional-Equational Theories.* Universität Passau, MIP - 8502, Research Report, 2nd edition, Passau, 1986.
5. J.-P. Jouannaud, M. Okada: *Executable Higher-Order Algebraic Specification Languages.* Proc. 6th IEEE Symp. Logic in Computer Science, Amsterdam 1991.
6. D. Miller: *A Logic Programming Language with Lambda-Abstraction, Function Variables and Simple Unification.* Journal of Logic Computation, Volume 1, No. 4, 1991, 497 - 536.
7. B. Möller, A. Tarlecki, M. Wirsing: *Algebraic Specification of Reachable Higher-Order Algebras.* In: D. Sannella, A. Tarlecki (eds.): Recent Trends in Data Type Specification: 5th Workshop on Specification of Abstract Data Types - Selected Papers. Lecture Notes in Computer Science 332, Springer, Berlin, 1988, 154 - 169.
8. B. Reus: *Algebraische Spezifikation mit Funktionen höherer Ordnung.* Diploma Thesis, Fakultät für Mathematik und Informatik, Passau, 1990.

Implementing Attribute Grammars by Computational Models *

Jaak Vilo

Department of Computer Science, University of Helsinki
Teollisuuskatu 23, SF-00510 Helsinki, Finland
e-mail: vilo@cs.Helsinki.FI

Abstract. We describe the implementation of attribute grammars with the knowledge-based system NUT. NUT uses intuitionistic propositional calculus for automatic synthesis of programs [2]. Penjam [3] discussed the connection between two formalisms – computational models, used in NUT system, and attribute grammars. We have developed this relation further. The system we are presenting is the extension of NUT and it allows automatic transformation from AG-representation to equivalent computational model (we call that the language model). NUT can then be used for automatic synthesis of tree-decoration algorithms for both – dynamic and static tree evaluation. For latter the algorithm synthesised is the multi-visit tree decoration algorithm.

Computational Models

Programming by means of computational models (for an overview see [4]) can be viewed as special kind of logic programming where the intuitionistic propositional calculus is used, instead of first order predicate calculus as in Prolog. The computational models are the set of computability statements which are logically implications. There are two kinds of these statements. Using $\overline{A}$ to denote $A_1 \& A_2 \& \ldots \& A_k$, we have the statement

$$\vdash \overline{A} \underset{f}{\rightarrow} B, \tag{1}$$

that can usually be understood as: "Knowing values of $A_1, A_2, \ldots, A_k$ one can compute the value of B by program f," and

$$\vdash \overline{(\overline{A} \underset{g}{\rightarrow} B)} \longrightarrow (\overline{C} \underset{F(g)}{\longrightarrow} D), \tag{2}$$

that can similarly be interpreted as: "Knowing how to compute the values B_i, $i = 1, \ldots, m$ from values $\overline{A_i}$ (by functions g_i) one can compute also the value of D from values $\overline{C}$ by program $F(g)$." It means that if all the subproblems can be solved then also D can be computed provided the solutions to subproblems. The function F can be viewed as a higher order function, taking as parameter the list of functions $g = g_1, \ldots, g_m$ that are the solutions to the subproblems.

Computational *problems* are usually presented as "given initial values and knowledge implied by computational models compute the desired values." The algorithm for solving such problems can be synthesized automatically. Synthesis is done during the constructive proof of the existence of solution. Set of inference rules, called structural synthesis rules (SSR), is used for the proof.

* This work was done in part at the Institute of Cybernetics, Tallinn, Estonia. Work partially supported by Academy of Finland

Implementation of Attribute Grammars

For implementation of languages the computational problems can be formalized as follows: "given derivation tree of language compute the synthesized attributes of the root." The language model for such task can be just the set of computability statements of type (1) between the attributes of the derivation tree. By such method we can dynamically implement the ***partial relational attribute grammars.***

For static realization of attribute grammars we build the language model from submodels. Submodels correspond to possible elementary trees of the grammar. Each such submodel contains relations between attributes of the elementary tree and the conditional computability statements of type (2) that introduce the possible dependencies on all possible subtrees. From such language model NUT is able to synthesize a recursive algorithm for evaluating the synthesized attributes of the start symbol of the grammar. The derived algorithm implements the multi-visit strategy for attribute evaluation [1]. Given such an algorithm all, derivation trees of the language can be decorated. The algorithm just has to check what is the actual structure of derivation tree in order to call right functions for evaluating the attributes.

System Description

Our system [6] takes as input the language description by means of attribute grammars. It produces automatically the corresponding language model and a parser for the language. The first is NUT and the latter is YACC program. The parser obtained for the language generates the derivation tree that is also a NUT class (NUT is object oriented). The algorithms for decorating the derivation tree are generated by NUT and the actual computation of the decoration is also done by this system.

Conclusions.

In our work we have shown the appropriateness of formal calculus as used in system NUT [5] for language implementation. Much of work has to be done for really building the effective language development environments that uses this kind of approach. However, it could be quite desirable to enrich systems, such as NUT with tools suitable for developing small problem-oriented languages.

References

1. Engelfriet, J. and Filé, G.: Passes, Sweeps and Visits in Attribute Grammars. Journal of the ACM. Vol 36, No. 4. Oct. 1989 841–869.
2. Mints, G.: Propositional Logic Programming. Machine Intelligence. **12**:17–38, 1991. Oxford University Press.
3. Penjam, J.: Computational and Attribute Models of Formal Languages. Theoretical Computer Science. **71** (1990) 241–264.
4. Tyugu, E.: Knowledge Based Programming. Turing Institute Press, Addison Wesley, Glasgow, 1987.
5. Tyugu, E.: Modularity of Knowledge. Machine Intelligence. **12**:3–16, 1991. Oxford University Press.
6. Vilo, J.: Attribute Grammars and Computational Models as Combined Language Development Tools. CS-43/92. Institute of Cybernetics, Tallinn 1992.

This article was processed using the LaTeX macro package with LLNCS style

ProQuery: Logical Access to an OODB

Chu Min Li & Paul Y Gloess

Heudiasyc
Département de Génie Informatique
U.R.A. C.N.R.S. N°817, BP 649
Université de Technologie de Compiègne
F-60206 Compiègne Cédex - France
Tel: (33) 44 23 44 63, Fax: (33) 44 23 44 77
e-mail: cli@hds.univ-compiegne.fr

LaBRI
U.R.A. C.N.R.S. n°1304
ENSERB, Université Bordeaux I
351, Cours de la Libération
F-33405 Talence Cédex - France
Tel: (33) 56 84 69 27, Fax: (33) 56 84 66 69
e-mail: gloess@geocub.greco-prog.fr

ProQuery is an extension of Prolog implemented as a strong and dynamic interface between Prolog and an OODBMS. The foundation is the unified object logic theory [2]. The system provides, in a unified framework and in addition to the classical Prolog language, both type reasoning and efficient and incremental access to the database by means of *filters* and *relational literals* built upon an OODB model.

Consider the database which is an interpretation of a model

$$<\mathscr{C}, \leq, \mathscr{L}, \chi, \delta>$$

where $\mathscr{C}$ is the set of basic classes partially ordered by inheritance, $\mathscr{L}$ is the set of attributes, $\chi:\mathscr{C}\times\mathscr{L}\rightarrow\{T, F\}$ and $\delta:\mathscr{L}\rightarrow\mathscr{C}^*\cup\mathscr{B}$, where $\mathscr{B}$ is the set of primitive types such as *number* and *string*, specify type constraints in the following manner:

$\chi(c, \ell) =$ T if ℓ is allowed for class c; F otherwise.

Furthermore, χ respects attribute inheritance: if a class admits attribute ℓ, then all its subclasses, own this attribute.

The δ function associates with each label ℓ a primitive type or a sequence $(c_1 \ldots c_n)$ of classes which will be interpreted as a logical *or* of these classes. So the type of an attribute ℓ is the same for all classes that admit this attribute.

A filter consists of a boolean expression on basic classes and an association list of attribute/value. Given the following signature

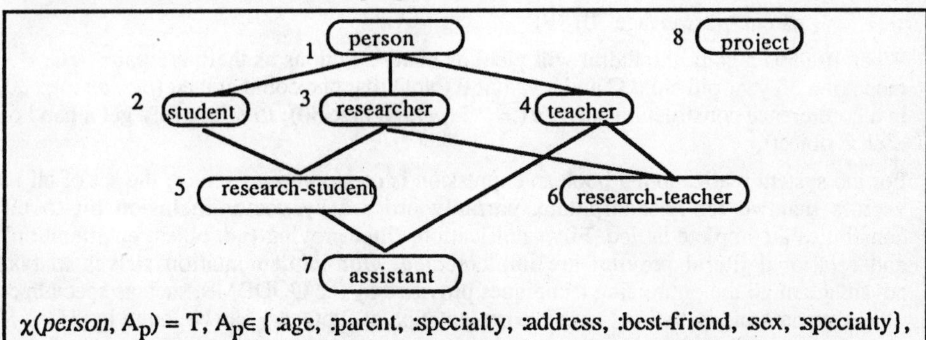

χ(*person*, A_p) = T, $A_p \in$ { :age, :parent, :specialty, :address, :best-friend, :sex, :specialty},
χ(*teacher*, A_t) = T, A_t=A_p or $\in$ { :salary}, χ(*project*, :title) = T,...;

δ(:age)=δ(:salary)=number, δ(:specialty)=δ(:sex)=δ(:title) = δ(:address) = string,
δ(:parent)=δ(:best_friend)=(person).

we can write two filters with their denotational semantics:

(*person* :age *30* :father (:= *X (*teacher* :specialty (*"computer science"*)))
:best_friend *X :address *Y)

represents the set of 30 year old persons whose best friend is their own father, a teacher whose specialty is "computer science". The construction allowing the Prolog variable *X to designate a teacher is called *coreference*, and allows the sharing of information. Here, the father and the best friend are the same person: the teacher. If we repeated the filter representing the teacher, instead of using the coreference, the father and the best friend would be different persons! The variable *Y does not specify a constraint; it is used for output purpose: we specifically want to know the address of the persons belonging to the filter denotation.

((or (and *student* (not *researcher*)) (and *teacher* (not *researcher*))) :specialty *S :sex "Male")

represents a subset of the faculty who are male and do not do research.

A filter can be used as a literal. Its proving allows to enumerate all objects contained in its denotation. For example we can ask:

;;; Who are faculty who are male and do not do research?
(? ((or (and *student* (not *researcher*))(and *teacher* (not *researcher*))) :specialty *S :sex "Male")

A filter can also be used as arguments of a literal. In this case, we can make type reasoning as defined in [1], which is in essence the possibility of providing a general answer to some question without looking for particular objects.

For example, we can define a predicate *teach* given the above signature:

(*teach* (*teacher*) (*student*)) ←;

The (*teacher*) and (*student*) filters are arguments and will just carry some type information; the same is true of the (*student*) filter in the goal below:

;;; Do some students teach some students?
(? (*teach* (*student*) (*student*)))

The resolution only needs filter unification to give the most general answer: assistants teach students. In fact, unification of the (*teacher*) and (*student*) filters gives the (*assistant*) filter, their greatest lower bound. The denotations of these filters are not actually needed to produce this answer to the query!

Any attribute can be used in a literal. For example, the following literal specifies a relation between all 30 year old persons and their parent:

(:parent (*person* :age 30) *P)

When used as a goal, the literal will yield as many solutions as there are pairs $< C, P >$ made of a 30 year old child C and a parent P (Note that one could embed (*person* :age 30) in a coreference construction such as (:= *C (*person* :age 30)) to effectively get a hand on each C object).

For the system realization, a boolean expression is coded into bit vector: the set of all bit vectors that we really manipulate, partially ordered by vector inclusion bit to bit, constitutes a complete lattice. Filter unification, filter proving (i.e. object enumeration), and relational literal proving are implemented. Our implementation strives to take advantage of all the optimizing techniques provided by the OODBMS, such as specialized object streams and statistics. Complete presentation of ProQuery can be found in [3].

References

[1] H. Gallaire, "Multiple Reasoning Styles in Logic Programming", in Proceedings of FGCS'88 Conference (ICOT), Tokyo, 1988.

[2] P.Y. Gloess, "U-Log, An Order Sorted Logic with Typed Attributes", Lecture Notes in Computer Science, Springer-Verlag, PLILP'91, Passau, FRG.

[3] C.M. Li, P.Y. Gloess, "Realizing an Efficient and Incremental Access to an Object Oriented Data Base with Prolog", Actes des Journées Francophone de la Programmation Logique, Lille, France, 1992.

Inference of Inheritance Relationships from Prolog Programs: a System Developed with PrologIII

Christine Solnon - Michel Rueher

I3S, University of Nice Sophia Antipolis - CNRS
06560 Valbonne, FRANCE
e-mail: solnon@mimosa.unice.fr

In order to support the object oriented design of reusable software components, we propose to extract an inheritance hierarchy from a Prolog prototype. The goal is to define a reverse engineering technique for recovering structural design information through the analysis of the Prolog prototype. Inheritance is an essential means in object oriented languages to express inclusion polymorphism (i.e., subtyping). Thus, to infer inheritance relationships from a Prolog program, we define a polymorphic type system for Prolog, and identify subtyping relations between these types.

We associate a type with each predicate and with each argument position in a predicate. The type of a term at position[1] i in a predicate p is noted $Tp(i)$, and is defined by:

$$\begin{aligned} Tp(i) = {} & \{A_i \mid p(\ldots,A_i,\ldots) \in denotation(p) \text{ and } A_i \text{ is a variable or a constant}\} \\ & \cup \{ f(A_1, \ldots ,A_n) \mid A_1 \in Tp(i.f(1)) \text{ and } \ldots \text{ and } A_n \in Tp(i.f(n)) \} \end{aligned}$$

The type of a predicate p of arity $n \geq 1$ is noted Tp, and is defined by:

$$Tp = \{ p(A_1, \ldots ,A_n) \mid A_1 \in Tp(1) \text{ and } \ldots \text{ and } A_n \in Tp(n) \}$$

In order to get independant of the test cases, we propose in [1] an algorithm that defines the types of a Prolog program by their relations with other types rather than by instances sets. The different kinds of type relations infered by this algorithm are:

- $Tp = p(Tp(1)\times \ldots \times Tp(n))$ that specifies that the type Tp of a predicate or a functional term p/n is defined by the composition of the types of its arguments $Tp(1)$, ..., $Tp(n)$.
- $T = T1 \cup \ldots \cup Tn$ that specifies that the type of an argument of a predicate is defined by the disjunction of the types of this argument in the different clauses that define this predicate.
- $T = T1 \cap \ldots \cap Tn$ that specifies that the type of a variable in the head of a clause is defined by the conjunction of the types associated with the occurences of this variable in the body of the clause.

[1]This position can be indexed in order to take into account functional terms which arity is different from zero: the position of a term X in a functional term $A=p(A1,...,An)$ is computed by using the following rules:
- $Position(X,A) = i$ if $X = Ai$
- $Position(X,A) = i.f(Position(X,Ai))$ if X appears in a functional term $Ai = f(..,X,..)$

- $T \subseteq T1 \cap \ldots \cap Tn$ that specifies that the type of a variable in the head of a clause is a specialization of the conjunction of the types associated with the occurences of this variable in the body of the clause. Indeed, the type of a variable can be restricted by another variable that occurs more than once in the body of the clause, a constant, or a functional term.

- T = *var_type(X)* that specifies that the type of a variable X that only occurs in the head of a clause is a parametric type.

- T = *instance(c)* that specifies that a constant c is instance of a type T.

From type relations, we infer inheritance relationships: $T1$ is an heir (i.e., a specialization) of $T2$ if $T1 \subseteq T2$. We compare types by using the two following rules:

$$T1 \cup \ldots \cup TN \subseteq U1 \cup \ldots \cup UM \text{ if } \forall i \in 1..N, \exists j \in 1..M \text{ so that } Ti \subseteq Uj$$
$$T1 \cap \ldots \cap TN \subseteq U1 \cap \ldots \cap UM \text{ if } \forall i \in 1..M, \exists j \in 1..N \text{ so that } Tj \subseteq Ui$$

The infered inheritance hierarchy is independant from the test cases: we do not consider the intances occuring in the type relations for comparing types (i.e., we do not suppose that the identity — resp. inclusion — of the sets of instances associated with two types implies the identity — resp. inclusion — of these types). We also infer an inheritance hierarchy dependant from test cases. For this, we take into account the instances occuring in the type relations when comparing types.

These two inheritance hierarchies exhibit the program structure at two different levels of abstraction: the first one explicits the relations expressed by "functional clauses" (i.e., clauses that describe the application), where as the second one explicits the relations expressed by "data clauses" (i.e., clauses that describe the data of the application). These inheritance hierarchies can be used to design an object oriented model of the application. Moreover, their comparison can outline an inconsistency between the implementation of the functionalities and the test cases. Thus, we provide a support to improve the Prolog prototype and to clarify the underlying data structure of the application to be developed. Our approach also enables one to take advantage of both logic and object-oriented paradigms and provides an alternative approach to the systems based on the integration of both paradigms.

The whole system has been implemented in PrologIII. Constraints on tuples allowed us to write a reversible parser in a very declarative way, whereas constraints on booleans provide a powerful and well suited mechanism for identifying inheritance relationships from type relations. Despite of some limits (e.g., difficulty for processing the resulting constraint system), PrologIII offered significantly more prototyping facilities than Prolog.

Different extensions of this work are considered. First of all, we plan to extend our system in order to better deal with generic clauses. In some cases, all type information is not present in the Prolog program. Thus, the infered inheritance hierarchy has to be interactively refined by the user, and a graphical editor would be useful. Further works concern also the reuse of the deduced type information in the Prolog prototype (e.g., introduction of types by means of constraints).

References

[1] C. Solnon, M. Rueher: *From a Prolog prototype to an object oriented model: an approach using relationships between types*, RR 92-21, I3S, 4 av. A. Einstein, 06560 Valbonne, France, 15p

CLP($\mathcal{PB}$)

A Meta-Interpreter in CLP($\mathcal{R}$)

Peter Barth

Max-Planck-Institut für Informatik
Im Stadtwald
W-6600 Saarbrücken, Germany
e-mail: Peter.Barth@mpi-sb.mpg.de

We present a prototype implementation of a new constraint logic programming language CLP($\mathcal{PB}$) [2]. The language is an instance of the general constraint logic programming scheme CLP($\mathcal{X}$) of [6]. The computational domain is the algebraic structure $\mathcal{PB}$ that allows us to handle equations and inequalities between pseudo-Boolean functions, where a *pseudo-Boolean function* is a mapping $g : \{0,1\}^n \to \mathcal{Z}$ of boolean variables to the ring $\mathcal{Z}$ of integer numbers. Additionally, optimization of pseudo-Boolean functions is available (constrained non-linear 0-1 programming). The implementation language CLP($\mathcal{R}$) [7] can handle linear equality and inequality constraints over the field $\mathcal{R}$ of real numbers.

For a detailed description see [1].

CLP-system design in CLP-systems

The main problem in implementing a CLP system is to provide a constraint solver and to ensure its incrementality. In [7] it is proposed to use an existing CLP($\mathcal{O}$) system as implementation language for a new CLP($\mathcal{N}$) system. This seems to be promising if the constraints in $\mathcal{N}$ can be expressed as constraints in $\mathcal{O}$ and the solutions of the transformed constraints in $\mathcal{O}$ can be identified with the original solutions in $\mathcal{N}$. This approach has the following advantages:

- We don't need to design a new constraint solver because the constraints are solved by the existing constraint solver for the domain $\mathcal{O}$.
- Incrementality is automatically provided.

Suppose that there are two computational domains $\mathcal{N}$ and $\mathcal{O}$ and their sets of possible constraints are $C(\mathcal{N})$ and $C(\mathcal{O})$. If there exist functions $\phi : C(\mathcal{N}) \to C(\mathcal{O})$ and $\psi : C(\mathcal{O}) \to C(\mathcal{N})$ such that

$$\forall p \in C(\mathcal{N}) : p \text{ is solvable in } \mathcal{N} \iff \phi(p) \text{ is solvable in } \mathcal{O}$$

$$\forall p \in C(\mathcal{N}) : \; S \text{ is solution of } \phi(p) \implies \psi(S) \text{ is solution of } p$$

then $C(\mathcal{N})$ is called *expressible* in $C(\mathcal{O})$.

Obviously, every constraint in a CLP($\mathcal{N}$) program can be translated by ϕ into a constraint of CLP($\mathcal{O}$). After executing the resulting CLP($\mathcal{O}$) program we obtain a solution which can be translated back by ψ into a solution of the CLP($\mathcal{N}$) program.

Example: Let $\mathcal{N}$ be $\mathcal{PB}$ and $\mathcal{O}$ be $\mathcal{R}$, then ϕ has to restrict every (real) variable to take its value in $\{0,1\}$; $\phi(c) = \{c\} \cup \bigcup_{X \in \mathcal{V}ar(c)} \{X * (X-1) = 0\}$. The function ψ is simply the identity.

This technique can be applied to various other CLP-languages and gives with a small effort prototypes of new CLP-languages.

Implementation

The prototype is implemented as meta-interpreter on top of CLP($\mathcal{R}$) [5]. Because solving polynomial constraints over $\mathcal{R}$ is very hard in general, we don't use the function ϕ as explained in the previous section. Instead, we first solve the *linear programming relaxation* (replace $X \in \{0,1\}$ by $0 \leq X \leq 1$) of the problem and then enumerate at the end the possible solutions by a branch and bound algorithm. This well known technique tends to be quite efficient in practice.

The current prototype consists of only 200 lines of source code and can be seen as an easily extensible platform for testing new heuristics and improvements of branch and bound algorithms for constrained non-linear 0-1 programming.

The following improvements have already been implemented.

- a variant of the Jeroslow-Wang heuristic [8] as variable selection rule. (adapted to the pseudo-Boolean case)
- Fortet's linearization [3]

The prototype has been tested on some of the well known satisfiability problems (pigeon hole, chess-board,...), as well as on some of the examples in [4] with promising results. Further testing of the prototype is in progress.

References

1. Peter Barth. CLP($\mathcal{PB}$) ; A Meta-Interpreter in CLP($\mathcal{R}$). Technical report, Max-Planck-Institut für Informatik, Saarbrücken, 1992.
2. A. Bockmayr. Logic programming with pseudo-boolean constraints. Technical Report mpii-91-227, Max-Planck-Institut für Informatik, Saarbrücken, 1991. to appear in: A. Colmerauer and F. Benhamou, editors, *Constraint Logic Programming – Selected Papers.*
3. R. Fortet. Applications de l'algèbre de boole en recherche opérationelle. *Rev. Française Recherche Opér.*, 4:17–26, 1960.
4. P.L. Hammer and S. Rudeanu. *Boolean Methods in Operations Research and Related Areas.* Springer-Verlag, 1968.
5. Nevin Heintze, Spiro Michaylov, Peter Stuckey, and Roland Yap. On meta-programming in CLP($\mathcal{R}$). In Ewing Lusk and Ross Overbeek, editors, *Logic Programming: Proceedings of the North Amercian Conference, 1989*, pages 52–68. MIT Press, October 1989.
6. Joxan Jaffar and Jean-Louis Lassez. Constraint logic programming. Technical Report 86/73, Monash University, Victoria, Australia, June 1986.
7. Joxan Jaffar, Spiro Michaylov, Peter Stuckey, and Roland Yap. The CLP($\mathcal{R}$) language and system. Technical Report RC 16292 (#72336) 11/15/90, IBM Research Division, November 1990.
8. R.E. Jeroslow and J. Wang. Solving propositional satisfiability problems. *Annals of Mathematics and AI*, 1, 1990.

Lecture Notes in Computer Science

For information about Vols. 1–544
please contact your bookseller or Springer-Verlag

Vol. 545: H. Alblas, B. Melichar (Eds.), Attribute Grammars , Applications and Systems. Proceedings, 1991. IX, 513 pages. 1991.

Vol. 546: O. Herzog, C.-R. Rollinger (Eds.), Text Understanding in LILOG. XI, 738 pages. 1991. (Subseries LNAI).

Vol. 547: D. W. Davies (Ed.), Advances in Cryptology – EUROCRYPT '91. Proceedings, 1991. XII, 556 pages. 1991.

Vol. 548: R. Kruse, P. Siegel (Eds.), Symbolic and Quantitative Approaches to Uncertainty. Proceedings, 1991. XI, 362 pages. 1991.

Vol. 549: E. Ardizzone, S. Gaglio, F. Sorbello (Eds.), Trends in Artificial Intelligence. Proceedings, 1991. XIV, 479 pages. 1991. (Subseries LNAI).

Vol. 550: A. van Lamsweerde, A. Fugetta (Eds.), ESEC '91. Proceedings, 1991. XII, 515 pages. 1991.

Vol. 551:S. Prehn, W. J. Toetenel (Eds.), VDM '91. Formal Software Development Methods. Volume 1. Proceedings, 1991. XIII, 699 pages. 1991.

Vol. 552: S. Prehn, W. J. Toetenel (Eds.), VDM '91. Formal Software Development Methods. Volume 2. Proceedings, 1991. XIV, 430 pages. 1991.

Vol. 553: H. Bieri, H. Noltemeier (Eds.), Computational Geometry - Methods, Algorithms and Applications '91. Proceedings, 1991. VIII, 320 pages. 1991.

Vol. 554: G. Grahne, The Problem of Incomplete Information in Relational Databases. VIII, 156 pages. 1991.

Vol. 555: H. Maurer (Ed.), New Results and New Trends in Computer Science. Proceedings, 1991. VIII, 403 pages. 1991.

Vol. 556: J.-M. Jacquet, Conclog: A Methodological Approach to Concurrent Logic Programming. XII, 781 pages. 1991.

Vol. 557: W. L. Hsu, R. C. T. Lee (Eds.), ISA '91 Algorithms. Proceedings, 1991. X, 396 pages. 1991.

Vol. 558: J. Hooman, Specification and Compositional Verification of Real-Time Systems. VIII, 235 pages. 1991.

Vol. 559: G. Butler, Fundamental Algorithms for Permutation Groups. XII, 238 pages. 1991.

Vol. 560: S. Biswas, K. V. Nori (Eds.), Foundations of Software Technology and Theoretical Computer Science. Proceedings, 1991. X, 420 pages. 1991.

Vol. 561: C. Ding, G. Xiao, W. Shan, The Stability Theory of Stream Ciphers. IX, 187 pages. 1991.

Vol. 562: R. Breu, Algebraic Specification Techniques in Object Oriented Programming Environments. XI, 228 pages. 1991.

Vol. 563: A. Karshmer, J. Nehmer (Eds.), Operating Systems of the 90s and Beyond. Proceedings, 1991. X, 285 pages. 1991.

Vol. 564: I. Herman, The Use of Projective Geometry in Computer Graphics. VIII, 146 pages. 1992.

Vol. 565: J. D. Becker, I. Eisele, F. W. Mündemann (Eds.), Parallelism, Learning, Evolution. Proceedings, 1989. VIII, 525 pages. 1991. (Subseries LNAI).

Vol. 566: C. Delobel, M. Kifer, Y. Masunaga (Eds.), Deductive and Object-Oriented Databases. Proceedings, 1991. XV, 581 pages. 1991.

Vol. 567: H. Boley, M. M. Richter (Eds.), Processing Declarative Kowledge. Proceedings, 1991. XII, 427 pages. 1991. (Subseries LNAI).

Vol. 568: H.-J. Bürckert, A Resolution Principle for a Logic with Restricted Quantifiers. X, 116 pages. 1991. (Subseries LNAI).

Vol. 569: A. Beaumont, G. Gupta (Eds.), Parallel Execution of Logic Programs. Proceedings, 1991. VII, 195 pages. 1991.

Vol. 570: R. Berghammer, G. Schmidt (Eds.), Graph-Theoretic Concepts in Computer Science. Proceedings, 1991. VIII, 253 pages. 1992.

Vol. 571: J. Vytopil (Ed.), Formal Techniques in Real-Time and Fault-Tolerant Systems. Proceedings, 1992. IX, 620 pages. 1991.

Vol. 572: K. U. Schulz (Ed.), Word Equations and Related Topics. Proceedings, 1990. VII, 256 pages. 1992.

Vol. 573: G. Cohen, S. N. Litsyn, A. Lobstein, G. Zémor (Eds.), Algebraic Coding. Proceedings, 1991. X, 158 pages. 1992.

Vol. 574: J. P. Banâtre, D. Le Métayer (Eds.), Research Directions in High-Level Parallel Programming Languages. Proceedings, 1991. VIII, 387 pages. 1992.

Vol. 575: K. G. Larsen, A. Skou (Eds.), Computer Aided Verification. Proceedings, 1991. X, 487 pages. 1992.

Vol. 576: J. Feigenbaum (Ed.), Advances in Cryptology - CRYPTO '91. Proceedings. X, 485 pages. 1992.

Vol. 577: A. Finkel, M. Jantzen (Eds.), STACS 92. Proceedings, 1992. XIV, 621 pages. 1992.

Vol. 578: Th. Beth, M. Frisch, G. J. Simmons (Eds.), Public-Key Cryptography: State of the Art and Future Directions. XI, 97 pages. 1992.

Vol. 579: S. Toueg, P. G. Spirakis, L. Kirousis (Eds.), Distributed Algorithms. Proceedings, 1991. X, 319 pages. 1992.

Vol. 580: A. Pirotte, C. Delobel, G. Gottlob (Eds.), Advances in Database Technology – EDBT '92. Proceedings. XII, 551 pages. 1992.

Vol. 581: J.-C. Raoult (Ed.), CAAP '92. Proceedings. VIII, 361 pages. 1992.

Vol. 582: B. Krieg-Brückner (Ed.), ESOP '92. Proceedings. VIII, 491 pages. 1992.

Vol. 583: I. Simon (Ed.), LATIN '92. Proceedings. IX, 545 pages. 1992.

Vol. 584: R. E. Zippel (Ed.), Computer Algebra and Parallelism. Proceedings, 1990. IX, 114 pages. 1992.

Vol. 585: F. Pichler, R. Moreno Díaz (Eds.), Computer Aided System Theory – EUROCAST '91. Proceedings. X, 761 pages. 1992.

Vol. 586: A. Cheese, Parallel Execution of Parlog. IX, 184 pages. 1992.

Vol. 587: R. Dale, E. Hovy, D. Rösner, O. Stock (Eds.), Aspects of Automated Natural Language Generation. Proceedings, 1992. VIII, 311 pages. 1992. (Subseries LNAI).

Vol. 588: G. Sandini (Ed.), Computer Vision – ECCV '92. Proceedings. XV, 909 pages. 1992.

Vol. 589: U. Banerjee, D. Gelernter, A. Nicolau, D. Padua (Eds.), Languages and Compilers for Parallel Computing. Proceedings, 1991. IX, 419 pages. 1992.

Vol. 590: B. Fronhöfer, G. Wrightson (Eds.), Parallelization in Inference Systems. Proceedings, 1990. VIII, 372 pages. 1992. (Subseries LNAI).

Vol. 591: H. P. Zima (Ed.), Parallel Computation. Proceedings, 1991. IX, 451 pages. 1992.

Vol. 592: A. Voronkov (Ed.), Logic Programming. Proceedings, 1991. IX, 514 pages. 1992. (Subseries LNAI).

Vol. 593: P. Loucopoulos (Ed.), Advanced Information Systems Engineering. Proceedings. XI, 650 pages. 1992.

Vol. 594: B. Monien, Th. Ottmann (Eds.), Data Structures and Efficient Algorithms. VIII, 389 pages. 1992.

Vol. 595: M. Levene, The Nested Universal Relation Database Model. X, 177 pages. 1992.

Vol. 596: L.-H. Eriksson, L. Hallnäs, P. Schroeder-Heister (Eds.), Extensions of Logic Programming. Proceedings, 1991. VII, 369 pages. 1992. (Subseries LNAI).

Vol. 597: H. W. Guesgen, J. Hertzberg, A Perspective of Constraint-Based Reasoning. VIII, 123 pages. 1992. (Subseries LNAI).

Vol. 598: S. Brookes, M. Main, A. Melton, M. Mislove, D. Schmidt (Eds.), Mathematical Foundations of Programming Semantics. Proceedings, 1991. VIII, 506 pages. 1992.

Vol. 599: Th. Wetter, K.-D. Althoff, J. Boose, B. R. Gaines, M. Linster, F. Schmalhofer (Eds.), Current Developments in Knowledge Acquisition - EKAW '92. Proceedings. XIII, 444 pages. 1992. (Subseries LNAI).

Vol. 600: J. W. de Bakker, C. Huizing, W. P. de Roever, G. Rozenberg (Eds.), Real-Time: Theory in Practice. Proceedings, 1991. VIII, 723 pages. 1992.

Vol. 601: D. Dolev, Z. Galil, M. Rodeh (Eds.), Theory of Computing and Systems. Proceedings, 1992. VIII, 220 pages. 1992.

Vol. 602: I. Tomek (Ed.), Computer Assisted Learning. Proceedings, 1992. X, 615 pages. 1992.

Vol. 603: J. van Katwijk (Ed.), Ada: Moving Towards 2000. Proceedings, 1992. VIII, 324 pages. 1992.

Vol. 604: F. Belli, F.-J. Radermacher (Eds.), Industrial and Engineering Applications of Artificial Intelligence and Expert Systems. Proceedings, 1992. XV, 702 pages. 1992. (Subseries LNAI).

Vol. 605: D. Etiemble, J.-C. Syre (Eds.), PARLE '92. Parallel Architectures and Languages Europe. Proceedings, 1992. XVII, 984 pages. 1992.

Vol. 606: D. E. Knuth, Axioms and Hulls. IX, 109 pages. 1992.

Vol. 607: D. Kapur (Ed.), Automated Deduction – CADE-11. Proceedings, 1992. XV, 793 pages. 1992. (Subseries LNAI).

Vol. 608: C. Frasson, G. Gauthier, G. I. McCalla (Eds.), Intelligent Tutoring Systems. Proceedings, 1992. XIV, 686 pages. 1992.

Vol. 609: G. Rozenberg (Ed.), Advances in Petri Nets 1992. VIII, 472 pages. 1992.

Vol. 610: F. von Martial, Coordinating Plans of Autonomous Agents. XII, 246 pages. 1992. (Subseries LNAI).

Vol. 611: M. P. Papazoglou, J. Zeleznikow (Eds.), The Next Generation of Information Systems: From Data to Knowledge. VIII, 310 pages. 1992. (Subseries LNAI).

Vol. 612: M. Tokoro, O. Nierstrasz, P. Wegner (Eds.), Object-Based Concurrent Computing. Proceedings, 1991. X, 265 pages. 1992.

Vol. 613: J. P. Myers, Jr., M. J. O'Donnell (Eds.), Constructivity in Computer Science. Proceedings, 1991. X, 247 pages. 1992.

Vol. 614: R. G. Herrtwich (Ed.), Network and Operating System Support for Digital Audio and Video. Proceedings, 1991. XII, 403 pages. 1992.

Vol. 615: O. Lehrmann Madsen (Ed.), ECOOP '92. European Conference on Object Oriented Programming. Proceedings. X, 426 pages. 1992.

Vol. 616: K. Jensen (Ed.), Application and Theory of Petri Nets 1992. Proceedings, 1992. VIII, 398 pages. 1992.

Vol. 617: V. Mařík, O. Štěpánková, R. Trappl (Eds.), Advanced Topics in Artificial Intelligence. Proceedings, 1992. IX, 484 pages. 1992. (Subseries LNAI).

Vol. 618: P. M. D. Gray, R. J. Lucas (Eds.), Advanced Database Systems. Proceedings, 1992. X, 260 pages. 1992.

Vol. 619: D. Pearce, H. Wansing (Eds.), Nonclassical Logics and Information Proceedings. Proceedings, 1990. VII, 171 pages. 1992. (Subseries LNAI).

Vol. 620: A. Nerode, M. Taitslin (Eds.), Logical Foundations of Computer Science – Tver '92. Proceedings. IX, 514 pages. 1992.

Vol. 621: O. Nurmi, E. Ukkonen (Eds.), Algorithm Theory – SWAT '92. Proceedings. VIII, 434 pages. 1992.

Vol. 622: F. Schmalhofer, G. Strube, Th. Wetter (Eds.), Contemporary Knowledge Engineering and Cognition. Proceedings, 1991. XII, 258 pages. 1992. (Subseries LNAI).

Vol. 623: W. Kuich (Ed.), Automata, Languages and Programming. Proceedings, 1992. XII, 721 pages. 1992.

Vol. 624: A. Voronkov (Ed.), Logic Programming and Automated Reasoning. Proceedings, 1992. XIV, 509 pages. 1992. (Subseries LNAI).

Vol. 625: W. Vogler, Modular Construction and Partial Order Semantics of Petri Nets. IX, 252 pages. 1992.

Vol. 626: E. Börger, G. Jäger, H. Kleine Büning, M. M. Richter (Eds.), Computer Science Logic. Proceedings, 1991. VIII, 428 pages. 1992.

Vol. 628: G. Vosselman, Relational Matching. IX, 190 pages. 1992.

Vol. 629: I. M. Havel, V. Koubek (Eds.), Mathematical Foundations of Computer Science 1992. Proceedings. IX, 521 pages. 1992.

Vol. 630: W. R. Cleaveland (Ed.), CONCUR '92. Proceedings. X, 580 pages. 1992.

Vol. 631: M. Bruynooghe, M. Wirsing (Eds.), Programming Language Implementation and Logic Programming. Proceedings, 1992. XI, 492 pages. 1992.

QMW LIBRARY
(MILE END)